COMPUTER ORGANIZATION
AND EMBEDDED SYSTEMS

COMPUTER ORGANIZATION
AND EMBEDDED SYSTEMS

SIXTH EDITION

Carl Hamacher
Queen's University

Zvonko Vranesic
University of Toronto

Safwat Zaky
University of Toronto

Naraig Manjikian
Queen's University

The McGraw-Hill Companies

Mc Graw Hill · Connect Learn Succeed™

COMPUTER ORGANIZATION AND EMBEDDED SYSTEMS, SIXTH EDITION

Published by McGraw-Hill, a business unit of The McGraw-Hill Companies, Inc., 1221 Avenue of the Americas, New York, NY 10020. Copyright © 2012 by The McGraw-Hill Companies, Inc. All rights reserved. Previous editions 2002, 1996, and 1990. No part of this publication may be reproduced or distributed in any form or by any means, or stored in a database or retrieval system, without the prior written consent of The McGraw-Hill Companies, Inc., including, but not limited to, in any network or other electronic storage or transmission, or broadcast for distance learning.

Some ancillaries, including electronic and print components, may not be available to customers outside the United States.

This book is printed on acid-free paper.

2 3 4 5 6 7 8 9 0 LCR 21 20 19 18 17

ISBN 978–0–07–338065–0
MHID 0–07–338065–2

Vice President & Editor-in-Chief: *Marty Lange*
Vice President EDP/Central Publishing Services: *Kimberly Meriwether David*
Publisher: *Raghothaman Srinivasan*
Senior Sponsoring Editor: *Peter E. Massar*
Developmental Editor: *Darlene M. Schueller*
Senior Marketing Manager: *Curt Reynolds*
Senior Project Manager: *Lisa A. Bruflodt*
Buyer: *Laura Fuller*
Design Coordinator: *Brenda A. Rolwes*
Media Project Manager: *Balaji Sundararaman*
Cover Design: *Studio Montage, St. Louis, Missouri*
Cover Image: *© Royalty-Free/CORBIS*
Compositor: *Techsetters, Inc.*
Typeface: *10/12 Times Roman*
Printer: *LSC Communications/Crawfordsville, IN*

Library of Congress Cataloging-in-Publication Data

Computer organization and embedded systems / Carl Hamacher ... [et al.]. – 6th ed.
     p. cm.
  Includes bibliographical references.
  ISBN-13: 978-0-07-338065-0 (alk. paper)
  ISBN-10: 0-07-338065-2 (alk. paper)
1. Computer organization. 2. Embedded computer systems. I. Hamacher, V. Carl.
  QA76.9.C643.H36 2012
  004.2'2–dc22
                              2010050243

www.mhhe.com

To our families

ABOUT THE AUTHORS

Carl Hamacher received the B.A.Sc. degree in Engineering Physics from the University of Waterloo, Canada, the M.Sc. degree in Electrical Engineering from Queen's University, Canada, and the Ph.D. degree in Electrical Engineering from Syracuse University, New York. From 1968 to 1990 he was at the University of Toronto, Canada, where he was a Professor in the Department of Electrical Engineering and the Department of Computer Science. He served as director of the Computer Systems Research Institute during 1984 to 1988, and as chairman of the Division of Engineering Science during 1988 to 1990. In 1991 he joined Queen's University, where is now Professor Emeritus in the Department of Electrical and Computer Engineering. He served as Dean of the Faculty of Applied Science from 1991 to 1996. During 1978 to 1979, he was a visiting scientist at the IBM Research Laboratory in San Jose, California. In 1986, he was a research visitor at the Laboratory for Circuits and Systems associated with the University of Grenoble, France. During 1996 to 1997, he was a visiting professor in the Computer Science Department at the University of California at Riverside and in the LIP6 Laboratory of the University of Paris VI.

His research interests are in multiprocessors and multicomputers, focusing on their interconnection networks.

Zvonko Vranesic received his B.A.Sc., M.A.Sc., and Ph.D. degrees, all in Electrical Engineering, from the University of Toronto. From 1963 to 1965 he worked as a design engineer with the Northern Electric Co. Ltd. in Bramalea, Ontario. In 1968 he joined the University of Toronto, where he is now a Professor Emeritus in the Department of Electrical & Computer Engineering. During the 1978–79 academic year, he was a Senior Visitor at the University of Cambridge, England, and during 1984-85 he was at the University of Paris, 6. From 1995 to 2000 he served as Chair of the Division of Engineering Science at the University of Toronto. He is also involved in research and development at the Altera Toronto Technology Center.

His current research interests include computer architecture and field-programmable VLSI technology.

He is a coauthor of four other books: *Fundamentals of Digital Logic with VHDL Design*, 3rd ed.; *Fundamentals of Digital Logic with Verilog Design*, 2nd ed.; *Microcomputer Structures*; and *Field-Programmable Gate Arrays*. In 1990, he received the Wighton Fellowship for "innovative and distinctive contributions to undergraduate laboratory instruction." In 2004, he received the Faculty Teaching Award from the Faculty of Applied Science and Engineering at the University of Toronto.

Safwat Zaky received his B.Sc. degree in Electrical Engineering and B.Sc. in Mathematics, both from Cairo University, Egypt, and his M.A.Sc. and Ph.D. degrees in Electrical Engineering from the University of Toronto. From 1969 to 1972 he was with Bell Northern Research, Bramalea, Ontario, where he worked on applications of electro-optics and magnetics in mass storage and telephone switching. In 1973, he joined the University of Toronto, where he is now Professor Emeritus in the Department of Electrical and Computer Engineering. He served as Chair of the Department from 1993 to 2003 and as Vice-Provost from 2003 to 2009. During 1980 to 1981, he was a senior visitor at the Computer Laboratory, University of Cambridge, England.

He is a Fellow of the Canadian Academy of Engineering. His research interests are in the areas of computer architecture, digital-circuit design, and electromagnetic compatibility. He is a coauthor of the book *Microcomputer Structures* and is a recipient of the IEEE Third Millennium Medal and of the Vivek Goel Award for distinguished service to the University of Toronto.

Naraig Manjikian received his B.A.Sc. degree in Computer Engineering and M.A.Sc. degree in Electrical Engineering from the University of Waterloo, Canada, and his Ph.D. degree in Electrical Engineering from the University of Toronto. In 1997, he joined Queen's University, Kingston, Canada, where he is now an Associate Professor in the Department of Electrical and Computer Engineering. From 2004 to 2006, he served as Undergraduate Chair for Computer Engineering. From 2006 to 2007, he served as Acting Head of the Department of Electrical and Computer Engineering, and from 2007 until 2009, he served as Associate Head for Student and Alumni Affairs. During 2003 to 2004, he was a visiting professor at McGill University, Montreal, Canada, and the University of British Columbia. During 2010 to 2011, he was a visiting professor at McGill University.

His research interests are in the areas of computer architecture, multiprocessor systems, field-programmable VLSI technology, and applications of parallel processing.

PREFACE

This book is intended for use in a first-level course on computer organization and embedded systems in electrical engineering, computer engineering, and computer science curricula. The book is self-contained, assuming only that the reader has a basic knowledge of computer programming in a high-level language. Many students who study computer organization will have had an introductory course on digital logic circuits. Therefore, this subject is not covered in the main body of the book. However, we have provided an extensive appendix on logic circuits for those students who need it.

The book reflects our experience in teaching three distinct groups of students: electrical and computer engineering undergraduates, computer science undergraduates, and engineering science undergraduates. We have always approached the teaching of courses on computer organization from a practical point of view. Thus, a key consideration in shaping the contents of the book has been to carefully explain the main principles, supported by examples drawn from commercially available processors. Our main commercial examples are based on: Altera's Nios II, Freescale's ColdFire, ARM, and Intel's IA-32 architectures.

It is important to recognize that digital system design is not a straightforward process of applying optimal design algorithms. Many design decisions are based largely on heuristic judgment and experience. They involve cost/performance and hardware/software tradeoffs over a range of alternatives. It is our goal to convey these notions to the reader.

The book is aimed at a one-semester course in engineering or computer science programs. It is suitable for both hardware- and software-oriented students. Even though the emphasis is on hardware, we have addressed a number of relevant software issues.

McGraw-Hill maintains a Website with support material for the book at http://www.mhhe.com/hamacher.

SCOPE OF THE BOOK

The first three chapters introduce the basic structure of computers, the operations that they perform at the machine-instruction level, and input/output methods as seen by a programmer. The fourth chapter provides an overview of the system software needed to translate programs written in assembly and high-level languages into machine language and to manage their execution. The remaining eight chapters deal with the organization, interconnection, and performance of hardware units in modern computers, including a coverage of embedded systems.

Five substantial appendices are provided. The first appendix covers digital logic circuits. Then, four current commercial instruction set architectures—Altera's Nios II, Freescale's ColdFire, ARM, and Intel's IA-32—are described in separate appendices.

Chapter 1 provides an overview of computer hardware and informally introduces terms that are discussed in more depth in the remainder of the book. This chapter discusses the basic functional units and the ways they interact to form a complete computer system. Number and character representations are discussed, along with basic arithmetic operations. An introduction to performance issues and a brief treatment of the history of computer development are also provided.

Chapter 2 gives a methodical treatment of machine instructions, addressing techniques, and instruction sequencing. Program examples at the machine-instruction level, expressed in a generic assembly language, are used to discuss concepts that include loops, subroutines, and stacks. The concepts are introduced using a RISC-style instruction set architecture. A comparison with CISC-style instruction sets is also included.

Chapter 3 presents a programmer's view of basic input/output techniques. It explains how program-controlled I/O is performed using polling, as well as how interrupts are used in I/O transfers.

Chapter 4 considers system software. The tasks performed by compilers, assemblers, linkers, and loaders are explained. Utility programs that trace and display the results of executing a program are described. Operating system routines that manage the execution of user programs and their input/output operations, including the handling of interrupts, are also described.

Chapter 5 explores the design of a RISC-style processor. This chapter explains the sequence of processing steps needed to fetch and execute the different types of machine instructions. It then develops the hardware organization needed to implement these processing steps. The differing requirements of CISC-style processors are also considered.

Chapter 6 provides coverage of the use of pipelining and multiple execution units in the design of high-performance processors. A pipelined version of the RISC-style processor design from Chapter 5 is used to illustrate pipelining. The role of the compiler and the relationship between pipelined execution and instruction set design are explored. Superscalar processors are discussed.

Input/output hardware is considered in **Chapter 7**. Interconnection networks, including the bus structure, are discussed. Synchronous and asynchronous operation is explained. Interconnection standards, including USB and PCI Express, are also presented.

Semiconductor memories, including SDRAM, Rambus, and Flash memory implementations, are discussed in **Chapter 8**. Caches are explained as a way for increasing the memory bandwidth. They are discussed in some detail, including performance modeling. Virtual-memory systems, memory management, and rapid address-translation techniques are also presented. Magnetic and optical disks are discussed as components in the memory hierarchy.

Chapter 9 explores the implementation of the arithmetic unit of a computer. Logic design for fixed-point add, subtract, multiply, and divide hardware, operating on 2's-complement numbers, is described. Carry-lookahead adders and high-speed multipliers are explained, including descriptions of the Booth multiplier recoding and carry-save addition techniques. Floating-point number representation and operations, in the context of the IEEE Standard, are presented.

Today, far more processors are in use in embedded systems than in general-purpose computers. **Chapters 10 and 11** are dedicated to the subject of embedded systems. First, basic aspects of system integration, component interconnections, and real-time operation are presented in Chapter 10. The use of microcontrollers is discussed. Then, Chapter 11 concentrates on system-on-a-chip (SoC) implementations, in which a single chip integrates the processing, memory, I/O, and timer functionality needed to satisfy application-specific requirements. A substantial example shows how FPGAs and modern design tools can be used in this environment.

Chapter 12 focuses on parallel processing and performance. Hardware multithreading and vector processing are introduced as enhancements in a single processor. Shared-memory multiprocessors are then described, along with the issue of cache coherence. Interconnection networks for multiprocessors are presented.

Appendix A provides extensive coverage of logic circuits, intended for a reader who has not taken a course on the design of such circuits.

Appendices B, C, D, and E illustrate how the instruction set concepts introduced in Chapters 2 and 3 are implemented in four commercial processors: Nios II, ColdFire, ARM, and Intel IA-32. The Nios II and ARM processors illustrate the RISC design style. ColdFire has an easy-to-teach CISC design, while the IA-32 CISC architecture represents the most successful commercial design. The presentation for each processor includes assembly-language examples from Chapters 2 and 3, implemented in the context of that processor. The details given in these appendices are not essential for understanding the material in the main body of the book. It is sufficient to cover only one of these appendices to gain an appreciation for commercial processor instruction sets. The choice of a processor to use as an example is likely to be influenced by the equipment in an accompanying laboratory. Instructors may wish to use more that one processor to illustrate the different design approaches.

CHANGES IN THE SIXTH EDITION

Substantial changes in content and organization have been made in preparing the sixth edition of this book. They include the following:

- The basic concepts of instruction set architecture are now covered using the RISC-style approach. This is followed by a comparative examination of the CISC-style approach.

- The processor design discussion is focused on a RISC-style implementation, which leads naturally to pipelined operation.

- Two chapters on embedded systems are included: one dealing with the basic structure of such systems and the use of microcontrollers, and the other dealing with system-on-a-chip implementations.

- Appendices are used to give examples of four commercial processors. Each appendix includes the essential information about the instruction set architecture of the given processor.

- Solved problems have been included in a new section toward the end of chapters and appendices. They provide the student with solutions that can be expected for typical problems.

DIFFICULTY LEVEL OF PROBLEMS

The problems at the end of chapters and appendices have been classified as easy (E), medium (M), or difficult (D). These classifications should be interpreted as follows:

- Easy—Solutions can be derived in a few minutes by direct application of specific information presented in one place in the relevant section of the book.

- Medium—Use of the book material in a way that does not directly follow any examples presented is usually needed. In some cases, solutions may follow the general pattern of an example, but will take longer to develop than those for easy problems.

- Difficult—Some additional insight is needed to solve these problems. If a solution requires a program to be written, its underlying algorithm or form may be quite different from that of any program example given in the book. If a hardware design is required, it may involve an arrangement and interconnection of basic logic circuit components that is quite different from any design shown in the book. If a performance analysis is needed, it may involve the derivation of an algebraic expression.

WHAT CAN BE COVERED IN A ONE-SEMESTER COURSE

This book is suitable for use at the university or college level as a text for a one-semester course in computer organization. It is intended for the first course that students will take on computer organization.

There is more than enough material in the book for a one-semester course. The core material on computer organization and relevant software issues is given in Chapters 1 through 9. For students who have not had a course in logic circuits, the material in Appendix A should be studied near the beginning of a course and certainly prior to covering Chapter 5.

A course aimed at embedded systems should include Chapters 1, 2, 3, 4, 7, 8, 10 and 11.

Use of the material on commercial processor examples in Appendices B through E can be guided by instructor and student interest, as well as by relevance to any hardware laboratory associated with a course.

ACKNOWLEDGMENTS

We wish to express our thanks to many people who have helped us during the preparation of this sixth edition of the book.

Our colleagues Daniel Etiemble of University of Paris South and Glenn Gulak of University of Toronto provided numerous comments and suggestions that helped significantly in shaping the material.

Blair Fort and Dan Vranesic provided valuable help with some of the programming examples.

Warren R. Carithers of Rochester Institute of Technology, Krishna M. Kavi of University of North Texas, and Nelson Luiz Passos of Midwestern State University provided reviews of material from both the fifth and sixth editions of the book.

The following people provided reviews of material from the fifth edition of the book: Goh Hock Ann of Multimedia University, Joseph E. Beaini of University of Colorado Denver, Kalyan Mohan Goli of Jawaharlal Nehru Technological University, Jaimon Jacob of Model Engineering College Ernakulam, M. Kumaresan of Anna University Coimbatore,

Kenneth K. C. Lee of City University of Hong Kong, Manoj Kumar Mishra of Institute of Technical Education and Research, Junita Mohamad-Saleh of Universiti Sains Malaysia, Prashanta Kumar Patra of College of Engineering and Technology Bhubaneswar, Shanq-Jang Ruan of National Taiwan University of Science and Technology, S. D. Samantaray of G. B. Pant University of Agriculture and Technology, Shivakumar Sastry of University of Akron, Donatella Sciuto of Politecnico of Milano, M. P. Singh of National Institute of Technology Patna, Albert Starling of University of Arkansas, Shannon Tauro of University of California Irvine, R. Thangarajan of Kongu Engineering College, Ashok Kunar Turuk of National Institute of Technology Rourkela, and Philip A. Wilsey of University of Cincinnati.

Finally, we truly appreciate the support of Raghothaman Srinivasan, Peter E. Massar, Darlene M. Schueller, Lisa Bruflodt, Curt Reynolds, Brenda Rolwes, and Laura Fuller at McGraw-Hill.

Carl Hamacher
Zvonko Vranesic
Safwat Zaky
Naraig Manjikian

McGraw-Hill Create[TM] Craft your teaching resources to match the way you teach! With McGraw-Hill Create, www.mcgrawhillcreate.com, you can easily rearrange chapters, combine material from other content sources, and quickly upload content you have written like your course syllabus or teaching notes. Find the content you need in Create by searching through thousands of leading McGraw-Hill textbooks. Arrange your book to fit your teaching style. Create even allows you to personalize your book's appearance by selecting the cover and adding your name, school, and course information. Order a Create book and you'll receive a complimentary print review copy in 3-5 business days or a complimentary electronic review copy (eComp) via email in minutes. Go to www.mcgrawhillcreate.com today and register to experience how McGraw-Hill Create empowers you to teach your students your way.

Do More

McGraw-Hill Higher Education and Blackboard® have teamed up.

Blackboard, the Web-based course management system, has partnered with McGraw-Hill to better allow students and faculty to use online materials and activities to complement face-to-face teaching. Blackboard features exciting social learning and teaching tools that foster more logical, visually impactful and active learning opportunities for students. You'll transform your closed-door classrooms into communities where students remain connected to their educational experience 24 hours a day.

This partnership allows you and your students access to McGraw-Hill's Create right from within your Blackboard course - all with one single sign-on. McGraw-Hill and Blackboard can now offer you easy access to industry leading technology and content, whether your campus hosts it, or we do. Be sure to ask your local McGraw-Hill representative for details.

CONTENTS

chapter

1

BASIC STRUCTURE OF COMPUTERS

CHAPTER OBJECTIVES

In this chapter you will be introduced to:

- The different types of computers
- The basic structure of a computer and its operation
- Machine instructions and their execution
- Number and character representations
- Addition and subtraction of binary numbers
- Basic performance issues in computer systems
- A brief history of computer development

This book is about computer organization. It explains the function and design of the various units of digital computers that store and process information. It also deals with the input units of the computer which receive information from external sources and the output units which send computed results to external destinations. The input, storage, processing, and output operations are governed by a list of instructions that constitute a program.

Most of the material in the book is devoted to *computer hardware* and *computer architecture*. Computer hardware consists of electronic circuits, magnetic and optical storage devices, displays, electromechanical devices, and communication facilities. Computer architecture encompasses the specification of an instruction set and the functional behavior of the hardware units that implement the instructions.

Many aspects of programming and software components in computer systems are also discussed in the book. It is important to consider both hardware and software aspects of the design of the various computer components in order to gain a good understanding of computer systems.

1.1   COMPUTER TYPES

Since their introduction in the 1940s, digital computers have evolved into many different types that vary widely in size, cost, computational power, and intended use. Modern computers can be divided roughly into four general categories:

•   *Embedded computers* are integrated into a larger device or system in order to automatically monitor and control a physical process or environment. They are used for a specific purpose rather than for general processing tasks. Typical applications include industrial and home automation, appliances, telecommunication products, and vehicles. Users may not even be aware of the role that computers play in such systems.

•   *Personal computers* have achieved widespread use in homes, educational institutions, and business and engineering office settings, primarily for dedicated individual use. They support a variety of applications such as general computation, document preparation, computer-aided design, audiovisual entertainment, interpersonal communication, and Internet browsing. A number of classifications are used for personal computers. *Desktop computers* serve general needs and fit within a typical personal workspace. *Workstation computers* offer higher computational capacity and more powerful graphical display capabilities for engineering and scientific work. Finally, *Portable* and *Notebook computers* provide the basic features of a personal computer in a smaller lightweight package. They can operate on batteries to provide mobility.

•   *Servers* and *Enterprise systems* are large computers that are meant to be shared by a potentially large number of users who access them from some form of personal computer over a public or private network. Such computers may host large databases and provide information processing for a government agency or a commercial organization.

•   *Supercomputers* and *Grid computers* normally offer the highest performance. They are the most expensive and physically the largest category of computers. Supercomputers are used for the highly demanding computations needed in weather forecasting, engineering design and simulation, and scientific work. They have a high cost. Grid computers provide a more cost-effective alternative. They combine a large number of personal computers and disk storage units in a physically distributed high-speed network, called a grid, which is managed as a coordinated computing resource. By evenly distributing the computational workload across the grid, it is possible to achieve high performance on large applications ranging from numerical computation to information searching.

There is an emerging trend in access to computing facilities, known as *cloud computing*. Personal computer users access widely distributed computing and storage server resources for individual, independent, computing needs. The Internet provides the necessary communication facility. Cloud hardware and software service providers operate as a utility, charging on a pay-as-you-use basis.

1.2 FUNCTIONAL UNITS

A computer consists of five functionally independent main parts: input, memory, arithmetic and logic, output, and control units, as shown in Figure 1.1. The input unit accepts coded information from human operators using devices such as keyboards, or from other computers over digital communication lines. The information received is stored in the computer's memory, either for later use or to be processed immediately by the arithmetic and logic unit. The processing steps are specified by a program that is also stored in the memory. Finally, the results are sent back to the outside world through the output unit. All of these actions are coordinated by the control unit. An interconnection network provides the means for the functional units to exchange information and coordinate their actions. Later chapters will provide more details on individual units and their interconnections. We refer to the

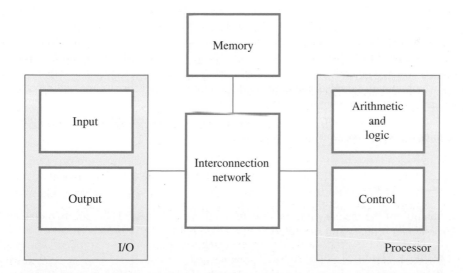

Figure 1.1 Basic functional units of a computer.

arithmetic and logic circuits, in conjunction with the main control circuits, as the *processor*. Input and output equipment is often collectively referred to as the *input-output* (I/O) unit.

We now take a closer look at the information handled by a computer. It is convenient to categorize this information as either instructions or data. *Instructions*, or *machine instructions*, are explicit commands that

- Govern the transfer of information within a computer as well as between the computer and its I/O devices
- Specify the arithmetic and logic operations to be performed

A *program* is a list of instructions which performs a task. Programs are stored in the memory. The processor fetches the program instructions from the memory, one after another, and performs the desired operations. The computer is controlled by the stored program, except for possible external interruption by an operator or by I/O devices connected to it. *Data* are numbers and characters that are used as operands by the instructions. Data are also stored in the memory.

The instructions and data handled by a computer must be encoded in a suitable format. Most present-day hardware employs digital circuits that have only two stable states. Each instruction, number, or character is encoded as a string of binary digits called *bits*, each having one of two possible values, 0 or 1, represented by the two stable states. Numbers are usually represented in positional binary notation, as discussed in Section 1.4. Alphanumeric characters are also expressed in terms of binary codes, as discussed in Section 1.5.

1.2.1   INPUT UNIT

Computers accept coded information through input units. The most common input device is the keyboard. Whenever a key is pressed, the corresponding letter or digit is automatically translated into its corresponding binary code and transmitted to the processor.

Many other kinds of input devices for human-computer interaction are available, including the touchpad, mouse, joystick, and trackball. These are often used as graphic input devices in conjunction with displays. Microphones can be used to capture audio input which is then sampled and converted into digital codes for storage and processing. Similarly, cameras can be used to capture video input.

Digital communication facilities, such as the Internet, can also provide input to a computer from other computers and database servers.

1.2.2   MEMORY UNIT

The function of the memory unit is to store programs and data. There are two classes of storage, called primary and secondary.

Primary Memory

Primary memory, also called *main memory*, is a fast memory that operates at electronic speeds. Programs must be stored in this memory while they are being executed. The memory consists of a large number of semiconductor storage cells, each capable of storing one bit of information. These cells are rarely read or written individually. Instead, they are handled in groups of fixed size called *words*. The memory is organized so that one word can be stored or retrieved in one basic operation. The number of bits in each word is referred to as the *word length* of the computer, typically 16, 32, or 64 bits.

To provide easy access to any word in the memory, a distinct *address* is associated with each word location. Addresses are consecutive numbers, starting from 0, that identify successive locations. A particular word is accessed by specifying its address and issuing a control command to the memory that starts the storage or retrieval process.

Instructions and data can be written into or read from the memory under the control of the processor. It is essential to be able to access any word location in the memory as quickly as possible. A memory in which any location can be accessed in a short and fixed amount of time after specifying its address is called a *random-access memory* (RAM). The time required to access one word is called the *memory access time*. This time is independent of the location of the word being accessed. It typically ranges from a few nanoseconds (ns) to about 100 ns for current RAM units.

Cache Memory

As an adjunct to the main memory, a smaller, faster RAM unit, called a *cache*, is used to hold sections of a program that are currently being executed, along with any associated data. The cache is tightly coupled with the processor and is usually contained on the same integrated-circuit chip. The purpose of the cache is to facilitate high instruction execution rates.

At the start of program execution, the cache is empty. All program instructions and any required data are stored in the main memory. As execution proceeds, instructions are fetched into the processor chip, and a copy of each is placed in the cache. When the execution of an instruction requires data located in the main memory, the data are fetched and copies are also placed in the cache.

Now, suppose a number of instructions are executed repeatedly as happens in a program loop. If these instructions are available in the cache, they can be fetched quickly during the period of repeated use. Similarly, if the same data locations are accessed repeatedly while copies of their contents are available in the cache, they can be fetched quickly.

Secondary Storage

Although primary memory is essential, it tends to be expensive and does not retain information when power is turned off. Thus additional, less expensive, permanent *secondary storage* is used when large amounts of data and many programs have to be stored, particularly for information that is accessed infrequently. Access times for secondary storage are longer than for primary memory. A wide selection of secondary storage devices is available, including *magnetic disks*, *optical disks* (DVD and CD), and *flash memory devices*.

1.2.3   ARITHMETIC AND LOGIC UNIT

Most computer operations are executed in the *arithmetic and logic unit* (ALU) of the processor. Any arithmetic or logic operation, such as addition, subtraction, multiplication, division, or comparison of numbers, is initiated by bringing the required operands into the processor, where the operation is performed by the ALU. For example, if two numbers located in the memory are to be added, they are brought into the processor, and the addition is carried out by the ALU. The sum may then be stored in the memory or retained in the processor for immediate use.

When operands are brought into the processor, they are stored in high-speed storage elements called *registers*. Each register can store one word of data. Access times to registers are even shorter than access times to the cache unit on the processor chip.

1.2.4   OUTPUT UNIT

The output unit is the counterpart of the input unit. Its function is to send processed results to the outside world. A familiar example of such a device is a *printer*. Most printers employ either photocopying techniques, as in laser printers, or ink jet streams. Such printers may generate output at speeds of 20 or more pages per minute. However, printers are mechanical devices, and as such are quite slow compared to the electronic speed of a processor.

Some units, such as graphic displays, provide both an output function, showing text and graphics, and an input function, through touchscreen capability. The dual role of such units is the reason for using the single name *input/output* (I/O) unit in many cases.

1.2.5   CONTROL UNIT

The memory, arithmetic and logic, and I/O units store and process information and perform input and output operations. The operation of these units must be coordinated in some way. This is the responsibility of the control unit. The control unit is effectively the nerve center that sends control signals to other units and senses their states.

I/O transfers, consisting of input and output operations, are controlled by program instructions that identify the devices involved and the information to be transferred. Control circuits are responsible for generating the *timing signals* that govern the transfers and determine when a given action is to take place. Data transfers between the processor and the memory are also managed by the control unit through timing signals. It is reasonable to think of a control unit as a well-defined, physically separate unit that interacts with other parts of the computer. In practice, however, this is seldom the case. Much of the control circuitry is physically distributed throughout the computer. A large set of control lines (wires) carries the signals used for timing and synchronization of events in all units.

The operation of a computer can be summarized as follows:

- The computer accepts information in the form of programs and data through an input unit and stores it in the memory.

- Information stored in the memory is fetched under program control into an arithmetic and logic unit, where it is processed.

- Processed information leaves the computer through an output unit.

- All activities in the computer are directed by the control unit.

1.3   BASIC OPERATIONAL CONCEPTS

In Section 1.2, we stated that the activity in a computer is governed by instructions. To perform a given task, an appropriate program consisting of a list of instructions is stored in the memory. Individual instructions are brought from the memory into the processor, which executes the specified operations. Data to be used as instruction operands are also stored in the memory.

A typical instruction might be

Load   R2, LOC

This instruction reads the contents of a memory location whose address is represented symbolically by the label LOC and loads them into processor register R2. The original contents of location LOC are preserved, whereas those of register R2 are overwritten. Execution of this instruction requires several steps. First, the instruction is fetched from the memory into the processor. Next, the operation to be performed is determined by the control unit. The operand at LOC is then fetched from the memory into the processor. Finally, the operand is stored in register R2.

After operands have been loaded from memory into processor registers, arithmetic or logic operations can be performed on them. For example, the instruction

Add   R4, R2, R3

adds the contents of registers R2 and R3, then places their sum into register R4. The operands in R2 and R3 are not altered, but the previous value in R4 is overwritten by the sum.

After completing the desired operations, the results are in processor registers. They can be transferred to the memory using instructions such as

Store   R4, LOC

This instruction copies the operand in register R4 to memory location LOC. The original contents of location LOC are overwritten, but those of R4 are preserved.

For Load and Store instructions, transfers between the memory and the processor are initiated by sending the address of the desired memory location to the memory unit and asserting the appropriate control signals. The data are then transferred to or from the memory.

Figure 1.2 shows how the memory and the processor can be connected. It also shows some components of the processor that have not been discussed yet. The interconnections between these components are not shown explicitly since we will only discuss their functional characteristics here. Chapter 5 describes the details of the interconnections as part of processor organization.

In addition to the ALU and the control circuitry, the processor contains a number of registers used for several different purposes. The *instruction register* (IR) holds the instruction that is currently being executed. Its output is available to the control circuits, which generate the timing signals that control the various processing elements involved in executing the instruction. The *program counter* (PC) is another specialized register. It

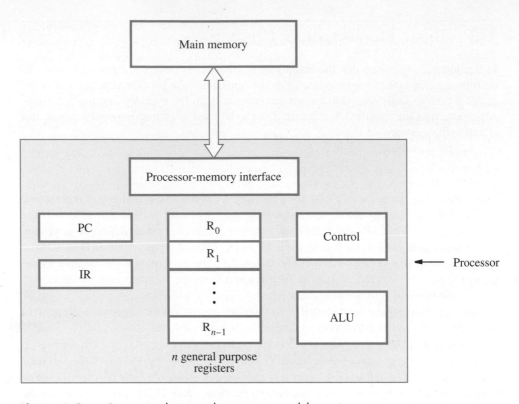

Figure 1.2   Connection between the processor and the main memory.

contains the memory address of the next instruction to be fetched and executed. During the execution of an instruction, the contents of the PC are updated to correspond to the address of the next instruction to be executed. It is customary to say that the PC *points* to the next instruction that is to be fetched from the memory. In addition to the IR and PC, Figure 1.2 shows *general-purpose registers* R_0 through R_{n-1}, often called processor registers. They serve a variety of functions, including holding operands that have been loaded from the memory for processing. The roles of the general-purpose registers are explained in detail in Chapter 2.

The processor-memory interface is a circuit which manages the transfer of data between the main memory and the processor. If a word is to be read from the memory, the interface sends the address of that word to the memory along with a Read control signal. The interface waits for the word to be retrieved, then transfers it to the appropriate processor register. If a word is to be written into memory, the interface transfers both the address and the word to the memory along with a Write control signal.

Let us now consider some typical operating steps. A program must be in the main memory in order for it to be executed. It is often transferred there from secondary storage through the input unit. Execution of the program begins when the PC is set to point to the first instruction of the program. The contents of the PC are transferred to the memory along with a Read control signal. When the addressed word (in this case, the first instruction of the program) has been fetched from the memory it is loaded into register IR. At this point, the instruction is ready to be interpreted and executed.

Instructions such as Load, Store, and Add perform data transfer and arithmetic operations. If an operand that resides in the memory is required for an instruction, it is fetched by sending its address to the memory and initiating a Read operation. When the operand has been fetched from the memory, it is transferred to a processor register. After operands have been fetched in this way, the ALU can perform a desired arithmetic operation, such as Add, on the values in processor registers. The result is sent to a processor register. If the result is to be written into the memory with a Store instruction, it is transferred from the processor register to the memory, along with the address of the location where the result is to be stored, then a Write operation is initiated.

At some point during the execution of each instruction, the contents of the PC are incremented so that the PC points to the next instruction to be executed. Thus, as soon as the execution of the current instruction is completed, the processor is ready to fetch a new instruction.

In addition to transferring data between the memory and the processor, the computer accepts data from input devices and sends data to output devices. Thus, some machine instructions are provided for the purpose of handling I/O transfers.

Normal execution of a program may be preempted if some device requires urgent service. For example, a monitoring device in a computer-controlled industrial process may detect a dangerous condition. In order to respond immediately, execution of the current program must be suspended. To cause this, the device raises an *interrupt* signal, which is a request for service by the processor. The processor provides the requested service by executing a program called an *interrupt-service routine*. Because such diversions may alter the internal state of the processor, its state must be saved in the memory before servicing the interrupt request. Normally, the information that is saved includes the contents of the PC, the contents of the general-purpose registers, and some control information. When the interrupt-service routine is completed, the state of the processor is restored from the memory so that the interrupted program may continue.

This section has provided an overview of the operation of a computer. Detailed discussion of these concepts is given in subsequent chapters, first from the point of view of the programmer in Chapters 2, 3, and 4, and then from the point of view of the hardware designer in later chapters.

1.4   NUMBER REPRESENTATION AND ARITHMETIC OPERATIONS

The most natural way to represent a number in a computer system is by a string of bits, called a binary number. We will first describe binary number representations for integers as well as arithmetic operations on them. Then we will provide a brief introduction to the representation of floating-point numbers.

1.4.1 INTEGERS

Consider an n-bit vector

$$B = b_{n-1} \ldots b_1 b_0$$

where $b_i = 0$ or 1 for $0 \le i \le n - 1$. This vector can represent an unsigned integer value $V(B)$ in the range 0 to $2^n - 1$, where

$$V(B) = b_{n-1} \times 2^{n-1} + \cdots + b_1 \times 2^1 + b_0 \times 2^0$$

We need to represent both positive and negative numbers. Three systems are used for representing such numbers:

- Sign-and-magnitude
- 1's-complement
- 2's-complement

In all three systems, the leftmost bit is 0 for positive numbers and 1 for negative numbers. Figure 1.3 illustrates all three representations using 4-bit numbers. Positive values have identical representations in all systems, but negative values have different representations. In the *sign-and-magnitude* system, negative values are represented by changing the most

B	Values represented		
$b_3 b_2 b_1 b_0$	Sign and magnitude	1's complement	2's complement
0 1 1 1	+ 7	+ 7	+ 7
0 1 1 0	+ 6	+ 6	+ 6
0 1 0 1	+ 5	+ 5	+ 5
0 1 0 0	+ 4	+ 4	+ 4
0 0 1 1	+ 3	+ 3	+ 3
0 0 1 0	+ 2	+ 2	+ 2
0 0 0 1	+ 1	+ 1	+ 1
0 0 0 0	+ 0	+ 0	+ 0
1 0 0 0	− 0	− 7	− 8
1 0 0 1	− 1	− 6	− 7
1 0 1 0	− 2	− 5	− 6
1 0 1 1	− 3	− 4	− 5
1 1 0 0	− 4	− 3	− 4
1 1 0 1	− 5	− 2	− 3
1 1 1 0	− 6	− 1	− 2
1 1 1 1	− 7	− 0	− 1

Figure 1.3   Binary, signed-integer representations.

significant bit (b_3 in Figure 1.3) from 0 to 1 in the B vector of the corresponding positive value. For example, +5 is represented by 0101, and −5 is represented by 1101.

In *1's-complement* representation, negative values are obtained by complementing each bit of the corresponding positive number. Thus, the representation for −3 is obtained by complementing each bit in the vector 0011 to yield 1100. The same operation, bit complementing, is done to convert a negative number to the corresponding positive value. Converting either way is referred to as forming the 1's-complement of a given number. For n-bit numbers, this operation is equivalent to subtracting the number from $2^n - 1$. In the case of the 4-bit numbers in Figure 1.3, we subtract from $2^4 - 1 = 15$, or 1111 in binary.

Finally, in the *2's-complement* system, forming the 2's-complement of an n-bit number is done by subtracting the number from 2^n. Hence, the 2's-complement of a number is obtained by adding 1 to the 1's-complement of that number.

Note that there are distinct representations for +0 and −0 in both the sign-and-magnitude and 1's-complement systems, but the 2's-complement system has only one representation for 0. For 4-bit numbers, as shown in Figure 1.3, the value −8 is representable in the 2's-complement system but not in the other systems. The sign-and-magnitude system seems the most natural, because we deal with sign-and-magnitude decimal values in manual computations. The 1's-complement system is easily related to this system, but the 2's-complement system may appear somewhat unnatural. However, we will show that the 2's-complement system leads to the most efficient way to carry out addition and subtraction operations. It is the one most often used in modern computers.

Addition of Unsigned Integers

Addition of 1-bit numbers is illustrated in Figure 1.4. The sum of 1 and 1 is the 2-bit vector 10, which represents the value 2. We say that the *sum* is 0 and the *carry-out* is 1. In order to add multiple-bit numbers, we use a method analogous to that used for manual computation with decimal numbers. We add bit pairs starting from the low-order (right) end of the bit vectors, propagating carries toward the high-order (left) end. The carry-out from a bit pair becomes the *carry-in* to the next bit pair to the left. The carry-in must be added to a bit pair in generating the sum and carry-out at that position. For example, if both bits of a pair are 1 and the carry-in is 1, then the sum is 1 and the carry-out is 1, which represents the value 3.

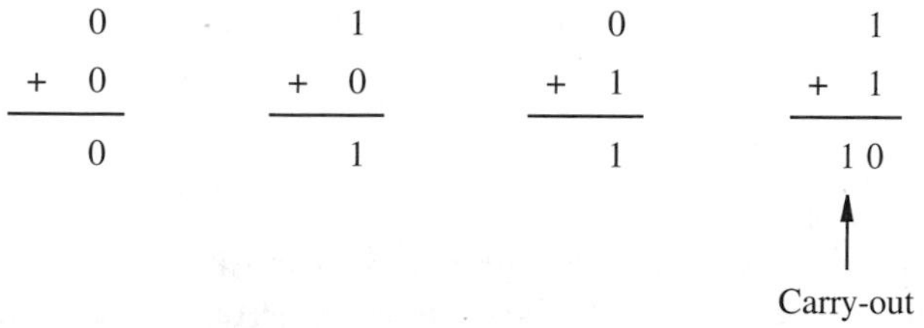

```
    0            1            0            1
 +  0         +  0         +  1         +  1
 ____         ____         ____         ____
    0            1            1          1 0
                                          ↑
                                          |
                                      Carry-out
```

Figure 1.4   Addition of 1-bit numbers.

Addition and Subtraction of Signed Integers

We introduced three systems for representing positive and negative numbers, or, simply, *signed numbers*. These systems differ only in the way they represent negative values. Their relative merits from the standpoint of ease of performing arithmetic operations can be summarized as follows. The sign-and-magnitude system is the simplest representation, but it is also the most awkward for addition and subtraction operations. The 1's-complement method is somewhat better. The 2's-complement system is the most efficient method for performing addition and subtraction operations.

To understand 2's-complement arithmetic, consider addition modulo N (abbreviated as mod N). A helpful graphical device for the description of addition of unsigned integers mod N is a circle with the values 0 through $N-1$ marked along its perimeter, as shown in Figure 1.5a. Consider the case $N = 16$, shown in part (b) of the figure. The decimal values 0 through 15 are represented by their 4-bit binary values 0000 through 1111 around the outside of the circle. In terms of decimal values, the operation $(7 + 5)$ mod 16 yields the value 12. To perform this operation graphically, locate 7 (0111) on the outside of the circle and then move 5 units in the clockwise direction to arrive at the answer 12 (1100). Similarly, $(9 + 14)$ mod $16 = 7$; this is modeled on the circle by locating 9 (1001) and moving 14 units in the clockwise direction past the zero position to arrive at the answer 7 (0111). This graphical technique works for the computation of $(a + b)$ mod 16 for any unsigned integers a and b; that is, to perform addition, locate a and move b units in the clockwise direction to arrive at $(a + b)$ mod 16.

Now consider a different interpretation of the mod 16 circle. We will reinterpret the binary vectors outside the circle to represent the signed integers from -8 through $+7$ in the 2's-complement representation as shown inside the circle.

Let us apply the mod 16 addition technique to the example of adding $+7$ to -3. The 2's-complement representation for these numbers is 0111 and 1101, respectively. To add these numbers, locate 0111 on the circle in Figure 1.5b. Then move 1101 (13) steps in the clockwise direction to arrive at 0100, which yields the correct answer of $+4$. Note that the 2's-complement representation of -3 is interpreted as an unsigned value for the number of steps to move.

If we perform this addition by adding bit pairs from right to left, we obtain

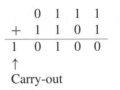

$$
\begin{array}{cccc}
  & 0 & 1 & 1 & 1 \\
+ & 1 & 1 & 0 & 1 \\
\hline
1 & 0 & 1 & 0 & 0 \\
\end{array}
$$

↑
Carry-out

If we ignore the carry-out from the fourth bit position in this addition, we obtain the correct answer. In fact, this is always the case. Ignoring this carry-out is a natural result of using mod N arithmetic. As we move around the circle in Figure 1.5b, the value next to 1111 would normally be 10000. Instead, we go back to the value 0000.

The rules governing addition and subtraction of n-bit signed numbers using the 2's-complement representation system may be stated as follows:

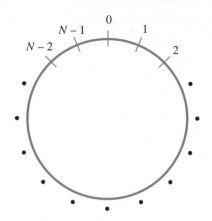

(a) Circle representation of integers mod N

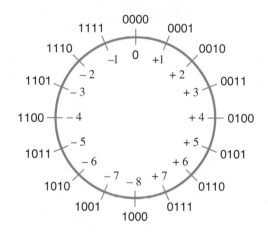

(b) Mod 16 system for 2's-complement numbers

Figure 1.5   Modular number systems and the 2's-complement system.

- To *add* two numbers, add their n-bit representations, ignoring the carry-out bit from the most significant bit (MSB) position. The sum will be the algebraically correct value in 2's-complement representation if the actual result is in the range -2^{n-1} through $+2^{n-1} - 1$.

- To *subtract* two numbers X and Y, that is, to perform $X - Y$, form the 2's-complement of Y, then add it to X using the *add* rule. Again, the result will be the algebraically correct value in 2's-complement representation if the actual result is in the range -2^{n-1} through $+2^{n-1} - 1$.

Figure 1.6 shows some examples of addition and subtraction in the 2's-complement system. In all of these 4-bit examples, the answers fall within the representable range of -8 through $+7$. When answers do not fall within the representable range, we say that *arithmetic overflow* has occurred. A later subsection discusses such situations. The four addition operations (*a*) through (*d*) in Figure 1.6 follow the add rule, and the six subtraction operations (*e*) through (*j*) follow the subtract rule. The subtraction operation requires forming the 2's-complement of the subtrahend (the bottom value). This operation

(a)	0 0 1 0	(+2)	(b)	0 1 0 0	(+4)	
	+ 0 0 1 1	(+3)		+ 1 0 1 0	(−6)	
	0 1 0 1	(+5)		1 1 1 0	(−2)	
(c)	1 0 1 1	(−5)	(d)	0 1 1 1	(+7)	
	+ 1 1 1 0	(−2)		+ 1 1 0 1	(−3)	
	1 0 0 1	(−7)		0 1 0 0	(+4)	
(e)	1 1 0 1	(−3)	⟹	1 1 0 1		
	− 1 0 0 1	(−7)		+ 0 1 1 1		
				0 1 0 0	(+4)	
(f)	0 0 1 0	(+2)	⟹	0 0 1 0		
	− 0 1 0 0	(+4)		+ 1 1 0 0		
				1 1 1 0	(−2)	
(g)	0 1 1 0	(+6)	⟹	0 1 1 0		
	− 0 0 1 1	(+3)		+ 1 1 0 1		
				0 0 1 1	(+3)	
(h)	1 0 0 1	(−7)	⟹	1 0 0 1		
	− 1 0 1 1	(−5)		+ 0 1 0 1		
				1 1 1 0	(−2)	
(i)	1 0 0 1	(−7)	⟹	1 0 0 1		
	− 0 0 0 1	(+1)		+ 1 1 1 1		
				1 0 0 0	(−8)	
(j)	0 0 1 0	(+2)	⟹	0 0 1 0		
	− 1 1 0 1	(−3)		+ 0 0 1 1		
				0 1 0 1	(+5)	

Figure 1.6   2's-complement Add and Subtract operations.

is done in exactly the same manner for both positive and negative numbers. To form the 2's-complement of a number, form the bit complement of the number and add 1.

The simplicity of adding and subtracting signed numbers in 2's-complement representation is the reason why this number representation is used in modern computers. It might seem that the 1's-complement representation would be just as good as the 2's-complement system. However, although complementation is easy, the result obtained after an addition operation is not always correct. The carry-out, c_n, cannot be ignored. If $c_n = 0$, the result obtained is correct. If $c_n = 1$, then a 1 must be added to the result to make it correct. The need for this correction operation means that addition and subtraction cannot be implemented as conveniently in the 1's-complement system as in the 2's-complement system.

Sign Extension

We often need to represent a value given in a certain number of bits by using a larger number of bits. For a positive number, this is achieved by adding 0s to the left. For a negative number in 2's-complement representation, the leftmost bit, which indicates the sign of the number, is a 1. A longer number with the same value is obtained by replicating the sign bit to the left as many times as needed. To see why this is correct, examine the mod 16 circle of Figure 1.5*b*. Compare it to larger circles for the mod 32 or mod 64 cases. The representations for the values -1, -2, etc., are exactly the same, with 1s added to the left. In summary, to represent a signed number in 2's-complement form using a larger number of bits, repeat the sign bit as many times as needed to the left. This operation is called *sign extension*.

Overflow in Integer Arithmetic

Using 2's-complement representation, n bits can represent values in the range -2^{n-1} to $+2^{n-1} - 1$. For example, the range of numbers that can be represented by 4 bits is -8 through $+7$, as shown in Figure 1.3. When the actual result of an arithmetic operation is outside the representable range, an *arithmetic overflow* has occurred.

When adding unsigned numbers, a carry-out of 1 from the most significant bit position indicates that an overflow has occurred. However, this is not always true when adding signed numbers. For example, using 2's-complement representation for 4-bit signed numbers, if we add $+7$ and $+4$, the sum vector is 1011, which is the representation for -5, an incorrect result. In this case, the carry-out bit from the MSB position is 0. If we add -4 and -6, we get $0110 = +6$, also an incorrect result. In this case, the carry-out bit is 1. Hence, the value of the carry-out bit from the sign-bit position is not an indicator of overflow. Clearly, overflow may occur only if both summands have the same sign. The addition of numbers with different signs cannot cause overflow because the result is always within the representable range.

These observations lead to the following way to detect overflow when adding two numbers in 2's-complement representation. Examine the signs of the two summands and the sign of the result. When both summands have the same sign, an overflow has occurred when the sign of the sum is not the same as the signs of the summands.

When subtracting two numbers, the testing method needed for detecting overflow has to be modified somewhat; but it is still quite straightforward. See Problem 1.10.

1.4.2   FLOATING-POINT NUMBERS

Until now we have only considered integers, which have an implied binary point at the right end of the number, just after bit b_0. If we use a full word in a 32-bit word length computer to represent a signed integer in 2's-complement representation, the range of values that can be represented is -2^{31} to $+2^{31} - 1$. In decimal terms, this range is somewhat smaller than -10^{10} to $+10^{10}$.

The same 32-bit patterns can also be interpreted as fractions in the range -1 to $+1 - 2^{-31}$ if we assume that the implied binary point is just to the right of the sign bit; that is, between bit b_{31} and bit b_{30} at the left end of the 32-bit representation. In this case, the magnitude of the smallest fraction representable is approximately 10^{-10}.

Neither of these two *fixed-point* number representations has a range that is sufficient for many scientific and engineering calculations. For convenience, we would like to have a binary number representation that can easily accommodate both very large integers and very small fractions. To do this, a computer must be able to represent numbers and operate on them in such a way that the position of the binary point is variable and is automatically adjusted as computation proceeds. In this case, the binary point is said to *float*, and the numbers are called *floating-point numbers*.

Since the position of the binary point in a floating-point number varies, it must be indicated explicitly in the representation. For example, in the familiar decimal scientific notation, numbers may be written as 6.0247×10^{23}, 3.7291×10^{-27}, -1.0341×10^2, -7.3000×10^{-14}, and so on. We say that these numbers have been given to 5 *significant digits* of precision. The *scale factors* 10^{23}, 10^{-27}, 10^2, and 10^{-14} indicate the actual position of the decimal point with respect to the significant digits. The same approach can be used to represent binary floating-point numbers in a computer, except that it is more appropriate to use 2 as the base of the scale factor. Because the base is fixed, it does not need to be given in the representation. The exponent may be positive or negative.

We conclude that a binary floating-point number can be represented by:

* a sign for the number
* some significant bits
* a signed scale factor exponent for an implied base of 2

An established international IEEE (Institute of Electrical and Electronics Engineers) standard for 32-bit floating-point number representation uses a sign bit, 23 significant bits, and 8 bits for a signed exponent of the scale factor, which has an implied base of 2. In decimal terms, the range of numbers represented is roughly $\pm 10^{-38}$ to $\pm 10^{38}$, which is adequate for most scientific and engineering calculations. The same IEEE standard also defines a 64-bit representation to accommodate more significant bits and more bits for the signed exponent, resulting in much higher precision and a much larger range of values.

Floating-point number representation and arithmetic operations on floating-point numbers are considered in detail in Chapter 9. Some of the commercial processors described in Appendices B to E include operations on floating-point numbers in their instruction sets and have processor registers dedicated to holding floating-point numbers.

1.5 CHARACTER REPRESENTATION

The most common encoding scheme for characters is ASCII (American Standard Code for Information Interchange). Alphanumeric characters, operators, punctuation symbols, and control characters are represented by 7-bit codes as shown in Table 1.1. It is convenient to use an 8-bit *byte* to represent and store a character. The code occupies the low-order seven bits. The high-order bit is usually set to 0. Note that the codes for the alphabetic and numeric characters are in increasing sequential order when interpreted as unsigned binary numbers. This facilitates sorting operations on alphabetic and numeric data.

The low-order four bits of the ASCII codes for the decimal digits 0 to 9 are the first ten values of the binary number system. This 4-bit encoding is referred to as the *binary-coded decimal* (BCD) code.

1.6 PERFORMANCE

The most important measure of the performance of a computer is how quickly it can execute programs. The speed with which a computer executes programs is affected by the design of its instruction set, its hardware and its software, including the operating system, and the technology in which the hardware is implemented. Because programs are usually written in a high-level language, performance is also affected by the compiler that translates programs into machine language. We do not describe the details of compilers or operating systems in this book. However, Chapter 4 provides an overview of software, including a discussion of the role of compilers and operating systems. This book concentrates on the design of instruction sets, along with memory, processor, and I/O hardware, and the organization of both small and large computers. Section 1.2.2 describes how caches can improve memory performance. Some performance aspects of instruction sets are discussed in Chapter 2. In this section, we give an overview of how performance is affected by technology, as well as processor and system organization.

1.6.1 TECHNOLOGY

The technology of Very Large Scale Integration (VLSI) that is used to fabricate the electronic circuits for a processor on a single chip is a critical factor in the speed of execution of machine instructions. The speed of switching between the 0 and 1 states in logic circuits is largely determined by the size of the transistors that implement the circuits. Smaller transistors switch faster. Advances in fabrication technology over several decades have reduced transistor sizes dramatically. This has two advantages: instructions can be executed faster, and more transistors can be placed on a chip, leading to more logic functionality and more memory storage capacity.

Table 1.1   The 7-bit ASCII code.

Bit positions 3210	Bit positions 654							
	000	001	010	011	100	101	110	111
0000	NUL	DLE	SPACE	0	@	P	´	p
0001	SOH	DC1	!	1	A	Q	a	q
0010	STX	DC2	"	2	B	R	b	r
0011	ETX	DC3	#	3	C	S	c	s
0100	EOT	DC4	$	4	D	T	d	t
0101	ENQ	NAK	%	5	E	U	e	u
0110	ACK	SYN	&	6	F	V	f	v
0111	BEL	ETB	'	7	G	W	g	w
1000	BS	CAN	(	8	H	X	h	x
1001	HT	EM	)	9	I	Y	i	y
1010	LF	SUB	*	:	J	Z	j	z
1011	VT	ESC	+	;	K	[	k	{
1100	FF	FS	,	<	L	/	l		
1101	CR	GS	-	=	M	]	m	}
1110	SO	RS	.	>	N	^	n	~
1111	SI	US	/	?	O	—	o	DEL

NUL	Null/Idle	SI	Shift in
SOH	Start of header	DLE	Data link escape
STX	Start of text	DC1-DC4	Device control
ETX	End of text	NAK	Negative acknowledgment
EOT	End of transmission	SYN	Synchronous idle
ENQ	Enquiry	ETB	End of transmitted block
ACK	Acknowledgment	CAN	Cancel (error in data)
BEL	Audible signal	EM	End of medium
BS	Back space	SUB	Special sequence
HT	Horizontal tab	ESC	Escape
LF	Line feed	FS	File separator
VT	Vertical tab	GS	Group separator
FF	Form feed	RS	Record separator
CR	Carriage return	US	Unit separator
SO	Shift out	DEL	Delete/Idle

Bit positions of code format = | 6 | 5 | 4 | 3 | 2 | 1 | 0 |

1.6.2 PARALLELISM

Performance can be increased by performing a number of operations in parallel. Parallelism can be implemented on many different levels.

Instruction-level Parallelism

The simplest way to execute a sequence of instructions in a processor is to complete all steps of the current instruction before starting the steps of the next instruction. If we overlap the execution of the steps of successive instructions, total execution time will be reduced. For example, the next instruction could be fetched from memory at the same time that an arithmetic operation is being performed on the register operands of the current instruction. This form of parallelism is called *pipelining*. It is discussed in detail in Chapter 6.

Multicore Processors

Multiple processing units can be fabricated on a single chip. In technical literature, the term *core* is used for each of these processors. The term processor is then used for the complete chip. Hence, we have the terminology *dual-core*, *quad-core*, and *octo-core* processors for chips that have two, four, and eight cores, respectively.

Multiprocessors

Computer systems may contain many processors, each possibly containing multiple cores. Such systems are called *multiprocessors*. These systems either execute a number of different application tasks in parallel, or they execute subtasks of a single large task in parallel. All processors usually have access to all of the memory in such systems, and the term *shared-memory multiprocessor* is often used to make this clear. The high performance of these systems comes with much higher complexity and cost, arising from the use of multiple processors and memory units, along with more complex interconnection networks.

In contrast to multiprocessor systems, it is also possible to use an interconnected group of complete computers to achieve high total computational power. The computers normally have access only to their own memory units. When the tasks they are executing need to share data, they do so by exchanging *messages* over a communication network. This property distinguishes them from shared-memory multiprocessors, leading to the name *message-passing multicomputers*.

Multiprocessors and multicomputers are described in Chapter 12.

1.7 HISTORICAL PERSPECTIVE

Electronic digital computers as we know them today have been developed since the 1940s. A long, slow evolution of mechanical calculating devices preceded the development of electronic computers. Here, we briefly sketch the history of computer development. A more extensive coverage can be found in Hayes [1].

In the 300 years before the mid-1900s, a series of increasingly complex mechanical devices, constructed from gear wheels, levers, and pulleys, were used to perform the basic operations of addition, subtraction, multiplication, and division. Holes on punched cards were mechanically sensed and used to control the automatic sequencing of a list of calculations, which essentially provided a programming capability. These devices enabled the computation of complete mathematical tables of logarithms and trigonometric functions as approximated by polynomials. Output results were punched on cards or printed on paper. Electromechanical relay devices, such as those used in early telephone switching systems, provided the means for performing logic functions in computers built in the late 1930s and early 1940s.

During World War II, the first electronic computer was designed and built at the University of Pennsylvania, using the vacuum tube technology developed for radios and military radar equipment. Vacuum tube circuits were used to perform logic operations and to store data. This technology initiated the modern era of electronic digital computers.

Development of the technologies used to fabricate processors, memories, and I/O units of computers has been divided into four generations: the first generation, 1945 to 1955; the second generation, 1955 to 1965; the third generation, 1965 to 1975; and the fourth generation, 1975 to the present.

1.7.1 THE FIRST GENERATION

The key concept of a stored program was introduced at the same time as the development of the first electronic digital computer. Programs and their data were located in the same memory, as they are today. This facilitates changing existing programs and data or preparing and loading new programs and data. Assembly language was used to prepare programs and was translated into machine language for execution.

Basic arithmetic operations were performed in a few milliseconds, using vacuum tube technology to implement logic functions. This provided a 100- to 1000-fold increase in speed relative to earlier mechanical and electromechanical technology. Mercury delay-line memory was used at first. I/O functions were performed by devices similar to typewriters. Magnetic core memories and magnetic tape storage devices were also developed.

1.7.2 THE SECOND GENERATION

The transistor was invented at AT&T Bell Laboratories in the late 1940s and quickly replaced the vacuum tube in implementing logic functions. This fundamental technology shift marked the start of the second generation. Magnetic core memories and magnetic drum storage devices were widely used in the second generation. Magnetic disk storage devices were developed in this generation. The earliest high-level languages, such as Fortran, were developed, making the preparation of application programs much easier. Compilers were developed to translate these high-level language programs into assembly language, which was then translated into executable machine-language form. IBM became a major computer manufacturer during this time.

1.7.3 THE THIRD GENERATION

Texas Instruments and Fairchild Semiconductor developed the ability to fabricate many transistors on a single silicon chip, called integrated-circuit technology. This enabled faster and less costly processors and memory elements to be built. Integrated-circuit memories began to replace magnetic core memories. This technological development marked the beginning of the third generation. Other developments included the introduction of microprogramming, parallelism, and pipelining. Operating system software allowed efficient sharing of a computer system by several user programs. Cache and virtual memories were developed. Cache memory makes the main memory appear faster than it really is, and virtual memory makes it appear larger. System 360 mainframe computers from IBM and the line of PDP minicomputers from Digital Equipment Corporation were dominant commercial products of the third generation.

1.7.4 THE FOURTH GENERATION

By the early 1970s, integrated-circuit fabrication techniques had evolved to the point where complete processors and large sections of the main memory of small computers could be implemented on single chips. This marked the start of the fourth generation. Tens of thousands of transistors could be placed on a single chip, and the name Very Large Scale Integration (VLSI) was coined to describe this technology. A complete processor fabricated on a single chip became known as a microprocessor. Companies such as Intel, National Semiconductor, Motorola, Texas Instruments, and Advanced Micro Devices have been the driving forces of this technology. Current VLSI technology enables the integration of multiple processors (cores) and cache memories on a single chip.

A particular form of VLSI technology, called Field Programmable Gate Arrays (FP-GAs), has allowed system developers to design and implement processor, memory, and I/O circuits on a single chip to meet the requirements of specific applications, especially in embedded computer systems. Sophisticated computer-aided-design tools make it possible to develop FPGA-based products quickly. Companies such as Altera and Xilinx provide this technology, along with the required software development systems.

Embedded computer systems, portable notebook computers, and versatile mobile telephone handsets are now in widespread use. Desktop personal computers and workstations interconnected by wired or wireless local area networks and the Internet, with access to database servers and search engines, provide a variety of powerful computing platforms.

Organizational concepts such as parallelism and hierarchical memories have evolved to produce the high-performance computing systems of today as the fourth generation has matured. Supercomputers and Grid computers, at the upper end of high-performance computing, are used for weather forecasting, scientific and engineering computations, and simulations.

1.8   CONCLUDING REMARKS

This chapter has introduced basic concepts about the structure of computers and their operation. Machine instructions and programs have been described briefly. The addition and subtraction of binary numbers has been explained. Much of the terminology needed to deal with these subjects has been defined. Subsequent chapters provide detailed explanations of these terms and concepts, with an emphasis on architecture and hardware.

1.9   SOLVED PROBLEMS

This section presents some examples of the types of problems that a student may be asked to solve, and shows how such problems can be solved.

Example 1.1   **Problem:** List the steps needed to execute the machine instruction

Load   R2, LOC

in terms of transfers between the components shown in Figure 1.2 and some simple control commands. An overview of the steps needed is given in Section 1.3. Assume that the address of the memory location containing this instruction is initially in register PC.

Solution: The required steps are:

- Send the address of the instruction word from register PC to the memory and issue a Read control command.
- Wait until the requested word has been retrieved from the memory, then load it into register IR, where it is interpreted (decoded) by the control circuitry to determine the operation to be performed.
- Increment the contents of register PC to point to the next instruction in memory.
- Send the address value LOC from the instruction in register IR to the memory and issue a Read control command.
- Wait until the requested word has been retrieved from the memory, then load it into register R2.

Example 1.2   **Problem:** Quantify the effect on performance that results from the use of a cache in the case of a program that has a total of 500 instructions, including a 100-instruction loop that is executed 25 times. Determine the ratio of execution time without the cache to execution time with the cache. This ratio is called the *speedup*.

Assume that main memory accesses require 10 units of time and cache accesses require 1 unit of time. We also make the following further assumptions so that we can simplify calculations in order to easily illustrate the advantage of using a cache:

- Program execution time is proportional to the total amount of time needed to fetch instructions from either the main memory or the cache, with operand data accesses being ignored.

- Initially, all instructions are stored in the main memory, and the cache is empty.

- The cache is large enough to contain all of the loop instructions.

Solution: Execution time without the cache is

$$T = 400 \times 10 + 100 \times 10 \times 25 = 29,000$$

Execution time with the cache is

$$T_{cache} = 500 \times 10 + 100 \times 1 \times 24 = 7,400$$

Therefore, the speedup is

$$T/T_{cache} = 3.92$$

Problem: Convert the following pairs of decimal numbers to 5-bit 2's-complement numbers, then perform addition and subtraction on each pair. Indicate whether or not overflow occurs for each case.

Example 1.3

(*a*) 7 and 13

(*b*) -12 and 9

Solution: The conversion and operations are:

(*a*) $7_{10} = 00111_2$ and $13_{10} = 01101_2$

Adding these two positive numbers, we obtain 10100, which is a negative number. Therefore, overflow has occurred.

To subtract them, we first form the 2's-complement of 01101, which is 10011. Then we perform addition with 00111 to obtain 11010, which is -6_{10}, the correct answer.

(*b*) $-12_{10} = 10100_2$ and $9_{10} = 01001_2$

Adding these two numbers, we obtain $11101 = -3_{10}$, the correct answer.

To subtract them, we first form the 2's-complement of 01001, which is 10111. Then we perform addition of the two negative numbers 10100 and 10111 to obtain 01011, which is a positive number. Therefore, overflow has occurred.

PROBLEMS

1.1   [E] Repeat Example 1.1 for the machine instruction

Add   R4, R2, R3

which is discussed in Section 1.3.

1.2   [E] Repeat Example 1.1 for the machine instruction

Store   R4, LOC

which is discussed in Section 1.3.

1.3   [M] (*a*) Give a short sequence of machine instructions for the task "Add the contents of memory location A to those of location B, and place the answer in location C". Instructions

Load   R*i*, LOC

and

Store   R*i*, LOC

are the only instructions available to transfer data between the memory and the general-purpose registers. Add instructions are described in Section 1.3. Do not change the contents of either location A or B.

(*b*) Suppose that Move and Add instructions are available with the formats

Move   Location1, Location2

and

Add   Location1, Location2

These instructions move or add a copy of the operand at the second location to the first location, overwriting the original operand at the first location. Either or both of the operands can be in the memory or the general-purpose registers. Is it possible to use fewer instructions of these types to accomplish the task in part (*a*)? If yes, give the sequence.

1.4   [M] (*a*) A program consisting of a total of 300 instructions contains a 50-instruction loop that is executed 15 times. The processor contains a cache, as described in Section 1.2.2. Fetching and executing an instruction that is in the main memory requires 20 time units. If the instruction is found in the cache, fetching and executing it requires only 2 time units. Ignoring operand data accesses, calculate the ratio of program execution time without the cache to execution time with the cache. This ratio is called the *speedup* due to the use of the cache. Assume that the cache is initially empty, that it is large enough to hold the loop, and that the program starts with all instructions in the main memory.

(*b*) Generalize part (*a*) by replacing the constants 300, 50, 15, 20, and 2 with the variables w, x, y, m, and c. Develop an expression for speedup.

(*c*) For the values $w = 300, x = 50, m = 20$, and $c = 2$ what value of y results in a speedup of 5?

(*d*) Consider the form of the expression for speedup developed in part (*b*). What is the upper limit on speedup as the number of loop iterations, *y*, becomes larger and larger?

1.5 **[M]** (*a*) A processor cache is discussed in Section 1.2.2. Suppose that execution time for a program is proportional to instruction fetch time. Assume that fetching an instruction from the cache takes 1 time unit, but fetching it from the main memory takes 10 time units. Also, assume that a requested instruction is found in the cache with probability 0.96. Finally, assume that if an instruction is not found in the cache it must first be fetched from the main memory into the cache and then fetched from the cache to be executed. Compute the ratio of program execution time without the cache to program execution time with the cache. This ratio is called the *speedup* resulting from the presence of the cache.

(*b*) If the size of the cache is doubled, assume that the probability of not finding a requested instruction there is cut in half. Repeat part (*a*) for a doubled cache size.

1.6 **[E]** Extend Figure 1.4 to incorporate both possibilities for a carry-in (0 or 1) to each of the four cases shown in the figure. Specify both the sum and carry-out bits for each of the eight new cases.

1.7 **[M]** Convert the following pairs of decimal numbers to 5-bit 2's-complement numbers, then add them. State whether or not overflow occurs in each case.

(*a*) 4 and 11
(*b*) 6 and 14
(*c*) −13 and 12
(*d*) −4 and 8
(*e*) −2 and −9
(*f*) −9 and −14

1.8 **[M]** Repeat Problem 1.7 for the subtract operation, where the second number of each pair is to be subtracted from the first number. State whether or not overflow occurs in each case.

1.9 **[E]** A memory byte location contains the pattern 01010011. What decimal value does this pattern represent when interpreted as a binary number? What does it represent as an ASCII code?

1.10 **[E]** A way to detect overflow when adding two 2's-complement numbers is given at the end of Section 1.4.1. State how to detect overflow when subtracting two such numbers.

REFERENCES

1. J. P. Hayes, *Computer Architecture and Organization*, 3rd Ed., McGraw-Hill, New York, 1998.

2

INSTRUCTION SET ARCHITECTURE

CHAPTER OBJECTIVES

In this chapter you will learn about:

- Machine instructions and program execution
- Addressing methods for accessing register and memory operands
- Assembly language for representing machine instructions, data, and programs
- Stacks and subroutines

This chapter considers the way programs are executed in a computer from the machine instruction set viewpoint. Chapter 1 introduced the general concept that both program instructions and data operands are stored in the memory. In this chapter, we discuss how instructions are composed and study the ways in which sequences of instructions are brought from the memory into the processor and executed to perform a given task. The addressing methods that are commonly used for accessing operands in memory locations and processor registers are also presented.

The emphasis here is on basic concepts. We use a generic style to describe machine instructions and operand addressing methods that are typical of those found in commercial processors. A sufficient number of instructions and addressing methods are introduced to enable us to present complete, realistic programs for simple tasks. These generic programs are specified at the assembly-language level, where machine instructions and operand addressing information are represented by symbolic names. A complete instruction set, including operand addressing methods, is often referred to as the *instruction set architecture* (ISA) of a processor. For the discussion of basic concepts in this chapter, it is not necessary to define a complete instruction set, and we will not attempt to do so. Instead, we will present enough examples to illustrate the capabilities of a typical instruction set.

The concepts introduced in this chapter and in Chapter 3, which deals with input/output techniques, are essential for understanding the functionality of computers. Our choice of the generic style of presentation makes the material easy to read and understand. Also, this style allows a general discussion that is not constrained by the characteristics of a particular processor.

Since it is interesting and important to see how the concepts discussed are implemented in a real computer, we supplement our presentation in Chapters 2 and 3 with four examples of popular commercial processors. These processors are presented in Appendices B to E. Appendix B deals with the Nios II processor from Altera Corporation. Appendix C presents the ColdFire processor from Freescale Semiconductor, Inc. Appendix D discusses the ARM processor from ARM Ltd. Appendix E presents the basic architecture of processors made by Intel Corporation. The generic programs in Chapters 2 and 3 are presented in terms of the specific instruction sets in each of the appendices.

The reader can choose only one processor and study the material in the corresponding appendix to get an appreciation for commercial ISA design. However, knowledge of the material in these appendices is not essential for understanding the material in the main body of the book.

The vast majority of programs are written in high-level languages such as C, C++, or Java. To execute a high-level language program on a processor, the program must be translated into the machine language for that processor, which is done by a compiler program. Assembly language is a readable symbolic representation of machine language. In this book we make extensive use of assembly language, because this is the best way to describe how computers work.

We will begin the discussion in this chapter by considering how instructions and data are stored in the memory and how they are accessed for processing.

2.1   MEMORY LOCATIONS AND ADDRESSES

We will first consider how the memory of a computer is organized. The memory consists of many millions of storage *cells*, each of which can store a *bit* of information having the value 0 or 1. Because a single bit represents a very small amount of information, bits are seldom handled individually. The usual approach is to deal with them in groups of fixed size. For this purpose, the memory is organized so that a group of *n* bits can be stored or retrieved in a single, basic operation. Each group of *n* bits is referred to as a *word* of information, and *n* is called the *word length*. The memory of a computer can be schematically represented as a collection of words, as shown in Figure 2.1.

Modern computers have word lengths that typically range from 16 to 64 bits. If the word length of a computer is 32 bits, a single word can store a 32-bit signed number or four ASCII-encoded characters, each occupying 8 bits, as shown in Figure 2.2. A unit of 8 bits is called a *byte*. Machine instructions may require one or more words for their representation. We will discuss how machine instructions are encoded into memory words in a later section, after we have described instructions at the assembly-language level.

Accessing the memory to store or retrieve a single item of information, either a word or a byte, requires distinct names or *addresses* for each location. It is customary to use numbers from 0 to $2^k - 1$, for some suitable value of *k*, as the addresses of successive locations in the memory. Thus, the memory can have up to 2^k addressable locations. The 2^k addresses constitute the *address space* of the computer. For example, a 24-bit address generates an address space of 2^{24} (16,777,216) locations. This number is usually written as 16M (16 mega), where 1M is the number 2^{20} (1,048,576). A 32-bit address creates an address space of 2^{32} or 4G (4 giga) locations, where 1G is 2^{30}. Other notational conventions

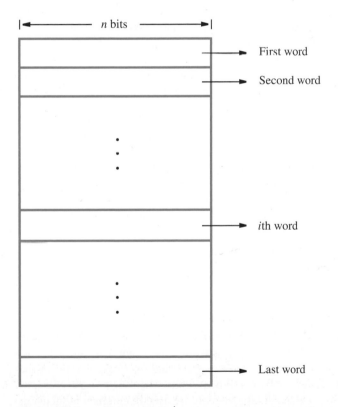

Figure 2.1   Memory words.

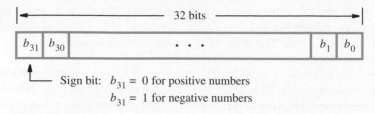

Sign bit: $b_{31} = 0$ for positive numbers
$b_{31} = 1$ for negative numbers

(a) A signed integer

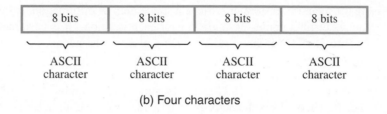

(b) Four characters

Figure 2.2   Examples of encoded information in a 32-bit word.

that are commonly used are K (kilo) for the number 2^{10} (1,024), and T (tera) for the number 2^{40}.

2.1.1   BYTE ADDRESSABILITY

We now have three basic information quantities to deal with: bit, byte, and word. A byte is always 8 bits, but the word length typically ranges from 16 to 64 bits. It is impractical to assign distinct addresses to individual bit locations in the memory. The most practical assignment is to have successive addresses refer to successive byte locations in the memory. This is the assignment used in most modern computers. The term *byte-addressable memory* is used for this assignment. Byte locations have addresses 0, 1, 2, ... Thus, if the word length of the machine is 32 bits, successive words are located at addresses 0, 4, 8, . . . , with each word consisting of four bytes.

2.1.2   BIG-ENDIAN AND LITTLE-ENDIAN ASSIGNMENTS

There are two ways that byte addresses can be assigned across words, as shown in Figure 2.3. The name *big-endian* is used when lower byte addresses are used for the more significant bytes (the leftmost bytes) of the word. The name *little-endian* is used for the opposite ordering, where the lower byte addresses are used for the less significant bytes (the rightmost bytes) of the word. The words "more significant" and "less significant" are used in relation to the weights (powers of 2) assigned to bits when the word represents a number. Both little-endian and big-endian assignments are used in commercial machines. In both cases, byte addresses 0, 4, 8, . . . , are taken as the addresses of successive words in the memory

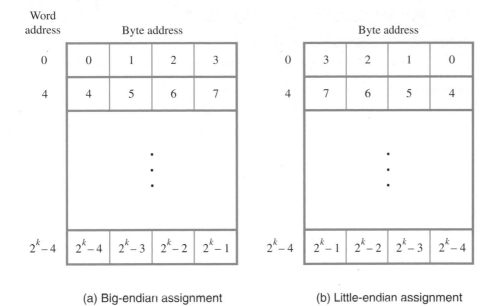

(a) Big-endian assignment   (b) Little-endian assignment

Figure 2.3   Byte and word addressing.

of a computer with a 32-bit word length. These are the addresses used when accessing the memory to store or retrieve a word.

In addition to specifying the address ordering of bytes within a word, it is also necessary to specify the labeling of bits within a byte or a word. The most common convention, and the one we will use in this book, is shown in Figure 2.2a. It is the most natural ordering for the encoding of numerical data. The same ordering is also used for labeling bits within a byte, that is, $b_7, b_6, \ldots, b_0$, from left to right.

2.1.3 WORD ALIGNMENT

In the case of a 32-bit word length, natural word boundaries occur at addresses 0, 4, 8, ..., as shown in Figure 2.3. We say that the word locations have *aligned* addresses if they begin at a byte address that is a multiple of the number of bytes in a word. For practical reasons associated with manipulating binary-coded addresses, the number of bytes in a word is a power of 2. Hence, if the word length is 16 (2 bytes), aligned words begin at byte addresses 0, 2, 4, ..., and for a word length of 64 (2^3 bytes), aligned words begin at byte addresses 0, 8, 16, ...

There is no fundamental reason why words cannot begin at an arbitrary byte address. In that case, words are said to have *unaligned* addresses. But, the most common case is to use aligned addresses, which makes accessing of memory operands more efficient, as we will see in Chapter 8.

2.1.4 ACCESSING NUMBERS AND CHARACTERS

A number usually occupies one word, and can be accessed in the memory by specifying its word address. Similarly, individual characters can be accessed by their byte address.

For programming convenience it is useful to have different ways of specifying addresses in program instructions. We will deal with this issue in Section 2.4.

2.2   MEMORY OPERATIONS

Both program instructions and data operands are stored in the memory. To execute an instruction, the processor control circuits must cause the word (or words) containing the instruction to be transferred from the memory to the processor. Operands and results must also be moved between the memory and the processor. Thus, two basic operations involving the memory are needed, namely, *Read* and *Write*.

The Read operation transfers a copy of the contents of a specific memory location to the processor. The memory contents remain unchanged. To start a Read operation, the processor sends the address of the desired location to the memory and requests that its contents be read. The memory reads the data stored at that address and sends them to the processor.

The Write operation transfers an item of information from the processor to a specific memory location, overwriting the former contents of that location. To initiate a Write operation, the processor sends the address of the desired location to the memory, together with the data to be written into that location. The memory then uses the address and data to perform the write.

The details of the hardware implementation of these operations are treated in Chapters 5 and 6. In this chapter, we consider all operations from the viewpoint of the ISA, so we concentrate on the logical handling of instructions and operands.

2.3   INSTRUCTIONS AND INSTRUCTION SEQUENCING

The tasks carried out by a computer program consist of a sequence of small steps, such as adding two numbers, testing for a particular condition, reading a character from the keyboard, or sending a character to be displayed on a display screen. A computer must have instructions capable of performing four types of operations:

- Data transfers between the memory and the processor registers
- Arithmetic and logic operations on data
- Program sequencing and control
- I/O transfers

We begin by discussing instructions for the first two types of operations. To facilitate the discussion, we first need some notation.

2.3.1   REGISTER TRANSFER NOTATION

We need to describe the transfer of information from one location in a computer to another. Possible locations that may be involved in such transfers are memory locations, processor registers, or registers in the I/O subsystem. Most of the time, we identify such locations symbolically with convenient names. For example, names that represent the addresses of memory locations may be LOC, PLACE, A, or VAR2. Predefined names for the processor registers may be R0 or R5. Registers in the I/O subsystem may be identified by names such as DATAIN or OUTSTATUS. To describe the transfer of information, the contents of any location are denoted by placing square brackets around its name. Thus, the expression

$$R2 \leftarrow [LOC]$$

means that the contents of memory location LOC are transferred into processor register R2.

As another example, consider the operation that adds the contents of registers R2 and R3, and places their sum into register R4. This action is indicated as

$$R4 \leftarrow [R2] + [R3]$$

This type of notation is known as *Register Transfer Notation* (RTN). Note that the right-hand side of an RTN expression always denotes a value, and the left-hand side is the name of a location where the value is to be placed, overwriting the old contents of that location.

In computer jargon, the words "transfer" and "move" are commonly used to mean "copy." Transferring data from a *source* location A to a *destination* location B means that the contents of location A are read and then written into location B. In this operation, only the contents of the destination will change. The contents of the source will stay the same.

2.3.2   ASSEMBLY-LANGUAGE NOTATION

We need another type of notation to represent machine instructions and programs. For this, we use *assembly language*. For example, a generic instruction that causes the transfer described above, from memory location LOC to processor register R2, is specified by the statement

$$\text{Load} \quad R2, LOC$$

The contents of LOC are unchanged by the execution of this instruction, but the old contents of register R2 are overwritten. The name Load is appropriate for this instruction, because the contents read from a memory location are *loaded* into a processor register.

The second example of adding two numbers contained in processor registers R2 and R3 and placing their sum in R4 can be specified by the assembly-language statement

$$\text{Add} \quad R4, R2, R3$$

In this case, registers R2 and R3 hold the source operands, while R4 is the destination.

An *instruction* specifies an operation to be performed and the operands involved. In the above examples, we used the English words Load and Add to denote the required operations. In the assembly-language instructions of actual (commercial) processors, such operations are defined by using *mnemonics*, which are typically abbreviations of the words describing the operations. For example, the operation Load may be written as LD, while the operation Store, which transfers a word from a processor register to the memory, may be written as STR or ST. Assembly languages for different processors often use different mnemonics for a given operation. To avoid the need for details of a particular assembly language at this early stage, we will continue the presentation in this chapter by using English words rather than processor-specific mnemonics.

2.3.3   RISC AND CISC INSTRUCTION SETS

One of the most important characteristics that distinguish different computers is the nature of their instructions. There are two fundamentally different approaches in the design of instruction sets for modern computers. One popular approach is based on the premise that higher performance can be achieved if each instruction occupies exactly one word in memory, and all operands needed to execute a given arithmetic or logic operation specified by an instruction are already in processor registers. This approach is conducive to an implementation of the processing unit in which the various operations needed to process a sequence of instructions are performed in "pipelined" fashion to overlap activity and reduce total execution time of a program, as we will discuss in Chapter 6. The restriction that each instruction must fit into a single word reduces the complexity and the number of different types of instructions that may be included in the instruction set of a computer. Such computers are called *Reduced Instruction Set Computers* (RISC).

An alternative to the RISC approach is to make use of more complex instructions which may span more than one word of memory, and which may specify more complicated operations. This approach was prevalent prior to the introduction of the RISC approach in the 1970s. Although the use of complex instructions was not originally identified by any particular label, computers based on this idea have been subsequently called *Complex Instruction Set Computers* (CISC).

We will start our presentation by concentrating on RISC-style instruction sets because they are simpler and therefore easier to understand. Later we will deal with CISC-style instruction sets and explain the key differences between the two approaches.

2.3.4   INTRODUCTION TO RISC INSTRUCTION SETS

Two key characteristics of RISC instruction sets are:

- Each instruction fits in a single word.
- A *load/store architecture* is used, in which
    - Memory operands are accessed only using Load and Store instructions.
    - All operands involved in an arithmetic or logic operation must either be in processor registers, or one of the operands may be given explicitly within the instruction word.

At the start of execution of a program, all instructions and data used in the program are stored in the memory of a computer. Processor registers do not contain valid operands at that time. If operands are expected to be in processor registers before they can be used by an instruction, then it is necessary to first bring these operands into the registers. This task is done by Load instructions which copy the contents of a memory location into a processor register. Load instructions are of the form

Load   destination, source

or more specifically

Load   processor_register, memory_location

The memory location can be specified in several ways. The term *addressing modes* is used to refer to the different ways in which this may be accomplished, as we will discuss in Section 2.4.

Let us now consider a typical arithmetic operation. The operation of adding two numbers is a fundamental capability in any computer. The statement

$$C = A + B$$

in a high-level language program instructs the computer to add the current values of the two variables called A and B, and to assign the sum to a third variable, C. When the program containing this statement is compiled, the three variables, A, B, and C, are assigned to distinct locations in the memory. For simplicity, we will refer to the addresses of these locations as A, B, and C, respectively. The contents of these locations represent the values of the three variables. Hence, the above high-level language statement requires the action

$$C \leftarrow [A] + [B]$$

to take place in the computer. To carry out this action, the contents of memory locations A and B are fetched from the memory and transferred into the processor where their sum is computed. This result is then sent back to the memory and stored in location C.

The required action can be accomplished by a sequence of simple machine instructions. We choose to use registers R2, R3, and R4 to perform the task with four instructions:

Load	R2, A
Load	R3, B
Add	R4, R2, R3
Store	R4, C

We say that Add is a *three-operand*, or a *three-address*, instruction of the form

Add   destination, source1, source2

The Store instruction is of the form

Store   source, destination

where the source is a processor register and the destination is a memory location. Observe that in the Store instruction the source and destination are specified in the reverse order from the Load instruction; this is a commonly used convention.

Note that we can accomplish the desired addition by using only two registers, R2 and R3, if one of the source registers is also used as the destination for the result. In this case the addition would be performed as

Add   R3, R2, R3

and the last instruction would become

Store   R3, C

2.3.5 INSTRUCTION EXECUTION AND STRAIGHT-LINE SEQUENCING

In the preceding subsection, we used the task C = A + B, implemented as C ← [A] + [B], as an example. Figure 2.4 shows a possible program segment for this task as it appears in the memory of a computer. We assume that the word length is 32 bits and the memory is byte-addressable. The four instructions of the program are in successive word locations, starting at location i. Since each instruction is 4 bytes long, the second, third, and fourth instructions are at addresses $i + 4$, $i + 8$, and $i + 12$. For simplicity, we assume that a desired

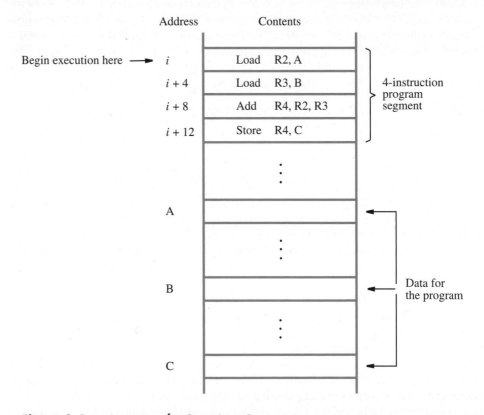

Figure 2.4   A program for C ← [A] + [B].

memory address can be directly specified in Load and Store instructions, although this is not possible if a full 32-bit address is involved. We will resolve this issue later in Section 2.4.

Let us consider how this program is executed. The processor contains a register called the *program counter* (PC), which holds the address of the next instruction to be executed. To begin executing a program, the address of its first instruction (i in our example) must be placed into the PC. Then, the processor control circuits use the information in the PC to fetch and execute instructions, one at a time, in the order of increasing addresses. This is called *straight-line sequencing*. During the execution of each instruction, the PC is incremented by 4 to point to the next instruction. Thus, after the Store instruction at location $i + 12$ is executed, the PC contains the value $i + 16$, which is the address of the first instruction of the next program segment.

Executing a given instruction is a two-phase procedure. In the first phase, called *instruction fetch*, the instruction is fetched from the memory location whose address is in the PC. This instruction is placed in the *instruction register* (IR) in the processor. At the start of the second phase, called *instruction execute*, the instruction in IR is examined to determine which operation is to be performed. The specified operation is then performed by the processor. This involves a small number of steps such as fetching operands from the memory or from processor registers, performing an arithmetic or logic operation, and storing the result in the destination location. At some point during this two-phase procedure, the contents of the PC are advanced to point to the next instruction. When the execute phase of an instruction is completed, the PC contains the address of the next instruction, and a new instruction fetch phase can begin.

2.3.6   BRANCHING

Consider the task of adding a list of n numbers. The program outlined in Figure 2.5 is a generalization of the program in Figure 2.4. The addresses of the memory locations containing the n numbers are symbolically given as NUM1, NUM2, ..., NUMn, and separate Load and Add instructions are used to add each number to the contents of register R2. After all the numbers have been added, the result is placed in memory location SUM.

Instead of using a long list of Load and Add instructions, as in Figure 2.5, it is possible to implement a program loop in which the instructions read the next number in the list and add it to the current sum. To add all numbers, the loop has to be executed as many times as there are numbers in the list. Figure 2.6 shows the structure of the desired program. The body of the loop is a straight-line sequence of instructions executed repeatedly. It starts at location LOOP and ends at the instruction Branch_if_[R2]>0. During each pass through this loop, the address of the next list entry is determined, and that entry is loaded into R5 and added to R3. The address of an operand can be specified in various ways, as will be described in Section 2.4. For now, we concentrate on how to create and control a program loop.

Assume that the number of entries in the list, n, is stored in memory location N, as shown. Register R2 is used as a counter to determine the number of times the loop is executed. Hence, the contents of location N are loaded into register R2 at the beginning of the program. Then, within the body of the loop, the instruction

Subtract   R2, R2, #1

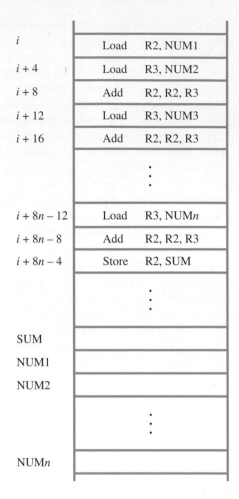

i	Load	R2, NUM1
$i + 4$	Load	R3, NUM2
$i + 8$	Add	R2, R2, R3
$i + 12$	Load	R3, NUM3
$i + 16$	Add	R2, R2, R3
	⋮	
$i + 8n - 12$	Load	R3, NUMn
$i + 8n - 8$	Add	R2, R2, R3
$i + 8n - 4$	Store	R2, SUM
	⋮	
SUM		
NUM1		
NUM2		
	⋮	
NUMn		

Figure 2.5   A program for adding n numbers.

reduces the contents of R2 by 1 each time through the loop. (We will explain the significance of the number sign '#' in Section 2.4.1.) Execution of the loop is repeated as long as the contents of R2 are greater than zero.

We now introduce *branch* instructions. This type of instruction loads a new address into the program counter. As a result, the processor fetches and executes the instruction at this new address, called the *branch target*, instead of the instruction at the location that follows the branch instruction in sequential address order. A *conditional branch* instruction causes a branch only if a specified condition is satisfied. If the condition is not satisfied, the PC is incremented in the normal way, and the next instruction in sequential address order is fetched and executed.

In the program in Figure 2.6, the instruction

Branch_if_[R2]>0   LOOP

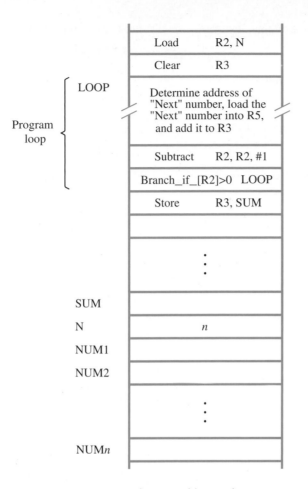

Figure 2.6   Using a loop to add *n* numbers.

is a conditional branch instruction that causes a branch to location LOOP if the contents of register R2 are greater than zero. This means that the loop is repeated as long as there are entries in the list that are yet to be added to R3. At the end of the *n*th pass through the loop, the Subtract instruction produces a value of zero in R2, and, hence, branching does not occur. Instead, the Store instruction is fetched and executed. It moves the final result from R3 into memory location SUM.

The capability to test conditions and subsequently choose one of a set of alternative ways to continue computation has many more applications than just loop control. Such a capability is found in the instruction sets of all computers and is fundamental to the programming of most nontrivial tasks.

One way of implementing conditional branch instructions is to compare the contents of two registers and then branch to the target instruction if the comparison meets the specified requirement. For example, the instruction that implements the action

Branch_if_[R4]>[R5]   LOOP

may be written in generic assembly language as

Branch_greater_than   R4, R5, LOOP

or using an actual mnemonic as

BGT   R4, R5, LOOP

It compares the contents of registers R4 and R5, without changing the contents of either register. Then, it causes a branch to LOOP if the contents of R4 are greater than the contents of R5.

A different way of implementing branch instructions uses the concept of condition codes, which we will discuss in Section 2.10.2.

2.3.7   GENERATING MEMORY ADDRESSES

Let us return to Figure 2.6. The purpose of the instruction block starting at LOOP is to add successive numbers from the list during each pass through the loop. Hence, the Load instruction in that block must refer to a different address during each pass. How are the addresses specified? The memory operand address cannot be given directly in a single Load instruction in the loop. Otherwise, it would need to be modified on each pass through the loop. As one possibility, suppose that a processor register, Ri, is used to hold the memory address of an operand. If it is initially loaded with the address NUM1 before the loop is entered and is then incremented by 4 on each pass through the loop, it can provide the needed capability.

This situation, and many others like it, give rise to the need for flexible ways to specify the address of an operand. The instruction set of a computer typically provides a number of such methods, called *addressing modes*. While the details differ from one computer to another, the underlying concepts are the same. We will discuss these in the next section.

2.4   ADDRESSING MODES

We have now seen some simple examples of assembly-language programs. In general, a program operates on data that reside in the computer's memory. These data can be organized in a variety of ways that reflect the nature of the information and how it is used. Programmers use *data structures* such as lists and arrays for organizing the data used in computations.

Programs are normally written in a high-level language, which enables the programmer to conveniently describe the operations to be performed on various data structures. When translating a high-level language program into assembly language, the compiler generates appropriate sequences of low-level instructions that implement the desired operations. The

Table 2.1   RISC-type addressing modes.

Name	Assembler syntax	Addressing function
Immediate	#Value	Operand = Value
Register	Ri	EA = Ri
Absolute	LOC	EA = LOC
Register indirect	(Ri)	EA = [Ri]
Index	X(Ri)	EA = [Ri] + X
Base with index	(Ri,Rj)	EA = [Ri] + [Rj]

EA = effective address
Value = a signed number
X = index value

different ways for specifying the locations of instruction operands are known as *addressing modes*. In this section we present the basic addressing modes found in RISC-style processors. A summary is provided in Table 2.1, which also includes the assembler syntax we will use for each mode. The assembler syntax defines the way in which instructions and the addressing modes of their operands are specified; it is discussed in Section 2.5.

2.4.1   IMPLEMENTATION OF VARIABLES AND CONSTANTS

Variables are found in almost every computer program. In assembly language, a variable is represented by allocating a register or a memory location to hold its value. This value can be changed as needed using appropriate instructions.

The program in Figure 2.5 uses only two addressing modes to access variables. We access an operand by specifying the name of the register or the address of the memory location where the operand is located. The precise definitions of these two modes are:

Register mode—The operand is the contents of a processor register; the name of the register is given in the instruction.

Absolute mode—The operand is in a memory location; the address of this location is given explicitly in the instruction.

Since in a RISC-style processor an instruction must fit in a single word, the number of bits that can be used to give an absolute address is limited, typically to 16 bits if the word length is 32 bits. To generate a 32-bit address, the 16-bit value is usually extended to 32 bits by replicating bit b_{15} into bit positions b_{31-16} (as in sign extension). This means that an absolute address can be specified in this manner for only a limited range of the full address space. We will deal with the issue of specifying full 32-bit addresses in Section 2.9. To keep our examples simple, we will assume for now that all addresses of memory locations involved in a program can be specified in 16 bits.

The instruction

$$\text{Add}\quad \text{R4, R2, R3}$$

uses the Register mode for all three operands. Registers R2 and R3 hold the two source operands, while R4 is the destination.

The Absolute mode can represent global variables in a program. A declaration such as

$$\text{Integer}\quad \text{NUM1, NUM2, SUM;}$$

in a high-level language program will cause the compiler to allocate a memory location to each of the variables NUM1, NUM2, and SUM. Whenever they are referenced later in the program, the compiler can generate assembly-language instructions that use the Absolute mode to access these variables.

The Absolute mode is used in the instruction

$$\text{Load}\quad \text{R2, NUM1}$$

which loads the value in the memory location NUM1 into register R2.

Constants representing data or addresses are also found in almost every computer program. Such constants can be represented in assembly language using the Immediate addressing mode.

Immediate mode—The operand is given explicitly in the instruction.

For example, the instruction

$$\text{Add}\quad \text{R4, R6, 200}_{\text{immediate}}$$

adds the value 200 to the contents of register R6, and places the result into register R4. Using a subscript to denote the Immediate mode is not appropriate in assembly languages. A common convention is to use the number sign (#) in front of the value to indicate that this value is to be used as an immediate operand. Hence, we write the instruction above in the form

$$\text{Add}\quad \text{R4, R6, \#200}$$

In the addressing modes that follow, the instruction does not give the operand or its address explicitly. Instead, it provides information from which an *effective address* (EA) can be derived by the processor when the instruction is executed. The effective address is then used to access the operand.

2.4.2 INDIRECTION AND POINTERS

The program in Figure 2.6 requires a capability for modifying the address of the memory operand during each pass through the loop. A good way to provide this capability is to use a processor register to hold the address of the operand. The contents of the register are then changed (incremented) during each pass to provide the address of the next number in the list that has to be accessed. The register acts as a *pointer* to the list, and we say that an item

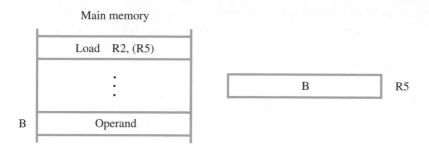

Figure 2.7 Register indirect addressing.

in the list is accessed *indirectly* by using the address in the register. The desired capability is provided by the indirect addressing mode.

> *Indirect mode*—The effective address of the operand is the contents of a register that is specified in the instruction.

We denote indirection by placing the name of the register given in the instruction in parentheses as illustrated in Figure 2.7 and Table 2.1.

To execute the Load instruction in Figure 2.7, the processor uses the value B, which is in register R5, as the effective address of the operand. It requests a Read operation to fetch the contents of location B in the memory. The value from the memory is the desired operand, which the processor loads into register R2. Indirect addressing through a memory location is also possible, but it is found only in CISC-style processors.

Indirection and the use of pointers are important and powerful concepts in programming. They permit the same code to be used to operate on different data. For example, register R5 in Figure 2.7 serves as a pointer for the Load instruction to load an operand from the memory into register R2. At one time, R5 may point to location B in memory. Later, the program may change the contents of R5 to point to a different location, in which case the same Load instruction will load the value from that location into R2. Thus, a program segment that includes this Load instruction is conveniently reused with only a change in the pointer value.

Let us now return to the program in Figure 2.6 for adding a list of numbers. Indirect addressing can be used to access successive numbers in the list, resulting in the program shown in Figure 2.8. Register R4 is used as a pointer to the numbers in the list, and the operands are accessed indirectly through R4. The initialization section of the program loads the counter value n from memory location N into R2. Then, it uses the Clear instruction to clear R3 to 0. The next instruction uses the Immediate addressing mode to place the address value NUM1, which is the address of the first number in the list, into R4. Observe that we cannot use the Load instruction to load the desired immediate value, because the Load instruction can operate only on memory source operands. Instead, we use the Move instruction

Move   R4, #NUM1

	Load	R2, N	Load the size of the list.
	Clear	R3	Initialize sum to 0.
	Move	R4, #NUM1	Get address of the first number.
LOOP:	Load	R5, (R4)	Get the next number.
	Add	R3, R3, R5	Add this number to sum.
	Add	R4, R4, #4	Increment the pointer to the list.
	Subtract	R2, R2, #1	Decrement the counter.
	Branch_if_[R2]>0	LOOP	Branch back if not finished.
	Store	R3, SUM	Store the final sum.

Figure 2.8   Use of indirect addressing in the program of Figure 2.6.

In many RISC-type processors, one general-purpose register is dedicated to holding a constant value zero. Usually, this is register R0. Its contents cannot be changed by a program instruction. We will assume that R0 is used in this manner in our discussion of RISC-style processors. Then, the above Move instruction can be implemented as

$$\text{Add} \quad \text{R4, R0, \#NUM1}$$

It is often the case that Move is provided as a *pseudoinstruction* for the convenience of programmers, but it is actually implemented using the Add instruction.

The first three instructions in the loop in Figure 2.8 implement the unspecified instruction block starting at LOOP in Figure 2.6. The first time through the loop, the instruction

$$\text{Load} \quad \text{R5, (R4)}$$

fetches the operand at location NUM1 and loads it into R5. The first Add instruction adds this number to the sum in register R3. The second Add instruction adds 4 to the contents of the pointer R4, so that it will contain the address value NUM2 when the Load instruction is executed in the second pass through the loop.

As another example of pointers, consider the C-language statement

$$A = {}^*B;$$

where B is a pointer variable and the '*' symbol is the operator for indirect accesses. This statement causes the contents of the memory location pointed to by B to be loaded into memory location A. The statement may be compiled into

Load	R2, B
Load	R3, (R2)
Store	R3, A

Indirect addressing through registers is used extensively. The program in Figure 2.8 shows the flexibility it provides.

2.4.3 INDEXING AND ARRAYS

The next addressing mode we discuss provides a different kind of flexibility for accessing operands. It is useful in dealing with lists and arrays.

Index mode—The effective address of the operand is generated by adding a constant value to the contents of a register.

For convenience, we will refer to the register used in this mode as the *index register*. Typically, this is just a general-purpose register. We indicate the Index mode symbolically as

$$X(Ri)$$

where X denotes a constant signed integer value contained in the instruction and Ri is the name of the register involved. The effective address of the operand is given by

$$EA = X + [Ri]$$

The contents of the register are not changed in the process of generating the effective address.

In an assembly-language program, whenever a constant such as the value X is needed, it may be given either as an explicit number or as a symbolic name representing a numerical value. The way in which a symbolic name is associated with a specific numerical value will be discussed in Section 2.5. When the instruction is translated into machine code, the constant X is given as a part of the instruction and is restricted to fewer bits than the word length of the computer. Since X is a signed integer, it must be sign-extended (see Section 1.4) to the register length before being added to the contents of the register.

Figure 2.9 illustrates two ways of using the Index mode. In Figure 2.9a, the index register, R5, contains the address of a memory location, and the value X defines an *offset* (also called a *displacement*) from this address to the location where the operand is found. An alternative use is illustrated in Figure 2.9b. Here, the constant X corresponds to a memory address, and the contents of the index register define the offset to the operand. In either case, the effective address is the sum of two values; one is given explicitly in the instruction, and the other is held in a register.

To see the usefulness of indexed addressing, consider a simple example involving a list of test scores for students taking a given course. Assume that the list of scores, beginning at location LIST, is structured as shown in Figure 2.10. A four word memory block comprises a record that stores the relevant information for each student. Each record consists of the student's identification number (ID), followed by the scores the student earned on three tests. There are n students in the class, and the value n is stored in location N immediately in front of the list. The addresses given in the figure for the student IDs and test scores assume that the memory is byte addressable and that the word length is 32 bits.

We should note that the list in Figure 2.10 represents a two-dimensional array having n rows and four columns. Each row contains the entries for one student, and the columns give the IDs and test scores.

Suppose that we wish to compute the sum of all scores obtained on each of the tests and store these three sums in memory locations SUM1, SUM2, and SUM3. A possible

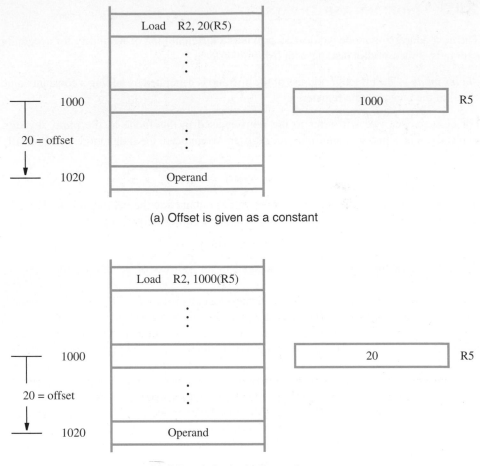

(a) Offset is given as a constant

(b) Offset is in the index register

Figure 2.9   Indexed addressing.

program for this task is given in Figure 2.11. In the body of the loop, the program uses the Index addressing mode in the manner depicted in Figure 2.9*a* to access each of the three scores in a student's record. Register R2 is used as the index register. Before the loop is entered, R2 is set to point to the ID location of the first student record which is the address LIST.

On the first pass through the loop, test scores of the first student are added to the running sums held in registers R3, R4, and R5, which are initially cleared to 0. These scores are accessed using the Index addressing modes 4(R2), 8(R2), and 12(R2). The index register R2 is then incremented by 16 to point to the ID location of the second student. Register R6, initialized to contain the value *n*, is decremented by 1 at the end of each pass through the loop. When the contents of R6 reach 0, all student records have been accessed, and

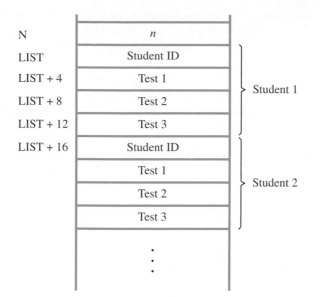

N	n
LIST	Student ID
LIST + 4	Test 1
LIST + 8	Test 2
LIST + 12	Test 3
LIST + 16	Student ID
	Test 1
	Test 2
	Test 3

Student 1

Student 2

Figure 2.10   A list of students' marks.

	Move	R2, #LIST	Get the address LIST.
	Clear	R3	
	Clear	R4	
	Clear	R5	
	Load	R6, N	Load the value n.
LOOP:	Load	R7, 4(R2)	Add the mark for next student's
	Add	R3, R3, R7	Test 1 to the partial sum.
	Load	R7, 8(R2)	Add the mark for that student's
	Add	R4, R4, R7	Test 2 to the partial sum.
	Load	R7, 12(R2)	Add the mark for that student's
	Add	R5, R5, R7	Test 3 to the partial sum.
	Add	R2, R2, #16	Increment the pointer.
	Subtract	R6, R6, #1	Decrement the counter.
	Branch_if_[R6]>0	LOOP	Branch back if not finished.
	Store	R3, SUM1	Store the total for Test 1.
	Store	R4, SUM2	Store the total for Test 2.
	Store	R5, SUM3	Store the total for Test 3.

Figure 2.11   Indexed addressing used in accessing test scores in the list in Figure 2.10.

the loop terminates. Until then, the conditional branch instruction transfers control back to the start of the loop to process the next record. The last three instructions transfer the accumulated sums from registers R3, R4, and R5, into memory locations SUM1, SUM2, and SUM3, respectively.

It should be emphasized that the contents of the index register, R2, are not changed when it is used in the Index addressing mode to access the scores. The contents of R2 are changed only by the last Add instruction in the loop, to move from one student record to the next.

In general, the Index mode facilitates access to an operand whose location is defined relative to a reference point within the data structure in which the operand appears. In the example just given, the ID locations of successive student records are the reference points, and the test scores are the operands accessed by the Index addressing mode.

We have introduced the most basic form of indexed addressing that uses a register Ri and a constant offset X. Several variations of this basic form provide for efficient access to memory operands in practical programming situations (although they may not be included in some processors). For example, a second register Rj may be used to contain the offset X, in which case we can write the Index mode as

$$(Ri,Rj)$$

The effective address is the sum of the contents of registers Ri and Rj. The second register is usually called the *base* register. This form of indexed addressing provides more flexibility in accessing operands, because both components of the effective address can be changed.

Yet another version of the Index mode uses two registers plus a constant, which can be denoted as

$$X(Ri,Rj)$$

In this case, the effective address is the sum of the constant X and the contents of registers Ri and Rj. This added flexibility is useful in accessing multiple components inside each item in a record, where the beginning of an item is specified by the (Ri,Rj) part of the addressing mode.

Finally, we should note that in the basic Index mode

$$X(Ri)$$

if the contents of the register are equal to zero, then the effective address is just equal to the sign-extended value of X. This has the same effect as the Absolute mode. If register R0 always contains the value zero, then the Absolute mode is implemented simply as

$$X(R0)$$

2.5 ASSEMBLY LANGUAGE

Machine instructions are represented by patterns of 0s and 1s. Such patterns are awkward to deal with when discussing or preparing programs. Therefore, we use symbolic names to represent the patterns. So far, we have used normal words, such as Load, Store, Add, and

Branch, for the instruction operations to represent the corresponding binary code patterns. When writing programs for a specific computer, such words are normally replaced by acronyms called *mnemonics*, such as LD, ST, ADD, and BR. A shorthand notation is also useful when identifying registers, such as R3 for register 3. Finally, symbols such as LOC may be defined as needed to represent particular memory locations. A complete set of such symbolic names and rules for their use constitutes a programming language, generally referred to as an *assembly language*. The set of rules for using the mnemonics and for specification of complete instructions and programs is called the *syntax* of the language.

Programs written in an assembly language can be automatically translated into a sequence of machine instructions by a program called an *assembler*. The assembler program is one of a collection of utility programs that are a part of the system software of a computer. The assembler, like any other program, is stored as a sequence of machine instructions in the memory of the computer. A user program is usually entered into the computer through a keyboard and stored either in the memory or on a magnetic disk. At this point, the user program is simply a set of lines of alphanumeric characters. When the assembler program is executed, it reads the user program, analyzes it, and then generates the desired machine-language program. The latter contains patterns of 0s and 1s specifying instructions that will be executed by the computer. The user program in its original alphanumeric text format is called a *source program*, and the assembled machine-language program is called an *object program*. We will discuss how the assembler program works in Section 2.5.2 and in Chapter 4. First, we present a few aspects of assembly language itself.

The assembly language for a given computer may or may not be case sensitive, that is, it may or may not distinguish between capital and lower-case letters. In this section, we use capital letters to denote all names and labels in our examples to improve the readability of the text. For example, we write a Store instruction as

ST   R2, SUM

The mnemonic ST represents the binary pattern, or *operation (OP) code*, for the operation performed by the instruction. The assembler translates this mnemonic into the binary OP code that the computer recognizes.

The OP-code mnemonic is followed by at least one blank space or tab character. Then the information that specifies the operands is given. In the Store instruction above, the source operand is in register R2. This information is followed by the specification of the destination operand, separated from the source operand by a comma. The destination operand is in the memory location that has its binary address represented by the name SUM.

Since there are several possible addressing modes for specifying operand locations, an assembly-language instruction must indicate which mode is being used. For example, a numerical value or a name used by itself, such as SUM in the preceding instruction, may be used to denote the Absolute mode. The number sign usually denotes an immediate operand. Thus, the instruction

ADD   R2, R3, #5

adds the number 5 to the contents of register R3 and puts the result into register R2. The number sign is not the only way to denote the Immediate addressing mode. In some assembly languages, the Immediate addressing mode is indicated in the OP-code mnemonic.

For example, the previous Add instruction may be written as

ADDI   R2, R3, 5

The suffix I in the mnemonic ADDI states that the second source operand is given in the Immediate addressing mode.

Indirect addressing is usually specified by putting parentheses around the name or symbol denoting the pointer to the operand. For example, if register R2 contains the address of a number in the memory, then this number can be loaded into register R3 using the instruction

LD   R3, (R2)

2.5.1 ASSEMBLER DIRECTIVES

In addition to providing a mechanism for representing instructions in a program, assembly language allows the programmer to specify other information needed to translate the source program into the object program. We have already mentioned that we need to assign numerical values to any names used in a program. Suppose that the name TWENTY is used to represent the value 20. This fact may be conveyed to the assembler program through an *equate* statement such as

TWENTY   EQU   20

This statement does not denote an instruction that will be executed when the object program is run; in fact, it will not even appear in the object program. It simply informs the assembler that the name TWENTY should be replaced by the value 20 wherever it appears in the program. Such statements, called *assembler directives* (or *commands*), are used by the assembler while it translates a source program into an object program.

To illustrate the use of assembly language further, let us reconsider the program in Figure 2.8. In order to run this program on a computer, it is necessary to write its source code in the required assembly language, specifying all of the information needed to generate the corresponding object program. Suppose that each instruction and each data item occupies one word of memory. Also assume that the memory is byte-addressable and that the word length is 32 bits. Suppose also that the object program is to be loaded in the main memory as shown in Figure 2.12. The figure shows the memory addresses where the machine instructions and the required data items are to be found after the program is loaded for execution. If the assembler is to produce an object program according to this arrangement, it has to know

• How to interpret the names

• Where to place the instructions in the memory

• Where to place the data operands in the memory

To provide this information, the source program may be written as shown in Figure 2.13. The program begins with the assembler directive, ORIGIN, which tells the assembler program where in the memory to place the instructions that follow. It specifies that the instructions

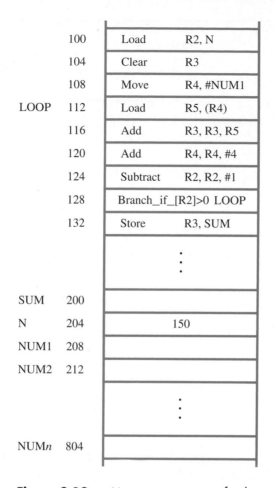

	100	Load	R2, N
	104	Clear	R3
	108	Move	R4, #NUM1
LOOP	112	Load	R5, (R4)
	116	Add	R3, R3, R5
	120	Add	R4, R4, #4
	124	Subtract	R2, R2, #1
	128	Branch_if_[R2]>0 LOOP	
	132	Store	R3, SUM
		⋮	
SUM	200		
N	204	150	
NUM1	208		
NUM2	212		
		⋮	
NUMn	804		

Figure 2.12   Memory arrangement for the program in Figure 2.8.

of the object program are to be loaded in the memory starting at address 100. It is followed by the source program instructions written with the appropriate mnemonics and syntax. Note that we use the statement

BGT   R2, R0, LOOP

to represent an instruction that performs the operation

Branch_if_[R2]>0   LOOP

The second ORIGIN directive tells the assembler program where in the memory to place the data block that follows. In this case, the location specified has the address 200. This is intended to be the location in which the final sum will be stored. A 4-byte space for the sum is reserved by means of the assembler directive RESERVE. The next word, at address 204, has to contain the value 150 which is the number of entries in the list.

	Memory address label	Operation	Addressing or data information
Assembler directive		ORIGIN	100
Statements that generate machine instructions		LD	R2, N
		CLR	R3
		MOV	R4, #NUM1
	LOOP:	LD	R5, (R4)
		ADD	R3, R3, R5
		ADD	R4, R4, #4
		SUB	R2, R2, #1
		BGT	R2, R0, LOOP
		ST	R3, SUM
		next instruction	
Assembler directives		ORIGIN	200
	SUM:	RESERVE	4
	N:	DATAWORD	150
	NUM1:	RESERVE	600
		END	

Figure 2.13   Assembly language representation for the program in Figure 2.12.

The DATAWORD directive is used to inform the assembler of this requirement. The next RESERVE directive declares that a memory block of 600 bytes is to be reserved for data. This directive does not cause any data to be loaded in these locations. Data may be loaded in the memory using an input procedure, as we will explain in Chapter 3. The last statement in the source program is the assembler directive END, which tells the assembler that this is the end of the source program text.

We previously described how the EQU directive can be used to associate a specific value, which may be an address, with a particular name. A different way of associating addresses with names or labels is illustrated in Figure 2.13. Any statement that results in instructions or data being placed in a memory location may be given a memory address label. The assembler automatically assigns the address of that location to the label. For example, in the data block that follows the second ORIGIN directive, we used the labels SUM, N, and NUM1. Because the first RESERVE statement after the ORIGIN directive is given the label SUM, the name SUM is assigned the value 200. Whenever SUM is encountered in the program, it will be replaced with this value. Using SUM as a label in this manner is equivalent to using the assembler directive

$$\text{SUM} \quad \text{EQU} \quad 200$$

Similarly, the labels N and NUM1 are assigned the values 204 and 208, respectively, because they represent the addresses of the two word locations immediately following the word location with address 200.

Most assembly languages require statements in a source program to be written in the form

$$\text{Label:} \quad \text{Operation} \quad \text{Operand(s)} \quad \text{Comment}$$

These four *fields* are separated by an appropriate delimiter, perhaps one or more blank or tab characters. The Label is an optional name associated with the memory address where the machine-language instruction produced from the statement will be loaded. Labels may also be associated with addresses of data items. In Figure 2.13 there are four labels: LOOP, SUM, N, and NUM1.

The Operation field contains an assembler directive or the OP-code mnemonic of the desired instruction. The Operand field contains addressing information for accessing the operands. The Comment field is ignored by the assembler program. It is used for documentation purposes to make the program easier to understand.

We have introduced only the very basic characteristics of assembly languages. These languages differ in detail and complexity from one computer to another.

2.5.2 ASSEMBLY AND EXECUTION OF PROGRAMS

A source program written in an assembly language must be assembled into a machine-language object program before it can be executed. This is done by the assembler program, which replaces all symbols denoting operations and addressing modes with the binary codes used in machine instructions, and replaces all names and labels with their actual values.

The assembler assigns addresses to instructions and data blocks, starting at the addresses given in the ORIGIN assembler directives. It also inserts constants that may be given in DATAWORD commands, and it reserves memory space as requested by RESERVE commands.

A key part of the assembly process is determining the values that replace the names. In some cases, where the value of a name is specified by an EQU directive, this is a straightforward task. In other cases, where a name is defined in the Label field of a given instruction, the value represented by the name is determined by the location of this instruction in the assembled object program. Hence, the assembler must keep track of addresses as it generates the machine code for successive instructions. For example, the names LOOP and SUM in the program of Figure 2.13 will be assigned the values 112 and 200, respectively.

In some cases, the assembler does not directly replace a name representing an address with the actual value of this address. For example, in a branch instruction, the name that specifies the location to which a branch is to be made (the branch target) is not replaced by the actual address. A branch instruction is usually implemented in machine code by specifying the branch target as the distance (in bytes) from the present address in the Program Counter to the target instruction. The assembler computes this *branch offset*, which can be positive or negative, and puts it into the machine instruction. We will show how branch instructions may be implemented in Section 2.13.

The assembler stores the object program on the secondary storage device available in the computer, usually a magnetic disk. The object program must be loaded into the main memory before it is executed. For this to happen, another utility program called a *loader* must already be in the memory. Executing the loader performs a sequence of input operations needed to transfer the machine-language program from the disk into a specified place in the memory. The loader must know the length of the program and the address in the memory where it will be stored. The assembler usually places this information in a header preceding the object code. Having loaded the object code, the loader starts execution of the object program by branching to the first instruction to be executed, which may be identified by an address label such as START. The assembler places that address in the header of the object code for the loader to use at execution time.

When the object program begins executing, it proceeds to completion unless there are logical errors in the program. The user must be able to find errors easily. The assembler can only detect and report syntax errors. To help the user find other programming errors, the system software usually includes a *debugger* program. This program enables the user to stop execution of the object program at some points of interest and to examine the contents of various processor registers and memory locations.

In this section, we introduced some important issues in assembly and execution of programs. Chapter 4 provides a more detailed discussion of these issues.

2.5.3 NUMBER NOTATION

When dealing with numerical values, it is often convenient to use the familiar decimal notation. Of course, these values are stored in the computer as binary numbers. In some situations, it is more convenient to specify the binary patterns directly. Most assemblers allow numerical values to be specified in different ways, using conventions that are defined by the assembly-language syntax. Consider, for example, the number 93, which is represented by the 8-bit binary number 01011101. If this value is to be used as an immediate operand, it can be given as a decimal number, as in the instruction

ADDI   R2, R3, 93

or as a binary number identified by an assembler-specific prefix symbol such as a percent sign, as in

ADDI   R2, R3, %01011101

Binary numbers can be written more compactly as *hexadecimal*, or *hex*, numbers, in which four bits are represented by a single hex digit. The first ten patterns 0000, 0001, . . . , 1001, referred to as *binary-coded decimal* (BCD), are represented by the digits 0, 1, . . . , 9. The remaining six 4-bit patterns, 1010, 1011, . . . , 1111, are represented by the letters A, B, . . . , F. In hexadecimal representation, the decimal value 93 becomes 5D. In assembly language, a hex representation is often identified by the prefix 0x (as in the C language) or by a dollar sign prefix. Thus, we would write

$$\text{ADDI} \quad \text{R2, R3, 0x5D}$$

2.6 STACKS

Data operated on by a program can be organized in a variety of ways. We have already encountered data structured as lists. Now, we consider an important data structure known as a stack. A *stack* is a list of data elements, usually words, with the accessing restriction that elements can be added or removed at one end of the list only. This end is called the top of the stack, and the other end is called the bottom. The structure is sometimes referred to as a *pushdown* stack. Imagine a pile of trays in a cafeteria; customers pick up new trays from the top of the pile, and clean trays are added to the pile by placing them onto the top of the pile. Another descriptive phrase, *last-in–first-out* (LIFO) stack, is also used to describe this type of storage mechanism; the last data item placed on the stack is the first one removed when retrieval begins. The terms *push* and *pop* are used to describe placing a new item on the stack and removing the top item from the stack, respectively.

In modern computers, a stack is implemented by using a portion of the main memory for this purpose. One processor register, called the *stack pointer* (SP), is used to point to a particular stack structure called the *processor stack*, whose use will be explained shortly.

Data can be stored in a stack with successive elements occupying successive memory locations. Assume that the first element is placed in location BOTTOM, and when new elements are pushed onto the stack, they are placed in successively lower address locations. We use a stack that grows in the direction of decreasing memory addresses in our discussion, because this is a common practice.

Figure 2.14 shows an example of a stack of word data items. The stack contains numerical values, with 43 at the bottom and -28 at the top. The stack pointer, SP, is used to keep track of the address of the element of the stack that is at the top at any given time. If we assume a byte-addressable memory with a 32-bit word length, the push operation can be implemented as

$$\begin{array}{ll} \text{Subtract} & \text{SP, SP, \#4} \\ \text{Store} & \text{R}j, \text{(SP)} \end{array}$$

where the Subtract instruction subtracts 4 from the contents of SP and places the result in SP. Assuming that the new item to be pushed on the stack is in processor register Rj, the Store instruction will place this value on the stack. These two instructions copy the word from Rj onto the top of the stack, decrementing the stack pointer by 4 before the store (push) operation. The pop operation can be implemented as

$$\begin{array}{ll} \text{Load} & \text{R}j, \text{(SP)} \\ \text{Add} & \text{SP, SP, \#4} \end{array}$$

These two instructions load (pop) the top value from the stack into register Rj and then increment the stack pointer by 4 so that it points to the new top element. Figure 2.15 shows the effect of each of these operations on the stack in Figure 2.14.

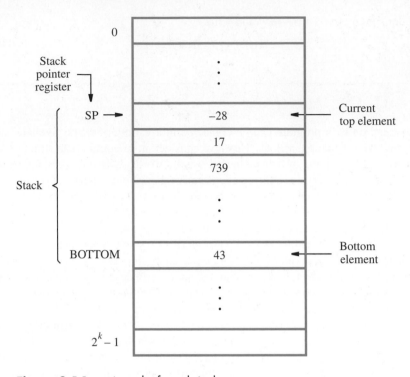

Figure 2.14   A stack of words in the memory.

2.7 SUBROUTINES

In a given program, it is often necessary to perform a particular task many times on different data values. It is prudent to implement this task as a block of instructions that is executed each time the task has to be performed. Such a block of instructions is usually called a *subroutine*. For example, a subroutine may evaluate a mathematical function, or it may sort a list of values into increasing or decreasing order.

It is possible to reproduce the block of instructions that constitute a subroutine at every place where it is needed in the program. However, to save space, only one copy of this block is placed in the memory, and any program that requires the use of the subroutine simply branches to its starting location. When a program branches to a subroutine we say that it is *calling* the subroutine. The instruction that performs this branch operation is named a Call instruction.

After a subroutine has been executed, the calling program must resume execution, continuing immediately after the instruction that called the subroutine. The subroutine is said to *return* to the program that called it, and it does so by executing a Return instruction. Since the subroutine may be called from different places in a calling program, provision must be made for returning to the appropriate location. The location where the calling

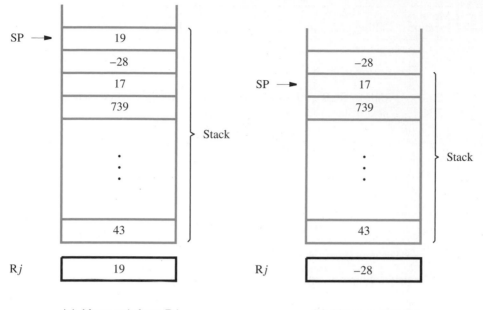

Figure 2.15   Effect of stack operations on the stack in Figure 2.14.

program resumes execution is the location pointed to by the updated program counter (PC) while the Call instruction is being executed. Hence, the contents of the PC must be saved by the Call instruction to enable correct return to the calling program.

The way in which a computer makes it possible to call and return from subroutines is referred to as its *subroutine linkage* method. The simplest subroutine linkage method is to save the return address in a specific location, which may be a register dedicated to this function. Such a register is called the *link register*. When the subroutine completes its task, the Return instruction returns to the calling program by branching indirectly through the link register.

The Call instruction is just a special branch instruction that performs the following operations:

- Store the contents of the PC in the link register
- Branch to the target address specified by the Call instruction

The Return instruction is a special branch instruction that performs the operation

- Branch to the address contained in the link register

Figure 2.16 illustrates how the PC and the link register are affected by the Call and Return instructions.

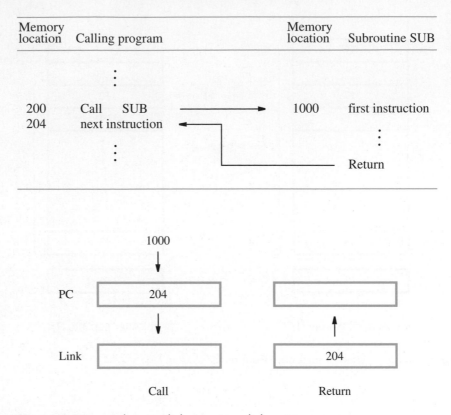

Memory location	Calling program		Memory location	Subroutine SUB
	⋮			
200	Call SUB	⟶	1000	first instruction
204	next instruction	←		⋮
	⋮			Return

Figure 2.16   Subroutine linkage using a link register.

2.7.1 SUBROUTINE NESTING AND THE PROCESSOR STACK

A common programming practice, called *subroutine nesting*, is to have one subroutine call another. In this case, the return address of the second call is also stored in the link register, overwriting its previous contents. Hence, it is essential to save the contents of the link register in some other location before calling another subroutine. Otherwise, the return address of the first subroutine will be lost.

Subroutine nesting can be carried out to any depth. Eventually, the last subroutine called completes its computations and returns to the subroutine that called it. The return address needed for this first return is the last one generated in the nested call sequence. That is, return addresses are generated and used in a last-in–first-out order. This suggests that the return addresses associated with subroutine calls should be pushed onto the processor stack.

Correct sequencing of nested calls is achieved if a given subroutine SUB1 saves the return address currently in the link register on the stack, accessed through the stack pointer, SP, before it calls another subroutine SUB2. Then, prior to executing its own Return instruction, the subroutine SUB1 has to pop the saved return address from the stack and load it into the link register.

2.7.2 Parameter Passing

When calling a subroutine, a program must provide to the subroutine the parameters, that is, the operands or their addresses, to be used in the computation. Later, the subroutine returns other parameters, which are the results of the computation. This exchange of information between a calling program and a subroutine is referred to as *parameter passing*. Parameter passing may be accomplished in several ways. The parameters may be placed in registers or in memory locations, where they can be accessed by the subroutine. Alternatively, the parameters may be placed on the processor stack.

Passing parameters through processor registers is straightforward and efficient. Figure 2.17 shows how the program in Figure 2.8 for adding a list of numbers can be implemented as a subroutine, LISTADD, with the parameters passed through registers. The size of the list, n, contained in memory location N, and the address, NUM1, of the first number, are passed through registers R2 and R4. The sum computed by the subroutine is passed back to the calling program through register R3. The first four instructions in Figure 2.17 constitute the relevant part of the calling program. The first two instructions load n and NUM1 into

---

Calling program

Load	R2, N	Parameter 1 is list size.
Move	R4, #NUM1	Parameter 2 is list location.
Call	LISTADD	Call subroutine.
Store	R3, SUM	Save result.

⋮

Subroutine

LISTADD:	Subtract	SP, SP, #4	Save the contents of
	Store	R5, (SP)	R5 on the stack.
	Clear	R3	Initialize sum to 0.
LOOP:	Load	R5, (R4)	Get the next number.
	Add	R3, R3, R5	Add this number to sum.
	Add	R4, R4, #4	Increment the pointer by 4.
	Subtract	R2, R2, #1	Decrement the counter.
	Branch_if_[R2]>0	LOOP	
	Load	R5, (SP)	Restore the contents of R5.
	Add	SP, SP, #4	
	Return		Return to calling program.

Figure 2.17   Program of Figure 2.8 written as a subroutine; parameters passed through registers.

R2 and R4. The Call instruction branches to the subroutine starting at location LISTADD. This instruction also saves the return address (i.e., the address of the Store instruction in the calling program) in the link register. The subroutine computes the sum and places it in R3. After the Return instruction is executed by the subroutine, the sum in R3 is stored in memory location SUM by the calling program.

In addition to registers R2, R3, and R4, which are used for parameter passing, the subroutine also uses R5. Since R5 may be used in the calling program, its contents are saved by pushing them onto the processor stack upon entry to the subroutine and restored before returning to the calling program.

If many parameters are involved, there may not be enough general-purpose registers available for passing them to the subroutine. The processor stack provides a convenient and flexible mechanism for passing an arbitrary number of parameters. Figure 2.18 shows the program of Figure 2.8 rewritten as a subroutine, LISTADD, which uses the processor stack for parameter passing. The address of the first number in the list and the number of entries are pushed onto the processor stack pointed to by register SP. The subroutine is then called. The computed sum is placed on the stack before the return to the calling program.

Figure 2.19 shows the stack entries for this example. Assume that before the subroutine is called, the top of the stack is at level 1. The calling program pushes the address NUM1 and the value n onto the stack and calls subroutine LISTADD. The top of the stack is now at level 2. The subroutine uses four registers while it is being executed. Since these registers may contain valid data that belong to the calling program, their contents should be saved at the beginning of the subroutine by pushing them onto the stack. The top of the stack is now at level 3. The subroutine accesses the parameters n and NUM1 from the stack using indexed addressing with offset values relative to the new top of the stack (level 3). Note that it does not change the stack pointer because valid data items are still at the top of the stack. The value n is loaded into R2 as the initial value of the count, and the address NUM1 is loaded into R4, which is used as a pointer to scan the list entries.

At the end of the computation, register R3 contains the sum. Before the subroutine returns to the calling program, the contents of R3 are inserted into the stack, replacing the parameter NUM1, which is no longer needed. Then the contents of the four registers used by the subroutine are restored from the stack. Also, the stack pointer is incremented to point to the top of the stack that existed when the subroutine was called, namely the parameter n at level 2. After the subroutine returns, the calling program stores the result in location SUM and lowers the top of the stack to its original level by incrementing the SP by 8.

Observe that for subroutine LISTADD in Figure 2.18, we did not use a pair of instructions

Subtract	SP, SP, #4
Store	Rj, (SP)

to push the contents of each register on the stack. Since we have to save four registers, this would require eight instructions. We needed only five instructions by adjusting SP immediately to point to the top of stack that will be in effect once all four registers are saved. Then, we used the Index mode to store the contents of registers. We used the same optimization when restoring the registers before returning from the subroutine.

Assume top of stack is at level 1 in Figure 2.19.

	Move	R2, #NUM1	Push parameters onto stack.
	Subtract	SP, SP, #4	
	Store	R2, (SP)	
	Load	R2, N	
	Subtract	SP, SP, #4	
	Store	R2, (SP)	
	Call	LISTADD	Call subroutine
			(top of stack is at level 2).
	Load	R2, 4(SP)	Get the result from the stack
	Store	R2, SUM	and save it in SUM.
	Add	SP, SP, #8	Restore top of stack
			(top of stack is at level 1).
	⋮		
LISTADD:	Subtract	SP, SP, #16	Save registers
	Store	R2, 12(SP)	
	Store	R3, 8(SP)	
	Store	R4, 4(SP)	
	Store	R5, (SP)	(top of stack is at level 3).
	Load	R2, 16(SP)	Initialize counter to n.
	Load	R4, 20(SP)	Initialize pointer to the list.
	Clear	R3	Initialize sum to 0.
LOOP:	Load	R5, (R4)	Get the next number.
	Add	R3, R3, R5	Add this number to sum.
	Add	R4, R4, #4	Increment the pointer by 4.
	Subtract	R2, R2, #1	Decrement the counter.
	Branch_if_[R2]>0	LOOP	
	Store	R3, 20(SP)	Put result in the stack.
	Load	R5, (SP)	Restore registers.
	Load	R4, 4(SP)	
	Load	R3, 8(SP)	
	Load	R2, 12(SP)	
	Add	SP, SP, #16	(top of stack is at level 2).
	Return		Return to calling program.

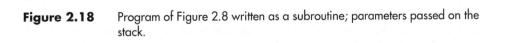

Figure 2.18   Program of Figure 2.8 written as a subroutine; parameters passed on the stack.

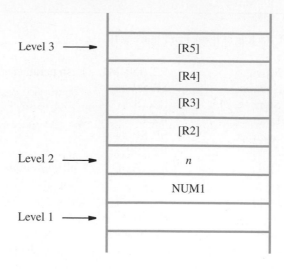

Figure 2.19   Stack contents for the program in Figure 2.18.

We should also note that some computers have special instructions for loading and storing multiple registers. For example, the four registers in Figure 2.18 may be saved on the stack by using the instruction

StoreMultiple   R2−R5, −(SP)

The source registers are specified by the range R2−R5. The notation −(SP) specifies that the stack pointer must be adjusted accordingly. The minus sign in front indicates that SP must be decremented (by 4) before the contents of each register are placed on the stack.

Similarly, the instruction

LoadMultiple   R2−R5, (SP)+

will load registers R2, R3, R4, and R5, in reverse order, with the values that were saved on the stack. The notation (SP)+ indicates that the stack pointer must be incremented (by 4) after each value has been loaded into the corresponding register. We will discuss the addressing modes denoted by −(SP) and (SP)+ in more detail in Section 2.9.1.

Parameter Passing by Value and by Reference

Note the nature of the two parameters, NUM1 and n, passed to the subroutines in Figures 2.17 and 2.18. The purpose of the subroutines is to add a list of numbers. Instead of passing the actual list entries, the calling program passes the address of the first number in the list. This technique is called *passing by reference*. The second parameter is *passed by value*, that is, the actual number of entries, n, is passed to the subroutine.

2.7.3   THE STACK FRAME

Now, observe how space is used in the stack in the example in Figures 2.18 and 2.19. During execution of the subroutine, six locations at the top of the stack contain entries that are needed by the subroutine. These locations constitute a private work space for the subroutine, allocated at the time the subroutine is entered and deallocated when the subroutine returns control to the calling program. Such space is called a *stack frame*. If the subroutine requires more space for local memory variables, the space for these variables can also be allocated on the stack.

Figure 2.20 shows an example of a commonly used layout for information in a stack frame. In addition to the stack pointer SP, it is useful to have another pointer register, called the *frame pointer* (FP), for convenient access to the parameters passed to the subroutine and to the local memory variables used by the subroutine. In the figure, we assume that four parameters are passed to the subroutine, three local variables are used within the subroutine, and registers R2, R3, and R4 need to be saved because they will also be used within the subroutine. When nested subroutines are used, the stack frame of the calling subroutine would also include the return address, as we will see in the example that follows.

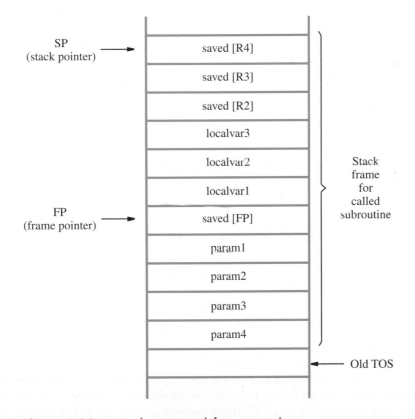

Figure 2.20   A subroutine stack frame example.

With the FP register pointing to the location just above the stored parameters, as shown in Figure 2.20, we can easily access the parameters and the local variables by using the Index addressing mode. The parameters can be accessed by using addresses 4(FP), 8(FP), ... The local variables can be accessed by using addresses −4(FP), −8(FP), ... The contents of FP remain fixed throughout the execution of the subroutine, unlike the stack pointer SP, which must always point to the current top element in the stack.

Now let us discuss how the pointers SP and FP are manipulated as the stack frame is allocated, used, and deallocated for a particular invocation of a subroutine. We begin by assuming that SP points to the old top-of-stack (TOS) element in Figure 2.20. Before the subroutine is called, the calling program pushes the four parameters onto the stack. Then the Call instruction is executed. At this time, SP points to the last parameter that was pushed on the stack. If the subroutine is to use the frame pointer, it should first save the contents of FP by pushing them on the stack, because FP is usually a general-purpose register and it may contain information of use to the calling program. Then, the contents of SP, which now points to the saved value of FP, are copied into FP.

Thus, the first three instructions executed in the subroutine are

$$
\begin{array}{ll}
\text{Subtract} & \text{SP, SP, \#4} \\
\text{Store} & \text{FP, (SP)} \\
\text{Move} & \text{FP, SP}
\end{array}
$$

The Move instruction copies the contents of SP into FP. After these instructions are executed, both SP and FP point to the saved FP contents. Space for the three local variables is now allocated on the stack by executing the instruction

$$
\text{Subtract} \quad \text{SP, SP, \#12}
$$

Finally, the contents of processor registers R2, R3, and R4 are saved by pushing them onto the stack. At this point, the stack frame has been set up as shown in Figure 2.20.

The subroutine now executes its task. When the task is completed, the subroutine pops the saved values of R4, R3, and R2 back into those registers, deallocates the local variables from the stack frame by executing the instruction

$$
\text{Add} \quad \text{SP, SP, \#12}
$$

and pops the saved old value of FP back into FP. At this point, SP points to the last parameter that was placed on the stack. Next, the Return instruction is executed, transferring control back to the calling program.

The calling program is responsible for deallocating the parameters from the stack frame, some of which may be results passed back by the subroutine. After deallocation of the parameters, the stack pointer points to the old TOS, and we are back to where we started.

Stack Frames for Nested Subroutines

When nested subroutines are used, it is necessary to ensure that the return addresses are properly saved. When a calling program calls a subroutine, say SUB1, the return address is saved in the link register. Now, if SUB1 calls another subroutine, SUB2, it must save the current contents of the link register before it makes the call to SUB2. The appropriate place for saving this return address is within the stack frame for SUB1. If SUB2 then calls SUB3, it must save the current contents of the link register within the stack frame associated with SUB2, and so on.

An example of a main program calling a first subroutine SUB1, which then calls a second subroutine SUB2, is shown in Figure 2.21. The stack frames corresponding to these two nested subroutines are shown in Figure 2.22. All parameters involved in this example are passed on the stack. The two figures only show the flow of control and data among the main program and the two subroutines. The actual computations are not shown.

The flow of execution is as follows. The main program pushes the two parameters *param2* and *param1* onto the stack, in that order, and then calls SUB1. This first subroutine is responsible for computing a single result and passing it back to the main program on the stack. During the course of its computations, SUB1 calls the second subroutine, SUB2, in order to perform some other subtask. SUB1 passes a single parameter *param3* to SUB2, and the result is passed back to it via the same location on the stack. After SUB2 executes its Return instruction, SUB1 loads this result into register R4. SUB1 then continues its computations and eventually passes the required answer back to the main program on the stack. When SUB1 executes its return to the main program, the main program stores this answer in memory location RESULT, restores the stack level, then continues with its computations at the next instruction at address 2040. Note how the return address to the calling program, 2028, is stored within the stack frame for SUB1 in Figure 2.22.

The comments in Figure 2.21 provide the details of how this flow of execution is managed. The first action performed by each subroutine is to save on the stack the contents of all registers used in the subroutine, including the frame pointer and link register (if needed). This is followed by initializing the frame pointer. SUB1 uses four registers, R2 to R5, and SUB2 uses two registers, R2 and R3. These registers, the frame pointer, and the link register in the case of SUB1, are restored just before the Return instructions are executed.

The Index addressing mode involving the frame pointer register FP is used to load parameters from the stack and place answers back on the stack. The byte offsets used in these operations are always $4, 8, \ldots$, as discussed for the general stack frame in Figure 2.20. Finally, note that each calling routine is responsible for removing its own parameters from the stack. This is done by the Add instructions, which lower the top of the stack.

2.8 ADDITIONAL INSTRUCTIONS

So far, we have introduced the following instructions: Load, Store, Move, Clear, Add, Subtract, Branch, Call, and Return. These instructions, along with the addressing modes in Table 2.1, have allowed us to write programs to illustrate machine instruction sequencing, including branching and subroutine linkage. In this section we introduce a few more instructions that are found in most instruction sets.

Memory location	Instructions		Comments
Main program			
⋮			
2000	Load	R2, PARAM2	Place parameters on stack.
2004	Subtract	SP, SP, #4	
2008	Store	R2, (SP)	
2012	Load	R2, PARAM1	
2016	Subtract	SP, SP, #4	
2020	Store	R2, (SP)	
2024	Call	SUB1	Call the subroutine.
2028	Load	R2, (SP)	Store result.
2032	Store	R2, RESULT	
2036	Add	SP, SP, #8	Restore stack level.
2040	next instruction		
⋮			
First subroutine			
2100 SUB1:	Subtract	SP, SP, #24	Save registers.
2104	Store	LINK_reg, 20(SP)	
2108	Store	FP, 16(SP)	
2112	Store	R2, 12(SP)	
2116	Store	R3, 8(SP)	
2120	Store	R4, 4(SP)	
2124	Store	R5, (SP)	
2128	Add	FP, SP, #16	Initialize the frame pointer.
2132	Load	R2, 8(FP)	Get first parameter.
2136	Load	R3, 12(FP)	Get second parameter.
⋮			
	Load	R4, PARAM3	Place a parameter on stack.
	Subtract	SP, SP, #4	
	Store	R4, (SP)	
	Call	SUB2	
	Load	R4, (SP)	Get result from SUB2.
	Add	SP, SP, #4	
⋮			
	Store	R5, 8(FP)	Place answer on stack.
	Load	R5, (SP)	Restore registers.
	Load	R4, 4(SP)	
	Load	R3, 8(SP)	
	Load	R2, 12(SP)	
	Load	FP, 16(SP)	
	Load	LINK_reg, 20(SP)	
	Add	SP, SP, #24	
	Return		Return to Main program.
...continued in part *b*.			

Figure 2.21   Nested subroutines (part *a*).

Memory location		Instructions		Comments

Second subroutine

3000	SUB2:	Subtract	SP, SP, #12	Save registers.
3004		Store	FP, 8(SP)	
		Store	R2, 4(SP)	
		Store	R3, (SP)	
		Add	FP, SP, #8	Initialize the frame pointer.
		Load	R2, 4(FP)	Get the parameter.
		⋮		
		Store	R3, 4(FP)	Place SUB2 result on stack.
		Load	R3, (SP)	Restore registers.
		Load	R2, 4(SP)	
		Load	FP, 8(SP)	
		Add	SP, SP, #12	
		Return		Return to Subroutine 1.

Figure 2.21   Nested subroutines (part *b*).

2.8.1 LOGIC INSTRUCTIONS

Logic operations such as AND, OR, and NOT, applied to individual bits, are the basic building blocks of digital circuits, as described in Appendix A. It is also useful to be able to perform logic operations in software, which is done using instructions that apply these operations to all bits of a word or byte independently and in parallel. For example, the instruction

$$\text{And} \quad \text{R4, R2, R3}$$

computes the bit-wise AND of operands in registers R2 and R3, and leaves the result in R4. An immediate form of this instruction may be

$$\text{And} \quad \text{R4, R2, #Value}$$

where Value is a 16-bit logic value that is extended to 32 bits by placing zeros into the 16 most-significant bit positions.

Consider the following application for this logic instruction. Suppose that four ASCII characters are contained in the 32-bit register R2. In some task, we wish to determine if the rightmost character is Z. If it is, then a conditional branch to FOUNDZ is to be made. From Table 1.1 in Chapter 1, we find that the ASCII code for Z is 01011010, which is expressed in hexadecimal notation as 5A. The three-instruction sequence

And	R2, R2, #0xFF
Move	R3, #0x5A
Branch_if_[R2]=[R3]	FOUNDZ

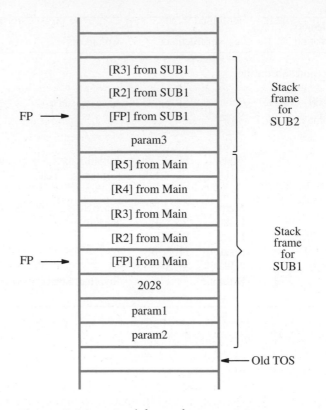

Figure 2.22   Stack frames for Figure 2.21.

implements the desired action. The And instruction clears all bits in the leftmost three character positions of R2 to zero, leaving the rightmost character unchanged. This is the result of using an immediate operand that has eight 1s at its right end, and 0s in the 24 bits to the left. The Move instruction loads the hex value 5A into R3. Since both R2 and R3 have 0s in the leftmost 24 bits, the Branch instruction compares the remaining character at the right end of R2 with the binary representation for the character Z, and causes a branch to FOUNDZ if there is a match.

2.8.2 SHIFT AND ROTATE INSTRUCTIONS

There are many applications that require the bits of an operand to be shifted right or left some specified number of bit positions. The details of how the shifts are performed depend on whether the operand is a signed number or some more general binary-coded information. For general operands, we use a logical shift. For a signed number, we use an arithmetic shift, which preserves the sign of the number.

Logical Shifts

Two logical shift instructions are needed, one for shifting left (LShiftL) and another for shifting right (LShiftR). These instructions shift an operand over a number of bit positions specified in a count operand contained in the instruction. The general form of a Logical-shift-left instruction is

LShiftL   R*i*, R*j*, count

which shifts the contents of register R*j* left by a number of bit positions given by the count operand, and places the result in register R*i*, without changing the contents of R*j*. The count operand may be given as an immediate operand, or it may be contained in a processor register. To complete the description of the shift left operation, we need to specify the bit values brought into the vacated positions at the right end of the destination operand, and to determine what happens to the bits shifted out of the left end. Vacated positions are filled with zeros. In computers that do not use condition code flags, the bits shifted out are simply dropped. In computers that use condition code flags, which will be discussed in Section 2.10.2, these bits are passed through the Carry flag, C, and then dropped. Involving the C flag in shifts is useful in performing arithmetic operations on large numbers that occupy more than one word. Figure 2.23*a* shows an example of shifting the contents of register R3 left by two bit positions. The Logical-shift-right instruction, LShiftR, works in the same manner except that it shifts to the right. Figure 2.23*b* illustrates this operation.

Digit-Packing Example

Consider the following short task that illustrates the use of both shift operations and logic operations. Suppose that two decimal digits represented in ASCII code are located in the memory at byte locations LOC and LOC + 1. We wish to represent each of these digits in the 4-bit BCD code and store both of them in a single byte location PACKED. The result is said to be in *packed-BCD* format. Table 1.1 in Chapter 1 shows that the rightmost four bits of the ASCII code for a decimal digit correspond to the BCD code for the digit. Hence, the required task is to extract the low-order four bits in LOC and LOC + 1 and concatenate them into the single byte at PACKED.

The instruction sequence shown in Figure 2.24 accomplishes the task using register R2 as a pointer to the ASCII characters in memory, and using registers R3 and R4 to develop the BCD digit codes. The program uses the LoadByte instruction, which loads a byte from the memory into the rightmost eight bit positions of a 32-bit processor register and clears the remaining higher-order bits to zero. The StoreByte instruction writes the rightmost byte in the source register into the specified destination location, but does not affect any other byte locations. The value 0xF in the And instruction is used to clear to zero all but the four rightmost bits in R4. Note that the immediate source operand is written as 0xF, which, interpreted as a 32-bit pattern, has 28 zeros in the most-significant bit positions.

Arithmetic Shifts

In an arithmetic shift, the bit pattern being shifted is interpreted as a signed number. A study of the 2's-complement binary number representation in Figure 1.3 reveals that shifting a number one bit position to the left is equivalent to multiplying it by 2, and shifting it to the right is equivalent to dividing it by 2. Of course, overflow might occur on shifting left, and the remainder is lost when shifting right. Another important observation is that on a right shift the sign bit must be repeated as the fill-in bit for the vacated position as a requirement of the 2's-complement representation for numbers. This requirement when shifting right distinguishes arithmetic shifts from logical shifts in which the fill-in

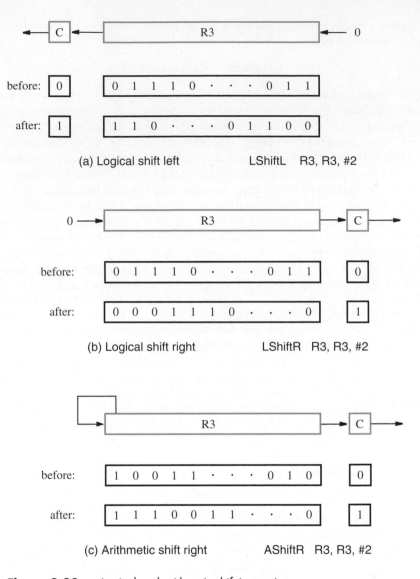

Figure 2.23   Logical and arithmetic shift instructions.

bit is always 0. Otherwise, the two types of shifts are the same. An example of an Arithmetic-shift-right instruction, AShiftR, is shown in Figure 2.23*c*. The Arithmetic-shift-left is exactly the same as the Logical-shift-left.

Rotate Operations

In the shift operations, the bits shifted out of the operand are lost, except for the last bit shifted out which is retained in the Carry flag C. For situations where it is desirable to preserve all of the bits, rotate instructions may be used instead. These are instructions that

Move	R2, #LOC	R2 points to data.
LoadByte	R3, (R2)	Load first byte into R3.
LShiftL	R3, R3, #4	Shift left by 4 bit positions.
Add	R2, R2, #1	Increment the pointer.
LoadByte	R4, (R2)	Load second byte into R4.
And	R4, R4, #0xF	Clear high-order bits to zero.
Or	R3, R3, R4	Concatenate the BCD digits.
StoreByte	R3, PACKED	Store the result.

Figure 2.24   A routine that packs two BCD digits into a byte.

move the bits shifted out of one end of the operand into the other end. Two versions of both the Rotate-left and Rotate-right instructions are often provided. In one version, the bits of the operand are simply rotated. In the other version, the rotation includes the C flag. Figure 2.25 shows the left and right rotate operations with and without the C flag being included in the rotation. Note that when the C flag is not included in the rotation, it still retains the last bit shifted out of the end of the register. The OP codes RotateL, RotateLC, RotateR, and RotateRC, denote the instructions that perform the rotate operations.

2.8.3 Multiplication and Division

Two signed integers can be multiplied or divided by machine instructions with the same format as we saw earlier for an Add instruction. The instruction

$$\text{Multiply} \quad Rk, Ri, Rj$$

performs the operation

$$Rk \leftarrow [Ri] \times [Rj]$$

The product of two n-bit numbers can be as large as $2n$ bits. Therefore, the answer will not necessarily fit into register Rk. A number of instruction sets have a Multiply instruction that computes the low-order n bits of the product and places it in register Rk, as indicated. This is sufficient if it is known that all products in some particular application task will fit into n bits. To accommodate the general $2n$-bit product case, some processors produce the product in two registers, usually adjacent registers Rk and $R(k + 1)$, with the high-order half being placed in register $R(k + 1)$.

An instruction set may also provide a signed integer Divide instruction

$$\text{Divide} \quad Rk, Ri, Rj$$

which performs the operation

$$Rk \leftarrow [Rj]/[Ri]$$

placing the quotient in Rk. The remainder may be placed in $R(k + 1)$, or it may be lost.

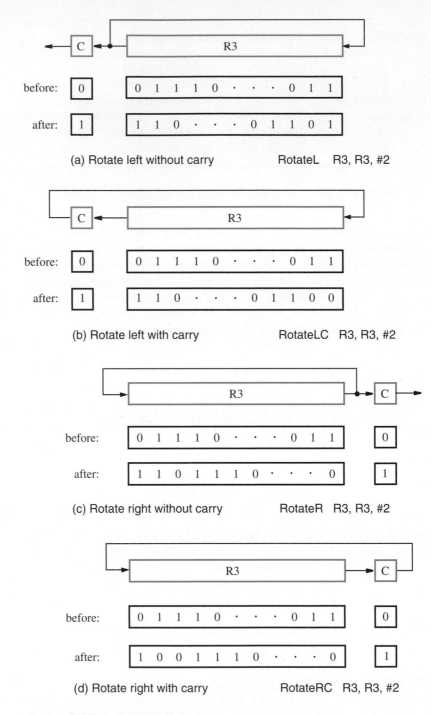

(a) Rotate left without carry   RotateL   R3, R3, #2

(b) Rotate left with carry   RotateLC   R3, R3, #2

(c) Rotate right without carry   RotateR   R3, R3, #2

(d) Rotate right with carry   RotateRC   R3, R3, #2

Figure 2.25    Rotate instructions.

Computers that do not have Multiply and Divide instructions can perform these and other arithmetic operations by using sequences of more basic instructions such as Add, Subtract, Shift, and Rotate. This will become more apparent when we describe the implementation of arithmetic operations in Chapter 9.

2.9   DEALING WITH 32-BIT IMMEDIATE VALUES

In the discussion of addressing modes, in Section 2.4.1, we raised the question of how a 32-bit value that represents a constant or a memory address can be loaded into a processor register. The Immediate and Absolute modes in a RISC-style processor restrict the operand size to 16 bits. Therefore, a 32-bit value cannot be given explicitly in a single instruction that must fit in a 32-bit word.

A possible solution is to use two instructions for this purpose. One approach found in RISC-style processors uses instructions that perform two different logical-OR operations. The instruction

Or   Rdst, Rsrc, #Value

extends the 16-bit immediate operand by placing zeros into the high-order bit positions to form a 32-bit value, which is then ORed with the contents of register Rsrc. If Rsrc contains zero, then Rdst will just be loaded with the extended 32-bit value. Another instruction

OrHigh   Rdst, Rsrc, #Value

forms a 32-bit value by taking the 16-bit immediate operand as the high-order bits and appending zeros as the low-order bits. This value is then ORed with the contents of Rsrc. Using these instructions, and assuming that R0 contains the value 0, we can load the 32-bit value 0x20004FF0 into register R2 as follows:

OrHigh   R2, R0, #0x2000
Or   R2, R2, #0x4FF0

To make it easier to write programs, a RISC-style instruction set may include pseudoinstructions that indicate an action that requires more than one machine instruction. Such pseudoinstructions are replaced with the corresponding machine-instruction sequence by the assembler program. For example, the pseudoinstruction

MoveImmediateAddress   R2, LOC

could be used to load a 32-bit address represented by the symbol LOC into register R2. In the assembled program, it would be replaced with two instructions using 16-bit values as shown above.

An alternative to using two instructions to load a 32-bit address into a register is to use more than one word per instruction. In that case, a two-word instruction could give the OP code and register specification in the first word, and include a 32-bit value in the second word. This is the approach found in CISC-style processors.

Finally, note that in the previous sections we always assumed that single Load and Store instructions can be used to access memory locations represented by symbolic names. This makes the example programs simpler and easier to read. The programs will run correctly if the required memory addresses can be specified in 16 bits. If longer addresses are involved, then the approach described above to construct 32-bit addresses must be used.

2.10   CISC INSTRUCTION SETS

In preceding sections, we introduced the RISC style of instruction sets. Now we will examine some important characteristics of *Complex Instruction Set Computers* (CISC).

One key difference is that CISC instruction sets are not constrained to the *load/store architecture*, in which arithmetic and logic operations can be performed only on operands that are in processor registers. Another key difference is that instructions do not necessarily have to fit into a single word. Some instructions may occupy a single word, but others may span multiple words.

Instructions in modern CISC processors typically do not use a three-address format. Most arithmetic and logic instructions use the *two-address* format

$$\text{Operation} \quad \text{destination, source}$$

An Add instruction of this type is

$$\text{Add} \quad \text{B, A}$$

which performs the operation $B \leftarrow [A] + [B]$ on memory operands. When the sum is calculated, the result is sent to the memory and stored in location B, replacing the original contents of this location. This means that memory location B is both a source and a destination.

Consider again the task of adding two numbers

$$C = A + B$$

where all three operands may be in memory locations. Obviously, this cannot be done with a single two-address instruction. The task can be performed by using another two-address instruction that copies the contents of one memory location into another. Such an instruction is

$$\text{Move} \quad \text{C, B}$$

which performs the operation $C \leftarrow [B]$, leaving the contents of location B unchanged. The operation $C \leftarrow [A] + [B]$ can now be performed by the two-instruction sequence

$$\text{Move} \quad \text{C, B}$$
$$\text{Add} \quad \text{C, A}$$

Observe that by using this sequence of instructions the contents of neither A nor B locations are overwritten.

In some CISC processors one operand may be in the memory but the other must be in a register. In this case, the instruction sequence for the required task would be

$$
\begin{array}{ll}
\text{Move} & \text{R}i, \text{A} \\
\text{Add} & \text{R}i, \text{B} \\
\text{Move} & \text{C}, \text{R}i
\end{array}
$$

The general form of the Move instruction is

$$\text{Move} \quad \text{destination, source}$$

where both the source and destination may be either a memory location or a processor register. The Move instruction includes the functionality of the Load and Store instructions we used previously in the discussion of RISC-style processors. In the Load instruction, the source is a memory location and the destination is a processor register. In the Store instruction, the source is a register and the destination is a memory location. While Load and Store instructions are restricted to moving operands between memory and processor registers, the Move instruction has a wider scope. It can be used to move immediate operands and to transfer operands between two memory locations or between two registers.

2.10.1   ADDITIONAL ADDRESSING MODES

Most CISC processors have all of the five basic addressing modes—Immediate, Register, Absolute, Indirect, and Index. Three additional addressing modes are often found in CISC processors.

Autoincrement and Autodecrement Modes

There are two modes that are particularly convenient for accessing data items in successive locations in the memory and for implementation of stacks.

Autoincrement mode—The effective address of the operand is the contents of a register specified in the instruction. After accessing the operand, the contents of this register are automatically incremented to point to the next operand in memory.

We denote the Autoincrement mode by putting the specified register in parentheses, to show that the contents of the register are used as the effective address, followed by a plus sign to indicate that these contents are to be incremented after the operand is accessed. Thus, the Autoincrement mode is written as

$$(\text{R}i)+$$

To access successive words in a byte-addressable memory with a 32-bit word length, the increment amount must be 4. Computers that have the Autoincrement mode automatically increment the contents of the register by a value that corresponds to the size of the accessed operand. Thus, the increment is 1 for byte-sized operands, 2 for 16-bit operands, and 4 for 32-bit operands. Since the size of the operand is usually specified as part of the operation code of an instruction, it is sufficient to indicate the Autoincrement mode as $(\text{R}i)+$.

As a companion for the Autoincrement mode, another useful mode accesses the memory locations in the reverse order:

Autodecrement mode—The contents of a register specified in the instruction are first automatically decremented and are then used as the effective address of the operand.

We denote the Autodecrement mode by putting the specified register in parentheses, preceded by a minus sign to indicate that the contents of the register are to be decremented before being used as the effective address. Thus, we write

$$-(Ri)$$

In this mode, operands are accessed in descending address order.

The reader may wonder why the address is decremented before it is used in the Autodecrement mode, and incremented after it is used in the Autoincrement mode. The main reason for this is to make it easy to use these modes together to implement a stack structure. Instead of needing two instructions

Subtract	SP, #4
Move	(SP), NEWITEM

to push a new item on the stack, we can use just one instruction

Move   −(SP), NEWITEM

Similarly, instead of needing two instructions

Move	ITEM, (SP)
Add	SP, #4

to pop an item from the stack, we can use just

Move   ITEM, (SP)+

Relative Mode

We have defined the Index mode by using general-purpose processor registers. Some computers have a version of this mode in which the program counter, PC, is used instead of a general-purpose register. Then, X(PC) can be used to address a memory location that is X bytes away from the location presently pointed to by the program counter. Since the addressed location is identified *relative* to the program counter, which always identifies the current execution point in a program, the name Relative mode is associated with this type of addressing.

Relative mode—The effective address is determined by the Index mode using the program counter in place of the general-purpose register Ri.

2.10.2   CONDITION CODES

Operations performed by the processor typically generate results such as numbers that are positive, negative, or zero. The processor can maintain the information about these results for use by subsequent conditional branch instructions. This is accomplished by recording the required information in individual bits, often called *condition code flags*. These flags are usually grouped together in a special processor register called the *condition code register* or *status register*. Individual condition code flags are set to 1 or cleared to 0, depending on the outcome of the operation performed.

Four commonly used flags are

N (negative)	Set to 1 if the result is negative; otherwise, cleared to 0
Z (zero)	Set to 1 if the result is 0; otherwise, cleared to 0
V (overflow)	Set to 1 if arithmetic overflow occurs; otherwise, cleared to 0
C (carry)	Set to 1 if a carry-out results from the operation; otherwise, cleared to 0

The N and Z flags record whether the result of an arithmetic or logic operation is negative or zero. In some computers, they may also be affected by the value of the operand of a Move instruction. This makes it possible for a later conditional branch instruction to cause a branch based on the sign and value of the operand that was moved. Some computers also provide a special Test instruction that examines a value in a register or in the memory without modifying it, and sets or clears the N and Z flags accordingly.

The V flag indicates whether overflow has taken place. As explained in Section 1.4, overflow occurs when the result of an arithmetic operation is outside the range of values that can be represented by the number of bits available for the operands. The processor sets the V flag to allow the programmer to test whether overflow has occurred and branch to an appropriate routine that deals with the problem. Instructions such as Branch_if_overflow are usually provided for this purpose.

The C flag is set to 1 if a carry occurs from the most-significant bit position during an arithmetic operation. This flag makes it possible to perform arithmetic operations on operands that are longer than the word length of the processor. Such operations are used in multiple-precision arithmetic, which is discussed in Chapter 9.

Consider the Branch instruction in Figure 2.6. If condition codes are used, then the Subtract instruction would cause both N and Z flags to be cleared to 0 if the contents of register R2 are still greater than 0. The desired branching could be specified simply as

Branch>0   LOOP

without indicating the register involved in the test. This instruction causes a branch if neither N nor Z is 1, that is, if the result produced by the Subtract instruction is neither negative nor equal to zero. Many conditional branch instructions are provided in the instruction set of a computer to enable a variety of conditions to be tested. The conditions are defined as logic expressions involving the condition code flags.

To illustrate the use of condition codes, consider again the program in Figure 2.8, which adds a list of numbers using RISC-style instructions. Using a CISC-style instruction set, this task can be implemented with fewer instructions, as shown in Figure 2.26. The

	Move	R2, N	Load the size of the list.
	Clear	R3	Initialize sum to 0.
	Move	R4, #NUM1	Load address of the first number.
LOOP:	Add	R3, (R4)+	Add the next number to sum.
	Subtract	R2, #1	Decrement the counter.
	Branch>0	LOOP	Loop back if not finished.
	Move	SUM, R3	Store the final sum.

Figure 2.26   A CISC version of the program of Figure 2.8.

Add instruction uses the pointer register (R4) to access successive numbers in the list and add them to the sum in register R3. After accessing the source operand, the processor automatically increments the pointer, because the Autoincrement addressing mode is used to specify the source operand. The Subtract instruction sets the condition codes, which are then used by the Branch instruction.

2.11   RISC AND CISC STYLES

RISC and CISC are two different styles of instruction sets. We introduced RISC first because it is simpler and easier to understand. Having looked at some basic features of both styles, we should summarize their main characteristics.

RISC style is characterized by:

*   Simple addressing modes
*   All instructions fitting in a single word
*   Fewer instructions in the instruction set, as a consequence of simple addressing modes
*   Arithmetic and logic operations that can be performed only on operands in processor registers
*   Load/store architecture that does not allow direct transfers from one memory location to another; such transfers must take place via a processor register
*   Simple instructions that are conducive to fast execution by the processing unit using techniques such as pipelining which is presented in Chapter 6
*   Programs that tend to be larger in size, because more, but simpler instructions are needed to perform complex tasks

CISC style is characterized by:

*   More complex addressing modes
*   More complex instructions, where an instruction may span multiple words

- Many instructions that implement complex tasks
- Arithmetic and logic operations that can be performed on memory operands as well as operands in processor registers
- Transfers from one memory location to another by using a single Move instruction
- Programs that tend to be smaller in size, because fewer, but more complex instructions are needed to perform complex tasks

Before the 1970s, all computers were of CISC type. An important objective was to simplify the development of software by making the hardware capable of performing fairly complex tasks, that is, to move the complexity from the software level to the hardware level. This is conducive to making programs simpler and shorter, which was important when computer memory was smaller and more expensive to provide. Today, memory is inexpensive and most computers have large amounts of it.

RISC-style designs emerged as an attempt to achieve very high performance by making the hardware very simple, so that instructions can be executed very quickly in pipelined fashion as will be discussed in Chapter 6. This results in moving complexity from the hardware level to the software level. Sophisticated compilers were developed to optimize the code consisting of simple instructions. The size of the code became less important as memory capacities increased.

While the RISC and CISC styles seem to define two significantly different approaches, today's processors often exhibit what may seem to be a compromise between these approaches. For example, it is attractive to add some non-RISC instructions to a RISC processor in order to reduce the number of instructions executed, as long as the execution of these new instructions is fast. We will deal with the performance issues in detail in Chapter 6 where we discuss the concept of pipelining.

2.12   EXAMPLE PROGRAMS

In this section we present two examples that further illustrate the use of machine instructions. The examples are representative of numeric and nonnumeric applications.

2.12.1   VECTOR DOT PRODUCT PROGRAM

The first example is a numerical application that is an extension of previous programs for adding numbers. In calculations that involve vectors and matrices, it is often necessary to compute the dot product of two vectors. Let A and B be two vectors of length n. Their dot product is defined as

$$\text{Dot Product} = \sum_{i=0}^{n-1} A(i) \times B(i)$$

Figures 2.27 and 2.28 show RISC- and CISC-style programs for computing the dot product and storing it in memory location DOTPROD. The first elements of each vector, $A(0)$ and

	Move	R2, #AVEC	R2 points to vector A.
	Move	R3, #BVEC	R3 points to vector B.
	Load	R4, N	R4 serves as a counter.
	Clear	R5	R5 accumulates the dot product.
LOOP:	Load	R6, (R2)	Get next element of vector A.
	Load	R7, (R3)	Get next element of vector B.
	Multiply	R8, R6, R7	Compute the product of next pair.
	Add	R5, R5, R8	Add to previous sum.
	Add	R2, R2, #4	Increment pointer to vector A.
	Add	R3, R3, #4	Increment pointer to vector B.
	Subtract	R4, R4, #1	Decrement the counter.
	Branch_if_[R4]>0	LOOP	Loop again if not done.
	Store	R5, DOTPROD	Store dot product in memory.

Figure 2.27   A RISC-style program for computing the dot product of two vectors.

	Move	R2, #AVEC	R2 points to vector A.
	Move	R3, #BVEC	R3 points to vector B.
	Move	R4, N	R4 serves as a counter.
	Clear	R5	R5 accumulates the dot product.
LOOP:	Move	R6, (R2)+	Compute the product of
	Multiply	R6, (R3)+	next components.
	Add	R5, R6	Add to previous sum.
	Subtract	R4, #1	Decrement the counter.
	Branch>0	LOOP	Loop again if not done.
	Move	DOTPROD, R5	Store dot product in memory.

Figure 2.28   A CISC-style program for computing the dot product of two vectors.

$B(0)$, are stored at memory locations AVEC and BVEC, with the remaining elements in the following word locations.

The task of accumulating a sum of products occurs in many signal-processing applications. In this case, one of the vectors consists of the most recent n signal samples in a continuing time sequence of inputs to a signal-processing unit. The other vector is a set of n weights. The n signal samples are multiplied by the weights, and the sum of these products constitutes an output signal sample.

Some computer instruction sets combine the operations of the Multiply and Add instructions used in the programs in Figures 2.27 and 2.28 into a single MultiplyAccumulate instruction. This is done in the ARM processor presented in Appendix D.

2.12.2 STRING SEARCH PROGRAM

As an example of a non-numerical application, let us consider the problem of string search. Given two strings of ASCII-encoded characters, a long string T and a short string P, we want to determine if the pattern P is contained in the target T. Since P may be found in T in several places, we will simplify our task by being interested only in the first occurrence of P in T when T is searched from left to right. Let T and P consist of n and m characters, respectively, where $n > m$. The characters are stored in memory in consecutive byte locations. Assume that the required data are located as follows:

- T is the address of $T(0)$, which is the first character in string T.
- N is the address of a 32-bit word that contains the value n.
- P is the address of $P(0)$, which is the first character in string P.
- M is the address of a 32-bit word that contains the value m.
- RESULT is the address of a word in which the result of the search is to be stored. If the substring P is found in T, then the address of the corresponding location in T will be stored in RESULT; otherwise, the value -1 will be stored.

String search is an important and well-researched problem. Many algorithms have been developed. Since our main purpose is to illustrate the use of assembly-language instructions, we will use the simplest algorithm which is known as the *brute-force* algorithm. It is given in Figure 2.29.

In a RISC-style computer, the algorithm can be implemented as shown in Figure 2.30. The comments explain the use of various processor registers. Note that in the case of a failed search, the immediate value -1 will cause the contents of R8 to become equal to 0xFFFFFFFF, which represents -1 in 2's complement.

Figure 2.31 shows how the algorithm may be implemented in a CISC-style computer. Observe that the first instruction in LOOP2 loads a character from string T into register R8, which is followed by an instruction that compares this character with a character in string P. The reader may wonder why is it not possible to use a single instruction

$$\text{CompareByte} \quad (R6)+, (R7)+$$

to achieve the same effect. While CISC-style instruction sets allow operations that involve memory operands, they typically require that if one operand is in the memory, the other

---

for $\quad i \leftarrow 0$ to $n - m$ do
$\quad\quad j \leftarrow 0$
$\quad\quad$ **while** $j < m$ **and** $P[j] = T[i + j]$ **do**
$\quad\quad\quad j \leftarrow j + 1$
$\quad\quad$ **if** $j = m$ **return** i
return -1

Figure 2.29 A brute-force string search algorithm.

	Move	R2, #T	R2 points to string T.
	Move	R3, #P	R3 points to string P.
	Load	R4, N	Get the value n.
	Load	R5, M	Get the value m.
	Subtract	R4, R4, R5	Compute $n - m$.
	Add	R4, R2, R4	The address of $T(n - m)$.
	Add	R5, R3, R5	The address of $P(m)$.
LOOP1:	Move	R6, R2	Use R6 to scan through string T.
	Move	R7, R3	Use R7 to scan through string P.
LOOP2:	LoadByte	R8, (R6)	Compare a pair of
	LoadByte	R9, (R7)	characters in
	Branch_if_[R8]≠[R9]	NOMATCH	strings T and P.
	Add	R6, R6, #1	Point to next character in T.
	Add	R7, R7, #1	Point to next character in P.
	Branch_if_[R5]>[R7]	LOOP2	Loop again if not done.
	Store	R2, RESULT	Store the address of $T(i)$.
	Branch	DONE	
NOMATCH:	Add	R2, R2, #1	Point to next character in T.
	Branch_if_[R4]≥[R2]	LOOP1	Loop again if not done.
	Move	R8, #−1	Write −1 to indicate that
	Store	R8, RESULT	no match was found.
DONE:	next instruction		

Figure 2.30   A RISC-style program for string search.

operand must be in a processor register. A common exception is the Move instruction, which may involve two memory operands. This provides a simple way of moving data between different memory locations.

2.13   ENCODING OF MACHINE INSTRUCTIONS

In this chapter, we have introduced a variety of useful instructions and addressing modes. We have used a generic form of assembly language to emphasize basic concepts without relying on processor-specific acronyms or mnemonics. Assembly-language instructions symbolically express the actions that must be performed by the processor circuitry. To be executed in a processor, assembly-language instructions must be converted by the assembler program, as described in Section 2.5, into machine instructions that are encoded in a compact binary pattern.

Let us now examine how machine instructions may be formed. The Add instruction

Add   Rdst, Rsrc1, Rsrc2

	Move	R2, #T	R2 points to string T.
	Move	R3, #P	R3 points to string P.
	Move	R4, N	Get the value n.
	Move	R5, M	Get the value m.
	Subtract	R4, R5	Compute $n - m$.
	Add	R4, R2	The address of $T(n - m)$.
	Add	R5, R3	The address of $P(m)$.
LOOP1:	Move	R6, R2	Use R6 to scan through string T.
	Move	R7, R3	Use R7 to scan through string P.
LOOP2:	MoveByte	R8, (R6)+	Compare a pair of
	CompareByte	R8, (R7)+	characters in
	Branch≠0	NOMATCH	strings T and P.
	Compare	R5, R7	Check if at $P(m)$.
	Branch>0	LOOP2	Loop again if not done.
	Move	RESULT, R2	Store the address of $T(i)$.
	Branch	DONE	
NOMATCH:	Add	R2, #1	Point to next character in T.
	Compare	R4, R2	Check if at $T(n - m)$.
	Branch≥0	LOOP1	Loop again if not done.
	Move	RESULT, #−1	No match was found.
DONE:	next instruction		

Figure 2.31   A CISC-style program for string search.

is representative of a class of three-operand instructions that use operands in processor registers. Registers Rdst, Rsrc1, and Rsrc2 hold the destination and two source operands. If a processor has 32 registers, then it is necessary to use five bits to specify each of the three registers in such instructions. If each instruction is implemented in a 32-bit word, the remaining 17 bits can be used to specify the OP code that indicates the operation to be performed. A possible format is shown in Figure 2.32a.

Now consider instructions in which one operand is given using the Immediate addressing mode, such as

Add   Rdst, Rsrc, #Value

Of the 32 bits available, ten bits are needed to specify the two registers. The remaining 22 bits must give the OP code and the value of the immediate operand. The most useful sizes of immediate operands are 32, 16, and 8 bits. Since 32 bits are not available, a good choice is to allocate 16 bits for the immediate operand. This leaves six bits for specifying the OP code. A possible format is presented in Figure 2.32b. This format can also be used for Load and Store instructions, where the Index addressing mode uses the 16-bit field to specify the offset that is added to the contents of the index register.

The format in Figure 2.32b can also be used to encode the Branch instructions. Consider the program in Figure 2.12. The Branch-greater-than instruction at memory address 128

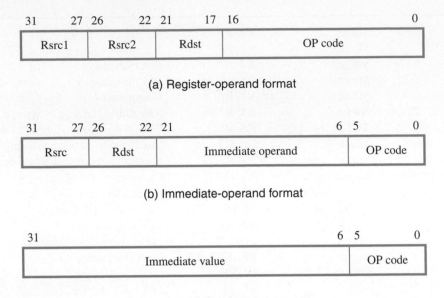

(a) Register-operand format

(b) Immediate-operand format

(c) Call format

Figure 2.32   Possible instruction formats.

could be written in a specific assembly language as

BGT   R2, R0, LOOP

if the contents of register R0 are zero. The registers R2 and R0 can be specified in the two register fields in Figure 2.32b. The six-bit OP code has to identify the BGT operation. The 16-bit immediate field can be used to provide the information needed to determine the branch target address, which is the location of the instruction with the label LOOP. The target address generally comprises 32 bits. Since there is no space for 32 bits, the BGT instruction makes use of the immediate field to give an offset from the location of this instruction in the program to the required branch target. At the time the BGT instruction is being executed, the program counter, PC, has been incremented to point to the next instruction, which is the Store instruction at address 132. Therefore, the branch offset is $132 - 112 = 20$. Since the processor computes the target address by adding the current contents of the PC and the branch offset, the required offset in this example is negative, namely -20.

Finally, we should consider the Call instruction, which is used to call a subroutine. It only needs to specify the OP code and an immediate value that is used to determine the address of the first instruction in the subroutine. If six bits are used for the OP code, then the remaining 26 bits can be used to denote the immediate value. This gives the format shown in Figure 2.32c.

In this section, we introduced the basic concept of encoding the machine instructions. Different commercial processors have instruction sets that vary in the details of implementation. Appendices B to E present the instruction sets of four processors that we have chosen as examples.

2.14   CONCLUDING REMARKS

This chapter introduced the representation and execution of instructions and programs at the assembly and machine level as seen by the programmer. The discussion emphasized the basic principles of addressing techniques and instruction sequencing. The programming examples illustrated the basic types of operations implemented by the instruction set of any modern computer. Commonly used addressing modes were introduced. The subroutine concept and the instructions needed to implement it were discussed. In the discussion in this chapter, we provided the contrast between two different approaches to the design of machine instruction sets—the RISC and CISC approaches.

2.15   SOLVED PROBLEMS

This section presents some examples of the types of problems that a student may be asked to solve, and shows how such problems can be solved.

Problem: Assume that there is a string of ASCII-encoded characters stored in memory starting at address STRING. The string ends with the Carriage Return (CR) character. Write a RISC-style program to determine the length of the string and store it in location LENGTH.

Example 2.1

Solution: Figure 2.33 presents a possible program. The characters in the string are compared to CR (ASCII code 0x0D), and a counter is incremented until the end of the string is reached.

	Move	R2, #STRING	R2 points to the start of the string.
	Clear	R3	R3 is a counter that is cleared to 0.
	Move	R4, #0x0D	ASCII code for Carriage Return.
LOOP:	LoadByte	R5, (R2)	Get the next character.
	Branch_if_[R5]=[R4]	DONE	Finished if character is CR.
	Add	R2, R2, #1	Increment the string pointer.
	Add	R3, R3, #1	Increment the counter.
	Branch	LOOP	Not finished, loop back.
DONE:	Store	R3, LENGTH	Store the count in location LENGTH.

Figure 2.33   Program for Example 2.1.

LIST	EQU	1000	Starting address of the list.
	ORIGIN	400	
	Move	R2, #LIST	R2 points to the start of the list.
	Load	R3, 4(R2)	R3 is a counter, initialize it with n.
	Add	R4, R2, #8	R4 points to the first number.
	Load	R5, (R4)	R5 holds the smallest number found so far.
LOOP:	Subtract	R3, R3, #1	Decrement the counter.
	Branch_if_[R3]=0	DONE	Finished if R3 is equal to 0.
	Add	R4, R4, #4	Increment the list pointer.
	Load	R6, (R4)	Get the next number.
	Branch_if_[R5]≤[R6]	LOOP	Check if smaller number found.
	Move	R5, R6	Update the smallest number found.
	Branch	LOOP	
DONE:	Store	R5, (R2)	Store the smallest number into SMALL.
	ORIGIN	1000	
SMALL:	RESERVE	4	Space for the smallest number found.
N:	DATAWORD	7	Number of entries in the list.
ENTRIES:	DATAWORD 4,5,3,6,1,8,2		Entries in the list.
	END		

Figure 2.34   Program for Example 2.2.

Example 2.2   **Problem:** We want to find the smallest number in a list of 32-bit positive integers. The word at address 1000 is to hold the value of the smallest number after it has been found. The next word contains the number of entries, n, in the list. The following n words contain the numbers in the list. The program is to start at address 400. Write a RISC-style program to find the smallest number and include the assembler directives needed to organize the program and data as specified. While the program has to be able to handle lists of different lengths, include in your code a small list of sample data comprising seven integers.

Solution: The program in Figure 2.34 accomplishes the required task. Comments in the program explain how this task is performed.

Example 2.3   **Problem:** Write a RISC-style program that converts an n-digit decimal integer into a binary number. The decimal number is given as n ASCII-encoded characters, as would be the case if the number is entered by typing it on a keyboard. Memory location N contains n, the ASCII string starts at DECIMAL, and the converted number is stored at BINARY.

Solution: Consider a four-digit decimal number, $D = d_3 d_2 d_1 d_0$. The value of this number is $((d_3 \times 10 + d_2) \times 10 + d_1) \times 10 + d_0$. This representation of the number is the basis for the conversion technique used in the program in Figure 2.35. Note that each ASCII-encoded

	Load	R2, N	Initialize counter R2 with n.
	Move	R3, #DECIMAL	R3 points to the ASCII digits.
	Clear	R4	R4 will hold the binary number.
LOOP:	LoadByte	R5, (R3)	Get the next ASCII digit.
	And	R5, R5, #0x0F	Form the BCD digit.
	Add	R4, R4, R5	Add to the intermediate result.
	Add	R3, R3, #1	Increment the digit pointer.
	Subtract	R2, R2, #1	Decrement the counter.
	Branch_if_[R2]=0	DONE	
	Multiply	R4, R4, #10	Multiply by 10.
	Branch	LOOP	Loop back if not done.
DONE:	Store	R4, BINARY	Store result in location BINARY.

Figure 2.35   Program for Example 2.3.

character is converted into a Binary Coded Decimal (BCD) digit before it is used in the computation. It is assumed that the converted value can be represented in no more than 32 bits.

Problem: Consider an array of numbers $A(i,j)$, where $i = 0$ through $n - 1$ is the row index, and $j = 0$ through $m - 1$ is the column index. The array is stored in the memory of a computer one row after another, with elements of each row occupying m successive word locations. Assume that the memory is byte-addressable and that the word length is 32 bits. Write a RISC-style subroutine for adding column x to column y, element by element, leaving the sum elements in column y. The indices x and y are passed to the subroutine in registers R2 and R3. The parameters n and m are passed to the subroutine in registers R4 and R5, and the address of element $A(0,0)$ is passed in register R6.

Example 2.4

Solution: A possible program is given in Figure 2.36. We have assumed that the values x, y, n, and m are stored in memory locations X, Y, N, and M. Also, the elements of the array are stored in successive words that begin at location ARRAY, which is the address of the element $A(0,0)$. Comments in the program indicate the purpose of individual instructions.

Problem: We want to sort a list of characters stored in memory. The list consists of n bytes, not necessarily distinct, and each byte contains the ASCII code for a character from the set of letters A through Z. In the ASCII code, presented in Chapter 1, the letters A, B, ..., Z, are represented by 7-bit patterns that have increasing values when interpreted as binary numbers. When an ASCII character is stored in a byte location, it is customary to set the most-significant bit position to 0. Using this code, we can sort a list of characters alphabetically by sorting their codes in increasing numerical order, considering them as positive numbers.

Example 2.5

	Load	R2, X	Load the value x.
	Load	R3, Y	Load the value y.
	Load	R4, N	Load the value n.
	Load	R5, M	Load the value m.
	Move	R6, #ARRAY	Load the address of A(0,0).
	Call	SUB	
	next instruction		
	⋮		
SUB:	Subtract	SP, SP, #4	
	Store	R7, (SP)	Save register R7.
	LShiftL	R5, R5, #2	Determine the distance in bytes between successive elements in a column.
	Subtract	R3, R3, R2	Form $y - x$.
	LShiftL	R3, R3, #2	Form $4(y - x)$.
	LShiftL	R2, R2, #2	Form $4x$.
	Add	R6, R6, R2	R6 points to A(0,x).
	Add	R7, R6, R3	R7 points to A(0,y).
LOOP:	Load	R2, (R6)	Get the next number in column x.
	Load	R3, (R7)	Get the next number in column y.
	Add	R2, R2, R3	Add the numbers and
	Store	R2, (R7)	store the sum.
	Add	R6, R6, R5	Increment pointer to column x.
	Add	R7, R7, R5	Increment pointer to column y.
	Subtract	R4, R4, #1	Decrement the row counter.
	Branch_if_[R4]>0	LOOP	Loop back if not done.
	Load	R7, (SP)	Restore R7.
	Add	SP, SP, #4	
	Return		Return to the calling program.

Figure 2.36   Program for Example 2.4.

Let the list be stored in memory locations LIST through LIST $+ n - 1$, and let n be a 32-bit value stored at address N. The sorting is to be done in place, that is, the sorted list is to occupy the same memory locations as the original list.

We can sort the list using a straight-selection sort algorithm. First, the largest number is found and placed at the end of the list in location LIST $+ n - 1$. Then the largest number in the remaining sublist of $n - 1$ numbers is placed at the end of the sublist in location LIST $+ n - 2$. The procedure is repeated until the list is sorted. A C-language program for this sorting algorithm is shown in Figure 2.37, where the list is treated as a one-dimensional array LIST(0) through LIST($n - 1$). For each sublist LIST(j) through LIST(0), the number in LIST(j) is compared with each of the other numbers in the sublist. Whenever a larger number is found in the sublist, it is interchanged with the number in LIST(j).

for   (j = n−1; j > 0; j = j − 1)
         { for (k = j−1; k > = 0; k = k − 1)
              { if   (LIST[k] > LIST[j])
                     { TEMP = LIST[k];
                             LIST[k] = LIST[j];
                             LIST[j] = TEMP;
                     }
              }
         }

Figure 2.37   C-language program for sorting.

	Move	R2, #LIST	Load LIST into base register R2.
	Move	R3, N	Initialize outer loop index
	Subtract	R3, #1	register R3 to $j = n - 1$.
OUTER:	Move	R4, R3	Initialize inner loop index
	Subtract	R4, #1	register R4 to $k = j - 1$.
	MoveByte	R5, (R2,R3)	Load LIST(j) into R5, which holds
			current maximum in sublist.
INNER:	CompareByte	(R2,R4), R5	If LIST(k) ≤ [R5],
	Branch≤0	NEXT	do not exchange.
	MoveByte	R6, (R2,R4)	Otherwise, exchange LIST(k)
	MoveByte	(R2,R4), R5	with LIST(j) and load
	MoveByte	(R2,R3), R6	new maximum into R5.
	MoveByte	R5, R6	Register R6 serves as TEMP.
NEXT:	Decrement	R4	Decrement index registers R4 and
	Branch≥0	INNER	R3, which also serve as
	Decrement	R3	loop counters, and branch
	Branch>0	OUTER	back if loops not finished.

Figure 2.38   A byte-sorting program.

Note that the C-language program traverses the list backwards. This order of traversal simplifies loop termination when a machine language program is written, because the loop is exited when an index is decremented to 0.

Write a CISC-style program that implements this sorting task.

Solution: A possible program is given in Figure 2.38.

PROBLEMS

2.1 **[E]** Given a binary pattern in some memory location, is it possible to tell whether this pattern represents a machine instruction or a number?

2.2 **[E]** Consider a computer that has a byte-addressable memory organized in 32-bit words according to the big-endian scheme. A program reads ASCII characters entered at a keyboard and stores them in successive byte locations, starting at location 1000. Show the contents of the two memory words at locations 1000 and 1004 after the word "Computer" has been entered.

2.3 **[E]** Repeat Problem 2.2 for the little-endian scheme.

2.4 **[E]** Registers R4 and R5 contain the decimal numbers 2000 and 3000 before each of the following addressing modes is used to access a memory operand. What is the effective address (EA) in each case?

(*a*) 12(R4)

(*b*) (R4,R5)

(*c*) 28(R4,R5)

(*d*) (R4)+

(*e*) −(R4)

2.5 **[E]** Write a RISC-style program that computes the expression SUM = 580 + 68400 + 80000.

2.6 **[E]** Write a CISC-style program for the task in Problem 2.5.

2.7 **[E]** Write a RISC-style program that computes the expression ANSWER = A × B + C × D.

2.8 **[E]** Write a CISC-style program for the task in Problem 2.7.

2.9 **[M]** Rewrite the addition loop in Figure 2.8 so that the numbers in the list are accessed in the reverse order; that is, the first number accessed is the last one in the list, and the last number accessed is at memory location NUM1. Try to achieve the most efficient way to determine loop termination. Would your loop execute faster than the loop in Figure 2.8?

2.10 **[M]** The list of student marks shown in Figure 2.10 is changed to contain j test scores for each student. Assume that there are n students. Write a RISC-style program for computing the sums of the scores on each test and store these sums in the memory word locations at addresses SUM, SUM + 4, SUM + 8, ... The number of tests, j, is larger than the number of registers in the processor, so the type of program shown in Figure 2.11 for the 3-test case cannot be used. Use two nested loops. The inner loop should accumulate the sum for a particular test, and the outer loop should run over the number of tests, j. Assume that the memory area used to store the sums has been cleared to zero initially.

2.11 **[M]** Write a RISC-style program that finds the number of negative integers in a list of n 32-bit integers and stores the count in location NEGNUM. The value n is stored in memory location N, and the first integer in the list is stored in location NUMBERS. Include the necessary assembler directives and a sample list that contains six numbers, some of which are negative.

2.12 **[E]** Both of the following statement segments cause the value 300 to be stored in location 1000, but at different times.

$$\begin{array}{ll} \text{ORIGIN} & 1000 \\ \text{DATAWORD} & 300 \end{array}$$

and

$$\begin{array}{ll} \text{Move} & \text{R2, \#1000} \\ \text{Move} & \text{R3, \#300} \\ \text{Store} & \text{R3, (R2)} \end{array}$$

Explain the difference.

2.13 **[E]** Write an assembly-language program in the style of Figure 2.13 for the program in Figure 2.11. Assume the data layout of Figure 2.10.

2.14 **[E]** Write a CISC-style program for the task in Example 2.1. At most one operand of an instruction can be in the memory.

2.15 **[E]** Write a CISC-style program for the task in Example 2.2. At most one operand of an instruction can be in the memory.

2.16 **[M]** Write a CISC-style program for the task in Example 2.3. At most one operand of an instruction can be in the memory.

2.17 **[M]** Write a CISC-style program for the task in Example 2.4. At most one operand of an instruction can be in the memory.

2.18 **[M]** Write a RISC-style program for the task in Example 2.5.

2.19 **[E]** Register R5 is used in a program to point to the top of a stack containing 32-bit numbers. Write a sequence of instructions using the Index, Autoincrement, and Autodecrement addressing modes to perform each of the following tasks:

(*a*) Pop the top two items off the stack, add them, then push the result onto the stack.

(*b*) Copy the fifth item from the top into register R3.

(*c*) Remove the top ten items from the stack.

For each case, assume that the stack contains ten or more elements.

2.20 **[M]** Show the processor stack contents and the contents of the stack pointer, SP, immediately after each of the following instructions in the program in Figure 2.18 is executed. Assume that [SP] = 1000 at Level 1, before execution of the calling program begins.

(*a*) The second Store instruction in the subroutine

(*b*) The last Load instruction in the subroutine

(*c*) The last Store instruction in the calling program

2.21 **[M]** Consider the following possibilities for saving the return address of a subroutine:

(*a*) In a processor register

(*b*) In a memory location associated with the call, so that a different location is used when the subroutine is called from different places

(*c*) On a stack

Which of these possibilities supports subroutine nesting and which supports subroutine recursion (that is, a subroutine that calls itself)?

2.22   [M] In addition to the processor stack, it may be convenient to use another stack in some programs. The second stack is usually allocated a fixed amount of space in the memory. In this case, it is important to avoid pushing an item onto the stack when the stack has reached its maximum size. Also, it is important to avoid attempting to pop an item off an empty stack, which could result from a programming error. Write two short RISC-style routines, called SAFEPUSH and SAFEPOP, for pushing onto and popping off this stack structure, while guarding against these two possible errors. Assume that the element to be pushed/popped is located in register R2, and that register R5 serves as the stack pointer for this user stack. The stack is full if its topmost element is stored in location TOP, and it is empty if the last element popped was stored in location BOTTOM. The routines should branch to FULLERROR and EMPTYERROR, respectively, if errors occur. All elements are of word size, and the stack grows toward lower-numbered address locations.

2.23   [M] Repeat Problem 2.22 for CISC-style routines that can use Autoincrement and Autodecrement addressing modes.

2.24   [D] Another useful data structure that is similar to the stack is called a *queue*. Data are stored in and retrieved from a queue on a first-in–first-out (FIFO) basis. Thus, if we assume that the queue grows in the direction of increasing addresses in the memory, which is a common practice, new data are added at the back (high-address end) and retrieved from the front (low-address end) of the queue.

There are two important differences between how a stack and a queue are implemented. One end of the stack is fixed (the bottom), while the other end rises and falls as data are pushed and popped. A single pointer is needed to point to the top of the stack at any given time. On the other hand, both ends of a queue move to higher addresses as data are added at the back and removed from the front. So two pointers are needed to keep track of the two ends of the queue.

A FIFO queue of bytes is to be implemented in the memory, occupying a fixed region of k bytes. The necessary pointers are an IN pointer and an OUT pointer. The IN pointer keeps track of the location where the next byte is to be appended to the back of the queue, and the OUT pointer keeps track of the location containing the next byte to be removed from the front of the queue.

(*a*) As data items are added to the queue, they are added at successively higher addresses until the end of the memory region is reached. What happens next, when a new item is to be added to the queue?

(*b*) Choose a suitable definition for the IN and OUT pointers, indicating what they point to in the data structure. Use a simple diagram to illustrate your answer.

(*c*) Show that if the state of the queue is described only by the two pointers, the situations when the queue is completely full and completely empty are indistinguishable.

(*d*) What condition would you add to solve the problem in part (*c*)?

(*e*) Propose a procedure for manipulating the two pointers IN and OUT to append and remove items from the queue.

2.25   **[M]** Consider the queue structure described in Problem 2.24. Write APPEND and RE-MOVE routines that transfer data between a processor register and the queue. Be careful to inspect and update the state of the queue and the pointers each time an operation is attempted and performed.

2.26   **[M]** The dot-product computation is discussed in Section 2.12.1. This type of computation can be used in the following signal-processing task. An input signal time sequence IN(0), IN(1), IN(2), IN(3), ..., is processed by a 3-element weight vector (WT(0), WT(1), WT(2)) = (1/8, 1/4, 1/2) to produce an output signal time sequence OUT(0), OUT(1), OUT(2), OUT(3), ..., as follows:

$$OUT(0) = WT(0) \times IN(0) + WT(1) \times IN(1) + WT(2) \times IN(2)$$
$$OUT(1) = WT(0) \times IN(1) + WT(1) \times IN(2) + WT(2) \times IN(3)$$
$$OUT(2) = WT(0) \times IN(2) + WT(1) \times IN(3) + WT(2) \times IN(4)$$
$$OUT(3) = WT(0) \times IN(3) + WT(1) \times IN(4) + WT(2) \times IN(5)$$
$$\vdots$$

All signal and weight values are 32-bit signed numbers. The weights, inputs, and outputs, are stored in the memory starting at locations WT, IN, and OUT, respectively. Write a RISC-style program to calculate and store the output values for the first n outputs, where n is stored at location N.

Hint: Arithmetic right shifts can be used to do the multiplications.

2.27   **[M]** Write a subroutine MEMCPY for copying a sequence of bytes from one area in the main memory to another area. The subroutine should accept three input parameters in registers representing the *from* address, the *to* address, and the *length* of the sequence to be copied. The two areas may overlap. In all but one case, the subroutine should copy the bytes in the order of increasing addresses. However, in the case where the *to* address falls within the sequence of bytes to be copied, i.e., when the *to* address is between *from* and *from+length*−1, the subroutine must copy the bytes in the order of decreasing addresses by starting at the end of the sequence of bytes to be copied in order to avoid overwriting bytes that have not yet been copied.

2.28   **[M]** Write a subroutine MEMCMP for performing a byte-by-byte comparison of two sequences of bytes in the main memory. The subroutine should accept three input parameters in registers representing the *first* address, the *second* address, and the *length* of the sequences to be compared. It should use a register to return the count of the number of comparisons that do not match.

2.29   **[M]** Write a subroutine called EXCLAIM that accepts a single parameter in a register representing the starting address STRNG in the main memory for a string of ASCII characters in successive bytes representing an arbitrary collection of sentences, with the NUL control character (value 0) at the end of the string. The subroutine should scan the string beginning at address STRNG and replace every occurrence of a period ('.') with an exclamation mark ('!').

2.30   **[M]** Write a subroutine called ALLCAPS that accepts a parameter in a register representing the starting address STRNG in the main memory for a string of ASCII characters in successive bytes, with the NUL control character (value 0) at the end of the string. The subroutine should scan the string beginning at address STRNG and replace every occurrence of a lower-case letter ('a'–'z') with the corresponding upper-case letter ('A'–'Z').

2.31   **[M]** Write a subroutine called WORDS that accepts a parameter in a register representing the starting address STRNG in the main memory for a string of ASCII characters in successive bytes, with the NUL control character (value 0) at the end of the string. The string represents English text with the space character between words. The subroutine has to determine the number of words in the string (excluding the punctuation characters). It must return the result to the calling program in a register.

2.32   **[D]** Write a subroutine called INSERT that places a number in the correct ordered position within a list of positive numbers that are stored in increasing order of value. Three input parameters should be passed to the subroutine in processor registers, representing the starting address of the ordered list of numbers, the length of the list, and the new value to be inserted into the list. The subroutine should locate the appropriate position for the new value in the list, then shift all of the larger numbers up by one position to create space for storing the new value in the list.

2.33   **[D]** Write a subroutine called INSERTSORT that repeatedly uses the INSERT subroutine in Problem 2.32 to take an unordered list of numbers and create a new list with the same numbers in increasing order. The subroutine should accept three input parameters in registers representing the starting address OLDLIST for the unordered sequence of numbers, the length of the list, and the starting address NEWLIST for the ordered sequence of numbers.

chapter

3

BASIC INPUT/OUTPUT

CHAPTER OBJECTIVES

In this chapter you will learn about:

- Transferring data between a processor and input/output (I/O) devices
- The programmer's view of I/O transfers
- How program-controlled I/O is performed using polling
- How interrupts are used in I/O transfers

One of the basic features of a computer is its ability to exchange data with other devices. This communication capability enables a human operator, for example, to use a keyboard and a display screen to process text and graphics. We make extensive use of computers to communicate with other computers over the Internet and access information around the globe. In other applications, computers are less visible but equally important. They are an integral part of home appliances, manufacturing equipment, transportation systems, banking, and point-of-sale terminals. In such applications, input to a computer may come from a sensor switch, a digital camera, a microphone, or a fire alarm. Output may be a sound signal sent to a speaker, or a digitally coded command that changes the speed of a motor, opens a valve, or causes a robot to move in a specified manner. In short, computers should have the ability to exchange digital and analog information with a wide range of devices in many different environments.

In this chapter we will consider the input/output (I/O) capability of computers as seen from the programmer's point of view. We will present only basic I/O operations, which are provided in all computers. This knowledge will enable the reader to perform interesting and useful exercises on equipment found in a typical teaching laboratory environment. More complex I/O schemes, as well as the hardware needed to implement the I/O capability, are discussed in Chapter 7.

3.1   ACCESSING I/O DEVICES

The components of a computer system communicate with each other through an interconnection network, as shown in Figure 3.1. The interconnection network consists of circuits needed to transfer information between the processor, the memory unit, and a number of I/O devices.

In Chapter 2, we described the concept of an address space and how the processor may access individual memory locations within such an address space. Load and Store instructions use addressing modes to generate effective addresses that identify the desired locations. This idea of using addresses to access various locations in the memory can be

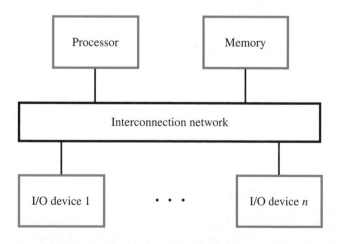

Figure 3.1   A computer system.

extended to deal with the I/O devices as well. For this purpose, each I/O device must appear to the processor as consisting of some addressable locations, just like the memory. Some addresses in the address space of the processor are assigned to these I/O locations, rather than to the main memory. These locations are usually implemented as bit storage circuits (flip-flops) organized in the form of registers. It is customary to refer to them as *I/O registers*. Since the I/O devices and the memory share the same address space, this arrangement is called *memory-mapped I/O*. It is used in most computers.

With memory-mapped I/O, any machine instruction that can access memory can be used to transfer data to or from an I/O device. For example, if DATAIN is the address of a register in an input device, the instruction

Load   R2, DATAIN

reads the data from the DATAIN register and loads them into processor register R2. Similarly, the instruction

Store   R2, DATAOUT

sends the contents of register R2 to location DATAOUT, which is a register in an output device.

3.1.1   I/O DEVICE INTERFACE

An I/O device is connected to the interconnection network by using a circuit, called the *device interface*, which provides the means for data transfer and for the exchange of status and control information needed to facilitate the data transfers and govern the operation of the device. The interface includes some registers that can be accessed by the processor. One register may serve as a buffer for data transfers, another may hold information about the current status of the device, and yet another may store the information that controls the operational behavior of the device. These *data*, *status*, and *control* registers are accessed by program instructions as if they were memory locations. Typical transfers of information are between I/O registers and the registers in the processor. Figure 3.2 illustrates how the keyboard and display devices are connected to the processor from the software point of view.

3.1.2   PROGRAM-CONTROLLED I/O

Let us begin the discussion of input/output issues by looking at two essential I/O devices for human-computer interaction—keyboard and display. Consider a task that reads characters typed on a keyboard, stores these data in the memory, and displays the same characters on a display screen. A simple way of implementing this task is to write a program that performs all functions needed to realize the desired action. This method is known as *program-controlled I/O*.

In addition to transferring each character from the keyboard into the memory, and then to the display, it is necessary to ensure that this happens at the right time. An input character must be read in response to a key being pressed. For output, a character must be sent to

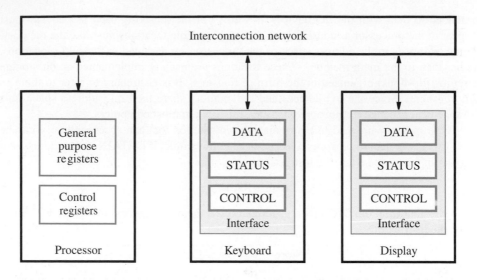

Figure 3.2   The connection for processor, keyboard, and display.

the display only when the display device is able to accept it. The rate of data transfer from the keyboard to a computer is limited by the typing speed of the user, which is unlikely to exceed a few characters per second. The rate of output transfers from the computer to the display is much higher. It is determined by the rate at which characters can be transmitted to and displayed on the display device, typically several thousand characters per second. However, this is still much slower than the speed of a processor that can execute billions of instructions per second. The difference in speed between the processor and I/O devices creates the need for mechanisms to synchronize the transfer of data between them.

One solution to this problem involves a signaling protocol. On output, the processor sends the first character and then waits for a signal from the display that the next character can be sent. It then sends the second character, and so on. An input character is obtained from the keyboard in a similar way. The processor waits for a signal indicating that a key has been pressed and that a binary code that represents the corresponding character is available in an I/O register associated with the keyboard. Then the processor proceeds to read that code.

The keyboard includes a circuit that responds to a key being pressed by producing the code for the corresponding character that can be used by the computer. We will assume that ASCII code (presented in Table 1.1) is used, in which each character code occupies one byte. Let KBD_DATA be the address label of an 8-bit register that holds the generated character. Also, let a signal indicating that a key has been pressed be provided by setting to 1 a flip-flop called KIN, which is a part of an eight-bit status register, KBD_STATUS. The processor can read the *status flag* KIN to determine when a character code has been placed in KBD_DATA. When the processor reads the status flag to determine its state, we say that the processor *polls* the I/O device.

The display includes an 8-bit register, which we will call DISP_DATA, used to receive characters from the processor. It also must be able to indicate that it is ready to receive the

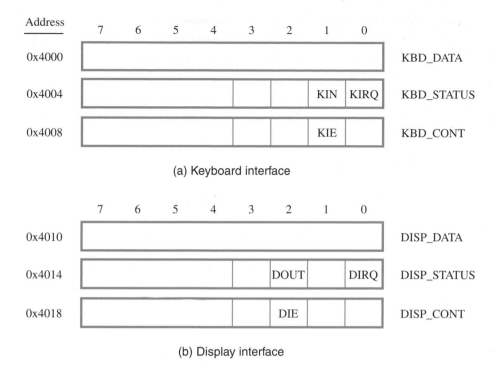

Figure 3.3   Registers in the keyboard and display interfaces.

next character; this can be done by using a status flag called DOUT, which is one bit in a status register, DISP_STATUS.

Figure 3.3 illustrates how these registers may be organized. The interface for each device also includes a control register, which we will discuss in Section 3.2. We have identified only a few bits in the registers, those that are pertinent to the discussion in this chapter. Other bits can be used for other purposes, or perhaps simply ignored.

If the registers in I/O interfaces are to be accessed as if they are memory locations, each register must be assigned a specific address that will be recognized by the interface circuit. In Figure 3.3, we assigned hexadecimal numbers 4000 and 4010 as base addresses for the keyboard and display, respectively. These are the addresses of the data registers. The addresses of the status registers are four bytes higher, and the control registers are eight bytes higher. This makes all addresses word-aligned in a 32-bit word computer, which is usually done in practice. Assigning the addresses to registers in this manner makes the I/O registers accessible in a program executed by the processor. This is the programmer's view of the device.

A program is needed to perform the task of reading the characters produced by the keyboard, storing these characters in the memory, and sending them to the display. To perform I/O transfers, the processor must execute machine instructions that check the state of the status flags and transfer data between the processor and the I/O devices.

Let us consider the details of the input process. When a key is pressed, the keyboard circuit places the ASCII-encoded character into the KBD_DATA register. At the same time, the circuit sets the KIN flag to 1. Meanwhile, the processor is executing the I/O program which continuously checks the state of the KIN flag. When it detects that KIN is set to 1, it transfers the contents of KBD_DATA into a processor register. Once the contents of KBD_DATA are read, KIN must be cleared to 0, which is usually done automatically by the interface circuit. If a second character is entered at the keyboard, KIN is again set to 1 and the process repeats. The desired action can be achieved by performing the operations:

> READWAIT   Read the KIN flag
> Branch to READWAIT if KIN = 0
> Transfer data from KBD_DATA to R5

which reads the character into processor register R5.

An analogous process takes place when characters are transferred from the processor to the display. When DOUT is equal to 1, the display is ready to receive a character. Under program control, the processor monitors DOUT, and when DOUT is equal to 1, the processor transfers an ASCII-encoded character to DISP_DATA. The transfer of a character to DISP_DATA clears DOUT to 0. When the display device is ready to receive a second character, DOUT is again set to 1. This can be achieved by performing the operations:

> WRITEWAIT   Read the DOUT flag
> Branch to WRITEWAIT if DOUT = 0
> Transfer data from R5 to DISP_DATA

The wait loop is executed repeatedly until the status flag DOUT is set to 1 by the display when it is free to receive a character. Then, the character from R5 is transferred to DISP_DATA to be displayed, which also clears DOUT to 0.

We assume that the initial state of KIN is 0 and the initial state of DOUT is 1. This initialization is normally performed by the device control circuits when power is turned on.

In computers that use memory-mapped I/O, in which some addresses are used to refer to registers in I/O interfaces, data can be transferred between these registers and the processor using instructions such as Load, Store, and Move. For example, the contents of the keyboard character buffer KBD_DATA can be transferred to register R5 in the processor by the instruction

> LoadByte   R5, KBD_DATA

Similarly, the contents of register R5 can be transferred to DISP_DATA by the instruction

> StoreByte   R5, DISP_DATA

The LoadByte and StoreByte operation codes signify that the operand size is a byte, to distinguish them from the Load and Store operation codes that we have used for word operands.

The Read operation described above may be implemented by the RISC-style instructions:

```
READWAIT:    LoadByte           R4, KBD_STATUS
             And                R4, R4, #2
             Branch_if_[R4]=0   READWAIT
             LoadByte           R5, KBD_DATA
```

The And instruction is used to test the KIN flag, which is bit b_1 of the status information in R4 that was read from the KBD_STATUS register. As long as $b_1 = 0$, the result of the AND operation leaves the value in R4 equal to zero, and the READWAIT loop continues to be executed.

Similarly, the Write operation may be implemented as:

```
WRITEWAIT:   LoadByte           R4, DISP_STATUS
             And                R4, R4, #4
             Branch_if_[R4]=0   WRITEWAIT
             StoreByte          R5, DISP_DATA
```

Observe that the And instruction in this case uses the immediate value 4 to test the display's status bit, b_2.

3.1.3   AN EXAMPLE OF A RISC-STYLE I/O PROGRAM

We can now put together a complete program for a typical I/O task, as shown in Figure 3.4. The program uses the program-controlled I/O approach described above to read, store, and display a line of characters typed at the keyboard. As the characters are read in, one by one, they are stored in the memory and then *echoed* back to the display. The program finishes when the carriage return character, CR, is encountered. The address of the first byte location of the memory where the line is to be stored is LOC. Register R2 is used to point to this part of the memory, and it is initially loaded with the address LOC by the first instruction in the program. R2 is incremented for each character read and displayed.

3.1.4   AN EXAMPLE OF A CISC-STYLE I/O PROGRAM

Let us now perform the same task using CISC-style instructions. In CISC instruction sets it is possible to perform some arithmetic and logic operations directly on operands in the memory. So, it is possible to have the instruction

$$\text{TestBit} \quad \text{destination, \#k}$$

which tests bit b_k of the destination operand and sets the condition flag Z (Zero) to 1 if $b_k = 0$ and to 0 otherwise. Since the operand can be in a memory location, we can use the instruction

$$\text{TestBit} \quad \text{KBD\_STATUS, \#1}$$

	Move	R2, #LOC	Initialize pointer register R2 to point to the address of the first location in main memory where the characters are to be stored.
	MoveByte	R3, #CR	Load ASCII code for Carriage Return into R3.
READ:	LoadByte	R4, KBD_STATUS	Wait for a character to be entered.
	And	R4, R4, #2	Check the KIN flag.
	Branch_if_[R4]=0	READ	
	LoadByte	R5, KBD_DATA	Read the character from KBD_DATA (this clears KIN to 0).
	StoreByte	R5, (R2)	Write the character into the main memory and increment the pointer to main memory.
	Add	R2, R2, #1	
ECHO:	LoadByte	R4, DISP_STATUS	Wait for the display to become ready.
	And	R4, R4, #4	Check the DOUT flag.
	Branch_if_[R4]=0	ECHO	
	StoreByte	R5, DISP_DATA	Move the character just read to the display buffer register (this clears DOUT to 0).
	Branch_if_[R5]≠[R3]	READ	Check if the character just read is the Carriage Return. If it is not, then branch back and read another character.

Figure 3.4   A RISC-style program that reads a line of characters and displays it.

to test the state of the KIN flag in the keyboard interface. A Branch instruction that checks the state of the Z flag can then be used to cause a branch to the beginning of the wait loop.

Figure 3.5 gives a CISC-style program that reads and displays a line of characters. Observe that the first MoveByte instruction transfers each character directly from KBD_DATA to the memory location pointed to by R2. A Compare instruction

Compare   destination, source

performs the comparison by subtracting the contents of the source from the contents of the destination, and then sets the condition flags based on the result. It does not change the contents of either the source or the destination. Note that the CompareByte instruction in Figure 3.5 uses the autoincrement addressing mode, which automatically increments the value of the pointer R2 after the comparison has been made. In the RISC-style program in Figure 3.4 the pointer has to be incremented using a separate Add instruction.

We have discussed the memory-mapped I/O scheme, which is used in most computers. There is an alternative that can be found in some processors where there exist special In and Out instructions to perform I/O transfers. In this case, there exists a separate I/O address space used only by these instructions. When building a computer system that uses these processors, the designer has the option of connecting I/O devices to use the special I/O address space or simply incorporating them as part of the memory address space.

	Move	R2, #LOC	Initialize pointer register R2 to point to the address of the first location in main memory where the characters are to be stored.
READ:	TestBit	KBD_STATUS, #1	Wait for a character to be entered
	Branch=0	READ	in the keyboard buffer KBD_DATA.
	MoveByte	(R2), KBD_DATA	Transfer the character from KBD_DATA into the main memory (this clears KIN to 0).
ECHO:	TestBit	DISP_STATUS, #2	Wait for the display to become ready.
	Branch=0	ECHO	
	MoveByte	DISP_DATA, (R2)	Move the character just read to the display buffer register (this clears DOUT to 0).
	CompareByte	(R2)+, #CR	Check if the character just read is CR (carriage return). If it is not CR, then
	Branch≠0	READ	branch back and read another character. Also, increment the pointer to store the next character.

Figure 3.5   A CISC-style program that reads a line of characters and displays it.

Program-controlled I/O requires continuous involvement of the processor in the I/O activities. Almost all of the execution time for the programs in Figures 3.4 and 3.5 is spent in the two wait loops, while the processor waits for a key to be pressed or for the display to become available. Wasting the processor execution time in this manner can be avoided by using the concept of interrupts.

3.2 INTERRUPTS

In the examples in Figures 3.4 and 3.5, the program enters a wait loop in which it repeatedly tests the device status. During this period, the processor is not performing any useful computation. There are many situations where other tasks can be performed while waiting for an I/O device to become ready. To allow this to happen, we can arrange for the I/O device to alert the processor when it becomes ready. It can do so by sending a hardware signal called an *interrupt request* to the processor. Since the processor is no longer required to continuously poll the status of I/O devices, it can use the waiting period to perform other useful tasks. Indeed, by using interrupts, such waiting periods can ideally be eliminated.

Consider a task that requires continuous extensive computations to be performed and the results to be displayed on a display device. The displayed results must be updated every ten seconds. The ten-second intervals can be determined by a simple timer circuit, which

Example 3.1

generates an appropriate signal. The processor treats the timer circuit as an input device that produces a signal that can be interrogated. If this is done by means of polling, the processor will waste considerable time checking the state of the signal. A better solution is to have the timer circuit raise an interrupt request once every ten seconds. In response, the processor displays the latest results.

The task can be implemented with a program that consists of two routines, COMPUTE and DISPLAY. The processor continuously executes the COMPUTE routine. When it receives an interrupt request from the timer, it suspends the execution of the COMPUTE routine and executes the DISPLAY routine which sends the latest results to the display device. Upon completion of the DISPLAY routine, the processor resumes the execution of the COMPUTE routine. Since the time needed to send the results to the display device is very small compared to the ten-second interval, the processor in effect spends almost all of its time executing the COMPUTE routine.

This example illustrates the concept of interrupts. The routine executed in response to an interrupt request is called the *interrupt-service routine*, which is the DISPLAY routine in our example. Interrupts bear considerable resemblance to subroutine calls. Assume that an interrupt request arrives during execution of instruction i in Figure 3.6. The processor first completes execution of instruction i. Then, it loads the program counter with the address of the first instruction of the interrupt-service routine. For the time being, let us assume that this address is hardwired in the processor. After execution of the interrupt-service routine, the processor returns to instruction $i + 1$. Therefore, when an interrupt occurs, the current contents of the PC, which point to instruction $i + 1$, must be put in temporary storage in a known location. A Return-from-interrupt instruction at the end of the interrupt-service routine reloads the PC from that temporary storage location, causing execution to resume at

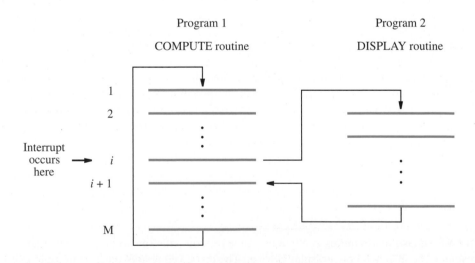

Figure 3.6   Transfer of control through the use of interrupts.

instruction $i + 1$. The *return address* must be saved either in a designated general-purpose register or on the processor stack.

We should note that as part of handling interrupts, the processor must inform the device that its request has been recognized so that it may remove its interrupt-request signal. This can be accomplished by means of a special control signal, called *interrupt acknowledge*, which is sent to the device through the interconnection network. An alternative is to have the transfer of data between the processor and the I/O device interface accomplish the same purpose. The execution of an instruction in the interrupt-service routine that accesses the status or data register in the device interface implicitly informs the device that its interrupt request has been recognized.

So far, treatment of an interrupt-service routine is very similar to that of a subroutine. An important departure from this similarity should be noted. A subroutine performs a function required by the program from which it is called. As such, potential changes to status information and contents of registers are anticipated. However, an interrupt-service routine may not have any relation to the portion of the program being executed at the time the interrupt request is received. Therefore, before starting execution of the interrupt-service routine, status information and contents of processor registers that may be altered in unanticipated ways during the execution of that routine must be saved. This saved information must be restored before execution of the interrupted program is resumed. In this way, the original program can continue execution without being affected in any way by the interruption, except for the time delay.

The task of saving and restoring information can be done automatically by the processor or by program instructions. Most modern processors save only the minimum amount of information needed to maintain the integrity of program execution. This is because the process of saving and restoring registers involves memory transfers that increase the total execution time, and hence represent execution overhead. Saving registers also increases the delay between the time an interrupt request is received and the start of execution of the interrupt-service routine. This delay is called *interrupt latency*. In some applications, a long interrupt latency is unacceptable. For these reasons, the amount of information saved automatically by the processor when an interrupt request is accepted should be kept to a minimum. Typically, the processor saves only the contents of the program counter and the processor status register. Any additional information that needs to be saved must be saved by explicit instructions at the beginning of the interrupt-service routine and restored at the end of the routine. In some earlier processors, particularly those with a small number of registers, all registers are saved automatically by the processor hardware at the time an interrupt request is accepted. The data saved are restored to their respective registers as part of the execution of the Return-from-interrupt instruction.

Some computers provide two types of interrupts. One saves all register contents, and the other does not. A particular I/O device may use either type, depending upon its response-time requirements. Another interesting approach is to provide duplicate sets of processor registers. In this case, a different set of registers can be used by the interrupt-service routine, thus eliminating the need to save and restore registers. The duplicate registers are sometimes called the *shadow registers*.

An interrupt is more than a simple mechanism for coordinating I/O transfers. In a general sense, interrupts enable transfer of control from one program to another to be initiated by an event external to the computer. Execution of the interrupted program resumes after the execution of the interrupt-service routine has been completed. The concept of interrupts is used in operating systems and in many control applications where processing of certain routines must be accurately timed relative to external events. The latter type of application is referred to as *real-time processing*.

3.2.1 ENABLING AND DISABLING INTERRUPTS

The facilities provided in a computer must give the programmer complete control over the events that take place during program execution. The arrival of an interrupt request from an external device causes the processor to suspend the execution of one program and start the execution of another. Because interrupts can arrive at any time, they may alter the sequence of events from that envisaged by the programmer. Hence, the interruption of program execution must be carefully controlled. A fundamental facility found in all computers is the ability to enable and disable such interruptions as desired.

There are many situations in which the processor should ignore interrupt requests. For instance, the timer circuit in Example 3.1 should raise interrupt requests only when the COMPUTE routine is being executed. It should be prevented from doing so when some other task is being performed. In another case, it may be necessary to guarantee that a particular sequence of instructions is executed to the end without interruption because the interrupt-service routine may change some of the data used by the instructions in question. For these reasons, some means for enabling and disabling interrupts must be available to the programmer.

It is convenient to be able to enable and disable interrupts at both the processor and I/O device ends. The processor can either accept or ignore interrupt requests. An I/O device can either be allowed to raise interrupt requests or prevented from doing so. A commonly used mechanism to achieve this is to use some control bits in registers that can be accessed by program instructions.

The processor has a *status register* (PS), which contains information about its current state of operation. Let one bit, IE, of this register be assigned for enabling/disabling interrupts. Then, the programmer can set or clear IE to cause the desired action. When IE = 1, interrupt requests from I/O devices are accepted and serviced by the processor. When IE = 0, the processor simply ignores all interrupt requests from I/O devices.

The interface of an I/O device includes a control register that contains the information that governs the mode of operation of the device. One bit in this register may be dedicated to interrupt control. The I/O device is allowed to raise interrupt requests only when this bit is set to 1. We will discuss this arrangement in Section 3.2.3.

Let us now consider the specific case of a single interrupt request from one device. When a device activates the interrupt-request signal, it keeps this signal activated until it learns that the processor has accepted its request. This means that the interrupt-request signal will be active during execution of the interrupt-service routine, perhaps until an instruction is reached that accesses the device in question. It is essential to ensure that this active request signal does not lead to successive interruptions, causing the system to enter an infinite loop from which it cannot recover.

A good choice is to have the processor automatically disable interrupts before starting the execution of the interrupt-service routine. The processor saves the contents of the program counter and the processor status register. After saving the contents of the PS register, with the IE bit equal to 1, the processor clears the IE bit in the PS register, thus disabling further interrupts. Then, it begins execution of the interrupt-service routine. When a Return-from-interrupt instruction is executed, the saved contents of the PS register are restored, setting the IE bit back to 1. Hence, interrupts are again enabled.

Before proceeding to study more complex aspects of interrupts, let us summarize the sequence of events involved in handling an interrupt request from a single device. Assuming that interrupts are enabled in both the processor and the device, the following is a typical scenario:

1. The device raises an interrupt request.

2. The processor interrupts the program currently being executed and saves the contents of the PC and PS registers.

3. Interrupts are disabled by clearing the IE bit in the PS to 0.

4. The action requested by the interrupt is performed by the interrupt-service routine, during which time the device is informed that its request has been recognized, and in response, it deactivates the interrupt-request signal.

5. Upon completion of the interrupt-service routine, the saved contents of the PC and PS registers are restored (enabling interrupts by setting the IE bit to 1), and execution of the interrupted program is resumed.

3.2.2 HANDLING MULTIPLE DEVICES

Let us now consider the situation where a number of devices capable of initiating interrupts are connected to the processor. Because these devices are operationally independent, there is no definite order in which they will generate interrupts. For example, device X may request an interrupt while an interrupt caused by device Y is being serviced, or several devices may request interrupts at exactly the same time. This gives rise to a number of questions:

1. How can the processor determine which device is requesting an interrupt?

2. Given that different devices are likely to require different interrupt-service routines, how can the processor obtain the starting address of the appropriate routine in each case?

3. Should a device be allowed to interrupt the processor while another interrupt is being serviced?

4. How should two or more simultaneous interrupt requests be handled?

The means by which these issues are handled vary from one computer to another, and the approach taken is an important consideration in determining the computer's suitability for a given application.

When an interrupt request is received it is necessary to identify the particular device that raised the request. Furthermore, if two devices raise interrupt requests at the same time, it must be possible to break the tie and select one of the two requests for service. When the interrupt-service routine for the selected device has been completed, the second request can be serviced.

The information needed to determine whether a device is requesting an interrupt is available in its status register. When the device raises an interrupt request, it sets to 1 a bit in its status register, which we will call the IRQ bit. The simplest way to identify the interrupting device is to have the interrupt-service routine poll all I/O devices in the system. The first device encountered with its IRQ bit set to 1 is the device that should be serviced. An appropriate subroutine is then called to provide the requested service.

The polling scheme is easy to implement. Its main disadvantage is the time spent interrogating the IRQ bits of devices that may not be requesting any service. An alternative approach is to use vectored interrupts, which we describe next.

Vectored Interrupts

To reduce the time involved in the polling process, a device requesting an interrupt may identify itself directly to the processor. Then, the processor can immediately start executing the corresponding interrupt-service routine. The term *vectored interrupts* refers to interrupt-handling schemes based on this approach.

A device requesting an interrupt can identify itself if it has its own interrupt-request signal, or if it can send a special code to the processor through the interconnection network. The processor's circuits determine the memory address of the required interrupt-service routine. A commonly used scheme is to allocate permanently an area in the memory to hold the addresses of interrupt-service routines. These addresses are usually referred to as *interrupt vectors*, and they are said to constitute the *interrupt-vector table*. For example, 128 bytes may be allocated to hold a table of 32 interrupt vectors. Typically, the interrupt-vector table is in the lowest-address range. The interrupt-service routines may be located anywhere in the memory. When an interrupt request arrives, the information provided by the requesting device is used as a pointer into the interrupt-vector table, and the address in the corresponding interrupt vector is automatically loaded into the program counter.

Interrupt Nesting

We suggested in Section 3.2.1 that interrupts should be disabled during the execution of an interrupt-service routine, to ensure that a request from one device will not cause more than one interruption. The same arrangement is often used when several devices are involved, in which case execution of a given interrupt-service routine, once started, always continues to completion before the processor accepts an interrupt request from a second device. Interrupt-service routines are typically short, and the delay they may cause is acceptable for most simple devices.

For some devices, however, a long delay in responding to an interrupt request may lead to erroneous operation. Consider, for example, a computer that keeps track of the time of day using a real-time clock. This is a device that sends interrupt requests to the processor at regular intervals. For each of these requests, the processor executes a short interrupt-service routine to increment a set of counters in the memory that keep track of time in seconds, minutes, and so on. Proper operation requires that the delay in responding to an interrupt request from the real-time clock be small in comparison with the interval between two successive requests. To ensure that this requirement is satisfied in the presence of other interrupting devices, it may be necessary to accept an interrupt request from the clock during the execution of an interrupt-service routine for another device, i.e., to nest interrupts.

This example suggests that I/O devices should be organized in a priority structure. An interrupt request from a high-priority device should be accepted while the processor is servicing a request from a lower-priority device.

A multiple-level priority organization means that during execution of an interrupt-service routine, interrupt requests will be accepted from some devices but not from others, depending upon the device's priority. To implement this scheme, we can assign a priority level to the processor that can be changed under program control. The priority level of the processor is the priority of the program that is currently being executed. The processor accepts interrupts only from devices that have priorities higher than its own. At the time that execution of an interrupt-service routine for some device is started, the priority of the processor is raised to that of the device either automatically or with special instructions. This action disables interrupts from devices that have the same or lower level of priority. However, interrupt requests from higher-priority devices will continue to be accepted. The processor's priority can be encoded in a few bits of the processor status register. While this scheme is used in some processors, we will use a simpler scheme in later examples.

Finally, we should point out that if nested interrupts are allowed, then each interrupt-service routine must save on the stack the saved contents of the program counter and the status register. This has to be done before the interrupt-service routine enables nesting by setting the IE bit in the staus register to 1.

Simultaneous Requests

We also need to consider the problem of simultaneous arrivals of interrupt requests from two or more devices. The processor must have some means of deciding which request to service first. Polling the status registers of the I/O devices is the simplest such mechanism. In this case, priority is determined by the order in which the devices are polled. When vectored interrupts are used, we must ensure that only one device is selected to send its interrupt vector code. This is done in hardware, by using arbitration circuits which we will discuss in Chapter 7.

3.2.3 CONTROLLING I/O DEVICE BEHAVIOR

It is important to ensure that interrupt requests are generated only by those I/O devices that the processor is currently willing to recognize. Hence, we need a mechanism in the interface circuits of individual devices to control whether a device is allowed to interrupt the processor. The control needed is usually provided in the form of an *interrupt-enable* bit in the device's interface circuit.

I/O devices vary in complexity from simple to quite complex. Simple devices, such as a keyboard, require little in the way of control. Complex devices may have a number of possible modes of operation, which must be controlled. A commonly used approach is to provide a control register in the device interface, which holds the information needed to control the behavior of the device. This register is accessed as an addressable location, just like the data and status registers that we discussed before. One bit in the register serves as the interrupt-enable bit, IE. When it is set to 1 by an instruction that writes new information into the control register, the device is placed into a mode in which it is allowed to interrupt the processor whenever it is ready for an I/O transfer.

Figure 3.3 shows the registers that may be used in the interfaces of keyboard and display devices. Since these devices transfer character-based data, handling one character at a time, it is appropriate to use an eight-bit data register. We have assumed that the status and control registers are also eight bits long. Only one or two bits in these registers are needed in handling the I/O transfers. The remaining bits can be used to specify other aspects of the operation of the device, or ignored if they are not needed. The keyboard status register includes bits KIN and KIRQ. We have already discussed the use of the KIN bit in Section 3.1.2. The KIRQ bit is set to 1 if an interrupt request has been raised, but not yet serviced. The keyboard may raise interrupt requests only when the interrupt-enable bit, KIE, in its control register is set to 1. Thus, when both KIE and KIN bits are equal to 1, an interrupt request is raised and the KIRQ bit is set to 1. Similarly, the DIRQ bit in the status register of the display interface indicates whether an interrupt request has been raised. Bit DIE in the control register of this interface is used to enable interrupts. Observe that we have placed KIN and KIE in bit position 1, and DOUT and DIE in position 2. This is an arbitrary choice that makes the program examples that follow easier to understand.

3.2.4 PROCESSOR CONTROL REGISTERS

We have already discussed the need for a status register in the processor. To deal with interrupts it is useful to have some other control registers. Figure 3.7 depicts one possibility, where there are four processor control registers. The status register, PS, includes the interrupt-enable bit, IE, in addition to other status information. Recall that the processor will accept interrupts only when this bit is set to 1. The IPS register is used to automatically

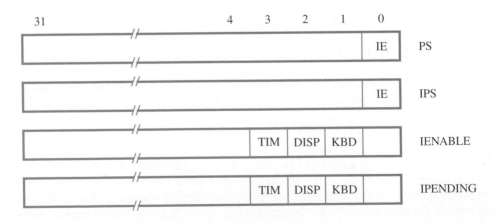

Figure 3.7 Control registers in the processor.

save the contents of PS when an interrupt request is received and accepted. At the end of the interrupt-service routine, the previous state of the processor is automatically restored by transferring the contents of IPS into PS. Since there is only one register available for storing the previous status information, it becomes necessary to save the contents of IPS on the stack if nested interrupts are allowed.

The IENABLE register allows the processor to selectively respond to individual I/O devices. A bit may be assigned for each device, as shown in the figure for the keyboard, display, and a timer circuit that we will use in a later example. When a bit is set to 1, the processor will accept interrupt requests from the corresponding device. The IPENDING register indicates the active interrupt requests. This is convenient when multiple devices may raise requests at the same time. Then, a program can decide which interrupt should be serviced first.

In a 32-bit processor, the control registers are 32 bits long. Using the structure in Figure 3.7, it is possible to accommodate 32 I/O devices in a straightforward manner.

Assembly-language instructions can refer to processor control registers by using names such as those in Figure 3.7. But, these registers cannot be accessed in the same way as the general-purpose registers. They cannot be accessed by arithmetic and logic instructions. They also cannot be accessed by Load and Store instructions that use the encoding format depicted in Figure 2.32c, because a five-bit field is used to specify a source or a destination register in these instructions, which makes it possible to specify only 32 general-purpose registers. Special instructions or special addressing modes may be provided to access the processor control registers. In a RISC-style processor, the special instructions may be of the type

MoveControl   R2, PS

which loads the contents of the program status register into register R2, and

MoveControl   IENABLE, R3

which places the contents of R3 into the IENABLE register. These instructions perform transfers between control and general-purpose registers.

3.2.5 EXAMPLES OF INTERRUPT PROGRAMS

Having presented the basic aspects of interrupts, we can now give some illustrative examples. We will use the keyboard and display devices with the register structure given in Figure 3.3.

Let us consider again the task of reading a line of characters typed on a keyboard, storing the characters in the main memory, and displaying them on a display device. In Figures 3.4 and 3.5, we showed how this task may be performed by using the polling approach to detect when the I/O devices are ready for data transfer. Now, we will use interrupts with the keyboard, but polling with the display.   **Example 3.2**

We assume for now that a specific memory location, ILOC, is dedicated for dealing with interrupts, and that it contains the first instruction of the interrupt-service routine. Whenever an interrupt request arrives at the processor, and processor interrupts are enabled, the processor will automatically:

- Save the contents of the program counter, either in a processor register that holds the return address or on the processor stack.
- Save the contents of the status register PS by transferring them into the IPS register, and clear the IE bit in the PS.
- Load the address ILOC into the program counter.

Assume that in the Main program we wish to read a line from the keyboard and store the characters in successive byte locations in the memory, starting at location LINE. Also, assume that the interrupt-service routine has been loaded in the memory, starting at location ILOC. The Main program has to initialize the interrupt process as follows:

1. Load the address LINE into a memory location PNTR. The interrupt-service routine will use this location as a pointer to store the input characters in the memory.
2. Enable interrupts in the keyboard interface by setting to 1 the KIE bit in the KBD_CONT register.
3. Enable the processor to accept interrupts from the keyboard by setting to 1 the KBD bit in its control register IENABLE.
4. Enable the processor to respond to interrupts in general by setting to 1 the IE bit in the processor status register, PS.

Once this initialization is completed, typing a character on the keyboard will cause an interrupt request to be generated by the keyboard interface. The program being executed at that time will be interrupted and the interrupt-service routine will be executed. This routine must perform the following tasks:

1. Read the input character from the keyboard input data register. This will cause the interface circuit to remove its interrupt request.
2. Store the character in the memory location pointed to by PNTR, and increment PNTR.
3. Display the character using the polling approach.
4. When the end of the line is reached, disable keyboard interrupts and inform the Main program.
5. Return from interrupt.

A RISC-style program that performs these tasks is shown in Figure 3.8. The comments in the program explain the relevant details. When the end of the input line is detected, the interrupt-service routine clears the KIE bit in register KBD_CONT, as no further input is expected. It also sets to 1 the variable EOL (End Of Line), which was initially cleared to 0. We assume that it is checked periodically by the Main program to determine when the input line is ready for processing. The EOL variable provides a means of signaling between the Main program and the interrupt-service routine.

Interrupt-service routine

ILOC:	Subtract	SP, SP, #8	Save registers.
	Store	R2, 4(SP)	
	Store	R3, (SP)	
	Load	R2, PNTR	Load address pointer.
	LoadByte	R3, KBD_DATA	Read character from keyboard.
	StoreByte	R3, (R2)	Write the character into memory
	Add	R2, R2, #1	and increment the pointer.
	Store	R2, PNTR	Update the pointer in memory.
ECHO:	LoadByte	R2, DISP_STATUS	Wait for display to become ready.
	And	R2, R2, #4	
	Branch_if_[R2]=0	ECHO	
	StoreByte	R3, DISP_DATA	Display the character just read.
	Move	R2, #CR	ASCII code for Carriage Return.
	Branch_if_[R3]≠[R2]	RTRN	Return if not CR.
	Move	R2, #1	
	Store	R2, EOL	Indicate end of line.
	Clear	R2	Disable interrupts in
	StoreByte	R2, KBD_CONT	the keyboard interface.
RTRN:	Load	R3, (SP)	Restore registers.
	Load	R2, 4(SP)	
	Add	SP, SP, #8	
	Return-from-interrupt		

Main program

START:	Move	R2, #LINE	
	Store	R2, PNTR	Initialize buffer pointer.
	Clear	R2	
	Store	R2, EOL	Clear end-of-line indicator.
	Move	R2, #2	Enable interrupts in
	StoreByte	R2, KBD_CONT	the keyboard interface.
	MoveControl	R2, IENABLE	
	Or	R2, R2, #2	Enable keyboard interrupts in
	MoveControl	IENABLE, R2	the processor control register.
	MoveControl	R2, PS	
	Or	R2, R2, #1	
	MoveControl	PS, R2	Set interrupt-enable bit in PS.
	next instruction		

Figure 3.8   A RISC-style program that reads a line of characters using interrupts, and displays the line using polling.

Observe that the last three instructions in the Main program are used to set to 1 the interrupt-enable bit in PS. Since only MoveControl instructions can access the contents of a control register, the contents of PS are loaded into a general-purpose register, R2, modified and then written back into PS. Using the Or instruction to modify the contents affects only the IE bit and leaves the rest of the bits in PS unchanged.

When multiple I/O devices raise interrupt requests, it is necessary to determine which device has requested an interrupt. This can be done in software by checking the information in the IPENDING control register and choosing the interrupt-service routine that should be executed.

Example 3.3   In Example 3.2, we used interrupts with the keyboard only. The display device can also use interrupts. Suppose a program needs to display a page of text stored in the memory. This can be done by having the processor send a character whenever the display interface is ready, which may be indicated by an interrupt request. Assume that both the display and the keyboard are used by this program, and that both are enabled to raise interrupt requests. Using the register structure in Figures 3.3 and 3.7, the initialization of interrupts and the processing of requests can be done as indicated in Figure 3.9.

The Main program must initialize any variables needed by the interrupt-service routines, such as the memory buffer pointers. Then, it enables interrupts in both the keyboard and display interfaces. Next, it enables interrupts in the processor control register IEN-ABLE. Note that the immediate value 6, which is loaded into this register, sets bits KBD and DISP to 1. Finally, the processor is enabled to respond to interrupts in general by setting to 1 the IE bit in the processor status register, PS.

Again, we assume that whenever an interrupt request arrives, the processor will automatically save the contents of the program counter (PC) and then load the address ILOC into PC. It will also save the contents of the status register (PS) by transferring them into the IPS register, and disable interrupts. Unlike Example 3.2, where we assumed that there is only one device that can raise interrupt requests, now we cannot go directly to the desired interrupt-service routine. First, it is necessary to identify the interrupting device. The needed information is found in the processor control register IPENDING. Since the interrupt-service routine uses registers R2 and R3 in this process, the contents of these registers must be saved on the stack and later restored. It is also necessary to save the contents of the subroutine linkage register, LINK_reg, because an interrupt can occur while some subroutine is being executed and the interrupt-service routine calls a subroutine. The circuit that detects interrupts sets to 1 the appropriate bit in IPENDING for each pending request. In Figure 3.9, the contents of IPENDING are loaded into general purpose register R2, and then examined to determine which interrupts are pending. If the display has a pending interrupt, then its interrupt-service routine is executed. If not, then a check is made for the keyboard. This may be followed by checking any other devices that could have pending requests. The order in which the bits in IPENDING are checked establishes a priority for the interrupting devices in case of simultaneous requests.

Interrupt handler

ILOC:	Subtract	SP, SP, #12	Save registers.
	Store	LINK_reg, 8(SP)	
	Store	R2, 4(SP)	
	Store	R3, (SP)	
	MoveControl	R2, IPENDING	Check contents of IPENDING.
	And	R3, R2, #4	Check if display raised the request.
	Branch_if_[R3]=0	TESTKBD	If not, check if keyboard.
	Call	DISR	Call the display ISR.
TESTKBD:	And	R3, R2, #2	Check if keyboard raised the request.
	Branch_if_[R3]=0	NEXT	If not, then check next device.
	Call	KISR	Call the keyboard ISR.
NEXT:	...		Check for other interrupts.
	Load	R3, (SP)	Restore registers.
	Load	R2, 4(SP)	
	Load	LINK_reg, 8(SP)	
	Add	SP, SP, #12	
	Return-from-interrupt		

Main program

START:	...		Set up parameters for ISRs.
	Move	R2, #2	Enable interrupts in
	StoreByte	R2, KBD_CONT	the keyboard interface.
	Move	R2, #4	Enable interrupts in
	StoreByte	R2, DISP_CONT	the display interface.
	MoveControl	R2, IENABLE	
	Or	R2, R2, #6	Enable interrupts in
	MoveControl	IENABLE, R2	the processor control register.
	MoveControl	R2, PS	
	Or	R2, R2, #1	
	MoveControl	PS, R2	Set interrupt-enable bit in PS.
	next instruction		

Keyboard interrupt-service routine

KISR:	...
	:
	Return

Display interrupt-service routine

DISR:	...
	:
	Return

Figure 3.9 A RISC-style program that initializes and handles interrupts.

The program parts that handle interrupt requests and provide the corresponding service to the requesting devices are often referred to as the *interrupt handler*. Note that while the interrupt handler starts at the fixed address ILOC, the individual interrupt-service routines are just subroutines that can be placed anywhere in the memory.

In Figure 3.9, we used a software approach to determine the interrupting device. In processors that use vectored interrupts, the circuit that detects interrupt requests automatically loads a different address into the program counter for each interrupt that is assigned a specific location in the interrupt-vector table. A separate interrupt-service routine is executed to completion for each pending request, even if multiple interrupt requests are raised at the same time.

CISC-style Examples of Interrupts

The above tasks can be implemented using CISC-style instructions using the same basic approach. The main difference is that some operations, such as testing a bit in an I/O register, can be done directly. The tasks in Examples 3.2 and 3.3 can be realized using the programs in Figures 3.10 and 3.11, respectively. The TestBit instruction is used to test the status flags. The SetBit and ClearBit instructions are used to set an individual bit in an I/O register to 1 and 0, respectively. The comments in the programs provide explanations of how the desired tasks are realized.

Input/output operations in a computer system are usually much more involved than our simple examples suggest. As we will describe in Chapter 4, the operating system of the computer performs these operations on behalf of user programs. In Chapter 7, we will discuss in detail the hardware used in I/O operations.

3.2.6   EXCEPTIONS

An interrupt is an event that causes the execution of one program to be suspended and the execution of another program to begin. So far, we have dealt only with interrupts caused by events associated with I/O data transfers. However, the interrupt mechanism is used in a number of other situations.

The term *exception* is often used to refer to any event that causes an interruption. Hence, I/O interrupts are one example of an exception. We now describe a few other kinds of exceptions.

Recovery from Errors

Computers use a variety of techniques to ensure that all hardware components are operating properly. For example, many computers include an error-checking code in the main memory, which allows detection of errors in the stored data. If an error occurs, the control hardware detects it and informs the processor by raising an interrupt.

The processor may also interrupt a program if it detects an error or an unusual condition while executing the instructions of this program. For example, the OP-code field of an instruction may not correspond to any legal instruction, or an arithmetic instruction may attempt a division by zero.

When exception processing is initiated as a result of such errors, the processor proceeds in exactly the same manner as in the case of an I/O interrupt request. It suspends the program

Interrupt-service routine

ILOC:	Move	−(SP), R2	Save register.
	Move	R2, PNTR	Load address pointer.
	MoveByte	(R2), KBD_DATA	Write the character into memory
	Add	PNTR, #1	and increment the pointer.
ECHO:	TestBit	DISP_STATUS, #2	Wait for the display to become ready.
	Branch=0	ECHO	
	MoveByte	DISP_DATA, (R2)	Display the character just read.
	CompareByte	(R2), #CR	Check if the character just read is CR.
	Branch≠0	RTRN	Return if not CR.
	Move	EOL, #1	Indicate end of line.
	ClearBit	KBD_CONT, #1	Disable interrupts in keyboard interface.
RTRN:	Move	R2, (SP)+	Restore register.
	Return-from-interrupt		

Main program

START:	Move	PNTR, #LINE	Initialize buffer pointer.
	Clear	EOL	Clear end-of-line indicator.
	SetBit	KBD_CONT, #1	Enable interrupts in keyboard interface.
	Move	R2, #2	Enable keyboard interrupts in
	MoveControl	IENABLE, R2	the processor control register.
	MoveControl	R2, PS	
	Or	R2, #1	
	MoveControl	PS, R2	Set interrupt-enable bit in PS.
	next instruction		

Figure 3.10   A CISC-style program that reads a line of characters using interrupts, and displays the line using polling.

being executed and starts an exception-service routine, which takes appropriate action to recover from the error, if possible, or to inform the user about it. Recall that in the case of an I/O interrupt, we assumed that the processor completes execution of the instruction in progress before accepting the interrupt. However, when an interrupt is caused by an error associated with the current instruction, that instruction cannot usually be completed, and the processor begins exception processing immediately.

Debugging

Another important type of exception is used as an aid in debugging programs. System software usually includes a program called a *debugger*, which helps the programmer find errors in a program. The debugger uses exceptions to provide two important facilities: trace mode and breakpoints. These facilities are described in detail in Chapter 4.

Interrupt handler

ILOC:	Move	– (SP), R2	Save registers.
	Move	– (SP), LINK_reg	
	MoveControl	R2, IPENDING	Check contents of IPENDING.
	TestBit	R2, #2	Check if display raised the request.
	Branch=0	TESTKBD	If not, check if keyboard.
	Call	DISR	Call the display ISR.
TESTKBD:	TestBit	R2, #1	Check if keyboard raised the request.
	Branch=0	NEXT	If not, then check next device.
	Call	KISR	Call the keyboard ISR.
NEXT:	⋯		Check for other interrupts.
	Move	LINK_reg, (SP)+	Restore registers.
	Move	R2, (SP)+	
	Return-from-interrupt		

Main program

START:	⋯		Set up parameters for ISRs.
	SetBit	KBD_CONT, #1	Enable interrupts in keyboard interface.
	SetBit	DISP_CONT, #2	Enable interrupts in display interface.
	MoveControl	R2, IENABLE	
	Or	R2, #6	Enable interrupts in
	MoveControl	IENABLE, R2	the processor control register.
	MoveControl	R2, PS	
	Or	R2, #1	
	MoveControl	PS, R2	Set interrupt-enable bit in PS.
	next instruction		

Keyboard interrupt-service routine

KISR:	⋯
	⋮
	Return

Display interrupt-service routine

DISR:	⋯
	⋮
	Return

Figure 3.11   A CISC-style program that initializes and handles interrupts.

Use of Exceptions in Operating Systems

The operating system (OS) software coordinates the activities within a computer. It uses exceptions to communicate with and control the execution of user programs. It uses hardware interrupts to perform I/O operations. This topic is discussed in Chapter 4.

3.3 CONCLUDING REMARKS

In this chapter, we discussed two basic approaches to I/O transfers. The simplest technique is programmed I/O, in which the processor performs all of the necessary functions under direct control of program instructions. The second approach is based on the use of interrupts; this mechanism makes it possible to interrupt the normal execution of programs in order to service higher-priority requests that require more urgent attention. Although all computers have a mechanism for dealing with such situations, the complexity and sophistication of interrupt-handling schemes vary from one computer to another.

We dealt with the I/O issues from the programmer's point of view. In Chapter 7 we will consider the hardware aspects and some commonly used I/O standards.

3.4 SOLVED PROBLEMS

This section presents some examples of problems that a student may be asked to solve, and shows how such problems can be solved.

Example 3.4

Problem: Assume that a memory location BINARY contains a 32-bit pattern. It is desired to display these bits as eight hexadecimal digits on a display device that has the interface depicted in Figure 3.3. Write a program that accomplishes this task.

Solution: First it is necessary to convert the 32-bit pattern into hex digits that are represented as ASCII-encoded characters. A simple way of doing the conversion is to use the *table-lookup* approach. A 16-entry table has to be constructed to provide the ASCII code for each possible hex digit. Then, for each four-bit segment of the pattern in BINARY, the corresponding character can be looked up in the table and stored in a block of memory bytes starting at location HEX. Finally, the eight characters starting at HEX are sent to the display.

Figures 3.12 and 3.13 give RISC- and CISC-style programs, respectively, for the required task. The comments describe the detailed actions taken.

	Load	R2, BINARY	Load the binary number.
	Move	R3, #8	R3 is a digit counter that is set to 8.
	Move	R4, #HEX	R4 points to the hex digits.
LOOP:	RotateL	R2, R2, #4	Rotate the high-order digit
			into low-order position.
	And	R5, R2, #0xF	Extract next digit.
	LoadByte	R6, TABLE(R5)	Get ASCII code for the digit and
	StoreByte	R6, (R4)	store it in HEX number location.
	Subtract	R3, R3, #1	Decrement the digit counter.
	Add	R4, R4, #1	Increment the pointer to hex digits.
	Branch_if_[R3]>0	LOOP	Loop back if not the last digit.
DISPLAY:	Move	R3, #8	
	Move	R4, #HEX	
DLOOP:	LoadByte	R5, DISP_STATUS	Wait for display to become ready.
	And	R5, R5, #4	Check the DOUT flag.
	Branch_if_[R5]=0	DLOOP	
	LoadByte	R6, (R4)	Get the next ASCII character
	StoreByte	R6, DISP_DATA	and send it to the display.
	Subtract	R3, R3, #1	Decrement the counter.
	Add	R4, R4, #1	Increment the character pointer.
	Branch_if_[R3]>0	DLOOP	Loop until all characters displayed.
	next instruction		
	ORIGIN	1000	
HEX:	RESERVE	8	Space for ASCII-encoded digits.
TABLE:	DATABYTE	0x30,0x31,0x32,0x33	Table for conversion
	DATABYTE	0x34,0x35,0x36,0x37	to ASCII code.
	DATABYTE	0x38,0x39,0x41,0x42	
	DATABYTE	0x43,0x44,0x45,0x46	

Figure 3.12   A RISC-style program for Example 3.4.

Example 3.5   **Problem:** Consider the task described in Example 3.1. Assume that the timer circuit includes a 32-bit up/down counter driven by a 100-MHz clock. The counter can be set to count from a specified initial count value. The timer I/O interface is shown in Figure 3.14. It contains four registers.

- TIM_STATUS indicates the current status of the timer where:

    – The TON bit is set to 1 when the counter is running.

    – The ZERO bit is set to 1 when the counter reaches the count of zero.

    – The TIRQ bit is set to 1 when the timer raises an interrupt request, which happens when the counter contents reach zero and the timer interrupts are enabled.

```
              Move         R2, BINARY              Load the binary number.
              Move         R3, #8                  R3 is a digit counter that is set to 8.
              Move         R4, #HEX                R4 points to the hex digits.
LOOP:         RotateL      R2, #4                  Rotate the high-order digit
                                                      into low-order position.

              Move         R5, R2
              And          R5, #0xF                Extract next digit.
              MoveByte     (R4)+, TABLE(R5)        Get ASCII code for the digit and
                                                      store it in HEX number location.

              Subtract     R3, #1                  Decrement the digit counter.
              Branch>0     LOOP                    Loop back if not the last digit.
DISPLAY:      Move         R3, #8
              Move         R4, #HEX
DLOOP:        TestBit      DISP_STATUS, #2         Wait for display to become ready.
              Branch=0     DLOOP
              MoveByte     DISP_DATA, (R4)+        Send next character to display.
              Subtract     R3, #1                  Decrement the counter.
              Branch>0     DLOOP                   Loop until all characters displayed.
              next instruction


              ORIGIN       1000
HEX:          RESERVE      8                       Space for ASCII-encoded digits.
TABLE:        DATABYTE     0x30,0x31,0x32,0x33     Table for conversion
              DATABYTE     0x34,0x35,0x36,0x37      to ASCII code.
              DATABYTE     0x38,0x39,0x41,0x42
              DATABYTE     0x43,0x44,0x45,0x46
```

Figure 3.13   A CISC-style program for Example 3.4.

The action of reading the status register automatically clears the ZERO and TIRQ bits to 0.

- TIM_CONT controls the mode of operation, where:
    - The UP bit is set to 1 to cause the counter to count by incrementing its contents; when this bit is cleared to zero, the counter contents are decremented.
    - The FREE bit is set to 1 to cause a continuously running mode, where the counter is automatically reloaded with the initial count value whenever the actual count reaches zero.
    - The RUN bit is set to 1 to cause the counter to count; it is cleared to 0 to stop the counter.
    - The TIE bit is set to 1 to enable timer interrupts.
- TIM_INIT holds the initial count value.
- TIM_COUNT holds the current count value.

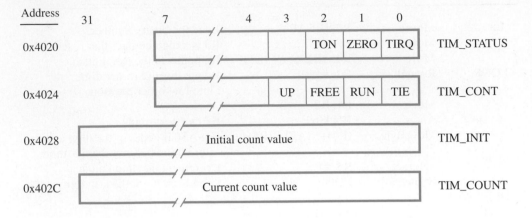

Figure 3.14 Registers in the timer interface.

Write a program to implement the desired task. Use the processor control registers depicted in Figure 3.7.

Solution: To obtain an interrupt request every ten seconds, it is necessary to count 10^9 clock cycles. This can be accomplished by writing this value into the TIM_INIT register, and then making the counter decrement its count and raise an interrupt when the count reaches zero. The value 10^9 can be represented by the hexadecimal number 3B9ACA00. To achieve the desired operation the FREE, RUN, and TIE bits must be set to 1, while the UP bit must be equal to 0.

Using the scheme outlined in Figure 3.9, we can implement the required task using a RISC-style program shown in Figure 3.15. Note that the initial count, which is a 32-bit immediate value, is loaded into R2 using the approach explained in Section 2.9.

Figure 3.16 gives a CISC-style program that uses the scheme outlined in Figure 3.11. In this case, the 32-bit immediate operand can be specified in a single instruction.

Example 3.6 **Problem:** A commonly used output device in digital systems is a seven-segment display, depicted in Figure 3.17. The device consists of seven independent segments which can be illuminated by applying electrical signals to them. Assume that each segment is illuminated when a logic value 1 is applied to it. The figure shows the bit patterns needed to display numbers 0 to 9.

Write a program that displays the number represented by an ASCII-encoded character stored in memory location DIGIT at address 0x800. Assume that the display has an I/O interface consisting of an eight-bit data register, SEVEN, where the segments a to g are connected to bits $SEVEN_{6-0}$. Let the bit $SEVEN_7$ be equal to 0. Also, assume that the address of register SEVEN is 0x4030. If the ASCII code in location DIGIT represents a

Interrupt handler

ILOC:	Subtract	SP, SP, #8	Save registers.
	Store	LINK_reg, 4(SP)	
	Store	R2, (SP)	
	MoveControl	R2, IPENDING	Check contents of IPENDING.
	And	R2, R2, #8	Check if request from timer.
	Branch_if_[R2]=0	NEXT	
	LoadByte	R2, TIM_STATUS	Clear TIRQ and ZERO bits.
	Call	DISPLAY	Call the DISPLAY routine.
NEXT:	· · ·		Check for other interrupts.
	Load	R2, (SP)	Restore registers.
	Load	LINK_reg, 4(SP)	
	Add	SP, SP, #8	
	Return-from-interrupt		

Main program

START:	· · ·		Set up parameters for ISRs.
	OrHigh	R2, R0, #0x3B9A	Prepare the initial
	Or	R2, R2, #0xCA00	count value.
	Store	R2, TIM_INIT	Set the initial count value.
	Move	R2, #7	Set the timer to free run
	StoreByte	R2, TIM_CONT	and enable interupts.
	MoveControl	R2, IENABLE	
	Or	R2, R2, #8	Enable timer interrupts in
	MoveControl	IENABLE, R2	the processor control register.
	MoveControl	R2, PS	
	Or	R2, R2, #1	
	MoveControl	PS, R2	Set interrupt-enable bit in PS.
COMPUTE:	next instruction		

Figure 3.15   A RISC-style program for Example 3.5.

character that is not a number in the range 0 to 9, then the display should be blank, where all segments are turned off.

Solution: A look-up table can be used to hold the seven-segment bit patterns that correspond to the numbers 0 to 9. The ASCII-encoded digit is converted into a four-bit number that is used as an index into the table, by using the AND operation. Also, it is necessary to check that the high-order four bits of ASCII code are 0011. Note that all three addresses DIGIT, SEVEN, and TABLE can be represented in 16 bits.

Figures 3.18 and 3.19 give possible RISC- and CISC-style programs, respectively.

Interrupt handler

ILOC:	Move	$-$(SP), R2	Save registers.
	Move	$-$(SP), LINK_reg	
	MoveControl	R2, IPENDING	Check contents of IPENDING.
	TestBit	R2, #3	Check if request from timer.
	Branch=0	NEXT	
	MoveByte	R2, TIM_STATUS	Clear TIRQ and ZERO bits.
	Call	DISPLAY	Call the DISPLAY routine.
NEXT:	$\cdots$		Check for other interrupts.
	Move	LINK_reg, (SP)+	Restore registers.
	Move	R2, (SP)+	
	Return-from-interrupt		

Main program

START:	$\cdots$		Set up parameters for ISRs.
	Move	TIM_INIT, #0x3B9ACA00	Set the initial count value.
	MoveByte	TIM_CON, #7	Set the timer to free run and enable interupts.
	MoveControl	R2, IENABLE	
	Or	R2, #8	Enable timer interrupts in
	MoveControl	IENABLE, R2	the processor control register.
	MoveControl	R2, PS	
	Or	R2, #1	
	MoveControl	PS, R2	Set interrupt-enable bit in PS.
COMPUTE:	next instruction		

Figure 3.16   A CISC-style program for Example 3.5.

Number	a	b	c	d	e	f	g
0	1	1	1	1	1	1	0
1	0	1	1	0	0	0	0
2	1	1	0	1	1	0	1
3	1	1	1	1	0	0	1
4	0	1	1	0	0	1	1
5	1	0	1	1	0	1	1
6	1	0	1	1	1	1	1
7	1	1	1	0	0	0	0
8	1	1	1	1	1	1	1
9	1	1	1	1	0	1	1

Figure 3.17   Seven-segment display.

DIGIT	EQU	0x800	Location of ASCII-encoded digit.
SEVEN	EQU	0x4030	Address of 7-segment display.
	LoadByte	R2, DIGIT	Load the ASCII-encoded digit.
	And	R3, R2, #0xF0	Extract high-order bits of ASCII.
	And	R2, R2, #0x0F	Extract the decimal number.
	Move	R4, #0x30	Check if high-order bits of
	Branch_if_[R3]=[R4]	HIGH3	ASCII code are 0011.
	Move	R2, #0x0F	Not a digit, display a blank.
HIGH3:	LoadByte	R5, TABLE(R2)	Get the 7-segment pattern.
	StoreByte	R5, SEVEN	Display the digit.
	ORIGIN	0x1000	
TABLE:	DATABYTE	0x7E,0x30,0x6D,0x79	Table that contains
	DATABYTE	0x33,0x5B,0x5F,0x70	the necessary
	DATABYTE	0x7F,0x7B,0x00,0x00	7-segment patterns.
	DATABYTE	0x00,0x00,0x00,0x00	

Figure 3.18 A RISC-style program for Example 3.6.

DIGIT	EQU	0x800	Location of ASCII-encoded digit.
SEVEN	EQU	0x4030	Address of 7-segment display.
	Move	R2, DIGIT	Load the ASCII-encoded digit.
	Move	R3, R2	
	And	R3, #0xF0	Extract high-order bits of ASCII.
	And	R2, #0x0F	Extract the decimal number.
	CompareByte	R3, #0x30	Check if high-order bits of
	Branch=0	HIGH3	ASCII code are 0011.
	Move	R2, #0x0F	Not a digit, display a blank.
HIGH3:	MoveByte	SEVEN, TABLE(R2)	Display the digit.
	ORIGIN	0x1000	
TABLE:	DATABYTE	0x7E,0x30,0x6D,0x79	Table that contains
	DATABYTE	0x33,0x5B,0x5F,0x70	the necessary
	DATABYTE	0x7F,0x7B,0x00,0x00	7-segment patterns.
	DATABYTE	0x00,0x00,0x00,0x00	

Figure 3.19 A CISC-style program for Example 3.6.

PROBLEMS

3.1 **[E]** The input status bit in an interface circuit is cleared as soon as the input data register is read. Why is this important?

3.2 **[E]** Write a program that displays the contents of ten bytes of the main memory in hexadecimal format on a line of a display device. The ten bytes start at location LOC in the memory, and there are two hex characters per byte. The contents of successive bytes should be separated by a space when displayed.

3.3 **[E]** What is the difference between a subroutine and an interrupt-service routine?

3.4 **[E]** In the first And instruction in Figure 3.4 the immediate value 2 is used when checking the KIN flag, but in Figure 3.5 the immediate value 1 is used in the first TestBit instruction when checking the same flag. Explain the difference.

3.5 **[D]** A computer is required to accept characters from the keyboard input of 20 terminals. The main memory area to be used for storing data for each terminal is pointed to by a pointer PNTRn, where $n = 1$ through 20. Input data must be collected from the terminals while another program PROG is being executed. This may be accomplished in one of two ways:

(*a*) Every T seconds, program PROG calls a polling subroutine POLL. This subroutine checks the status of each of the 20 terminals in sequence and transfers any input characters to the memory. Then it returns to PROG.

(*b*) Whenever a character is ready in any of the interface buffers of the terminals, an interrupt request is generated. This causes the interrupt routine INTERRUPT to be executed. INTERRUPT polls the status registers to find the first ready character, transfers it, and then returns to PROG.

Write the routines POLL and INTERRUPT. Let the maximum character rate for any terminal be c characters per second, with an average rate equal to rc, where $r \leq 1$. In method (*a*), what is the maximum value of T for which it is still possible to guarantee that no input characters will be lost? What is the equivalent value for method (*b*)? Estimate, on the average, the percentage of time spent in servicing the terminals for methods (*a*) and (*b*), for $c = 100$ characters per second and $r = 0.01, 0.1, 0.5$, and 1. Assume that POLL takes 800 ns to poll all 20 devices and that an interrupt from a device requires 200 ns to process.

3.6 **[E]** In Figure 3.9, the interrupt-enable bit in the PS is set last in the START section of the Main program. Why? Does the order matter for earlier operations in START? Why or why not?

3.7 **[E]** Even if multiple interrupt requests are pending, only one request will be handled for each entry into ILOC in Figure 3.9. True or false? Explain.

3.8 **[E]** A user program could check for a zero divisor immediately preceding each division operation, and then take appropriate action without invoking the OS. Give reasons why this may or may not be preferable to allowing an exception interrupt to occur on an actual divide by zero situation in a user program.

3.9   **[M]** Assume that a memory location BINARY contains a 16-bit pattern. It is desired to display these bits as a string of 0s and 1s on a display device that has the interface depicted in Figure 3.3. Write a RISC-style program that accomplishes this task.

3.10   **[M]** Write a CISC-style program for the task in Problem 3.9.

3.11   **[E]** Modify the program in Figure 3.18 if the address of TABLE is 0x10100.

3.12   **[E]** Modify the program in Figure 3.19 if the address of TABLE is 0x10100.

3.13   **[M]** Using the seven-segment display in Figure 3.17 and the timer interface registers in Figure 3.14, write a RISC-style program that flashes decimal digits in the repeating sequence $0, 1, 2, \ldots, 9, 0, \ldots$. Each digit is to be displayed for one second. Assume that the counter in the timer circuit is driven by a 100-MHz clock.

3.14   **[M]** Write a CISC-style program for the task in Problem 3.13.

3.15   **[D]** Using two 7-segment displays of the type shown in Figure 3.17, and the timer interface registers in Figure 3.14, write a RISC-style program that flashes the repeating sequence of numbers $0, 1, 2, \ldots, 98, 99, 0, \ldots$. Each number is to be displayed for one second. Assume that the counter in the timer circuit is driven by a 100-MHz clock.

3.16   **[D]** Write a CISC-style program for the task in Problem 3.15.

3.17   **[D]** Write a RISC-style program that computes wall clock time and displays the time in hours (0 to 23) and minutes (0 to 59). The display consists of four 7-segment display devices of the type shown in Figure 3.17. A timer circuit that has the interface registers given in Figure 3.14 is available. Its counter is driven by a 100-MHz clock.

3.18   **[D]** Write a CISC-style program for the task in Problem 3.17.

3.19   **[M]** Write a RISC-style program that displays the name of the user backwards. The program should display a prompt requesting that the characters in the user's name be entered on the keyboard, followed by the carriage return (CR). The program should accept a sequence of characters and store them in the main memory. It should then display a message to indicate that the user's name will be displayed backwards, followed by the display of the characters from the user's name in reverse order.

3.20   **[M]** Write a CISC-style program for the task in Problem 3.19.

3.21   **[M]** Write a RISC style program that determines whether a word entered by a user on the keyboard is a palindrome, i.e., a word that is same when its characters are written in normal and reverse order. The program should display a prompt requesting that the user enter the characters of an arbitrary word on the keyboard, followed by the carriage return (CR). The program should read the characters and store them in the main memory. It should then analyze the word to determine whether it is a palindrome. Finally, the program should display a message to indicate the result of the analysis.

3.22   **[M]** Write a CISC-style program for the task in Problem 3.21.

3.23   **[D]** Write a RISC-style program that displays a string of characters centered horizontally on a standard 80-character line and enclosed in a box, as shown below:

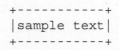

```
+-----------+
|sample text|
+-----------+
```

The string of characters is located in the main memory beginning at address STRING. There is a NUL control character (value 0) at the end of the string of characters. If the string has more than 78 characters (including spaces), the program should truncate the displayed string to 78 characters. The program for determining the length of a character string in Example 2.1 can be adapted as a subroutine for use by the program in this problem. Assume that the display device has the interface depicted in Figure 3.3.

3.24   **[D]** Write a CISC-style program for the task in Problem 3.23.

3.25   **[D]** Write a RISC-style program that displays a long sequence of text encoded in ASCII characters with automatic wraparound to fit within 80-character lines. Before displaying the next word, the program must determine whether there is sufficient space remaining on the line. If not, the word should appear at the beginning of the next line. The display process must continue until the NUL control character (value 0) is reached at the end of the sequence of characters to be displayed. Assume that the sequence of characters uses no control characters other than the NUL character at the end, hence words are separated only by a space character. Assume that the display device has the interface depicted in Figure 3.3.

3.26   **[D]** Write a CISC-style program for the task in Problem 3.25.

chapter

4

SOFTWARE

CHAPTER OBJECTIVES

In this chapter you will learn about:

- Software needed to prepare and run programs
- Assemblers
- Loaders
- Linkers
- Compilers
- Debuggers
- Interaction between assembly language and C language
- Operating systems

Chapter 2 introduced the instruction set of a computer and illustrated how programs can be written in assembly language. Chapter 3 showed how to write programs that perform input/output operations. In this chapter, we will give an overview of the software needed to prepare and run programs.

Assembly-language programs are written using a symbolic notation, which is easily understood by the programmer. These programs must be translated into machine-language code before they can be executed in the computer, as explained in Section 2.5. This is done by the assembler program, which interprets the mnemonics representing machine instructions and the assembler directives for data declarations.

Having presented how assembly-language programs can be written, we will now discuss the complete process of preparing programs for execution. We will describe:

- How the assembler translates a source program written in assembly language into an object program consisting of machine instructions and data in binary form
- How object programs are loaded into the memory of a computer
- How program execution is initiated and terminated
- How larger programs can be formed by linking together several related programs
- How programming errors can be identified during the execution of a program

Then, we will consider some issues involved when programs are prepared in a high-level language, such as C. Finally, we will consider the role of operating system software in managing and coordinating the use of computer resources.

4.1   THE ASSEMBLY PROCESS

To prepare a source program, the programmer uses a utility program called a *text editor* which allows the statements of a source program to be entered at a keyboard and saved in a *file*. The file containing the source program is a sequence of binary-encoded alphanumeric characters. The file is identified by a name chosen by the user. Files are normally stored in a secondary storage device, such as a magnetic disk.

After preparing the source file, the programmer uses another utility program called the *assembler*. It translates source programs written in an assembly language into object programs that comprise machine instructions. This process is often referred to as *assembling* a program. The assembler also converts the assembly-language representation of data into binary patterns that are part of the object program. After loading a source file from the disk into the memory and translating it into an object program, the assembler stores the object program in a separate file on the disk.

The source program uses mnemonics to represent OP codes in machine instructions. A set of syntax rules governs the specification of addressing modes for the data operands of these instructions. The assembler generates the binary encoding for the OP code and other instruction fields.

The assembler recognizes directives that specify numbers and characters and directives that allocate memory space for data areas. Using EQU (equate) directives, the programmer can define names that represent constants. These names can then appear in the source program as operands in instructions. Names can also be defined as address labels for branch targets, entry points of subroutines, or data locations in the memory. Address labels are assigned values based on their position relative to the beginning of an assembled program.

As the assembler scans through the source program, it keeps track of all names and their corresponding values in a *symbol table*. Each time a name appears, it is replaced with its value from the table.

4.1.1   TWO-PASS ASSEMBLER

A problem arises when a name appears as an operand before its value is defined. For example, this happens if a forward branch is required to an address label that appears later in the program. As discussed in Section 2.5.2, an offset for the branch is calculated by the assembler using the address of the branch target. With a forward branch, the assembler cannot determine the address of the branch target, because the value of the address label has not yet been recorded in the symbol table.

A commonly-used solution to this problem is to have the assembler scan through the source program twice. During the first pass, it creates the symbol table. For EQU directives, each name and its defined value are recorded in the symbol table. For address labels, the assembler determines the value of each name from its position relative to the start of the source program. The value is determined by summing the sizes of all machine instructions processed before the definition of the name. At the end of the first pass, all names appearing in the source program will have been assigned numerical values in the symbol table. The assembler then makes a second pass through the source program, looks up each name it encounters in the symbol table, and substitutes the corresponding numerical value. Such a *two-pass* assembler produces a complete object program.

4.2   LOADING AND EXECUTING OBJECT PROGRAMS

Object programs generated by the assembler are stored in files on a disk. To execute a specific object program, it is first loaded from the disk into the memory. Then, the address of the first instruction to be executed is loaded into the program counter. A utility program called the *loader* is used to perform these operations.

The loader is invoked when a user enters a command to execute an object program that is stored on the disk. The user command specifies the name of the object file, which enables the loader to find the file on the disk. The loader transfers the object program from the disk into a specified place in the memory. It must know the length of the program and the address in the memory where it will be loaded. The assembler usually places this information in a header in the object file, preceding the machine instructions and data of the object program.

One way of entering the user commands is by typing them on the keyboard. A more commonly used alternative is to use a *graphical user interface* (GUI). In this case, the user uses a mouse to select the desired object file. Then, the GUI software passes to the loader the information about the location of the object file on the disk.

Once the object program has been loaded into the memory, the loader starts its execution by branching to the first instruction to be executed. In the source program, the programmer indicates the first instruction with a special address label such as START. The assembler includes the value of this address label in the header of the object program.

When an object program completes its task, its execution has to be terminated in a well-defined manner. This permits the space in the memory containing the object program to be recovered, and enables the user to enter a new command to execute another object program. These issues are normally addressed by the operating system (OS) software, which is discussed in Section 4.9.

4.3   THE LINKER

In the preceding sections we assumed that all instructions and data for a particular program are specified in a single source file from which the assembler generates an object program. In many cases, a programmer may wish to call subroutines created by other programmers. It is not convenient or practical to gather all of the desired subroutines from possibly many separate source files into a single source file for processing by the assembler.

Instead, a common procedure is to use the assembler on each of the source files separately. In this case, each individual output file will not be a complete object program. Each program may contain references to *external names*, which are address labels defined in other source files. When processing a source file, the assembler identifies such external references and builds a list of these names and the instructions that refer to them. It includes this list in the object file that it generates from the source file.

A utility program called the *linker* is used to combine the contents of separate object files into one object program. It resolves references to external names using the information recorded in each object file. The linker needs the relative positions of address labels defined in the source files, so that it can determine the absolute address values when it combines the separate object files. Information on address labels that may be referenced in other source files must be *exported* from each source file to aid in this task. Normally, the programmer is required to indicate the specific labels to be exported. The exported names are included by the assembler in each object file that it generates, along with a list of the external names used in the program and the instructions referring to them.

The linker uses the information in each object file and the known sizes of machine-language programs to build a memory map of the final combined object file. The final values corresponding to exported address labels are determined once all of the individual object files are collected together and assigned to their final locations in memory. At this point, references to external names can be resolved. The final address values determined by the linker are substituted in the specific instructions that contain external references. Once all external references are resolved, the final object program is complete.

The programmer may choose to determine some of the addresses of instructions and data explicitly in an object file. This may be done using directives such as ORIGIN in an assembly-language source file. In this case, the programmer must ensure that instructions and data from different object files do not overlap in memory. A more flexible approach is not to use ORIGIN directives, giving the linker the freedom to select the starting address for the object program and to assign absolute addresses accordingly. The linker ensures that different object files do not overlap with each other or with special locations in memory such as interrupt vectors.

4.4 LIBRARIES

Subroutines written for one application program may be useful for other application programs. It is a common practice to collect object files containing such subroutines into a *library* file stored on the disk. The subroutines in the library can then be linked with other object files for any application program. A utility program called an *archiver* is used to create a library file. This file includes information needed by the linker to resolve references to external names in a program that calls library routines.

When invoking the linker, the programmer specifies the desired library files. The linker extracts the relevant object files from the library and includes them in the final object program.

4.5 THE COMPILER

Assembly-language programming requires knowledge of machine-specific details that vary from one computer to another. Programming in a high-level language such as C, C++, or Java does not require such knowledge. Before a program written in a high-level language can be executed in a computer, it must be translated first into assembly language and then into the machine language of the computer. A utility program called a *compiler* performs the first task. A source file in a high-level language is prepared by the programmer and stored on the disk. From this source file, the compiler generates assembly-language instructions and directives, and writes them into an output file. Then, the compiler invokes the assembler to assemble this file.

It is often convenient to partition a high-level source program into multiple files, grouping subroutines together based on related tasks. In each source file, the names of external subroutines and data variables in other files must be declared. This is necessary to enable the compiler to check data types and detect any errors. For each source file, the compiler generates an assembly-language file, then invokes the assembler to generate an object file. The linker combines all object files, including any library routines, to create the final object program.

An important benefit of programming in a high-level language is that the compiler automates many of the tedious tasks that a programmer has to do when programming in assembly language. For example, when generating the assembly-language representation of subroutines, the compiler performs all tasks related to managing stack frames.

4.5.1 COMPILER OPTIMIZATIONS

If the compiler uses a straightforward approach to generate an assembly-language program from a source file written in a high-level language, it may not necessarily produce the most efficient program in terms of its execution time or its size. Improved performance can be achieved if the compiler uses techniques such as reordering the instructions produced from a straightforward approach. A compiler with such capabilities is called an *optimizing* compiler.

Because much of the execution time of a program is spent in loops, compilers may apply optimizations that are particularly effective for loops. For example, a high-level source program may use a memory variable as a loop counter. This variable needs to be read and written to increment its value in each pass through the loop. A straightforward assembly-language implementation of this task consists of Load, Add, and Store instructions within the loop. A better implementation is produced by a compiler that recognizes that the counter value may be maintained in a register while executing the loop. In this case, the Load and Store instructions are not needed within the loop. A Load instruction may be used before entering the loop to place an initial value into the register. A Store instruction may be needed after exiting the loop to record the final value of the counter.

4.5.2 COMBINING PROGRAMS WRITTEN IN DIFFERENT LANGUAGES

Section 4.3 describes the linker, which links several object files to generate the object program. In some cases, a programmer may wish to combine object files produced from source files written in a high-level language and source files written in assembly language. For example, the programmer may prepare special assembly-language subroutines that have been carefully crafted to achieve high performance. A high-level language source program may then call these assembly-language subroutines. Similarly, an assembly-language program can call high-level language subroutines.

Figure 4.1 illustrates the complete flow for generating an object program from multiple source files and library routines.

4.6 THE DEBUGGER

An object program is generated successfully when there are no syntax errors or unknown names in the source files for the program. Such problems are detected and reported by the assembler, compiler, or linker. The programmer then makes the necessary corrections in the source files.

However, when an object program is executed, it may produce incorrect results due to programming errors, or *bugs*, that are often difficult to isolate. To help the programmer identify such errors, a utility program called the *debugger* can be used. It enables the programmer to stop execution of the object program at some points of interest and to

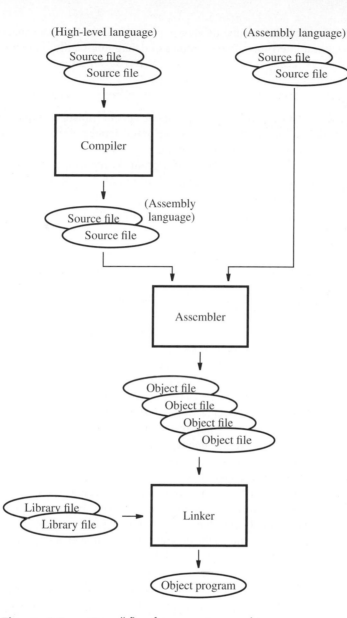

Figure 4.1 Overall flow for generating an object program.

examine the contents of various processor registers and memory locations. In this manner, the programmer can compare computed values with the expected results at any point of execution to determine where a programming error may exist. With that information, the programmer can then revise the erroneous source file.

To support the functions of the debugger, processors usually have special modes of operation and special interrupts. Two examples of debugging facilities are trace mode and breakpoints.

Trace Mode

When a processor is operating in the *trace* mode, an interrupt occurs after the execution of every instruction. An interrupt-service routine in the debugger program is invoked each time this interrupt occurs. It allows the debugger to assume execution control, enabling the user to enter commands for examining the contents of registers and memory locations. When the user enters a command to resume execution of the object program, a Return-from-interrupt instruction is executed. The next instruction in the program being debugged is executed, then the debugger is activated again with another interrupt. The trace-mode interrupt is automatically disabled when the debugger routine is entered, and re-enabled upon return to the object program.

Breakpoints

Breakpoints provide a similar interrupt-based debugging facility, except that the object program being debugged is interrupted only at specific points indicated by the programmer. For example, the programmer may set a breakpoint to determine whether a particular subroutine in the object program is ever reached. If it is, the debugger is activated through an interrupt. The programmer can then examine the state of processing at that point. The advantage of using a breakpoint is that execution proceeds at full speed until the breakpoint is encountered.

A special instruction called Trap or Software-interrupt is usually used to implement breakpoints. Execution of this instruction results in the same actions as when a hardware-interrupt request is received. When the debugger has execution control, it allows the user to set a breakpoint that interrupts execution just before instruction i in the object program. The debugger saves instruction i in a temporary location, and replaces it with a Software-interrupt instruction. The user then enters a command to resume execution of the object program. The debugger executes a Return-from-interrupt instruction. Instructions from the object program are processed normally until the Software-interrupt instruction is encountered. At that point, interrupt processing causes the debugger to be activated again, allowing the user to examine the state of processing.

When the user enters the command to resume execution, the debugger must perform several tasks, not only to execute instruction i but also to set the same breakpoint again. It must first restore instruction i to its original location in the program. This will be the first instruction to be executed when the program resumes execution. Then, the debugger has to reinstall the breakpoint. It needs to arrange for a second interrupt to occur after instruction i is executed. To do so, it may enable the trace mode, if available. Alternatively, it may place a temporary breakpoint at the location of instruction $i + 1$, then resume execution of the program being debugged. After instruction i is executed, a second interrupt occurs because of the temporary breakpoint in place of instruction $i + 1$. This time, the debugger restores instruction $i + 1$, reinstalls the breakpoint at instruction i, and resumes execution of the interrupted program.

4.7 USING A HIGH-LEVEL LANGUAGE FOR I/O TASKS

The compiler, the assembler, and the linker provide considerable flexibility for the programmer. Source programs may be written entirely in assembly language, entirely in a high-level language, or in a mixture of languages. Using a high-level language is preferable in most applications, because the development time is shorter and the desired code is easier to generate and maintain. In this section and the next one, we will show some example programs for I/O tasks using the C programming language to illustrate this approach.

Consider the following I/O task. A program uses the polling approach to read 8-bit characters from a keyboard and send them to a display as they are entered by a user. Chapter 3 presents examples of memory-mapped interfaces for such devices. Figure 4.2 shows an assembly-language program for this I/O task using the interfaces in Figure 3.3.

Figure 4.3 gives a C-language program that performs the same task. In the C language, a pointer may be set to any memory location, including a memory-mapped I/O location. The value of such a pointer is the address of the location in question. If the contents of this location are to be treated as a character, the pointer should be declared to be of character type. This defines the contents as being one byte in length, which is the size of the I/O registers in Figure 3.3. The *define* statements in Figure 4.3 are used to associate the required address constants with the symbolic names of the pointers. These statements serve the same purpose as the EQU statements in Figure 4.2. They enable the compiler to replace the symbolic names in the program with numeric values. The *define* statements also indicate the data type for the pointers. The compiler can then generate assembly-language instructions with known values and correct data sizes.

```
KBD_DATA       EQU           0x4000           Keyboard data register (8 bits).
KBD_STATUS     EQU           0x4004           Keyboard status register (bit 1 is KIN flag).
DISP_DATA      EQU           0x4010           Display data register (8 bits).
DISP_STATUS    EQU           0x4014           Display status register (bit 2 is DOUT flag).

               Move          R2, #KBD_DATA    Pointer to keyboard device interface.
               Move          R3, #DISP_DATA   Pointer to display device interface.

KBD_LOOP:      LoadByte      R4, 4(R2)        Check if there is a character
               And           R4, R4, #2          from the keyboard.
               Branch_if_[R4]=0  KBD_LOOP
               LoadByte      R5, (R2)         Read the received character.
DISP_LOOP:     LoadByte      R4, 4(R3)        Check if the display
               And           R4, R4, #4          is ready for a character.
               Branch_if_[R4]=0  DISP_LOOP
               StoreByte     R5, (R3)         Write the received character to the display.
               Branch        KBD_LOOP
```

Figure 4.2 Assembly-language program for transferring characters from a keyboard to a display.

```
/* Define register addresses. */
#define    KBD_DATA        (volatile char *) 0x4000
#define    KBD_STATUS      (volatile char *) 0x4004
#define    DISP_DATA       (volatile char *) 0x4010
#define    DISP_STATUS     (volatile char *) 0x4014

void main()
{
    char ch;

    /* Transfer the characters. */
    while (1) {                               /* Infinite loop. */
        while ((*KBD_STATUS & 0x2) == 0);     /* Wait for a new character. */
        ch = *KBD_DATA;                       /* Read the character from the keyboard. */
        while ((*DISP_STATUS & 0x4) == 0);    /* Wait for display to become ready. */
        *DISP_DATA = ch;                      /* Transfer the character to the display. */
    }
}
```

Figure 4.3   C program that performs the same task as the assembly-language program in Figure 4.2.

Note that the KBD_STATUS and DISP_STATUS pointers are declared as being *volatile*. This is necessary because the program only reads the contents of the corresponding locations. No data are written to those locations. An optimizing compiler may remove program statements that appear to have no impact, which include statements referring to locations in memory that are read but never written. Since the contents of the memory-mapped KBD_STATUS and DISP_STATUS registers change under influences external to the program, it is essential to inform the compiler of this fact. The compiler will not remove statements that involve pointers or other variables that are declared to be volatile.

For a computer that includes a cache memory, some compilers have an additional interpretation for volatile pointers or variables. The cache is a small, fast memory that holds copies of data in the main memory. Instructions that refer to locations in memory are executed more quickly when data are available in the cache. However, data from memory-mapped I/O registers should not be kept in the cache because the contents of those registers change under external influences. Thus, references to these locations should *bypass* the cache and directly access the I/O registers. Declaring pointers to such locations as volatile can inform a compiler to not only prevent unwanted optimizations, but also to generate memory-access instructions that bypass the cache.

In Figure 4.3, we included numeric constants for the specific values that represent the bit positions in the two status registers. For example, the constant 0x2 in the statement

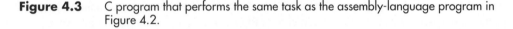

$$\text{while ((*KBD\_STATUS \& 0x2) == 0);}$$

is used to detect whether bit b_1 in the KBD_STATUS register is set. This approach is used here to make it easier to compare the given values with the specification of the device interfaces in Figure 3.3. A more usual approach in writing C programs is to include *define* statements to associate meaningful names with such constant values and then use the names in the rest of the program.

4.8   INTERACTION BETWEEN ASSEMBLY LANGUAGE AND C LANGUAGE

Occasionally, a program may require access to control registers in a processor. For example, this is needed in the initialization for an interrupt-service routine. Based on a statement in a high-level language, a compiler cannot generate assembly-language instructions that access control registers in a processor. Since assembly-language instructions are needed for this purpose, the compiler allows assembly-language instructions to be included directly in a high-level language program. This section illustrates this approach.

Consider an I/O task to transfer characters from a keyboard to a display. Let interrupts be used to receive characters from the keyboard interface. To make the example simple, assume that the interrupt-service routine sends each received character directly to the display interface without polling its status. This assumes that the characters are received at a rate that is low enough for the display to handle.

The initialization in the program for this task requires accessing I/O registers and processor control registers. The I/O interface in Figure 3.3 should be configured to raise an interrupt request when KIN = 1. The corresponding interrupt-enable bit in the KBD_CONT register, KIE, has to be set to 1. It is also necessary to enable interrupts in the processor by setting to 1 the IE bit in the processor status (PS) register and the KBD bit in the IENABLE control register in Figure 3.7.

Chapter 3 describes different methods of identifying the starting address of an interrupt-service routine that has to be executed when a particular interrupt is raised. The method of vectored interrupts for different sources uses predetermined memory locations that hold the addresses of the corresponding interrupt-service routines. In this section, we will assume for simplicity that there is a single interrupt vector, IVECT, at address 0x20 for all interrupts. This vector must be initialized with the address of the interrupt-service routine.

Figure 4.4 shows an assembly-language program that uses interrupts to read characters from the keyboard. The main program loads the address of the interrupt-service routine into location IVECT. It sets to 1 the KIN bit in the control register of the keyboard interface, and the interrupt-enable bits in the IENABLE and PS registers of the processor. On each interrupt from the keyboard interface, the interrupt-service routine reads the input character, then sends it to the display.

Consider now using a C program to accomplish the same I/O task. A high-level language such as C is not designed to handle hardware features such as interrupts. To write a C program that uses interrupts we need to address two questions:

- How do we access processor control registers?
- How do we write an interrupt-service routine?

IVECT	EQU	0x20	Vector for interrupt-service routine.
KBD_DATA	EQU	0x4000	Keyboard data register (8 bits).
KBD_STATUS	EQU	0x4004	Keyboard status register (bit 1 is KIN flag).
KBD_CONT	EQU	0x4008	Keyboard control register (bit 1 is KIE flag).
DISP_DATA	EQU	0x4010	Display data register (8 bits).
DISP_STATUS	EQU	0x4014	Display status register (bit 2 is DOUT flag).

Main program

MAIN:	Move	R2, #KBD_DATA	Pointer to keyboard interface.
	Move	R3, #0x2	
	StoreByte	R3, 8(R2)	Configure the keyboard to cause interrupts.
	Move	R2, #IVECT	Pointer to vector.
	Move	R3, #INTSERV	Start of interrupt-service routine.
	Store	R3, (R2)	Set interrupt vector.
	Move	R2, #0x2	Allow the processor to recognize keyboard
	MoveControl	IENABLE, R2	interrupts.
	Move	R2, #0x1	Set the interrupt-enable bit for the processor.
	MoveControl	PS, R2	
LOOP:	Branch	LOOP	Continuous wait loop.

Interrupt-service routine

INTSERV:	Subtract	SP, SP, #8	Save registers.
	Store	R2, 4(SP)	
	Store	R3, (SP)	
	Move	R2, #KBD_DATA	Pointer to keyboard interface.
	LoadByte	R3, (R2)	Read next character.
	Move	R2, #DISP_DATA	Pointer to display interface.
	StoreByte	R3, (R2)	Write the received character to the display.
	Load	R2, 4(SP)	Restore registers.
	Load	R3, (SP)	
	Add	SP, SP, #8	
	Return-from-interrupt		

Figure 4.4   Assembly-language program for character transfer using interrupts.

The interrupt approach requires setting control bits in the IENABLE and PS registers as part of initialization. The pointer-based approach used in Figure 4.3 to access memory-mapped I/O registers cannot be used because the IENABLE and PS control registers do not have addresses. Instead, these registers can be accessed by including suitable assembly-language instructions directly in the C program. A special directive to the compiler makes this possible. For example, the statement

asm ("MoveControl   PS, R2");

```
#define    KBD_DATA     (volatile char *) 0x4000
#define    DISP_DATA    (volatile char *) 0x4010

void main()
{
        ⋮
}

void intserv()
{
    *DISP_DATA = *KBD_DATA;    /* Transfer a character. */
}
```

Figure 4.5   Representing an interrupt-service routine as a function in a C program.

causes the C compiler to insert the assembly-language instruction between the quotes into the compiled code. Since register R2 may already be used by compiler-generated instructions, its contents must not be corrupted by any inserted assembly-language instructions. A simple solution is to save the contents of R2 on the stack before R2 is modified for use by the MoveControl instruction, and then restore them after this instruction. We will use this approach. But, we should note that compilers provide more sophisticated methods for managing the use of registers specified in the *asm* directives.

The second issue is the interrupt-service routine. The C language requires this routine to be written as a function. However, the compiler implements all C functions as subroutines that implicitly end with a Return-from-subroutine instruction. Figure 4.5 gives an example. There is a main function that performs some unspecified task. The function named *intserv* transfers one character from the keyboard to the display. The compiler-generated code for the function *intserv* is

```
<save registers>
LoadByte      R2, 0x4000(R0)
StoreByte     R2, 0x4010(R0)
<restore registers>
Return-from-subroutine
```

Since the I/O register addresses fit within 16 bits, the compiler can use the Absolute addressing mode, with register R0 which always contains the value zero, as discussed in Section 2.4.3.

To use the function *intserv* as an interrupt-service routine, it must end with a Return-from-interrupt instruction. This instruction is needed to restore the contents of the program counter and the processor status register to their values at the time the interrupt occurred. We can insert the Return-from-interrupt as the last statement of the *intserv* function in the program using the statement

asm ("Return-from-interrupt");

With this statement, the compiled code for the function will be

```
<save registers>
LoadByte        R2, 0x4000(R0)
StoreByte       R2, 0x4010(R0)
Return-from-interrupt
<restore registers>
Return-from-subroutine
```

The compiler still includes the code to restore registers and the Return-from-subroutine instruction at the end as it does for all functions. However, the inclusion of the Return-from-interrupt instruction means that the code after it will never be executed. Since interrupts can occur at any point in the program, failure to restore the original value of a register that is modified in the function causes the subsequent execution of the program to be incorrect. More critically, failure to restore the correct value of the stack pointer causes corruption of the stack frames for nested subroutines.

There are two approaches for correctly supporting interrupts in a high-level language such as C. The first approach requires extending the syntax of the language with a special keyword for identifying interrupt-service routines. For example, a C compiler may recognize the keyword *interrupt* at the beginning of a function definition, such as

interrupt void intserv () { . . . }

for the function in Figure 4.5. This keyword instructs the compiler to substitute the Return-from-interrupt instruction in place of the Return-from-subroutine instruction. Registers are still saved and restored as before. Not all C compilers provide this feature.

The second approach is to prepare an interrupt handler using assembly language and use the linker to link it to the C program. In this case, the handler must first save the link register, because the interrupt may occur after a subroutine call in the main program. After saving the link register, the interrupt handler can call a C-language subroutine that services the interrupt. In this manner, no special keyword is needed in the high-level language source file. Upon return from the subroutine, the link register is restored and the Return-from-interrupt instruction is executed.

We can now write a C program that uses interrupts to transfer characters from the keyboard to the display. Figure 4.6 gives a possible program that is equivalent to Figure 4.4. We use the approach based on the special keyword for the C compiler because it allows the entire program to be in a single high-level language source file. Note that the pointers to memory-mapped I/O registers are of character type because they point to locations that correspond to 8-bit registers in the device interfaces. The pointer IVECT is of unsigned integer type because it points to a memory location that stores a 4-byte interrupt vector.

```
#define    IVECT            (volatile unsigned int *) 0x20
#define    KBD_DATA         (volatile char *) 0x4000
#define    KBD_CONT         (volatile char *) 0x4008
#define    DISP_DATA        (volatile char *) 0x4010
#define    DISP_STATUS      (volatile char *) 0x4014

interrupt void intserv();    /* Forward declaration. */

void main()
{
    /* Initialize for interrupt-based character transfers. */
    *KBD_CONT = 0x2;                        /* Enable keyboard interrupts. */
    *IVECT = (unsigned int) &intserv;       /* Set interrupt vector. */
    asm ("Subtract    SP, SP, #4");         /* Save register R2. */
    asm ("Store    R2, (SP)");
    asm ("Move    R2, #0x2");               /* Allow processor to recognize keyboard interrupts. */
    asm ("MoveControl    IENABLE, R2");
    asm ("Move    R2, #0x1");               /* Enable interrupts for processor. */
    asm ("MoveControl    PS, R2");
    asm ("Load    R2, (SP)");               /* Restore register R2. */
    asm ("Add    SP, SP, #4");

    while (1)                               /* Continuous loop. */
    {
                                            /* Transfer the characters using interrupt-service routine. */
    }
}

interrupt void intserv()    /* Keyword instructs compiler to treat function as interrupt routine. */
{
    *DISP_DATA = *KBD_DATA;    /* Transfer a character. */
    /* Compiler will insert Return-from-interrupt instruction at end of function. */
}
```

Figure 4.6    C program for character transfer using interrupts.

4.9 THE OPERATING SYSTEM

The preceding sections describe how application programs are prepared and executed with the aid of various utility programs. All of the tasks described in this chapter are facilitated by the *operating system* (OS), which is a key software component in most computers. It is responsible for the coordination of all activities in a computer. The OS software normally consists of essential routines that always reside in the memory of the computer, and various utility programs that are stored on a magnetic disk to be loaded into the memory and executed when needed.

The OS manages the processing, memory, and input/output resources of the computer during the execution of programs. It interprets user commands, assigns memory and disk space, moves information between the memory and the disk, and handles I/O operations. It makes it possible for a user to use the text editor, compiler, assembler, and linker to prepare application programs. The loader is normally part of the OS, and it is invoked when a user enters a command to execute an application program. Our objective in this section is to provide a basic appreciation of the important functions performed by the OS. A more thorough discussion is outside the scope of this book (see Reference [1]).

4.9.1 THE BOOT-STRAPPING PROCESS

The OS for a general-purpose computer is a large and complex collection of software. All parts of the OS, including the portion that always resides in memory, are normally stored on the disk. A process called *boot-strapping* is used to load the memory-resident portion of the OS into the memory so that it can begin execution and assume control over the resources of the computer.

The boot-strapping process begins when the computer is turned on and the processor fetches the first instruction from a predetermined location. That location must be in a permanent portion of the memory that retains its contents when the computer is turned off. A small program placed at that location enables the processor to transfer progressively larger parts of the OS from the disk to the portion of the memory that is not permanent. Each program executed in this boot-strapping sequence transfers more of the OS from the disk into the memory, and performs any necessary initialization of the memory and I/O devices of the computer. Ultimately, the loader and the portion of the OS responsible for processing user commands are transferred into the memory. This enables the OS to begin accepting commands to load and execute application programs stored in files on the disk.

4.9.2 MANAGING THE EXECUTION OF APPLICATION PROGRAMS

To understand the basics of operating systems, let us consider a computer with a processor and I/O devices consisting of a keyboard, a display, a disk, and a printer. We first discuss the steps involved in running one application program. Then, we will describe how the OS manages the execution of multiple application programs.

To execute an application program stored in a file on the disk, the user enters a command that causes the loader to transfer this file into the memory. When the transfer is complete, execution of the program is started. Assume that the program's task involves reading a data file from the disk into the memory, performing some computation on the data, and printing the results. When execution of the program reaches the point where the data file is needed, the program requests the OS to transfer the data file from the disk to the memory. Once the data are transferred, the OS passes execution control back to the application program, which proceeds to perform the required computation. When the computation

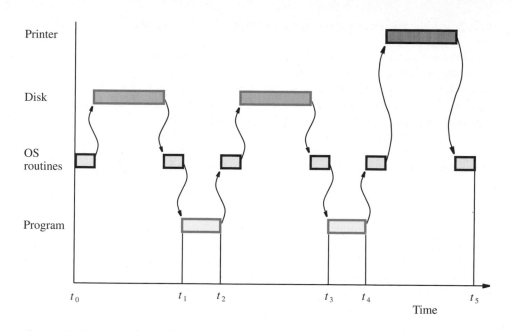

Figure 4.7 Time-line to illustrate execution control moving between user program and OS routines.

is completed and the results stored in memory are ready to be printed, the application program again sends a request to the OS. An OS routine is then executed to print the results.

Execution control passes back and forth between the application program and the OS routines, which share the processor to perform their respective tasks. A convenient way to illustrate this activity is with a time-line diagram, such as that shown in Figure 4.7. During the time period t_0 to t_1, the loader transfers the object program from the disk to the memory. At t_1, the OS passes execution control to the application program, which runs until it needs the data on the disk. The OS transfers the required data during the period t_2 to t_3. Finally, the OS prints the results stored in the memory during the period t_4 to t_5.

Computer resources can be used more efficiently if there are several application programs to be executed. Note that the disk and the processor are idle during most of the time period t_4 to t_5 in Figure 4.7. If the user is allowed to enter a command during this period, the OS can load and begin execution of another program while the printer is printing. The result is concurrent processing of the computation and I/O requests of the two programs when they are not competing for access to the same resource in the computer. The OS is responsible for managing the concurrent execution of several application programs to make the best possible use of all computer resources. This approach to concurrent execution is called *multiprogramming* or *multitasking*. It is a mode of operation in which the processor executes several programs in some interleaved time order, overlapped with tasks performed by different I/O devices.

4.9.3   USE OF INTERRUPTS IN OPERATING SYSTEMS

The operating system makes extensive use of interrupts to perform I/O operations, as well as to communicate with and control the execution of programs. The interrupt mechanism enables the OS to assign priorities, switch from one program to another, terminate programs, implement security and protection features, and coordinate I/O activities. We will discuss some of these aspects briefly to illustrate how interrupts are used.

The OS incorporates the interrupt-service routines for all devices connected to a computer that are capable of raising interrupts. In a general-purpose computer with an operating system, application programs do not directly perform I/O operations themselves. When an application program needs an input or an output operation, it points to the data to be transferred and asks the OS to perform the operation. The request from the application program is often made through a library subroutine that raises a software interrupt to enter the OS routines. The OS temporarily suspends the execution of the requesting program, then initiates the requested I/O operation. When the I/O operation is completed, the OS is normally informed of this condition through a hardware interrupt. The OS then allows the suspended program to resume execution. The OS and the application program pass control back and forth using software interrupts.

The OS provides a variety of services to application programs. To facilitate the implementation of these services, a processor may have several different Software-interrupt instructions, each with its own interrupt vector. They can be used to call different parts of the OS, depending on the service being requested. Alternatively, a processor may have only one Software-interrupt instruction, with an immediate operand to indicate the desired service.

The OS must ensure that the execution of an application program is terminated properly. Executing an appropriate Software-interrupt instruction at the end of the application program instructs the OS to assume control and complete the termination. Recall that information about the starting location and length of the program in the memory are included in the header of an object program. The OS uses this information to recover the space allocated to the program. The recovered space is then available for another application program.

To achieve multitasking, the OS accepts a new command from the user at any time. It loads and begins execution of the requested program when all the resources needed by that program are available.

Example of Multitasking

To illustrate the interaction between application programs and the OS, let us consider an example that involves multitasking. A common OS technique that makes this possible is called *time slicing*. Each program runs for a short period, τ, called a time slice. Then another program runs for its time slice, and so on. The period τ is determined by a continuously running hardware timer, which generates an interrupt every τ seconds.

Figure 4.8 describes the routines needed to implement some of the essential functions in a multitasking environment. At the time the operating system is started, an initialization routine, called OSINIT in Figure 4.8a, is executed. Among other things, this routine sets the interrupt vector locations in the memory. The values written to the vector locations

OSINIT	Set interrupt vectors:
	Timer interrupt ← SCHEDULER
	Software interrupt ← OSSERVICES
	I/O interrupt ← IODATA
	⋮
OSSERVICES	Examine stack or processor registers
	to determine requested operation.
	Call appropriate routine.
SCHEDULER	Save program state of current running process.
	Select another runnable process.
	Restore saved program state of new process.
	Return from interrupt.

(a) OS initialization, services, and scheduler

IOINIT	Set requesting process state to Blocked.
	Initialize memory buffer address pointer and counter.
	Call device driver to initialize driver
	and enable interrupts in the device interface.
	Return from subroutine.
IODATA	Poll devices to determine source of interrupt.
	Call appropriate driver.
	If END = 1, then set I/O-blocked process state to Runnable.
	Return from interrupt.

(b) I/O routines

KBDINIT	Enable interrupts.
	Return from subroutine.
KBDDATA	Check device status.
	If ready, then transfer character.
	If Character = CR, then {set End = 1; Disable interrupts}
	else set End = 0.
	Return from subroutine.

(c) Keyboard driver

Figure 4.8   Examples of operating system routines.

are the starting addresses of the interrupt-service routines for the corresponding interrupts. For example, OSINIT loads the starting address of a routine called SCHEDULER in the interrupt vector corresponding to the timer interrupt. Hence, at the end of each time slice, the timer interrupt causes this routine to be executed.

A program, together with any information that describes its current state of execution, is regarded as an entity called a *process*. A process can be in one of three states: Running, Runnable, or Blocked. The Running state means that the program is currently being executed. The process is Runnable if the program is ready and waiting to be selected for execution. The third state, Blocked, means that the program is not ready to resume execution for some reason. For example, it may be waiting for completion of an I/O operation that it requested earlier.

Assume that program A is in the Running state during a given time slice. At the end of that time slice, the timer interrupts the execution of this program and starts the execution of SCHEDULER. This is an operating system routine whose function is to determine which user program should run in the next time slice. It starts by saving all of the information that will be needed later when execution of program A is resumed. The information saved includes the contents of registers, including the program counter and the processor status register. Registers must be saved because they may contain intermediate results for a computation in progress at the time of interruption. The program counter points to the location where execution is to resume later. The processor status register reflects the current program state.

Then, SCHEDULER selects for execution some other program, B, that was suspended earlier and is in the Runnable state. It restores all information saved at the time program B was suspended, including the contents of the program counter and status register, and executes a Return-from-interrupt instruction. As a result, program B resumes execution for τ seconds, at the end of which the timer raises an interrupt again, and a *context switch* to another runnable program takes place.

Suppose that program A is currently executing and needs to read a line of characters from the keyboard. Instead of performing the operation itself, it requests I/O service from the operating system. It uses the stack or the processor registers to pass information to the OS describing the required operation, the I/O device, and the address of a buffer in the program data area where the characters from the keyboard should be placed. Then it raises a software interrupt. The corresponding interrupt vector points to the OSSERVICES routine in Figure 4.8*a*. This routine examines the information on the stack or in registers, and initiates the requested operation by calling an appropriate OS routine. In our example, it calls IOINIT in Figure 4.8*b*, which is a general routine responsible for starting I/O operations.

While an I/O operation is in progress, the program that requested it cannot continue execution. Hence, the IOINIT routine sets the process associated with program A into the Blocked state. The IOINIT routine carries out any preparations needed for the I/O operation, such as initializing address pointers and byte count, then calls a routine that initializes the specific device for the requested I/O operation.

It is common practice in OS design to encapsulate all software pertaining to a particular I/O device into a self-contained module called the *device driver*. Such a module can be easily added to or deleted from the OS. We have assumed that the device driver for the keyboard consists of two routines, KBDINIT and KBDDATA, as shown in Figure 4.8*c*.

The IOINIT routine calls KBDINIT, which performs any initialization operations needed by the device or its interface circuit. KBDINIT also enables interrupts in the interface circuit by setting the appropriate bit in its control register, and then it returns to IOINIT, which returns to OSSERVICES. The keyboard interface is now ready to participate in a data transfer operation. It will generate an interrupt request whenever a key is pressed.

Following the return to OSSERVICES, the SCHEDULER routine selects another user program to run. Of course, the scheduler will not select program A, because that program has requested an I/O operation and is now in the Blocked state. Instead, program B or some other program in the Runnable state is selected. The Return-from-interrupt instruction that causes the selected user program to begin execution will also re-enable interrupts in the processor by loading the saved contents into the processor status register. Thus, an interrupt request generated by the keyboard's interface will be accepted. The interrupt vector for this interrupt points to an OS routine called IODATA. Because there could be several devices requesting an interrupt, IODATA begins by polling these devices to identify the one requesting service. Then, it calls the appropriate device driver to service the request. In our example, the driver called will be KBDDATA, which will transfer one character of data. If the character is a Carriage Return, it will also set to 1 a flag called END, to inform IODATA that the requested I/O operation has been completed. At this point, the IODATA routine changes the state of process A from Blocked to Runnable, so that the scheduler may select it for execution in some future time slice.

4.10 CONCLUDING REMARKS

Software is the key factor contributing to the versatility and usefulness of a computer. Utility programs allow users to create, execute, and debug application software. Programmers have the flexibility to combine high-level language source files, assembly-language source files, and library files using the compiler, the assembler, and the linker to generate object programs. When necessary, assembly-language instructions may be included within a high-level language source file.

The power of a computer is greatly enhanced with the software of the operating system, which manages and coordinates all activities. Multitasking by the operating system permits different activities to proceed concurrently for multiple application programs, thus making the best use of the computer.

PROBLEMS

4.1 [E] Write a C program to perform the task described in Problem 3.2.

4.2 [M] Write a C program to perform the task described in Problem 3.9.

4.3 [M] Write a C program to perform the task described in Problem 3.13.

4.4 [D] Write a C program to perform the task described in Problem 3.15.

4.5   **[D]** Write a C program to perform the task described in Problem 3.17.

4.6   **[D]** Write a C program to perform the task described in Problem 3.17, but use an interrupt-service routine associated with the timer.

4.7   **[D]** Assume that the instruction set of a processor includes the instruction

$$\text{MultiplyAccumulate} \quad Ri, Rj, Rk$$

that performs the operation $Ri \leftarrow [Ri] + [Rj] \times [Rk]$ using processor registers Ri, Rj, and Rk. Such an instruction is described in Section 2.12.1.

Assume that the compiler does not use this instruction when it generates assembly-language output. Assume that there are three variables X, Y, and Z defined as global variables in a C program. Write a function *mult_acc_XYZ* in the C language that uses the Multiply-Accumulate instruction to compute $X = X + Y \times Z$. Note that the compiler-generated assembly-language instructions in this function and in the calling program may use processor registers to hold data.

4.8   **[D]** Section 4.9.2 discusses how the input and output steps of a collection of programs such as the one shown in Figure 4.7 could be overlapped to reduce the total time needed to execute them. Let each of the six OS routine execution intervals be 1 unit of time, with each disk operation requiring 3 units, printing requiring 3 units, and each program execution interval requiring 2 units. Compute the ratio of best overlapped time to non-overlapped time for a long sequence of programs. Ignore startup and ending transients.

4.9   **[D]** Section 4.9.2 indicated that program computation can be overlapped with either input or output operations or both. Ignoring the relatively short time needed for OS routines, what is the ratio of best overlapped time to non-overlapped time for completing the execution of a collection of programs, where each program has about equal balance among input, compute, and output activities?

4.10   **[M]** In the discussion of the three process states in Section 4.9.3, transitions from Runnable to Running, Running to Blocked, and Blocked to Runnable are described. What other direct transitions between these states are possible for a process? Which ones are not? Explain each of your choices briefly.

References

1. A. Silbershatz, P. B. Gavin, and G. Gagne, *Operating System Concepts*, 8th ed., John Wiley and Sons, Hoboken, New Jersey, 2008.

chapter

5

BASIC PROCESSING UNIT

CHAPTER OBJECTIVES

In this chapter you will learn about:

- Execution of instructions by a processor
- The functional units of a processor and how they are interconnected
- Hardware for generating control signals
- Microprogrammed control

In this chapter we focus on the processing unit, which executes machine-language instructions and coordinates the activities of other units in a computer. We examine its internal structure and show how it performs the tasks of fetching, decoding, and executing such instructions. The processing unit is often called the *central processing unit* (CPU). The term "central" is not as appropriate today as it was in the past, because today's computers often include several processing units. We will use the term *processor* in this discussion.

The organization of processors has evolved over the years, driven by developments in technology and the desire to provide high performance. To achieve high performance, it is prudent to make various functional units of a processor operate in parallel as much as possible. Such processors have a *pipelined* organization where the execution of an instruction is started before the execution of the preceding instruction is completed. Another approach, known as *superscalar* operation, is to fetch and start the execution of several instructions at the same time. Pipelining and superscalar approaches are discussed in Chapter 6. In this chapter, we concentrate on the basic ideas that are common to all processors.

5.1 SOME FUNDAMENTAL CONCEPTS

A typical computing task consists of a series of operations specified by a sequence of machine-language instructions that constitute a program. The processor fetches one instruction at a time and performs the operation specified. Instructions are fetched from successive memory locations until a branch or a jump instruction is encountered. The processor uses the *program counter*, PC, to keep track of the address of the next instruction to be fetched and executed. After fetching an instruction, the contents of the PC are updated to point to the next instruction in sequence. A branch instruction may cause a different value to be loaded into the PC.

When an instruction is fetched, it is placed in the *instruction register*, IR, from where it is interpreted, or decoded, by the processor's control circuitry. The IR holds the instruction until its execution is completed.

Consider a 32-bit computer in which each instruction is contained in one word in the memory, as in RISC-style instruction set architecture. To execute an instruction, the processor has to perform the following steps:

1. Fetch the contents of the memory location pointed to by the PC. The contents of this location are the instruction to be executed; hence they are loaded into the IR. In register transfer notation, the required action is

$$IR \leftarrow [[PC]]$$

2. Increment the PC to point to the next instruction. Assuming that the memory is byte addressable, the PC is incremented by 4; that is

$$PC \leftarrow [PC] + 4$$

3. Carry out the operation specified by the instruction in the IR.

Fetching an instruction and loading it into the IR is usually referred to as the *instruction fetch phase.* Performing the operation specified in the instruction constitutes the *instruction execution phase.*

With few exceptions, the operation specified by an instruction can be carried out by performing one or more of the following actions:

- Read the contents of a given memory location and load them into a processor register.
- Read data from one or more processor registers.
- Perform an arithmetic or logic operation and place the result into a processor register.
- Store data from a processor register into a given memory location.

The hardware components needed to perform these actions are shown in Figure 5.1. The processor communicates with the memory through the processor-memory interface, which transfers data from and to the memory during Read and Write operations. The instruction address generator updates the contents of the PC after every instruction is fetched. The register file is a memory unit whose storage locations are organized to form the processor's general-purpose registers. During execution, the contents of the registers named in an instruction that performs an arithmetic or logic operation are sent to the arithmetic and logic

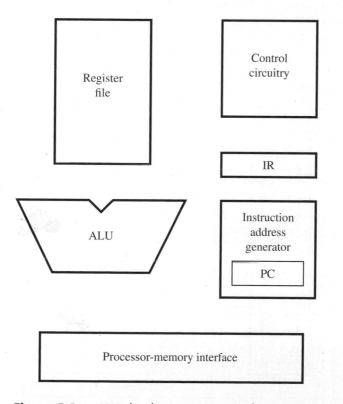

Figure 5.1   Main hardware components of a processor.

unit (ALU), which performs the required computation. The results of the computation are stored in a register in the register file.

Before we examine these units and their interaction in detail, it is helpful to consider the general structure of any data processing system.

Data Processing Hardware

A typical computation operates on data stored in registers. These data are processed by combinational circuits, such as adders, and the results are placed into a register. Figure 5.2 illustrates this structure. A clock signal is used to control the timing of data transfers. The registers comprise edge-triggered flip-flops into which new data are loaded at the active edge of the clock. In this chapter, we assume that the rising edge of the clock is the active edge. The clock period, which is the time between two successive rising edges, must be long enough to allow the combinational circuit to produce the correct result.

The operation performed by the combinational block in Figure 5.2 may be quite complex. It can often be broken down into several simpler steps, where each step is performed by a subcircuit of the original circuit. These subcircuits can then be cascaded into a multi-stage structure as shown in Figure 5.3. Then, if n stages are used, the operation will be completed in n clock cycles. Since these combinational subcircuits are smaller, they can complete their operation in less time, and hence a shorter clock period can be used. A key advantage of the multi-stage structure is that it is suitable for pipelined operation, as will be discussed in Chapter 6. Such a structure is particularly useful for implementing processors that have a RISC-style instruction set. The discussion in the remainder of this chapter focuses on processors that use a multi-stage structure of this type. In Section 5.7 we will consider a more traditional alternative that is suitable for CISC-style processors.

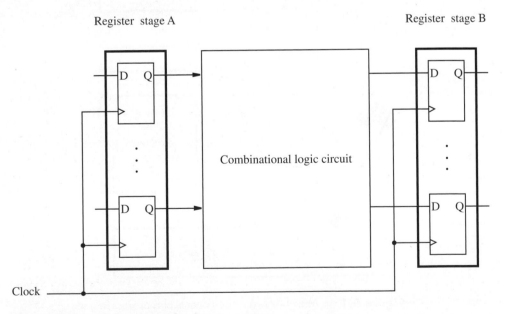

Figure 5.2   Basic structure for data processing.

Register stage A   Register stage B

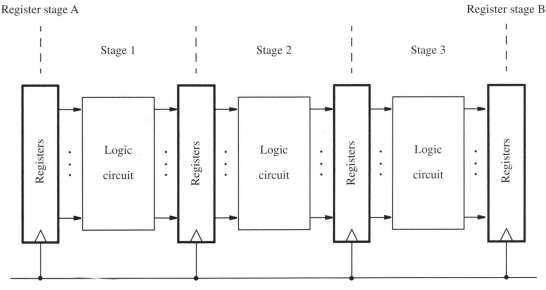

Figure 5.3 A hardware structure with multiple stages.

5.2 INSTRUCTION EXECUTION

Let us now examine the actions involved in fetching and executing instructions. We illustrate these actions using a few representative RISC-style instructions.

5.2.1 LOAD INSTRUCTIONS

Consider the instruction

$$\text{Load} \quad \text{R5, X(R7)}$$

which uses the Index addressing mode to load a word of data from memory location X + [R7] into register R5. Execution of this instruction involves the following actions.

- Fetch the instruction from the memory.
- Increment the program counter.
- Decode the instruction to determine the operation to be performed.
- Read register R7.
- Add the immediate value X to the contents of R7.
- Use the sum X + [R7] as the effective address of the source operand, and read the contents of that location in the memory.
- Load the data received from the memory into the destination register, R5.

Depending on how the hardware is organized, some of these actions can be performed at the same time. In the discussion that follows, we will assume that the processor has five hardware stages, which is a commonly used arrangement in RISC-style processors. Execution of each instruction is divided into five steps, such that each step is carried out by one hardware stage. In this case, fetching and executing the Load instruction above can be completed as follows:

1. Fetch the instruction and increment the program counter.
2. Decode the instruction and read the contents of register R7 in the register file.
3. Compute the effective address.
4. Read the memory source operand.
5. Load the operand into the destination register, R5.

5.2.2   ARITHMETIC AND LOGIC INSTRUCTIONS

Instructions that involve an arithmetic or logic operation can be executed using similar steps. They differ from the Load instruction in two ways:

- There are either two source registers, or a source register and an immediate source operand.
- No access to memory operands is required.

A typical instruction of this type is

$$\text{Add} \quad \text{R3, R4, R5}$$

It requires the following steps:

1. Fetch the instruction and increment the program counter.
2. Decode the instruction and read the contents of source registers R4 and R5.
3. Compute the sum [R4] + [R5].
4. Load the result into the destination register, R3.

The Add instruction does not require access to an operand in the memory, and therefore could be completed in four steps instead of the five steps needed for the Load instruction. However, as we will see in the next chapter, it is advantageous to use the same multistage processing hardware for as many instructions as possible. This can be achieved if we arrange for all instructions to be executed in the same number of steps. To this end, the Add instruction should be extended to five steps, patterned along the steps of the Load instruction. Since no access to memory operands is required, we can insert a step in which no action takes place between steps 3 and 4 above. The Add instruction would then be performed as follows:

1. Fetch the instruction and increment the program counter.
2. Decode the instruction and read registers R4 and R5.
3. Compute the sum [R4] + [R5].

4.   No action.

5.   Load the result into the destination register, R3.

If the instruction uses an immediate operand, as in

Add   R3, R4, #1000

the immediate value is given in the instruction word. Once the instruction is loaded into the IR, the immediate value is available for use in the addition operation. The same five-step sequence can be used, with steps 2 and 3 modified as:

2.   Decode the instruction and read register R4.

3.   Compute the sum [R4] + 1000.

5.2.3   STORE INSTRUCTIONS

The five-step sequence used for the Load and Add instructions is also suitable for Store instructions, except that the final step of loading the result into a destination register is not required. The hardware stage responsible for this step takes no action. For example, the instruction

Store   R6, X(R8)

stores the contents of register R6 into memory location X + [R8]. It can be implemented as follows:

1.   Fetch the instruction and increment the program counter.

2.   Decode the instruction and read registers R6 and R8.

3.   Compute the effective address X + [R8].

4.   Store the contents of register R6 into memory location X + [R8].

5.   No action.

After reading register R8 in step 2, the memory address is computed in step 3 using the immediate value, X, in the IR. In step 4, the contents of R6 are sent to the memory to be stored. No action is taken in step 5.

In summary, the five-step sequence of actions given in Figure 5.4 is suitable for all instructions in a RISC-style instruction set. RISC-style instructions are one word long and only Load and Store instructions access operands in the memory, as explained in Chapter 2. Instructions that perform computations use data that are either stored in general-purpose registers or given as immediate data in the instruction.

The five-step sequence is suitable for all Load and Store instructions, because the addressing modes that can be used in these instructions are special cases of the Index mode. Most RISC-style processors provide one general-purpose register, usually register R0, that always contains the value zero. When R0 is used as the index register, the effective address of the operand is the immediate value X. This is the Absolute addressing mode. Alternatively, if the offset X is set to zero, the effective address is the contents of the index register, Ri. This is the Indirect addressing mode. Thus, only one addressing mode, the Index mode,

Step	Action
1	Fetch an instruction and increment the program counter.
2	Decode the instruction and read registers from the register file.
3	Perform an ALU operation.
4	Read or write memory data if the instruction involves a memory operand.
5	Write the result into the destination register, if needed.

Figure 5.4   A five-step sequence of actions to fetch and execute an instruction.

needs to be implemented, resulting in a significant simplification of the processor hardware. The task of selecting R0 as the index register or setting X to zero is left to the assembler or the compiler. This is consistent with the RISC philosophy of aiming for simple and fast hardware at the expense of higher compiler complexity and longer compilation time. The result is a net gain in the time needed to perform various tasks on a computer, because programs are compiled much less frequently than they are executed.

5.3 HARDWARE COMPONENTS

The discussion above indicates that all instructions of a RISC-style processor can be executed using the five-step sequence in Figure 5.4. Hence, the processor hardware may be organized in five stages, such that each stage performs the actions needed in one of the steps. We now examine the components in Figure 5.1 to see how they may be organized in the multi-stage structure of Figure 5.3.

5.3.1 REGISTER FILE

General-purpose registers are usually implemented in the form of a register file, which is a small and fast memory block. It consists of an array of storage elements, with access circuitry that enables data to be read from or written into any register. The access circuitry is designed to enable two registers to be read at the same time, making their contents available at two separate outputs, A and B. The register file has two address inputs that select the two registers to be read. These inputs are connected to the fields in the IR that specify the source registers, so that the required registers can be read. The register file also has a data input, C, and a corresponding address input to select the register into which data are to be written. This address input is connected to the IR field that specifies the destination register of the instruction.

The inputs and outputs of any memory unit are often called input and output *ports*. A memory unit that has two output ports is said to be *dual-ported*. Figure 5.5 shows two ways

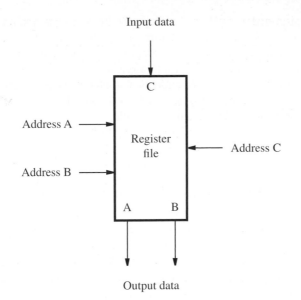

(a) Single memory block

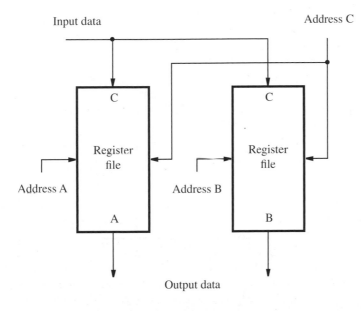

(b) Two memory blocks

Figure 5.5   Two alternatives for implementing a dual-ported register file.

of realizing a dual-ported register file. One possibility is to use a single set of registers with duplicate data paths and access circuitry that enable two registers to be read at the same time. An alternative is to use two memory blocks, each containing one copy of the register file. Whenever data are written into a register, they are written into both copies of that register. Thus, the two files have identical contents. When an instruction requires data from two registers, one register is accessed in each file. In effect, the two register files together function as a single dual-ported register file.

5.3.2 ALU

The arithmetic and logic unit is used to manipulate data. It performs arithmetic operations such as addition and subtraction, and logic operations such as AND, OR, and XOR. Conceptually, the register file and the ALU may be connected as shown in Figure 5.6. When an instruction that performs an arithmetic or logic operation is being executed, the contents of the two registers specified in the instruction are read from the register file and become

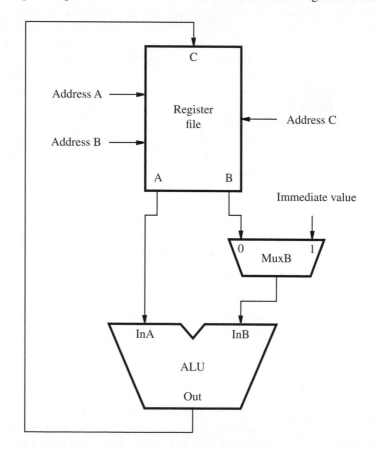

Figure 5.6   Conceptual view of the hardware needed for computation.

available at outputs A and B. Output A is connected directly to the first input of the ALU, InA, and output B is connected to a multiplexer, MuxB. The multiplexer selects either output B of the register file or the immediate value in the IR to be connected to the second ALU input, InB. The output of the ALU is connected to the data input, C, of the register file so that the results of a computation can be loaded into the destination register.

5.3.3 DATAPATH

Instruction processing consists of two phases: the fetch phase and the execution phase. It is convenient to divide the processor hardware into two corresponding sections. One section fetches instructions and the other executes them. The section that fetches instructions is also responsible for decoding them and for generating the control signals that cause appropriate actions to take place in the execution section. The execution section reads the data operands specified in an instruction, performs the required computations, and stores the results.

We now need to organize the hardware into a multi-stage structure similar to that in Figure 5.3, with stages corresponding to the five steps in Figure 5.4. A possible structure is shown in Figure 5.7. The actions taken in each of the five stages are completed in one clock cycle. An instruction is fetched in step 1 by hardware stage 1 and placed into the IR. It is decoded, and its source registers are read in step 2. The information in the IR is used to generate the control signals for all subsequent steps. Therefore, the IR must continue to hold the instruction until its execution is completed.

It is necessary to insert registers between stages. Inter-stage registers hold the results produced in one stage so that they can be used as inputs to the next stage during the next clock cycle. This leads to the organization in Figure 5.8. The hardware in the figure is often referred to as the *datapath*. It corresponds to stages 2 to 5 in Figure 5.7. Data read from the register file are placed in registers RA and RB. Register RA provides the data to input InA of the ALU. Multiplexer MuxB forwards either the contents of RB or the immediate value in the IR to the ALU's second input, InB. The ALU constitutes stage 3, and the result of the computation it performs is placed in register RZ.

Recall that for computational instructions, such as an Add instruction, no processing actions take place in step 4. During that step, multiplexer MuxY in Figure 5.8 selects register RZ to transfer the result of the computation to RY. The contents of RY are transferred to the register file in step 5 and loaded into the destination register. For this reason, the register file is in both stages 2 and 5. It is a part of stage 2 because it contains the source registers and a part of stage 5 because it contains the destination register.

For Load and Store instructions, the effective address of the memory operand is computed by the ALU in step 3 and loaded into register RZ. From there, it is sent to the memory, which is stage 4. In the case of a Load instruction, the data read from the memory are selected by multiplexer MuxY and placed in register RY, to be transferred to the register file in the next clock cycle. For a Store instruction, data are read from the register file, which is part of stage 2, and placed in register RB. Since memory access is done in stage 4, another inter-stage register is needed to maintain correct data flow in the multi-stage structure. Register RM is introduced for this purpose. The data to be stored are moved from RB to RM in step 3, and from there to the memory in step 4. No action is taken in step 5 in this case.

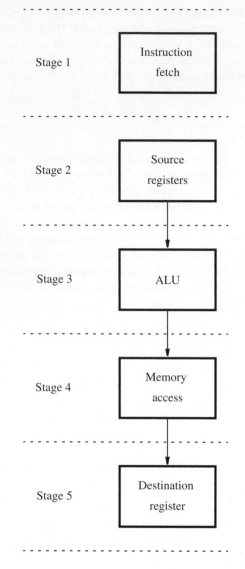

Figure 5.7   A five-stage organization.

The subroutine call instructions introduced in Section 2.7 save the return address in a general-purpose register, which we call LINK for ease of reference. Similarly, interrupt processing requires a return address to be saved, as described in Section 3.2. Assume that another general-purpose register, IRA, is used for this purpose. Both of these actions require the contents of the program counter to be sent to the register file. For this reason, multiplexer MuxY has a third input through which the return address can be routed to register RY, from where it can be sent to the register file. The return address is produced by the instruction address generator, as we will explain later.

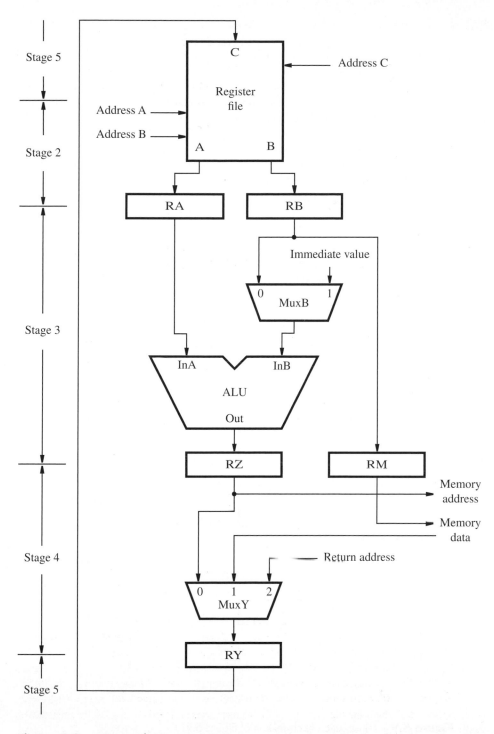

Figure 5.8 Datapath in a processor.

5.3.4 INSTRUCTION FETCH SECTION

The organization of the instruction fetch section of the processor is illustrated in Figure 5.9. The addresses used to access the memory come from the PC when fetching instructions and from register RZ in the datapath when accessing instruction operands. Multiplexer MuxMA selects one of these two sources to be sent to the processor-memory interface. The PC is included in a larger block, the instruction address generator, which updates the contents of the PC after each instruction is fetched. The instruction read from the memory is loaded into the IR, where it stays until its execution is completed and the next instruction is fetched.

The contents of the IR are examined by the control circuitry to generate the signals needed to control all the processor's hardware. They are also used by the block labeled Immediate. As described in Chapter 2, an immediate value may be included in some instructions. A 16-bit immediate value is extended to 32 bits. The extended value is then used either directly as an operand or to compute the effective address of an operand. For some instructions, such as those that perform arithmetic operations, the immediate value is sign-extended; for others, such as logic instructions, it is padded with zeros. The Immediate block in Figure 5.9 generates the extended value and forwards it to MuxB in Figure 5.8 to be used in an ALU computation. It also generates the extended value to be used in computing the target address of branch instructions.

The address generator circuit is shown in Figure 5.10. An adder is used to increment the PC by 4 during straight-line execution. It is also used to compute a new value to be

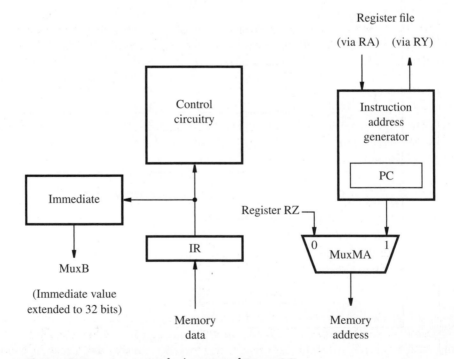

Figure 5.9   Instruction fetch section of Figure 5.7.

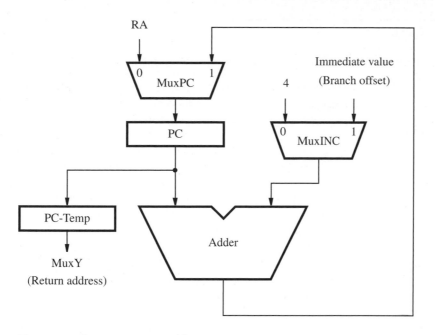

Figure 5.10   Instruction address generator.

loaded into the PC when executing branch and subroutine call instructions. One adder input is connected to the PC. The second input is connected to a multiplexer, MuxINC, which selects either the constant 4 or the branch offset to be added to the PC. The branch offset is given in the immediate field of the IR and is sign-extended to 32 bits by the Immediate block in Figure 5.9. The output of the adder is routed to the PC via a second multiplexer, MuxPC, which selects between the adder and the output of register RA. The latter connection is needed when executing subroutine linkage instructions. Register PC-Temp is needed to hold the contents of the PC temporarily during the process of saving the subroutine or interrupt return address.

5.4   INSTRUCTION FETCH AND EXECUTION STEPS

We now examine the process of fetching and executing instructions in more detail, using the datapath in Figure 5.8. Consider again the instruction

$$\text{Add}\quad \text{R3, R4, R5}$$

The steps for fetching and executing this instruction are given in Figure 5.11. Assume that the instruction is encoded using the format in Figure 2.32, which is reproduced here as Figure 5.12. After the instruction has been fetched from the memory and placed in the IR, the source register addresses are available in fields IR_{31-27} and IR_{26-22}. These two fields

Step	Action
1	Memory address ← [PC], Read memory, IR ← Memory data, PC ← [PC] + 4
2	Decode instruction, RA ← [R4], RB ← [R5]
3	RZ ← [RA] + [RB]
4	RY ← [RZ]
5	R3 ← [RY]

Figure 5.11   Sequence of actions needed to fetch and execute the instruction: Add R3, R4, R5.

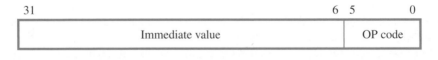

(a) Register-operand format

(b) Immediate-operand format

(c) Call format

Figure 5.12   Instruction encoding.

are connected to the address inputs for ports A and B of the register file. As a result, registers R4 and R5 are read and their contents placed in registers RA and RB, respectively, at the end of step 2. In the next step, the control circuitry sets MuxB to select input 0, thus connecting register RB to input InB of the ALU. At the same time, it causes the ALU to perform an addition operation. Since register RA is connected to input InA, the ALU produces the required sum [RA] + [RB], which is loaded into register RZ at the end of step 3.

In step 4, multiplexer MuxY selects input 0, thus causing the contents of RZ to be transferred to RY. The control circuitry connects the destination address field of the Add instruction, IR_{21-17}, to the address input for port C of the register file. In step 5, it issues

Step	Action
1	Memory address ← [PC], Read memory, IR ← Memory data, PC ← [PC] + 4
2	Decode instruction, RA ← [R7]
3	RZ ← [RA] + Immediate value X
4	Memory address ← [RZ], Read memory, RY ← Memory data
5	R5 ← [RY]

Figure 5.13   Sequence of actions needed to fetch and execute the instruction: Load R5, X(R7).

Step	Action
1	Memory address ← [PC], Read memory, IR ← Memory data, PC ← [PC] + 4
2	Decode instruction, RA ← [R8], RB ← [R6]
3	RZ ← [RA] + Immediate value X, RM ← [RB]
4	Memory address ← [RZ], Memory data ← [RM], Write memory
5	No action

Figure 5.14   Sequence of actions needed to fetch and execute the instruction: Store R6, X(R8).

a Write command to the register file, causing the contents of register RY to be written into register R3.

Load and Store instructions are executed in a similar manner. In this case, the address of the destination register is given in bit field IR_{26-22}. The control hardware connects this field to the address input corresponding to input C of the register file. The steps involved in executing these instructions are given in Figures 5.13 and 5.14. In both examples, the memory address is specified using the Index mode, in which the index value X is given as an immediate value in the instruction. The immediate field of IR, extended as appropriate by the Immediate block in Figure 5.9, is selected by MuxB in step 3 and added to the contents of register RA. The resulting sum is the effective address of the operand.

Some Observations

In the discussion above, we assumed that memory Read and Write operations can be completed in one clock cycle. Is this a realistic assumption? In general, accessing the main memory of a computer takes significantly longer than reading the contents of a register in the register file. However, most modern processors use cache memories, which will be discussed in detail in Chapter 8. A cache memory is much faster than the main memory.

It is usually implemented on the same chip as the processor, making it about as fast as the register file. Thus, a memory Read or Write operation can be completed in one clock cycle when the data involved are available in the cache. When the operation requires access to the main memory, the processor must wait for that operation to be completed. We will discuss how slower memory accesses are handled in Section 5.4.2.

We also assumed that the processor reads the source registers of the instruction in step 2, while it is still decoding the OP code of the instruction that has just been loaded into the IR. Can these two tasks be completed in the same step? How can the control hardware know which registers to read before it completes decoding the instruction? This is possible because source register addresses are specified using the same bit positions in all instructions. The hardware reads the registers whose addresses are in these bit positions once the instruction is loaded into the IR. Their contents are loaded into registers RA and RB at the end of step 2. If these data are needed by the instruction, they will be available for use in step 3. If not, they will be ignored by subsequent hardware stages.

Note that the actions described in Figures 5.11, 5.13, and 5.14 do not show two registers being read in step 2 in every case. To avoid confusion, only the registers needed by the specific instruction described in the figure are mentioned, even though two registers are always read.

5.4.1   BRANCHING

Instructions are fetched from sequential word locations in the memory during straight-line program execution. Whenever an instruction is fetched, the processor increments the PC by 4 to point to the next word. This execution pattern continues until a branch or subroutine call instruction loads a new address into the PC. Subroutine call instructions also save the return address, to be used when returning to the calling program. In this section we examine the actions needed to implement these instructions. Interrupts from I/O devices and software interrupt instructions are handled in a similar manner.

Branch instructions specify the branch target address relative to the PC. A branch offset given as an immediate value in the instruction is added to the current contents of the PC. The number of bits used for this offset is considerably less than the word length of the computer, because space is needed within the instruction to specify the OP code and the branch condition. Hence, the range of addresses that can be reached by a branch instruction is limited.

Subroutine call instructions can reach a larger range of addresses. Because they do not include a condition, more bits are available to specify the target address. Also, most RISC-style computers have Jump and Call instructions that use a general-purpose register to specify a full 32-bit address. The details vary from one computer to another, as the example processors introduced in Appendices B to E illustrate.

Branch Instructions

The sequence of steps for implementing an unconditional branch instruction is given in Figure 5.15. The instruction is fetched and the PC is incremented as usual in step 1. After the instruction has been decoded in step 2, multiplexer MuxINC selects the branch offset in

Step	Action
1	Memory address ← [PC], Read memory, IR ← Memory data, PC ← [PC] + 4
2	Decode instruction
3	PC ← [PC] + Branch offset
4	No action
5	No action

Figure 5.15   Sequence of actions needed to fetch and execute an unconditional branch instruction.

the IR to be added to the PC in step 3. This is the address that will be used to fetch the next instruction. Execution of a Branch instruction is completed in step 3. No action is taken in steps 4 and 5.

We explained in Section 2.13 that the branch offset is the distance between the branch target and the memory location following the branch instruction. The reason for this can be seen clearly in Figure 5.15. The PC is incremented by 4 in step 1, at the time the branch instruction is fetched. Then, the branch target address is computed in step 3 by adding the branch offset to the updated contents of the PC.

The sequence in Figure 5.15 can be readily modified to implement conditional branch instructions. In processors that do not use condition-code flags, the branch instruction specifies a compare-and-test operation that determines the branch condition. For example, the instruction

$$\text{Branch\_if\_[R5]=[R6]} \quad \text{LOOP}$$

results in a branch if the contents of registers R5 and R6 are identical. When this instruction is executed, the register contents are compared, and if they are equal, a branch is made to location LOOP.

Figure 5.16 shows how this instruction may be executed. Registers R5 and R6 are read in step 2, as usual, and compared in step 3. The comparison could be done by performing the subtraction operation [R5] − [R6] in the ALU. The ALU generates signals that indicate whether the result of the subtraction is positive, negative, or zero. The ALU may also generate signals to show whether arithmetic overflow has occurred and whether the operation produced a carry-out. The control circuitry examines these signals to test the condition given in the branch instruction. In the example above, it checks whether the result of the subtraction is equal to zero. If it is, the branch target address is loaded into the PC, to be used to fetch the next instruction. Otherwise, the contents of the PC remain at the incremented value computed in step 1, and straight-line execution continues.

According to the sequence of steps in Figure 5.16, the two actions of comparing the register contents and testing the result are both carried out in step 3. Hence, the clock cycle must be long enough for the two actions to be completed, one after the other. For this reason, it is desirable that the comparison be done as quickly as possible. A subtraction

Step	Action
1	Memory address ← [PC], Read memory, IR ← Memory data, PC ← [PC] + 4
2	Decode instruction, RA ← [R5], RB ← [R6]
3	Compare [RA] to [RB], If [RA] = [RB], then PC ← [PC] + Branch offset
4	No action
5	No action

Figure 5.16   Sequence of actions needed to fetch and execute the instruction: Branch_if_[R5]=[R6] LOOP.

operation in the ALU is time consuming, and is not needed in this case. A simpler and faster comparator circuit can examine the contents of registers RA and RB and produce the required condition signals, which indicate the conditions greater than, equal, less than, etc. A comparator is not shown separately in Figure 5.8 as it can be a part of the ALU block. Example 5.3 shows how a comparator circuit can be designed.

Subroutine Call Instructions

Subroutine calls and returns are implemented in a similar manner to branch instructions. The address of the subroutine may either be computed using an immediate value given in the instruction or it may be given in full in one of the general-purpose registers. Figure 5.17 gives the sequence of actions for the instruction

Call_Register   R9

which calls a subroutine whose address is in register R9. The contents of that register are read and placed in RA in step 2. During step 3, multiplexer MuxPC selects its 0 input, thus transferring the data in register RA to be loaded into the PC.

Step	Action
1	Memory address ← [PC], Read memory, IR ← Memory data, PC ← [PC] + 4
2	Decode instruction, RA ← [R9]
3	PC-Temp ← [PC], PC ← [RA]
4	RY ← [PC-Temp]
5	Register LINK ← [RY]

Figure 5.17   Sequence of actions needed to fetch and execute the instruction: Call_Register R9.

Assume that the return address of the subroutine, which is the previous contents of the PC, is to be saved in a general-purpose register called LINK in the register file. Data are written into the register file in step 5. Hence, it is not possible to send the return address directly to the register file in step 3. To maintain correct data flow in the five-stage structure, the processor saves the return address in a temporary register, PC-Temp. From there, the return address is transferred to register RY in step 4, then to register LINK in step 5. The address LINK is built into the control circuitry.

Subroutine return instructions transfer the value saved in register LINK back to the PC. The encoding of the Return-from-subroutine instruction is such that the address of register LINK appears in bits IR_{31-27}. This is the field connected to Address A of the register file. Hence, once the instruction is fetched, register LINK is read and its contents are placed in RA, from where they can be transferred to the PC via MuxPC in Figure 5.10. Return-from-interrupt instructions are handled in a similar manner, except that a different register is used to hold the return address.

5.4.2 WAITING FOR MEMORY

The role of the processor-memory interface circuit is to control data transfers between the processor and the memory. We pointed out earlier that modern processors use fast, on-chip cache memories. Most of the time, the instruction or data referenced in memory Read and Write operations are found in the cache, in which case the operation is completed in one clock cycle. When the requested information is not in the cache and has to be fetched from the main memory, several clock cycles may be needed. The interface circuit must inform the processor's control circuitry about such situations, to delay subsequent execution steps until the memory operation is completed.

Assume that the processor-memory interface circuit generates a signal called Memory Function Completed (MFC). It asserts this signal when a requested memory Read or Write operation has been completed. The processor's control circuitry checks this signal during any processing step in which it issues a memory Read or Write request, to determine when it can proceed to the next step. When the requested data are found in the cache, the interface circuit asserts the MFC signal before the end of the same clock cycle in which the memory request is issued. Hence, instruction execution continues uninterrupted. If access to the main memory is required, the interface circuit delays asserting MFC until the operation is completed. In this case, the processor's control circuitry must extend the duration of the execution step for as many clock cycles as needed, until MFC is asserted. We will use the command Wait for MFC to indicate that a given execution step must be extended, if necessary, until a memory operation is completed. When MFC is received, the actions specified in the step are completed, and the processor proceeds to the next step in the execution sequence.

Step 1 of the execution sequence of any instruction involves fetching the instruction from the memory. Therefore, it must include a Wait for MFC command, as follows:

Memory address ← [PC], Read memory, Wait for MFC,
IR ← Memory data, PC ← [PC] + 4

The Wait for MFC command is also needed in step 4 of Load and Store instructions in Figures 5.13 and 5.14. Most of the time, the requested information is found in the cache, so the MFC signal is generated quickly, and the step is completed in one clock cycle. When an access involves the main memory, the MFC response is delayed, and the step is extended to several clock cycles.

5.5   CONTROL SIGNALS

The operation of the processor's hardware components is governed by *control signals*. These signals determine which multiplexer input is selected, what operation is performed by the ALU, and so on. In this section we discuss the signals needed to control the operation of the components in Figures 5.8 to 5.10.

It is instructive to begin by recalling how data flow through the four stages of the datapath, as described in Section 5.3.3. In each clock cycle, the results of the actions that take place in one stage are stored in inter-stage registers, to be available for use by the next stage in the next clock cycle. Since data are transferred from one stage to the next in every clock cycle, inter-stage registers are always enabled. This is the case for registers RA, RB, RZ, RY, RM, and PC-Temp. The contents of the other registers, namely, the PC, the IR, and the register file, must not be changed in every clock cycle. New data are loaded into these registers only when called for in a particular processing step. They must be enabled only at those times.

The role of the multiplexers is to select the data to be operated on in any given stage. For example, MuxB in stage 3 of Figure 5.8 selects the immediate field in the IR for instructions that use an immediate source operand. It also selects that field for instructions that use immediate data as an offset when computing the effective address of a memory operand. Otherwise, it selects register RB. The data selected by the multiplexer are used by the ALU. Examination of Figures 5.11, 5.13, and 5.14 shows that the ALU is used only in step 3, and hence the selection made by MuxB matters only during that step. To simplify the required control circuit, the same selection can be maintained in all execution steps. A similar observation can be made about MuxY. However, MuxMA in Figure 5.9 must change its selection in different execution steps. It selects the PC as the source of the memory address during step 1, when a new instruction is being fetched. During step 4 of Load and Store instructions, it selects register RZ, which contains the effective address of the memory operand.

Figures 5.18, 5.19, and 5.20 show the required control signals. The register file has three 5-bit address inputs, allowing access to 32 general-purpose registers. Two of these inputs, Address A and Address B, determine which registers are to be read. They are connected to fields IR_{31-27} and IR_{26-22} in the instruction register. The third address input, Address C, selects the destination register, into which the input data at port C are to be written. Multiplexer MuxC selects the source of that address. We have assumed that three-register instructions use bits IR_{21-17} and other instructions use IR_{26-22} to specify the destination register, as in Figure 5.12. The third input of the multiplexer is the address of the link register used in subroutine linkage instructions. New data are loaded into the selected register only when the control signal RF_write is asserted.

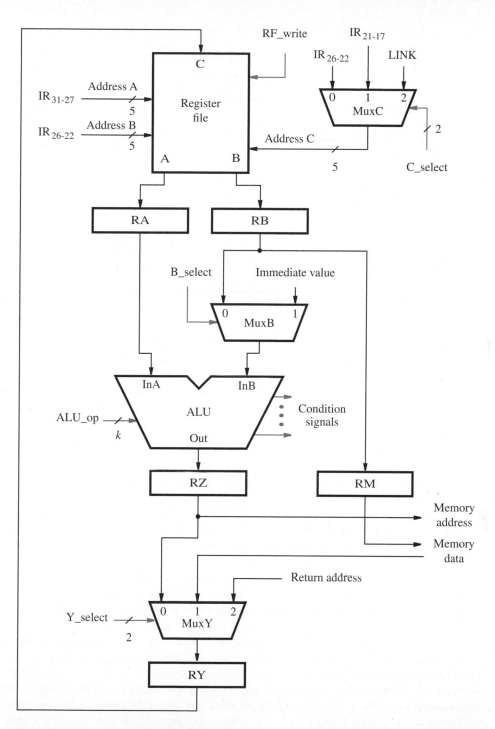

Figure 5.18 Control signals for the datapath.

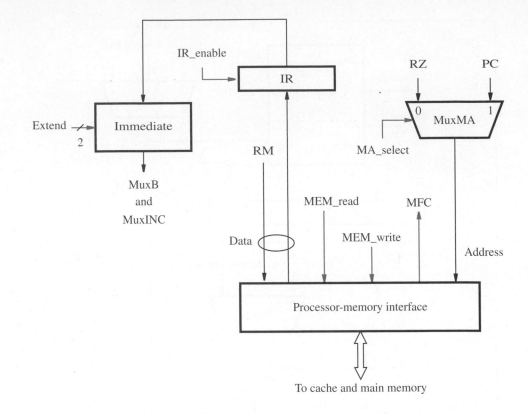

Figure 5.19   Processor-memory interface and IR control signals.

Multiplexers are controlled by signals that select which input data appear at the multiplexer's output. For example, when B_select is equal to 0, MuxB selects the contents of register RB to be available at input InB of the ALU. Note that two bits are needed to control MuxC and MuxY, because each multiplexer selects one of three inputs.

The operation performed by the ALU is determined by a k-bit control code, ALU_op, which can specify up to 2^k distinct operations, such as Add, Subtract, AND, OR, and XOR. When an instruction calls for two values to be compared, a comparator performs the comparison specified, as mentioned earlier. The comparator generates condition signals that indicate the result of the comparison. These signals are examined by the control circuitry during the execution of conditional branch instructions to determine whether the branch condition is true or false.

The interface between the processor and the memory and the control signals associated with the instruction register are presented in Figure 5.19. Two signals, MEM_read and MEM_write are used to initiate a memory Read or a memory Write operation. When the requested operation has been completed, the interface asserts the MFC signal. The instruction register has a control signal, IR_enable, which enables a new instruction to be loaded into the register. During a fetch step, it must be activated only after the MFC signal is asserted.

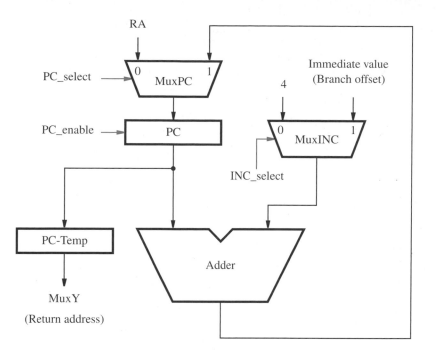

Figure 5.20   Control signals for the instruction address generator.

We have assumed that the Immediate block handles three possible formats for the immediate value: a sign-extended 16-bit value, a zero-extended 16-bit value, and a 26-bit value that is handled in a special way (see Problem 5.14). Hence, its control signal, Extend, comprises two bits.

The signals that control the operation of the instruction address generator are shown in Figure 5.20. The INC_select signal selects the value to be added to the PC, either the constant 4 or the branch offset specified in the instruction. The PC_select signal selects either the updated address or the contents of register RA to be loaded into the PC when the PC enable control signal is activated.

5.6   HARDWIRED CONTROL

Previous sections described the actions needed to fetch and execute instructions. We now examine how the processor generates the control signals that cause these actions to take place in the correct sequence and at the right time. There are two basic approaches: hardwired control and microprogrammed control. Hardwired control is discussed in this section.

An instruction is executed in a sequence of steps, where each step requires one clock cycle. Hence, a step counter may be used to keep track of the progress of execution. Several actions are performed in each step, depending on the instruction being executed. In some cases, such as for branch instructions, the actions taken depend on tests applied to the result of a computation or a comparison operation. External signals, such as interrupt requests, may also influence the actions to be performed. Thus, the setting of the control signals depends on:

- Contents of the step counter
- Contents of the instruction register
- The result of a computation or a comparison operation
- External input signals, such as interrupt requests

The circuitry that generates the control signals may be organized as shown in Figure 5.21. The instruction decoder interprets the OP-code and addressing mode information in the IR and sets to 1 the corresponding INSi output. During each clock cycle, one of the outputs T1 to T5 of the step counter is set to 1 to indicate which of the five steps involved in fetching and executing instructions is being carried out. Since all instructions are completed in five steps, a modulo-5 counter may be used. The control signal generator is a combinational circuit that produces the necessary control signals based on all its inputs. The required settings of the control signals can be determined from the action sequences that implement each of the instructions represented by the signals INS1 to INSm.

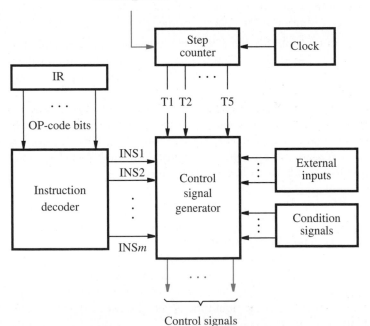

Figure 5.21   Generation of the control signals.

As an example, consider step 1 in the instruction execution process. This is the step in which a new instruction is fetched from the memory. It is identified by signal T1 being asserted. During that clock period, the MA_select signal in Figure 5.19 is set to 1 to select the PC as the source of the memory address, and MEM_read is activated to initiate a memory Read operation. The data received from the memory are loaded into the IR by activating IR_enable when the memory's response signal, MFC, is asserted. At the same time, the PC is incremented by 4, by setting the INC_select signal in Figure 5.20 to 0 and PC_select to 1. The PC_enable signal is activated to cause the new value to be loaded into the PC at the positive edge of the clock marking the end of step T1.

5.6.1 DATAPATH CONTROL SIGNALS

Instructions that handle data include Load, Store, and all computational instructions. They perform various data movement and manipulation operations using the processor's datapath, whose control signals are shown in Figures 5.18 and 5.19. Once an instruction is loaded into the IR, the instruction decoder interprets its contents to determine the actions needed. At the same time, the source registers are read and their contents become available at the A and B outputs of the register file. As mentioned earlier, inter-stage registers RA, RB, RZ, RM, and RY are always enabled. This means that data flow automatically from one datapath stage to the next on every active edge of the clock signal.

The desired setting of various control signals can be determined by examining the actions taken in each execution step of every instruction. For example, the RF_write signal is set to 1 in step T5 during execution of an instruction that writes data into the register file. It may be generated by the logic expression

$$RF\_write = T5 \cdot (ALU + Load + Call)$$

where ALU stands for all instructions that perform arithmetic or logic operations, Load stands for all Load instructions, and Call stands for all subroutine-call and software-interrupt instructions. The RF_write signal is a function of both the instruction and the timing signals. But, as mentioned earlier, the setting of some of the multiplexers need not change from one timing step to another. In this case, the multiplexer's select signal can be implemented as a function of the instruction only. For example,

$$B\_select = Immediate$$

where Immediate stands for all instructions that use an immediate value in the IR. We encourage the reader to examine other control signals and derive the appropriate logic expressions for them, based on the execution steps of various instructions.

5.6.2 DEALING WITH MEMORY DELAY

The timing signals T1 to T5 are asserted in sequence as the step counter is advanced. Most of the time, the step counter is incremented at the end of every clock cycle. However, a step in which a MEM_read or a MEM_write command is issued does not end until the MFC signal is asserted, indicating that the requested memory operation has been completed.

To extend the duration of an execution step to more than one clock cycle, we need to disable the step counter. Assume that the counter is incremented when enabled by a control signal called Counter_enable. Let the need to wait for a memory operation to be completed be indicated by a control signal called WMFC, which is activated during any execution step in which the Wait for MFC command is issued. Counter_enable should be set to 1 in any step in which WMFC is not asserted. Otherwise, it should be set to 1 when MFC is asserted. This means that

$$\text{Counter\_enable} = \overline{\text{WMFC}} + \text{MFC}$$

A new value is loaded into the PC at the end of any clock cycle in which the PC_enable signal in Figure 5.20 is activated. We must ensure that the PC is incremented only once when an execution step is extended for more than one clock cycle. Hence, when fetching an instruction, the PC should be enabled only when MFC is received. It is also enabled in step 3 of instructions that cause branching. Let BR denote all instructions in this group. Then, PC_enable may be realized as

$$\text{PC\_enable} = \text{T1} \cdot \text{MFC} + \text{T3} \cdot \text{BR}$$

5.7   CISC-STYLE PROCESSORS

We saw in the previous sections that a RISC-style instruction set is conducive to a multistage implementation of the processor. All instructions can be executed in a uniform manner using the same five-stage hardware. As a result, the hardware is simple and well suited to pipelined operation. Also, the control signals are easy to generate.

CISC-style instruction sets are more complex because they allow much greater flexibility in accessing instruction operands. Unlike RISC-style instruction sets, where only Load and Store instructions access data in the memory, CISC instructions can operate directly on memory operands. Also, they are not restricted to one word in length. An instruction may use several words to specify operand addresses and the actions to be performed, as explained in Section 2.10. Therefore, CISC-style instructions require a different organization of the processor hardware.

Figure 5.22 shows a possible processor organization. The main difference between this organization and the five-stage structure discussed earlier is that the Interconnect block, which provides interconnections among other blocks, does not prescribe any particular structure or pattern of data flow. It provides paths that make it possible to transfer data between any two components, as needed to implement instructions. The multi-stage structure of Figure 5.8 uses inter-stage registers, such as RZ and RY. These are not needed in the organization of Figure 5.22. Instead, some registers are needed to hold intermediate results during instruction execution. The temporary registers block in the figure is provided for this purpose. It includes two temporary registers, Temp1 and Temp2. The need for these registers will become apparent from the examples given later.

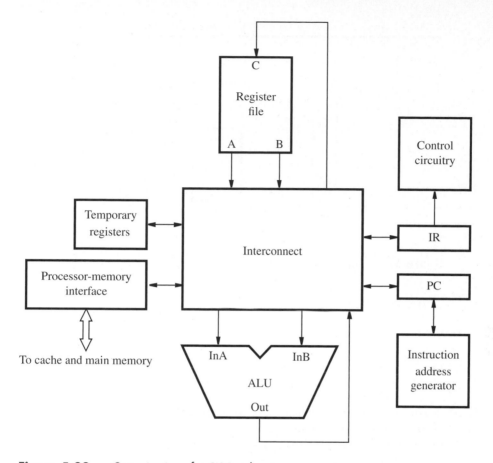

Figure 5.22 Organization of a CISC-style processor.

A traditional approach to the implementation of the Interconnect is to use buses. A *bus* consists of a set of lines to which several devices may be connected, enabling data to be transferred from any one device to any other. A logic gate that sends a signal over a bus line is called a *bus driver* Since all devices connected to the bus have the ability to send data, we must ensure that only one of them is driving the bus at any given time. For this reason, the bus driver is a special type of logic gate called a *tri-state gate*. It has a control input that turns it on or off. When turned on, the gate places a logic signal of 0 or 1 on the bus, according to the value of its input. When turned off, the gate is electrically disconnected from the bus, as explained in Appendix A.

Figure 5.23 shows how a flip-flop that forms one bit of a data register can be connected to a bus line. There are two control signals, R_{in} and R_{out}. When R_{in} is equal to 1 the multiplexer selects the data on the bus line to be loaded into the flip-flop. Setting R_{in} to 0 causes the flip-flop to maintain its present value. The output of the flip-flop is connected to the bus line through a tri-state gate, which is turned on when R_{out} is asserted. At other times, the tri-state gate is turned off, allowing other components to drive the bus line.

Bus

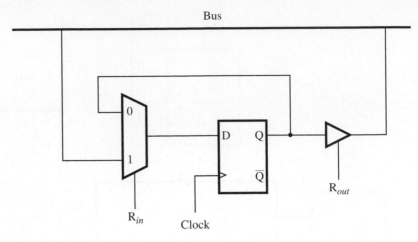

Figure 5.23   Input and output gating for one register bit.

5.7.1   AN INTERCONNECT USING BUSES

The Interconnect in Figure 5.22 may be implemented using one or more buses. Figure 5.24 shows a three-bus implementation. All registers are assumed to be edge-triggered. That is, when a register is enabled, data are loaded into it on the active edge of the clock at the end of the clock period. Addresses for the three ports of the register file are provided by the Control block. These connections are not shown to keep the figure simple. Also not shown is the Immediate block through which the IR is connected to bus B. This is the circuit that extends an immediate operand in the IR to 32 bits.

Consider the two-operand instruction

$$\text{Add} \quad \text{R5, R6}$$

which performs the operation

$$\text{R5} \leftarrow [\text{R5}] + [\text{R6}]$$

Fetching and executing this instruction using the hardware in Figure 5.24 can be performed in three steps, as shown in Figure 5.25. Each step, except for the step involving access to the memory, is completed in one clock cycle. In step 1, bus B is used to send the contents of the PC to the processor-memory interface, which sends them on the memory address lines and initiates a memory Read operation. The data received from the memory, which represent an instruction to be executed, are sent to the IR over bus C. The command Wait for MFC is included to accommodate the possibility that memory access may take more than one clock cycle, as explained in Section 5.4.2. The instruction is decoded in step 2 and the control circuitry begins reading the source registers, R5 and R6. However, the contents of the registers do not become available at the A and B outputs of the register file until step 3. They are sent to the ALU using buses A and B. The ALU performs the addition operation, and the sum is sent back to the ALU over bus C, to be written into register R5 at the end of the clock cycle.

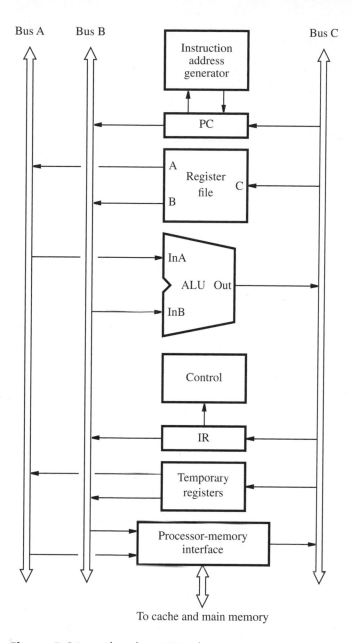

Figure 5.24 Three-bus CISC-style processor organization.

Note that reading the source registers is completed in step 2 in Figure 5.11. In that case, the action of reading the registers proceeds in parallel with the action of decoding the instruction, because the location of the bit fields containing register addresses in a RISC-style instruction is known. Since CISC-style instructions do not always use the same

Step	Action
1	Memory address ← [PC], Read memory, Wait for MFC, IR ← Memory data, PC ← [PC] + 4
2	Decode instruction
3	R5 ← [R5] + [R6]

Figure 5.25   Sequence of actions needed to fetch and execute the instruction: Add R5, R6.

instruction fields to specify register addresses, the action of reading the source registers does not begin until the instruction has been at least partially decoded. Hence, it may not be possible to complete reading the source registers in step 2.

Next, consider the instruction

$$\text{And}\quad \text{X(R7), R9}$$

which performs the logical AND operation on the contents of register R9 and memory location X + [R7] and stores the result back in the same memory location. Assume that the index offset X is a 32-bit value given as the second word of the instruction. To execute this instruction, it is necessary to access the memory four times. First, the OP-code word is fetched. Then, when the instruction decoding circuit recognizes the Index addressing mode, the index offset X is fetched. Next, the memory operand is fetched and the AND operation is performed. Finally, the result is stored back into the memory.

Figure 5.26 gives the steps needed to execute the instruction. After decoding the instruction in step 2, the second word of the instruction is read in step 3. The data received,

Step	Action
1	Memory address ← [PC], Read memory, Wait for MFC, IR ← Memory data, PC ← [PC] + 4
2	Decode instruction
3	Memory address ← [PC], Read memory, Wait for MFC, Temp1 ← Memory data, PC ← [PC] + 4
4	Temp2 ← [Temp1] + [R7]
5	Memory address ← [Temp2], Read memory, Wait for MFC, Temp1 ← Memory data
6	Temp1 ← [Temp1] AND [R9]
7	Memory address ← [Temp2], Memory data ← [Temp1], Write memory, Wait for MFC

Figure 5.26   Sequence of actions needed to fetch and execute the instruction: And X(R7), R9.

which represent the offset X, are stored temporarily in register Temp1, to be used in the next step for computing the effective address of the memory operand. In step 4, the contents of registers Temp1 and R7 are sent to the ALU inputs over buses A and B. The effective address is computed and placed into register Temp2, then used to read the operand in step 5. Register Temp1 is used again during step 5, this time to hold the data operand received from the memory. The computation is performed in step 6, and the result is placed back in register Temp1. In the final step, the result is sent to be stored in the memory at the operand address, which is still available in register Temp2.

The two examples in Figures 5.25 and 5.26 illustrate the variability in the number of execution steps in CISC-style instructions. There is no uniform sequence of actions that can be followed for all instructions in the same way as was demonstrated for RISC instructions in Section 5.2.

5.7.2   MICROPROGRAMMED CONTROL

The control signals needed to control the operation of the components in Figures 5.22 and 5.24 can be generated using the hardwired approach described in Section 5.6. But, there is an interesting alternative that was popular in the past, which we describe next.

Control signals are generated for each execution step based on the instruction in the IR. In hardwired control, these signals are generated by circuits that interpret the contents of the IR as well as the timing signals derived from a step counter. Instead of employing such circuits, it is possible to use a "software" approach, in which the desired setting of the control signals in each step is determined by a program stored in a special memory. The control program is called a *microprogram* to distinguish it from the program being executed by the processor. The microprogram is stored on the processor chip in a small and fast memory called the *microprogram memory* or the *control store*.

Suppose that n control signals are needed. Let each control signal be represented by a bit in an n-bit word, which is often referred to as a *control word* or a *microinstruction*. Each bit in that word specifies the setting of the corresponding signal for a particular step in the execution flow. One control word is stored in the microprogram memory for each step in the execution sequence of an instruction. For example, the action of reading an instruction or a data operand from the memory requires use of the MEM_read and WMFC signals introduced in Sections 5.5 and 5.6.2, respectively. These signals are asserted by setting the corresponding bits in the control word to 1 for steps 1, 3, and 5 in Figure 5.26. When a microinstruction is read from the control store, each control signal takes on the value of its corresponding bit.

The sequence of microinstructions corresponding to a given machine instruction constitutes the *microroutine* that implements that instruction. The first two steps in Figures 5.25 and 5.26 specify the actions for fetching and decoding an instruction. They are common to all instructions. The microroutine that is specific to a given machine instruction starts with step 3.

Figure 5.27 depicts a typical organization of the hardware needed for microprogrammed control. It consists of a microinstruction address generator, which generates the address

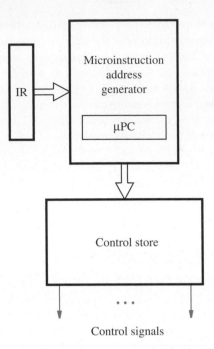

Figure 5.27   Microprogrammed control unit organization.

to be used for reading microinstructions from the control store. The address generator uses a *microprogram counter*, μPC, to keep track of control store addresses when reading microinstructions from successive locations. During step 2 in Figures 5.25 and 5.26, the microinstruction address generator decodes the instruction in the IR to obtain the starting address of the corresponding microroutine and loads that address into the μPC. This is the address that will be used in the following clock cycle to read the control word corresponding to step 3. As execution proceeds, the microinstruction address generator increments the μPC to read microinstructions from successive locations in the control store. One bit in the microinstruction, which we will call End, is used to mark the last microinstruction in a given microroutine. When End is equal to 1, as would be the case in step 3 in Figure 5.25 and step 7 in Figure 5.26, the address generator returns to the microinstruction corresponding to step 1, which causes a new machine instruction to be fetched.

Microprogrammed control can be viewed as having a control processor within the main processor. Microinstructions are fetched and executed much like machine instructions. Their function is to direct the actions of the main processor's hardware components, by indicating which control signals need to be active during each execution step.

Microprogrammed control is simple to implement and provides considerable flexibility in controlling the execution of machine instructions. But, it is slower than hardwired control. Also, the flexibility it provides is not needed in RISC-style processors. As the discussion in this chapter illustrates, the control signals needed to implement RISC-style instructions are quite simple to generate. Since the cost of logic circuitry is no longer a significant factor, hardwired control has become the preferred choice.

5.8   CONCLUDING REMARKS

This chapter explained the basic structure of a processor and how it executes instructions. Modern processors have a multi-stage organization because this is a structure that is well-suited to pipelined operation. Each stage implements the actions needed in one of the execution steps of an instruction. A five-step sequence in which each step is completed in one clock cycle has been demonstrated. Such an approach is commonly used in processors that have a RISC-style instruction set.

The discussion in this chapter assumed that the execution of one instruction is completed before the next instruction is fetched. Only one of the five hardware stages is used at any given time, as execution moves from one stage to the next in each clock cycle. We will show in the next chapter that it is possible to overlap the execution steps of successive instructions, resulting in much better performance. This leads to a pipelined organization.

5.9   SOLVED PROBLEMS

This section presents some examples of the types of problems that a student may be asked to solve, and shows how such problems can be solved.

Problem: Figure 5.11 shows an Add instruction being executed in five steps, but no processing actions take place in step 4. If it is desired to eliminate that step, what changes have to be made in the datapath in Figure 5.8 to make this possible?

Example 5.1

Solution: Step 4 can be skipped by sending the output of the ALU in Figure 5.8 directly to register RY. This can be accomplished by adding one more input to multiplexer MuxY and connecting that input to the output of the ALU. Thus, the result of a computation at the output of the ALU is loaded into both registers RZ and RY at the end of step 3. For an Add instruction, or any other computational instruction, the register file control signal RF_write can be enabled in step 4 to load the contents of RY into the register file.

Problem: Assume that all memory access operations are completed in one clock cycle in a processor that has a 1-GHz clock. What is the frequency of memory access operations if Load and Store instructions constitute 20 percent of the dynamic instruction count in a program? (The dynamic count is the number of instruction executions, including the effect of program loops, which may cause some instructions to be executed more than once.) Assume that all instructions are executed in 5 clock cycles.

Example 5.2

Solution: There is one memory access to fetch each instruction. Then, 20 percent of the instructions have a second memory access to read or write a memory operand. On average, each instruction has 1.2 memory accesses in 5 clock cycles. Therefore, the frequency of memory accesses is $(1.2/5) \times 10^9$, or 240 million accesses per second.

Example 5.3   **Problem:** Derive the logic expressions for a circuit that compares two unsigned numbers: $X = x_2 x_1 x_0$ and $Y = y_2 y_1 y_0$ and generates three outputs: XGY, XEY, and XLY. One of these outputs is set to 1 to indicate that X is greater than, equal to, or less than Y, respectively.

Solution: To compare two unsigned numbers, we need to compare individual bit locations, starting with the most significant bit. If $x_2 = 1$ and $y_2 = 0$, then X is greater than Y. If $x_2 = y_2$, then we need to compare the next lower bit location, and so on. Thus, the logic expressions for the three outputs may be written as follows:

$$XGY = x_2 \bar{y}_2 + \overline{(x_2 \oplus y_2)} \cdot (x_1 \bar{y}_1 + \overline{(x_1 \oplus y_1)} \, x_0 \bar{y}_0)$$

$$XEY = \overline{(x_2 \oplus y_2)} \cdot \overline{(x_1 \oplus y_1)} \cdot \overline{(x_0 \oplus y_0)}$$

$$XLY = \overline{XGY + XEY}$$

Example 5.4   **Problem:** Give the sequence of actions for a Return-from-subroutine instruction in a RISC processor. Assume that the address LINK of the general-purpose register in which the subroutine return address is stored is given in the instruction field connected to address A of the register file (IR_{31-27}).

Solution: Whenever an instruction is loaded into the IR, the contents of the general-purpose register whose address is given in bits IR_{31-27} are read and placed into register RA (see Figure 5.18). Hence, a Return-from-subroutine instruction will cause the contents of register LINK to be read and placed in register RA. Execution proceeds as follows:

1. Memory address ← [PC],   Read memory,   Wait for MFC,   IR ← Memory data, PC ← [PC] + 4
2. Decode instruction, RA ← [LINK]
3. PC ← [RA]
4. No action
5. No action

Example 5.5   **Problem:** A processor has the following interrupt structure. When an interrupt is received, the interrupt return address is saved in a general-purpose register called IRA. The current contents of the processor status register, PS, are saved in a special register called IPS, which is not a general-purpose register. The interrupt-service routine starts at address ILOC.

Assume that the processor checks for interrupts in the last execution step of every instruction. If an interrupt request is present and interrupts are enabled, the request is accepted. Instead of fetching the next instruction, the processor saves the PC and the PS and branches to ILOC. Give a suitable sequence of steps for performing these actions. What additional hardware is needed in Figures 5.18 to 5.20 to support interrupt processing?

Solution: The first two steps of instruction execution, in which an instruction is fetched and decoded, are not needed in the case of an interrupt. They may be skipped, or they would take no action if it is desired to maintain a 5-step sequence. Saving the PC can be done in exactly the same manner as for a subroutine call instruction. Another input to MuxC in Figure 5.18 is needed to which the address of register IRA should be connected. To load the starting address of the interrupt-service routine into the PC, an additional input to MuxPC in Figure 5.20 is needed, to which the value ILOC should be connected. Registers PS and IPS should be connected directly to each other to enable data to be transferred between them. The execution steps required are:

3.   PC-Temp ← [PC],   PC ← ILOC,   IPS ← [PS],   Disable interrupts

4.   RY ← [PC-Temp]

5.   IRA ← [RY]

These actions are reversed by a Return-from-interrupt instruction. See Problem 5.8.

Problem: Example 5.5 illustrates how the contents of the PC and the PS are saved when an interrupt request is accepted. In order to support interrupt nesting, it is necessary for the interrupt-service routine to save these registers on the processor stack, as described in Section 3.2. To do so, the contents of the PS, which are saved in register IPS at the time the interrupt is accepted, need to be moved to one of the general-purpose registers, from where they can be saved on the stack. Assume that two special instructions

Example 5.6

MoveControl   Ri, IPS

and

MoveControl   IPS, Ri

are available to save and restore the contents of IPS, respectively. Suggest changes to the hardware in Figures 5.8 and 5.10 to implement these instructions.

Solution: A possible organization is shown in Figure 5.28. To save the contents of IPS, its output is connected to an additional input on MuxY. When restoring its contents, MuxIPS selects register RA.

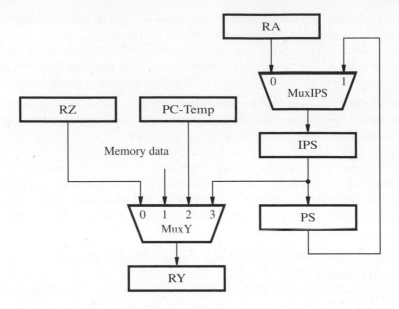

Figure 5.28   Connection of IPS for Example 5.6.

PROBLEMS

5.1 **[M]** The propagation delay through the combinational circuit in Figure 5.2 is 600 ps (picoseconds). The registers have a setup time requirement of 50 ps, and the maximum propagation delay from the clock input to the Q outputs is 70 ps.

(*a*) What is the minimum clock period required for correct operation of this circuit?

(*b*) Assume that the circuit is reorganized into three stages as in Figure 5.3, such that the combinational circuit in each stage has a delay of 200 ps. What is the minimum clock period in this case?

5.2 **[M]** At the time the instruction

Load   R6, 1000(R9)

is fetched, R6 and R9 contain the values 4200 and 85320, respectively. Memory location 86320 contains 75900. Show the contents of the interstage registers in Figure 5.8 during each of the 5 execution steps of this instruction.

5.3 **[E]** Figure 5.12 shows the bit fields assigned to register addresses for different groups of instructions. Why is it important to use the same field locations for all instructions?

5.4 **[M]** At some point in the execution of a program, registers R4, R6, and R7 contain the values 1000, 7500, and 2500, respectively. Show the contents of registers RA, RB, RZ,

RY, and R6 in Figure 5.8 during steps 3 to 5 as the instruction

$$\text{Subtract} \quad \text{R6, R4, R7}$$

is fetched and executed, and also during step 1 of the instruction that is fetched next.

5.5 **[M]** The instruction

$$\text{And} \quad \text{R4, R4, R8}$$

is stored in location 0x37C00 in the memory. At the time this instruction is fetched, registers R4 and R8 contain the values 0x1000 and 0xB2500, respectively. Give the values in registers PC, R4, RA, RM, RZ, and RY of Figures 5.8 and 5.10 in each clock cycle as this instruction is executed, and also in the first clock cycle of the next instruction.

5.6 **[D]** Modify the expressions given in Example 5.3 to compare two, 4-bit, signed numbers in 2's-complement representation.

5.7 **[E]** The subroutine-call instructions described in Chapter 2 always use the same general-purpose register, LINK, to store the return address. Hence, the return register address is not included in the instruction. However, the address LINK is included in bits IR_{31-27} of subroutine-return instructions (see Section 5.4.1 and Example 5.4). Why are the two instructions treated differently?

5.8 **[M]** Give the execution sequence for the Return-from-interrupt instruction for a processor that has the interrupt structure given in Example 5.5. Assume that the address of register IRA is given in bits IR_{31-27} of the instruction.

5.9 **[D]** Consider an instruction set in which instruction encoding is such that register addresses for different instructions are not always in the same bit locations. What effect would that have on the execution steps of the instructions? What would you do to maintain a five-step execution sequence in this case? Assume the same hardware structure as in Figure 5.8.

5.10 **[M]** Assume that immediate operands occupy bits IR_{21-6} of the instruction. The immediate value is sign-extended to 32 bits in arithmetic instructions, such as Add, and padded with zeros in logic instructions, such as Or. Design a suitable implementation for the Immediate block in Figure 5.9.

5.11 **[M]** A RISC processor that uses the five-step sequence in Figure 5.4 is driven by a 1-GHz clock. Instruction statistics in a large program are as follows:

Branch	20%
Load	20%
Store	10%
Computational instructions	50%

Estimate the rate of instruction execution in each of the following cases:

(*a*) Access to the memory is always completed in 1 clock cycle.

(*b*) 90% of instruction fetch operations are completed in one clock cycle and 10% are completed in 4 clock cycles. On average, access to the data operands of a Load or Store instruction is completed in 3 clock cycles.

5.12 **[E]** The execution of computational instructions follows the pattern given in Figure 5.11 for the Add instruction, in which no processing actions are performed in step 4. Consider a program that has the instruction statistics given in Problem 5.11. Estimate the increase in instruction execution rate if this step is eliminated, assuming that all execution steps are completed in one clock cycle.

5.13 **[D]** Figure 5.16 shows that step 3 of a conditional branch instruction may result in a new value being loaded into the PC. In pipelined processors, it is desirable to determine the outcome of a conditional branch as early as possible in the execution sequence. What hardware changes would be needed to make it possible to move the actions in step 3 to step 2? Examine all the actions involved in these two steps and show which actions can be carried out in parallel and which must be completed sequentially.

5.14 **[M]** The instructions of a computer are encoded as shown in Figure 5.12. When an immediate value is given in an instruction, it has to be extended to a 32-bit value. Assume that the immediate value is used in three different ways:

(*a*) A 16-bit value is sign-extended for use in arithmetic operations.

(*b*) A 16-bit value is padded with zeros to the left for use in logic operations.

(*c*) A 26-bit value is padded with 2 zeros to the right and the 4 high-order bits of the PC are appended to the left for use in subroutine-call instructions.

Show an implementation for the Immediate block in Figure 5.19 that would perform the required extensions.

5.15 **[E]** We have seen how all RISC-style instructions can be executed using the steps in Figure 5.4 on the multi-stage hardware of Figure 5.8. Autoincrement and Autodecrement addressing modes are not included in RISC-style instruction sets. Explain why the instruction

$$\text{Load} \quad \text{R3, (R5)+}$$

cannot be executed on the hardware in Figure 5.8.

5.16 **[E]** Section 2.9 describes how the two instructions Or and OrHigh can be used to load a 32-bit value into a register. What additional functionality is needed in the processor's datapath to implement the OrHigh instruction? Give the sequence of actions needed to fetch and execute the instruction.

5.17 **[E]** During step 1 of instruction processing, a memory Read operation is started to fetch an instruction at location 0x46000. However, as the instruction is not found in the cache, the Read operation is delayed, and the MFC signal does not become active until the fourth clock cycle. Assume that the delay is handled as described in Section 5.6.2. Show the contents of the PC during each of the four clock cycles of step 1, and also during step 2.

5.18 **[M]** Give the sequence of steps needed to fetch and execute the two special instructions

$$\text{MoveControl} \quad \text{R}i, \text{IPS}$$

and

$$\text{MoveControl} \quad \text{IPS, R}i$$

used in Example 5.6.

5.19   **[D]** What are the essential differences between the hardware structures in Figures 5.8 and 5.22? Illustrate your answer by identifying the difficulties that would be encountered if one attempts to execute the instruction

$$\text{Subtract} \quad \text{LOC, R5}$$

on the hardware in Figure 5.8. This instruction performs the operation

$$\text{LOC} \leftarrow [\text{LOC}] - [\text{R5}]$$

where LOC is a memory location whose address is given as the second word of a two-word instruction.

5.20   **[M]** Consider the actions needed to execute the instructions given in Section 5.4.1. Derive the logic expressions to generate the signals C_select, MA_select, and Y_select in Figures 5.18 and 5.19 for these instructions.

5.21   **[E]** Why is it necessary to include both WMFC and MFC in the logic expression for Counter_enable given in Section 5.6.2?

5.22   **[E]** Explain what would happen if the MFC variable is omitted from the expression for PC_enable given in Section 5.6.2.

5.23   **[M]** Derive the logic expressions to generate the signals PC_select and INC_select shown in Figure 5.20, taking into account the actions needed when executing the following instructions:

Branch: All branch instructions, with a 16-bit branch offset given in the instruction

Call_register: A subroutine-call instruction with the subroutine address given in a general-purpose register

Other: All other instructions that do not involve branching

5.24   **[M]** A microprogrammed processor has the following parameters. Generating the starting address of the microroutine of an instruction takes 2.1 ns, and reading a microinstruction from the control store takes 1.5 ns. Performing an operation in the ALU requires a maximum of 2.2 ns, and access to the cache memory requires 1.7 ns. Assume that all instructions and data are in the cache.

(a) Determine the minimum time needed for each of the steps in Figure 5.26.

(b) Ignoring all other delays, what is the minimum clock cycle that can be used for this processor?

5.25   **[M]** Give the sequence of steps needed to fetch and execute the instruction

$$\text{Load} \quad \text{R3, (R5)+}$$

on the processor of Figure 5.24. Assume 32-bit operands.

5.26   **[M]** Consider a CISC-style processor that saves the return address of a subroutine on the processor stack instead of in the predefined register LINK. Give the sequence of actions needed to execute a Call_Register instruction on the processor of Figure 5.24.

PIPELINING

CHAPTER OBJECTIVES

In this chapter you will learn about:

- Pipelining as a means for improving performance by overlapping the execution of machine instructions

- Hazards that limit performance gains in pipelined processors and means for mitigating their effect

- Hardware and software implications of pipelining

- Influence of pipelining on instruction set design

- Superscalar processors

Chapter 5 introduced the organization of a processor for executing instructions one at a time. In this chapter, we discuss the concept of pipelining, which overlaps the execution of successive instructions to achieve high performance. We begin by explaining the basics of pipelining and how it can lead to improved performance. Then we examine hazards that cause performance degradation and techniques to alleviate their effect on performance. We discuss the role of *optimizing compilers*, which rearrange the sequence of instructions to maximize the benefits of pipelined execution. For further performance improvement, we also consider replicating hardware units in a *superscalar* processor so that multiple pipelines can operate concurrently.

6.1   BASIC CONCEPT—THE IDEAL CASE

The speed of execution of programs is influenced by many factors. One way to improve performance is to use faster circuit technology to implement the processor and the main memory. Another possibility is to arrange the hardware so that more than one operation can be performed at the same time. In this way, the number of operations performed per second is increased, even though the time needed to perform any one operation is not changed.

Pipelining is a particularly effective way of organizing concurrent activity in a computer system. The basic idea is very simple. It is frequently encountered in manufacturing plants, where pipelining is commonly known as an assembly-line operation. Readers are undoubtedly familiar with the assembly line used in automobile manufacturing. The first station in an assembly line may prepare the automobile chassis, the next station adds the body, the next one installs the engine, and so on. While one group of workers is installing the engine on one automobile, another group is fitting a body on the chassis of a second automobile, and yet another group is preparing a new chassis for a third automobile. Although it may take hours or days to complete one automobile, the assembly-line operation makes it possible to have a new automobile rolling off the end of the assembly line every few minutes.

Consider how the idea of pipelining can be used in a computer. The five-stage processor organization in Figure 5.7 and the corresponding datapath in Figure 5.8 allow instructions to be fetched and executed one at a time. It takes five clock cycles to complete the execution of each instruction. Rather than wait until each instruction is completed, instructions can be fetched and executed in a pipelined manner, as shown in Figure 6.1. The five stages corresponding to those in Figure 5.7 are labeled as Fetch, Decode, Compute, Memory, and Write. Instruction I_j is fetched in the first cycle and moves through the remaining stages in the following cycles. In the second cycle, instruction I_{j+1} is fetched while instruction I_j is in the Decode stage where its operands are also read from the register file. In the third cycle, instruction I_{j+2} is fetched while instruction I_{j+1} is in the Decode stage and instruction I_j is in the Compute stage where an arithmetic or logic operation is performed on its operands. Ideally, this overlapping pattern of execution would be possible for all instructions. Although any one instruction takes five cycles to complete its execution, instructions are completed at the rate of one per cycle.

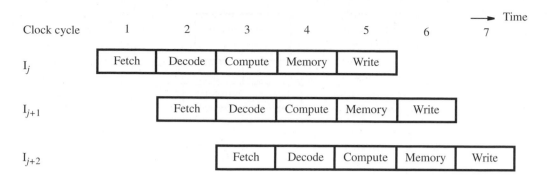

Figure 6.1   Pipelined execution—the ideal case.

6.2   PIPELINE ORGANIZATION

Figure 6.2 indicates how the five-stage organization in Figures 5.7 and 5.8 can be pipelined. In the first stage of the pipeline, the program counter (PC) is used to fetch a new instruction. As other instructions are fetched, execution proceeds through successive stages. At any given time, each stage of the pipeline is processing a different instruction. Information such as register addresses, immediate data, and the operations to be performed must be carried through the pipeline as each instruction proceeds from one stage to the next. This information is held in *interstage buffers*. These include registers RA, RB, RM, RY, and RZ in Figure 5.8, the IR and PC-Temp registers in Figures 5.9 and 5.10, and additional storage. The interstage buffers are used as follows:

- Interstage buffer B1 feeds the Decode stage with a newly-fetched instruction.

- Interstage buffer B2 feeds the Compute stage with the two operands read from the register file, the source/destination register identifiers, the immediate value derived from the instruction, the incremented PC value used as the return address for a subroutine call, and the settings of control signals determined by the instruction decoder. The settings for control signals move through the pipeline to determine the ALU operation, the memory operation, and a possible write into the register file.

- Interstage buffer B3 holds the result of the ALU operation, which may be data to be written into the register file or an address that feeds the Memory stage. In the case of a write access to memory, buffer B3 holds the data to be written. These data were read from the register file in the Decode stage. The buffer also holds the incremented PC value passed from the previous stage, in case it is needed as the return address for a subroutine-call instruction.

- Interstage buffer B4 feeds the Write stage with a value to be written into the register file. This value may be the ALU result from the Compute stage, the result of the Memory access stage, or the incremented PC value that is used as the return address for a subroutine-call instruction.

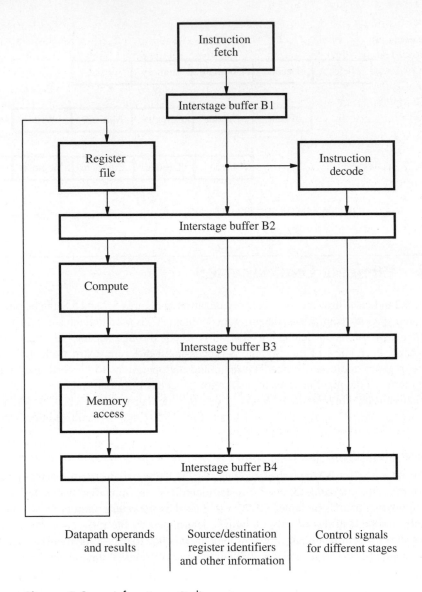

Figure 6.2   A five-stage pipeline.

6.3   PIPELINING ISSUES

Figure 6.1 depicts the ideal overlap of three successive instructions. But, there are times when it is not possible to have a new instruction enter the pipeline in every cycle. Consider the case of two instructions, I_j and I_{j+1}, where the destination register for instruction I_j is a source register for instruction I_{j+1}. The result of instruction I_j is not written into the register file until cycle 5, but it is needed earlier in cycle 3 when the source operand is read for instruction I_{j+1}. If execution proceeds as shown in Figure 6.1, the result of instruction I_{j+1} would be incorrect because the arithmetic operation would be performed using the old value of the register in question. To obtain the correct result, it is necessary to wait until the new value is written into the register by instruction I_j. Hence, instruction I_{j+1} cannot read its operand until cycle 6, which means it must be *stalled* in the Decode stage for three cycles. While instruction I_{j+1} is stalled, instruction I_{j+2} and all subsequent instructions are similarly delayed. New instructions cannot enter the pipeline, and the total execution time is increased.

Any condition that causes the pipeline to stall is called a *hazard*. We have just described an example of a *data hazard*, where the value of a source operand of an instruction is not available when needed. Other hazards arise from memory delays, branch instructions, and resource limitations. The next several sections describe these hazards in more detail, along with techniques to mitigate their impact on performance.

6.4 DATA DEPENDENCIES

Consider the two instructions in Figure 6.3:

Add   R2, R3, #100
Subtract   R9, R2, #30

The destination register R2 for the Add instruction is a source register for the Subtract instruction. There is a *data dependency* between these two instructions, because register R2 carries data from the first instruction to the second. Pipelined execution of these two instructions is depicted in Figure 6.3. The Subtract instruction is stalled for three cycles to delay reading register R2 until cycle 6 when the new value becomes available.

We now explain the stall in more detail. The control circuit must first recognize the data dependency when it decodes the Subtract instruction in cycle 3 by comparing its source register identifier from interstage buffer B1 with the destination register identifier of the Add instruction that is held in interstage buffer B2. Then, the Subtract instruction must be held in interstage buffer B1 during cycles 3 to 5. Meanwhile, the Add instruction proceeds through the remaining pipeline stages. In cycles 3 to 5, as the Add instruction moves ahead, control

Figure 6.3   Pipeline stall due to data dependency.

signals can be set in interstage buffer B2 for an implicit NOP (No-operation) instruction that does not modify the memory or the register file. Each NOP creates one clock cycle of idle time, called a *bubble*, as it passes through the Compute, Memory, and Write stages to the end of the pipeline.

6.4.1 OPERAND FORWARDING

Pipeline stalls due to data dependencies can be alleviated through the use of *operand forwarding*. Consider the pair of instructions discussed above, where the pipeline is stalled for three cycles to enable the Subtract instruction to use the new value in register R2. The desired value is actually available at the end of cycle 3, when the ALU completes the operation for the Add instruction. This value is loaded into register RZ in Figure 5.8, which is a part of interstage buffer B3. Rather than stall the Subtract instruction, the hardware can *forward* the value from register RZ to where it is needed in cycle 4, which is the ALU input. Figure 6.4 shows pipelined execution when forwarding is implemented. The arrow shows that the ALU result from cycle 3 is used as an input to the ALU in cycle 4.

Figure 6.5 shows the modification needed in the datapath of Figure 5.8 to make this forwarding possible. A new multiplexer, MuxA, is inserted before input InA of the ALU, and the existing multiplexer MuxB is expanded with another input. The multiplexers select either a value read from the register file in the normal manner, or the value available in register RZ.

Forwarding can also be extended to a result in register RY in Figure 5.8. This would handle a data dependency such as the one involving register R2 in the following sequence of instructions:

$$
\begin{array}{ll}
\text{Add} & \text{R2, R3, \#100} \\
\text{Or} & \text{R4, R5, R6} \\
\text{Subtract} & \text{R9, R2, \#30}
\end{array}
$$

When the Subtract instruction is in the Compute stage of the pipeline, the Or instruction is in the Memory stage (where no operation is performed), and the Add instruction is in the Write stage. The new value of register R2 generated by the Add instruction is now in register RY. Forwarding this value from register RY to ALU input InA makes it possible

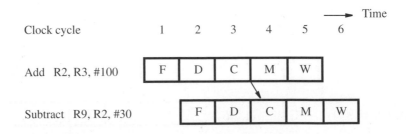

Figure 6.4   Avoiding a stall by using operand forwarding.

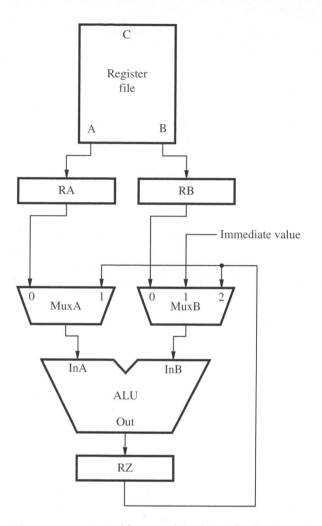

Figure 6.5   Modification of the datapath of Figure 5.8 to support data forwarding from register RZ to the ALU inputs.

to avoid stalling the pipeline. MuxA requires another input for the value of RY. Similarly, MuxB is extended with another input.

6.4.2   HANDLING DATA DEPENDENCIES IN SOFTWARE

Figures 6.3 and 6.4 show how data dependencies may be handled by the processor hardware, either by stalling the pipeline or by forwarding data. An alternative approach is to leave the task of detecting data dependencies and dealing with them to the compiler. When the

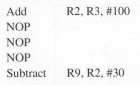

(a) Insertion of NOP instructions for a data dependency

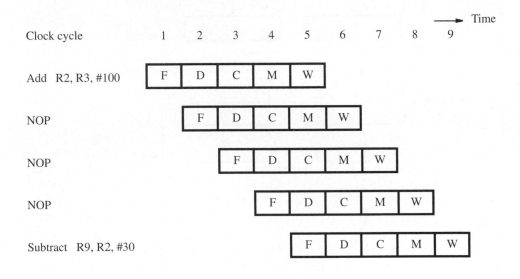

(b) Pipelined execution of instructions

Figure 6.6   Using NOP instructions to handle a data dependency in software.

compiler identifies a data dependency between two successive instructions I_j and I_{j+1}, it can insert three explicit NOP (No-operation) instructions between them. The NOPs introduce the necessary delay to enable instruction I_{j+1} to read the new value from the register file after it is written. For the instructions in Figure 6.4, the compiler would generate the instruction sequence in Figure 6.6a. Figure 6.6b shows that the three NOP instructions have the same effect on execution time as the stall in Figure 6.3.

Requiring the compiler to identify dependencies and insert NOP instructions simplifies the hardware implementation of the pipeline. However, the code size increases, and the execution time is not reduced as it would be with operand forwarding. The compiler can attempt to *optimize* the code to improve performance and reduce the code size by reordering instructions to move useful instructions into the NOP slots. In doing so, the compiler must consider data dependencies between instructions, which constrain the extent to which the NOP slots can be usefully filled.

6.5   MEMORY DELAYS

Delays arising from memory accesses are another cause of pipeline stalls. For example, a Load instruction may require more than one clock cycle to obtain its operand from memory. This may occur because the requested instruction or data are not found in the cache, resulting in a *cache miss*. Figure 6.7 shows the effect of a delay in accessing data in the memory on pipelined execution. A memory access may take ten or more cycles. For simplicity, the figure shows only three cycles. A cache miss causes all subsequent instructions to be delayed. A similar delay can be caused by a cache miss when fetching an instruction.

There is an additional type of memory-related stall that occurs when there is a data dependency involving a Load instruction. Consider the instructions:

> Load   R2, (R3)
> Subtract   R9, R2, #30

Assume that the data for the Load instruction is found in the cache, requiring only one cycle to access the operand. The destination register R2 for the Load instruction is a source register for the Subtract instruction. Operand forwarding cannot be done in the same manner as Figure 6.4, because the data read from memory (the cache, in this case) are not available until they are loaded into register RY at the beginning of cycle 5. Therefore, the Subtract instruction must be stalled for one cycle, as shown in Figure 6.8, to delay the ALU operation. The memory operand, which is now in register RY, can be forwarded to the ALU input in cycle 5.

The compiler can eliminate the one-cycle stall for this type of data dependency by reordering instructions to insert a useful instruction between the Load instruction and the instruction that depends on the data read from the memory. The inserted instruction fills the bubble that would otherwise be created. If a useful instruction cannot be found by the compiler, then the hardware introduces the one-cycle stall automatically. If the processor hardware does not deal with dependencies, then the compiler must insert an explicit NOP instruction.

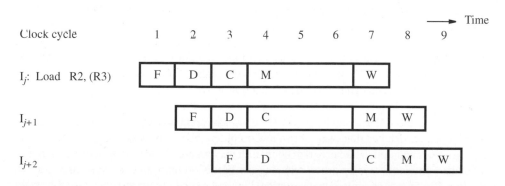

Figure 6.7   Stall caused by a memory access delay for a Load instruction.

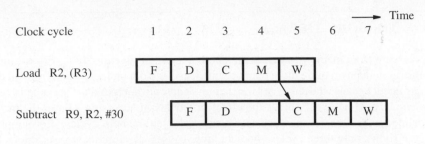

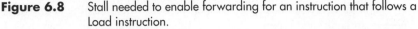

Figure 6.8   Stall needed to enable forwarding for an instruction that follows a Load instruction.

6.6   BRANCH DELAYS

In ideal pipelined execution a new instruction is fetched every cycle, while the preceding instruction is still being decoded. Branch instructions can alter the sequence of execution, but they must first be executed to determine whether and where to branch. We now examine the effect of branch instructions and the techniques that can be used for mitigating their impact on pipelined execution.

6.6.1   UNCONDITIONAL BRANCHES

Figure 6.9 shows the pipelined execution of a sequence of instructions, beginning with an unconditional branch instruction, I_j. The next two instructions, I_{j+1} and I_{j+2}, are stored in successive memory addresses following I_j. The target of the branch is instruction I_k. According to Figure 5.15, the branch instruction is fetched in cycle 1 and decoded in cycle 2, and the target address is computed in cycle 3. Hence, instruction I_k is fetched in cycle 4, after the program counter has been updated with the target address. In pipelined execution, instructions I_{j+1} and I_{j+2} are fetched in cycles 2 and 3, respectively, before the branch instruction is decoded and its target address is known. They must be discarded. The resulting two-cycle delay constitutes a *branch penalty*.

Branch instructions occur frequently. In fact, they represent about 20 percent of the dynamic instruction count of most programs. (The dynamic count is the number of in-struction executions, taking into account the fact that some instructions in a program are executed many times, because of loops.) With a two-cycle branch penalty, the relatively high frequency of branch instructions could increase the execution time for a program by as much as 40 percent. Therefore, it is important to find ways to mitigate this impact on performance.

Reducing the branch penalty requires the branch target address to be computed earlier in the pipeline. Rather than wait until the Compute stage, it is possible to determine the target address and update the program counter in the Decode stage. Thus, instruction I_k can be fetched one clock cycle earlier, reducing the branch penalty to one cycle, as shown in Figure 6.10. This time, only one instruction, I_{j+1}, is fetched incorrectly, because the target address is determined in the Decode stage.

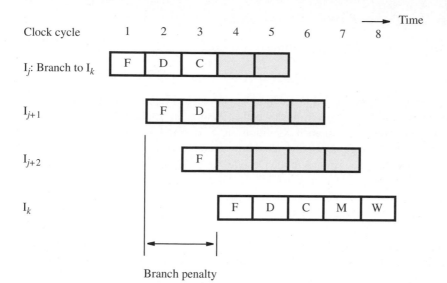

Figure 6.9 Branch penalty when the target address is determined in the Compute stage of the pipeline.

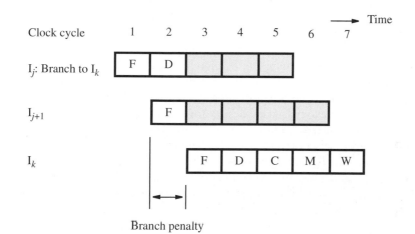

Figure 6.10 Branch penalty when the target address is determined in the Decode stage of the pipeline.

The hardware in Figure 5.10 must be modified to implement this change. The adder in the figure is needed to increment the PC in every cycle. A second adder is needed in the Decode stage to compute a branch target address for every instruction. When the instruction decoder determines that the instruction is indeed a branch instruction, the computed target address will be available before the end of the cycle. It can then be used to fetch the target instruction in the next cycle.

6.6.2   CONDITIONAL BRANCHES

Consider a conditional branch instruction such as

$$\text{Branch\_if\_}[R5]{=}[R6] \quad \text{LOOP}$$

The execution steps for this instruction are shown in Figure 5.16. The result of the comparison in the third step determines whether the branch is taken.

For pipelining, the branch condition must be tested as early as possible to limit the branch penalty. We have just described how the target address for an unconditional branch instruction can be determined in the Decode stage. Similarly, the comparator that tests the branch condition can also be moved to the Decode stage, enabling the conditional branch decision to be made at the same time that the target address is determined. In this case, the comparator uses the values from outputs A and B of the register file directly.

Moving the branch decision to the Decode stage ensures a common branch penalty of only one cycle for all branch instructions. In the next two sections, we discuss additional techniques that can be used to further mitigate the effect of branches on execution time.

6.6.3   THE BRANCH DELAY SLOT

Consider the program fragment shown in Figure 6.11a. Assume that the branch target address and the branch decision are determined in the Decode stage, at the same time that instruction I_{j+1} is fetched. The branch instruction may cause instruction I_{j+1} to be discarded, after the branch condition is evaluated. If the condition is true, then there is a branch penalty of one cycle before the correct target instruction I_k is fetched. If the condition is false, then instruction I_{j+1} is executed, and there is no penalty. In both of these cases, the instruction immediately following the branch instruction is always fetched. Based on this observation, we describe a technique to reduce the penalty for branch instructions.

The location that follows a branch instruction is called the *branch delay slot*. Rather than conditionally discard the instruction in the delay slot, we can arrange to have the pipeline always execute this instruction, whether or not the branch is taken. The instruction in the delay slot cannot be I_{j+1}, the one that may be discarded depending on the branch condition. Instead, the compiler attempts to find a suitable instruction to occupy the delay slot, one that needs to be executed even when the branch is taken. It can do so by moving one of the instructions preceding the branch instruction to the delay slot. Of course, this can only be done if any data dependencies involving the instruction being moved are preserved. If a useful instruction is found, then there will be no branch penalty. If no useful instruction can be placed in the delay slot because of constraints arising from data dependencies, a NOP must be placed there instead. In this case, there will be a penalty of one cycle whether or not the branch is taken.

For the instructions in Figure 6.11a, the Add instruction can safely be moved into the branch delay slot, as shown in Figure 6.11b. The Add instruction is always fetched and executed, even if the branch is taken. Instruction I_{j+1} is fetched only if the branch is not taken. Logically, execution proceeds as though the branch instruction were placed after the

Add   R7, R8, R9
Branch_if_[R3]=0   TARGET
I_{j+1}

⋮

TARGET: I_k

(a) Original sequence of instructions containing
a conditional branch instruction

Branch_if_[R3]=0   TARGET
Add   R7, R8, R9
I_{j+1}

⋮

TARGET: I_k

(b) Placing the Add instruction in the branch delay
slot where it is always executed

Figure 6.11   Filling the branch delay slot with a useful instruction.

Add instruction. That is, branching takes place one instruction later than where the branch instruction appears in the instruction sequence. This technique is called *delayed branching*.

The effectiveness of delayed branching depends on how often the compiler can reorder instructions to usefully fill the delay slot. Experimental data collected from many programs indicate that the compiler can fill a branch delay slot in 70 percent or more of the cases.

6.6.4   BRANCH PREDICTION

The discussion above shows that making the branch decision in cycle 2 of the execution of a branch instruction reduces the branch penalty. But, even then, the instruction immediately following the branch instruction is still fetched in cycle 2 and may have to be discarded. The decision to fetch this instruction is actually made in cycle 1, when the PC is incremented while the branch instruction itself is being fetched. Thus, to reduce the branch penalty further, the processor needs to anticipate that an instruction being fetched is a branch instruction and *predict* its outcome to determine which instruction should be fetched in cycle 2. In this section, we first describe different methods for branch prediction. Then, we discuss how the prediction is made in cycle 1 while a branch instruction is being fetched.

Static Branch Prediction

The simplest form of branch prediction is to assume that the branch will not be taken and to fetch the next instruction in sequential address order. If the prediction is correct, the fetched instruction is allowed to complete and there is no penalty. However, if it is determined that the branch is to be taken, the instruction that has been fetched is discarded and the correct branch target instruction is fetched. Misprediction incurs the full branch penalty. This simple approach is a form of *static branch prediction*. The same choice (assume not-taken) is used every time a conditional branch is encountered.

If branch outcomes were random, then half of all conditional branches would be taken. In this case, always assuming that branches will not be taken results in a prediction accuracy of 50 percent. However, a backward branch at the end of a loop is taken most of the time. For such a branch, better accuracy can be achieved by predicting that the branch is likely to be taken. Thus, instructions are fetched using the branch target address as soon as it is known. Similarly, for a forward branch at the beginning of a loop, the not-taken prediction leads to good prediction accuracy. The processor can determine the static prediction of taken or not-taken by checking the sign of the branch offset. Alternatively, the machine encoding of a branch instruction may include one bit that indicates whether the branch should be predicted as taken or nor taken. The setting of this bit can be specified by the compiler.

Dynamic Branch Prediction

To improve prediction accuracy further, we can use actual branch behavior to influence the prediction, resulting in *dynamic branch prediction*. The processor hardware assesses the likelihood of a given branch being taken by keeping track of branch decisions every time that a branch instruction is executed.

In its simplest form, a dynamic prediction algorithm can use the result of the most recent execution of a branch instruction. The processor assumes that the next time the instruction is executed, the branch decision is likely to be the same as the last time. Hence, the algorithm may be described by the two-state machine in Figure 6.12*a*. The two states are:

LT   -   Branch is likely to be taken
LNT   -   Branch is likely not to be taken

Suppose that the algorithm is started in state LNT. When the branch instruction is executed and the branch is taken, the machine moves to state LT. Otherwise, it remains in state LNT. The next time the same instruction is encountered, the branch is predicted as taken if the state machine is in state LT. Otherwise it is predicted as not taken.

This simple scheme, which requires only a single bit to represent the history of execution for a branch instruction, works well inside program loops. Once a loop is entered, the decision for the branch instruction that controls looping will always be the same except for the last pass through the loop. Hence, each prediction for the branch instruction will be correct except in the last pass. The prediction in the last pass will be incorrect, and the branch history state machine will be changed to the opposite state. Unfortunately, this means that the next time this same loop is entered—and assuming that there will be more than one pass through the loop—the state machine will lead to the wrong prediction for the

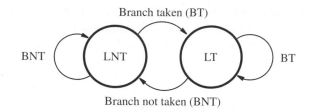

(a) A 2-state algorithm

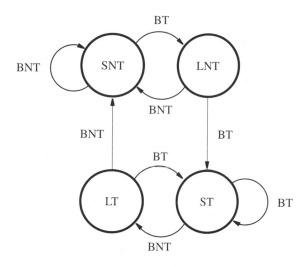

(b) A 4-state algorithm

Figure 6.12   State-machine representation of branch prediction algorithms.

first pass. Thus, repeated execution of the same loop results in mispredictions in the first pass and the last pass.

Better prediction accuracy can be achieved by keeping more information about execution history. An algorithm that uses four states is shown in Figure 6.12*b*. The four states are:

ST   -   Strongly likely to be taken
LT   -   Likely to be taken
LNT   -   Likely not to be taken
SNT   -   Strongly likely not to be taken

Again assume that the state of the algorithm is initially set to LNT. After the branch instruction is executed, and if the branch is actually taken, the state is changed to ST; otherwise, it is changed to SNT. As program execution progresses and the same branch instruction is encountered multiple times, the state of the prediction algorithm changes as shown. The branch is predicted as taken if the state is either ST or LT. Otherwise, the branch is predicted as not taken.

Let us reconsider what happens when executing a program loop. Assume that the branch instruction is at the end of the loop and that the processor sets the initial state of the algorithm to LNT. In the first pass, the prediction (not taken) will be wrong, and hence the state will be changed to ST. In all subsequent passes, the prediction will be correct, except for the last pass. At that time, the state will change to LT. When the loop is entered a second time, the prediction in the first pass will be to take the branch, which will be correct if there is more than one iteration. Thus, repeated execution of the same loop now results in only one misprediction in the last pass.

Branch Target Buffer for Dynamic Prediction

In earlier discussion, we pointed out that the branch target address and the branch decision can both be determined in the Decode stage of the pipeline, which is cycle 2 of instruction execution. The instruction being fetched in the same cycle may or may not be the one that has to be executed after the branch instruction. It may have to be discarded, in which case the correct instruction will be fetched in cycle 3. How can branch prediction be used to obtain better performance?

The key to improving performance is to increase the likelihood that the instruction fetched in cycle 2 is the correct one. This can be achieved only if branch prediction takes place in cycle 1, at the same time that the branch instruction is being fetched. To make this possible, the processor needs to keep more information about the history of execution. The required information is usually stored in a small, fast memory called the *branch target buffer*.

The branch target buffer identifies branch instructions by their addresses. As each branch instruction is executed, the processor records the address of the instruction and the outcome of the branch decision in the buffer. The information is organized in the form of a lookup table, in which each entry includes:

- the address of the branch instruction
- one or two state bits for the branch prediction algorithm
- the branch target address

With this information, the processor is able to identify branch instructions and obtain the corresponding branch prediction state bits based on the address of the instruction being fetched.

Every time the processor fetches a new instruction, it checks the branch target buffer for an entry containing the same instruction address. If an entry with that address is found, this means that the instruction being fetched is a branch instruction. The processor is then able to use the state bits to predict whether that branch is likely to be taken. At the same time, the target address is also obtained. The processor is able to obtain this information as the branch instruction is being fetched in cycle 1. In cycle 2, the processor uses the predicted outcome of the branch to fetch the next instruction. Of course, it must also determine the actual branch decision and target address to determine whether the predicted values were correct. If they are, execution continues without penalty. Otherwise, the instruction that has just been fetched is discarded, and the correct instruction is fetched in cycle 3. The main value of the branch target buffer is that the state information needed for branch prediction and the target address of a branch instruction are both obtained at the same time the branch instruction is being fetched.

Large programs have many branch instructions. A branch target buffer with enough storage to accommodate information for all of them would be large, and searching it quickly would be difficult. For this reason, the table has a limited size, containing information for only the most recently executed branch instructions. Entries in the table are replaced as other branch instructions are executed. Typically, the table contains on the order of 1024 entries.

6.7   RESOURCE LIMITATIONS

Pipelining enables overlapped execution of instructions, but the pipeline stalls when there are insufficient hardware resources to permit all actions to proceed concurrently. If two instructions need to access the same resource in the same clock cycle, one instruction must be stalled to allow the other instruction to use the resource. This can be prevented by providing additional hardware.

Such stalls can occur in a computer that has a single cache that supports only one access per cycle. If both the Fetch and Memory stages of the pipeline are connected to the cache, then it is not possible for activity in both stages to proceed simultaneously. Normally, the Fetch stage accesses the cache in every cycle. However, this activity must be stalled for one cycle when there is a Load or Store instruction in the Memory stage also needing to access the cache. If 25 percent of all instructions executed are Load or Store instructions, these stalls increase the execution time by 25 percent. Using separate caches for instructions and data allows the Fetch and Memory stages to proceed simultaneously without stalling.

6.8   PERFORMANCE EVALUATION

For a non-pipelined processor, the execution time, T, of a program that has a dynamic instruction count of N is given by

$$T = \frac{N \times S}{R}$$

where S is the average number of clock cycles it takes to fetch and execute one instruction, and R is the clock rate in cycles per second. This is often referred to as the *basic performance equation*. A useful performance indicator is the *instruction throughput*, which is the number of instructions executed per second. For non-pipelined execution, the throughput, P_{np}, is given by

$$P_{np} = \frac{R}{S}$$

The processor presented in Chapter 5 uses five cycles to execute all instructions. Thus, if there are no cache misses, S is equal to 5.

Pipelining improves performance by overlapping the execution of successive instructions, which increases instruction throughput even though an individual instruction is still executed in the same number of cycles. For the five-stage pipeline described in this chapter, each instruction is executed in five cycles, but a new instruction can ideally enter the pipeline every cycle. Thus, in the absence of stalls, S is equal to 1, and the ideal throughput with pipelining is

$$P_p = R$$

A five-stage pipeline can potentially increase the throughput by a factor of five. In general, an n-stage pipeline has the potential to increase throughput n times. Thus, it would appear that the higher the value of n, the larger the performance gain. This leads to two questions:

- How much of this potential increase in instruction throughput can actually be realized in practice?
- What is a good value for n?

Any time a pipeline is stalled or instructions are discarded, the instruction throughput is reduced below its ideal value. Hence, the performance of a pipeline is highly influenced by factors such as stalls due to data dependencies between instructions and penalties due to branches. Cache misses increase the execution time even further. We discuss these issues first, and then we return to the question of how many pipeline stages should be used.

6.8.1   EFFECTS OF STALLS AND PENALTIES

The effects of stalls and penalties have been examined qualitatively in the previous sections. We now consider these effects in quantitative terms.

The five-stage pipeline involves memory-access operations in the Fetch and Memory stages, and ALU operations in the Compute stage. The operations with the longest delay dictate the cycle time, and hence the clock rate R. For a processor that has on-chip caches, memory-access operations have a small delay when the desired instructions or data are found in the cache. The delay through the ALU is likely to be the critical parameter. If this delay is 2 ns, then $R = 500$ MHz, and the ideal pipelined instruction throughput is $P_p = 500$ MIPS (million instructions per second).

Consider a processor with operand forwarding in hardware, as explained in Section 6.4.1. This means that there are no penalties due to data dependencies, except in the case of Load instructions. To evaluate the effect of stalls not related to cache misses, we can consider how often a Load instruction is immediately followed by another instruction that uses the result of the memory access. Section 6.5 explained that a one-cycle stall is necessary in such cases. While ideal pipelined execution has $S = 1$, stalls due to such Load instructions have the effect of increasing S by an amount δ_{stall}. For example, assume that Load instructions constitute 25 percent of the dynamic instruction count, and assume that 40 percent of these Load instructions are followed by a dependent instruction. A one-cycle stall is needed in such cases. Hence, the increase over the ideal case of $S = 1$ is

$$\delta_{\text{stall}} = 0.25 \times 0.40 \times 1 = 0.10$$

That is, the execution time T is increased by 10 percent, and throughput is reduced to

$$P_p = \frac{R}{1 + \delta_{\text{stall}}} = \frac{R}{1.1} = 0.91R$$

The compiler can improve performance by reducing the number of times that a Load instruction is immediately followed by a dependent instruction. A stall is eliminated each time the compiler can safely move a nearby instruction to a position between the Load instruction and the dependent instruction.

Now, consider the penalties due to mispredicting branches during program execution. When both the branch decision and the branch target address are determined in the Decode stage of the pipeline, the branch penalty is one cycle. Assume that branches constitute 20 percent of the dynamic instruction count of a program, and that the average prediction accuracy for branch instructions is 90 percent. In other words, 10 percent of all branch instructions that are executed incur a one-cycle penalty due to misprediction. The increase in the average number of cycles per instruction due to branch penalties is

$$\delta_{\text{branch\_penalty}} = 0.20 \times 0.10 \times 1 = 0.02$$

High prediction accuracy is beneficial in limiting the adverse impact of this penalty on performance.

The stalls related to Load instructions and the penalties from branch misprediction are independent. Hence, their effect on performance is additive. The sum of δ_{stall} and $\delta_{\text{branch\_penalty}}$ determines the increase in the number of cycles, S, the increase in the execution time, T, and the reduction in the throughput, P_p.

The effect of cache misses on performance can be assessed by considering the frequency of their occurrence. The time to access the slower main memory is a penalty that stalls the pipeline for p_m cycles every time there is a cache miss. A fraction m_i of all instructions that are fetched incur a cache miss. A fraction d of all instructions are Load or Store instructions, and a fraction m_d of these instructions incur a cache miss. The increase over the ideal case of $S = 1$ due to cache misses is

$$\delta_{\text{miss}} = (m_i + d \times m_d) \times p_m$$

Suppose that 5 percent of all fetched instructions incur a cache miss, 30 percent of all instructions executed are Load or Store instructions, and 10 percent of their data-operand accesses incur a cache miss. Assume that the penalty to access the main memory for a cache miss is 10 cycles. The increase over the ideal case of $S = 1$ due to cache misses in this case is given by

$$\delta_{\text{miss}} = (0.05 + 0.30 \times 0.10) \times 10 = 0.8$$

Compared to δ_{stall} for data dependencies and $\delta_{\text{branch\_penalty}}$ for mispredicted branches, the effect of a slow main memory for cache misses is more significant in this example. When all factors are combined, S is increased from the ideal value of 1 to $1 + \delta_{\text{stall}} + \delta_{\text{branch\_penalty}} + \delta_{\text{miss}}$. The contribution of cache misses is often the dominant one.

6.8.2 NUMBER OF PIPELINE STAGES

The fact that an n-stage pipeline may increase instruction throughput by a factor of n suggests that we should use a large number of stages. However, as the number of pipeline stages increases, there are more instructions being executed concurrently. Consequently, there are more potential dependencies between instructions that may lead to pipeline stalls. Furthermore, the branch penalty may be larger than one cycle if a longer pipeline moves the branch decision to a later stage. For these reasons, the gain in throughput from increasing the value of n begins to diminish, and the cost of a deeper pipeline may not be justified.

Another important factor is the inherent delay in the basic operations performed by the processor. The most important among these is the ALU delay. In many processors, the cycle time of the processor clock is chosen such that one ALU operation can be completed in one cycle. Other operations, including accesses to a cache memory, are typically divided into steps that each take about the same time as an ALU operation. Further reductions in the clock cycle time are possible if a pipelined ALU is used. Some recent processor implementations have used twenty or more pipeline stages to aggressively reduce the cycle time. Implementing such long pipelines using modern technology allows for clock rates of several GHz.

6.9 SUPERSCALAR OPERATION

The maximum throughput of a pipelined processor is one instruction per clock cycle. A more aggressive approach is to equip the processor with multiple execution units, each of which may be pipelined, to increase the processor's ability to handle several instructions in parallel. With this arrangement, several instructions start execution in the same clock cycle, but in different execution units, and the processor is said to use *multiple-issue*. Such processors can achieve an instruction execution throughput of more than one instruction per cycle. They are known as *superscalar* processors. Many modern high-performance processors use this approach.

To enable multiple-issue execution, a superscalar processor has a more elaborate *fetch unit* that fetches two or more instructions per cycle before they are needed and places them in an instruction queue. A separate unit, called the *dispatch unit*, takes two or more instructions from the front of the queue, decodes them, and sends them to the appropriate execution units. At the end of the pipeline, another unit is responsible for writing results into the register file. Figure 6.13 shows a superscalar processor with this organization. It incorporates two execution units, one for arithmetic instructions and another for Load and Store instructions. Arithmetic operations normally require only one cycle, hence the first execution unit is simple. Because Load and Store instructions involve an address calculation for the Index mode before each memory access, the Load/Store unit has a two-stage pipeline.

The organization in Figure 6.13 raises some important implications for the register file. An arithmetic instruction and a Load or Store instruction must obtain all their operands from the register file when they are dispatched in the same cycle to the two execution units. The register file must now have four output ports instead of the two output ports needed in

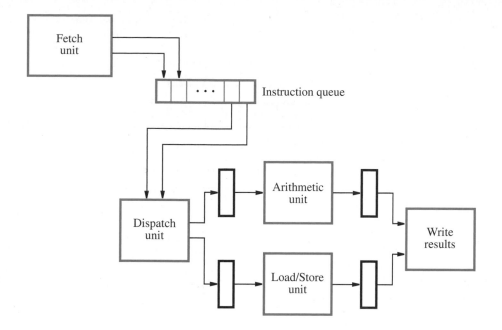

Figure 6.13   A superscalar processor with two execution units.

the simple pipeline. Similarly, an arithmetic instruction and a Load instruction must write their results into the register file when they complete in the same cycle. Thus, the register file must now have two input ports instead of the single input port for the simple pipeline. There is also the potential complication of two instructions completing at the same time with the same destination register for their results. This complication is avoided, if possible, by dispatching the instructions in a manner that prevents its occurrence. Otherwise, one instruction is stalled to ensure that results are written into the destination register in the same order as in the original instruction sequence of the program.

To illustrate superscalar execution in the processor in Figure 6.13, consider the following sequence of instructions:

Add	R2, R3, #100
Load	R5, 16(R6)
Subtract	R7, R8, R9
Store	R10, 24(R11)

Figure 6.14 shows how these instructions would be executed. The fetch unit fetches two instructions every cycle. The instructions are decoded and their source registers are read in the next cycle. Then, they are dispatched to the arithmetic and Load/Store units. Arithmetic operations can be initiated every cycle. A Load or Store instruction can also be initiated every cycle, because the two-stage pipeline overlaps the address calculation for one Load or Store instruction with the memory access for the preceding Load or Store instruction.

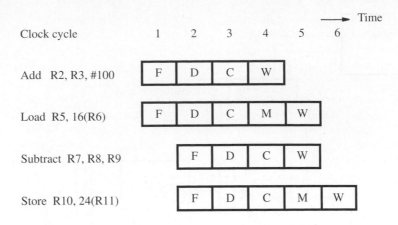

Figure 6.14   An example of instruction flow in the processor of Figure 6.13.

As instructions complete execution in each unit, the register file allows two results to be written in the same cycle because the destination registers are different.

6.9.1 BRANCHES AND DATA DEPENDENCIES

In the absence of any branch instructions and any data dependencies between instructions, throughput is maximized by interleaving instructions that can be dispatched simultaneously to different execution units. However, programs contain branch instructions that change the execution flow, and data dependencies between instructions that impose sequential ordering constraints. A superscalar processor must ensure that instructions are executed in the proper sequence. Furthermore, memory delays due to cache misses may occasionally stall the fetching and dispatching of instructions. As a result, actual throughput is typically below the maximum that is possible. The challenges presented by branch instructions and data dependencies can be addressed with additional hardware. We first consider branch instructions and then consider the issues stemming from data dependencies.

The fetch unit handles branch instructions as it determines which instructions to place in the queue for dispatching. It must determine both the branch decision and the target for each branch instruction. The branch decision may depend on the result of an earlier instruction that is either still queued or newly dispatched. Stalling the fetch unit until the result is available can significantly reduce the throughput and is therefore not a desirable approach. Instead, it is better to employ branch prediction. Since the aim is to achieve high throughput, prediction is also combined with a technique called *speculative execution*. In this technique, subsequent instructions based on an unconfirmed prediction are fetched, dispatched, and possibly executed, but are labeled as being speculative so that they and their results may be discarded if the prediction is incorrect. Additional hardware is required to maintain information about speculatively executed instructions and to ensure that registers or memory locations are not modified until the validity of the prediction is confirmed.

Additional hardware is also needed to ensure that the correct instructions are fetched and dispatched in the event of misprediction.

Data dependencies between instructions impose ordering constraints. A simple approach is to dispatch dependent instructions in sequence to the same execution unit, where their order would be preserved. However, dependent instructions may be dispatched to different execution units. For example, the result of a Load instruction dispatched to the Load/Store unit in Figure 6.13 may be needed by an Add instruction dispatched to the arithmetic unit. Because the units operate independently and because other instructions may have already been dispatched to them, there is no guarantee as to when the result needed by the Add instruction is generated by the Load instruction. A mechanism is needed to ensure that a dependent instruction waits for its operands to become available. When an instruction is dispatched to an execution unit, it is buffered until all necessary results from other instructions have been generated. Such buffers are called *reservation stations*, and they are used to hold information and operands relevant to each dispatched instruction. Results from each execution unit are broadcast to all reservation stations with each result tagged with a register identifier. This enables the reservation stations to recognize a result on which a buffered instruction depends. When there is a matching tag, the hardware copies the result into the reservation station containing the instruction. The control circuit begins the execution of a buffered instruction only when it has all of its operands.

In a superscalar processor using multiple-issue, the detrimental effect of stalls becomes even more pronounced than in a single-issue pipelined processor. The compiler can avoid many stalls through judicious selection and ordering of instructions. For example, for the processor in Figure 6.13, the compiler should strive to interleave arithmetic and memory instructions. This enables the dispatch unit to keep both units busy most of the time.

6.9.2 OUT-OF-ORDER EXECUTION

The instructions in Figure 6.14 are dispatched in the same order as they appear in the program. However, their execution may be completed out of order. For example, the Subtract instruction writes to register R7 in the same cycle as the Load instruction that was fetched earlier writes to register R5. If the memory access for the Load instruction requires more than one cycle to complete, execution of the Subtract instruction would be completed before the Load instruction. Does this type of situation lead to problems?

We have already discussed the issues arising from dependencies among instructions. For example, if an instruction I_{j+1} depends on the result of instruction I_j, the execution of I_{j+1} will be delayed if the result is not available when it is needed. As long as such dependencies are handled correctly, there is no reason to delay the execution of an unrelated instruction. If there is no dependency between a pair of instructions, the order in which execution is completed does not matter.

However, a new complication arises when we consider the possibility of an instruction causing an exception. For example, the Load instruction in Figure 6.14 may attempt an illegal unaligned memory access for a data operand. By the time this illegal operation is recognized, the Subtract instruction that is fetched after the Load instruction may have already modified its destination register. Program execution is now in an inconsistent state. The instruction that caused the exception in the original sequence is identified, but a succeeding instruction in that sequence has been executed to completion. If such a situation is permitted, the processor is said to have *imprecise exceptions*.

The alternative of *precise exceptions* requires additional hardware. To guarantee a consistent state when exceptions occur, the results of the execution of instructions must be written into the destination locations strictly in program order. This means that we must delay writing into register R7 for the Subtract instruction in Figure 6.14 until after register R5 for the Load instruction has been updated. Either the arithmetic unit in Figure 6.13 must retain the result of the Subtract instruction, or the result must be buffered in a temporary register until preceding instructions have written their results. If an exception occurs during the execution of an instruction, all subsequent instructions and their buffered results are discarded.

It is easier to provide precise exceptions in the case of external interrupts. When an external interrupt is received, the dispatch unit stops reading new instructions from the instruction queue, and the instructions remaining in the queue are discarded. All instructions whose execution is pending continue to completion. At this point, the processor and all its registers are in a consistent state, and interrupt processing can begin.

6.9.3 EXECUTION COMPLETION

To improve performance, an execution unit should be allowed to execute any instructions whose operands are ready in its reservation station. This may lead to out-of-order execution of instructions. However, instructions must be completed in program order to allow precise exceptions. These seemingly conflicting requirements can be resolved if execution is allowed to proceed out of order, but the results are written into temporary registers. The contents of these registers are later transferred to the permanent registers in correct program order. This last step is often called the *commitment* step, because the effect of an instruction cannot be reversed after that point. If an instruction causes an exception, the results of any subsequent instructions that have been executed would still be in temporary registers and can be safely discarded. Results that would normally be written to memory would also be buffered temporarily, and they can be safely discarded as well.

A temporary register that is assigned for the result of an instruction assumes the role of the permanent register whose data it is holding. Its contents are forwarded to any subsequent instruction that refers to the original permanent register during that period. This technique is called *register renaming*. There may be as many temporary registers as there are permanent registers, or there may be fewer temporary registers that are allocated as needed for association with different permanent registers.

When out-of-order execution is allowed, a special control unit is needed to guarantee in-order commitment. This is called the *commitment unit*. It uses a separate queue called the *reorder buffer* to determine which instruction(s) should be committed next. Instructions are entered in the queue strictly in program order as they are dispatched for execution. When an instruction reaches the head of this queue and the execution of that instruction has been completed, the corresponding results are transferred from the temporary registers to the permanent registers and the instruction is removed from the queue. All resources that were assigned to the instruction, including the temporary registers, are released. The instruction is said to have been *retired* at this point. Because an instruction is retired only when it is at the head of the queue, all instructions that were dispatched before it must also have been retired. Hence, instructions may complete execution out of order, but they are retired in program order.

6.9.4   DISPATCH OPERATION

We now return to the dispatch operation. When dispatching decisions are made, the dispatch unit must ensure that all the resources needed for the execution of an instruction are available. For example, since the results of an instruction may have to be written in a temporary register, there should be one available, and it is reserved for use by that instruction as a part of the dispatch operation. There must be space available in the reservation station of an appropriate execution unit. Finally, a location in the reorder buffer for later commitment of results must also be available for the instruction. When all the resources needed are assigned, the instruction is dispatched.

Should instructions be dispatched out of order? For example, the dispatch of the Load instruction in Figure 6.14 may be delayed because there is no space in the reservation station of the Load/Store unit as a result of a cache miss in a previously dispatched instruction. Should the Subtract instruction be dispatched instead? In principle this is possible, provided that all the resources needed by the Load instruction, including a place in the reorder buffer, are reserved for it. This is essential to ensure that all instructions are ultimately retired in the correct order and that no deadlocks occur.

A *deadlock* is a situation that can arise when two units, A and B, use a shared resource. Suppose that unit B cannot complete its operation until unit A completes its operation. At the same time, unit B has been assigned a resource that unit A needs. If this happens, neither unit can complete its operation. Unit A is waiting for the resource it needs, which is being held by unit B. At the same time, unit B is waiting for unit A to finish before it can complete its operation and release that resource.

As an example of a deadlock when dispatching instructions out of order, consider a superscalar processor that has only one temporary register. When the Subtract instruction in Figure 6.14 is dispatched before the Load instruction, the temporary register is reserved for it. The Load instruction cannot be dispatched because it is waiting for the same temporary register, which, in turn, will not become free until the Subtract instruction is retired. Since the Subtract instruction cannot be retired before the Load instruction, we have a deadlock.

To prevent deadlocks, the dispatch unit must take many factors into account. Hence, issuing instructions out of order is likely to increase the complexity of the dispatch unit significantly. It may also mean that more time is required to make dispatching decisions. Dispatching instructions in order avoids this complexity. In this case, the program order of instructions is enforced at the time instructions are dispatched and again at the time they are retired. Between these two events, the execution of several instructions across multiple execution units can proceed out of order, subject only to interdependencies among them.

A final comment on superscalar processors concerns the number of execution units. The processor in Figure 6.13 has one arithmetic unit and one Load/Store unit. For higher performance, modern superscalar processors often have two arithmetic units for integer operations, as well as a separate arithmetic unit for floating-point operations. The floating-point unit has its own register file. Many processors also include a vector unit for integer or floating-point arithmetic, which typically performs two to eight operations in parallel. Such a unit may also have a dedicated register file. A single Load/Store unit typically supports all memory accesses to or from the register files for integer, floating-point, or vector units. To keep many execution units busy, modern processors may fetch four or more instructions at the same time to place at the tail of the instruction queue, and similarly four or more instructions may be dispatched to the execution units from the head of the instruction queue.

6.10   PIPELINING IN CISC PROCESSORS

The instruction set of a RISC processor makes pipelining relatively easy to implement. All instructions are one word in size, and operand information is typically located in the same position within a word for different instructions. No instruction requires more than one memory operand. Only Load and Store instructions access memory operands, typically using only indexed addressing. All other instructions operate on register operands. The five-stage pipeline described in this chapter is tailored for these characteristics of RISC-style instructions.

For pipelining in CISC processors, complications arise due to instructions that are variable in size, have multiple memory operands and complex addressing modes, and use condition codes. Instructions that occupy more than one word may take several cycles to fetch. Furthermore, variability in instruction size and format complicates both decoding and operand access, as well as management of the dispatch queue in a superscalar processor.

The availability of more complex addressing modes such as Autoincrement or Autodecrement introduces *side effects* when executing instructions. A side effect occurs when a location other than that of the destination operand is also affected. For example, the instruction

Move   R5, (R8)+

has a side effect. Not only is the destination register R5 affected, but source register R8 is also affected by the autoincrement operation. Should a later instruction depend on the value in register R8, this dependency must be handled with additional hardware in the same manner as a dependency involving the destination register, R5. It may require stalling the pipeline or forwarding the new value. In a superscalar processor, such a dependency requires the use of temporary registers and register renaming as discussed in Section 6.9.3.

Condition codes also introduce side effects. For example, in the sequence of instructions

Compare   R7, R8
Branch>0   TARGET

the result of the Compare instruction affects the condition code flags as a side effect. The Branch instruction, in turn, implicitly depends on this side effect. A condition code register can be included with relative ease in a simple pipeline such as the one shown in Figure 6.2, because only one ALU operation is performed in any cycle. However, in a superscalar processor with multiple execution units, many instructions may be in various stages of execution, and two or more ALU operations may be performed in each cycle. Dependencies arising from side effects related to the condition codes require the use of additional temporary registers and register renaming.

Finally, consider the following sequence of CISC-style instructions:

Move   (R2), (R3)
Move   (R4), R5

The first Move instruction requires two operand accesses to the memory, while the second Move instruction requires only one. Executing these instructions in a pipeline such as the one in Figure 6.2 requires additional hardware to stall the second Move instruction so that the first Move instruction can complete its two operand accesses to the memory. In a superscalar processor such as the one in Figure 6.13, the Load/Store unit must similarly stall its internal pipeline.

CISC-style instructions complicate pipelining. This was one of the main reasons for developing the RISC approach. Nonetheless, pipelined processors have been implemented for CISC-style instruction sets, which were initially introduced before the widespread use of pipelining. Examples include processors based on the ColdFire and Intel instruction sets discussed in Appendices C and E. ColdFire processors are primarily intended for embedded applications, while Intel processors serve general-purpose needs. Consequently, the extent to which pipelining is used in ColdFire processors is less than that in Intel processors.

6.10.1 PIPELINING IN COLDFIRE PROCESSORS

ColdFire processor implementations labeled as versions V1 and V2 have two pipelines in series with a first-in first-out (FIFO) buffer between them. A two-stage instruction fetch pipeline prefetches instructions into the buffer. This buffer then feeds a two-stage pipeline that executes instructions. Instructions that involve register-only or register-to-memory operations pass once through the two execution stages. Instructions that involve memory-to-register or memory-to-memory operations must make two passes through the execution stages.

Later versions of ColdFire processor implementations use a similar buffer arrangement between two pipelines, but they incorporate various enhancements for higher performance. For example, the instruction fetch pipeline in version V4 is extended to four stages and includes branch prediction. The execution pipeline is extended to five stages. The early stages are used for address calculation, and the later stages are used for arithmetic/logic operations. This separation of functions enables a limited form of superscalar processing. In certain cases, a Move instruction and another instruction can be issued to the execution pipeline in the same cycle. Version V5 implementations have two distinct execution pipelines based on the V4 organization. They provide true superscalar processing.

6.10.2 PIPELINING IN INTEL PROCESSORS

Intel processors achieve high performance with superscalar execution and deep pipelines. For example, the Core 2 and Core i7 architectures have a multiple-issue width of four instructions and a 14-stage pipeline. Branch prediction, register renaming, out-of-order execution, and other techniques are used.

To reduce internal complexity, CISC-style instructions are dynamically converted by the hardware into simpler RISC-style micro-operations. These micro-operations are then issued to the execution units to complete the tasks specified by the original CISC-style instructions. This approach preserves code compatibility while making it possible to use the aggressive performance enhancement techniques that have been developed for RISC-style instruction sets. In some cases, micro-operations are fused back together into macro-operations for more efficient handling. For example, in a program containing original CISC-style instructions, a comparison instruction that affects condition codes is often followed by a branch instruction. The hardware may initially convert the comparison and branch instructions into separate micro-operations, but would then fuse them into a combined compare-and-branch operation, whose function reflects what is typically found in a RISC-style instruction set.

6.11 CONCLUDING REMARKS

Two important features for performance enhancement have been introduced in this chapter, pipelining and multiple-issue. Pipelining enables processors to have instruction throughput approaching one instruction per clock cycle. Multiple-issue combined with pipelining makes possible superscalar operation, with instruction throughput of several instructions per clock cycle.

The potential gain in performance can only be realized by careful attention to three aspects:

• The instruction set of the processor

• The design of the pipeline hardware

• The design of the associated compiler

It is important to appreciate that there are strong interactions among all three aspects. High performance is critically dependent on the extent to which these interactions are taken into account in the design of a processor. Instruction sets that are particularly well-suited for pipelined execution are key features of modern processors.

There are many sources that provide additional details on the topics presented in this chapter. Reference [1] covers pipelining and Reference [2] covers superscalar processors.

6.12 EXAMPLES OF SOLVED PROBLEMS

This section presents some examples of the types of problems that a student may be asked to solve, and shows how such problems can be solved.

Problem: Consider the pipelined execution of the following sequence of instructions:

Example 6.1

Add	R4, R3, R2
Or	R7, R6, R5
Subtract	R8, R7, R4

Initially, registers R2 and R3 contain 4 and 8, respectively. Registers R5 and R6 contain 128 and 2, respectively. Assume that the pipeline provides forwarding paths to the ALU from registers RY and RZ in Figure 5.8. The first instruction is fetched in cycle 1, and the remaining instructions are fetched in successive cycles.

Draw a diagram similar to Figure 6.1 to show the pipelined execution of these instructions assuming that the processor uses operand forwarding. Then, with reference to Figure 5.8, describe the contents of registers RY and RZ during cycles 4 to 7.

Solution: There are data dependencies involving registers R4 and R7. The Subtract instruction needs the new values for these registers before they are written to the register file. Hence, those values need to be forwarded to the ALU inputs when the Subtract instruction is in the Compute stage of the pipeline. Figure 6.15 shows the execution with forwarding. One arrow represents the new value of register R7 being forwarded from register RZ, and the other arrow represents the new value of register R4 being forwarded from register RY.

As for the contents of registers RY and RZ during cycles 4 to 7, the following description provides the answer.

- Using the initial values for registers R2 and R3, the Add instruction generates the result of 12 in cycle 3. That result is available in register RZ during cycle 4. The value in register RY during cycle 4 is the result for the unspecified instruction preceding the Add instruction.

- In cycle 4, the Or instruction generates the result of 130. That result is placed in register RZ to be available during cycle 5. The result of 12 for the Add instruction is in register RY during cycle 5.

- In cycle 5, the Subtract instruction is in the Compute stage. To generate a correct result, forwarding is used to provide the value of 130 in register RY and the value of

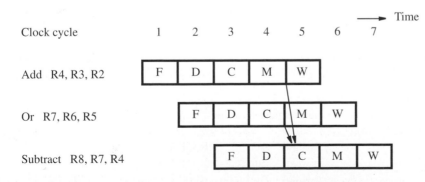

Figure 6.15 Pipelined execution of instructions for Example 6.1.

12 in register RZ. The result from the ALU is $130 - 12 = 118$. This result is available in register RZ during cycle 6. The result of the Or instruction, 130, is in register RY during in cycle 6.

- In cycle 6, the Subtract instruction is in the Memory stage. The unspecified instruction following the Subtract instruction is generating a result in the Compute stage. In cycle 7, the result of the unspecified instruction is in register RZ, and the result of the Subtract instruction is in register RY.

Example 6.2   **Problem:** Assume that 20 percent of the dynamic count of the instructions executed for a program are branch instructions. There are no pipeline stalls due to data dependencies. Static branch prediction is used with a not-taken assumption.

    (*a*) Determine the execution times for two cases: when 30 percent of the branches are taken, and when 70 percent of the branches are taken.

    (*b*) Determine the speedup for one case relative to the other. Express the speedup as a percentage relative to 1.

Solution: Section 6.8.1 describes the calculation of $\delta_{\text{branch\_penalty}}$ to consider the effect of branch penalties.

    (*a*) The value of $\delta_{\text{branch\_penalty}}$ is $0.20 \times 0.30 = 0.06$ for the first case and $0.20 \times 0.70 = 0.14$ for the second case. Using $S = 1 + \delta_{\text{branch\_penalty}}$, the execution time for the first case is $(1.06 \times N)/R$ and $(1.14 \times N)/R$ for the second case.

    (*b*) Because the execution time for the first case is smaller, the performance improvement as a speedup percentage is

$$\left(\frac{1.14}{1.06} - 1 \right) \times 100 = 7.5 \text{ percent}$$

PROBLEMS

6.1   [M] Consider the following instructions at the given addresses in the memory:

1000	Add	R3, R2, #20
1004	Subtract	R5, R4, #3
1008	And	R6, R4, #0x3A
1012	Add	R7, R2, R4

Initially, registers R2 and R4 contain 2000 and 50, respectively. These instructions are executed in a computer that has a five-stage pipeline as shown in Figure 6.2. The first instruction is fetched in clock cycle 1, and the remaining instructions are fetched in successive cycles.

(*a*) Draw a diagram similar to Figure 6.1 that represents the flow of the instructions through the pipeline. Describe the operation being performed by each pipeline stage during clock cycles 1 through 8.

(*b*) With reference to Figures 5.8 and 5.9, describe the contents of registers IR, PC, RA, RB, RY, and RZ in the pipeline during cycles 2 to 8.

6.2   [M] Repeat Problem 6.1 for the following program:

1000	Add	R3, R2, #20
1004	Subtract	R5, R4, #3
1008	And	R6, R3, #0x3A
1012	Add	R7, R2, R4

Assume that the pipeline provides forwarding paths to the ALU from registers RY and RZ in Figure 5.8 and that the processor uses forwarding of operands.

6.3   [M] Consider the loop in the program of Figure 2.8. Assume it is executed in a five-stage pipeline with forwarding paths to the ALU from registers RY and RZ in Figure 5.8. Assume that the pipeline uses static branch prediction with a not-taken assumption. Draw a diagram similar to Figure 6.1 for the execution of two successive iterations of the loop.

6.4   [D] Repeat Problem 6.3, but first reorder the instructions to optimize performance as the compiler would do.

6.5   [D] Repeat Problem 6.3 for a pipeline that uses delayed branching with one delay slot. Reorder the instructions as needed to improve performance.

6.6   [M] The forwarding path in Figure 6.5 allows the contents of register RZ to be used directly in an ALU operation. The result of that operation is stored in register RZ, replacing its previous contents. This problem involves tracing the contents of register RZ over multiple cycles. Consider the two instructions

I_1:	Add	R3, R2, R1
I_2:	LShiftL	R3, R3, #1

While instruction I_1 is being fetched in cycle 1, a previously fetched instruction is performing an ALU operation that gives a result of 17. Then, while instruction I_1 is being decoded in cycle 2, another previously fetched instruction is performing an ALU operation that gives a result of 198. Also during cycle 2, registers R1, R2, and R3 contain the values 30, 100, and 45, respectively. Using this information, draw a timing diagram that shows the contents of register RZ during cycles 2 to 5.

6.7   [M] Assume that 20 percent of the dynamic count of the instructions executed for a program are branch instructions. Delayed branching is used, with one delay slot. Assume that there are no stalls caused by other factors. First, derive an expression for the execution time in cycles if all delay slots are filled with NOP instructions. Then, derive another expression that reflects the execution time with 70 percent of delay slots filled with useful instructions by the optimizing compiler. From these expressions, determine the compiler's contribution to the increase in performance, expressed as a speedup percentage.

6.8 **[D]** Repeat Problem 6.7, but this time for a pipelined processor with two branch delay slots. The output from the optimizing compiler is such that the first delay slot is filled with a useful instruction 70 percent of the time, but the second slot is filled with a useful instruction only 10 percent of the time.

Compare the compiler-optimized execution time for this case with the compiler-optimized execution time for Problem 6.7. Assume that the two processors have the same clock rate. Indicate which processor/compiler combination is faster, and determine the speedup percentage by which it is faster.

6.9 **[D]** Assume that 20 percent of the dynamic count of the instructions executed for a program are branch instructions. Assume further that 75 percent of branches are actually taken. The program is executed in two different processors that have the same clock rate. One uses static branch prediction with the assume-not-taken approach. The other uses dynamic branch prediction based on the states in Figure 6.12a. The branch target buffer is used in the manner described in Section 6.6.4.

(a) With no pipeline stalls due to other causes, what must be the minimum prediction accuracy for the processor using dynamic branch prediction to perform at least as well as the processor using static branch prediction?

(b) If the dynamic prediction accuracy is actually 90 percent, what is the speedup relative to using static prediction?

6.10 **[M]** Additional control logic is required in the pipeline to forward the value of register RZ as shown in Figure 6.5. What specific conditions must this additional logic check to determine the settings of the multiplexers feeding the ALU inputs in the Compute stage of the pipeline?

6.11 **[M]** Repeat Problem 6.10 for the specific conditions related to forwarding of the contents of register RY in Figure 5.8 to the multiplexers feeding the inputs of the ALU.

6.12 **[D]** As a continuation of Problems 6.10 and 6.11, consider the following sequence of instructions:

$$\begin{array}{ll} \text{Add} & \text{R3, R2, R1} \\ \text{Subtract} & \text{R3, R5, R4} \\ \text{Or} & \text{R8, R3, \#1} \end{array}$$

Describe the manner in which forwarding must be handled for this situation. How should the conditions developed in Problems 6.10 and 6.11 be modified?

6.13 **[M]** Consider a program that consists of four memory-access instructions and four arithmetic instructions. Assume that there are no data dependencies between the instructions. Two versions of this program are executed on the superscalar processor shown in Figure 6.13. The first version has the four memory-access instructions in sequence, followed by the four arithmetic instructions. The second version has the memory-access instructions interleaved with the arithmetic instructions. Draw two diagrams similar to Figure 6.14 to compare the execution of these two versions of the program.

6.14   **[E]** Assume that a program contains no branch instructions. It is executed on the superscalar processor shown in Figure 6.13. What is the best execution time in cycles that can be expected if the mix of instructions consists of 75 percent arithmetic instructions and 25 percent memory-access instructions? How does this time compare to the best execution time on the simpler processor in Figure 6.2 using the same clock?

6.15   **[M]** Repeat Problem 6.14 to find the best possible execution times for the processors in Figures 6.2 and 6.13, assuming that the mix of instructions consists of 15 percent branch instructions that are never taken, 65 percent arithmetic instructions, and 20 percent memory-access instructions. Assume a prediction accuracy of 100 percent for all branch instructions.

6.16   **[E]** Consider a processor that uses the branch prediction scheme represented in Figure 6.12*b*. The instruction set for the processor is enhanced with a feature that enables the compiler to specify the initial prediction state as either LT or LNT for each branch instruction. This initial state is used by the processor at execution time when information about the branch instruction is not found in the branch target buffer. Discuss how the compiler should use this feature when generating code for the following cases:

(*a*) A loop with a conditional branch instruction at the end to branch to the start of the loop

(*b*) A loop with a conditional branch at the beginning of the loop to exit the loop, and an unconditional branch at the end of the loop to branch to the start

6.17   **[M]** Assume that a processor has the feature described in Problem 6.16 for specifying the initial prediction state for branch instructions. Consider a statement of the form

$$IF \ A>B \ THEN \ A = A + 1 \ ELSE \ B = B + 1$$

(*a*) Generate assembly-language code for the statement above.

(*b*) In the absence of any other information, discuss how the compiler should specify the initial prediction state for the branch instructions in the assembly code.

(*c*) A study of the execution behavior of the program containing the above statement reveals that the value of variable A is often larger than the value of variable B. If this information is made available to the compiler, discuss how it would influence the initial prediction state for the branch instructions.

6.18   **[M]** Consider a statement of the form

$$IF \ A>B \ THEN \ A = A + 1 \ ELSE \ B = B + 1$$

(*a*) Consider a processor that has the pipelined organization shown in Figure 6.2, with static branch prediction that uses a not-taken assumption. Write assembly-language code for the statement above. Draw diagrams similar to Figure 6.1 to show the pipelined execution of the instructions for different branch decisions and determine the execution times in cycles.

(*b*) Now assume that delayed branching is used. Write assembly-language code for the statement above. Draw diagrams to show the pipelined execution of the instructions for different branch decisions and compare the execution times in cycles with the times for the previous case.

REFERENCES

1. D. A. Patterson and J. L. Hennessy, *Computer Organization and Design: The Hardware/Software Interface*, 4th edition, Morgan Kaufmann, Burlington, Massachusetts, 2009.

2. J. P. Shen and M. H. Lipasti, *Modern Processor Design: Fundamentals of Superscalar Processors*, McGraw-Hill, New York, 2005.

INPUT/OUTPUT ORGANIZATION

CHAPTER OBJECTIVES

In this chapter you will learn about:

- Hardware needed to access I/O devices
- Synchronous and asynchronous bus operation
- Interface circuits
- Commercial standards, such as USB, SAS, and PCI Express

One of the basic features of a computer is its ability to transfer data to and from I/O devices. This communication capability enables a human operator, for example, to use a keyboard and a display screen to process text and graphics. We make extensive use of computers to communicate with other computers over the Internet and access information around the globe. In embedded applications, computers are less visible but equally important. They are an integral part of home appliances, manufacturing equipment, vehicle systems, cell phones, and banking and point-of-sale terminals. In such applications, input to a computer may come from a touch panel, a sensor switch, a digital camera, a microphone, or a fire alarm. Output may be characters or numbers to be displayed, a sound signal to be sent to a speaker, or a digitally-coded command to change the speed of a motor, open a valve, or cause a robot to move in a specified manner.

A computer should have the ability to exchange information with a wide variety of devices. In many cases, the processor is fully involved in these exchanges. However, data transfers may also take place directly between I/O devices, such as magnetic hard disks, and the main memory, with only minimal involvement of the processor. This possibility will be explored in the next chapter on the memory system.

Chapter 3 presents the programmer's view of input/output data transfers that take place between the processor and the registers in I/O device interfaces. In this chapter, we discuss the details of the hardware needed to make such transfers possible.

An interconnection network is used to transfer data among the processor, memory, and I/O devices. We describe below a commonly used interconnection network called a *bus*.

7.1   BUS STRUCTURE

The bus shown in Figure 7.1 is a simple structure that implements the interconnection network in Figure 3.1. Only one source/destination pair of units can use this bus to transfer data at any one time.

The bus consists of three sets of lines used to carry address, data, and control signals. I/O device interfaces are connected to these lines, as shown in Figure 7.2 for an input device. Each I/O device is assigned a unique set of addresses for the registers in its interface. When the processor places a particular address on the address lines, it is examined by the address

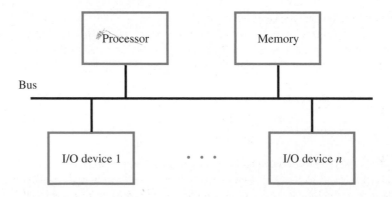

Figure 7.1   A single-bus structure.

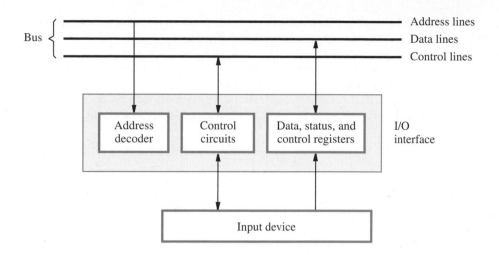

Figure 7.2 I/O interface for an input device.

decoders of all devices on the bus. The device that recognizes this address responds to the commands issued on the control lines. The processor uses the control lines to request either a Read or a Write operation, and the requested data are transferred over the data lines.

When I/O devices and the memory share the same address space, the arrangement is called *memory-mapped I/O,* as described in Section 3.1. Any machine instruction that can access memory can be used to transfer data to or from an I/O device. For example, if the input device in Figure 7.2 is a keyboard and if DATAIN is its data register, the instruction

Load   R2, DATAIN

reads the data from DATAIN and stores them into processor register R2. Similarly, the instruction

Store   R2, DATAOUT

sends the contents of register R2 to location DATAOUT, which may be the data register of a display device interface. The status and control registers contain information relevant to the operation of the I/O device. The address decoder, the data and status registers, and the control circuitry required to coordinate I/O transfers constitute the device's interface circuit.

7.2 BUS OPERATION

A bus requires a set of rules, often called a *bus protocol*, that govern how the bus is used by various devices. The bus protocol determines when a device may place information on the bus, when it may load the data on the bus into one of its registers, and so on. These rules are implemented by control signals that indicate what and when actions are to be taken.

One control line, usually labelled R/$\overline{\text{W}}$, specifies whether a Read or a Write operation is to be performed. As the label suggests, it specifies Read when set to 1 and Write when set to 0. When several data sizes are possible, such as byte, halfword, or word, the required size is indicated by other control lines. The bus control lines also carry timing information. They specify the times at which the processor and the I/O devices may place data on or receive data from the data lines. A variety of schemes have been devised for the timing of data transfers over a bus. These can be broadly classified as either synchronous or asynchronous schemes.

In any data transfer operation, one device plays the role of a *master*. This is the device that initiates data transfers by issuing Read or Write commands on the bus. Normally, the processor acts as the master, but other devices may also become masters as we will see in Section 7.3. The device addressed by the master is referred to as a *slave*.

7.2.1 SYNCHRONOUS BUS

On a *synchronous* bus, all devices derive timing information from a control line called the *bus clock*, shown at the top of Figure 7.3. The signal on this line has two *phases*: a high level followed by a low level. The two phases constitute a *clock cycle*. The first half of the cycle between the low-to-high and high-to-low transitions is often referred to as a clock pulse.

The address and data lines in Figure 7.3 are shown as if they are carrying both high and low signal levels at the same time. This is a common convention for indicating that

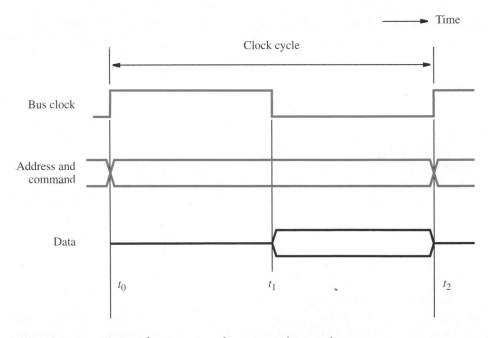

Figure 7.3   Timing of an input transfer on a synchronous bus.

some lines are high and some low, depending on the particular address or data values being transmitted. The crossing points indicate the times at which these patterns change. A signal line at a level half-way between the low and high signal levels indicates periods during which the signal is unreliable, and must be ignored by all devices.

Let us consider the sequence of signal events during an input (Read) operation. At time t_0, the master places the device address on the address lines and sends a command on the control lines indicating a Read operation. The command may also specify the length of the operand to be read. Information travels over the bus at a speed determined by its physical and electrical characteristics. The clock pulse width, $t_1 - t_0$, must be longer than the maximum propagation delay over the bus. Also, it must be long enough to allow all devices to decode the address and control signals, so that the addressed device (the slave) can respond at time t_1 by placing the requested input data on the data lines. At the end of the clock cycle, at time t_2, the master loads the data on the data lines into one of its registers. To be loaded correctly into a register, data must be available for a period greater than the setup time of the register (see Appendix A). Hence, the period $t_2 - t_1$ must be greater than the maximum propagation time on the bus plus the setup time of the master's register.

A similar procedure is followed for a Write operation. The master places the output data on the data lines when it transmits the address and command information. At time t_2, the addressed device loads the data into its data register.

The timing diagram in Figure 7.3 is an idealized representation of the actions that take place on the bus lines. The exact times at which signals change state are somewhat different from those shown, because of propagation delays on bus wires and in the circuits of the devices. Figure 7.4 gives a more realistic picture of what actually happens. It shows two views of each signal, except the clock. Because signals take time to travel from one device to another, a given signal transition is seen by different devices at different times. The top view shows the signals as seen by the master and the bottom view as seen by the slave. We assume that the clock changes are seen at the same time by all devices connected to the bus. System designers spend considerable effort to ensure that the clock signal satisfies this requirement.

The master sends the address and command signals on the rising edge of the clock at the beginning of the clock cycle (at t_0). However, these signals do not actually appear on the bus until t_{AM}, largely due to the delay in the electronic circuit output from the master to the bus lines. A short while later, at t_{AS}, the signals reach the slave. The slave decodes the address, and at t_1 sends the requested data. Here again, the data signals do not appear on the bus until t_{DS}. They travel toward the master and arrive at t_{DM}. At t_2, the master loads the data into its register. Hence the period $t_2 - t_{DM}$ must be greater than the setup time of that register. The data must continue to be valid after t_2 for a period equal to the hold time requirement of the register (see Appendix A for hold time).

Timing diagrams often show only the simplified picture in Figure 7.3, particularly when the intent is to give the basic idea of how data are transferred. But, actual signals will always involve delays as shown in Figure 7.4.

Multiple-Cycle Data Transfer

The scheme described above results in a simple design for the device interface. However, it has some limitations. Because a transfer has to be completed within one clock cycle,

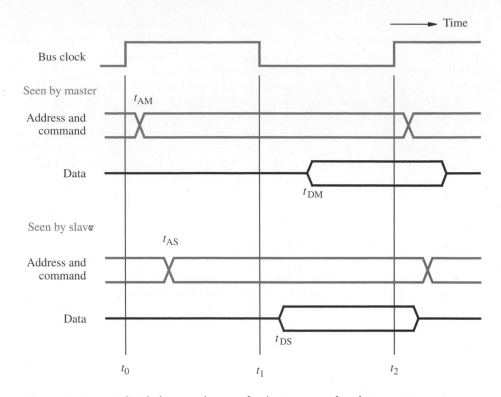

Figure 7.4   A detailed timing diagram for the input transfer of Figure 7.3.

the clock period, $t_2 - t_0$, must be chosen to accommodate the longest delays on the bus and the slowest device interface. This forces all devices to operate at the speed of the slowest device.

Also, the processor has no way of determining whether the addressed device has actually responded. At t_2, it simply assumes that the input data are available on the data lines in a Read operation, or that the output data have been received by the I/O device in a Write operation. If, because of a malfunction, a device does not operate correctly, the error will not be detected.

To overcome these limitations, most buses incorporate control signals that represent a response from the device. These signals inform the master that the slave has recognized its address and that it is ready to participate in a data transfer operation. They also make it possible to adjust the duration of the data transfer period to match the response speeds of different devices. This is often accomplished by allowing a complete data transfer operation to span several clock cycles. Then, the number of clock cycles involved can vary from one device to another.

An example of this approach is shown in Figure 7.5. During clock cycle 1, the master sends address and command information on the bus, requesting a Read operation. The slave receives this information and decodes it. It begins to access the requested data on the active

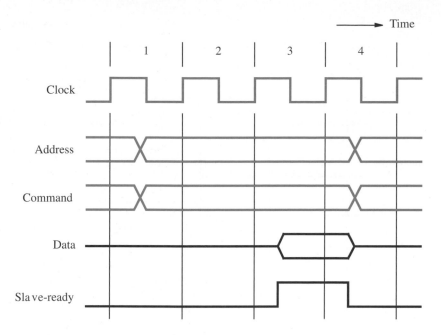

Figure 7.5   An input transfer using multiple clock cycles.

edge of the clock at the beginning of clock cycle 2. We have assumed that due to the delay involved in getting the data, the slave cannot respond immediately. The data become ready and are placed on the bus during clock cycle 3. The slave asserts a control signal called Slave-ready at the same time. The master, which has been waiting for this signal, loads the data into its register at the end of the clock cycle. The slave removes its data signals from the bus and returns its Slave-ready signal to the low level at the end of cycle 3. The bus transfer operation is now complete, and the master may send new address and command signals to start a new transfer in clock cycle 4.

The Slave-ready signal is an acknowledgment from the slave to the master, confirming that the requested data have been placed on the bus. It also allows the duration of a bus transfer to change from one device to another. In the example in Figure 7.5, the slave responds in cycle 3. A different device may respond in an earlier or a later cycle. If the addressed device does not respond at all, the master waits for some predefined maximum number of clock cycles, then aborts the operation. This could be the result of an incorrect address or a device malfunction.

We will now present a different approach that does not use a clock signal at all.

7.2.2 Asynchronous Bus

An alternative scheme for controlling data transfers on a bus is based on the use of a *handshake* protocol between the master and the slave. A handshake is an exchange of

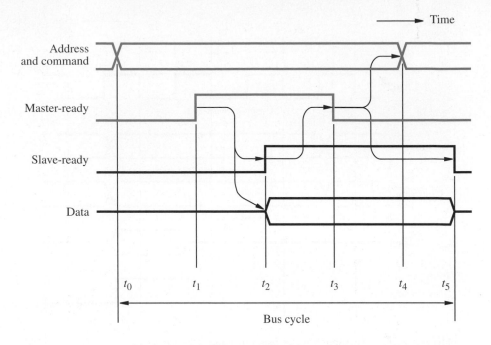

Figure 7.6   Handshake control of data transfer during an input operation.

command and response signals between the master and the slave. It is a generalization of the way the Slave-ready signal is used in Figure 7.5. A control line called Master-ready is asserted by the master to indicate that it is ready to start a data transfer. The Slave responds by asserting Slave-ready.

A data transfer controlled by a handshake protocol proceeds as follows. The master places the address and command information on the bus. Then it indicates to all devices that it has done so by activating the Master-ready line. This causes all devices to decode the address. The selected slave performs the required operation and informs the processor that it has done so by activating the Slave-ready line. The master waits for Slave-ready to become asserted before it removes its signals from the bus. In the case of a Read operation, it also loads the data into one of its registers.

An example of the timing of an input data transfer using the handshake protocol is given in Figure 7.6, which depicts the following sequence of events:

t_0—The master places the address and command information on the bus, and all devices on the bus decode this information.

t_1—The master sets the Master-ready line to 1 to inform the devices that the address and command information is ready. The delay $t_1 - t_0$ is intended to allow for any *skew* that may occur on the bus. Skew occurs when two signals transmitted simultaneously from one source arrive at the destination at different times. This happens because different lines of the bus may have different propagation speeds. Thus, to guarantee that the Master-ready signal does not arrive at any device ahead of the address and command information, the delay $t_1 - t_0$ should be longer than the maximum possible bus skew. (Note that bus skew is a part of the maximum propagation delay in the synchronous case.) Sufficient time should be allowed for the device interface circuitry to decode the address. The delay needed can be included in the period $t_1 - t_0$.

t_2—The selected slave, having decoded the address and command information, performs the required input operation by placing its data on the data lines. At the same time, it sets the Slave-ready signal to 1. If extra delays are introduced by the interface circuitry before it places the data on the bus, the slave must delay the Slave-ready signal accordingly. The period $t_2 - t_1$ depends on the distance between the master and the slave and on the delays introduced by the slave's circuitry.

t_3—The Slave-ready signal arrives at the master, indicating that the input data are available on the bus. The master must allow for bus skew. It must also allow for the setup time needed by its register. After a delay equivalent to the maximum bus skew and the minimum setup time, the master loads the data into its register. Then, it drops the Master-ready signal, indicating that it has received the data.

t_4—The master removes the address and command information from the bus. The delay between t_3 and t_4 is again intended to allow for bus skew. Erroneous addressing may take place if the address, as seen by some device on the bus, starts to change while the Master-ready signal is still equal to 1.

t_5—When the device interface receives the 1-to-0 transition of the Master-ready signal, it removes the data and the Slave-ready signal from the bus. This completes the input transfer.

The timing for an output operation, illustrated in Figure 7.7, is essentially the same as for an input operation. In this case, the master places the output data on the data lines at the same time that it transmits the address and command information. The selected slave loads the data into its data register when it receives the Master-ready signal and indicates that it has done so by setting the Slave-ready signal to 1. The remainder of the cycle is similar to the input operation.

The handshake signals in Figures 7.6 and 7.7 are said to be *fully interlocked*, because a change in one signal is always in response to a change in the other. Hence, this scheme is known as a *full handshake*. It provides the highest degree of flexibility and reliability.

Discussion

Many variations of the bus protocols just described are found in commercial computers. The choice of a particular design involves trade-offs among factors such as:

- Simplicity of the device interface
- Ability to accommodate device interfaces that introduce different amounts of delay
- Total time required for a bus transfer
- Ability to detect errors resulting from addressing a nonexistent device or from an interface malfunction

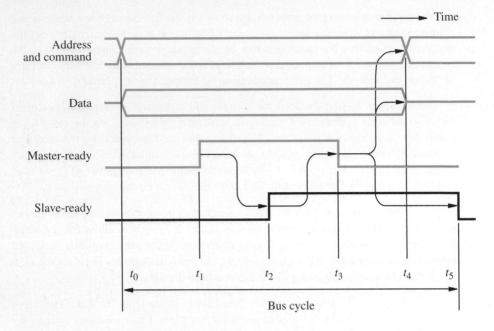

Figure 7.7   Handshake control of data transfer during an output operation.

The main advantage of the asynchronous bus is that the handshake protocol eliminates the need for distribution of a single clock signal whose edges should be seen by all devices at about the same time. This simplifies timing design. Delays, whether introduced by the interface circuits or by propagation over the bus wires, are readily accommodated. These delays are likely to differ from one device to another, but the timing of data transfers adjusts automatically. For a synchronous bus, clock circuitry must be designed carefully to ensure proper timing, and delays must be kept within strict bounds.

The rate of data transfer on an asynchronous bus controlled by the handshake protocol is limited by the fact that each transfer involves two round-trip delays (four end-to-end delays). This can be seen in Figures 7.6 and 7.7 as each transition on Slave-ready must wait for the arrival of a transition on Master-ready, and vice versa. On synchronous buses, the clock period need only accommodate one round trip delay. Hence, faster transfer rates can be achieved. To accommodate a slow device, additional clock cycles are used, as described above. Most of today's high-speed buses use the synchronous approach.

7.2.3 ELECTRICAL CONSIDERATIONS

A bus is an interconnection medium to which several devices may be connected. It is essential to ensure that only one device can place data on the bus at any given time. A logic gate that places data on the bus is called a *bus driver*. All devices connected to the bus, except the one that is currently sending data, must have their bus drivers turned off. A special type of logic gate, known as a *tri-state gate*, is used for this purpose. A tri-state gate has a control input that is used to turn the gate on or off. When turned on, or enabled, it drives the bus with 1 or 0, corresponding to the value of its input signal. When turned off, or disabled, it is effectively disconnected from the bus. From an electrical point of view, its output goes into a high-impedance state that does not affect the signal on the bus.

7.3 ARBITRATION

There are occasions when two or more entities contend for the use of a single resource in a computer system. For example, two devices may need to access a given slave at the same time. In such cases, it is necessary to decide which device will access the slave first. The decision is usually made in an arbitration process performed by an *arbiter* circuit. The arbitration process starts by each device sending a *request* to use the shared resource. The arbiter associates priorities with individual requests. If it receives two requests at the same time, it *grants* the use of the slave to the device having the higher priority first.

To illustrate the arbitration process, we consider the case where a single bus is the shared resource. The device that initiates data transfer requests on the bus is the bus master. In Section 7.2, the discussion involved only one bus master—the processor. It is possible that several devices in a computer system need to be bus masters to transfer data. For example, an I/O device needs to be a bus master to transfer data directly to or from the computer's memory. Since the bus is a single shared facility, it is essential to provide orderly access to it by the bus masters.

A device that wishes to use the bus sends a request to the arbiter. When multiple requests arrive at the same time, the arbiter selects one request and grants the bus to the corresponding device. For some devices, a delay in gaining access to the bus may lead to an error. Such devices must be given high priority. If there is no particular urgency among requests, the arbiter may grant the bus using a simple round-robin scheme.

Figure 7.8 illustrates an arrangement for bus arbitration involving two masters. There are two Bus-request lines, BR1 and BR2, and two Bus-grant lines, BG1 and BG2, connecting

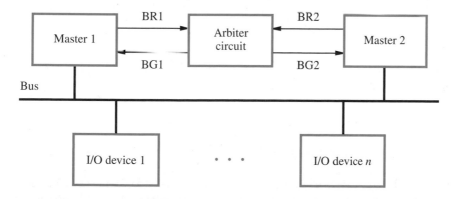

Figure 7.8   Bus arbitration.

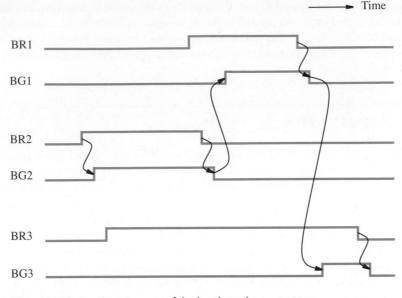

Figure 7.9   Granting use of the bus based on priorities.

the arbiter to the masters. A master requests use of the bus by activating its Bus-request line. If a single Bus-request is activated, the arbiter activates the corresponding Bus-grant. This indicates to the selected master that it may now use the bus for transferring data. When the transfer is completed, that master deactivates its Bus-request, and the arbiter deactivates its Bus-grant.

Figure 7.9 illustrates a possible sequence of events for the case of three masters. Assume that master 1 has the highest priority, followed by the others in increasing numerical order. Master 2 sends a request to use the bus first. Since there are no other requests, the arbiter grants the bus to this master by asserting BG2. When master 2 completes its data transfer operation, it releases the bus by deactivating BR2. By that time, both masters 1 and 3 have activated their request lines. Since device 1 has a higher priority, the arbiter activates BG1 after it deactivates BG2, thus granting the bus to master 1. Later, when master 1 releases the bus by deactivating BR1, the arbiter deactivates BG1 and activates BG3 to grant the bus to master 3. Note that the bus is granted to master 1 before master 3 even though master 3 activated its request line before master 1.

7.4   Interface Circuits

The I/O interface of a device consists of the circuitry needed to connect that device to the bus. On one side of the interface are the bus lines for address, data, and control. On the other side are the connections needed to transfer data between the interface and the I/O device. This side is called a *port,* and it can be either a parallel or a serial port. A parallel port transfers multiple bits of data simultaneously to or from the device. A serial port sends and receives data one bit at a time. Communication with the processor is the same for both formats; the conversion from a parallel to a serial format and vice versa takes place inside the interface circuit.

Before we present specific circuit examples, let us recall the functions of an I/O interface. According to the discussion in Section 3.1, an I/O interface does the following:

1. Provides a register for temporary storage of data

2. Includes a status register containing status information that can be accessed by the processor

3. Includes a control register that holds the information governing the behavior of the interface

4. Contains address-decoding circuitry to determine when it is being addressed by the processor

5. Generates the required timing signals

6. Performs any format conversion that may be necessary to transfer data between the processor and the I/O device, such as parallel-to-serial conversion in the case of a serial port

7.4.1 PARALLEL INTERFACE

We now explain the key aspects of interface design by means of examples. First, we describe an interface circuit for an 8-bit input port that can be used for connecting a simple input device, such as a keyboard. Then, we describe an interface circuit for an 8-bit output port, which can be used with an output device such as a display. We assume that these interface circuits are connected to a 32-bit processor that uses memory-mapped I/O and the asynchronous bus protocol depicted in Figures 7.6 and 7.7.

Input Interface

Figure 7.10 shows a circuit that can be used to connect a keyboard to a processor. The registers in this circuit correspond to those given in Figure 3.3. Assume that interrupts are not used, so there is no need for a control register. There are only two registers: a data register, KBD_DATA, and a status register, KBD_STATUS. The latter contains the keyboard status flag, KIN.

A typical keyboard consists of mechanical switches that are normally open. When a key is pressed, its switch closes and establishes a path for an electrical signal. This signal is detected by an encoder circuit that generates the ASCII code for the corresponding character. A difficulty with such mechanical pushbutton switches is that the contacts *bounce* when a key is pressed, resulting in the electrical connection being made then broken several times before the switch settles in the closed position. Although bouncing may last only one or two milliseconds, this is long enough for the computer to erroneously interpret a single pressing of a key as the key being pressed and released several times. The effect of bouncing can be eliminated using a simple debouncing circuit, which could be part of the keyboard hardware

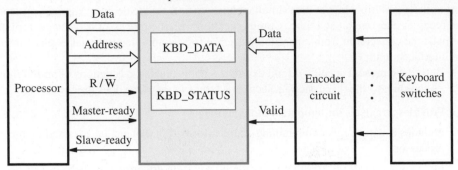

Figure 7.10   Keyboard to processor connection.

or may be incorporated in the encoder circuit. Alternatively, switch bouncing can be dealt with in software. The software detects that a key has been pressed when it observes that the keyboard status flag, KIN, has been set to 1. The I/O routine can then introduce sufficient delay before reading the contents of the input buffer, KBD_DATA, to ensure that bouncing has subsided. When debouncing is implemented in hardware, the I/O routine can read the input character as soon as it detects that KIN is equal to 1.

The output of the encoder in Figure 7.10 consists of one byte of data representing the encoded character and one control signal called Valid. When a key is pressed, the Valid signal changes from 0 to 1, causing the ASCII code of the corresponding character to be loaded into the KBD_DATA register and the status flag KIN to be set to 1. The status flag is cleared to 0 when the processor reads the contents of the KBD_DATA register. The interface circuit is shown connected to an asynchronous bus on which transfers are controlled by the handshake signals Master-ready and Slave-ready, as in Figure 7.6. The bus has one other control line, $R/\overline{W}$, which indicates a Read operation when equal to 1.

Figure 7.11 shows a possible circuit for the input interface. There are two addressable locations in this interface, KBD_DATA and KBD_STATUS. They occupy adjacent word locations in the address space, as in Figure 3.3. Only one bit, b_1, in the status register actually contains useful information. This is the keyboard status flag, KIN. When the status register is read by the processor, all other bit locations appear as containing zeros.

When the processor requests a Read operation, it places the address of the appropriate register on the address lines of the bus. The address decoder in the interface circuit examines bits A_{31-3}, and asserts its output, My-address, when one of the two registers KBD_DATA or KBD_STATUS is being addressed. Bit A_2 determines which of the two registers is involved. Hence, a multiplexer is used to select the register to be connected to the bus based on address bit A_2. The two least-significant address bits, A_1 and A_0, are not used, because we have assumed that all addresses are word-aligned.

The output of the multiplexer is connected to the data lines of the bus through a set of tri-state gates. The interface circuit turns the tri-state gates on only when the three signals Master-ready, My_address, and $R/\overline{W}$ are all equal to 1, indicating a Read operation. The

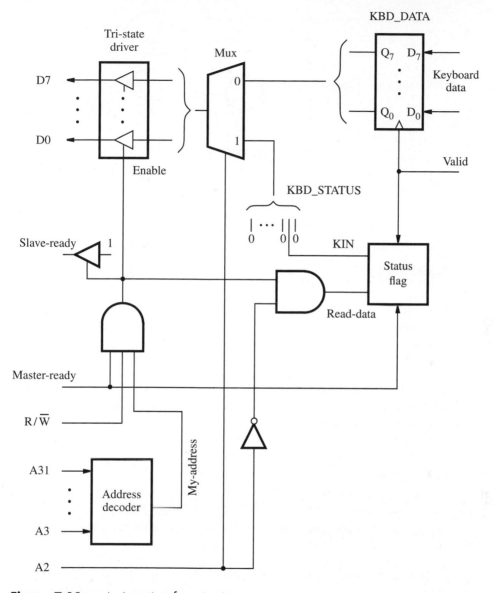

Figure 7.11   An input interface circuit.

Slave-ready signal is asserted at the same time, to inform the processor that the requested data or status information has been placed on the data lines. When address bit A_2 is equal to 0, Read-data is also asserted. This signal is used to reset the KIN flag.

A possible implementation of the status flag circuit is given in Figure 7.12. The KIN flag is the output of a NOR latch connected as shown. A flip-flop is set to 1 by the rising edge on the Valid signal line. This event changes the state of the NOR latch to set KIN to

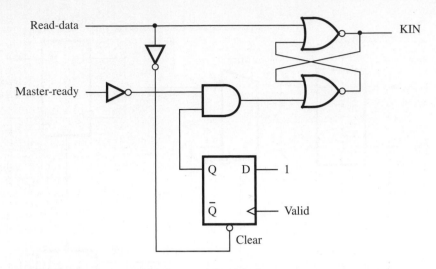

Figure 7.12   Circuit for the status flag block in Figure 7.11.

1, but only when Master-ready is low. The reason for this additional condition is to ensure that KIN does not change state while being read by the processor. Both the flip-flop and the latch are reset to 0 when Read-data becomes equal to 1, indicating that KBD_DATA is being read.

The circuits shown in Figures 7.11 and 7.12 are intended to illustrate the various functions that an interface circuit needs to perform. A designer using modern computer-aided design tools would specify these functions using a hardware description language such as VHDL or Verilog. The resulting circuits would depend on the technology used and may or may not be the same as the circuits shown in these figures.

Output Interface

Let us now consider the output interface shown in Figure 7.13, which can be used to connect an output device such as a display. We have assumed that the display uses two handshake signals, New-data and Ready, in a manner similar to the handshake between the bus signals Master-ready and Slave-ready. When the display is ready to accept a character, it asserts its Ready signal, which causes the DOUT flag in the DISP_STATUS register to be set to 1. When the I/O routine checks DOUT and finds it equal to 1, it sends a character to DISP_DATA. This clears the DOUT flag to 0 and sets the New-data signal to 1. In response, the display returns Ready to 0 and accepts and displays the character in DISP_DATA. When it is ready to receive another character, it asserts Ready again, and the cycle repeats.

Figure 7.14 shows an implementation of this interface. Its operation is similar to that of the input interface of Figure 7.11, except that it responds to both Read and Write operations. A Write operation in which $A_2 = 0$ loads a byte of data into register DISP_DATA. A Read operation in which $A_2 = 1$ reads the contents of the status register DISP_STATUS. In this case, only the DOUT flag, which is bit b_2 of the status register, is sent by the interface. The remaining bits of DISP_STATUS are not used. The state of the status flag is determined

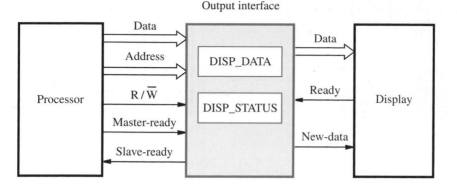

Figure 7.13 Display to processor connection.

by the handshake control circuit. A state diagram describing the behavior of this circuit is given as Example 7.4 at the end of the chapter.

7.4.2 SERIAL INTERFACE

A serial interface is used to connect the processor to I/O devices that transmit data one bit at a time. Data are transferred in a bit-serial fashion on the device side and in a bit-parallel fashion on the processor side. The transformation between the parallel and serial formats is achieved with shift registers that have parallel access capability. A block diagram of a typical serial interface is shown in Figure 7.15. The input shift register accepts bit-serial input from the I/O device. When all 8 bits of data have been received, the contents of this shift register are loaded in parallel into the DATAIN register. Similarly, output data in the DATAOUT register are transferred to the output shift register, from which the bits are shifted out and sent to the I/O device.

The part of the interface that deals with the bus is the same as in the parallel interface described earlier. Two status flags, which we will refer to as SIN and SOUT, are maintained by the Status and control block. The SIN flag is set to 1 when new data are loaded into DATAIN from the shift register, and cleared to 0 when these data are read by the processor. The SOUT flag indicates whether the DATAOUT register is available. It is cleared to 0 when the processor writes new data into DATAOUT and set to 1 when data are transferred from DATAOUT to the output shift register.

The double buffering used in the input and output paths in Figure 7.15 is important. It is possible to implement DATAIN and DATAOUT themselves as shift registers, thus obviating the need for separate shift registers. However, this would impose awkward restrictions on the operation of the I/O device. After receiving one character from the serial line, the interface would not be able to start receiving the next character until the processor reads the contents of DATAIN. Thus, a pause would be needed between two characters to give the processor time to read the input data. With double buffering, the transfer of the second character can begin as soon as the first character is loaded from the shift register into the

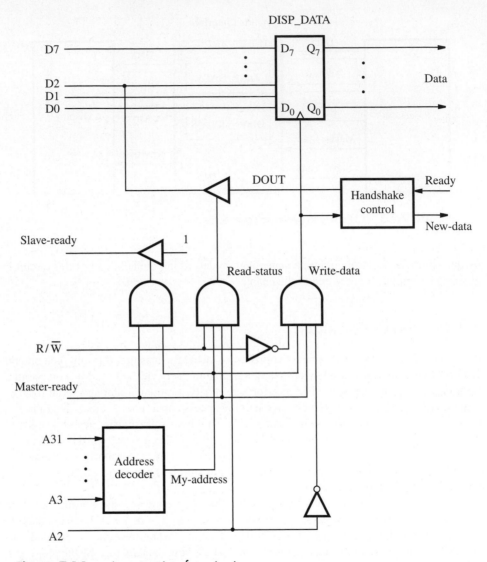

Figure 7.14   An output interface circuit.

DATAIN register. Thus, provided the processor reads the contents of DATAIN before the serial transfer of the second character is completed, the interface can receive a continuous stream of input data over the serial line. An analogous situation occurs in the output path of the interface.

During serial transmission, the receiver needs to know when to shift each bit into its input shift register. Since there is no separate line to carry a clock signal from the transmitter to the receiver, the timing information needed must be embedded into the transmitted data using an encoding scheme. There are two basic approaches. The first is known as

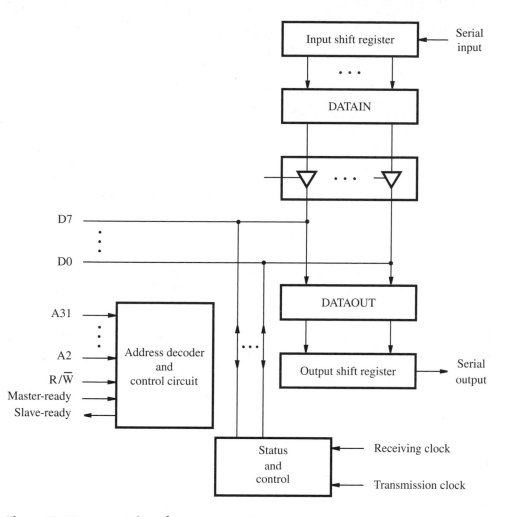

Figure 7.15 A serial interface.

asynchronous transmission, because the receiver uses a clock that is not synchronized with the transmitter clock. In the second approach, the receiver is able to generate a clock that is synchronized with the transmitter clock. Hence it is called synchronous transmission. These approaches are described briefly below.

Asynchronous Transmission

This approach uses a technique called *start-stop* transmission. Data are organized in small groups of 6 to 8 bits, with a well-defined beginning and end. In a typical arrangement, alphanumeric characters encoded in 8 bits are transmitted as shown in Figure 7.16. The line connecting the transmitter and the receiver is in the 1 state when idle. A character is transmitted as a 0 bit, referred to as the Start bit, followed by 8 data bits and 1 or 2 Stop bits. The Stop bits have a logic value of 1. The 1-to-0 transition at the beginning of the

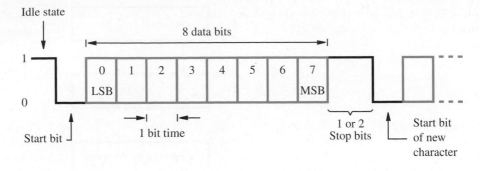

Figure 7.16   Asynchronous serial character transmission.

Start bit alerts the receiver that data transmission is about to begin. Using its own clock, the receiver determines the position of the next 8 bits, which it loads into its input register. The Stop bits following the transmitted character, which are equal to 1, ensure that the Start bit of the next character will be recognized. When transmission stops, the line remains in the 1 state until another character is transmitted.

To ensure correct reception, the receiver needs to sample the incoming data as close to the center of each bit as possible. It does so by using a clock signal whose frequency, f_R, is substantially higher than the transmission clock, f_T. Typically, $f_R = 16f_T$. This means that 16 pulses of the local clock occur during each data bit interval. This clock is used to increment a modulo-16 counter, which is cleared to 0 when the leading edge of a Start bit is detected. The middle of the Start bit is reached at the count of 8. The state of the input line is sampled again at this point to confirm that it is a valid Start bit (a zero), and the counter is cleared to 0. From this point onward, the incoming data signal is sampled whenever the count reaches 16, which should be close to the middle of each incoming bit. Therefore, as long as $f_R/16$ is sufficiently close to f_T, the receiver will correctly load the bits of the incoming character.

Synchronous Transmission

In the start-stop scheme described above, the position of the 1-to-0 transition at the beginning of the start bit in Figure 7.16 is the key to obtaining correct timing information. This scheme is useful only where the speed of transmission is sufficiently low and the conditions on the transmission link are such that the square waveforms shown in the figure maintain their shape. For higher speed a more reliable method is needed for the receiver to recover the timing information.

In synchronous transmission, the receiver generates a clock that is synchronized to that of the transmitter by observing successive 1-to-0 and 0-to-1 transitions in the received signal. It adjusts the position of the active edge of the clock to be in the center of the bit position. A variety of encoding schemes are used to ensure that enough signal transitions occur to enable the receiver to generate a synchronized clock and to maintain synchronization. Once synchronization is achieved, data transmission can continue indefinitely. Encoded data are usually transmitted in large blocks consisting of several hundreds or several thousands of bits. The beginning and end of each block are marked by appropriate codes, and data within a block are organized according to an agreed upon set of rules. Synchronous transmission enables very high data transfer rates.

7.5   INTERCONNECTION STANDARDS

A typical desktop or notebook computer has several ports that can be used to connect I/O devices, such as a mouse, a memory key, or a disk drive. Standard interfaces have been developed to enable I/O devices to use interfaces that are independent of any particular processor. For example, a memory key that has a USB connector can be used with any computer that has a USB port. In this section, we describe briefly some of the widely used interconnection standards.

Most standards are developed by a collaborative effort among a number of companies. In many cases, the IEEE (Institute of Electrical and Electronics Engineers) develops these standards further and publishes them as IEEE Standards.

7.5.1   UNIVERSAL SERIAL BUS (USB)

The Universal Serial Bus (USB) [1] is the most widely used interconnection standard. A large variety of devices are available with a USB connector, including mice, memory keys, disk drives, printers, cameras, and many more. The commercial success of the USB is due to its simplicity and low cost. The original USB specification supports two speeds of operation, called low-speed (1.5 Megabits/s) and full-speed (12 Megabits/s). Later, USB 2, called High-Speed USB, was introduced. It enables data transfers at speeds up to 480 Megabits/s. As I/O devices continued to evolve with even higher speed requirements, USB 3 (called Superspeed) was developed. It supports data transfer rates up to 5 Gigabits/s.

The USB has been designed to meet several key objectives:

- Provide a simple, low-cost, and easy to use interconnection system

- Accommodate a wide range of I/O devices and bit rates, including Internet connections, and audio and video applications

- Enhance user convenience through a "plug-and-play" mode of operation

We will elaborate on some of these objectives before discussing the technical details of the USB.

Device Characteristics

The kinds of devices that may be connected to a computer cover a wide range of functionality. The speed, volume, and timing constraints associated with data transfers to and from these devices vary significantly.

In the case of a keyboard, one byte of data is generated every time a key is pressed, which may happen at any time. These data should be transferred to the computer promptly. Since the event of pressing a key is not synchronized to any other event in a computer system, the data generated by the keyboard are called *asynchronous*. Furthermore, the rate at which the data are generated is quite low. It is limited by the speed of the human operator to about 10 bytes per second, which is less than 100 bits per second.

A variety of simple devices that may be attached to a computer generate data of a similar nature—low speed and asynchronous. Computer mice and some of the controls and manipulators used with video games are good examples.

Consider now a different source of data. Many computers have a microphone, either externally attached or built in. The sound picked up by the microphone produces an analog electrical signal, which must be converted into a digital form before it can be handled by the computer. This is accomplished by sampling the analog signal periodically. For each sample, an analog-to-digital (A/D) converter generates an n-bit number representing the magnitude of the sample. The number of bits, n, is selected based on the desired precision with which to represent each sample. Later, when these data are sent to a speaker, a digital-to-analog (D/A) converter is used to restore the original analog signal from the digital format. A similar approach is used with video information from a camera.

The sampling process yields a continuous stream of digitized samples that arrive at regular intervals, synchronized with the sampling clock. Such a data stream is called *isochronous,* meaning that successive events are separated by equal periods of time. A signal must be sampled quickly enough to track its highest-frequency components. In general, if the sampling rate is s samples per second, the maximum frequency component captured by the sampling process is $s/2$. For example, human speech can be captured adequately with a sampling rate of 8 kHz, which will record sound signals having frequencies up to 4 kHz. For higher-quality sound, as needed in a music system, higher sampling rates are used. A standard sampling rate for digital sound is 44.1 kHz. Each sample is represented by 4 bytes of data to accommodate the wide range in sound volume (dynamic range) that is necessary for high-quality sound reproduction. This yields a data rate of about 1.4 Megabits/s.

An important requirement in dealing with sampled voice or music is to maintain precise timing in the sampling and replay processes. A high degree of jitter (variability in sample timing) is unacceptable. Hence, the data transfer mechanism between a computer and a music system must maintain consistent delays from one sample to the next. Otherwise, complex buffering and retiming circuitry would be needed. On the other hand, occasional errors or missed samples can be tolerated. They either go unnoticed by the listener or they may cause an unobtrusive click. No sophisticated mechanisms are needed to ensure perfectly correct data delivery.

Data transfers for images and video have similar requirements, but require much higher data transfer rates. To maintain the picture quality of commercial television, an image should be represented by about 160 kilobytes and transmitted 30 times per second. Together with control information, this yields a total bit rate of 44 Megabits/s. Higher-quality images, as in HDTV (High Definition TV), require higher rates.

Large storage devices such as magnetic and optical disks present different requirements. These devices are part of the computer's memory hierarchy, as will be discussed in Chapter 8. Their connection to the computer requires a data transfer bandwidth of at least 40 or 50 Megabits/s. Delays on the order of milliseconds are introduced by the movement of the mechanical components in the disk mechanism. Hence, a small additional delay introduced while transferring data to or from the computer is not important, and jitter is not an issue. However, the transfer mechanism must guarantee data correctness.

Plug-and-Play

When an I/O device is connected to a computer, the operating system needs some information about it. It needs to know what type of device it is so that it can use the appropriate device driver. It also needs to know the addresses of the registers in the device's interface to be able to communicate with it. The USB standard defines both the USB hardware and the software that communicates with it. Its *plug-and-play* feature means that when a new device is connected, the system detects its existence automatically. The software determines the kind of device and how to communicate with it, as well as any special requirements it might have. As a result, the user simply plugs in a USB device and begins to use it, without having to get involved in any of these details.

The USB is also hot-pluggable, which means a device can be plugged into or removed from a USB port while power is turned on.

USB Architecture

The USB uses point-to-point connections and a serial transmission format. When multiple devices are connected, they are arranged in a tree structure as shown in Figure 7.17. Each node of the tree has a device called a *hub,* which acts as an intermediate transfer point between the host computer and the I/O devices. At the root of the tree, a *root hub* connects the entire tree to the host computer. The leaves of the tree are the I/O devices: a mouse, a keyboard, a printer, an Internet connection, a camera, or a speaker. The tree structure makes it possible to connect many devices using simple point-to-point serial links.

If I/O devices are allowed to send messages at any time, two messages may reach the hub at the same time and interfere with each other. For this reason, the USB operates strictly on the basis of polling. A device may send a message only in response to a poll message from the host processor. Hence, no two devices can send messages at the same time. This restriction allows hubs to be simple, low-cost devices.

Each device on the USB, whether it is a hub or an I/O device, is assigned a 7-bit address. This address is local to the USB tree and is not related in any way to the processor's address space. The root hub of the USB, which is attached to the processor, appears as a single device. The host software communicates with individual devices by sending information to the root hub, which it forwards to the appropriate device in the USB tree.

When a device is first connected to a hub, or when it is powered on, it has the address 0. Periodically, the host polls each hub to collect status information and learn about new devices that may have been added or disconnected. When the host is informed that a new device has been connected, it reads the information in a special memory in the device's USB interface to learn about the device's capabilities. It then assigns the device a unique USB address and writes that address in one of the device's interface registers. It is this initial connection procedure that gives the USB its plug-and-play capability.

Isochronous Traffic on USB

An important feature of the USB is its ability to support the transfer of isochronous data in a simple manner. As mentioned earlier, isochronous data need to be transferred at precisely timed regular intervals. To accommodate this type of traffic, the root hub transmits a uniquely recognizable sequence of bits over the USB tree every millisecond. This sequence of bits, called a Start of Frame character, acts as a marker indicating the

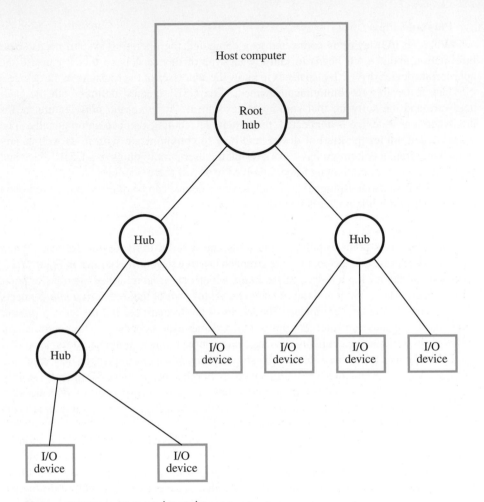

Figure 7.17   Universal Serial Bus tree structure.

beginning of isochronous data, which are transmitted after this character. Thus, digitized audio and video signals can be transferred in a regular and precisely timed manner.

Electrical Characteristics

USB connections consist of four wires, of which two carry power, +5 V and Ground, and two carry data. Thus, I/O devices that do not have large power requirements can be powered directly from the USB. This obviates the need for a separate power supply for simple devices such as a memory key or a mouse.

Two methods are used to send data over a USB cable. When sending data at low speed, a high voltage relative to Ground is transmitted on one of the two data wires to represent a 0 and on the other to represent a 1. The Ground wire carries the return current in both cases. Such a scheme in which a signal is injected on a wire relative to ground is referred to as *single-ended* transmission.

The speed at which data can be sent on any cable is limited by the amount of electrical noise present. The term *noise* refers to any signal that interferes with the desired data signal and hence could cause errors. Single-ended transmission is highly susceptible to noise. The voltage on the ground wire is common to all the devices connected to the computer. Signals sent by one device can cause small variations in the voltage on the ground wire, and hence can interfere with signals sent by another device. Interference can also be caused by one wire picking up noise from nearby wires.

The High-Speed USB uses an alternative arrangement known as *differential signaling*. The data signal is injected between two data wires twisted together. The ground wire is not involved. The receiver senses the voltage difference between the two signal wires directly, without reference to ground. This arrangement is very effective in reducing the noise seen by the receiver, because any noise injected on one of the two wires of the twisted pair is also injected on the other. Since the receiver is sensitive only to the voltage difference between the two wires, the noise component is cancelled out. The ground wire acts as a shield for the data on the twisted pair against interference from nearby wires. Differential signaling allows much lower voltages and much higher speeds to be used compared to single-ended signaling.

7.5.2 FIREWIRE

FireWire is another popular interconnection standard. It was originally developed by Apple and has been adopted as IEEE Standard 1394 [2]. Like the USB, it uses differential point-to-point serial links. The following are some of the salient differences between FireWire and USB.

- Devices are organized in a daisy chain manner on a FireWire bus, instead of the tree structure of USB. One device is connected to the computer, a second device is connected to the first one, a third device is connected to the second one, and so on.

- FireWire is well suited for connecting audio and video equipment. It can be operated in an isochronous mode that is highly optimized for carrying high-speed isochronous traffic.

- I/O devices connected to the USB communicate with the host computer. If data are to be transferred from one device to another, for example from a camera to a display or printer, they are first read by the host then sent to the display or printer. FireWire, on the other hand, supports a mode of operation called *peer-to-peer*. This means that data may be transferred directly from one I/O device to another, without the host's involvement.

- The basic FireWire connector has six pins. There are two pairs of data wires, one for transmission in each direction, and two for power and ground. Higher-speed versions use a nine-pin connector, with three ground wires added to shield the data wires against interference.

- The FireWire bus can deliver considerably more power than the USB. Hence, it can support devices with moderate power requirements.

FireWire is widely used with audio and video devices. For example, most camcorders have a FireWire port. Several versions of the standard have been defined, which can operate at speeds ranging from 400 Megabits/s to 3.6 Gigabits/s.

7.5.3   PCI BUS

The PCI (Peripheral Component Interconnect) bus [3] was developed as a low-cost, processor-independent bus. It is housed on the motherboard of a computer and used to connect I/O interfaces for a wide variety of devices. A device connected to the PCI bus appears to the processor as if it is connected directly to the processor bus. Its interface registers are assigned addresses in the address space of the processor.

We will start by describing how the PCI bus operates, then discuss some of its features.

Bus Structure

The use of the PCI bus in a computer system is illustrated in Figure 7.18. The PCI bus is connected to the processor bus via a controller called a bridge. The bridge has a special port for connecting the computer's main memory. It may also have another special high-speed port for connecting graphics devices. The bridge translates and relays commands and responses from one bus to the other and transfers data between them. For example, when

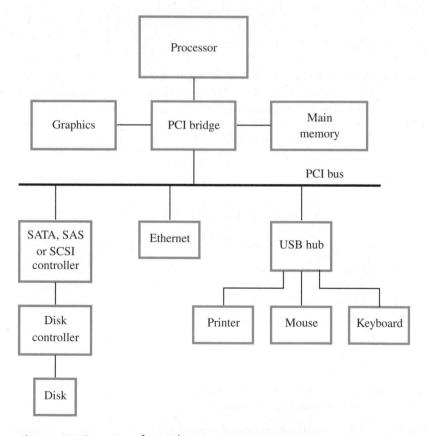

Figure 7.18   Use of a PCI bus in a computer system.

the processor sends a Read request to an I/O device, the bridge forwards the command and address to the PCI bus. When the bridge receives the device's response, it forwards the data to the processor using the processor bus. I/O devices are connected to the PCI bus, possibly through ports that use standards such as Ethernet, USB, SATA, SCSI, or SAS.

The PCI bus supports three independent address spaces: memory, I/O, and configuration. The system designer may choose to use memory-mapped I/O even with a processor that has a separate I/O address space. In fact, this is the approach recommended by the PCI standard for wider compatibility. The configuration space is intended to give the PCI its plug-and-play capability, as we will explain shortly. A 4-bit command that accompanies the address identifies which of the three spaces is being used in a given data transfer operation.

Data transfers on a computer bus often involve bursts of data rather than individual words. Words stored in successive memory locations are transferred directly between the memory and an I/O device such as a disk or an Ethernet connection. Data transfers are initiated by the interface of the I/O device, which acts as a bus master. This way of transferring data directly between the memory and I/O devices is discussed in detail in Chapter 8. The PCI bus is designed primarily to support multiple-word transfers. A Read or a Write operation involving a single word is simply treated as a burst of length one.

The signaling convention on the PCI bus is similar to that used in Figure 7.5, with one important difference. The PCI bus uses the same lines to transfer both address and data. In Figure 7.5, we assumed that the master maintains the address information on the bus until the data transfer is completed. But, this is not necessary. The address is needed only long enough for the slave to be selected, freeing the lines for sending data in subsequent clock cycles. For transfers involving multiple words, the slave can store the address in an internal register and increment it to access successive address locations. A significant cost reduction can be realized in this manner, because the number of bus lines is an important factor affecting the cost of a computer system.

Data Transfer

To understand the operation of the bus and its various features, we will examine a typical bus transaction. The bus master, which is the device that initiates data transfers by issuing Read and Write commands, is called the *initiator* in PCI terminology. The addressed device that responds to these commands is called a *target*. The main bus signals used for transferring data are listed in Table 7.1. There are 32 or 64 lines that carry address and data using a synchronous signaling scheme similar to that of Figure 7.5. The target-ready, TRDY#, signal is equivalent to the Slave ready signal in that figure. In addition, PCI uses an initiator-ready signal, IRDY#, to support burst transfers. We will describe these signals briefly, to provide the reader with an appreciation of the main features of the bus.

A complete transfer operation on the PCI bus, involving an address and a burst of data, is called a *transaction*. Consider a bus transaction in which an initiator reads four consecutive 32-bit words from the memory. The sequence of events on the bus is illustrated in Figure 7.19. All signal transitions are triggered by the rising edge of the clock. As in the case of Figure 7.5, we show the signals changing later in the clock cycle to indicate the delays they encounter. A signal whose name ends with the symbol # is asserted when in the low-voltage state.

Table 7.1   Data transfer signals on the PCI bus.

Name	Function
CLK	A 33-MHz or 66-MHz clock
FRAME#	Sent by the initiator to indicate the duration of a transmission
AD	32 address/data lines, which may be optionally increased to 64
C/BE#	4 command/byte-enable lines (8 for a 64-bit bus)
IRDY#, TRDY#	Initiator-ready and Target-ready signals
DEVSEL#	A response from the device indicating that it has recognized its address and is ready for a data transfer transaction
IDSEL#	Initialization Device Select

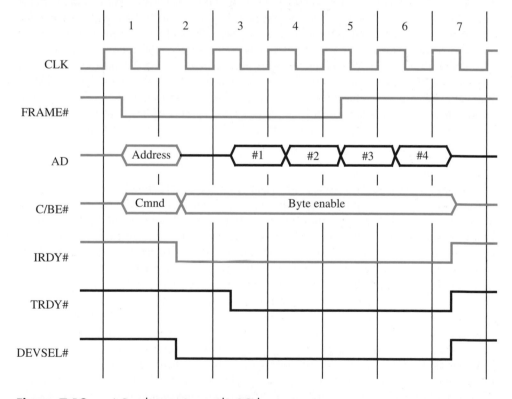

Figure 7.19   A Read operation on the PCI bus.

The bus master, acting as the initiator, asserts FRAME# in clock cycle 1 to indicate the beginning of a transaction. At the same time, it sends the address on the AD lines and a command on the C/BE# lines. In this case, the command will indicate that a Read operation is requested and that the memory address space is being used.

In clock cycle 2, the initiator removes the address, disconnects its drivers from the AD lines, and asserts IRDY# to indicate that it is ready to receive data. The selected target asserts DEVSEL# to indicate that it has recognized its address and is ready to respond. At the same time, it enables its drivers on the AD lines, so that it can send data to the initiator in subsequent cycles. Clock cycle 2 is used to accommodate the delays involved in turning the AD lines around, as the initiator turns its drivers off and the target turns its drivers on. The target asserts TRDY# in clock cycle 3 and begins to send data. It maintains DEVSEL# in the asserted state until the end of the transaction.

We have assumed that the target is ready to send data in clock cycle 3. If not, it would delay asserting TRDY# until it is ready. The entire burst of data need not be sent in successive clock cycles. Either the initiator or the target may introduce a pause by deactivating its ready signal, then asserting it again when it is ready to resume the transfer of data.

The C/BE# lines, which are used to send a bus command in clock cycle 1, are used for a different purpose during the rest of the transaction. Each of these four lines is associated with one byte on the AD lines. The initiator asserts one or more of the C/BE# lines to indicate which byte lines are to be used for transferring data.

The initiator uses the FRAME# signal to indicate the duration of the burst. It deactivates this signal during the second-last word of the transfer. In Figure 7.19, the initiator maintains FRAME# in the asserted state until clock cycle 5, the cycle in which it receives the third word. In response, the target sends one more word in clock cycle 6, then stops. After sending the fourth word, the target deactivates TRDY# and DEVSEL# and disconnects its drivers on the AD lines.

Device Configuration

When an I/O device is connected to a computer, several actions are needed to configure both the device interface and the software that communicates with it. Like USB, PCI has a plug-and-play capability that greatly simplifies this process. In fact, the plug-and-play feature was pioneered by the PCI standard. A PCI interface includes a small configuration ROM memory that stores information about the I/O device connected to it. The configuration ROMs of all devices are accessible in the configuration address space, where they are read by the PCI initialization software whenever the system is powered up or reset. By reading the information in the configuration ROM, the software determines whether the device is a printer, a camera, an Ethernet interface, or a disk controller. It can further learn about various device options and characteristics.

Devices connected to the PCI bus are not assigned permanent addresses that are built into their I/O interface hardware. Instead, device addresses are assigned by software during the initial configuration process. This means that when power is turned on, devices cannot be accessed using their addresses in the usual way, as they have not yet been assigned any address. A different mechanism is used to select I/O devices at that time.

The PCI bus may have up to 21 connectors for I/O device interface cards to be plugged into. Each connector has a pin called Initialization Device Select (IDSEL#). This pin is connected to one of the upper 21 address/data lines, AD11 to AD31. A device interface responds to a configuration command if its IDSEL# input is asserted. The configuration software scans all 21 locations to identify where I/O device interfaces are present. For each location, it issues a configuration command using an address in which the AD line corresponding to that location is set to 1 and the remaining 20 lines are set to 0. If a device interface responds, it is assigned an address and that address is writen into one of its registers designated for this purpose. Using the same addressing mechanism, the processor reads the device's configuration ROM and carries out any necessary initialization. It uses the low-order address bits, AD0 to AD10, to access locations within the configuration ROM. This automated process means that the user simply plugs in the interface board and turns on the power. The software does the rest.

The PCI bus has gained great popularity, particularly in the PC world. It is also used in many other computers, to benefit from the wide range of I/O devices for which a PCI interface is available. Both a 32-bit and a 64-bit configuration are available, using either a 33-MHz or 66-MHz clock. A high-performance variant known as PCI-X is also available. It is a 64-bit bus that runs at 133 MHz. Yet higher performance versions of PCI-X run at speeds up to 533 MHz.

7.5.4   SCSI Bus

The acronym SCSI stands for Small Computer System Interface [4]. It refers to a standard bus defined by the American National Standards Institute (ANSI). The SCSI bus may be used to connect a variety of devices to a computer. It is particularly well-suited for use with disk drives. It is often found in installations such as institutional databases or email systems where many disks drives are used.

In the original specifications of the SCSI standard, devices are connected to a computer via a 50-wire cable, which can be up to 25 meters in length and can transfer data at rates of up to 5 Megabytes/s. The standard has undergone many revisions, and its data transfer capability has increased rapidly. SCSI-2 and SCSI-3 have been defined, and each has several options. Data are transferred either 8 bits or 16 bits in parallel, using clock speeds of up to 80 MHz. There are also several options for the electrical signaling scheme used. The bus may use single-ended transmission, where each signal uses one wire, with a common ground return for all signals. In another option, differential signaling is used, with a pair of wires for each signal.

Data Transfer

Devices connected to the SCSI bus are not part of the address space of the processor in the same way as devices connected to the processor bus or to the PCI bus. A SCSI bus may be connected directly to the processor bus, or more likely to another standard I/O bus such as PCI, through a SCSI controller. Data and commands are transferred in the form of multi-byte messages called packets. To send commands or data to a device, the processor assembles the information in the memory then instructs the SCSI controller to transfer it to the device. Similarly, when data are read from a device, the controller transfers the data to the memory and then informs the processor by raising an interrupt.

To illustrate the operation of the SCSI bus, let us consider how it may be used with a disk drive. Communication with a disk drive differs substantially from communication with the main memory. Data are stored on a disk in blocks called *sectors,* where each sector may contain several hundred bytes. When a data file is written on a disk, it is not always stored in contiguous sectors. Some sectors may already contain previously stored information; others may be defective and must be skipped. Hence, a Read or Write request may result in accessing several disk sectors that are not necessarily contiguous. Because of the constraints of the mechanical motion of the disk, there is a long delay, on the order of several milliseconds, before reaching the first sector to or from which data are to be transferred. Then, a burst of data are transferred at high speed. Another delay may ensue to reach the next sector, followed by a burst of data. A single Read or Write request may involve several such bursts. The SCSI protocol is designed to facilitate this mode of operation.

Let us examine a complete Read operation as an example. The following is a simplified high-level description, ignoring details and signaling conventions. Assume that the processor wishes to read a block of data from a disk drive and that these data are stored in two disk sectors that are not contiguous. The processor sends a command to the SCSI controller, which causes the following sequence of events to take place:

1. The SCSI controller contends for control of the SCSI bus.

2. When it wins the arbitration process, the SCSI controller sends a command to the disk controller, specifying the required Read operation.

3. The disk controller cannot start to transfer data immediately. It must first move the read head of the disk to the required sector. Hence, it sends a message to the SCSI controller indicating that it will temporarily suspend the connection between them. The SCSI bus is now free to be used by other devices.

4. The disk controller sends a command to the disk drive to move the read head to the first sector involved in the requested Read operation. It reads the data stored in that sector and stores them in a data buffer. When it is ready to begin transferring data, it requests control of the bus. After it wins arbitration, it re-establishes the connection with the SCSI controller, sends the contents of the data buffer, then suspends the connection again.

5. The process is repeated to read and transfer the contents of the second disk sector.

6. The SCSI controller transfers the requested data to the main memory and sends an interrupt to the processor indicating that the data are now available.

This scenario shows that the messages exchanged over the SCSI bus are at a higher level than those exchanged over the processor bus. Messages refer to more complex operations that may require several steps to complete, depending on the device. Neither the processor nor the SCSI controller need be aware of the details of the disk's operation and how it moves from one sector to the next.

The SCSI bus standard defines a wide range of control messages that can be used to handle different types of I/O devices. Messages are also defined to deal with various error or failure conditions that might arise during device operation or data transfer.

7.5.5 SATA

In the early days of the personal computer, the bus of a popular IBM computer called AT, which was based on Intel's 8080 microprocessor bus, became an industry standard. It was named ISA, for Industry Standard Architecture. An enhanced version, including a definition of the basic software needed to support disk drives, was later named ATA, for AT Attachment bus. A serial version of the same architecture became known as SATA [5], which is now widely used as an interface for disks. Like all standards, several versions of SATA have been developed with added features and higher speeds. The original parallel version has been renamed PATA, but it is no longer used in new equipment.

The basic SATA connector has 7 pins, connecting two twisted pairs and three ground wires. Differential transmission is used, with clock frequencies ranging from 1.5 to 6.0 Gigabits/s. Some of the recent versions provide an isochronous transmission feature to support audio and video devices.

7.5.6 SAS

This is a serial implementation of the SCSI bus, hence its name: Serially Attached SCSI [6]. It is primarily intended for connecting magnetic disks and CD and DVD drives. It uses serial, point-to-point links that are similar to SATA. A SAS link can transfer data in both directions simultaneously, at speeds up to 12 Gigabits/s. At the software level, SAS is fully compatible with SCSI.

7.5.7 PCI E<small>XPRESS</small>

The demands placed on I/O interconnections are ever increasing. Internet connections, sophisticated graphics devices, streaming video and high-definition television are examples of applications that involve data transfers at very high speed. The PCI Express interconnection standard (often called PCIe) [7] has been developed to meet these needs and to anticipate further increases in data transfer rates, which are inevitable as new applications are introduced.

PCI Express uses serial, point-to-point links interconnected via switches to form a tree structure, as shown in Figure 7.20. The root node of the tree, called the Root complex, is connected to the processor bus. The Root complex has a special port to connect the main memory. All other connections emanating from the Root complex are serial links to I/O devices. Some of these links may connect to a switch that leads to more serial branches, as shown in the figure. The switch may also connect to bridging interfaces that support other standards, such as PCI or USB. For example, one of the tree branches could be a PCI bus, to take advantage of the wide variety of devices for which PCI interfaces already exist.

The basic PCI Express link consists of two twisted pairs, one for each direction of transmission. Data are transmitted at the rate of of 2.5 Gigabits/s over each twisted pair, using the differential signaling scheme described in Section 7.5.1. Data may be transmitted in both directions at the same time. Also, links to different devices may be carrying data at the same time, because there is no shared bus as in the case of PCI or SCSI. Furthermore,

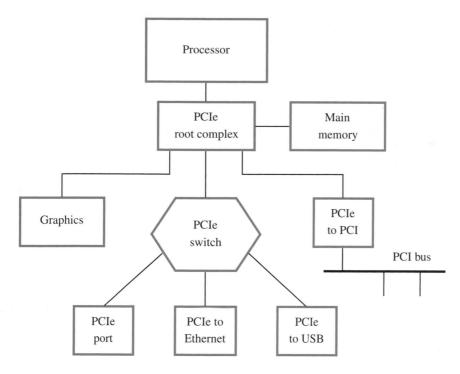

Figure 7.20   PCI Express connections.

a link may use more than one twisted pair in each direction. The basic arrangement with one twisted pair for each direction is called a lane and referred to as a X1 (read as by 1) connection. A link may use 2, 4, 8, or 16 lanes, in which case it is called a X2, X4, X8, or X16 link.

The receiver on a synchronous transmission link must synchronize its clock with that of the sender, as described in Section 7.4.2. To make this possible, the transmitted data are encoded to ensure that 0-to-1 and 1-to-0 transitions occur frequently enough. In the case of PCIe, each 8 bits of data are encoded using 10 bits. Other bits are inserted in the stream to perform various control functions, such as delineating address and data information. After accounting for the additional bits, a single twisted pair on which data are transmitted at 2.5 Gigabits/s actually delivers 1.6 Gigabits/s or 200 MByte/s of useful information. A X16 link transfers data at the rate of 3.2 Gigabyte/s in each direction. By comparison, a 64-bit PCI bus operating at 64 MHz has a peak aggregate data transfer rate of 512 Megabytes/s. PCI Express has the additional advantage of using a small number of wires, resulting in lower-cost hardware.

The PCI Express protocols are fully compatible with those of PCI. For example, the same initial configuration procedures are used. Thus, a computer that uses PCI Express can use existing operating systems and applications software that were developed for a PCI-based system.

7.6   CONCLUDING REMARKS

This chapter introduced the I/O structure of a computer from a hardware point of view. I/O devices connected to a bus are used as examples to illustrate the synchronous and asynchronous schemes for transferring data.

The architecture of interconnection networks for input and output devices has been a major area of development, driven by an ever-increasing need for transferring data at high speed, for reduced cost, and for features that enhance user convenience such as plug-and-play. Several I/O standards are described briefly in this chapter, illustrating the approaches used to meet these objectives. The current trend is to move away from parallel buses to serial point-to-point links. Serial links have lower cost and can transfer data at high speed.

7.7   SOLVED PROBLEMS

This section presents some examples of the types of problems that a student may be asked to solve, and shows how such problems can be solved.

Example 7.1

Problem: The I/O bus of a computer uses the synchronous protocol shown in Figure 7.4. Maximum propagation delay on this bus is 4 ns. The bus master takes 1.5 ns to place an address on the address lines. Slave devices require 3 ns to decode the address and a maximum of 5 ns to place the requested data on the data lines. Input registers connected to the bus have a minimum setup time of 1 ns. Assume that the bus clock has a 50% duty cycle; that is, the high and low phases of the clock are of equal duration. What is the maximum clock frequency for this bus?

Solution: The minimum time for the high phase of the clock is the time for the address to arrive and be decoded by the slave, which is $1.5 + 4 + 3 = 8.5$ ns. The minimum time for the low phase of the clock is the time for the slave to place data on the bus and for the master to load the data into a register, which is $5 + 4 + 1 = 10$ ns. Then, the minimum clock period is $2 \times 10 = 20$ ns, and the maximum clock frequency is 50 MHz.

Example 7.2

Problem: An arbiter receives three request signals, R1, R2, R3, and generates three grant signals, G1, G2, G3. Request R1 has the highest priority and request R3 the lowest priority. An example of the operation of such an arbiter is given in Figure 7.9. Give a state diagram that describes the behavior of this arbiter.

Solution: A state diagram is given in Figure 7.21. The arbiter starts in the idle state, A. When one or more of the request signals is asserted, the arbiter moves to one of the three states, B, C, or D, depending on which of the active requests has the highest priority. When it enters the new state, it asserts the corresponding grant signal. The arbiter remains in that state

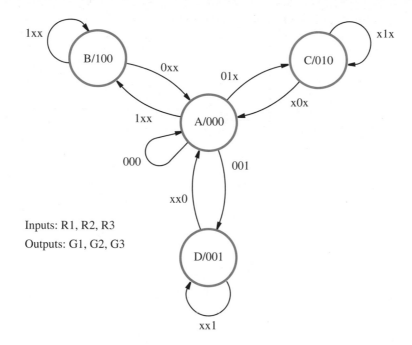

Figure 7.21   State diagram for Example 7.2.

until the device being served drops its request, at which time the arbiter returns to state A. Once it is back in state A, it will respond to any request that may be active at that time, or wait for a new request to be asserted.

Problem: Design an output interface circuit for a synchronous bus that uses the protocol of Figure 7.4. When data are written into the data register of this interface, the interface sends a pulse with a width of one clock cycle on a line called New-data. This pulse lets the output device connected to the interface know that new data are available.   **Example 7.3**

Solution: All events in a synchronous circuit are driven by a clock signal. A possible circuit for the interface is shown in Figure 7.22. The Write-data signal enables the data register, and data are loaded into it at the clock edge at the end of the clock cycle. At the same time, the New-data flip-flop is set to 1. The feedback connection from the $\overline{Q}$ output of the flip-flop clears the flip-flop to 0 on the following clock edge.

Problem: Draw a state diagram for a finite-state machine (FSM) that represents the behavior of the handshake control circuit in Figure 7.14.   **Example 7.4**

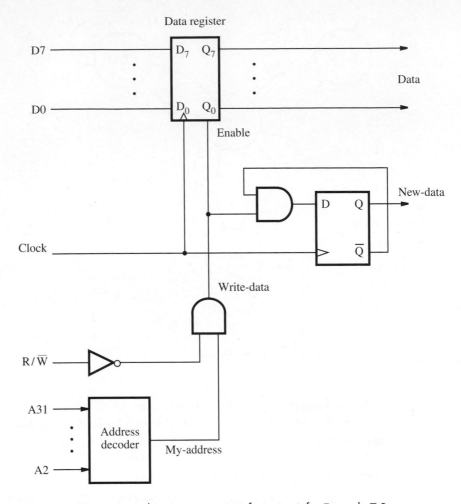

Figure 7.22   A synchronous output interface circuit for Example 7.3.

Solution: A state diagram is given in Figure 7.23. The circuit starts in state A, with the display device ready to receive new data. Thus, New-data = 0 and DOUT = 1. A Write operation causes Write-data to change to 1. This causes the state machine to move to state B, and its outputs change to 10. The machine stays in state B until Ready drops to 0, indicating that the display device recognized that new data are available. When that happens, the machine moves to state C to wait for the display to become ready again. It must also wait for Write-data to return to zero, if it has not done so already.

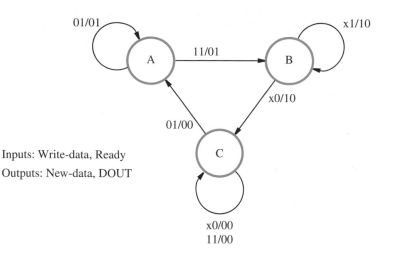

Inputs: Write-data, Ready

Outputs: New-data, DOUT

Figure 7.23   State diagram for Example 7.4.

PROBLEMS

7.1   **[E]** The input status bit in an interface circuit, which indicates that new data are available, is cleared as soon as the input data register is read. Why is this important?

7.2   **[E]** The address bus of a computer has 16 address lines, A_{15-0}. If the hexadecimal address assigned to one device is 7CA4 and the address decoder for that device ignores lines A_8 and A_9, what are all the addresses to which this device will respond?

7.3   **[M]** A processor has seven interrupt-request lines, INTR1 to INTR7. Line INTR7 has the highest priority and INTR1 the lowest priority. Design a priority encoder circuit that generates a 3-bit code representing the request with the highest priority.

7.4   **[M]** Figures 7.4, 7.5, and 7.6 show three protocols for transferring data between a master and a slave. What happens in each case if the addressed device does not respond due to a malfunction during a Read operation? What problems would this cause and what remedies are possible?

7.5   **[E]** In the timing diagram in Figure 7.5, the processor maintains the address on the bus until it receives a response from the device. Is this necessary? What additions are needed on the device side if the processor sends an address for one cycle only?

7.6   **[E]** How is the timing diagram in Figure 7.6 affected as the distance between the processor and the I/O device increases? How is increased distance accommodated in the case of Figure 7.4?

7.7   [E] Consider a synchronous bus that operates according to the timing diagram in Figure 7.5. The bus and the interface circuitry connected to it have the following parameters:

Bus driver delay	2 ns
Propagation delay on the bus	5 to 10 ns
Address decoder delay	6 ns
Time to fetch the requested data	0 to 25 ns
Setup time	1.5 ns

(*a*) What is the maximum clock speed at which this bus can operate?

(*b*) How many clock cycles are needed to complete an input operation?

7.8   [M] Consider the asynchronous bus protocol shown in Figure 7.6. Using the same parameters as in Problem 7.7, what are the minimum and maximum times to complete one bus transfer? Allow 1 ns for bus skew.

7.9   [M] The asynchronous bus protocol in Figure 7.6 uses a full-handshake, in which the master maintains an asserted signal on Master-ready until it receives Slave-ready, the slave keeps Slave-ready asserted until Master-ready becomes inactive, and so on. Consider an alternative protocol in which each of these signals is a pulse of a fixed width of 4 ns. Devices take action only on the rising edge of the pulse. Using the same parameters as in Problem 7.7, what is the minimum and maximum time to complete one bus transfer?

7.10   [M] In the arbiter protocol example depicted in Figure 7.9, the master that receives a bus grant maintains its request line in the asserted state until it is ready to relinquish bus mastership. Assume that a common line called Busy is available, which is asserted by the master that is currently using the bus. The arbiter grants the bus only when Busy is inactive. Once a master receives a grant, it asserts Busy and drops its request, and in response the arbiter drops the grant. The master deactivates Busy when it is finished using the bus. Draw a timing diagram equivalent to Figure 7.9 for this mode of operation.

7.11   [M] Modify the state diagram given in Example 7.2 for the mode of operation described in Problem 7.10.

7.12   [D] The arbiter of Example 7.2 controls access to a common resource. It does not allow preemption. This means that if a high-priority request is received after a lower-priority request has been granted, it must wait until service to the device that is currently using the common resource is completed. In some cases, it is desirable to allow preemption, to provide service to a high-priority device more quickly. Devices in such a system, must be able to stop and relinquish the use of the common resource when asked to do so by the arbiter. This must be done in a safe manner. A device that is using the resource must be allowed to reach a safe point at which service can be terminated. It would then signal to the arbiter that it has stopped using the resource.

(*a*) Suggest a suitable modification to the signaling protocol that enables the service in progress to be terminated safely.

(*b*) Modify the state diagram of the arbiter to implement the revised protocol.

7.13 **[E]** An arbiter controls access to a common resource. It uses a rotating-priority scheme in responding to requests on lines R1 through R4. Initially, R1 has the highest priority and R4 the lowest priority. After a request on one of the lines receives service, that line drops to the lowest priority, and the next line in sequence becomes the highest-priority line. For example, after R2 has been serviced, the priority order, starting with the highest, becomes R3, R4, R1, R2. What will be the sequence of grants for the following sequence of requests: R3, R1, R4, R2? Assume that the last three requests arrive while the first one is being serviced.

7.14 **[E]** Consider an arbiter that uses the priority scheme described in Problem 7.13. What happens if one device requests service repeatedly. Compare the behavior of this arbiter to one that uses a fixed-priority scheme.

7.15 **[E]** Give the logic expression for an address decoder that recognizes the 16-bit hexadecimal address FA68.

7.16 **[M]** An industrial plant uses several sensors to monitor temperature, pressure, and other factors. Each sensor includes a switch that moves to the ON position when the corresponding parameter exceeds a preset limit. Eight such sensors need to be connected to the bus of a 16-bit computer. Design an appropriate interface to enable the state of all eight switches to be read simultaneously as a single byte. Assume the bus is synchronous and that it uses the timing sequence of Figure 7.4.

7.17 **[E]** The bus protocol of Figure 7.4 specifies that the slave device should send its data only in the second phase of the clock.

(a) It is possible that some device may recognize its address and is ready to send data sooner. Why is it not allowed to do so? Would the processor receive wrong data?

(b) Would any other problem arise?

7.18 **[M]** Data are stored in a small memory in an input interface connected to a synchronous bus that uses the protocol of Figure 7.5. Read and Write operations on the bus are indicated by a Command line called R/$\overline{\text{W}}$. The speed of the memory is such that two clock cycles are required to read data from the memory. Design a circuit to generate the Slave-ready response of this interface.

7.19 **[E]** Each of the two signals DEVSEL# and TRDY# of the PCI protocol in Figure 7.19 represents a response from the initiator. How do the functions of these two signals differ?

7.20 **[E]** Consider the data transfer operation shown in Figure 7.19 for the PCI bus. How would this bus protocol handle a situation in which the target needs a delay of two clock cycles between words 2 and 3?

7.21 **[E]** Draw a timing diagram for transferring three words to an output device connected to the PCI bus.

REFERENCES

1. *Universal Serial Bus Specification,* available at www.usb.org/developers.
2. *IEEE Standard for a High-Performance Serial Bus*, IEEE Std. 1394-2008, October 2008.
3. Specifications and other information about the *PCI Local Bus* and *PCI Express* are available at www.pcisig.com/developers.
4. *SCSI-3 Architecture Model (SAM),* ANSI Standard X3.270, 1996. This and other SCSI documents are available on the web at www.ansi.org.
5. *SATA* specifications and related material are available at www.serialata.org.
6. Information about the *Serial SCSI (SAS)* standard is available at www.scsita.org.
7. A. Wilen, J. Schade, and R. Thornburg, *Introduction to PCI Express, A Hardware and Software Developer's Guide,* Intel Press, 2003.

8

THE MEMORY SYSTEM

CHAPTER OBJECTIVES

In this chapter you will learn about:

- Basic memory circuits
- Organization of the main memory
- Memory technology
- Direct memory access as an I/O mechanism
- Cache memory, which reduces the effective memory access time
- Virtual memory, which increases the apparent size of the main memory
- Magnetic and optical disks used for secondary storage

Programs and the data they operate on are held in the memory of the computer. In this chapter, we discuss how this vital part of the computer operates. By now, the reader appreciates that the execution speed of programs is highly dependent on the speed with which instructions and data can be transferred between the processor and the memory. It is also important to have sufficient memory to facilitate execution of large programs having large amounts of data.

Ideally, the memory would be fast, large, and inexpensive. Unfortunately, it is impossible to meet all three of these requirements simultaneously. Increased speed and size are achieved at increased cost. Much work has gone into developing structures that improve the effective speed and size of the memory, yet keep the cost reasonable.

The memory of a computer comprises a hierarchy, including a cache, the main memory, and secondary storage, as Chapter 1 explains. In this chapter, we describe the most common components and organizations used to implement these units. Direct memory access is introduced as a mechanism to transfer data between an I/O device, such as a disk, and the main memory, with minimal involvement from the processor. We examine memory speed and discuss how access times to memory data can be reduced by means of caches. Next, we present the virtual memory concept, which makes use of the large storage capacity of secondary storage devices to increase the effective size of the memory. We start with a presentation of some basic concepts, to extend the discussion in Chapters 1 and 2.

8.1   BASIC CONCEPTS

The maximum size of the memory that can be used in any computer is determined by the addressing scheme. For example, a computer that generates 16-bit addresses is capable of addressing up to $2^{16} = 64K$ (kilo) memory locations. Machines whose instructions generate 32-bit addresses can utilize a memory that contains up to $2^{32} = 4G$ (giga) locations, whereas machines with 64-bit addresses can access up to $2^{64} = 16E$ (exa) $\approx 16 \times 10^{18}$ locations. The number of locations represents the size of the address space of the computer.

The memory is usually designed to store and retrieve data in word-length quantities. Consider, for example, a byte-addressable computer whose instructions generate 32-bit addresses. When a 32-bit address is sent from the processor to the memory unit, the high-order 30 bits determine which word will be accessed. If a byte quantity is specified, the low-order 2 bits of the address specify which byte location is involved.

The connection between the processor and its memory consists of address, data, and control lines, as shown in Figure 8.1. The processor uses the address lines to specify the memory location involved in a data transfer operation, and uses the data lines to transfer the data. At the same time, the control lines carry the command indicating a Read or a Write operation and whether a byte or a word is to be transferred. The control lines also provide the necessary timing information and are used by the memory to indicate when it has completed the requested operation. When the processor-memory interface receives the memory's response, it asserts the MFC signal shown in Figure 5.19. This is the processor's internal control signal that indicates that the requested memory operation has been completed. When asserted, the processor proceeds to the next step in its execution sequence.

Processor-memory interface

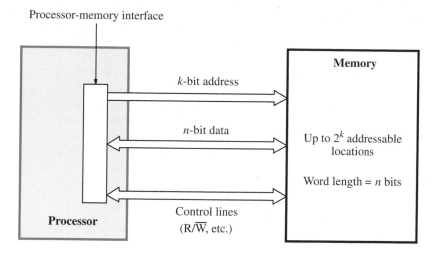

Figure 8.1   Connection of the memory to the processor.

A useful measure of the speed of memory units is the time that elapses between the initiation of an operation to transfer a word of data and the completion of that operation. This is referred to as the *memory access time.* Another important measure is the *memory cycle time,* which is the minimum time delay required between the initiation of two successive memory operations, for example, the time between two successive Read operations. The cycle time is usually slightly longer than the access time, depending on the implementation details of the memory unit.

A memory unit is called a *random-access memory* (RAM) if the access time to any location is the same, independent of the location's address. This distinguishes such memory units from serial, or partly serial, access storage devices such as magnetic and optical disks. Access time of the latter devices depends on the address or position of the data.

The technology for implementing computer memories uses semiconductor integrated circuits. The sections that follow present some basic facts about the internal structure and operation of such memories. We then discuss some of the techniques used to increase the effective speed and size of the memory.

Cache and Virtual Memory

The processor of a computer can usually process instructions and data faster than they can be fetched from the main memory. Hence, the memory access time is the bottleneck in the system. One way to reduce the memory access time is to use a *cache memory.* This is a small, fast memory inserted between the larger, slower main memory and the processor. It holds the currently active portions of a program and their data.

Virtual memory is another important concept related to memory organization. With this technique, only the active portions of a program are stored in the main memory, and the remainder is stored on the much larger secondary storage device. Sections of the program are transferred back and forth between the main memory and the secondary storage device in a manner that is transparent to the application program. As a result, the application program sees a memory that is much larger than the computer's physical main memory.

Block Transfers

The discussion above shows that data move frequently between the main memory and the cache and between the main memory and the disk. These transfers do not occur one word at a time. Data are always transferred in contiguous blocks involving tens, hundreds, or thousands of words. Data transfers between the main memory and high-speed devices such as a graphic display or an Ethernet interface also involve large blocks of data. Hence, a critical parameter for the performance of the main memory is its ability to read or write blocks of data at high speed. This is an important consideration that we will encounter repeatedly as we discuss memory technology and the organization of the memory system.

8.2   SEMICONDUCTOR RAM MEMORIES

Semiconductor random-access memories (RAMs) are available in a wide range of speeds. Their cycle times range from 100 ns to less than 10 ns. In this section, we discuss the main characteristics of these memories. We start by introducing the way that memory cells are organized inside a chip.

8.2.1   INTERNAL ORGANIZATION OF MEMORY CHIPS

Memory cells are usually organized in the form of an array, in which each cell is capable of storing one bit of information. A possible organization is illustrated in Figure 8.2. Each row of cells constitutes a memory word, and all cells of a row are connected to a common line referred to as the *word line,* which is driven by the address decoder on the chip. The cells in each column are connected to a Sense/Write circuit by two *bit lines,* and the Sense/Write circuits are connected to the data input/output lines of the chip. During a Read operation, these circuits sense, or read, the information stored in the cells selected by a word line and place this information on the output data lines. During a Write operation, the Sense/Write circuits receive input data and store them in the cells of the selected word.

Figure 8.2 is an example of a very small memory circuit consisting of 16 words of 8 bits each. This is referred to as a 16×8 organization. The data input and the data output of each Sense/Write circuit are connected to a single bidirectional data line that can be connected to the data lines of a computer. Two control lines, $R/\overline{W}$ and CS, are provided. The $R/\overline{W}$ (Read/Write) input specifies the required operation, and the CS (Chip Select) input selects a given chip in a multichip memory system.

The memory circuit in Figure 8.2 stores 128 bits and requires 14 external connections for address, data, and control lines. It also needs two lines for power supply and ground connections. Consider now a slightly larger memory circuit, one that has 1K (1024) memory cells. This circuit can be organized as a 128×8 memory, requiring a total of 19 external connections. Alternatively, the same number of cells can be organized into a $1K \times 1$ format. In this case, a 10-bit address is needed, but there is only one data line, resulting in 15 external

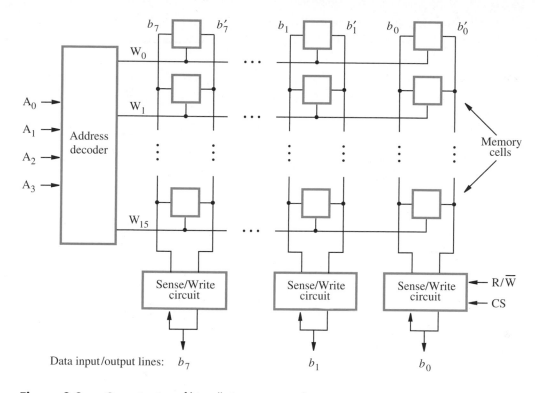

Figure 8.2 Organization of bit cells in a memory chip.

connections. Figure 8.3 shows such an organization. The required 10-bit address is divided into two groups of 5 bits each to form the row and column addresses for the cell array. A row address selects a row of 32 cells, all of which are accessed in parallel. But, only one of these cells is connected to the external data line, based on the column address.

Commercially available memory chips contain a much larger number of memory cells than the examples shown in Figures 8.2 and 8.3. We use small examples to make the figures easy to understand. Large chips have essentially the same organization as Figure 8.3, but use a larger memory cell array and have more external connections. For example, a 1G-bit chip may have a 256M $\times$ 4 organization, in which case a 28-bit address is needed and 4 bits are transferred to or from the chip.

8.2.2 STATIC MEMORIES

Memories that consist of circuits capable of retaining their state as long as power is applied are known as *static memories*. Figure 8.4 illustrates how a *static RAM* (SRAM) cell may be implemented. Two inverters are cross-connected to form a latch. The latch is connected to two bit lines by transistors T_1 and T_2. These transistors act as switches that can be opened or

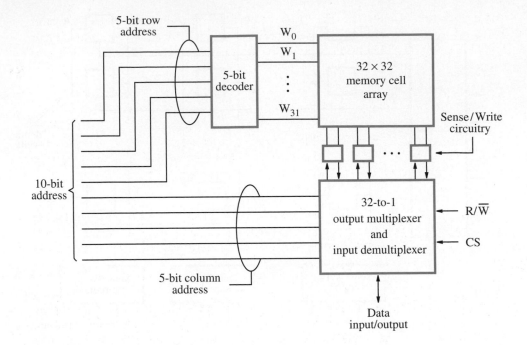

Figure 8.3   Organization of a 1K × 1 memory chip.

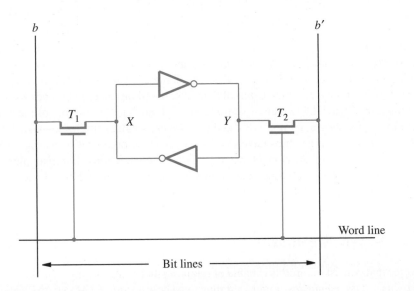

Figure 8.4   A static RAM cell.

closed under control of the word line. When the word line is at ground level, the transistors are turned off and the latch retains its state. For example, if the logic value at point X is 1 and at point Y is 0, this state is maintained as long as the signal on the word line is at ground level. Assume that this state represents the value 1.

Read Operation

In order to read the state of the SRAM cell, the word line is activated to close switches T_1 and T_2. If the cell is in state 1, the signal on bit line b is high and the signal on bit line b' is low. The opposite is true if the cell is in state 0. Thus, b and b' are always complements of each other. The Sense/Write circuit at the end of the two bit lines monitors their state and sets the corresponding output accordingly.

Write Operation

During a Write operation, the Sense/Write circuit drives bit lines b and b', instead of sensing their state. It places the appropriate value on bit line b and its complement on b' and activates the word line. This forces the cell into the corresponding state, which the cell retains when the word line is deactivated.

CMOS Cell

A CMOS realization of the cell in Figure 8.4 is given in Figure 8.5. Transistor pairs (T_3, T_5) and (T_4, T_6) form the inverters in the latch (see Appendix A). The state of the cell is read or written as just explained. For example, in state 1, the voltage at point X is maintained high by having transistors T_3 and T_6 on, while T_4 and T_5 are off. If T_1 and T_2 are turned on, bit lines b and b' will have high and low signals, respectively.

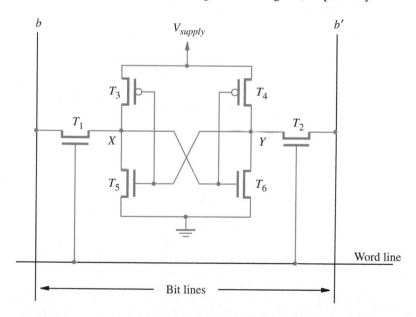

Figure 8.5 An example of a CMOS memory cell.

Continuous power is needed for the cell to retain its state. If power is interrupted, the cell's contents are lost. When power is restored, the latch settles into a stable state, but not necessarily the same state the cell was in before the interruption. Hence, SRAMs are said to be *volatile* memories because their contents are lost when power is interrupted.

A major advantage of CMOS SRAMs is their very low power consumption, because current flows in the cell only when the cell is being accessed. Otherwise, T_1, T_2, and one transistor in each inverter are turned off, ensuring that there is no continuous electrical path between V_{supply} and ground.

Static RAMs can be accessed very quickly. Access times on the order of a few nanoseconds are found in commercially available chips. SRAMs are used in applications where speed is of critical concern.

8.2.3 DYNAMIC RAMs

Static RAMs are fast, but their cells require several transistors. Less expensive and higher density RAMs can be implemented with simpler cells. But, these simpler cells do not retain their state for a long period, unless they are accessed frequently for Read or Write operations. Memories that use such cells are called *dynamic RAMs* (DRAMs).

Information is stored in a dynamic memory cell in the form of a charge on a capacitor, but this charge can be maintained for only tens of milliseconds. Since the cell is required to store information for a much longer time, its contents must be periodically *refreshed* by restoring the capacitor charge to its full value. This occurs when the contents of the cell are read or when new information is written into it.

An example of a dynamic memory cell that consists of a capacitor, C, and a transistor, T, is shown in Figure 8.6. To store information in this cell, transistor T is turned on and an appropriate voltage is applied to the bit line. This causes a known amount of charge to be stored in the capacitor.

After the transistor is turned off, the charge remains stored in the capacitor, but not for long. The capacitor begins to discharge. This is because the transistor continues to

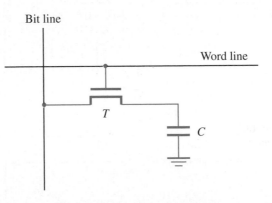

Figure 8.6   A single-transistor dynamic memory cell.

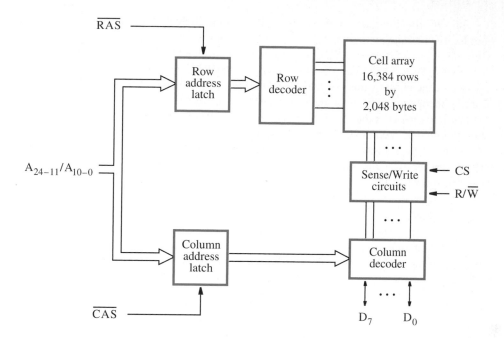

Figure 8.7   Internal organization of a 32M × 8 dynamic memory chip.

conduct a tiny amount of current, measured in picoamperes, after it is turned off. Hence, the information stored in the cell can be retrieved correctly only if it is read before the charge in the capacitor drops below some threshold value. During a Read operation, the transistor in a selected cell is turned on. A sense amplifier connected to the bit line detects whether the charge stored in the capacitor is above or below the threshold value. If the charge is above the threshold, the sense amplifier drives the bit line to the full voltage representing the logic value 1. As a result, the capacitor is recharged to the full charge corresponding to the logic value 1. If the sense amplifier detects that the charge in the capacitor is below the threshold value, it pulls the bit line to ground level to discharge the capacitor fully. Thus, reading the contents of a cell automatically refreshes its contents. Since the word line is common to all cells in a row, all cells in a selected row are read and refreshed at the same time.

A 256-Megabit DRAM chip, configured as 32M × 8, is shown in Figure 8.7. The cells are organized in the form of a 16K × 16K array. The 16,384 cells in each row are divided into 2,048 groups of 8, forming 2,048 bytes of data. Therefore, 14 address bits are needed to select a row, and another 11 bits are needed to specify a group of 8 bits in the selected row. In total, a 25-bit address is needed to access a byte in this memory. The high-order 14 bits and the low-order 11 bits of the address constitute the row and column addresses of a byte, respectively. To reduce the number of pins needed for external connections, the row and column addresses are multiplexed on 14 pins. During a Read or a Write operation, the row address is applied first. It is loaded into the row address latch in response to a signal pulse on an input control line called the Row Address Strobe (RAS). This causes a Read operation to be initiated, in which all cells in the selected row are read and refreshed.

Shortly after the row address is loaded, the column address is applied to the address pins and loaded into the column address latch under control of a second control line called the Column Address Strobe (CAS). The information in this latch is decoded and the appropriate group of 8 Sense/Write circuits is selected. If the R/$\overline{W}$ control signal indicates a Read operation, the output values of the selected circuits are transferred to the data lines, D_{7-0}. For a Write operation, the information on the D_{7-0} lines is transferred to the selected circuits, then used to overwrite the contents of the selected cells in the corresponding 8 columns. We should note that in commercial DRAM chips, the RAS and CAS control signals are active when low. Hence, addresses are latched when these signals change from high to low. The signals are shown in diagrams as $\overline{RAS}$ and $\overline{CAS}$ to indicate this fact.

The timing of the operation of the DRAM described above is controlled by the RAS and CAS signals. These signals are generated by a memory controller circuit external to the chip when the processor issues a Read or a Write command. During a Read operation, the output data are transferred to the processor after a delay equivalent to the memory's access time. Such memories are referred to as *asynchronous DRAMs*. The memory controller is also responsible for refreshing the data stored in the memory chips, as we describe later.

Fast Page Mode

When the DRAM in Figure 8.7 is accessed, the contents of all 16,384 cells in the selected row are sensed, but only 8 bits are placed on the data lines, D_{7-0}. This byte is selected by the column address, bits A_{10-0}. A simple addition to the circuit makes it possible to access the other bytes in the same row without having to reselect the row. Each sense amplifier also acts as a latch. When a row address is applied, the contents of all cells in the selected row are loaded into the corresponding latches. Then, it is only necessary to apply different column addresses to place the different bytes on the data lines.

This arrangement leads to a very useful feature. All bytes in the selected row can be transferred in sequential order by applying a consecutive sequence of column addresses under the control of successive CAS signals. Thus, a block of data can be transferred at a much faster rate than can be achieved for transfers involving random addresses. The block transfer capability is referred to as the *fast page mode* feature. (A large block of data is often called a page.)

It was pointed out earlier that the vast majority of main memory transactions involve block transfers. The faster rate attainable in the fast page mode makes dynamic RAMs particularly well suited to this environment.

8.2.4   SYNCHRONOUS DRAMs

In the early 1990s, developments in memory technology resulted in DRAMs whose operation is synchronized with a clock signal. Such memories are known as *synchronous DRAMs* (SDRAMs). Their structure is shown in Figure 8.8. The cell array is the same as in asynchronous DRAMs. The distinguishing feature of an SDRAM is the use of a clock signal, the availability of which makes it possible to incorporate control circuitry on the chip that provides many useful features. For example, SDRAMs have built-in refresh circuitry, with a refresh counter to provide the addresses of the rows to be selected for refreshing. As a result, the dynamic nature of these memory chips is almost invisible to the user.

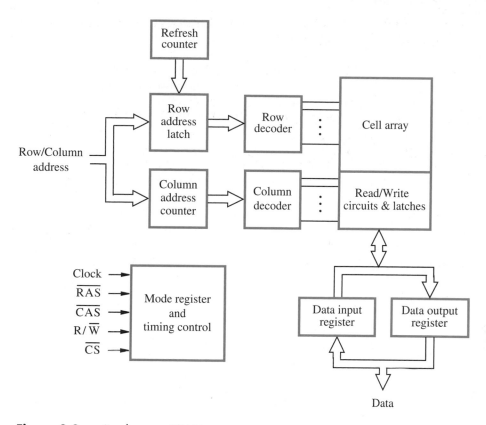

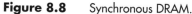

Figure 8.8   Synchronous DRAM.

The address and data connections of an SDRAM may be buffered by means of registers, as shown in the figure. Internally, the Sense/Write amplifiers function as latches, as in asynchronous DRAMs. A Read operation causes the contents of all cells in the selected row to be loaded into these latches. The data in the latches of the selected column are transferred into the data register, thus becoming available on the data output pins. The buffer registers are useful when transferring large blocks of data at very high speed. By isolating external connections from the chip's internal circuitry, it becomes possible to start a new access operation while data are being transferred to or from the registers.

SDRAMs have several different modes of operation, which can be selected by writing control information into a *mode* register. For example, burst operations of different lengths can be specified. It is not necessary to provide externally-generated pulses on the CAS line to select successive columns. The necessary control signals are generated internally using a column counter and the clock signal. New data are placed on the data lines at the rising edge of each clock pulse.

Figure 8.9 shows a timing diagram for a typical burst read of length 4. First, the row address is latched under control of the RAS signal. The memory typically takes 5 or 6 clock

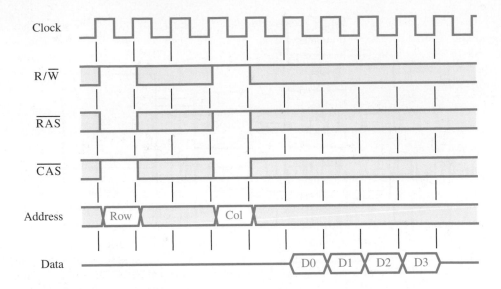

Figure 8.9   A burst read of length 4 in an SDRAM.

cycles (we use 2 in the figure for simplicity) to activate the selected row. Then, the column address is latched under control of the CAS signal. After a delay of one clock cycle, the first set of data bits is placed on the data lines. The SDRAM automatically increments the column address to access the next three sets of bits in the selected row, which are placed on the data lines in the next 3 clock cycles.

Synchronous DRAMs can deliver data at a very high rate, because all the control signals needed are generated inside the chip. The initial commercial SDRAMs in the 1990s were designed for clock speeds of up to 133 MHz. As technology evolved, much faster SDRAM chips were developed. Today's SDRAMs operate with clock speeds that can exceed 1 GHz.

Latency and Bandwidth

Data transfers to and from the main memory often involve blocks of data. The speed of these transfers has a large impact on the performance of a computer system. The memory access time defined earlier is not sufficient for describing the memory's performance when transferring blocks of data. During block transfers, *memory latency* is the amount of time it takes to transfer the first word of a block. The time required to transfer a complete block depends also on the rate at which successive words can be transferred and on the size of the block. The time between successive words of a block is much shorter than the time needed to transfer the first word. For instance, in the timing diagram in Figure 8.9, the access cycle begins with the assertion of the RAS signal. The first word of data is transferred five clock cycles later. Thus, the latency is five clock cycles. If the clock rate is 500 MHz, then the latency is 10 ns. The remaining three words are transferred in consecutive clock cycles, at the rate of one word every 2 ns.

The example above illustrates that we need a parameter other than memory latency to describe the memory's performance during block transfers. A useful performance measure is the number of bits or bytes that can be transferred in one second. This measure is often referred to as the memory *bandwidth*. It depends on the speed of access to the stored data and on the number of bits that can be accessed in parallel. The rate at which data can be transferred to or from the memory depends on the bandwidth of the system interconnections. For this reason, the interconnections used always ensure that the bandwidth available for data transfers between the processor and the memory is very high.

Double-Data-Rate SDRAM

In the continuous quest for improved performance, faster versions of SDRAMs have been developed. In addition to faster circuits, new organizational and operational features make it possible to achieve high data rates during block transfers. The key idea is to take advantage of the fact that a large number of bits are accessed at the same time inside the chip when a row address is applied. Various techniques are used to transfer these bits quickly to the pins of the chip. To make the best use of the available clock speed, data are transferred externally on both the rising and falling edges of the clock. For this reason, memories that use this technique are called *double-data-rate SDRAMs* (DDR SDRAMs).

Several versions of DDR chips have been developed. The earliest version is known as DDR. Later versions, called DDR2, DDR3, and DDR4, have enhanced capabilities. They offer increased storage capacity, lower power, and faster clock speeds. For example, DDR2 and DDR3 can operate at clock frequencies of 400 and 800 MHz, respectively. Therefore, they transfer data using the effective clock speeds of 800 and 1600 MHz, respectively.

Rambus Memory

The rate of transferring data between the memory and the processor is a function of both the bandwidth of the memory and the bandwidth of its connection to the processor. Rambus is a memory technology that achieves a high data transfer rate by providing a high-speed interface between the memory and the processor. One way for increasing the bandwidth of this connection is to use a wider data path. However, this requires more space and more pins, increasing system cost. The alternative is to use fewer wires with a higher clock speed. This is the approach taken by Rambus.

The key feature of Rambus technology is the use of a differential-signaling technique to transfer data to and from the memory chips. The basic idea of differential signaling is described in Section 7.5.1. In Rambus technology, signals are transmitted using small voltage swings of 0.1 V above and below a reference value. Several versions of this standard have been developed, with clock speeds of up to 800 MHz and data transfer rates of several gigabytes per second.

Rambus technology competes directly with the DDR SDRAM technology. Each has certain advantages and disadvantages. A nontechnical consideration is that the specification of DDR SDRAM is an open standard that can be used free of charge. Rambus, on the other hand, is a proprietary scheme that must be licensed by chip manufacturers.

8.2.5   STRUCTURE OF LARGER MEMORIES

We have discussed the basic organization of memory circuits as they may be implemented on a single chip. Next, we examine how memory chips may be connected to form a much larger memory.

Static Memory Systems

Consider a memory consisting of 2M words of 32 bits each. Figure 8.10 shows how this memory can be implemented using 512K × 8 static memory chips. Each column in the figure implements one byte position in a word, with four chips providing 2M bytes. Four columns implement the required 2M × 32 memory. Each chip has a control input called

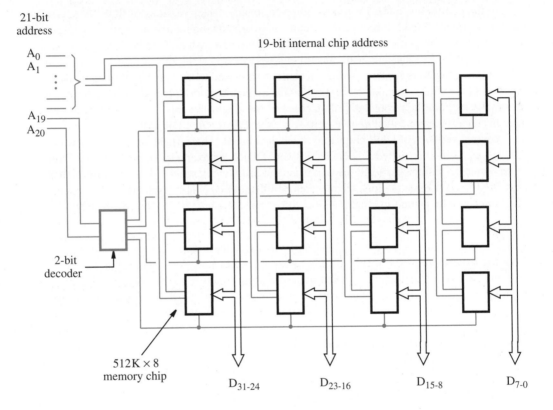

Figure 8.10   Organization of a 2M × 32 memory module using 512K × 8 static memory chips.

Chip-select. When this input is set to 1, it enables the chip to accept data from or to place data on its data lines. The data output for each chip is of the tri-state type described in Section 7.2.3. Only the selected chip places data on the data output line, while all other outputs are electrically disconnected from the data lines. Twenty-one address bits are needed to select a 32-bit word in this memory. The high-order two bits of the address are decoded to determine which of the four rows should be selected. The remaining 19 address bits are used to access specific byte locations inside each chip in the selected row. The $R/\overline{W}$ inputs of all chips are tied together to provide a common Read/Write control line (not shown in the figure).

Dynamic Memory Systems

Modern computers use very large memories. Even a small personal computer is likely to have at least 1G bytes of memory. Typical desktop computers may have 4G bytes or more of memory. A large memory leads to better performance, because more of the programs and data used in processing can be held in the memory, thus reducing the frequency of access to secondary storage.

Because of their high bit density and low cost, dynamic RAMs, mostly of the synchronous type, are widely used in the memory units of computers. They are slower than static RAMs, but they use less power and have considerably lower cost per bit. Available chips have capacities as high as 2G bits, and even larger chips are being developed. To reduce the number of memory chips needed in a given computer, a memory chip may be organized to read or write a number of bits in parallel, as in the case of Figure 8.7. Chips are manufactured in different organizations, to provide flexibility in designing memory systems. For example, a 1-Gbit chip may be organized as 256M $\times$ 4, or 128M $\times$ 8.

Packaging considerations have led to the development of assemblies known as memory modules. Each such module houses many memory chips, typically in the range 16 to 32, on a small board that plugs into a socket on the computer's motherboard. Memory modules are commonly called *SIMM*s (Single In-line Memory Modules) or *DIMM*s (Dual In-line Memory Modules), depending on the configuration of the pins. Modules of different sizes are designed to use the same socket. For example, 128M $\times$ 64, 256M $\times$ 64, and 512M $\times$ 64 bit DIMMs all use the same 240-pin socket. Thus, total memory capacity is easily expanded by replacing a smaller module with a larger one, using the same socket.

Memory Controller

The address applied to dynamic RAM chips is divided into two parts, as explained earlier. The high-order address bits, which select a row in the cell array, are provided first and latched into the memory chip under control of the RAS signal. Then, the low-order address bits, which select a column, are provided on the same address pins and latched under control of the CAS signal. Since a typical processor issues all bits of an address at the same time, a multiplexer is required. This function is usually performed by a *memory controller* circuit. The controller accepts a complete address and the $R/\overline{W}$ signal from the processor, under control of a *Request* signal which indicates that a memory access operation is needed. It forwards the $R/\overline{W}$ signals and the row and column portions of the address to the memory and generates the RAS and CAS signals, with the appropriate timing. When a memory includes multiple modules, one of these modules is selected based on the high-order bits of the address. The memory controller decodes these high-order bits and generates the chip-select signal for the appropriate module. Data lines are connected directly between the processor and the memory.

Dynamic RAMs must be refreshed periodically. The circuitry required to initiate refresh cycles is included as part of the internal control circuitry of synchronous DRAMs. However, a control circuit external to the chip is needed to initiate periodic Read cycles to refresh the cells of an asynchronous DRAM. The memory controller provides this capability.

Refresh Overhead

A dynamic RAM cannot respond to read or write requests while an internal refresh operation is taking place. Such requests are delayed until the refresh cycle is completed. However, the time lost to accommodate refresh operations is very small. For example, consider an SDRAM in which each row needs to be refreshed once every 64 ms. Suppose that the minimum time between two row accesses is 50 ns and that refresh operations are arranged such that all rows of the chip are refreshed in 8K (8192) refresh cycles. Thus, it takes $8192 \times 0.050 = 0.41$ ms to refresh all rows. The refresh overhead is $0.41/64 = 0.0064$, which is less than 1 percent of the total time available for accessing the memory.

Choice of Technology

The choice of a RAM chip for a given application depends on several factors. Foremost among these are the cost, speed, power dissipation, and size of the chip.

Static RAMs are characterized by their very fast operation. However, their cost and bit density are adversely affected by the complexity of the circuit that realizes the basic cell. They are used mostly where a small but very fast memory is needed. Dynamic RAMs, on the other hand, have high bit densities and a low cost per bit. Synchronous DRAMs are the predominant choice for implementing the main memory.

8.3 READ-ONLY MEMORIES

Both static and dynamic RAM chips are volatile, which means that they retain information only while power is turned on. There are many applications requiring memory devices that retain the stored information when power is turned off. For example, Chapter 4 describes the need to store a small program in such a memory, to be used to start the bootstrap process of loading the operating system from a hard disk into the main memory. The embedded applications described in Chapters 10 and 11 are another important example. Many embedded applications do not use a hard disk and require nonvolatile memories to store their software.

Different types of nonvolatile memories have been developed. Generally, their contents can be read in the same way as for their volatile counterparts discussed above. But, a special writing process is needed to place the information into a nonvolatile memory. Since its normal operation involves only reading the stored data, a memory of this type is called a *read-only memory* (ROM).

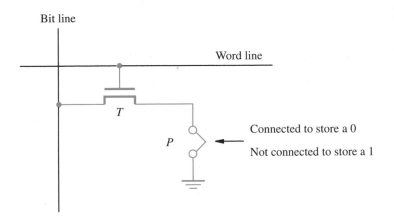

Figure 8.11   A ROM cell.

8.3.1   ROM

A memory is called a read-only memory, or ROM, when information can be written into it only once at the time of manufacture. Figure 8.11 shows a possible configuration for a ROM cell. A logic value 0 is stored in the cell if the transistor is connected to ground at point P; otherwise, a 1 is stored. The bit line is connected through a resistor to the power supply. To read the state of the cell, the word line is activated to close the transistor switch. As a result, the voltage on the bit line drops to near zero if there is a connection between the transistor and ground. If there is no connection to ground, the bit line remains at the high voltage level, indicating a 1. A sense circuit at the end of the bit line generates the proper output value. The state of the connection to ground in each cell is determined when the chip is manufactured, using a mask with a pattern that represents the information to be stored.

8.3.2   PROM

Some ROM designs allow the data to be loaded by the user, thus providing a *programmable ROM* (PROM). Programmability is achieved by inserting a fuse at point P in Figure 8.11. Before it is programmed, the memory contains all 0s. The user can insert 1s at the required locations by burning out the fuses at these locations using high-current pulses. Of course, this process is irreversible.

PROMs provide flexibility and convenience not available with ROMs. The cost of preparing the masks needed for storing a particular information pattern makes ROMs cost-effective only in large volumes. The alternative technology of PROMs provides a more convenient and considerably less expensive approach, because memory chips can be programmed directly by the user.

8.3.3   EPROM

Another type of ROM chip provides an even higher level of convenience. It allows the stored data to be erased and new data to be written into it. Such an *erasable*, reprogrammable ROM is usually called an *EPROM*. It provides considerable flexibility during the development phase of digital systems. Since EPROMs are capable of retaining stored information for a long time, they can be used in place of ROMs or PROMs while software is being developed. In this way, memory changes and updates can be easily made.

An EPROM cell has a structure similar to the ROM cell in Figure 8.11. However, the connection to ground at point P is made through a special transistor. The transistor is normally turned off, creating an open switch. It can be turned on by injecting charge into it that becomes trapped inside. Thus, an EPROM cell can be used to construct a memory in the same way as the previously discussed ROM cell. Erasure requires dissipating the charge trapped in the transistors that form the memory cells. This can be done by exposing the chip to ultraviolet light, which erases the entire contents of the chip. To make this possible, EPROM chips are mounted in packages that have transparent windows.

8.3.4   EEPROM

An EPROM must be physically removed from the circuit for reprogramming. Also, the stored information cannot be erased selectively. The entire contents of the chip are erased when exposed to ultraviolet light. Another type of erasable PROM can be programmed, erased, and reprogrammed electrically. Such a chip is called an *electrically erasable* PROM, or EEPROM. It does not have to be removed for erasure. Moreover, it is possible to erase the cell contents selectively. One disadvantage of EEPROMs is that different voltages are needed for erasing, writing, and reading the stored data, which increases circuit complexity. However, this disadvantage is outweighed by the many advantages of EEPROMs. They have replaced EPROMs in practice.

8.3.5   FLASH MEMORY

An approach similar to EEPROM technology has given rise to *flash memory* devices. A flash cell is based on a single transistor controlled by trapped charge, much like an EEPROM cell. Also like an EEPROM, it is possible to read the contents of a single cell. The key difference is that, in a flash device, it is only possible to write an entire block of cells. Prior to writing, the previous contents of the block are erased. Flash devices have greater density, which leads to higher capacity and a lower cost per bit. They require a single power supply voltage, and consume less power in their operation.

The low power consumption of flash memories makes them attractive for use in portable, battery-powered equipment. Typical applications include hand-held computers, cell phones, digital cameras, and MP3 music players. In hand-held computers and cell phones, a flash memory holds the software needed to operate the equipment, thus obviating the need for a disk drive. A flash memory is used in digital cameras to store picture data. In MP3 players, flash memories store the data that represent sound. Cell phones, digital cameras, and MP3 players are good examples of embedded systems, which are discussed in Chapters 10 and 11.

Single flash chips may not provide sufficient storage capacity for the applications mentioned above. Larger memory modules consisting of a number of chips are used where needed. There are two popular choices for the implementation of such modules: flash cards and flash drives.

Flash Cards

One way of constructing a larger module is to mount flash chips on a small card. Such flash cards have a standard interface that makes them usable in a variety of products. A card is simply plugged into a conveniently accessible slot. Flash cards with a USB interface are widely used and are commonly known as memory keys. They come in a variety of memory sizes. Larger cards may hold as much as 32 Gbytes. A minute of music can be stored in about 1 Mbyte of memory, using the MP3 encoding format. Hence, a 32-Gbyte flash card can store approximately 500 hours of music.

Flash Drives

Larger flash memory modules have been developed to replace hard disk drives, and hence are called flash drives. They are designed to fully emulate hard disks, to the point that they can be fitted into standard disk drive bays. However, the storage capacity of flash drives is significantly lower. Currently, the capacity of flash drives is on the order of 64 to 128 Gbytes. In contrast, hard disks have capacities exceeding a terabyte. Also, disk drives have a very low cost per bit.

The fact that flash drives are solid state electronic devices with no moving parts provides important advantages over disk drives. They have shorter access times, which result in a faster response. They are insensitive to vibration and they have lower power consumption, which makes them attractive for portable, battery-driven applications.

8.4 DIRECT MEMORY ACCESS

Blocks of data are often transferred between the main memory and I/O devices such as disks. This section discusses a technique for controlling such transfers without frequent, program-controlled intervention by the processor.

The discussion in Chapter 3 concentrates on single-word or single-byte data transfers between the processor and I/O devices. Data are transferred from an I/O device to the memory by first reading them from the I/O device using an instruction such as

Load   R2, DATAIN

which loads the data into a processor register. Then, the data read are stored into a memory location. The reverse process takes place for transferring data from the memory to an I/O device. An instruction to transfer input or output data is executed only after the processor determines that the I/O device is ready, either by polling its status register or by waiting for an interrupt request. In either case, considerable overhead is incurred, because several program instructions must be executed involving many memory accesses for each data word transferred. When transferring a block of data, instructions are needed to increment the memory address and keep track of the word count. The use of interrupts involves operating system routines which incur additional overhead to save and restore processor registers, the program counter, and other state information.

An alternative approach is used to transfer blocks of data directly between the main memory and I/O devices, such as disks. A special control unit is provided to manage the transfer, without continuous intervention by the processor. This approach is called *direct memory access*, or DMA. The unit that controls DMA transfers is referred to as a *DMA controller*. It may be part of the I/O device interface, or it may be a separate unit shared by a number of I/O devices. The DMA controller performs the functions that would normally be carried out by the processor when accessing the main memory. For each word transferred, it provides the memory address and generates all the control signals needed. It increments the memory address for successive words and keeps track of the number of transfers.

Although a DMA controller transfers data without intervention by the processor, its operation must be under the control of a program executed by the processor, usually an operating system routine. To initiate the transfer of a block of words, the processor sends to the DMA controller the starting address, the number of words in the block, and the direction of the transfer. The DMA controller then proceeds to perform the requested operation. When the entire block has been transferred, it informs the processor by raising an interrupt.

Figure 8.12 shows an example of the DMA controller registers that are accessed by the processor to initiate data transfer operations. Two registers are used for storing the starting address and the word count. The third register contains status and control flags. The R/$\overline{\text{W}}$ bit determines the direction of the transfer. When this bit is set to 1 by a program instruction, the controller performs a Read operation, that is, it transfers data from the memory to the I/O device. Otherwise, it performs a Write operation. Additional information is also transferred as may be required by the I/O device. For example, in the case of a disk, the processor provides the disk controller with information to identify where the data is located on the disk (see Section 8.10.1 for disk details).

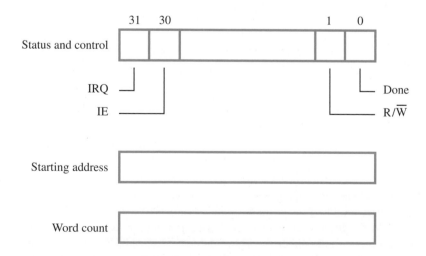

Figure 8.12   Typical registers in a DMA controller.

When the controller has completed transferring a block of data and is ready to receive another command, it sets the Done flag to 1. Bit 30 is the Interrupt-enable flag, IE. When this flag is set to 1, it causes the controller to raise an interrupt after it has completed transferring a block of data. Finally, the controller sets the IRQ bit to 1 when it has requested an interrupt.

Figure 8.13 shows how DMA controllers may be used in a computer system such as that in Figure 7.18. One DMA controller connects a high-speed Ethernet to the computer's I/O bus (a PCI bus in the case of Figure 7.18). The disk controller, which controls two disks, also has DMA capability and provides two DMA channels. It can perform two independent DMA operations, as if each disk had its own DMA controller. The registers needed to store the memory address, the word count, and so on, are duplicated, so that one set can be used with each disk.

To start a DMA transfer of a block of data from the main memory to one of the disks, an OS routine writes the address and word count information into the registers of the disk controller. The DMA controller proceeds independently to implement the specified operation. When the transfer is completed, this fact is recorded in the status and control register of the DMA channel by setting the Done bit. At the same time, if the IE bit is set, the controller sends an interrupt request to the processor and sets the IRQ bit. The status register may also be used to record other information, such as whether the transfer took place correctly or errors occurred.

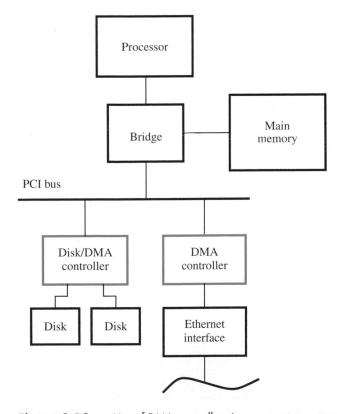

Figure 8.13   Use of DMA controllers in a computer system.

8.5   M EMORY H IERARCHY

We have already stated that an ideal memory would be fast, large, and inexpensive. From the discussion in Section 8.2, it is clear that a very fast memory can be implemented using static RAM chips. But, these chips are not suitable for implementing large memories, because their basic cells are larger and consume more power than dynamic RAM cells.

Although dynamic memory units with gigabyte capacities can be implemented at a reasonable cost, the affordable size is still small compared to the demands of large programs with voluminous data. A solution is provided by using secondary storage, mainly magnetic disks, to provide the required memory space. Disks are available at a reasonable cost, and they are used extensively in computer systems. However, they are much slower than semiconductor memory units. In summary, a very large amount of cost-effective storage can be provided by magnetic disks, and a large and considerably faster, yet affordable, main memory can be built with dynamic RAM technology. This leaves the more expensive and much faster static RAM technology to be used in smaller units where speed is of the essence, such as in cache memories.

All of these different types of memory units are employed effectively in a computer system. The entire computer memory can be viewed as the hierarchy depicted in Figure 8.14. The fastest access is to data held in processor registers. Therefore, if we consider the

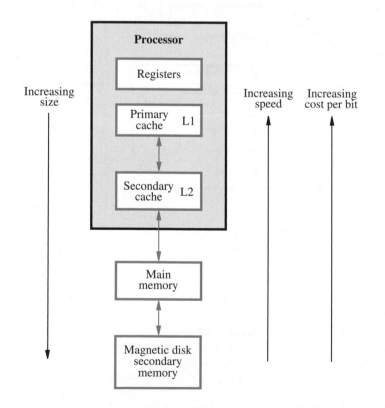

Figure 8.14   Memory hierarchy.

registers to be part of the memory hierarchy, then the processor registers are at the top in terms of speed of access. Of course, the registers provide only a minuscule portion of the required memory.

At the next level of the hierarchy is a relatively small amount of memory that can be implemented directly on the processor chip. This memory, called a *processor cache*, holds copies of the instructions and data stored in a much larger memory that is provided externally. The cache memory concept was introduced in Section 1.2.2 and is examined in detail in Section 8.6. There are often two or more levels of cache. A primary cache is always located on the processor chip. This cache is small and its access time is comparable to that of processor registers. The primary cache is referred to as the *level 1* (L1) cache. A larger, and hence somewhat slower, secondary cache is placed between the primary cache and the rest of the memory. It is referred to as the *level 2* (L2) cache. Often, the L2 cache is also housed on the processor chip.

Some computers have a *level 3* (L3) cache of even larger size, in addition to the L1 and L2 caches. An L3 cache, also implemented in SRAM technology, may or may not be on the same chip with the processor and the L1 and L2 caches.

The next level in the hierarchy is the *main memory*. This is a large memory implemented using dynamic memory components, typically assembled in memory modules such as DIMMs, as described in Section 8.2.5. The main memory is much larger but significantly slower than cache memories. In a computer with a processor clock of 2 GHz or higher, the access time for the main memory can be as much as 100 times longer than the access time for the L1 cache.

Disk devices provide a very large amount of inexpensive memory, and they are widely used as secondary storage in computer systems. They are very slow compared to the main memory. They represent the bottom level in the memory hierarchy.

During program execution, the speed of memory access is of utmost importance. The key to managing the operation of the hierarchical memory system in Figure 8.14 is to bring the instructions and data that are about to be used as close to the processor as possible. This is the main purpose of using cache memories, which we discuss next.

8.6 CACHE MEMORIES

The cache is a small and very fast memory, interposed between the processor and the main memory. Its purpose is to make the main memory appear to the processor to be much faster than it actually is. The effectiveness of this approach is based on a property of computer programs called *locality of reference*. Analysis of programs shows that most of their execution time is spent in routines in which many instructions are executed repeatedly. These instructions may constitute a simple loop, nested loops, or a few procedures that repeatedly call each other. The actual detailed pattern of instruction sequencing is not important—the point is that many instructions in localized areas of the program are executed repeatedly during some time period. This behavior manifests itself in two ways: temporal and spatial. The first means that a recently executed instruction is likely to be executed again very soon. The spatial aspect means that instructions close to a recently executed instruction are also likely to be executed soon.

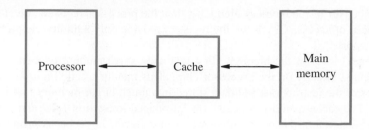

Figure 8.15   Use of a cache memory.

Conceptually, operation of a cache memory is very simple. The memory control circuitry is designed to take advantage of the property of locality of reference. Temporal locality suggests that whenever an information item, instruction or data, is first needed, this item should be brought into the cache, because it is likely to be needed again soon. Spatial locality suggests that instead of fetching just one item from the main memory to the cache, it is useful to fetch several items that are located at adjacent addresses as well. The term *cache block* refers to a set of contiguous address locations of some size. Another term that is often used to refer to a cache block is a *cache line*.

Consider the arrangement in Figure 8.15. When the processor issues a Read request, the contents of a block of memory words containing the location specified are transferred into the cache. Subsequently, when the program references any of the locations in this block, the desired contents are read directly from the cache. Usually, the cache memory can store a reasonable number of blocks at any given time, but this number is small compared to the total number of blocks in the main memory. The correspondence between the main memory blocks and those in the cache is specified by a *mapping function*. When the cache is full and a memory word (instruction or data) that is not in the cache is referenced, the cache control hardware must decide which block should be removed to create space for the new block that contains the referenced word. The collection of rules for making this decision constitutes the cache's *replacement algorithm*.

Cache Hits

The processor does not need to know explicitly about the existence of the cache. It simply issues Read and Write requests using addresses that refer to locations in the memory. The cache control circuitry determines whether the requested word currently exists in the cache. If it does, the Read or Write operation is performed on the appropriate cache location. In this case, a *read* or *write hit* is said to have occurred. The main memory is not involved when there is a cache hit in a Read operation. For a Write operation, the system can proceed in one of two ways. In the first technique, called the *write-through* protocol, both the cache location and the main memory location are updated. The second technique is to update only the cache location and to mark the block containing it with an associated flag bit, often called the *dirty* or *modified bit*. The main memory location of the word is updated later, when the block containing this marked word is removed from the cache to make room for a new block. This technique is known as the *write-back*, or *copy-back*, protocol.

The write-through protocol is simpler than the write-back protocol, but it results in unnecessary Write operations in the main memory when a given cache word is updated several times during its cache residency. The write-back protocol also involves unnecessary Write operations, because all words of the block are eventually written back, even if only a single word has been changed while the block was in the cache. The write-back protocol is used most often, to take advantage of the high speed with which data blocks can be transferred to memory chips.

Cache Misses

A Read operation for a word that is not in the cache constitutes a *Read miss*. It causes the block of words containing the requested word to be copied from the main memory into the cache. After the entire block is loaded into the cache, the particular word requested is forwarded to the processor. Alternatively, this word may be sent to the processor as soon as it is read from the main memory. The latter approach, which is called *load-through*, or *early restart*, reduces the processor's waiting time somewhat, at the expense of more complex circuitry.

When a *Write miss* occurs in a computer that uses the write-through protocol, the information is written directly into the main memory. For the write-back protocol, the block containing the addressed word is first brought into the cache, and then the desired word in the cache is overwritten with the new information.

Recall from Section 6.7 that resource limitations in a pipelined processor can cause instruction execution to stall for one or more cycles. This can occur if a Load or Store instruction requests access to data in the memory at the same time that a subsequent instruction is being fetched. When this happens, instruction fetch is delayed until the data access operation is completed. To avoid stalling the pipeline, many processors use separate caches for instructions and data, making it possible for the two operations to proceed in parallel.

8.6.1   MAPPING FUNCTIONS

There are several possible methods for determining where memory blocks are placed in the cache. It is instructive to describe these methods using a specific small example. Consider a cache consisting of 128 blocks of 16 words each, for a total of 2048 (2K) words, and assume that the main memory is addressable by a 16-bit address. The main memory has 64K words, which we will view as 4K blocks of 16 words each. For simplicity, we have assumed that consecutive addresses refer to consecutive words.

Direct Mapping

The simplest way to determine cache locations in which to store memory blocks is the *direct-mapping* technique. In this technique, block j of the main memory maps onto block j modulo 128 of the cache, as depicted in Figure 8.16. Thus, whenever one of the main memory blocks 0, 128, 256, ... is loaded into the cache, it is stored in cache block 0. Blocks 1, 129, 257, ... are stored in cache block 1, and so on. Since more than one memory block is mapped onto a given cache block position, contention may arise for that position even when the cache is not full. For example, instructions of a program may start in block 1 and continue in block 129, possibly after a branch. As this program is executed,

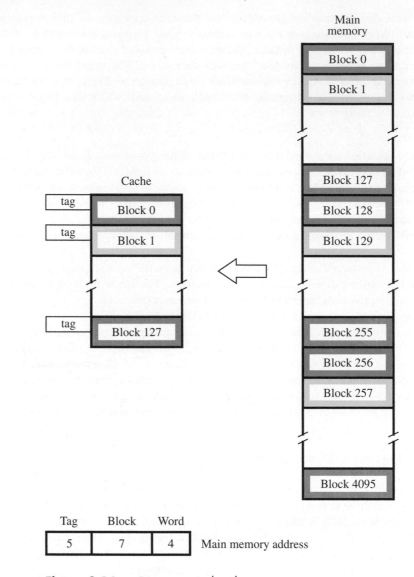

Figure 8.16   Direct-mapped cache.

both of these blocks must be transferred to the block-1 position in the cache. Contention is resolved by allowing the new block to overwrite the currently resident block.

With direct mapping, the replacement algorithm is trivial. Placement of a block in the cache is determined by its memory address. The memory address can be divided into three fields, as shown in Figure 8.16. The low-order 4 bits select one of 16 words in a block. When a new block enters the cache, the 7-bit cache block field determines the cache position in which this block must be stored. The high-order 5 bits of the memory address of the block are stored in 5 *tag* bits associated with its location in the cache. The tag bits identify which of the 32 main memory blocks mapped into this cache position is currently resident in the cache. As execution proceeds, the 7-bit cache block field of each address generated by the processor points to a particular block location in the cache. The high-order 5 bits of the address are compared with the tag bits associated with that cache location. If they match, then the desired word is in that block of the cache. If there is no match, then the block containing the required word must first be read from the main memory and loaded into the cache. The direct-mapping technique is easy to implement, but it is not very flexible.

Associative Mapping

Figure 8.17 shows the most flexible mapping method, in which a main memory block can be placed into any cache block position. In this case, 12 tag bits are required to identify a memory block when it is resident in the cache. The tag bits of an address received from the processor are compared to the tag bits of each block of the cache to see if the desired block is present. This is called the *associative-mapping* technique. It gives complete freedom in

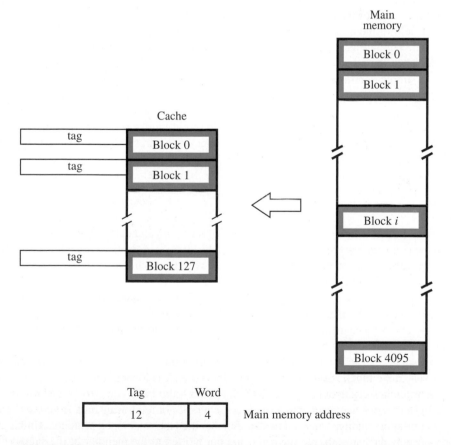

Figure 8.17   Associative-mapped cache.

choosing the cache location in which to place the memory block, resulting in a more efficient use of the space in the cache. When a new block is brought into the cache, it replaces (ejects) an existing block only if the cache is full. In this case, we need an algorithm to select the block to be replaced. Many replacement algorithms are possible, as we discuss in Section 8.6.2. The complexity of an associative cache is higher than that of a direct-mapped cache, because of the need to search all 128 tag patterns to determine whether a given block is in the cache. To avoid a long delay, the tags must be searched in parallel. A search of this kind is called an *associative search*.

Set-Associative Mapping

Another approach is to use a combination of the direct- and associative-mapping techniques. The blocks of the cache are grouped into sets, and the mapping allows a block of the main memory to reside in any block of a specific set. Hence, the contention problem of the direct method is eased by having a few choices for block placement. At the same time, the hardware cost is reduced by decreasing the size of the associative search. An example of this *set-associative-mapping* technique is shown in Figure 8.18 for a cache with two blocks per set. In this case, memory blocks 0, 64, 128, . . . , 4032 map into cache set 0, and they can occupy either of the two block positions within this set. Having 64 sets means that the 6-bit set field of the address determines which set of the cache might contain the desired block. The tag field of the address must then be associatively compared to the tags of the two blocks of the set to check if the desired block is present. This two-way associative search is simple to implement.

The number of blocks per set is a parameter that can be selected to suit the requirements of a particular computer. For the main memory and cache sizes in Figure 8.18, four blocks per set can be accommodated by a 5-bit set field, eight blocks per set by a 4-bit set field, and so on. The extreme condition of 128 blocks per set requires no set bits and corresponds to the fully-associative technique, with 12 tag bits. The other extreme of one block per set is the direct-mapping method. A cache that has k blocks per set is referred to as a k-way set-associative cache.

Stale Data

When power is first turned on, the cache contains no valid data. A control bit, usually called the *valid bit*, must be provided for each cache block to indicate whether the data in that block are valid. This bit should not be confused with the modified, or dirty, bit mentioned earlier. The valid bits of all cache blocks are set to 0 when power is initially applied to the system. Some valid bits may also be set to 0 when new programs or data are loaded from the disk into the main memory. Data transferred from the disk to the main memory using the DMA mechanism are usually loaded directly into the main memory, bypassing the cache. If the memory blocks being updated are currently in the cache, the valid bits of the corresponding cache blocks are set to 0. As program execution proceeds, the valid bit of a given cache block is set to 1 when a memory block is loaded into that location. The processor fetches data from a cache block only if its valid bit is equal to 1. The use of the valid bit in this manner ensures that the processor will not fetch *stale* data from the cache.

A similar precaution is needed in a system that uses the write-back protocol. Under this protocol, new data written into the cache are not written to the memory at the same time.

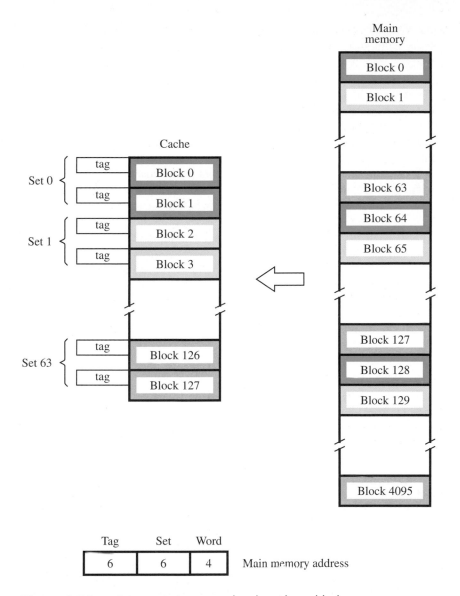

Figure 8.18   Set-associative-mapped cache with two blocks per set.

Hence, data in the memory do not always reflect the changes that may have been made in the cached copy. It is important to ensure that such stale data in the memory are not transferred to the disk. One solution is to *flush* the cache, by forcing all dirty blocks to be written back to the memory before performing the transfer. The operating system can do this by issuing a command to the cache before initiating the DMA operation that transfers the data to the disk. Flushing the cache does not affect performance greatly, because such disk transfers do not occur often. The need to ensure that two different entities (the processor and the DMA subsystems in this case) use identical copies of the data is referred to as a *cache-coherence* problem.

8.6.2   REPLACEMENT ALGORITHMS

In a direct-mapped cache, the position of each block is predetermined by its address; hence, the replacement strategy is trivial. In associative and set-associative caches there exists some flexibility. When a new block is to be brought into the cache and all the positions that it may occupy are full, the cache controller must decide which of the old blocks to overwrite. This is an important issue, because the decision can be a strong determining factor in system performance. In general, the objective is to keep blocks in the cache that are likely to be referenced in the near future. But, it is not easy to determine which blocks are about to be referenced. The property of locality of reference in programs gives a clue to a reasonable strategy. Because program execution usually stays in localized areas for reasonable periods of time, there is a high probability that the blocks that have been referenced recently will be referenced again soon. Therefore, when a block is to be overwritten, it is sensible to overwrite the one that has gone the longest time without being referenced. This block is called the *least recently used* (LRU) block, and the technique is called the *LRU replacement algorithm*.

To use the LRU algorithm, the cache controller must track references to all blocks as computation proceeds. Suppose it is required to track the LRU block of a four-block set in a set-associative cache. A 2-bit counter can be used for each block. When a hit occurs, the counter of the block that is referenced is set to 0. Counters with values originally lower than the referenced one are incremented by one, and all others remain unchanged. When a *miss* occurs and the set is not full, the counter associated with the new block loaded from the main memory is set to 0, and the values of all other counters are increased by one. When a miss occurs and the set is full, the block with the counter value 3 is removed, the new block is put in its place, and its counter is set to 0. The other three block counters are incremented by one. It can be easily verified that the counter values of occupied blocks are always distinct.

The LRU algorithm has been used extensively. Although it performs well for many access patterns, it can lead to poor performance in some cases. For example, it produces disappointing results when accesses are made to sequential elements of an array that is slightly too large to fit into the cache (see Section 8.6.3 and Problem 8.11). Performance of the LRU algorithm can be improved by introducing a small amount of randomness in deciding which block to replace.

Several other replacement algorithms are also used in practice. An intuitively reasonable rule would be to remove the "oldest" block from a full set when a new block must be brought in. However, because this algorithm does not take into account the recent pattern of access to blocks in the cache, it is generally not as effective as the LRU algorithm in choosing the best blocks to remove. The simplest algorithm is to randomly choose the block to be overwritten. Interestingly enough, this simple algorithm has been found to be quite effective in practice.

8.6.3 EXAMPLES OF MAPPING TECHNIQUES

We now consider a detailed example to illustrate the effects of different cache mapping techniques. Assume that a processor has separate instruction and data caches. To keep the example simple, assume the data cache has space for only eight blocks of data. Also assume that each block consists of only one 16-bit word of data and the memory is word-addressable with 16-bit addresses. (These parameters are not realistic for actual computers, but they allow us to illustrate mapping techniques clearly.) Finally, assume the LRU replacement algorithm is used for block replacement in the cache.

Let us examine changes in the data cache entries caused by running the following application. A 4×10 array of numbers, each occupying one word, is stored in main memory locations 7A00 through 7A27 (hex). The elements of this array, A, are stored in column order, as shown in Figure 8.19. The figure also indicates how tags for different cache mapping techniques are derived from the memory address. Note that no bits are needed to identify a word within a block, as was done in Figures 8.16 through 8.18, because we have assumed that each block contains only one word. The application normalizes the elements of the first row of A with respect to the average value of the elements in the row. Hence, we need to compute the average of the elements in the row and divide each element by that average. The required task can be expressed as

$$A(0, i) \leftarrow \frac{A(0, i)}{\left(\sum_{j=0}^{9} A(0, j)\right)/10} \qquad \text{for } i = 0, 1, \ldots, 9$$

	Memory address	Contents
(7A00)	0 1 1 1 1 0 1 0 0 0 0 0 0 0 0 0	A(0,0)
(7A01)	0 1 1 1 1 0 1 0 0 0 0 0 0 0 0 1	A(1,0)
(7A02)	0 1 1 1 1 0 1 0 0 0 0 0 0 0 1 0	A(2,0)
(7A03)	0 1 1 1 1 0 1 0 0 0 0 0 0 0 1 1	A(3,0)
(7A04)	0 1 1 1 1 0 1 0 0 0 0 0 0 1 0 0	A(0,1)
	⋮	
(7A24)	0 1 1 1 1 0 1 0 0 0 1 0 0 1 0 0	A(0,9)
(7A25)	0 1 1 1 1 0 1 0 0 0 1 0 0 1 0 1	A(1,9)
(7A26)	0 1 1 1 1 0 1 0 0 0 1 0 0 1 1 0	A(2,9)
(7A27)	0 1 1 1 1 0 1 0 0 0 1 0 0 1 1 1	A(3,9)

← Tag for direct mapped →

← Tag for set-associative →

← Tag for associative →

Figure 8.19 An array stored in the main memory.

```
SUM := 0
for j := 0 to 9 do
        SUM := SUM + A(0,j)
end
AVG := SUM/10
for i := 9 downto 0 do
        A(0,i) := A(0,i)/AVG
end
```

Figure 8.20   Task for example in Section 8.6.3.

Figure 8.20 gives the structure of a program that corresponds to this task. We use the variables SUM and AVE to hold the sum and average values, respectively. These variables, as well as index variables i and j, are held in processor registers during the computation.

Direct-Mapped Cache

In a direct-mapped data cache, the contents of the cache change as shown in Figure 8.21. The columns in the table indicate the cache contents after various passes through the two program loops in Figure 8.20 are completed. For example, after the second pass through the first loop ($j = 1$), the cache holds the elements $A(0, 0)$ and $A(0, 1)$. These elements are in block positions 0 and 4, as determined by the three least-significant bits of the address. During the next pass, the $A(0, 0)$ element is replaced by $A(0, 2)$, which maps into the same block position. Note that the desired elements map into only two positions in the cache, thus leaving the contents of the other six positions unchanged from whatever they were before the normalization task started.

Elements $A(0, 8)$ and $A(0, 9)$ are loaded into the cache during the ninth and tenth passes through the first loop ($j = 8, 9$). The second loop reverses the order in which the elements are handled. The first two passes through this loop ($i = 9, 8$) find the required data in the cache. When $i = 7$, element $A(0, 9)$ is replaced with $A(0, 7)$. When $i = 6$, element $A(0, 8)$

Block position	Contents of data cache after pass:								
	$j = 1$	$j = 3$	$j = 5$	$j = 7$	$j = 9$	$i = 6$	$i = 4$	$i = 2$	$i = 0$
0	A(0,0)	A(0,2)	A(0,4)	A(0,6)	A(0,8)	A(0,6)	A(0,4)	A(0,2)	A(0,0)
1									
2									
3									
4	A(0,1)	A(0,3)	A(0,5)	A(0,7)	A(0,9)	A(0,7)	A(0,5)	A(0,3)	A(0,1)
5									
6									
7									

Figure 8.21   Contents of a direct-mapped data cache.

is replaced with $A(0, 6)$, and so on. Thus, eight elements are replaced while the second loop is executed. In total, there are only two hits during execution of this task.

The reader should keep in mind that the tags must be kept in the cache for each block. They are not shown to keep the figure simple.

Associative-Mapped Cache

Figure 8.22 presents the changes in cache contents for the case of an associative-mapped cache. During the first eight passes through the first loop, the elements are brought into consecutive block positions, assuming that the cache was initially empty. During the ninth pass ($j = 8$), the LRU algorithm chooses $A(0, 0)$ to be overwritten by $A(0, 8)$. In the next and last pass through the j loop, element $A(0, 1)$ is replaced with $A(0, 9)$. Now, for the first eight passes through the second loop ($i = 9, 8, \ldots, 2$) all the required elements are found in the cache. When $i = 1$, the element needed is $A(0, 1)$, so it replaces the least recently used element, $A(0, 9)$. During the last pass, $A(0, 0)$ replaces $A(0, 8)$.

In this case, when the second loop is executed, only two elements are not found in the cache. In the direct-mapped case, eight of the elements had to be reloaded during the second loop. Obviously, the associative-mapped cache benefits from the complete freedom in mapping a memory block into any position in the cache. In both cases, better utilization of the cache is achieved by reversing the order in which the elements are handled in the second loop of the program. It is interesting to consider what would happen if the second loop dealt with the elements in the same order as in the first loop. Using either direct mapping or the LRU algorithm, all elements would be overwritten before they are used in the second loop (see Problem 8.10).

Set-Associative-Mapped Cache

For this example, we assume that a set-associative data cache is organized into two sets, each capable of holding four blocks. Thus, the least-significant bit of an address determines which set a memory block maps into, but the memory data can be placed in any of the four blocks of the set. The high-order 15 bits of the address constitute the tag.

Block position	Contents of data cache after pass:				
	$j = 7$	$j = 8$	$j = 9$	$i = 1$	$i = 0$
0	A(0,0)	A(0,8)	A(0,8)	A(0,8)	A(0,0)
1	A(0,1)	A(0,1)	A(0,9)	A(0,1)	A(0,1)
2	A(0,2)	A(0,2)	A(0,2)	A(0,2)	A(0,2)
3	A(0,3)	A(0,3)	A(0,3)	A(0,3)	A(0,3)
4	A(0,4)	A(0,4)	A(0,4)	A(0,4)	A(0,4)
5	A(0,5)	A(0,5)	A(0,5)	A(0,5)	A(0,5)
6	A(0,6)	A(0,6)	A(0,6)	A(0,6)	A(0,6)
7	A(0,7)	A(0,7)	A(0,7)	A(0,7)	A(0,7)

Figure 8.22   Contents of an associative-mapped data cache.

	Contents of data cache after pass:					
	$j = 3$	$j = 7$	$j = 9$	$i = 4$	$i = 2$	$i = 0$
Set 0	A(0,0)	A(0,4)	A(0,8)	A(0,4)	A(0,4)	A(0,0)
	A(0,1)	A(0,5)	A(0,9)	A(0,5)	A(0,5)	A(0,1)
	A(0,2)	A(0,6)	A(0,6)	A(0,6)	A(0,2)	A(0,2)
	A(0,3)	A(0,7)	A(0,7)	A(0,7)	A(0,3)	A(0,3)
Set 1						

Figure 8.23   Contents of a set-associative-mapped data cache.

Changes in the cache contents are depicted in Figure 8.23. Since all the desired blocks have even addresses, they map into set 0. In this case, six elements are reloaded during execution of the second loop.

Even though this is a simplified example, it illustrates that in general, associative mapping performs best, set-associative mapping is next best, and direct mapping is the worst. However, fully-associative mapping is expensive to implement, so set-associative mapping is a good practical compromise.

8.7   PERFORMANCE CONSIDERATIONS

Two key factors in the commercial success of a computer are performance and cost; the best possible performance for a given cost is the objective. A common measure of success is the *price/performance ratio*. Performance depends on how fast machine instructions can be brought into the processor and how fast they can be executed. Chapter 6 shows how pipelining increases the speed of program execution. In this chapter, we focus on the memory subsystem.

The memory hierarchy described in Section 8.5 results from the quest for the best price/performance ratio. The main purpose of this hierarchy is to create a memory that the processor sees as having a short access time and a large capacity. When a cache is used, the processor is able to access instructions and data more quickly when the data from the referenced memory locations are in the cache. Therefore, the extent to which caches improve performance is dependent on how frequently the requested instructions and data are found in the cache. In this section, we examine this issue quantitatively.

8.7.1 HIT RATE AND MISS PENALTY

An excellent indicator of the effectiveness of a particular implementation of the memory hierarchy is the success rate in accessing information at various levels of the hierarchy. Recall that a successful access to data in a cache is called a hit. The number of hits stated as a fraction of all attempted accesses is called the *hit rate*, and the *miss rate* is the number of misses stated as a fraction of attempted accesses.

Ideally, the entire memory hierarchy would appear to the processor as a single memory unit that has the access time of the cache on the processor chip and the size of the magnetic disk. How close we get to this ideal depends largely on the hit rate at different levels of the hierarchy. High hit rates well over 0.9 are essential for high-performance computers.

Performance is adversely affected by the actions that need to be taken when a miss occurs. A performance penalty is incurred because of the extra time needed to bring a block of data from a slower unit in the memory hierarchy to a faster unit. During that period, the processor is stalled waiting for instructions or data. The waiting time depends on the details of the operation of the cache. For example, it depends on whether or not the load-through approach is used. We refer to the total access time seen by the processor when a miss occurs as the *miss penalty*.

Consider a system with only one level of cache. In this case, the miss penalty consists almost entirely of the time to access a block of data in the main memory. Let h be the hit rate, M the miss penalty, and C the time to access information in the cache. Thus, the average access time experienced by the processor is

$$t_{avg} = hC + (1 - h)M$$

The following example illustrates how the values of these parameters affect the average access time.

Consider a computer that has the following parameters. Access times to the cache and the main memory are τ and 10τ, respectively. When a cache miss occurs, a block of 8 words is transferred from the main memory to the cache. It takes 10τ to transfer the first word of the block, and the remaining 7 words are transferred at the rate of one word every τ seconds. The miss penalty also includes a delay of τ for the initial access to the cache, which misses, and another delay of τ to transfer the word to the processor after the block is loaded into the cache (assuming no load-through). Thus, the miss penalty in this computer is given by: **Example 8.1**

$$M = \tau + 10\tau + 7\tau + \tau = 19\tau$$

Assume that 30 percent of the instructions in a typical program perform a Read or a Write operation, which means that there are 130 memory accesses for every 100 instructions executed. Assume that the hit rates in the cache are 0.95 for instructions and 0.9 for data. Assume further that the miss penalty is the same for both read and write accesses. Then, a rough estimate of the improvement in memory performance that results from using the cache can be obtained as follows:

$$\frac{\text{Time without cache}}{\text{Time with cache}} = \frac{130 \times 10\tau}{100(0.95\tau + 0.05 \times 19\tau) + 30(0.9\tau + 0.1 \times 19\tau)} = 4.7$$

This result shows that the cache makes the memory appear almost five times faster than it really is. The improvement factor increases as the speed of the cache increases relative to the main memory. For example, if the access time of the main memory is 20τ, the improvement factor becomes 7.3.

High hit rates are essential for the cache to be effective in reducing memory access time. Hit rates depend on the size of the cache, its design, and the instruction and data access patterns of the programs being executed. It is instructive to consider how effective the cache of this example is compared to the ideal case in which the hit rate is 100 percent. With ideal cache behavior, all memory references take one τ. Thus, an estimate of the increase in memory access time caused by misses in the cache is given by:

$$\frac{\text{Time for real cache}}{\text{Time for ideal cache}} = \frac{100(0.95\tau + 0.05 \times 19\tau) + 30(0.9\tau + 0.1 \times 19\tau)}{130\tau} = 2.1$$

In other words, a 100% hit rate in the cache would make the memory appear twice as fast as when realistic hit rates are used.

How can the hit rate be improved? One possibility is to make the cache larger, but this entails increased cost. Another possibility is to increase the cache block size while keeping the total cache size constant, to take advantage of spatial locality. If all items in a larger block are needed in a computation, then it is better to load these items into the cache in a single miss, rather than loading several smaller blocks as a result of several misses. The high data rate achievable during block transfers is the main reason for this advantage. But larger blocks are effective only up to a certain size, beyond which the improvement in the hit rate is offset by the fact that some items may not be referenced before the block is ejected (replaced). Also, larger blocks take longer to transfer, and hence increase the miss penalty. Since the performance of a computer is affected positively by increased hit rate and negatively by increased miss penalty, block size should be neither too small nor too large. In practice, block sizes in the range of 16 to 128 bytes are the most popular choices.

Finally, we note that the miss penalty can be reduced if the load-through approach is used when loading new blocks into the cache. Then, instead of waiting for an entire block to be transferred, the processor resumes execution as soon as the required word is loaded into the cache.

8.7.2 CACHES ON THE PROCESSOR CHIP

When information is transferred between different chips, considerable delays occur in driver and receiver gates on the chips. Thus, it is best to implement the cache on the processor chip. Most processor chips include at least one L1 cache. Often there are two separate L1 caches, one for instructions and another for data.

In high-performance processors, two levels of caches are normally used, separate L1 caches for instructions and data and a larger L2 cache. These caches are often implemented on the processor chip. In this case, the L1 caches must be very fast, as they determine the memory access time seen by the processor. The L2 cache can be slower, but it should be much larger than the L1 caches to ensure a high hit rate. Its speed is less critical because it only affects the miss penalty of the L1 caches. A typical computer may have L1 caches with capacities of tens of kilobytes and an L2 cache of hundreds of kilobytes or possibly several megabytes.

Including an L2 cache further reduces the impact of the main memory speed on the performance of a computer. Its effect can be assessed by observing that the average access time of the L2 cache is the miss penalty of either of the L1 caches. For simplicity, we will assume that the hit rates are the same for instructions and data. Thus, the average access time experienced by the processor in such a system is:

$$t_{avg} = h_1 C_1 + (1 - h_1)(h_2 C_2 + (1 - h_2)M)$$

where

h_1 is the hit rate in the L1 caches.

h_2 is the hit rate in the L2 cache.

C_1 is the time to access information in the L1 caches.

C_2 is the miss penalty to transfer information from the L2 cache to an L1 cache.

M is the miss penalty to transfer information from the main memory to the L2 cache.

Of all memory references made by the processor, the number of misses in the L2 cache is given by $(1 - h_1)(1 - h_2)$. If both h_1 and h_2 are in the 90 percent range, then the number of misses in the L2 cache will be less than one percent of all memory accesses. This makes the value of M, and in turn the speed of the main memory, less critical. See Problem 8.14 for a quantitative examination of this issue.

8.7.3 OTHER ENHANCEMENTS

In addition to the main design issues just discussed, several other possibilities exist for enhancing performance. We discuss three of them in this section.

Write Buffer

When the write-through protocol is used, each Write operation results in writing a new value into the main memory. If the processor must wait for the memory function to be completed, as we have assumed until now, then the processor is slowed down by all Write requests. Yet the processor typically does not need immediate access to the result of a Write operation; so it is not necessary for it to wait for the Write request to be completed.

To improve performance, a *Write buffer* can be included for temporary storage of Write requests. The processor places each Write request into this buffer and continues execution of the next instruction. The Write requests stored in the Write buffer are sent to the main memory whenever the memory is not responding to Read requests. It is important that the Read requests be serviced quickly, because the processor usually cannot proceed before receiving the data being read from the memory. Hence, these requests are given priority over Write requests.

The Write buffer may hold a number of Write requests. Thus, it is possible that a subsequent Read request may refer to data that are still in the Write buffer. To ensure correct operation, the addresses of data to be read from the memory are always compared with the addresses of the data in the Write buffer. In the case of a match, the data in the Write buffer are used.

A similar situation occurs with the write-back protocol. In this case, Write commands issued by the processor are performed on the word in the cache. When a new block of data is to be brought into the cache as a result of a Read miss, it may replace an existing block that has some dirty data. The dirty block has to be written into the main memory. If the required write-back is performed first, then the processor has to wait for this operation to be completed before the new block is read into the cache. It is more prudent to read the new block first. The dirty block being ejected from the cache is temporarily stored in the Write buffer and held there while the new block is being read. Afterwards, the contents of the buffer are written into the main memory. Thus, the Write buffer also works well for the write-back protocol.

Prefetching

In the previous discussion of the cache mechanism, we assumed that new data are brought into the cache when they are first needed. Following a Read miss, the processor has to pause until the new data arrive, thus incurring a miss penalty.

To avoid stalling the processor, it is possible to prefetch the data into the cache before they are needed. The simplest way to do this is through software. A special *prefetch* instruction may be provided in the instruction set of the processor. Executing this instruction causes the addressed data to be loaded into the cache, as in the case of a Read miss. A prefetch instruction is inserted in a program to cause the data to be loaded in the cache shortly before they are needed in the program. Then, the processor will not have to wait for the referenced data as in the case of a Read miss. The hope is that prefetching will take place while the processor is busy executing instructions that do not result in a Read miss, thus allowing accesses to the main memory to be overlapped with computation in the processor.

Prefetch instructions can be inserted into a program either by the programmer or by the compiler. Compilers are able to insert these instructions with good success for many applications. Software prefetching entails a certain overhead because inclusion of prefetch instructions increases the length of programs. Moreover, some prefetches may load into the cache data that will not be used by the instructions that follow. This can happen if the prefetched data are ejected from the cache by a Read miss involving other data. However, the overall effect of software prefetching on performance is positive, and many processors have machine instructions to support this feature. See Reference [1] for a thorough discussion of software prefetching.

Prefetching can also be done in hardware, using circuitry that attempts to discover a pattern in memory references and prefetches data according to this pattern. A number of schemes have been proposed for this purpose, as described in References [2] and [3].

Lockup-Free Cache

Software prefetching does not work well if it interferes significantly with the normal execution of instructions. This is the case if the action of prefetching stops other accesses to the cache until the prefetch is completed. While servicing a miss, the cache is said to be locked. This problem can be solved by modifying the basic cache structure to allow the processor to access the cache while a miss is being serviced. In this case, it is possible to have more than one outstanding miss, and the hardware must accommodate such occurrences.

A cache that can support multiple outstanding misses is called *lockup-free*. Such a cache must include circuitry that keeps track of all outstanding misses. This may be done with special registers that hold the pertinent information about these misses. Lockup-free caches were first used in the early 1980s in the Cyber series of computers manufactured by the Control Data company [4].

We have used software prefetching to motivate the need for a cache that is not locked by a Read miss. A much more important reason is that in a pipelined processor, which overlaps the execution of several instructions, a Read miss caused by one instruction could stall the execution of other instructions. A lockup-free cache reduces the likelihood of such stalls.

8.8 VIRTUAL MEMORY

In most modern computer systems, the physical main memory is not as large as the address space of the processor. For example, a processor that issues 32-bit addresses has an addressable space of 4G bytes. The size of the main memory in a typical computer with a 32-bit processor may range from 1G to 4G bytes. If a program does not completely fit into the main memory, the parts of it not currently being executed are stored on a secondary storage device, typically a magnetic disk. As these parts are needed for execution, they must first be brought into the main memory, possibly replacing other parts that are already in the memory. These actions are performed automatically by the operating system, using a scheme known as *virtual memory*. Application programmers need not be aware of the limitations imposed by the available main memory. They prepare programs using the entire address space of the processor.

Under a virtual memory system, programs, and hence the processor, reference instructions and data in an address space that is independent of the available physical main memory space. The binary addresses that the processor issues for either instructions or data are called *virtual* or *logical addresses*. These addresses are translated into physical addresses by a combination of hardware and software actions. If a virtual address refers to a part of the program or data space that is currently in the physical memory, then the contents of the appropriate location in the main memory are accessed immediately. Otherwise, the contents of the referenced address must be brought into a suitable location in the memory before they can be used.

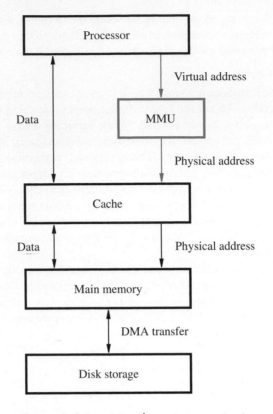

Figure 8.24   Virtual memory organization.

Figure 8.24 shows a typical organization that implements virtual memory. A special hardware unit, called the *Memory Management Unit* (MMU), keeps track of which parts of the virtual address space are in the physical memory. When the desired data or instructions are in the main memory, the MMU translates the virtual address into the corresponding physical address. Then, the requested memory access proceeds in the usual manner. If the data are not in the main memory, the MMU causes the operating system to transfer the data from the disk to the memory. Such transfers are performed using the DMA scheme discussed in Section 8.4.

8.8.1   ADDRESS TRANSLATION

A simple method for translating virtual addresses into physical addresses is to assume that all programs and data are composed of fixed-length units called *pages*, each of which consists of a block of words that occupy contiguous locations in the main memory. Pages commonly range from 2K to 16K bytes in length. They constitute the basic unit of information that is transferred between the main memory and the disk whenever the MMU determines that a transfer is required. Pages should not be too small, because the access time of a magnetic disk is much longer (several milliseconds) than the access time of the main memory. The reason for this is that it takes a considerable amount of time to locate the data on the disk, but once located, the data can be transferred at a rate of several megabytes per second. On the other hand, if pages are too large, it is possible that a substantial portion of a page may not be used, yet this unnecessary data will occupy valuable space in the main memory.

This discussion clearly parallels the concepts introduced in Section 8.6 on cache memory. The cache bridges the speed gap between the processor and the main memory and is implemented in hardware. The virtual-memory mechanism bridges the size and speed gaps between the main memory and secondary storage and is usually implemented in part by software techniques. Conceptually, cache techniques and virtual-memory techniques are very similar. They differ mainly in the details of their implementation.

A virtual-memory address-translation method based on the concept of fixed-length pages is shown schematically in Figure 8.25. Each virtual address generated by the proces-

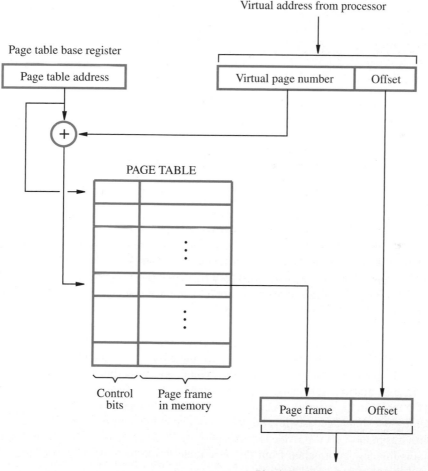

Figure 8.25   Virtual-memory address translation.

sor, whether it is for an instruction fetch or an operand load/store operation, is interpreted as a *virtual page number* (high-order bits) followed by an *offset* (low-order bits) that specifies the location of a particular byte (or word) within a page. Information about the main memory location of each page is kept in a *page table*. This information includes the main memory address where the page is stored and the current status of the page. An area in the main memory that can hold one page is called a *page frame*. The starting address of the page table is kept in a *page table base register*. By adding the virtual page number to the contents of this register, the address of the corresponding entry in the page table is obtained. The contents of this location give the starting address of the page if that page currently resides in the main memory.

Each entry in the page table also includes some control bits that describe the status of the page while it is in the main memory. One bit indicates the validity of the page, that is, whether the page is actually loaded in the main memory. It allows the operating system to invalidate the page without actually removing it. Another bit indicates whether the page has been modified during its residency in the memory. As in cache memories, this information is needed to determine whether the page should be written back to the disk before it is removed from the main memory to make room for another page. Other control bits indicate various restrictions that may be imposed on accessing the page. For example, a program may be given full read and write permission, or it may be restricted to read accesses only.

Translation Lookaside Buffer

The page table information is used by the MMU for every read and write access. Ideally, the page table should be situated within the MMU. Unfortunately, the page table may be rather large. Since the MMU is normally implemented as part of the processor chip, it is impossible to include the complete table within the MMU. Instead, a copy of only a small portion of the table is accommodated within the MMU, and the complete table is kept in the main memory. The portion maintained within the MMU consists of the entries corresponding to the most recently accessed pages. They are stored in a small table, usually called the *Translation Lookaside Buffer* (TLB). The TLB functions as a cache for the page table in the main memory. Each entry in the TLB includes a copy of the information in the corresponding entry in the page table. In addition, it includes the virtual address of the page, which is needed to search the TLB for a particular page. Figure 8.26 shows a possible organization of a TLB that uses the associative-mapping technique. Set-associative mapped TLBs are also found in commercial products.

Address translation proceeds as follows. Given a virtual address, the MMU looks in the TLB for the referenced page. If the page table entry for this page is found in the TLB, the physical address is obtained immediately. If there is a miss in the TLB, then the required entry is obtained from the page table in the main memory and the TLB is updated.

It is essential to ensure that the contents of the TLB are always the same as the contents of page tables in the memory. When the operating system changes the contents of a page table, it must simultaneously invalidate the corresponding entries in the TLB. One of the control bits in the TLB is provided for this purpose. When an entry is invalidated, the TLB acquires the new information from the page table in the memory as part of the MMU's normal response to access misses.

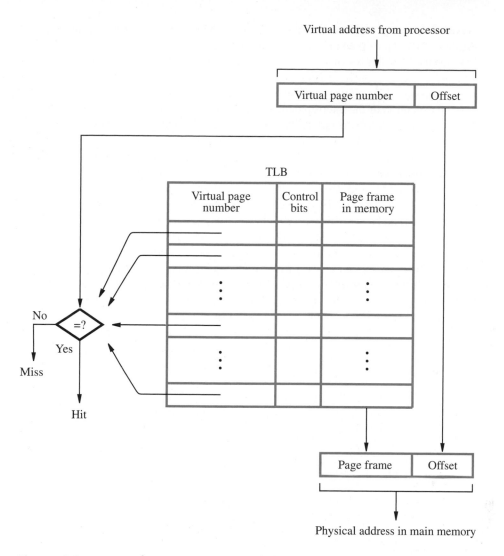

Figure 8.26   Use of an associative-mapped TLB.

Page Faults

When a program generates an access request to a page that is not in the main memory, a *page fault* is said to have occurred. The entire page must be brought from the disk into the memory before access can proceed. When it detects a page fault, the MMU asks the operating system to intervene by raising an exception (interrupt). Processing of the program that generated the page fault is interrupted, and control is transferred to the operating system. The operating system copies the requested page from the disk into the main memory. Since this process involves a long delay, the operating system may begin execution of another program whose pages are in the main memory. When page transfer is completed, the execution of the interrupted program is resumed.

When the MMU raises an interrupt to indicate a page fault, the instruction that requested the memory access may have been partially executed. It is essential to ensure that the interrupted program continues correctly when it resumes execution. There are two options. Either the execution of the interrupted instruction continues from the point of interruption, or the instruction must be restarted. The design of a particular processor dictates which of these two options is used.

If a new page is brought from the disk when the main memory is full, it must replace one of the resident pages. The problem of choosing which page to remove is just as critical here as it is in a cache, and the observation that programs spend most of their time in a few localized areas also applies. Because main memories are considerably larger than cache memories, it should be possible to keep relatively larger portions of a program in the main memory. This reduces the frequency of transfers to and from the disk. Concepts similar to the LRU replacement algorithm can be applied to page replacement, and the control bits in the page table entries can be used to record usage history. One simple scheme is based on a control bit that is set to 1 whenever the corresponding page is referenced (accessed). The operating system periodically clears this bit in all page table entries, thus providing a simple way of determining which pages have not been used recently.

A modified page has to be written back to the disk before it is removed from the main memory. It is important to note that the write-through protocol, which is useful in the framework of cache memories, is not suitable for virtual memory. The access time of the disk is so long that it does not make sense to access it frequently to write small amounts of data.

Looking up entries in the TLB introduces some delay, slowing down the operation of the MMU. Here again we can take advantage of the property of locality of reference. It is likely that many successive TLB translations involve addresses on the same program page. This is particularly likely when fetching instructions. Thus, address translation time can be reduced by keeping the most recently used TLB entries in a few special registers that can be accessed quickly.

8.9 MEMORY MANAGEMENT REQUIREMENTS

In our discussion of virtual-memory concepts, we have tacitly assumed that only one large program is being executed. If all of the program does not fit into the available physical memory, parts of it (pages) are moved from the disk into the main memory when they are to be executed. Although we have alluded to software routines that are needed to manage this movement of program segments, we have not been specific about the details.

Memory management routines are part of the operating system of the computer. It is convenient to assemble the operating system routines into a virtual address space, called the *system space*, that is separate from the virtual space in which user application programs reside. The latter space is called the *user space*. In fact, there may be a number of user spaces, one for each user. This is arranged by providing a separate page table for each user program. The MMU uses a page table base register to determine the address of the table to be used in the translation process. Hence, by changing the contents of this register, the operating system can switch from one space to another. The physical main memory is thus shared by the active pages of the system space and several user spaces. However, only the pages that belong to one of these spaces are accessible at any given time.

In any computer system in which independent user programs coexist in the main memory, the notion of *protection* must be addressed. No program should be allowed to destroy either the data or instructions of other programs in the memory. The needed protection can be provided in several ways. Let us first consider the most basic form of protection. Most processors can operate in one of two modes, the *supervisor mode* and the *user mode*. The processor is usually placed in the supervisor mode when operating system routines are being executed and in the user mode to execute user programs. In the user mode, some machine instructions cannot be executed. These are *privileged instructions*. They include instructions that modify the page table base register, which can only be executed while the processor is in the supervisor mode. Since a user program is executed in the user mode, it is prevented from accessing the page tables of other users or of the system space.

It is sometimes desirable for one application program to have access to certain pages belonging to another program. The operating system can arrange this by causing these pages to appear in both spaces. The shared pages will therefore have entries in two different page tables. The control bits in each table entry can be set to control the access privileges granted to each program. For example, one program may be allowed to read and write a given page, while the other program may be given only read access.

8.10 SECONDARY STORAGE

The semiconductor memories discussed in the previous sections cannot be used to provide all of the storage capability needed in computers. Their main limitation is the cost per bit of stored information. The large storage requirements of most computer systems are economically realized in the form of magnetic and optical disks, which are usually referred to as secondary storage devices.

8.10.1 MAGNETIC HARD DISKS

The storage medium in a magnetic-disk system consists of one or more disk platters mounted on a common spindle. A thin magnetic film is deposited on each platter, usually on both sides. The assembly is placed in a drive that causes it to rotate at a constant speed. The magnetized surfaces move in close proximity to read/write heads, as shown in Figure 8.27a. Data are stored on concentric tracks, and the read/write heads move radially to access different tracks.

Each read/write head consists of a magnetic yoke and a magnetizing coil, as indicated in Figure 8.27b. Digital information can be stored on the magnetic film by applying current pulses of suitable polarity to the magnetizing coil. This causes the magnetization of the film in the area immediately underneath the head to switch to a direction parallel to the applied

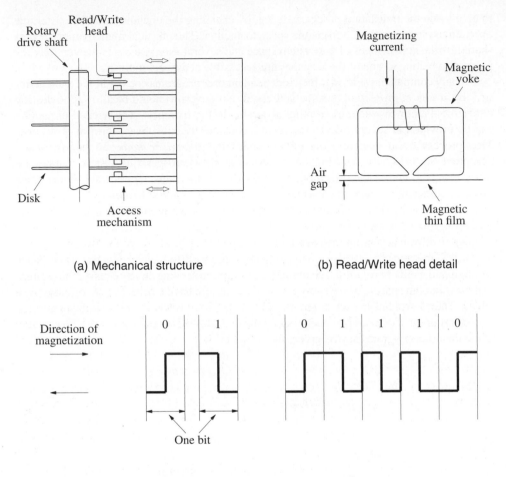

(a) Mechanical structure   (b) Read/Write head detail

(c) Bit representation by phase encoding

Figure 8.27   Magnetic disk principles.

field. The same head can be used for reading the stored information. In this case, changes in the magnetic field in the vicinity of the head caused by the movement of the film relative to the yoke induce a voltage in the coil, which now serves as a sense coil. The polarity of this voltage is monitored by the control circuitry to determine the state of magnetization of the film. Only changes in the magnetic field under the head can be sensed during the Read operation. Therefore, if the binary states 0 and 1 are represented by two opposite states of magnetization, a voltage is induced in the head only at 0-to-1 and at 1-to-0 transitions in the bit stream. A long string of 0s or 1s causes an induced voltage only at the beginning and end of the string. Therefore, to determine the number of consecutive 0s or 1s stored, a clock must provide information for synchronization.

In some early designs, a clock was stored on a separate track, on which a change in magnetization is forced for each bit period. Using the clock signal as a reference, the data stored on other tracks can be read correctly. The modern approach is to combine the clocking information with the data. Several different techniques have been developed for such encoding. One simple scheme, depicted in Figure 8.27c, is known as *phase encoding* or *Manchester encoding*. In this scheme, changes in magnetization occur for each data bit, as shown in the figure. Clocking information is provided by the change in magnetization at the midpoint of each bit period. The drawback of Manchester encoding is its poor bit-storage density. The space required to represent each bit must be large enough to accommodate two changes in magnetization. We use the Manchester encoding example to illustrate how a *self-clocking* scheme may be implemented, because it is easy to understand. Other, more compact codes have been developed. They are much more efficient and provide better storage density. They also require more complex control circuitry. The discussion of such codes is beyond the scope of this book.

Read/write heads must be maintained at a very small distance from the moving disk surfaces in order to achieve high bit densities and reliable Read and Write operations. When the disks are moving at their steady rate, air pressure develops between the disk surface and the head and forces the head away from the surface. This force is counterbalanced by a spring-loaded mounting arrangement that presses the head toward the surface. The flexible spring connection between the head and its arm mounting permits the head to fly at the desired distance away from the surface in spite of any small variations in the flatness of the surface.

In most modern disk units, the disks and the read/write heads are placed in a sealed, air-filtered enclosure. This approach is known as *Winchester technology*. In such units, the read/write heads can operate closer to the magnetized track surfaces, because dust particles, which are a problem in unsealed assemblies, are absent. The closer the heads are to a track surface, the more densely the data can be packed along the track, and the closer the tracks can be to each other. Thus, Winchester disks have a larger capacity for a given physical size compared to unsealed units. Another advantage of Winchester technology is that data integrity tends to be greater in sealed units, where the storage medium is not exposed to contaminating elements.

The read/write heads of a disk system are movable. There is one head per surface. All heads are mounted on a comb-like arm that can move radially across the stack of disks to provide access to individual tracks, as shown in Figure 8.27a. To read or write data on a given track, the read/write heads must first be positioned over that track.

The disk system consists of three key parts. One part is the assembly of disk platters, which is usually referred to as the *disk*. The second part comprises the electromechanical mechanism that spins the disk and moves the read/write heads; it is called the *disk drive*. The third part is the *disk controller*, which is the electronic circuitry that controls the operation of the system. The disk controller may be implemented as a separate module, or it may be incorporated into the enclosure that contains the entire disk system. We should note that the term disk is often used to refer to the combined package of the disk drive and the disk it contains. We will do so in the sections that follow, when there is no ambiguity in the meaning of the term.

Organization and Accessing of Data on a Disk

The organization of data on a disk is illustrated in Figure 8.28. Each surface is divided into concentric *tracks*, and each track is divided into *sectors*. The set of corresponding tracks on all surfaces of a stack of disks forms a logical *cylinder*. All tracks of a cylinder can be accessed without moving the read/write heads. Data are accessed by specifying the surface number, the track number, and the sector number. Read and Write operations always start at sector boundaries.

Data bits are stored serially on each track. Each sector may contain 512 or more bytes. The data are preceded by a *sector header* that contains identification (addressing) information used to find the desired sector on the selected track. Following the data, there are additional bits that constitute an *error-correcting code* (ECC). The ECC bits are used to detect and correct errors that may have occurred in writing or reading the data bytes. There is a small *inter-sector gap* that enables the disk control circuitry to distinguish easily between two consecutive sectors.

An unformatted disk has no information on its tracks. The formatting process writes markers that divide the disk into tracks and sectors. During this process, the disk controller may discover some sectors or even whole tracks that are defective. The disk controller keeps a record of such defects and excludes them from use. The formatting information comprises sector headers, ECC bits, and inter-sector gaps. The capacity of a formatted disk, after accounting for the formating information overhead, is the proper indicator of the disk's storage capability. After formatting, the disk is divided into logical partitions.

Figure 8.28 indicates that each track has the same number of sectors, which means that all tracks have the same storage capacity. In this case, the stored information is packed more densely on inner tracks than on outer tracks. It is also possible to increase the storage density by placing more sectors on the outer tracks, which have longer circumference. This would be at the expense of more complicated access circuitry.

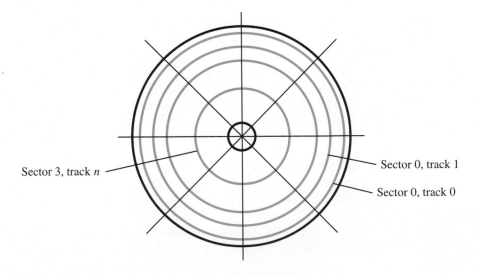

Figure 8.28   Organization of one surface of a disk.

Access Time

There are two components involved in the time delay between the disk receiving an address and the beginning of the actual data transfer. The first, called the *seek time*, is the time required to move the read/write head to the proper track. This time depends on the initial position of the head relative to the track specified in the address. Average values are in the 5- to 8-ms range. The second component is the *rotational delay*, also called *latency time*, which is the time taken to reach the addressed sector after the read/write head is positioned over the correct track. On average, this is the time for half a rotation of the disk. The sum of these two delays is called the disk *access time*. If only a few sectors of data are accessed in a single operation, the access time is at least an order of magnitude longer than the time it takes to transfer the data.

Data Buffer/Cache

A disk drive is connected to the rest of a computer system using some standard interconnection scheme, such as SCSI or SATA. The interconnection hardware is usually capable of transferring data at much higher rates than the rate at which data can be read from disk tracks. An efficient way to deal with the possible differences in transfer rates is to include a *data buffer* in the disk unit. The buffer is a semiconductor memory, capable of storing a few megabytes of data. The requested data are transferred between the disk tracks and the buffer at a rate dependent on the rotational speed of the disk. Transfers between the data buffer and the main memory can then take place at the maximum rate allowed by the interconnect between them.

The data buffer in the disk controller can also be used to provide a caching mechanism for the disk. When a Read request arrives at the disk, the controller can first check to see if the desired data are already available in the buffer. If so, the data are transferred to the memory in microseconds instead of milliseconds. Otherwise, the data are read from a disk track in the usual way, stored in the buffer, then transferred to the memory. Because of locality of reference, a subsequent request is likely to refer to data that sequentially follow the data specified in the current request. In anticipation of future requests, the disk controller may read more data than needed and place them into the buffer. When used as a cache, the buffer is typically large enough to store entire tracks of data. So, a possible strategy is to begin transferring the contents of the track into the data buffer as soon as the read/write head is positioned over the desired track.

Disk Controller

Operation of a disk drive is controlled by a *disk controller* circuit, which also provides an interface between the disk drive and the rest of the computer system. One disk controller may be used to control more than one drive.

A disk controller that communicates directly with the processor contains a number of registers that can be read and written by the operating system. Thus, communication between the OS and the disk controller is achieved in the same manner as with any I/O interface, as discussed in Chapter 7. The disk controller uses the DMA scheme to transfer data between the disk and the main memory. Actually, these transfers are from/to the data buffer, which is implemented as a part of the disk controller module. The OS initiates the transfers by issuing Read and Write requests, which entail loading the controller's registers with the necessary addressing and control information. Typically, this information includes:

Main memory address—The address of the first main memory location of the block of words involved in the transfer.

Disk address—The location of the sector containing the beginning of the desired block of words.

Word count—The number of words in the block to be transferred.

The disk address issued by the OS is a logical address. The corresponding physical address on the disk may be different. For example, bad sectors may be detected when the disk is formatted. The disk controller keeps track of such sectors and maintains the mapping between logical and physical addresses. Normally, a few spare sectors are kept on each track, or on another track in the same cylinder, to be used as substitutes for the bad sectors.

On the disk drive side, the controller's major functions are:

Seek—Causes the disk drive to move the read/write head from its current position to the desired track.

Read—Initiates a Read operation, starting at the address specified in the disk address register. Data read serially from the disk are assembled into words and placed into the data buffer for transfer to the main memory. The number of words is determined by the word count register.

Write—Transfers data to the disk, using a control method similar to that for Read operations.

Error checking—Computes the error correcting code (ECC) value for the data read from a given sector and compares it with the corresponding ECC value read from the disk. In the case of a mismatch, it corrects the error if possible; otherwise, it raises an interrupt to inform the OS that an error has occurred. During a Write operation, the controller computes the ECC value for the data to be written and stores this value on the disk.

Floppy Disks

The disks discussed above are known as hard or rigid disk units. *Floppy disks* are smaller, simpler, and cheaper disk units that consist of a flexible, removable, plastic *diskette* coated with magnetic material. The diskette is enclosed in a plastic jacket, which has an opening where the read/write head can be positioned. A hole in the center of the diskette allows a spindle mechanism in the disk drive to position and rotate the diskette.

The main feature of floppy disks is their low cost and shipping convenience. However, they have much smaller storage capacities, longer access times, and higher failure rates than hard disks. In recent years, they have largely been replaced by CDs, DVDs, and flash cards as portable storage media.

RAID Disk Arrays

Processor speeds have increased dramatically. At the same time, access times to disk drives are still on the order of milliseconds, because of the limitations of the mechanical motion involved. One way to reduce access time is to use multiple disks operating in parallel. In 1988, researchers at the University of California-Berkeley proposed such a storage system [5]. They called it RAID, for Redundant Array of Inexpensive Disks. (Since all disks are now inexpensive, the acronym was later reinterpreted as Redundant Array of Independent Disks.) Using multiple disks also makes it possible to improve the reliability of the overall system. Different configurations were proposed, and many more have been developed since.

The basic configuration, known as RAID 0, is simple. A single large file is stored in several separate disk units by dividing the file into a number of smaller pieces and storing these pieces on different disks. This is called *data striping*. When the file is accessed for a Read operation, all disks access their portions of the data in parallel. As a result, the rate at which the data can be transferred is equal to the data rate of individual disks times the number of disks. However, access time, that is, the seek and rotational delay needed to locate the beginning of the data on each disk, is not reduced. Since each disk operates independently, access times vary. Individual pieces of the data are buffered, so that the complete file can be reassembled and transferred to the memory as a single entity.

Various RAID configurations form a hierarchy, with each level in the hierarchy providing additional features. For example, RAID 1 is intended to provide better reliability by storing identical copies of the data on two disks rather than just one. The two disks are said to be mirrors of each other. If one disk drive fails, all Read and Write operations are directed to its mirror drive. Other levels of the hierarchy achieve increased reliability through various parity-checking schemes, without requiring a full duplication of disks. Some also have error-recovery capability.

The RAID concept has gained commercial acceptance. RAID systems are available from many manufacturers for use with a variety of operating systems.

8.10.2   OPTICAL DISKS

Storage devices can also be implemented using optical means. The familiar compact disk (CD), used in audio systems, was the first practical application of this technology. Soon after, the optical technology was adapted to the computer environment to provide a high-capacity read-only storage medium known as a CD-ROM.

The first generation of CDs was developed in the mid-1980s by the Sony and Philips companies. The technology exploited the possibility of using a digital representation for analog sound signals. To provide high-quality sound recording and reproduction, 16-bit samples of the analog signal are taken at a rate of 44,100 samples per second. Initially, CDs were designed to hold up to 75 minutes, requiring a total of about 3×10^9 bits (3 gigabits) of storage. Since then, higher-capacity devices have been developed.

CD Technology

The optical technology that is used for CD systems makes use of the fact that laser light can be focused on a very small spot. A laser beam is directed onto a spinning disk, with tiny indentations arranged to form a long spiral track on its surface. The indentations reflect the focused beam toward a photodetector, which detects the stored binary patterns.

The laser emits a coherent light beam that is sharply focused on the surface of the disk. Coherent light consists of synchronized waves that have the same wavelength. If a coherent light beam is combined with another beam of the same kind, and the two beams are in phase, the result is a brighter beam. But, if the waves of the two beams are 180 degrees out of phase, they cancel each other. Thus, a photodetector can be used to detect the beams. It will see a bright spot in the first case and a dark spot in the second case.

A cross-section of a small portion of a CD is shown in Figure 8.29a. The bottom layer is made of transparent polycarbonate plastic, which serves as a clear glass base. The surface of this plastic is programmed to store data by indenting it with *pits*. The unindented parts are called *lands*. A thin layer of reflecting aluminum material is placed on top of a programmed disk. The aluminum is then covered by a protective acrylic. Finally, the topmost layer is deposited and stamped with a label. The total thickness of the disk is 1.2 mm, almost all of it contributed by the polycarbonate plastic. The other layers are very thin.

The laser source and the photodetector are positioned below the polycarbonate plastic. The emitted beam travels through the plastic layer, reflects off the aluminum layer, and travels back toward the photodetector. Note that from the laser side, the pits actually appear as bumps rising above the lands.

Figure 8.29b shows what happens as the laser beam scans across the disk and encounters a transition from a pit to a land. Three different positions of the laser source and the detector are shown, as would occur when the disk is rotating. When the light reflects solely from a pit, or from a land, the detector sees the reflected beam as a bright spot. But, a different situation arises when the beam moves over the edge between a pit and the adjacent land. The pit is one quarter of a wavelength closer to the laser source. Thus, the reflected beams from the pit and the adjacent land will be 180 degrees out of phase, cancelling each other. Hence, the detector will not see a reflected beam at pit-land and land-pit transitions, and will detect a dark spot.

Figure 8.29c depicts several transitions between lands and pits. If each transition, detected as a dark spot, is taken to denote the binary value 1, and the flat portions represent 0s, then the detected binary pattern will be as shown in the figure. This pattern is not a direct representation of the stored data. CDs use a complex encoding scheme to represent data. Each byte of data is represented by a 14-bit code, which provides considerable error detection capability. We will not delve into details of this code.

The pits are arranged on a long track on the surface of the disk, spiraling from the middle of the disk toward the outer edge. But, it is customary to refer to each circular path spanning 360 degrees as a separate track, which is analogous to the terminology used for magnetic disks. The CD is 120 mm in diameter, with a 15-mm hole in the center. The tracks cover the area from a 25-mm radius to a 58-mm radius. The space between the tracks is 1.6 microns. Pits are 0.5 microns wide and 0.8 to 3 microns long. There are more than 15,000 tracks on a disk. If the entire track spiral were unraveled, it would be over 5 km long!

CD-ROM

Since CDs store information in a binary form, they are suitable for use as a storage medium in computer systems. The main challenge is to ensure the integrity of stored data.

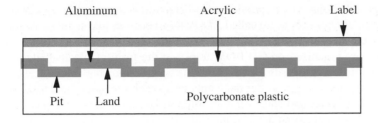

(a) Cross-section

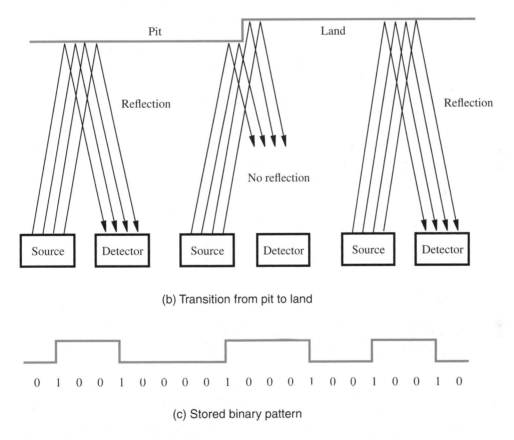

(b) Transition from pit to land

(c) Stored binary pattern

Figure 8.29 Optical disk.

Because the pits are very small, it is difficult to implement all of the pits perfectly. In audio and video applications, some errors in the data can be tolerated, because they are unlikely to affect the reproduced sound or image in a perceptible way. However, such errors are not acceptable in computer applications. Since physical imperfections cannot be avoided, it is necessary to use additional bits to provide error detection and correction capability. The CDs used to store computer data are called *CD-ROMs*, because, like semiconductor ROM chips, their contents can only be read.

Stored data are organized on CD-ROM tracks in the form of blocks called *sectors*. There are several different formats for a sector. One format, known as Mode 1, uses 2352-byte sectors. There is a 16-byte header that contains a synchronization field used to detect the beginning of the sector and addressing information used to identify the sector. This is followed by 2048 bytes of stored data. At the end of the sector, there are 288 bytes used to implement the error-correcting scheme. The number of sectors per track is variable; there are more sectors on the longer outer tracks. With the Mode 1 format, a CD-ROM has a storage capacity of about 650 Mbytes.

Error detection and correction is done at more than one level. As mentioned earlier, each byte of information stored on a CD is encoded using a 14-bit code that has some error-correcting capability. This code can correct single-bit errors. Errors that occur in short bursts, affecting several bits, are detected and corrected using the error-checking bits at the end of the sector.

CD-ROM drives operate at a number of different rotational speeds. The basic speed, known as 1X, is 75 sectors per second. This provides a data rate of 153,600 bytes/s (150 Kbytes/s), using the Mode 1 format. Higher speed CD-ROM drives are identified in relation to the basic speed. Thus, a 56X CD-ROM has a data transfer rate that is 56 times that of the 1X CD-ROM, or about 6 Mbytes/s. This transfer rate is considerably lower than the transfer rates of magnetic hard disks, which are in the range of tens of megabytes per second. Another significant difference in performance is the seek time, which in CD-ROMs may be several hundred milliseconds. So, in terms of performance, CD-ROMs are clearly inferior to magnetic disks. Their attraction lies in their small physical size, low cost, and ease of handling as a removable and transportable mass-storage medium. As a result, they are widely used for the distribution of software, textbooks, application programs, video games, and so on.

CD-Recordable

The CDs described above are read-only devices, in which the information is stored at the time of manufacture. First, a master disk is produced using a high-power laser to burn holes that correspond to the required pits. A mold is then made from the master disk, which has bumps in the place of holes. Copies are made by injecting molten polycarbonate plastic into the mold to make CDs that have the same pattern of holes (pits) as the master disk. This process is clearly suitable only for volume production of CDs containing the same information.

A new type of CD was developed in the late 1990s on which data can be easily recorded by a computer user. It is known as CD-Recordable (CD-R). A shiny spiral track covered by an organic dye is implemented on a disk during the manufacturing process. Then, a laser in a CD-R drive burns pits into the organic dye. The burned spots become opaque. They reflect less light than the shiny areas when the CD is being read. This process is irreversible, which means that the written data are stored permanently. Unused portions of a disk can be used to store additional data at a later time.

CD-Rewritable

The most flexible CDs are those that can be written multiple times by the user. They are known as CD-RWs (CD-ReWritables).

The basic structure of CD-RWs is similar to the structure of CD-Rs. Instead of using an organic dye in the recording layer, an alloy of silver, indium, antimony, and tellurium is used. This alloy has interesting and useful behavior when it is heated and cooled. If it is heated above its melting point (500 degrees C) and then cooled down, it goes into an amorphous state in which it absorbs light. But, if it is heated only to about 200 degrees C and this temperature is maintained for an extended period, a process known as *annealing* takes place, which leaves the alloy in a crystalline state that allows light to pass through. If the crystalline state represents land area, pits can be created by heating selected spots past the melting point. The stored data can be erased using the annealing process, which returns the alloy to a uniform crystalline state. A reflective material is placed above the recording layer to reflect the light when the disk is read.

A CD-RW drive uses three different laser powers. The highest power is used to record the pits. The middle power is used to put the alloy into its crystalline state; it is referred to as the "erase power." The lowest power is used to read the stored information.

CD drives designed to read and write CD-RW disks can usually be used with other compact disk media. They can read CD-ROMs and can read and write CD-Rs. They are designed to meet the requirements of standard interconnection interfaces, such as SATA and USB.

CD-RW disks provide low-cost storage media. They are suitable for archival storage of information that may range from databases to photographic images. They can be used for low-volume distribution of information, just like CD-Rs, and for backup purposes. The CD-RW technology has made CD-Rs less relevant because it offers superior capability at only slightly higher cost.

DVD Technology

The success of CD technology and the continuing quest for greater storage capability has led to the development of DVD (Digital Versatile Disk) technology. The first DVD standard was defined in 1996 by a consortium of companies, with the objective of being able to store a full-length movie on one side of a DVD disk.

The physical size of a DVD disk is the same as that of CDs. The disk is 1.2 mm thick, and it is 120 mm in diameter. Its storage capacity is made much larger than that of CDs by several design changes:

- A red-light laser with a wavelength of 635 nm is used instead of the infrared light laser used in CDs, which has a wavelength of 780 nm. The shorter wavelength makes it possible to focus the light to a smaller spot.
- Pits are smaller, having a minimum length of 0.4 micron.
- Tracks are placed closer together; the distance between tracks is 0.74 micron.

Using these improvements leads to a DVD capacity of 4.7 Gbytes.

Further increases in capacity have been achieved by going to two-layered and two-sided disks. The single-layered single-sided disk, defined in the standard as DVD-5, has a structure that is almost the same as the CD in Figure 8.29*a*. A double-layered disk makes use of two layers on which tracks are implemented on top of each other. The first layer is the clear base, as in CD disks. But, instead of using reflecting aluminum, the lands and pits of this layer are covered by a translucent material that acts as a semi-reflector. The surface of this material is then also programmed with indented pits to store data. A reflective material is placed on top of the second layer of pits and lands. The disk is read by focusing the laser beam on the desired layer. When the beam is focused on the first layer, sufficient light is reflected by the translucent material to detect the stored binary patterns. When the beam is focused on the second layer, the light reflected by the reflective material corresponds to the information stored on this layer. In both cases, the layer on which the beam is not focused reflects a much smaller amount of light, which is eliminated by the detector circuit as noise. The total storage capacity of both layers is 8.5 Gbytes. This disk is called DVD-9 in the standard.

Two single-sided disks can be put together to form a sandwich-like structure where the top disk is turned upside down. This can be done with single-layered disks, as specified in DVD-10, giving a composite disk with a capacity of 9.4 Gbytes. It can also be done with the double-layered disks, as specified in DVD-18, yielding a capacity of 17 Gbytes.

Access times for DVD drives are similar to CD drives. However, when the DVD disks rotate at the same speed, the data transfer rates are much higher because of the higher density of pits. Rewritable versions of DVD devices have also been developed, providing large storage capacities.

8.10.3   MAGNETIC TAPE SYSTEMS

Magnetic tapes are suited for off-line storage of large amounts of data. They are typically used for backup purposes and for archival storage. Magnetic-tape recording uses the same principle as magnetic disks. The main difference is that the magnetic film is deposited on a very thin 0.5- or 0.25-inch wide plastic tape. Seven or nine bits (corresponding to one character) are recorded in parallel across the width of the tape, perpendicular to the direction of motion. A separate read/write head is provided for each bit position on the tape, so that all bits of a character can be read or written in parallel. One of the character bits is used as a parity bit.

Data on the tape are organized in the form of *records* separated by gaps, as shown in Figure 8.30. Tape motion is stopped only when a record gap is underneath the read/write heads. The record gaps are long enough to allow the tape to attain its normal speed before the beginning of the next record is reached. If a coding scheme such as that in Figure 8.27*c* is used for recording data on the tape, record gaps are identified as areas where there is no change in magnetization. This allows record gaps to be detected independently of the recorded data. To help users organize large amounts of data, a group of related records is called a *file*. The beginning of a file is identified by a *file mark*, as shown in Figure 8.30. The file mark is a special single- or multiple-character record, usually preceded by a gap longer than the inter-record gap. The first record following a file mark can be used as a *header* or *identifier* for the file. This allows the user to search a tape containing a large number of files for a particular file.

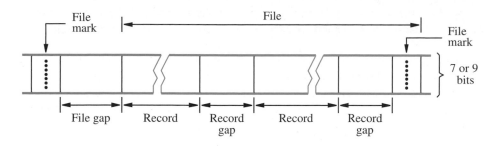

Figure 8.30   Organization of data on magnetic tape.

Cartridge Tape System

Tape systems have been developed for backup of on-line disk storage. One such system uses an 8-mm video-format tape housed in a cassette. These units are called cartridge tapes. They have capacities in the range of 2 to 5 gigabytes and handle data transfers at the rate of a few hundred kilobytes per second. Reading and writing is done by a helical scan system operating across the tape, similar to that used in video cassette tape drives. Bit densities of tens of millions of bits per square inch are achievable. Multiple-cartridge systems are available that automate the loading and unloading of cassettes so that tens of gigabytes of on-line storage can be backed up unattended.

8.11 CONCLUDING REMARKS

The design of the memory hierarchy is critical to the performance of a computer system. Modern operating systems and application programs place heavy demands on both the capacity and speed of the memory. In this chapter, we presented the most important technological and organizational details of memory systems and how they have evolved to meet these demands.

Developments in semiconductor technology have led to significant improvements in the speed and capacity of memory chips, accompanied by a large decrease in the cost per bit. The performance of computer memories is enhanced further by the use of a memory hierarchy. Today, a large yet affordable main memory is implemented with dynamic memory chips. One or more levels of cache memory are always provided. The introduction of the cache memory reduces significantly the effective memory access time seen by the processor. Virtual memory makes the main memory appear larger than the physical memory.

Magnetic disks continue to be the primary technology for secondary storage. They provide enormous storage capacity, reaching and exceeding a trillion bytes on a single drive, with a very low cost per bit. But, flash semiconductor technology is beginning to compete effectively in some applications.

8.12 SOLVED PROBLEMS

This section presents some examples of the types of problems that a student may be asked to solve, and shows how such problems can be solved.

Example 8.2 **Problem:** Describe a structure similar to the one in Figure 8.10 for an 8M × 32 memory using 512K × 8 memory chips.

Solution: The required structure is essentially the same as in Figure 8.10, except that 16 rows are needed, each with four 512 × 8 chips. Address lines A_{18-0} should be connected to all chips. Address lines A_{22-19} should be connected to a 4-bit decoder to select one of the 16 rows.

Example 8.3 **Problem:** A computer system uses 32-bit memory addresses and it has a main memory consisting of 1G bytes. It has a 4K-byte cache organized in the block-set-associative manner, with 4 blocks per set and 64 bytes per block.

(a) Calculate the number of bits in each of the Tag, Set, and Word fields of the memory address.

(b) Assume that the cache is initially empty. Suppose that the processor fetches 1088 words of four bytes each from successive word locations starting at location 0. It then repeats this fetch sequence nine more times. If the cache is 10 times faster than the memory, estimate the improvement factor resulting from the use of the cache. Assume that the LRU algorithm is used for block replacement.

Solution: Consecutive addresses refer to bytes.

(a) A block has 64 bytes; hence the Word field is 6 bits long. With $4 \times 64 = 256$ bytes in a set, there are 4K/256 = 16 sets, requiring a Set field of 4 bits. This leaves $32 - 4 - 6 = 22$ bits for the Tag field.

(b) The 1088 words constitute 68 blocks, occupying blocks 0 to 67 in the memory. The cache has space for 64 blocks. Hence, after blocks 0, 1, 2, . . . , 63 have been read from the memory into the cache on the first pass, the cache is full. The next four blocks, numbered 64 to 67, map to sets 0, 1, 2, and 3. Each of them will replace the least recently used cache block in its set, which is block 0. During the second pass, memory block 0 has to be reloaded into set 0 of the cache, since it has been overwritten by block 64. It will be placed in the least recently used block of set 0 at that point, which is block 1. Next, memory blocks 1, 2, and 3 will replace block 1 of sets 1, 2 and 3 in the cache, respectively. Memory blocks 4 to 15 will be found in the cache. Memory blocks 16 to 19, which were in block location 1 of sets 0 to 3, have now been overwritten, and will be reloaded in block location 2 of these sets.

As execution proceeds, all memory blocks that occupy the first four of the 16 cache sets are always overwritten before they can be used on a succeeding pass. Memory blocks 0, 16, 32, 48, and 64 continually displace each other as they compete for the 4 block positions in cache set 0. The same thing occurs in cache set 1 (memory blocks 1, 17, 33, 49, 65), cache set 2 (memory blocks 2, 18, 34, 50, 66), and cache set 3 (memory blocks 3, 19, 35, 51, 67). Memory blocks that occupy the last 12 sets (sets 4 through 15) are fetched once on the first pass and remain in the cache for the next 9 passes.

In summary, on the first pass, all 68 blocks of the loop are fetched from the memory. On each of the 9 successive passes, 48 blocks are found in sets 4 through 15 of the cache, and the remaining 20 blocks must be fetched from the memory. Let τ be the access time of the cache. Therefore,

$$\text{Improvement factor} = \frac{\text{Time without cache}}{\text{Time with cache}}$$

$$= \frac{10 \times 68 \times 10\tau}{1 \times 68 \times 11\tau + 9(20 \times 11\tau + 48\tau)}$$

$$= 2.15$$

This example illustrates a weakness of the LRU algorithm during the execution of program loops. See Problem 8.9 for the performance of an alternative algorithm in this case.

Problem: Suppose that a computer has a processor with two L1 caches, one for instructions and one for data, and an L2 cache. Let τ be the access time for the two L1 caches. The miss penalties are approximately 15τ for transferring a block from L2 to L1, and 100τ for transferring a block from the main memory to L2. For the purpose of this problem, assume that the hit rates are the same for instructions and data and that the hit rates in the L1 and L2 caches are 0.96 and 0.80, respectively.

Example 8.4

(a) What fraction of accesses miss in both the L1 and L2 caches, thus requiring access to the main memory?

(b) What is the average access time as seen by the processor?

(c) Suppose that the L2 cache has an ideal hit rate of 1. By what factor would this reduce the average memory access time as seen by the processor?

(d) Consider the following change to the memory hierarchy. The L2 cache is removed and the size of the L1 caches is increased so that their miss rate is cut in half. What is the average memory access time as seen by the processor in this case?

Solution: The average memory access time with one cache level is given in Section 8.7.1 as

$$t_{avg} = hC + (1 - h)M$$

With L1 and L2 caches, the average memory access time is given in Section 8.7.2 as

$$t_{avg} = h_1C_1 + (1 - h_1)(h_2C_2 + (1 - h_2)M)$$

(a) The fraction of memory accesses that miss in both the L1 and L2 caches is

$$(1 - h_1)(1 - h_2) = (1 - 0.96)(1 - 0.80) = 0.008$$

(b) The average memory access time using two cache levels is

$$t_{avg} = 0.96\tau + 0.04(0.80 \times 15\tau + 0.20 \times 100\tau)$$
$$= 2.24\tau$$

(c) With no misses in the L2 cache, we get:

$$t_{avg}(\text{ideal}) = 0.96\tau + 0.04 \times 15\tau = 1.56\tau$$

Therefore,

$$\frac{t_{avg}(\text{actual})}{t_{avg}(\text{ideal})} = \frac{2.24\tau}{1.56\tau} = 1.44$$

(d) With larger L1 caches and the L2 cache removed, the access time is

$$t_{avg} = 0.98\tau + 0.02 \times 100\tau = 2.98\tau$$

Example 8.5   **Problem:** A 1024×1024 array of 32-bit numbers is to be normalized as follows. For each column, the largest element is found and all elements of the column are divided by the value of this element. Assume that each page in the virtual memory consists of 4K bytes, and that 1M bytes of the main memory are allocated for storing array data during this computation. Assume that it takes 10 ms to load a page from the disk into the main memory when a page fault occurs.

(a) Assume that the array is processed one column at a time. How many page faults would occur and how long does it take to complete the normalization process if the elements of the array are stored in column order in the virtual memory?

(b) Repeat part (a) assuming the elements are stored in row order?

(c) Propose an alternative way for processing the array to reduce the number of page faults when the array is stored in the memory in row order. Estimate the number of page faults and the time needed for your solution.

Solution: Each 32-bit number comprises 4 bytes. Hence, each page holds 1024 numbers. There is space for 256 pages in the 1M-byte portion of the main memory that is allocated for storing data during the computation.

(a) Each column is stored in one page; there is a page fault to bring each column to the main memory, for a total of 1024 page faults.

Processing time $= 1024 \times 10$ ms $= 10.24$ s.

(b) Processing of each column requires two passes, the first to find the largest element and the second to perform the normalization. When processing the first column, each element access results in a page fault that brings all elements of the corresponding row into the main memory. After 256 elements have been examined, the main memory is full. Accessing the next 256 elements results in page faults that replace all the data in the memory, and the process repeats. Thus, a page fault occurs for every access to every element in the array.

Processing time $= 2 \times 1024 \times 1024 \times 10$ ms $= 20,972$ s $= 5.8$ hours.

(c) A more efficient alternative for this arrangement of the data is to complete the first pass for only one quarter of each column for all columns, then process the second quarter, and so on. The second pass is handled in the same way. In this case, each pass through the array results in 1024 page faults, for a total of 2048.

Processing time $= 2048 \times 10$ ms $= 20.48$ s.

This example illustrates how the number of page faults can increase dramatically in some cases when the size of the main memory is insufficient for the application. This behavior is called *thrashing*.

Problem: Consider a long sequence of accesses to a disk with an average seek time of 6 ms and an average rotational delay of 3 ms. The average size of a block being accessed is 8K bytes. The data transfer rate from the disk is 34 Mbytes/sec.   **Example 8.6**

(a) Assuming that the data blocks are randomly located on the disk, estimate the average percentage of the total time occupied by seek operations and rotational delays.

(b) Repeat part (a) for the situation in which disk accesses are arranged so that in 90 percent of the cases, the next access will be to a data block on the same cylinder.

Solution: It takes 8K/34M $= 0.23$ ms to transfer a block of data.

(a) The total time needed to access each block is $6 + 3 + 0.23 = 9.23$ ms. The portion of time occupied by seek and rotational delay is $9/9.23 = 0.97 = 97\%$.

(*b*) In 90% of the cases, only rotational delays are involved. Therefore, the average time to access a block is $0.9 \times 3 + 0.1 \times 9 + 0.23 = 3.89$ ms. The portion of time occupied by seek and rotational delay is $3.6/3.89 = 0.92 = 92\%$.

PROBLEMS

8.1 **[M]** Consider the dynamic memory cell of Figure 8.6. Assume that $C = 30$ femtofarads (10^{-15} F) and that leakage current through the transistor is about 0.25 picoamperes (10^{-12} A). The voltage across the capacitor when it is fully charged is 1.5 V. The cell must be refreshed before this voltage drops below 0.9 V. Estimate the minimum refresh rate.

8.2 **[M]** Consider a main memory built with SDRAM chips. Data are transferred in bursts as shown in Figure 8.9, except that the burst length is 8. Assume that 32 bits of data are transferred in parallel. If a 400-MHz clock is used, how much time does it take to transfer:

(*a*) 32 bytes of data

(*b*) 64 bytes of data

What is the latency in each case?

8.3 **[E]** Describe a structure similar to that in Figure 8.10 for a 16M × 32 memory using 1M × 4 memory chips.

8.4 **[E]** Give a critique of the following statement: "Using a faster processor chip results in a corresponding increase in performance of a computer even if the main memory speed remains the same."

8.5 **[M]** The memory of a computer is byte-addressable, and the word length is 32 bits. A program consists of two nested loops—a small inner loop and a much larger outer loop. The general structure of the program is given in Figure P8.1. The decimal memory addresses shown delineate the location of the two loops and the beginning and end of the total program. All memory locations in the various sections of the program, 8-52, 56-136, 140-240, and so on, contain instructions to be executed in straight-line sequencing. The program is to be run on a computer that has an instruction cache organized in the direct-mapped manner (see Figure 8.16) with the following parameters:

Cache size	1K bytes
Block size	128 bytes

The miss penalty in the instruction cache is 80τ, where τ is the access time of the cache. Compute the total time needed for instruction fetching during execution of the program in Figure P8.1.

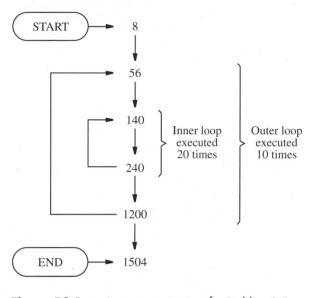

Figure P8.1   A program structure for Problem 8.5.

8.6   **[M]** A computer with a 16-bit word length has a direct-mapped cache, used for both instructions and data. Memory addresses are 16 bits long, and the memory is byte-addressable. The cache is small for illustrative purposes. It contains only four 16-bit words. Each word constitutes a cache block and has an associated 13-bit tag, as shown in Figure P8.2a. Words are accessed in the cache using the low-order 3 bits of an address. When a miss occurs during a Read operation for either an instruction or a data operand, the requested word is read from the main memory and sent to the processor. At the same time, it is copied into the cache, and its block number is stored in the associated tag. Consider the following short loop, in which all instructions are 16 bits long:

```
LOOP:      Add          R0, (R1)+
           Decrement    R2
           BNE          LOOP
```

Assume that, before this loop is entered, registers R0, R1, and R2 contain 0, 054E, and 3, respectively. Also assume that the main memory contains the data shown in Figure P8.2b, where all entries are given in hexadecimal notation. The loop starts at location LOOP = 02EC. The Autoincrement address mode in the Add instruction is used to access successive numbers in a 3-number list and add them into register R0. The counter register, R2, is decremented until it reaches 0, at which point an exit is made from the loop.

(*a*) Starting with an empty cache, show the contents of the cache, including the tags, at the end of each pass through the loop.

(*b*) Assume that the access times of the cache and the main memory are τ and 10τ, respectively. Calculate the execution time for each pass, counting only memory access times.

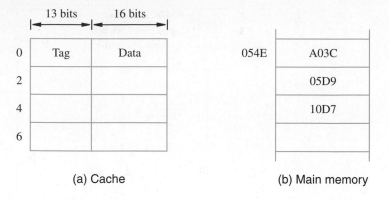

(a) Cache   (b) Main memory

Figure P8.2   Cache and main memory contents in Problem 8.6.

8.7   **[M]** Repeat Problem 8.6 assuming that only instructions are stored in the cache. Data operands are fetched directly from the main memory and not copied into the cache. Why does this choice lead to faster execution than when both instructions and data are loaded into the cache?

8.8   **[E]** A block-set-associative cache consists of a total of 64 blocks, divided into 4-block sets. The main memory contains 4096 blocks, each consisting of 32 words. Assuming a 32-bit byte-addressable address space, how many bits are there in each of the Tag, Set, and Word fields?

8.9   **[M]** Consider the cache in Example 8.3. Assume that whenever a block is to be brought from the main memory and the corresponding set in the cache is full, the new block replaces the most recently used block of this set. Derive the solution for part (*b*) in this case.

8.10   **[D]** Section 8.6.3 illustrates the effect of different cache-mapping techniques, using the program in Figure 8.20. Suppose that this program is changed so that in the second loop the elements are handled in the same order as in the first loop; that is, the control for the second loop is specified as

$$\textbf{for } i := 0 \textbf{ to } 9 \textbf{ do}$$

Derive the equivalents of Figures 8.21 through 8.23 for this program. What conclusions can be drawn from this exercise?

8.11   **[M]** A byte-addressable computer has a small data cache capable of holding eight 32-bit words. Each cache block consists of one 32-bit word. When a given program is executed, the processor reads data sequentially from the following hex addresses:

$$200, 204, 208, 20C, 2F4, 2F0, 200, 204, 218, 21C, 24C, 2F4$$

This pattern is repeated four times.

(*a*) Assume that the cache is initially empty. Show the contents of the cache at the end of each pass through the loop if a direct-mapped cache is used, and compute the hit rate.

(*b*) Repeat part (*a*) for an associative-mapped cache that uses the LRU replacement algorithm.

(*c*) Repeat part (*a*) for a four-way set-associative cache.

8.12 **[M]** Repeat Problem 8.11, assuming that each cache block consists of two 32-bit words. For part (*c*), use a two-way set-associative cache that uses the LRU replacement algorithm.

8.13 **[E]** The cache block size in many computers is in the range of 32 to 128 bytes. What would be the main advantages and disadvantages of making the size of cache blocks larger or smaller?

8.14 **[M]** A computer has two cache levels L1 and L2. Plot two graphs for the average memory access time (*y*-axis) versus hit rate h_1 (*x*-axis) for the two values $h_2 = 0.75$ and $h_2 = 0.85$. Use the values 0.90, 0.92, 0.94, and 0.96, for h_1. Assume that the miss penalties are 15τ and 100τ for the L1 and L2 caches, respectively, where τ is the access time of the L1 caches.

8.15 **[E]** Consider the two-level cache described in Example 8.4. The average access time is given in the solution to part (*b*) of the example as 2.24τ. What value for h_1 would be needed to reduce t_{avg} to 1.5τ, if all other parameters are the same as in the example? Can the same result be achieved by improving the hit rate of L2?

8.16 **[E]** Consider the following analogy for the concept of caching. A serviceman comes to a house to repair the heating system. He carries a toolbox that contains a number of tools that he has used recently in similar jobs. He uses these tools repeatedly, until he reaches a point where other tools are needed. It is likely that he has the required tools in his truck outside the house. But, if the needed tools are not in the truck, he must go to his shop to get them.

Suppose we argue that the toolbox, the truck, and the shop correspond to the L1 cache, the L2 cache, and the main memory of a computer. How good is this analogy? Discuss its correct and incorrect features.

8.17 **[E]** The purpose of using an L2 cache is to reduce the miss penalty of the L1 cache, and in turn to reduce the memory access time as seen by the processor. An alternative is to increase the size of the L1 cache to increase its hit rate. What limits the utility of this approach?

8.18 **[M]** Give a critique of the assumption made in Example 8.1, in Section 8.7.1, that the miss penalty is the same for both read and write accesses. Consider both the write-through and write-back cases, as described in Section 8.6, in formulating your answer.

8.19 **[M]** Consider a computer system in which the available pages in the physical memory are divided among several application programs. The operating system monitors the page transfer activity and dynamically adjusts the number of pages allocated to various programs. Suggest a suitable strategy that the operating system can use to minimize the overall rate of page transfers.

8.20 **[M]** In a computer with a virtual-memory system, the execution of an instruction may be interrupted by a page fault. What state information has to be saved so that this instruction can be resumed later? Note that bringing a new page into the main memory involves a DMA transfer, which requires execution of other instructions. Is it simpler to abandon the interrupted instruction and completely re-execute it later? Can this be done?

8.21 **[E]** When a program generates a reference to a page that does not reside in the physical main memory, execution of the program is suspended until the requested page is loaded into the main memory from a disk. What difficulties might arise when an instruction in one page has an operand in a different page? What capabilities must the processor have to handle this situation?

8.22 **[M]** A disk unit has 24 recording surfaces. It has a total of 14,000 cylinders. There is an average of 400 sectors per track. Each sector contains 512 bytes of data.

(*a*) What is the maximum number of bytes that can be stored in this unit?

(*b*) What is the data transfer rate in bytes per second at a rotational speed of 7200 rpm?

(*c*) Using a 32-bit word, suggest a suitable scheme for specifying the disk address.

8.23 **[M]** Consider a long sequence of accesses to a disk with 8 ms average seek time, 3 ms average rotational delay, and a data transfer rate of 60 Mbytes/sec. The average size of a block being accessed is 64 Kbytes. Assume that each data block is stored in contiguous sectors.

(*a*) Assuming that the blocks are randomly located on the disk, estimate the average percentage of the total time occupied by seek operations and rotational delays.

(*b*) Suppose that 20 blocks are transferred in sequence from adjacent cylinders, reducing seek time to 1 ms. The blocks are randomly located on these cylinders. What is the total transfer time?

8.24 **[M]** The average seek time and rotational delay in a disk system are 6 ms and 3 ms, respectively. The rate of data transfer to or from the disk is 30 Mbytes/sec, and all disk accesses are for 8 Kbytes of data, stored in contiguous sectors. Data blocks are stored at random locations on the disk. The disk controller has an 8-Kbyte buffer. The disk controller, the processor, and the main memory are all attached to a single bus. The bus data width is 32 bits, and a single bus transfer to or from the main memory takes 10 nanoseconds.

(*a*) What is the maximum number of disk units that can be simultaneously transferring data to or from the main memory?

(*b*) What percentage of main memory accesses are used by one disk unit, on average, over a long period of time during which a sequence of independent 8-Kbyte transfers takes place?

8.25 **[M]** Magnetic disks are used as the secondary storage for program and data files in most virtual-memory systems. Which disk parameter(s) should influence the choice of page size?

REFERENCES

1. T.C. Mowry, "Tolerating Latency through Software-Controlled Data Prefetching," *Tech. Report CSL-TR-94-628*, Stanford University, Calif., 1994.

2. J.L. Baer and T.F. Chen, "An Effective On-Chip Preloading Scheme to Reduce Data Access Penalty," *Proceedings of Supercomputing '91*, 1991, pp. 176–186.

3. J.W.C. Fu and J.H. Patel, "Stride Directed Prefetching in Scalar Processors," *Proceedings of the 24th International Symposium on Microarchitecture,* 1992, pp. 102–110.

4. D. Kroft, "Lockup-Free Instruction Fetch/Prefetch Cache Organization," *Proceedings of the 8th Annual International Symposium on Computer Architecture,* 1981, pp. 81–85.

5. D.A. Patterson, G.A. Gibson, and R.H. Katz, "A Case for Redundant Arrays of Inexpensive Disks (RAID)," *Proceedings of the ACM SIGMOD International Conference on Management of Data*, 1988, pp. 109-166.

9

ARITHMETIC

CHAPTER OBJECTIVES

In this chapter you will learn about:

- Adder and subtractor circuits
- High-speed adders based on carry-lookahead logic circuits
- The Booth algorithm for multiplication of signed numbers
- High-speed multipliers based on carry-save addition
- Logic circuits for division
- Arithmetic operations on floating-point numbers conforming to the IEEE standard

Addition and subtraction of two numbers are basic operations at the machine-instruction level in all computers. These operations, as well as other arithmetic and logic operations, are implemented in the arithmetic and logic unit (ALU) of the processor. In this chapter, we present the logic circuits used to implement arithmetic operations. The time needed to perform addition or subtraction affects the processor's performance. Multiply and divide operations, which require more complex circuitry than either addition or subtraction operations, also affect performance. We present some of the techniques used in modern computers to perform arithmetic operations at high speed. Operations on floating-point numbers are also described.

In Section 1.4 of Chapter 1, we described the representation of signed binary numbers, and showed that 2's-complement is the best representation from the standpoint of performing addition and subtraction operations. The examples in Figure 1.6 show that two, n-bit, signed numbers can be added using n-bit binary addition, treating the sign bit the same as the other bits. In other words, a logic circuit that is designed to add unsigned binary numbers can also be used to add signed numbers in 2's-complement. The first two sections of this chapter present logic circuits for addition and subtraction.

9.1 ADDITION AND SUBTRACTION OF SIGNED NUMBERS

Figure 9.1 shows the truth table for the sum and carry-out functions for adding equally weighted bits x_i and y_i in two numbers X and Y. The figure also shows logic expressions for these functions, along with an example of addition of the 4-bit unsigned numbers 7 and 6. Note that each stage of the addition process must accommodate a carry-in bit. We use c_i to represent the carry-in to stage i, which is the same as the carry-out from stage $(i-1)$.

The logic expression for s_i in Figure 9.1 can be implemented with a 3-input XOR gate, used in Figure 9.2a as part of the logic required for a single stage of binary addition. The carry-out function, c_{i+1}, is implemented with an AND-OR circuit, as shown. A convenient symbol for the complete circuit for a single stage of addition, called a *full adder* (FA), is also shown in the figure.

A cascaded connection of n full-adder blocks can be used to add two n-bit numbers, as shown in Figure 9.2b. Since the carries must propagate, or ripple, through this cascade, the configuration is called a *ripple-carry adder*.

The carry-in, c_0, into the *least-significant-bit* (LSB) position provides a convenient means of adding 1 to a number. For instance, forming the 2's-complement of a number involves adding 1 to the 1's-complement of the number. The carry signals are also useful for interconnecting k adders to form an adder capable of handling input numbers that are kn bits long, as shown in Figure 9.2c.

9.1.1 ADDITION/SUBTRACTION LOGIC UNIT

The n-bit adder in Figure 9.2b can be used to add 2's-complement numbers X and Y, where the x_{n-1} and y_{n-1} bits are the sign bits. The carry-out bit c_n is not part of the answer. Arithmetic overflow was discussed in Section 1.4. It occurs when the signs of the two

x_i	y_i	Carry-in c_i	Sum s_i	Carry-out c_{i+1}
0	0	0	0	0
0	0	1	1	0
0	1	0	1	0
0	1	1	0	1
1	0	0	1	0
1	0	1	0	1
1	1	0	0	1
1	1	1	1	1

$$s_i = \overline{x}_i\,\overline{y}_i\,c_i + \overline{x}_i\,y_i\,\overline{c}_i + x_i\,\overline{y}_i\,\overline{c}_i + x_i\,y_i\,c_i = x_i \oplus y_i \oplus c_i$$

$$c_{i+1} = y_i\,c_i + x_i\,c_i + x_i\,y_i$$

Example:

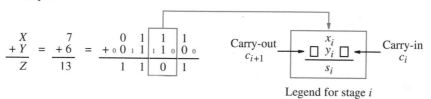

Figure 9.1   Logic specification for a stage of binary addition.

operands are the same, but the sign of the result is different. Therefore, a circuit to detect overflow can be added to the n-bit adder by implementing the logic expression

$$\text{Overflow} = x_{n-1}y_{n-1}\overline{s}_{n-1} + \overline{x}_{n-1}\overline{y}_{n-1}s_{n-1}$$

It can also be shown that overflow occurs when the carry bits c_n and c_{n-1} are different. (See Problem 9.5.) Therefore, a simpler circuit for detecting overflow can be obtained by implementing the expression $c_n \oplus c_{n-1}$ with an XOR gate.

In order to perform the subtraction operation $X - Y$ on 2's-complement numbers X and Y, we form the 2's-complement of Y and add it to X. The logic circuit shown in Figure 9.3 can be used to perform either addition or subtraction based on the value applied to the Add/Sub input control line. This line is set to 0 for addition, applying Y unchanged to one of the adder inputs along with a carry-in signal, c_0, of 0. When the Add/Sub control line is set to 1, the Y number is 1's-complemented (that is, bit-complemented) by the XOR gates and c_0 is set to 1 to complete the 2's-complementation of Y. Recall that 2's-complementing a negative number is done in exactly the same manner as for a positive number. An XOR gate can be added to Figure 9.3 to detect the overflow condition $c_n \oplus c_{n-1}$.

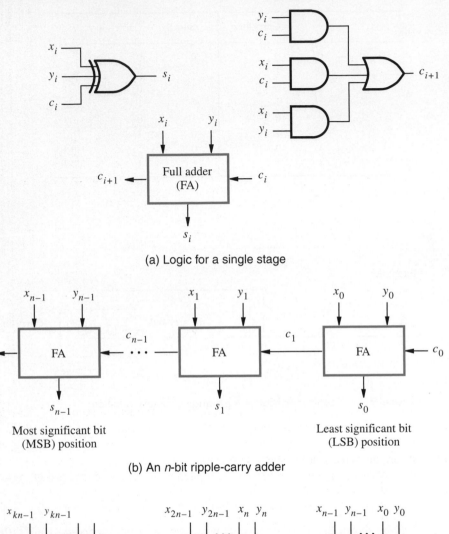

(a) Logic for a single stage

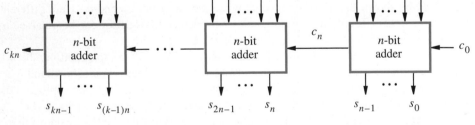

Most significant bit
(MSB) position

Least significant bit
(LSB) position

(b) An n-bit ripple-carry adder

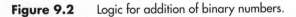

(c) Cascade of k n-bit adders

Figure 9.2   Logic for addition of binary numbers.

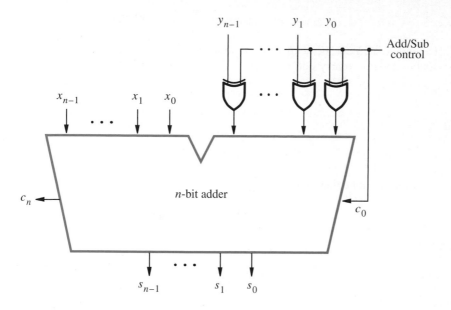

Figure 9.3   Binary addition/subtraction logic circuit.

9.2   DESIGN OF FAST ADDERS

If an n-bit ripple-carry adder is used in the addition/subtraction circuit of Figure 9.3, it may have too much delay in developing its outputs, s_0 through s_{n-1} and c_n. Whether or not the delay incurred is acceptable can be decided only in the context of the speed of other processor components and the data transfer times of registers and cache memories. The delay through a network of logic gates depends on the integrated circuit electronic technology used in fabricating the network and on the number of gates in the paths from inputs to outputs. The delay through any combinational circuit constructed from gates in a particular technology is determined by adding up the number of logic-gate delays along the longest signal propagation path through the circuit. In the case of the n-bit ripple-carry adder, the longest path is from inputs x_0, y_0, and c_0 at the LSB position to outputs c_n and s_{n-1} at the *most-significant-bit* (MSB) position.

Using the implementation indicated in Figure 9.2a, c_{n-1} is available in $2(n-1)$ gate delays, and s_{n-1} is correct one XOR gate delay later. The final carry-out, c_n, is available after $2n$ gate delays. Therefore, if a ripple-carry adder is used to implement the addition/subtraction unit shown in Figure 9.3, all sum bits are available in $2n$ gate delays, including the delay through the XOR gates on the Y input. Using the implementation $c_n \oplus c_{n-1}$ for overflow, this indicator is available after $2n + 2$ gate delays.

Two approaches can be taken to reduce delay in adders. The first approach is to use the fastest possible electronic technology. The second approach is to use a logic gate network called a carry-lookahead network, which is described in the next section.

9.2.1 CARRY-LOOKAHEAD ADDITION

A fast adder circuit must speed up the generation of the carry signals. The logic expressions for s_i (sum) and c_{i+1} (carry-out) of stage i (see Figure 9.1) are

$$s_i = x_i \oplus y_i \oplus c_i$$

and

$$c_{i+1} = x_i y_i + x_i c_i + y_i c_i$$

Factoring the second equation into

$$c_{i+1} = x_i y_i + (x_i + y_i)c_i$$

we can write

$$c_{i+1} = G_i + P_i c_i$$

where

$$G_i = x_i y_i \qquad \text{and} \qquad P_i = x_i + y_i$$

The expressions G_i and P_i are called the *generate* and *propagate* functions for stage i. If the generate function for stage i is equal to 1, then $c_{i+1} = 1$, independent of the input carry, c_i. This occurs when both x_i and y_i are 1. The propagate function means that an input carry will produce an output carry when either x_i is 1 or y_i is 1. All G_i and P_i functions can be formed independently and in parallel in one logic-gate delay after the X and Y operands are applied to the inputs of an n-bit adder. Each bit stage contains an AND gate to form G_i, an OR gate to form P_i, and a three-input XOR gate to form s_i. A simpler circuit can be derived by observing that an adequate propagate function can be realized as $P_i = x_i \oplus y_i$, which differs from $P_i = x_i + y_i$ only when $x_i = y_i = 1$. But, in this case $G_i = 1$, so it does not matter whether P_i is 0 or 1. Then, using a cascade of two 2-input XOR gates to realize the 3-input XOR function for s_i, the basic B cell in Figure 9.4a can be used in each bit stage.

Expanding c_i in terms of $i - 1$ subscripted variables and substituting into the c_{i+1} expression, we obtain

$$c_{i+1} = G_i + P_i G_{i-1} + P_i P_{i-1} c_{i-1}$$

Continuing this type of expansion, the final expression for any carry variable is

$$c_{i+1} = G_i + P_i G_{i-1} + P_i P_{i-1} G_{i-2} + \cdots + P_i P_{i-1} \cdots P_1 G_0 + P_i P_{i-1} \cdots P_0 c_0 \qquad (9.1)$$

Thus, all carries can be obtained three gate delays after the input operands X, Y, and c_0 are applied because only one gate delay is needed to develop all P_i and G_i signals, followed by two gate delays in the AND-OR circuit for c_{i+1}. After a further XOR gate delay, all sum bits are available. In total, the n-bit addition process requires only four gate delays, independent of n.

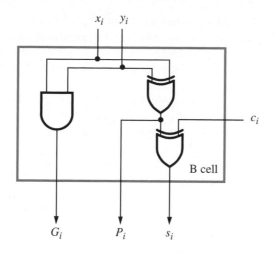

(a) Bit-stage cell

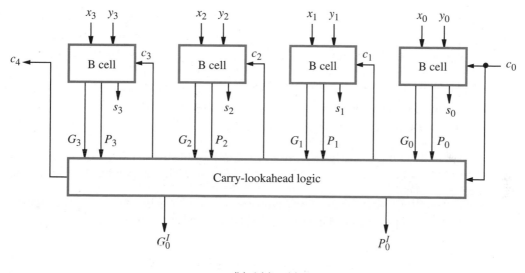

(b) 4-bit adder

Figure 9.4   A 4-bit carry-lookahead adder.

Let us consider the design of a 4-bit adder. The carries can be implemented as

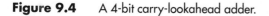

$$c_1 = G_0 + P_0 c_0$$
$$c_2 = G_1 + P_1 G_0 + P_1 P_0 c_0$$
$$c_3 = G_2 + P_2 G_1 + P_2 P_1 G_0 + P_2 P_1 P_0 c_0$$
$$c_4 = G_3 + P_3 G_2 + P_3 P_2 G_1 + P_3 P_2 P_1 G_0 + P_3 P_2 P_1 P_0 c_0$$

The complete 4-bit adder is shown in Figure 9.4b. The carries are produced in the block labeled carry-lookahead logic. An adder implemented in this form is called a *carry-lookahead adder*. Delay through the adder is 3 gate delays for all carry bits and 4 gate delays for all sum bits. In comparison, a 4-bit ripple-carry adder requires 7 gate delays for s_3 and 8 gate delays for c_4.

If we try to extend the carry-lookahead adder design of Figure 9.4b for longer operands, we encounter the problem of gate fan-in constraints. From Expression 9.1, we see that the last AND gate and the OR gate require a fan-in of $i + 2$ in generating c_{i+1}. A fan-in of 5 is required for c_4 in the 4-bit adder. This is about the limit for practical gates. So the adder design shown in Figure 9.4b cannot be extended easily for longer operands. However, it is possible to build longer adders by cascading a number of 4-bit adders, as shown in Figure 9.2c.

Eight, 4-bit, carry-lookahead adders can be connected as in Figure 9.2c to form a 32-bit adder. The delays in generating sum bits s_{31}, s_{30}, s_{29}, s_{28}, and carry bit c_{32} in the high-order 4-bit adder in this cascade are calculated as follows. The carry-out c_4 from the low-order adder is available 3 gate delays after the input operands X, Y, and c_0 are applied to the 32-bit adder. Then, c_8 is available at the output of the second adder after a further 2 gate delays, c_{12} is available after a further 2 gate delays, and so on. Finally, c_{28}, the carry-in to the high-order 4-bit adder, is available after a total of $(6 \times 2) + 3 = 15$ gate delays. Then, c_{32} and all carries inside the high-order adder are available after a further 2 gate delays, and all 4 sum bits are available after 1 more gate delay, for a total of 18 gate delays. This should be compared to total delays of 63 and 64 for s_{31} and c_{32} if a ripple-carry adder is used.

In the next section, we show how it is possible to improve upon the cascade structure just discussed, leading to further reduction in adder delay. The key idea is to generate the carries c_4, c_8, ... in parallel, similar to the way that c_1, c_2, c_3, and c_4, are generated in parallel in the 4-bit carry-lookahead adder.

Higher-Level Generate and Propagate Functions

In the 32-bit adder just discussed, the carries $c_4, c_8, c_{12}, \ldots$ ripple through the 4-bit adder blocks with two gate delays per block, analogous to the way that individual carries ripple through each bit stage in a ripple-carry adder. It is possible to use the lookahead approach to develop the carries c_4, c_8, c_{12}, ... in parallel by using higher-level block generate and propagate functions.

Figure 9.5 shows a 16-bit adder built from four 4-bit adder blocks. These blocks provide new output functions defined as G_k^I and P_k^I, where $k = 0$ for the first 4-bit block, $k = 1$ for the second 4-bit block, and so on, as shown in Figures 9.4b and 9.5. In the first block,

$$P_0^I = P_3 P_2 P_1 P_0$$

and

$$G_0^I = G_3 + P_3 G_2 + P_3 P_2 G_1 + P_3 P_2 P_1 G_0$$

The first-level G_i and P_i functions determine whether bit stage i generates or propagates a carry. The second-level G_k^I and P_k^I functions determine whether block k generates or propagates a carry. With these new functions available, it is not necessary to wait for carries to ripple through the 4-bit blocks. Carry c_{16} is formed by one of the carry-lookahead

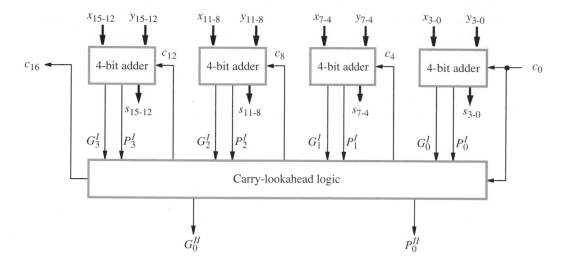

Figure 9.5   A 16-bit carry-lookahead adder built from 4-bit adders (see Figure 9.4*b*).

circuits in Figure 9.5 as

$$c_{16} = G_3^I + P_3^I G_2^I + P_3^I P_2^I G_1^I + P_3^I P_2^I P_1^I G_0^I + P_3^I P_2^I P_1^I P_0^I c_0$$

The input carries to the 4-bit blocks are formed in parallel by similar shorter expressions. Expressions for c_{16}, c_{12}, c_8, and c_4, are identical in form to the expressions for c_4, c_3, c_2, and c_1, respectively, implemented in the carry-lookahead circuits in Figure 9.4*b*. Only the variable names are different. Therefore, the structure of the carry-lookahead circuits in Figure 9.5 is identical to the carry-lookahead circuits in Figure 9.4*b*. However, the carries c_4, c_8, c_{12}, and c_{16}, generated internally by the 4-bit adder blocks, are not needed in Figure 9.5 because they are generated by the higher-level carry-lookahead circuits.

Now, consider the delay in producing outputs from the 16-bit carry-lookahead adder. The delay in developing the carries produced by the carry-lookahead circuits is two gate delays more than the delay needed to develop the G_k^I and P_k^I functions. The latter require two gate delays and one gate delay, respectively, after the generation of G_i and P_i. Therefore, all carries produced by the carry-lookahead circuits are available 5 gate delays after X, Y, and c_0 are applied as inputs. The carry c_{15} is generated inside the high-order 4-bit block in Figure 9.5 in two gate delays after c_{12}, followed by s_{15} in one further gate delay. Therefore, s_{15} is available after 8 gate delays. If a 16-bit adder is built by cascading 4-bit carry-lookahead adder blocks, the delays in developing c_{16} and s_{15} are 9 and 10 gate delays, respectively, as compared to 5 and 8 gate delays for the configuration in Figure 9.5.

Two 16-bit adder blocks can be cascaded to implement a 32-bit adder. In this configuration, the output c_{16} from the low-order block is the carry input to the high-order block. The delay is much lower than the delay through the 32-bit adder that we discussed earlier, which was built by cascading eight 4-bit adders. In that configuration, recall that s_{31} is available after 18 gate delays and c_{32} is available after 17 gate delays. The delay analysis for the cascade of two 16-bit adders is as follows. The carry c_{16} out of the low-order block is available after 5 gate delays, as calculated above. Then, both c_{28} and c_{32} are available in the high-order block after a further 2 gate delays, and c_{31} is available 2 gate delays after c_{28}. Therefore, c_{31} is available after a total of 9 gate delays, and s_{31} is available in 10 gate delays. Recapitulating, s_{31} and c_{32} are available after 10 and 7 gate delays, respectively, compared to 18 and 17 gate delays for the same outputs if the 32-bit adder is built from a cascade of eight 4-bit adders.

The same reasoning used in developing second-level G_k^I and P_k^I functions from first-level G_i and P_i functions can be used to develop third-level G_k^{II} and P_k^{II} functions from G_k^I and P_k^I functions. Two such third-level functions are shown as outputs from the carry-lookahead logic in Figure 9.5. A 64-bit adder can be built from four of the 16-bit adders shown in Figure 9.5, along with additional carry-lookahead logic circuits that produce carries c_{16}, c_{32}, c_{48}, and c_{64}. Delay through this adder can be shown to be 12 gate delays for s_{63} and 7 gate delays for c_{64}, using an extension of the reasoning used above for the 16-bit adder. (See Problem 9.7.)

9.3 MULTIPLICATION OF UNSIGNED NUMBERS

The usual algorithm for multiplying integers by hand is illustrated in Figure 9.6a for the binary system. The product of two, unsigned, n-digit numbers can be accommodated in $2n$ digits, so the product of the two 4-bit numbers in this example is accommodated in 8 bits, as shown. In the binary system, multiplication of the multiplicand by one bit of the multiplier is easy. If the multiplier bit is 1, the multiplicand is entered in the appropriate shifted position. If the multiplier bit is 0, then 0s are entered, as in the third row of the example. The product is computed one bit at a time by adding the bit columns from right to left and propagating carry values between columns.

9.3.1 ARRAY MULTIPLIER

Binary multiplication of unsigned operands can be implemented in a combinational, two-dimensional, logic array, as shown in Figure 9.6b for the 4-bit operand case. The main component in each cell is a full adder, FA. The AND gate in each cell determines whether a multiplicand bit, m_j, is added to the incoming partial-product bit, based on the value of the multiplier bit, q_i. Each row i, where $0 \leq i \leq 3$, adds the multiplicand (appropriately shifted) to the incoming partial product, PPi, to generate the outgoing partial product, PP$(i + 1)$, if $q_i = 1$. If $q_i = 0$, PPi is passed vertically downward unchanged. PP0 is all 0s, and PP4 is the desired product. The multiplicand is shifted left one position per row by the diagonal signal path. We note that the row-by-row addition done in the array circuit differs from the usual hand addition described previously, which is done column-by-column.

The worst-case signal propagation delay path is from the upper right corner of the array to the high-order product bit output at the bottom left corner of the array. This critical path consists of the staircase pattern that includes the two cells at the right end of each

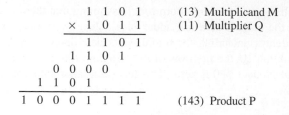

```
        1  1  0  1         (13)  Multiplicand M
     ×  1  0  1  1         (11)  Multiplier Q
     ─────────────
        1  1  0  1
     1  1  0  1
  0  0  0  0
  1  1  0  1
 ────────────────────
 1  0  0  0  1  1  1  1    (143)  Product P
```

(a) Manual multiplication algorithm

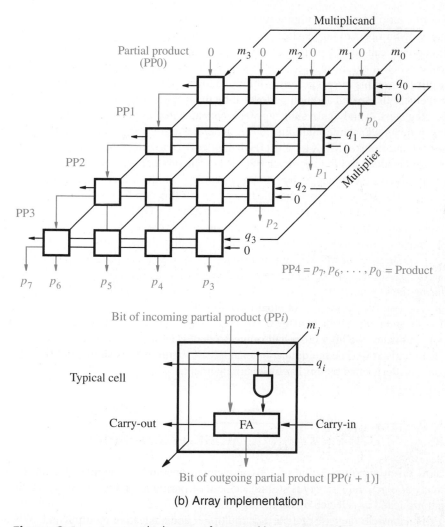

(b) Array implementation

Figure 9.6   Array multiplication of unsigned binary operands.

row, followed by all the cells in the bottom row. Assuming that there are two gate delays from the inputs to the outputs of a full-adder block, FA, the critical path has a total of $6(n - 1) - 1$ gate delays, including the initial AND gate delay in all cells, for an $n \times n$ array. (See Problem 9.8.) In the first row of the array, no full adders are needed, because the incoming partial product PP0 is zero. This has been taken into account in developing the delay expression.

9.3.2   Sequential Circuit Multiplier

The combinational array multiplier just described uses a large number of logic gates for multiplying numbers of practical size, such as 32- or 64-bit numbers. Multiplication of two n-bit numbers can also be performed in a sequential circuit that uses a single n-bit adder.

The block diagram in Figure 9.7a shows the hardware arrangement for sequential multiplication. This circuit performs multiplication by using a single n-bit adder n times to implement the spatial addition performed by the n rows of ripple-carry adders in Figure 9.6b. Registers A and Q are shift registers, concatenated as shown. Together, they hold partial product PPi while multiplier bit q_i generates the signal Add/Noadd. This signal causes the multiplexer MUX to select 0 when $q_i = 0$, or to select the multiplicand M when $q_i = 1$, to be added to PPi to generate PP$(i + 1)$. The product is computed in n cycles. The partial product grows in length by one bit per cycle from the initial vector, PP0, of n 0s in register A. The carry-out from the adder is stored in flip-flop C, shown at the left end of register A. At the start, the multiplier is loaded into register Q, the multiplicand into register M, and C and A are cleared to 0. At the end of each cycle, C, A, and Q are shifted right one bit position to allow for growth of the partial product as the multiplier is shifted out of register Q. Because of this shifting, multiplier bit q_i appears at the LSB position of Q to generate the Add/Noadd signal at the correct time, starting with q_0 during the first cycle, q_1 during the second cycle, and so on. After they are used, the multiplier bits are discarded by the right-shift operation. Note that the carry-out from the adder is the leftmost bit of PP$(i + 1)$, and it must be held in the C flip-flop to be shifted right with the contents of A and Q. After n cycles, the high-order half of the product is held in register A and the low-order half is in register Q. The multiplication example of Figure 9.6a is shown in Figure 9.7b as it would be performed by this hardware arrangement.

9.4   Multiplication of Signed Numbers

We now discuss multiplication of 2's-complement operands, generating a double-length product. The general strategy is still to accumulate partial products by adding versions of the multiplicand as selected by the multiplier bits.

First, consider the case of a positive multiplier and a negative multiplicand. When we add a negative multiplicand to a partial product, we must extend the sign-bit value of the multiplicand to the left as far as the product will extend. Figure 9.8 shows an example in which a 5-bit signed operand, -13, is the multiplicand. It is multiplied by $+11$ to get

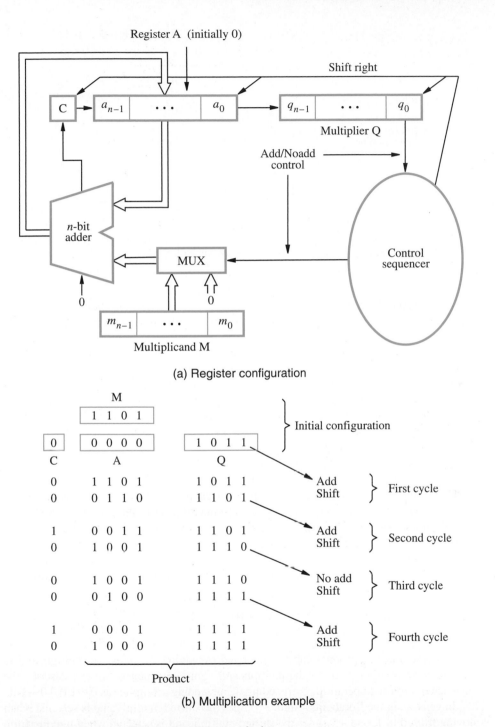

(a) Register configuration

(b) Multiplication example

Figure 9.7   Sequential circuit binary multiplier.

$$
\begin{array}{rrrrrrrrrrr}
 & & & & & 1 & 0 & 0 & 1 & 1 & (-13) \\
 & & & & \times & 0 & 1 & 0 & 1 & 1 & (+11) \\
\hline
 & 1 & 1 & 1 & 1 & 1 & 1 & 0 & 0 & 1 & 1 \\
 & 1 & 1 & 1 & 1 & 1 & 0 & 0 & 1 & 1 & \\
 & 0 & 0 & 0 & 0 & 0 & 0 & 0 & 0 & & \\
 & 1 & 1 & 1 & 0 & 0 & 1 & 1 & & & \\
 & 0 & 0 & 0 & 0 & 0 & 0 & & & & \\
\hline
 & 1 & 1 & 0 & 1 & 1 & 1 & 0 & 0 & 0 & 1 & (-143)
\end{array}
$$

Sign extension is shown in blue

Figure 9.8 Sign extension of negative multiplicand.

the 10-bit product, -143. The sign extension of the multiplicand is shown in blue. The hardware discussed earlier can be used for negative multiplicands if it is augmented to provide for sign extension of the partial products.

For a negative multiplier, a straightforward solution is to form the 2's-complement of both the multiplier and the multiplicand and proceed as in the case of a positive multiplier. This is possible because complementation of both operands does not change the value or the sign of the product. A technique that works equally well for both negative and positive multipliers, called the Booth algorithm, is described next.

9.4.1 THE BOOTH ALGORITHM

The Booth algorithm [1] generates a $2n$-bit product and treats both positive and negative 2's-complement n-bit operands uniformly. To understand the basis of this algorithm, consider a multiplication operation in which the multiplier is positive and has a single block of 1s, for example, 0011110. To derive the product, we could add four appropriately shifted versions of the multiplicand, as in the standard procedure. However, we can reduce the number of required operations by regarding this multiplier as the difference between two numbers:

$$
\begin{array}{ll}
 & 0100000 \quad (32) \\
- & 0000010 \quad (2) \\
\hline
 & 0011110 \quad (30)
\end{array}
$$

This suggests that the product can be generated by adding 2^5 times the multiplicand to the 2's-complement of 2^1 times the multiplicand. For convenience, we can describe the sequence of required operations by recoding the preceding multiplier as $0 +1\,0\,0\,0 -1\,0$.

In general, in the Booth algorithm, -1 times the shifted multiplicand is selected when moving from 0 to 1, and $+1$ times the shifted multiplicand is selected when moving from

1 to 0, as the multiplier is scanned from right to left. Figure 9.9 illustrates the normal and the Booth algorithms for the example just discussed. The Booth algorithm clearly extends to any number of blocks of 1s in a multiplier, including the situation in which a single 1 is considered a block. Figure 9.10 shows another example of recoding a multiplier. The case when the least significant bit of the multiplier is 1 is handled by assuming that an implied 0 lies to its right. The Booth algorithm can also be used directly for negative multipliers, as shown in Figure 9.11.

To demonstrate the correctness of the Booth algorithm for negative multipliers, we use the following property of negative-number representations in the 2's-complement system.

```
                    0   1   0   1   1   0   1
                    0   0 + 1 + 1 + 1 + 1   0
                   ─────────────────────────────
                    0   0   0   0   0   0   0
                0   1   0   1   1   0   1
            0   1   0   1   1   0   1
        0   1   0   1   1   0   1
    0   0   0   0   0   0   0
0   0   0   0   0   0   0
─────────────────────────────────────────────
0   0   0   1   0   1   0   1   0   0   0   1   1   0
```

```
                    0   1   0   1   1   0   1
                    0 + 1   0   0   0 - 1   0
0   0   0   0   0   0   0   0   0   0   0   0   0   0
1   1   1   1   1   1   1   0   1   0   0   1   1      ◄──  2's complement of
0   0   0   0   0   0   0   0   0   0   0   0              the multiplicand
0   0   0   0   0   0   0   0   0   0   0
0   0   0   0   0   0   0   0   0   0
0   0   0   1   0   1   1   0   1
0   0   0   0   0   0   0   0
──────────────────────────────────────────────
0   0   0   1   0   1   0   1   0   0   0   1   1   0
```

Figure 9.9　Normal and Booth multiplication schemes.

```
0   0   1   0   1   1   0   0   1   1   1   0   1   0   1   1   0   0

                            ⇓⇓

0  +1  -1  +1   0  -1   0  +1   0   0  -1  +1  -1  +1   0  -1   0   0
```

Figure 9.10　Booth recoding of a multiplier.

$$
\begin{array}{cc}
\begin{array}{ccccc}
0 & 1 & 1 & 0 & 1 \\
\times\, 1 & 1 & 0 & 1 & 0 \\
\end{array} & \begin{array}{c}(+13) \\ (-6)\end{array}
\end{array}
\qquad \Longrightarrow \qquad
\begin{array}{ccccc}
0 & 1 & 1 & 0 & 1 \\
0 & -1 & +1 & -1 & 0 \\
\end{array}
$$

```
                    0 0 0 0 0 0 0 0 0 0
                    1 1 1 1 1 0 0 1 1
                    0 0 0 0 1 1 0 1
                    1 1 1 0 0 1 1
                    0 0 0 0 0 0
                   ─────────────────────
                    1 1 1 0 1 1 0 0 1 0   (−78)
```

Figure 9.11   Booth multiplication with a negative multiplier.

Suppose that the leftmost 0 of a negative number, X, is at bit position k, that is,

$$X = 11\ldots10x_{k-1}\ldots x_0$$

Then the value of X is given by

$$V(X) = -2^{k+1} + x_{k-1} \times 2^{k-1} + \cdots + x_0 \times 2^0$$

The correctness of this expression for $V(X)$ is shown by observing that if X is formed as the sum of two numbers, as follows,

$$
\begin{array}{rl}
 & 11\ldots100000\ldots0 \\
+ & 00\ldots00x_{k-1}\ldots x_0 \\
\hline
X = & 11\ldots10x_{k-1}\ldots x_0 \\
\end{array}
$$

then the upper number is the 2's-complement representation of -2^{k+1}. The recoded multiplier now consists of the part corresponding to the lower number, with -1 added in position $k + 1$. For example, the multiplier 110110 is recoded as $0 -1 +1\, 0 -1\, 0$.

The Booth technique for recoding multipliers is summarized in Figure 9.12. The transformation $011\ldots110 \Rightarrow +1\,0\,0\ldots0 -1\,0$ is called *skipping over 1s*. This term is derived from the case in which the multiplier has its 1s grouped into a few contiguous blocks. Only a few versions of the shifted multiplicand (the summands) need to be added to generate the product, thus speeding up the multiplication operation. However, in the worst case—that of alternating 1s and 0s in the multiplier—each bit of the multiplier selects a summand. In fact, this results in more summands than if the Booth algorithm were not used. A 16-bit worst-case multiplier, an ordinary multiplier, and a good multiplier are shown in Figure 9.13.

The Booth algorithm has two attractive features. First, it handles both positive and negative multipliers uniformly. Second, it achieves some efficiency in the number of additions required when the multiplier has a few large blocks of 1s.

Multiplier		Version of multiplicand selected by bit i
Bit i	Bit $i-1$	
0	0	$0 \times M$
0	1	$+1 \times M$
1	0	$-1 \times M$
1	1	$0 \times M$

Figure 9.12 Booth multiplier recoding table.

Worst-case multiplier

0 1 0 1 0 1 0 1 0 1 0 1 0 1 0 1

+1 −1 +1 −1 +1 −1 +1 −1 +1 −1 +1 −1 +1 −1 +1 −1

Ordinary multiplier

1 1 0 0 0 1 0 1 1 0 1 1 1 1 0 0

0 −1 0 0 +1 −1 +1 0 −1 +1 0 0 0 −1 0 0

Good multiplier

0 0 0 0 1 1 1 1 1 0 0 0 0 1 1 1

0 0 0 +1 0 0 0 0 −1 0 0 0 +1 0 0 −1

Figure 9.13 Booth recoded multipliers.

9.5 FAST MULTIPLICATION

We now describe two techniques for speeding up the multiplication operation. The first technique guarantees that the maximum number of summands (versions of the multiplicand) that must be added is $n/2$ for n-bit operands. The second technique leads to adding the summands in parallel.

9.5.1 BIT-PAIR RECODING OF MULTIPLIERS

A technique called *bit-pair recoding* of the multiplier results in using at most one summand for each pair of bits in the multiplier. It is derived directly from the Booth algorithm. Group the Booth-recoded multiplier bits in pairs, and observe the following. The pair (+1 −1) is equivalent to the pair (0 +1). That is, instead of adding −1 times the multiplicand M at shift position i to +1 × M at position $i + 1$, the same result is obtained by adding +1 × M at position i. Other examples are: (+1 0) is equivalent to (0 +2), (−1 +1) is equivalent to (0 −1), and so on. Thus, if the Booth-recoded multiplier is examined two bits at a time, starting from the right, it can be rewritten in a form that requires at most one version of the multiplicand to be added to the partial product for each pair of multiplier bits. Figure 9.14*a* shows an example of bit-pair recoding of the multiplier in Figure 9.11, and Figure 9.14*b*

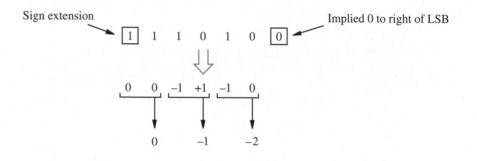

(a) Example of bit-pair recoding derived from Booth recoding

Multiplier bit-pair		Multiplier bit on the right	Multiplicand
$i + 1$	i	$i - 1$	selected at position i
0	0	0	$0 \times M$
0	0	1	$+1 \times M$
0	1	0	$+1 \times M$
0	1	1	$+2 \times M$
1	0	0	$-2 \times M$
1	0	1	$-1 \times M$
1	1	0	$-1 \times M$
1	1	1	$0 \times M$

(b) Table of multiplicand selection decisions

Figure 9.14   Multiplier bit-pair recoding.

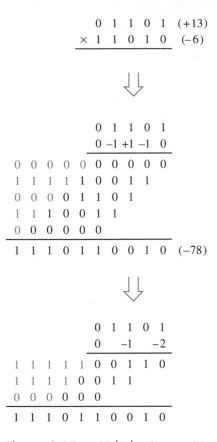

```
                  0  1  1  0  1   (+13)
              ×   1  1  0  1  0    (−6)
```

```
                  0  1  1  0  1
                  0 −1 +1 −1  0
      0  0  0  0  0  0  0  0  0  0
      1  1  1  1  1  0  0  1  1
      0  0  0  0  1  1  0  1
      1  1  1  0  0  1  1
      0  0  0  0  0  0
      ─────────────────────────────
      1  1  1  0  1  1  0  0  1  0   (−78)
```

```
                  0  1  1  0  1
                  0    −1    −2
      1  1  1  1  1  0  0  1  1  0
      1  1  1  1  0  0  1  1
      0  0  0  0  0  0
      ─────────────────────────────
      1  1  1  0  1  1  0  0  1  0
```

Figure 9.15   Multiplication requiring only $n/2$ summands.

shows a table of the multiplicand selection decisions for all possibilities. The multiplication operation in Figure 9.11 is shown in Figure 9.15 as it would be computed using bit-pair recoding of the multiplier.

9.5.2 CARRY-SAVE ADDITION OF SUMMANDS

Multiplication requires the addition of several summands. A technique called *carry-save addition* (CSA) can be used to speed up the process. Consider the 4×4 multiplication array shown in Figure 9.16a. This structure is in the form of the array shown in Figure 9.6, in which the first row consists of just the AND gates that produce the four inputs m_3q_0, m_2q_0, m_1q_0, and m_0q_0.

Instead of letting the carries ripple along the rows, they can be "saved" and introduced into the next row, at the correct weighted positions, as shown in Figure 9.16b. This frees up an input to each of three full adders in the first row. These inputs can be used to introduce

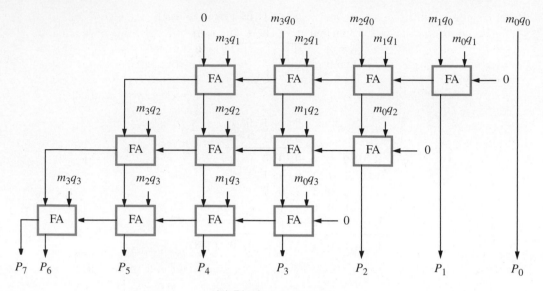

(a) Ripple-carry array

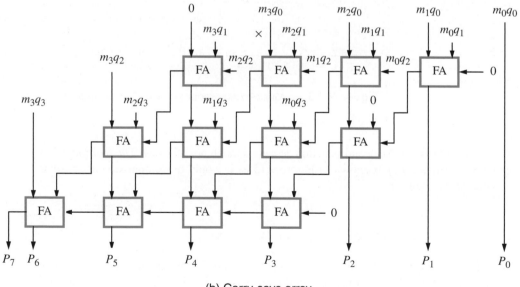

(b) Carry-save array

Figure 9.16 Ripple-carry and carry-save arrays for a 4 × 4 multiplier.

the third summand bits m_2q_2, m_1q_2, and m_0q_2. Now, two inputs of each of three full adders in the second row are fed by the sum and carry outputs from the first row. The third input is used to introduce the bits m_2q_3, m_1q_3, and m_0q_3 of the fourth summand. The high-order bits m_3q_2 and m_3q_3 of the third and fourth summands are introduced into the remaining free full-adder inputs at the left end in the second and third rows. The saved carry bits and the sum bits from the second row are now added in the third row, which is a ripple-carry adder, to produce the final product bits.

The delay through the carry-save array is somewhat less than the delay through the ripple-carry array. This is because the S and C vector outputs from each row are produced in parallel in one full-adder delay. The amount of reduction in delay is considered in Problem 9.15.

9.5.3 SUMMAND ADDITION TREE USING 3-2 REDUCERS

A more significant reduction in delay can be achieved when dealing with longer operands than those considered in Figure 9.16. We can group the summands in threes and perform carry-save addition on each of these groups in parallel to generate a set of S and C vectors in one full-adder delay. Here, we will refer to a full-adder circuit as simply an adder. Next, we group all the S and C vectors into threes, and perform carry-save addition on them, generating a further set of S and C vectors in one more adder delay. We continue with this process until there are only two vectors remaining. The adder at each bit position of the three summands is called a *3-2 reducer*, and the logic circuit structure that reduces a number of summands to two is called a *CSA tree*, as described by Wallace [2]. The final two S and C vectors can be added in a carry-lookahead adder to produce the desired product.

Consider the example shown in Figure 9.17. It involves adding the six shifted versions of the multiplicand for the case of multiplying two, 6-bit, unsigned numbers, where all six

						1	0	1	1	0	1			(45)	M
					×	1	1	1	1	1	1			(63)	Q
						1	0	1	1	0	1				A
					1	0	1	1	0	1					B
				1	0	1	1	0	1						C
			1	0	1	1	0	1							D
		1	0	1	1	0	1								E
	1	0	1	1	0	1									F
1	0	1	1	0	0	0	1	0	0	1	1			(2,835)	Product

Figure 9.17 A multiplication example used to illustrate carry-save addition as shown in Figure 9.18.

bits of the multiplier are equal to 1. The six summands, $A, B, \ldots, F$ are added by carry-save addition in Figure 9.18. The blue boxes in these two figures indicate the same operand bits, and show how they are reduced to sum and carry bits in Figure 9.18 by carry-save addition. Three levels of carry-save addition are performed, as shown schematically in Figure 9.19. This figure shows that the final two vectors S_4 and C_4 are available in three adder delays

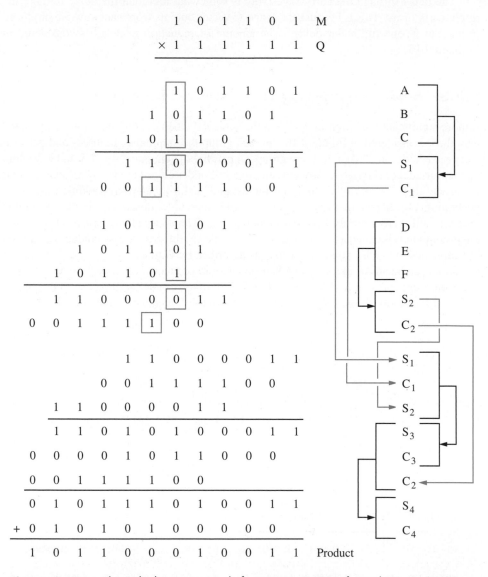

Figure 9.18   The multiplication example from Figure 9.17 performed using carry-save addition.

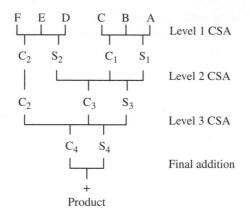

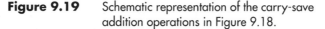

Figure 9.19   Schematic representation of the carry-save addition operations in Figure 9.18.

after the six input summands are applied to level 1. The final regular addition operation on S_4 and C_4, which produces the product, can be done with a carry-lookahead adder.

The multiplier delay is lower when using the tree structure illustrated in Figure 9.19 than when using the array structure illustrated in Figure 9.16*b*. When the number of summands is large, the reduction in delay is significant. For example, the addition of 32 summands following the pattern shown in Figure 9.19 requires only 8 levels of 3-2 reduction before the final Add operation. In general, it can be shown that approximately $1.7log_2k - 1.7$ levels of 3-2 reduction are needed to reduce k summands to 2 vectors, which, when added, produce the desired product. (See Example 9.3. in Section 9.10.)

We should note that negative summands are involved when signed-number multiplication and Booth recoding of multipliers is used. This requires sign extension of the summands before they are entered into the reduction tree. Also, the number of summands that need to be added is reduced if bit-pair recoding of the multiplier is done.

The 3-2 reducer is not the only logic circuit that can be used in building reduction trees. It is also possible to use 4-2 reducers and 7-3 reducers. The first of these possibilities is described in the next subsection, and the second is explored in Problem 9.17.

9.5.4   SUMMAND ADDITION TREE USING 4-2 REDUCERS

The interconnection pattern between levels in a CSA tree that uses 3-2 reducers is irregular, as can be seen in Figure 9.19. A more regularly structured tree can be obtained by using 4-2 reducers [3], especially for the case in which the number of summands to be reduced is a power of 2. This is the usual case for the multiplication operation in the ALU of a processor. For example, if 32 summands are reduced to 2 using 4-2 reducers at each reduction level, then only four levels are needed. The tree has a regular structure, with 16, 8, 4, and 2 summands at the outputs of the four levels. If 3-2 reducers are used, eight levels are required, and the wiring connections between levels are quite irregular. Regular tree structures facilitate logic circuit and wiring layout for VLSI circuit implementation.

Let us consider the design of a 4-2 reducer as developed in reference [3]. The addition of four equally-weighted bits, w, x, y, and z, from four summands, produces a value in the range 0 to 4. Such a value cannot be represented by a sum bit, s, and a single carry bit, c. However, a second carry bit, c_{out}, with the same weight as c, can be used along with s and c, to represent any value in the range 0 to 5. This is sufficient for our purposes here.

We do not want to send three output bits down to the next reduction level. That would implement a 4-3 reducer, which provides less reduction than a 3-2 reducer. The solution is to send c_{out} laterally to the 4-2 reducer in the next higher-weighted bit position on the same reduction level. Thus, each 4-2 reducer must have a fifth input, c_{in}, which is the c_{out} output from the 4-2 reducer in the next lower-weighted bit position on the same reduction level.

A final requirement on the design of the 4-2 reducer is that the value of c_{out} cannot depend on the value of c_{in}. This is a key requirement. Without it, carries would ripple laterally along a reduction level, defeating the purpose of parallel reduction of summands with short fixed delay. A 4-2 reducer block is shown in Figure 9.20.

In summary, the specification for a 4-2 reducer is as follows:

- The three outputs, s, c, and c_{out}, represent the arithmetic sum of the five inputs, that is

$$w + x + y + z + c_{in} = s + 2(c + c_{out})$$

where all operators here are arithmetic.

- Output s is the usual sum variable; that is, s is the XOR function of the five input variables.

- The lateral carry, c_{out}, must be independent of c_{in}. It is a function of only the four input variables w, x, y, and z.

There are different possibilities for specifying the two carry outputs in a way that meets the given conditions. We present one that is easy to describe. First, assign the lateral carry

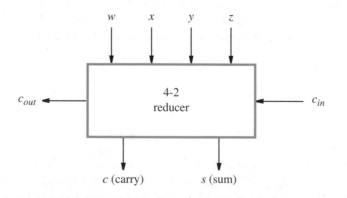

Figure 9.20   A 4-2 reducer block.

				$c_{in} = 0$		$c_{in} = 1$		
w	x	y	z	c	s	c	s	c_{out}
0	0	0	0	0	0	0	1	0
0	0	0	1	0	1	1	0	0
0	0	1	0	0	1	1	0	0
0	1	0	0	0	1	1	0	0
1	0	0	0	0	1	1	0	0
0	0	1	1	0	0	0	1	1
0	1	0	1	0	0	0	1	1
0	1	1	0	0	0	0	1	1
1	0	0	1	0	0	0	1	1
1	0	1	0	0	0	0	1	1
1	1	0	0	0	0	0	1	1
0	1	1	1	0	1	1	0	1
1	0	1	1	0	1	1	0	1
1	1	0	1	0	1	1	0	1
1	1	1	0	0	1	1	0	1
1	1	1	1	1	0	1	1	1

Figure 9.21   A 4-2 reducer truth table.

output, c_{out}, to be 1 when two or more of the input variables w, x, y, and z, are equal to 1. Then, the other carry output, c, is determined so as to satisfy the arithmetic condition. A complete truth table satisfying these conditions is given in Figure 9.21. The table is shown in a form that is different from the usual form used in Appendix A. The four inputs w, x, y, and z, are not listed in binary numerical order. They are listed in groups corresponding to the number of inputs that have the value 1. This makes it easy to see how the outputs are specified to meet the given conditions. A logic gate network can be derived from the table.

9.5.5 SUMMARY OF FAST MULTIPLICATION

We now summarize the techniques for high-speed multiplication. Bit-pair recoding of the multiplier, derived from the Booth algorithm, can be used to initially reduce the number of summands by a factor of two. The resulting summands can then be reduced to two in a reduction tree with a relatively small number of reduction levels. The final product can be generated by an addition operation that uses a carry-lookahead adder. All three of these techniques—bit-pair recoding of the multiplier, parallel reduction of summands, and carry-lookahead addition—have been used in various combinations by the designers of high-performance processors to reduce the time needed to perform multiplication.

9.6 INTEGER DIVISION

In Section 9.3, we discussed the multiplication of unsigned numbers by relating the way the multiplication operation is done manually to the way it is done in a logic circuit. We use the same approach here in discussing integer division. We discuss unsigned-number division in detail, and then make some general comments on the signed-number case.

Figure 9.22 shows examples of decimal division and binary division of the same values. Consider the decimal version first. The 2 in the quotient is determined by the following reasoning: First, we try to divide 13 into 2, and it does not work. Next, we try to divide 13 into 27. We go through the trial exercise of multiplying 13 by 2 to get 26, and, observing that $27 - 26 = 1$ is less than 13, we enter 2 as the quotient and perform the required subtraction. The next digit of the dividend, 4, is brought down, and we finish by deciding that 13 goes into 14 once, and the remainder is 1. We can discuss binary division in a similar way, with the simplification that the only possibilities for the quotient bits are 0 and 1.

A circuit that implements division by this longhand method operates as follows: It positions the divisor appropriately with respect to the dividend and performs a subtraction. If the remainder is zero or positive, a quotient bit of 1 is determined, the remainder is extended by another bit of the dividend, the divisor is repositioned, and another subtraction is performed. If the remainder is negative, a quotient bit of 0 is determined, the dividend is restored by adding back the divisor, and the divisor is repositioned for another subtraction. This is called the *restoring division* algorithm.

Restoring Division

Figure 9.23 shows a logic circuit arrangement that implements the restoring division algorithm just discussed. Note its similarity to the structure for multiplication shown in Figure 9.7. An n-bit positive divisor is loaded into register M and an n-bit positive dividend

$$
\begin{array}{r}
21 \\
13\overline{)274} \\
26 \\
\hline
14 \\
13 \\
\hline
1
\end{array}
\qquad\qquad
\begin{array}{r}
10101 \\
1101\overline{)100010010} \\
1101 \\
\hline
10000 \\
1101 \\
\hline
1110 \\
1101 \\
\hline
1
\end{array}
$$

Figure 9.22   Longhand division examples.

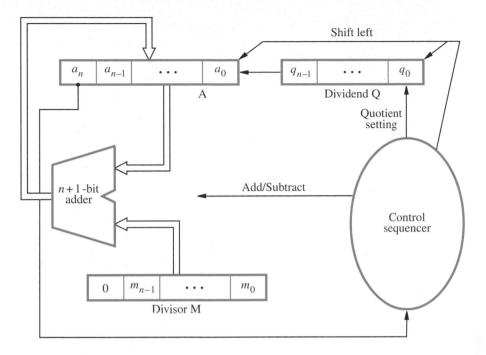

Figure 9.23   Circuit arrangement for binary division.

is loaded into register Q at the start of the operation. Register A is set to 0. After the division is complete, the n-bit quotient is in register Q and the remainder is in register A. The required subtractions are facilitated by using 2's-complement arithmetic. The extra bit position at the left end of both A and M accommodates the sign bit during subtractions. The following algorithm performs restoring division.

Do the following three steps n times:

1. Shift A and Q left one bit position.
2. Subtract M from A, and place the answer back in A.
3. If the sign of A is 1, set q_0 to 0 and add M back to A (that is, restore A); otherwise, set q_0 to 1.

Figure 9.24 shows a 4-bit example as it would be processed by the circuit in Figure 9.23.

Non-Restoring Division

The restoring division algorithm can be improved by avoiding the need for restoring A after an unsuccessful subtraction. Subtraction is said to be unsuccessful if the result is negative. Consider the sequence of operations that takes place after the subtraction operation in the preceding algorithm. If A is positive, we shift left and subtract M, that is, we perform $2A - M$. If A is negative, we restore it by performing $A + M$, and then we shift it left and subtract M. This is equivalent to performing $2A + M$. The q_0 bit is appropriately

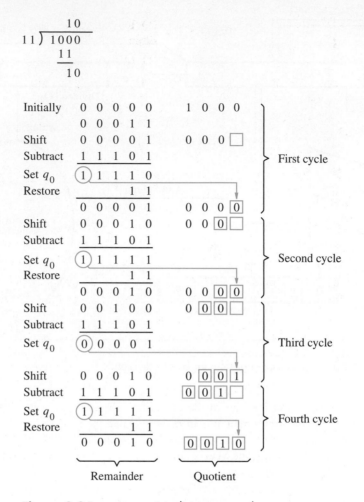

Figure 9.24   A restoring division example.

set to 0 or 1 after the correct operation has been performed. We can summarize this in the following algorithm for *non-restoring division*.

Stage 1: Do the following two steps n times:

1.   If the sign of A is 0, shift A and Q left one bit position and subtract M from A; otherwise, shift A and Q left and add M to A.
2.   Now, if the sign of A is 0, set q_0 to 1; otherwise, set q_0 to 0.

Stage 2: If the sign of A is 1, add M to A.

Stage 2 is needed to leave the proper positive remainder in A after the n cycles of Stage 1. The logic circuitry in Figure 9.23 can also be used to perform this algorithm, except that

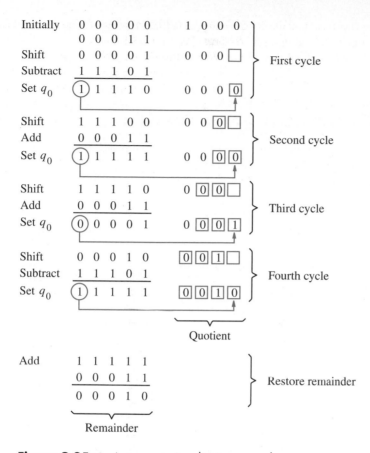

Figure 9.25   A non-restoring division example.

the Restore operations are no longer needed. One Add or Subtract operation is performed in each of the n cycles of stage 1, plus a possible final addition in Stage 2. Figure 9.25 shows how the division example in Figure 9.24 is executed by the non-restoring division algorithm.

There are no simple algorithms for directly performing division on signed operands that are comparable to the algorithms for signed multiplication. In division, the operands can be preprocessed to change them into positive values. After using one of the algorithms just discussed, the signs of the quotient and the remainder are adjusted as necessary.

9.7   FLOATING-POINT NUMBERS AND OPERATIONS

Chapter 1 provided the motivation for using floating-point numbers and indicated how they can be represented in a 32-bit binary format. In this chapter, we provide more detail on representation formats and arithmetic operations on floating-point numbers. The descriptions provided here are based on the 2008 version of IEEE (Institute of Electrical and Electronics Engineers) Standard 754, labeled 754-2008 [4].

Recall from Chapter 1 that a binary floating-point number can be represented by

- A sign for the number
- Some significant bits
- A signed scale factor exponent for an implied base of 2

The basic IEEE format is a 32-bit representation, shown in Figure 9.26a. The leftmost bit represents the sign, S, for the number. The next 8 bits, E', represent the signed exponent of the scale factor (with an implied base of 2), and the remaining 23 bits, M, are the

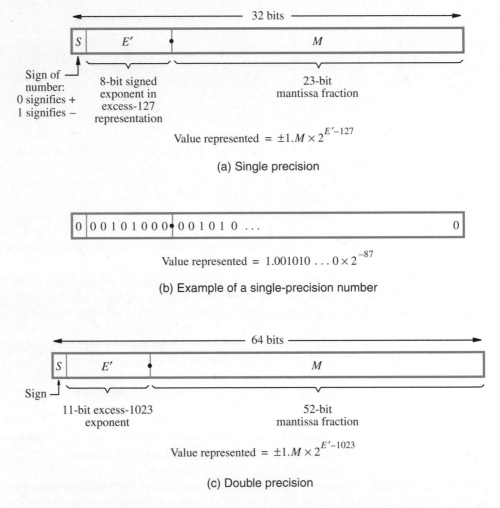

Value represented $= \pm 1.M \times 2^{E'-127}$

(a) Single precision

Value represented $= 1.001010 \ldots 0 \times 2^{-87}$

(b) Example of a single-precision number

Value represented $= \pm 1.M \times 2^{E'-1023}$

(c) Double precision

Figure 9.26   IEEE standard floating-point formats.

fractional part of the significant bits. The full 24-bit string, B, of significant bits, called the *mantissa*, always has a leading 1, with the binary point immediately to its right. Therefore, the mantissa

$$B = 1.M = 1.b_{-1}b_{-2}\ldots b_{-23}$$

has the value

$$V(B) = 1 + b_{-1} \times 2^{-1} + b_{-2} \times 2^{-2} + \cdots + b_{-23} \times 2^{-23}$$

By convention, when the binary point is placed to the right of the first significant bit, the number is said to be *normalized*. Note that the base, 2, of the scale factor and the leading 1 of the mantissa are both fixed. They do not need to appear explicitly in the representation.

Instead of the actual signed exponent, E, the value stored in the exponent field is an unsigned integer $E' = E + 127$. This is called the *excess*-127 format. Thus, E' is in the range $0 \le E' \le 255$. The end values of this range, 0 and 255, are used to represent special values, as described later. Therefore, the range of E' for normal values is $1 \le E' \le 254$. This means that the actual exponent, E, is in the range $-126 \le E \le 127$. The use of the excess-127 representation for exponents simplifies comparison of the relative sizes of two floating-point numbers. (See Problem 9.23.)

The 32-bit standard representation in Figure 9.26a is called a *single-precision* representation because it occupies a single 32-bit word. The scale factor has a range of 2^{-126} to 2^{+127}, which is approximately equal to $10^{\pm 38}$. The 24-bit mantissa provides approximately the same precision as a 7-digit decimal value. An example of a single-precision floating-point number is shown in Figure 9.26b.

To provide more precision and range for floating-point numbers, the IEEE standard also specifies a *double-precision* format, as shown in Figure 9.26c. The double-precision format has increased exponent and mantissa ranges. The 11-bit excess-1023 exponent E' has the range $1 \le E' \le 2046$ for normal values, with 0 and 2047 used to indicate special values, as before. Thus, the actual exponent E is in the range $-1022 \le E \le 1023$, providing scale factors of 2^{-1022} to 2^{1023} (approximately $10^{\pm 308}$). The 53-bit mantissa provides a precision equivalent to about 16 decimal digits.

A computer must provide at least single-precision representation to conform to the IEEE standard. Double-precision representation is optional. The standard also specifies certain optional extended versions of both of these formats. The extended versions provide increased precision and increased exponent range for the representation of intermediate values in a sequence of calculations. The use of extended formats helps to reduce the size of the accumulated round-off error in a sequence of calculations leading to a desired result. For example, the dot product of two vectors of numbers involves accumulating a sum of products. The input vector components are given in a standard precision, either single or double, and the final answer (the dot product) is truncated to the same precision. All intermediate calculations should be done using extended precision to limit accumulation of errors. Extended formats also enhance the accuracy of evaluation of elementary functions such as sine, cosine, and so on. This is because they are usually evaluated by adding up a number of terms in a series representation. In addition to requiring the four basic arithmetic operations, the standard requires three additional operations to be provided: remainder, square root, and conversion between binary and decimal representations.

excess-127 exponent

| 0 | 1 0 0 0 1 0 0 0 • 0 0 1 0 1 1 0 … |

(There is no implicit 1 to the left of the binary point.)

Value represented $= +0.0010110\ldots \times 2^9$

(a) Unnormalized value

| 0 | 1 0 0 0 0 1 0 1 • 0 1 1 0 … |

Value represented $= +1.0110\ldots \times 2^6$

(b) Normalized version

Figure 9.27   Floating-point normalization in IEEE single-precision format.

We note two basic aspects of operating with floating-point numbers. First, if a number is not normalized, it can be put in normalized form by shifting the binary point and adjusting the exponent. Figure 9.27 shows an unnormalized value, $0.0010110\ldots \times 2^9$, and its normalized version, $1.0110\ldots \times 2^6$. Since the scale factor is in the form 2^i, shifting the mantissa right or left by one bit position is compensated by an increase or a decrease of 1 in the exponent, respectively. Second, as computations proceed, a number that does not fall in the representable range of normal numbers might be generated. In single precision, this means that its normalized representation requires an exponent less than -126 or greater than $+127$. In the first case, we say that *underflow* has occurred, and in the second case, we say that *overflow* has occurred.

Special Values

The end values 0 and 255 of the excess-127 exponent E' are used to represent special values. When $E' = 0$ and the mantissa fraction M is zero, the value 0 is represented. When $E' = 255$ and $M = 0$, the value ∞ is represented, where ∞ is the result of dividing a normal number by zero. The sign bit is still used in these representations, so there are representations for ± 0 and $\pm \infty$.

When $E' = 0$ and $M \neq 0$, *denormal* numbers are represented. Their value is $\pm 0.M \times 2^{-126}$. Therefore, they are smaller than the smallest normal number. There is no implied one to the left of the binary point, and M is any nonzero 23-bit fraction. The purpose of introducing denormal numbers is to allow for *gradual underflow*, providing an extension of the range of normal representable numbers. This is useful in dealing with very small numbers, which may be needed in certain situations. When $E' = 255$ and $M \neq 0$, the value represented is called *Not a Number* (NaN). A NaN represents the result of performing an invalid operation such as $0/0$ or $\sqrt{-1}$.

Exceptions

In conforming to the IEEE Standard, a processor must set *exception* flags if any of the following conditions arise when performing operations: underflow, overflow, divide by zero, inexact, invalid. We have already mentioned the first three. *Inexact* is the name for a result that requires rounding in order to be represented in one of the normal formats. An *invalid* exception occurs if operations such as $0/0$ or $\sqrt{-1}$ are attempted. When an exception occurs, the result is set to one of the special values.

If interrupts are enabled for any of the exception flags, system or user-defined routines are entered when the associated exception occurs. Alternatively, the application program can test for the occurrence of exceptions, as necessary, and decide how to proceed.

9.7.1   Arithmetic Operations on Floating-Point Numbers

In this section, we outline the general procedures for addition, subtraction, multiplication, and division of floating-point numbers. The rules given below apply to the single-precision IEEE standard format. These rules specify only the major steps needed to perform the four operations; for example, the possibility that overflow or underflow might occur is not discussed. Furthermore, intermediate results for both mantissas and exponents might require more than 24 and 8 bits, respectively. These and other aspects of the operations must be carefully considered in designing an arithmetic unit that meets the standard. Although we do not provide full details in specifying the rules, we consider some aspects of implementation, including rounding, in later sections.

When adding or subtracting floating-point numbers, their mantissas must be shifted with respect to each other if their exponents differ. Consider a decimal example in which we wish to add 2.9400×10^2 to 4.3100×10^4. We rewrite 2.9400×10^2 as 0.0294×10^4 and then perform addition of the mantissas to get 4.3394×10^4. The rule for addition and subtraction can be stated as follows:

Add/Subtract Rule

1. Choose the number with the smaller exponent and shift its mantissa right a number of steps equal to the difference in exponents.

2. Set the exponent of the result equal to the larger exponent.

3. Perform addition/subtraction on the mantissas and determine the sign of the result.

4. Normalize the resulting value, if necessary.

Multiplication and division are somewhat easier than addition and subtraction, in that no alignment of mantissas is needed.

Multiply Rule

1. Add the exponents and subtract 127 to maintain the excess-127 representation.

2. Multiply the mantissas and determine the sign of the result.

3. Normalize the resulting value, if necessary.

Divide Rule

1. Subtract the exponents and add 127 to maintain the excess-127 representation.
2. Divide the mantissas and determine the sign of the result.
3. Normalize the resulting value, if necessary.

9.7.2 GUARD BITS AND TRUNCATION

Let us consider some important aspects of implementing the steps in the preceding algorithms. Although the mantissas of initial operands and final results are limited to 24 bits, including the implicit leading 1, it is important to retain extra bits, often called *guard* bits, during the intermediate steps. This yields maximum accuracy in the final results.

Removing guard bits in generating a final result requires that the extended mantissa be *truncated* to create a 24-bit number that approximates the longer version. This operation also arises in other situations, for instance, in converting from decimal to binary numbers. We should mention that the general term rounding is also used for the truncation operation, but a more restrictive definition of rounding is used here as one of the forms of truncation.

There are several ways to truncate. The simplest way is to remove the guard bits and make no changes in the retained bits. This is called *chopping*. Suppose we want to truncate a fraction from six to three bits by this method. All fractions in the range $0.b_{-1}b_{-2}b_{-3}000$ to $0.b_{-1}b_{-2}b_{-3}111$ are truncated to $0.b_{-1}b_{-2}b_{-3}$. The error in the 3-bit result ranges from 0 to 0.000111. In other words, the error in chopping ranges from 0 to almost 1 in the least significant position of the retained bits. In our example, this is the b_{-3} position. The result of chopping is a *biased* approximation because the error range is not symmetrical about 0.

The next simplest method of truncation is *von Neumann rounding*. If the bits to be removed are all 0s, they are simply dropped, with no changes to the retained bits. However, if any of the bits to be removed are 1, the least significant bit of the retained bits is set to 1. In our 6-bit to 3-bit truncation example, all 6-bit fractions with $b_{-4}b_{-5}b_{-6}$ not equal to 000 are truncated to $0.b_{-1}b_{-2}1$. The error in this truncation method ranges between -1 and $+1$ in the LSB position of the retained bits. Although the range of error is larger with this technique than it is with chopping, the maximum magnitude is the same, and the approximation is *unbiased* because the error range is symmetrical about 0.

Unbiased approximations are advantageous if many operands and operations are involved in generating a result, because positive errors tend to offset negative errors as the computation proceeds. Statistically, we can expect the results of a complex computation to be more accurate.

The third truncation method is a *rounding* procedure. Rounding achieves the closest approximation to the number being truncated and is an unbiased technique. The procedure is as follows: A 1 is added to the LSB position of the bits to be retained if there is a 1 in the MSB position of the bits being removed. Thus, $0.b_{-1}b_{-2}b_{-3}1\ldots$ is rounded to $0.b_{-1}b_{-2}b_{-3} + 0.001$, and $0.b_{-1}b_{-2}b_{-3}0\ldots$ is rounded to $0.b_{-1}b_{-2}b_{-3}$. This provides the desired approximation, except for the case in which the bits to be removed are $10\ldots0$. This is a tie situation; the longer value is halfway between the two closest truncated representations. To break the tie in an unbiased way, one possibility is to choose the retained bits to be the nearest even number. In terms of our 6-bit example, the value $0.b_{-1}b_{-2}0100$ is truncated to the value $0.b_{-1}b_{-2}0$, and $0.b_{-1}b_{-2}1100$ is truncated to $0.b_{-1}b_{-2}1 + 0.001$. The descriptive phrase "round to the nearest number or nearest even number in case of a tie" is sometimes used to refer to this truncation technique. The error range is approximately $-\frac{1}{2}$ to $+\frac{1}{2}$ in the LSB position of the retained bits. Clearly, this is the best method. However, it is also the most difficult to implement because it requires an addition operation and a possible renormalization. This rounding technique is the default mode for truncation specified in the IEEE floating-point standard. The standard also specifies other truncation methods, referring to all of them as rounding modes.

This discussion of errors that are introduced when guard bits are removed by truncation has treated the case of a single truncation operation. When a long series of calculations involving floating-point numbers is performed, the analysis that determines error ranges or bounds for the final results can be a complicated study. We do not discuss this aspect of numerical computation further, except to make a few comments on the way that guard bits and rounding are handled in the IEEE floating-point standard.

According to the standard, results of single operations must be computed to be accurate within half a unit in the LSB position. This means that rounding must be used as the truncation method. Implementing rounding requires only three guard bits to be carried along during the intermediate steps in performing an operation. The first two of these bits are the two most significant bits of the section of the mantissa to be removed. The third bit is the logical OR of all bits beyond these first two bits in the full representation of the mantissa. This bit is relatively easy to maintain during the intermediate steps of the operations to be performed. It should be initialized to 0. If a 1 is shifted out through this position while aligning mantissas, the bit becomes 1 and retains that value; hence, it is usually called the *sticky bit*.

9.7.3 IMPLEMENTING FLOATING-POINT OPERATIONS

The hardware implementation of floating-point operations involves a considerable amount of logic circuitry. These operations can also be implemented by software routines. In either case, the computer must be able to convert input and output from and to the user's decimal representation of numbers. In many general-purpose processors, floating-point operations are available at the machine-instruction level, implemented in hardware.

An example of the implementation of floating-point operations is shown in Figure 9.28. This is a block diagram of a hardware implementation for the addition and subtraction of 32-bit floating-point operands that have the format shown in Figure 9.26a. Following the Add/Subtract rule given in Section 9.7.1, we see that the first step is to compare exponents to determine how far to shift the mantissa of the number with the smaller exponent. The shift-count value, n, is determined by the 8-bit subtractor circuit in the upper left corner of the figure. The magnitude of the difference $E'_A - E'_B$, or n, is sent to the SHIFTER unit. If n is larger than the number of significant bits of the operands, then the answer is essentially the larger operand (except for guard and sticky-bit considerations in rounding), and shortcuts can be taken in deriving the result. We do not explore this in detail.

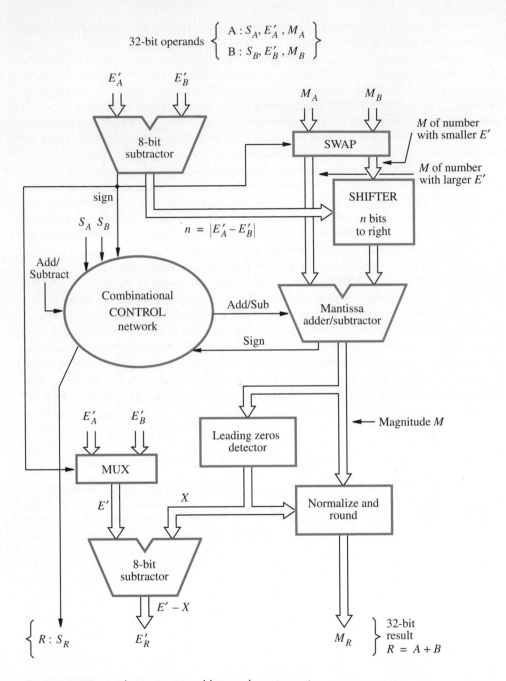

$$32\text{-bit operands} \begin{cases} A : S_A, E'_A, M_A \\ B : S_B, E'_B, M_B \end{cases}$$

Figure 9.28   Floating-point addition-subtraction unit.

The sign of the difference that results from comparing exponents determines which mantissa is to be shifted. Therefore, in step 1, the sign is sent to the SWAP network in the upper right corner of Figure 9.28. If the sign is 0, then $E'_A \geq E'_B$ and the mantissas M_A and M_B are sent straight through the SWAP network. This results in M_B being sent to the SHIFTER, to be shifted n positions to the right. The other mantissa, M_A, is sent directly to the mantissa adder/subtractor. If the sign is 1, then $E'_A < E'_B$ and the mantissas are swapped before they are sent to the SHIFTER.

Step 2 is performed by the two-way multiplexer, MUX, near the bottom left corner of the figure. The exponent of the result, E', is tentatively determined as E'_A if $E'_A \geq E'_B$, or E'_B if $E'_A < E'_B$, based on the sign of the difference resulting from comparing exponents in step 1.

Step 3 involves the major component, the mantissa adder/subtractor in the middle of the figure. The CONTROL logic determines whether the mantissas are to be added or subtracted. This is decided by the signs of the operands (S_A and S_B) and the operation (Add or Subtract) that is to be performed on the operands. The CONTROL logic also determines the sign of the result, S_R. For example, if A is negative ($S_A = 1$), B is positive ($S_B = 0$), and the operation is $A - B$, then the mantissas are added and the sign of the result is negative ($S_R = 1$). On the other hand, if A and B are both positive and the operation is $A - B$, then the mantissas are subtracted. The sign of the result, S_R, now depends on the mantissa subtraction operation. For instance, if $E'_A > E'_B$, then $M = M_A - (\text{shifted } M_B)$ and the resulting number is positive. But if $E'_B > E'_A$, then $M = M_B - (\text{shifted } M_A)$ and the result is negative. This example shows that the sign from the exponent comparison is also required as an input to the CONTROL network. When $E'_A = E'_B$ and the mantissas are subtracted, the sign of the mantissa adder/subtractor output determines the sign of the result. The reader should now be able to construct the complete truth table for the CONTROL network (see Problem 9.26).

Step 4 of the Add/Subtract rule consists of normalizing the result of step 3 by shifting M to the right or to the left, as appropriate. The number of leading zeros in M determines the number of bit shifts, X, to be applied to M. The normalized value is rounded to generate the 24-bit mantissa, M_R, of the result. The value X is also subtracted from the tentative result exponent E' to generate the true result exponent, E'_R. Note that only a single right shift might be needed to normalize the result. This would be the case if two mantissas of the form $1.xx\ldots$ were added. The vector M would then have the form $1x.xx\ldots$.

We have not given any details on the guard bits that must be carried along with intermediate mantissa values. In the IEEE standard, only a few bits are needed, as discussed earlier, to generate the 24-bit normalized mantissa of the result.

Let us consider the actual hardware that is needed to implement the blocks in Figure 9.28. The two 8-bit subtractors and the mantissa adder/subtractor can be implemented by combinational logic, as discussed earlier in this chapter. Because their outputs must be in sign-and-magnitude form, we must modify some of our earlier discussions. A combination of 1's-complement arithmetic and sign-and-magnitude representation is often used. Considerable flexibility is allowed in implementing the SHIFTER and the output normalization operation. The operations can be implemented with shift registers. However, they can also be built as combinational logic units for high-performance.

9.8 DECIMAL-TO-BINARY CONVERSION

In Chapter 1 and in this chapter, examples that involve decimal numbers have used small values. Conversion from decimal to binary representation has been easy to do based on the binary bit-position weights $1, 2, 4, 8, 16, \ldots$. However, it is useful to have a general method for converting decimal numbers to binary representation.

The fixed-point, unsigned, binary number

$$B = b_{n-1}b_{n-2}\ldots b_0.b_{-1}b_{-2}\ldots b_{-m}$$

has an n-bit integer part and an m-bit fraction part. Its value, $V(B)$, is given by

$$V(B) = b_{n-1} \times 2^{n-1} + b_{n-2} \times 2^{n-2} + \cdots + b_0 \times 2^0$$
$$+ b_{-1} \times 2^{-1} + b_{-2} \times 2^{-2} + \cdots + b_{-m} \times 2^{-m}$$

To convert a fixed-point decimal number into binary, the integer and fraction parts are handled separately. Conversion of the integer part starts by dividing it by 2. The remainder, which is either 0 or 1, is the least significant bit, b_0, of the integer part of B. The quotient is again divided by 2. The remainder is the next bit, b_1, of B. This process is repeated up to and including the step in which the quotient becomes 0.

Conversion of the fraction part starts by multiplying it by 2. The part of the product to the left of the decimal point, which is either 0 or 1, is bit b_{-1} of the fraction part of B. The fraction part of the product is again multiplied by 2, generating the next bit, b_{-2} of the fraction part of B. The process is repeated until the fraction part of the product becomes 0 or until the required accuracy is obtained.

Figure 9.29 shows an example of conversion from the decimal number 927.45 to binary. Note that conversion of the integer part is always exact and terminates when the quotient becomes 0. But an exact binary fraction may not exist for a given decimal fraction. For example, the decimal fraction 0.45 used in Figure 9.29 does not have an exact binary equivalent. This is obvious from the pattern developing in the figure. In such cases, the binary fraction is generated to some desired level of accuracy. Of course, some decimal fractions have an exact binary representation. For example, the decimal fraction 0.25 has a binary equivalent of 0.01.

9.9 CONCLUDING REMARKS

Computer arithmetic poses several interesting logic design problems. This chapter discussed some of the techniques that have proven useful in designing binary arithmetic units. The carry-lookahead technique is one of the major ideas in high-performance adder design. In the design of fast multipliers, bit-pair recoding of the multiplier, derived from the Booth algorithm, reduces the number of summands that must be added to generate the product. The parallel addition of summands using carry-save reduction trees substantially reduces

Convert $(927.45)_{10}$

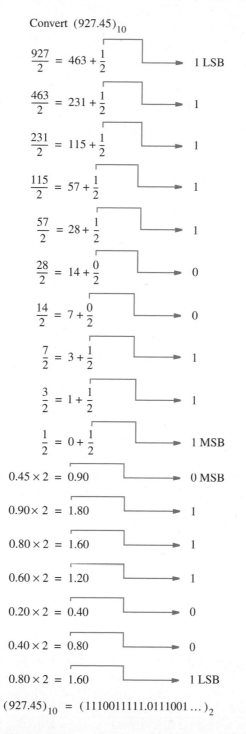

$$\frac{927}{2} = 463 + \frac{1}{2} \longrightarrow 1 \text{ LSB}$$

$$\frac{463}{2} = 231 + \frac{1}{2} \longrightarrow 1$$

$$\frac{231}{2} = 115 + \frac{1}{2} \longrightarrow 1$$

$$\frac{115}{2} = 57 + \frac{1}{2} \longrightarrow 1$$

$$\frac{57}{2} = 28 + \frac{1}{2} \longrightarrow 1$$

$$\frac{28}{2} = 14 + \frac{0}{2} \longrightarrow 0$$

$$\frac{14}{2} = 7 + \frac{0}{2} \longrightarrow 0$$

$$\frac{7}{2} = 3 + \frac{1}{2} \longrightarrow 1$$

$$\frac{3}{2} = 1 + \frac{1}{2} \longrightarrow 1$$

$$\frac{1}{2} = 0 + \frac{1}{2} \longrightarrow 1 \text{ MSB}$$

$$0.45 \times 2 = 0.90 \longrightarrow 0 \text{ MSB}$$

$$0.90 \times 2 = 1.80 \longrightarrow 1$$

$$0.80 \times 2 = 1.60 \longrightarrow 1$$

$$0.60 \times 2 = 1.20 \longrightarrow 1$$

$$0.20 \times 2 = 0.40 \longrightarrow 0$$

$$0.40 \times 2 = 0.80 \longrightarrow 0$$

$$0.80 \times 2 = 1.60 \longrightarrow 1 \text{ LSB}$$

$$(927.45)_{10} = (1110011111.0111001\ldots)_2$$

Figure 9.29   Conversion from decimal to binary.

the time needed to add the summands. The important IEEE floating-point number representation standard was described, and rules for performing the four standard operations were given.

9.10　SOLVED PROBLEMS

This section presents some examples of the types of problems that a student may be asked to solve, and shows how such problems can be solved.

Example 9.1　**Problem:** How many logic gates are needed to build the 4-bit carry-lookahead adder shown in Figure 9.4?

Solution: Each B cell requires 3 gates as shown in Figure 9.4a. Hence, 12 gates are needed for all four B cells.

　　The carries c_1, c_2, c_3, and c_4, produced by the carry-lookahead logic, require 2, 3, 4, and 5 gates, respectively, according to the four logic expressions in Section 9.2.1. The carry-lookahead logic also produces G_0^I, using 4 gates, and P_0^I, using 1 gate, as also shown in Section 9.2.1. Hence, a total of 19 gates are needed to implement the carry-lookahead logic.

　　The complete 4-bit adder requires $12 + 19 = 31$ gates, with a maximum fan-in of 5.

Example 9.2　**Problem:** Assuming 6-bit 2's-complement number representation, multiply the multiplicand $A = 110101$ by the multiplier $B = 011011$ using both the normal Booth algorithm and the bit-pair recoding Booth algorithm, following the pattern used in Figure 9.15.

Solution: The multiplications are performed as follows:

(a) Normal Booth algorithm

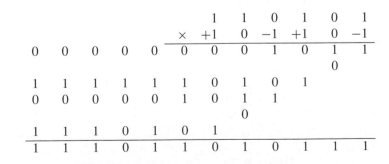

(*b*) Bit-pair recoding Booth algorithm

$$
\begin{array}{ccccccccccc}
 & & & & & 1 & 1 & 0 & 1 & 0 & 1 \\
 & & & & \times & & +2 & & -1 & & -1 \\
\hline
0 & 0 & 0 & 0 & 0 & 0 & 0 & 0 & 1 & 0 & 1 & 1 \\
0 & 0 & 0 & 0 & 0 & 0 & 1 & 0 & 1 & 1 \\
1 & 1 & 1 & 0 & 1 & 0 & 1 \\
\hline
1 & 1 & 1 & 0 & 1 & 1 & 0 & 1 & 0 & 1 & 1 & 1 \\
\end{array}
$$

Problem: How many levels of 4-2 reducers are needed to reduce k summands to 2 in a reduction tree? How many levels are needed if 3-2 reducers are used?   **Example 9.3**

Solution: Let the number of levels be L.
  For 4-2 reducers, we have

$$k(1/2)^L = 2$$

Take logarithms to the base 2 of each side of this equation to derive

$$log_2 k - L = 1$$

or

$$L = log_2 k - 1$$

  For 3-2 reducers, we have

$$k(2/3)^L = 2$$

As above, taking logarithms to the base 2, we derive

$$log_2 k + L(log_2 2 - log_2 3) = log_2 2$$
$$log_2 k + L(1 - 1.59) = 1$$
$$L = (1 - log_2 k)/(-0.59)$$
$$L = 1.7 log_2 k - 1.7$$

  These expressions are only approximations unless the number of input summands to each level is a multiple of 4 in the case of 4-2 reduction, or is a multiple of 3 in the case of 3-2 reduction.

Problem: Convert the decimal fraction 0.1 to a binary fraction. If the conversion is not exact, give the binary fraction approximation to 8 bits after the binary point using each of the three truncation methods discussed in Section 9.7.2.   **Example 9.4**

Solution: Use the conversion method given in Section 9.8. Multiplying the decimal fraction 0.1 by 2 repeatedly, as shown in Figure 9.29, generates the sequence of bits

$0, 0, 0, 1, 1, 0, 0, 1, 1, 0, 0, 1, 1, \ldots$ to the left of the decimal point, which continues in-definitely, repeating the pattern $0, 0, 1, 1$. Hence, the conversion is not exact.

- Truncation by chopping gives 0.00011001
- Truncation by von Neumann rounding gives 0.00011001
- Truncation by rounding gives 0.00011010

Example 9.5

Problem: Consider the following 12-bit floating-point number representation format that is manageable for working through numerical exercises. The first bit is the sign of the number. The next five bits represent an excess-15 exponent for the scale factor, which has an implied base of 2. The last six bits represent the fractional part of the mantissa, which has an implied 1 to the left of the binary point.

Perform Subtract and Multiply operations on the operands

$A =$	0	10001	011011

$B =$	1	01111	101010

which represent the numbers

$$A = 1.011011 \times 2^2$$

and

$$B = -1.101010 \times 2^0$$

Solution: The required operations are performed as follows:

- Subtraction
  According to the Add/Subtract rule in Section 9.7.1, we perform the following four steps:

  1. Shift the mantissa of B to the right by two bit positions, giving 0.01101010.
  2. Set the exponent of the result to 10001.
  3. Subtract the mantissa of B from the mantissa of A by adding mantissas, because B is negative, giving

$$
\begin{array}{r}
1\ .\ 0\ 1\ 1\ 0\ 1\ 1\ 0\ 0 \\
+\ 0\ .\ 0\ 1\ 1\ 0\ 1\ 0\ 1\ 0 \\
\hline
1\ .\ 1\ 1\ 0\ 1\ 0\ 1\ 1\ 0
\end{array}
$$

  and set the sign of the result to 0 (positive).

  4. The result is in normalized form, but the fractional part of the mantissa needs to be truncated to six bits. If this is done by rounding, the two bits to be removed represent the tie case, so we round to the nearest even number by adding 1, obtaining a result mantissa of 1.110110. The answer is

$A - B =$	0	10001	110110

- Multiplication

  According to the Multiplication rule in Section 9.7.1, we perform the following three steps:

1. Add the exponents and subtract 15 to obtain 10001 as the exponent of the result.

2. Multiply mantissas to obtain 10.010110101110 as the mantissa of the result. The sign of the result is set to 1 (negative).

3. Normalize the resulting mantissa by shifting it to the right by one bit position. Then add 1 to the exponent to obtain 10010 as the exponent of the result. Truncate the mantissa fraction to six bits by rounding to obtain the answer

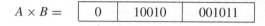

PROBLEMS

9.1 **[M]** A *half adder* is a combinational logic circuit that has two inputs, x and y, and two outputs, s and c, that are the sum and carry-out, respectively, resulting from the binary addition of x and y.

(*a*) Design a half adder as a two-level AND-OR circuit.

(*b*) Show how to implement a full adder, as shown in Figure 9.2*a*, by using two half adders and external logic gates, as necessary.

(*c*) Compare the longest logic delay path through the network derived in part (*b*) to that of the logic delay of the adder network shown in Figure 9.2*a*.

9.2 **[M]** The 1's-complement and 2's-complement binary representation methods are special cases of the $(b-1)$'s-complement and b's-complement representation techniques in base b number systems. For example, consider the decimal system. The sign-and-magnitude values $+526$, -526, $+70$, and -70 have 4-digit signed-number representations in each of the two complement systems, as shown in Figure P9.1. The 9's-complement is formed by

Representation	Examples			
Sign and magnitude	+526	−526	+70	−70
9's complement	0526	9473	0070	9929
10's complement	0526	9474	0070	9930

Figure P9.1   Signed numbers in base 10 used in Problem 9.2.

taking the complement of each digit position with respect to 9. The 10's-complement is formed by adding 1 to the 9's-complement. In each of the latter two representations, the leftmost digit is zero for a positive number and 9 for a negative number.

Now consider the base-3 (ternary) system, in which the unsigned, 5-digit number $t_4t_3t_2t_1t_0$ has the value $t_4 \times 3^4 + t_3 \times 3^3 + t_2 \times 3^2 + t_1 \times 3^1 + t_0 \times 3^0$, with $0 \leq t_i \leq 2$. Express the ternary sign-and-magnitude numbers $+11011$, -10222, $+2120$, -1212, $+10$, and -201 as 6-digit, signed, ternary numbers in the 3's-complement system.

9.3   **[M]**   Represent each of the decimal values 56, -37, 122, and -123 as signed 6-digit numbers in the 3's-complement ternary format, perform addition and subtraction on them in all possible pairwise combinations, and state whether or not arithmetic overflow occurs for each operation performed. (See Problem 9.2 for a definition of the ternary number system, and use a technique analogous to that given in Section 9.8 for decimal-to-ternary integer conversion.)

9.4   **[M]**   A modulo 10 adder is needed for adding BCD digits. Modulo 10 addition of two BCD digits, $A = A_3A_2A_1A_0$ and $B = B_3B_2B_1B_0$, can be achieved as follows: Add A to B (binary addition). Then, if the result is an illegal code that is greater than or equal to 10_{10}, add 6_{10}. (Ignore overflow from this addition.)

(*a*) When is the output carry equal to 1?

(*b*) Show that this algorithm gives correct results for:

(1) $A = 0101$ and $B = 0110$

(2) $A = 0011$ and $B = 0100$

(*c*) Design a BCD digit adder using a 4-bit binary adder and external logic gates as needed. The inputs are $A_3A_2A_1A_0$, $B_3B_2B_1B_0$, and a carry-in. The outputs are the sum digit $S_3S_2S_1S_0$ and the carry-out. A cascade of such blocks can form a ripple-carry BCD adder.

9.5   **[E]**   Show that the logic expression $c_n \oplus c_{n-1}$ is a correct indicator of overflow in the addition of 2's-complement integers by using an appropriate truth table.

9.6   **[E]**   Use appropriate parts of the solution in Example 9.1 to calculate how many logic gates are needed to build the 16-bit carry-lookahead adder shown in Figure 9.5.

9.7   **[M]**   Carry-lookahead adders and their delay are investigated in this problem.

(*a*) Design a 64-bit adder that uses four of the 16-bit carry-lookahead adders shown in Figure 9.5 along with additional logic circuits to generate c_{16}, c_{32}, c_{48}, and c_{64}, from c_0 and the G_i^{II} and P_i^{II} variables shown in the figure. What is the relationship of the additional circuits to the carry-lookahead logic circuits in the figure?

(*b*) Show that the delay through the 64-bit adder is 12 gate delays for s_{63} and 7 gate delays for c_{64}, as claimed at the end of Section 9.2.1.

(*c*) Compare the gate delays to produce s_{31} and c_{32} in the 64-bit adder of part (*a*) to the gate delays for the same variables in the 32-bit adder built from a cascade of two 16-bit adders, as discussed in Section 9.2.1.

9.8   **[M]**   Show that the worst case delay through an $n \times n$ array of the type shown in Figure 9.6*b* is $6(n-1) - 1$ gate delays, as claimed in Section 9.3.1.

9.9   **[E]** Multiply each of the following pairs of signed 2's-complement numbers using the Booth algorithm. In each case, assume that A is the multiplicand and B is the multiplier.

(*a*) $A = 010111$ and $B = 110110$

(*b*) $A = 110011$ and $B = 101100$

(*c*) $A = 001111$ and $B = 001111$

9.10   **[M]** Repeat Problem 9.9 using bit-pair recoding of the multiplier.

9.11   **[M]** Indicate generally how to modify the circuit diagram in Figure 9.7*a* to implement multiplication of 2's-complement *n*-bit numbers using the Booth algorithm, by clearly specifying inputs and outputs for the Control sequencer and any other changes needed around the adder and register A.

9.12   **[M]** Extend the Figure 9.14*b* table to 16 rows, indicating how to recode three multiplier bits: $i + 2$, $i + 1$, and i. Can all required versions of the multiplicand selected at position i be generated by shifting and/or negating the multiplicand M? If not, what versions cannot be generated this way, and for what cases are they required?

9.13   **[M]** If the product of two *n*-bit numbers in 2's-complement representation can be represented in *n* bits, the manual multiplication algorithm shown in Figure 9.6*a* can be used directly, treating the sign bits the same as the other bits. Try this on each of the following pairs of 4-bit signed numbers:

(*a*) Multiplicand $= 1110$ and Multiplier $= 1101$

(*b*) Multiplicand $= 0010$ and Multiplier $= 1110$

Why does this work correctly?

9.14   **[D]** An integer arithmetic unit that can perform addition and multiplication of 16-bit unsigned numbers is to be used to multiply two 32-bit unsigned numbers. All operands, intermediate results, and final results are held in 16-bit registers labeled R_0 through R_{15}. The hardware multiplier multiplies the contents of R_i (multiplicand) by R_j (multiplier) and stores the double-length 32-bit product in registers R_j and R_{j+1}, with the low-order half in R_j. When $j = i - 1$, the product overwrites both operands. The hardware adder adds the contents of R_i and R_j and puts the result in R_j. The input carry to an Add operation is 0, and the input carry to an Add-with-carry operation is the contents of a carry flag C. The output carry from the adder is always stored in C.

Specify the steps of a procedure for multiplying two 32-bit operands in registers R_1, R_0, and R_3, R_2, high-order halves first, leaving the 64-bit product in registers R_{15}, R_{14}, R_{13}, and R_{12}. Any of the registers R_{11} through R_4 may be used for intermediate values, if necessary. Each step in the procedure can be a multiplication, or an addition, or a register transfer operation.

9.15   **[M]** Delay in multiplier arrays is investigated in this problem.

(*a*) Calculate the delay, in terms of full-adder block delays, in producing product bit p_7 in each of the 4×4 multiplier arrays in Figure 9.16. Ignore the AND gate delay to generate all $m_i q_j$ products at the beginning.

(*b*) Develop delay expressions for each of the arrays in Figure 9.16 in terms of *n* for the $n \times n$ case, as an extension of part (*a*) of the problem. Then use these expressions to calculate delay for the 32×32 case for each array.

9.16 [M] Tree depth for carry-save reduction is analyzed in this problem.

(a) How many 3-2 reduction levels are needed to reduce 16 summands to 2 using a pattern similar to that shown in Figure 9.19?

(b) Repeat part (a) for reducing 32 summands to 2 to show that the claim of 8 levels in Section 9.5.3 is correct.

(c) Compare the exact answers in parts (a) and (b) to the results obtained by using the approximation developed in Example 9.3 in Section 9.10.

9.17 [M] Tree reduction of summands using 3-2 and 4-2 reducers was described in Sections 9.5.3 and 9.5.4. It is also possible to perform 7-3 reductions on each reduction level. When only three summands remain, a 3-2 reduction is performed, followed by addition of the final two summands.

(a) How many 7-3 reduction levels are needed to reduce 32 summands to three? Compare this to the seven levels needed to reduce 32 summands to three when using 3-2 reductions.

(b) Example 9.3 in Section 9.10 shows that $log_2 k - 1$ levels of 4-2 reduction are needed to reduce k summands to 2 in a reduction tree. How many levels of 7-3 reduction are needed to reduce k summands to 3?

9.18 [M] Show how to implement a 4-2 reducer by using two 3-2 reducers. The truth table for this implementation is different from that shown in Figure 9.21.

9.19 [E] Using manual methods, perform the operations $A \times B$ and $A \div B$ on the 5-bit unsigned numbers $A = 10101$ and $B = 00101$.

9.20 [M] Show how the multiplication and division operations in Problem 9.19 would be performed by the hardware in Figures 9.7a and 9.23, respectively, by constructing charts similar to those in Figures 9.7b and 9.25.

9.21 [D] In Section 9.7, we used the practical-sized 32-bit IEEE standard format for floating-point numbers. Here, we use a shortened format that retains all the pertinent concepts but is manageable for working through numerical exercises. Consider that floating-point numbers are represented in a 12-bit format as shown in Figure P9.2. The scale factor has an implied base of 2 and a 5-bit, excess-15 exponent, with the two end values of 0 and 31 used to signify exact 0 and infinity, respectively. The 6-bit mantissa is normalized as in the IEEE format, with an implied 1 to the left of the binary point.

(a) Represent the numbers $+1.7$, -0.012, $+19$, and $\frac{1}{8}$ in this format.

(b) What are the smallest and largest numbers representable in this format?

(c) How does the range calculated in part (b) compare to the ranges of a 12-bit signed integer and a 12-bit signed fraction?

(d) Perform Add, Subtract, Multiply, and Divide operations on the operands

$A =$	0	10000	011011

$B =$	1	01110	101010

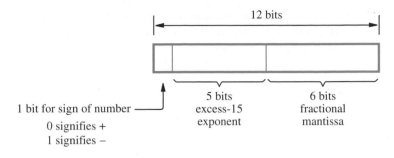

Figure P9.2   Floating-point format used in Problem 9.21.

9.22   **[D]** Consider a 16-bit, floating-point number in a format similar to that discussed in Problem 9.21, with a 6-bit exponent and a 9-bit mantissa fraction. The base of the scale factor is 2 and the exponent is represented in excess-31 format.

(*a*) Add the numbers A and B, formatted as follows:

$A =$	0	100001	111111110

$B =$	0	011111	001010101

Give the answer in normalized form. Remember that an implicit 1 is to the left of the binary point but is not included in the A and B formats. Use rounding as the truncation method when producing the final mantissa.

(*b*) Using decimal numbers w, x, y, and z, express the magnitude of the largest and smallest (nonzero) values representable in the preceding normalized floating-point format. Use the following form:

$$\text{Largest } = w \times 2^x$$
$$\text{Smallest} = y \times 2^{-z}$$

9.23   **[M]** How does the excess-x representation for exponents of the scale factor in the floating-point number representation of Figure 9.26*a* facilitate the comparison of the relative sizes of two floating-point numbers? (Hint: Assume that a combinational logic network that compares the relative sizes of two, 32 bit, unsigned integers is available. Use this network, along with external logic gates, as necessary, to design the required network for the comparison of floating-point numbers.)

9.24   **[D]** In Problem 9.21(*a*), conversion of the simple decimal numbers into binary floating-point format is straightforward. However, if the decimal numbers are given in floating-point format, conversion is not straightforward because we cannot separately convert the mantissa and the exponent of the scale factor because $10^x = 2^y$ does not, in general, allow both x and y to be integers. Suppose a table of binary, floating-point numbers t_i, such that $t_i = 10^{x_i}$ for x_i in the representable range, is stored in a computer. Give a procedure in general terms for converting a given decimal floating-point number into binary floating-point format. You may use both the integer and floating-point instructions available in the computer.

9.25   **[D]** Construct an example to show that three guard bits are needed to produce the correct answer when two positive numbers are subtracted.

9.26   **[M]** Derive logic expressions that specify the Add/Sub and S_R outputs of the combinational CONTROL network in Figure 9.28.

9.27   **[M]** If gate fan-in is limited to four, how can the SHIFTER in Figure 9.28 be implemented combinationally?

9.28   **[M]** Sketch a logic-gate network that implements the multiplexer MUX in Figure 9.28.

9.29   **[M]** Relate the structure of the SWAP network in Figure 9.28 to your solution to Problem 9.28.

9.30   **[M]** How can the leading zeros detector in Figure 9.28 be implemented combinationally?

9.31   **[M]** The mantissa adder-subtractor in Figure 9.28 operates on positive, unsigned binary fractions and must produce a sign-and-magnitude result. In the discussion accompanying Figure 9.28, we state that 1's-complement arithmetic is convenient because of the required format for input and output operands. When adding two signed numbers in 1's-complement notation, the carry-out from the sign position must be added to the result to obtain the correct signed answer. This is called *end-around carry correction*. Consider the two examples in Figure P9.3, which illustrate addition using signed, 4-bit encodings of operands and answers in the 1's-complement system.

The 1's-complement arithmetic system is convenient when a sign-and-magnitude result is to be generated because a negative number in 1's-complement notation can be converted to sign-and-magnitude form by complementing the bits to the right of the sign-bit position. Using 2's-complement arithmetic, addition of $+1$ is needed to convert a negative value into sign-and-magnitude notation. If a carry-lookahead adder is used, it is possible to incorporate the end-around carry operation required by 1's-complement arithmetic into the lookahead logic. With this discussion as a guide, give the complete design of the 1's-complement adder/subtractor required in Figure 9.28.

9.32   **[M]** Signed binary fractions in 2's-complement representation are discussed in Section 1.4.2.

(*a*) Express the decimal values 0.5, -0.123, -0.75, and -0.1 as signed 6-bit fractions. (See Section 9.8 for decimal-to-binary fraction conversion.)

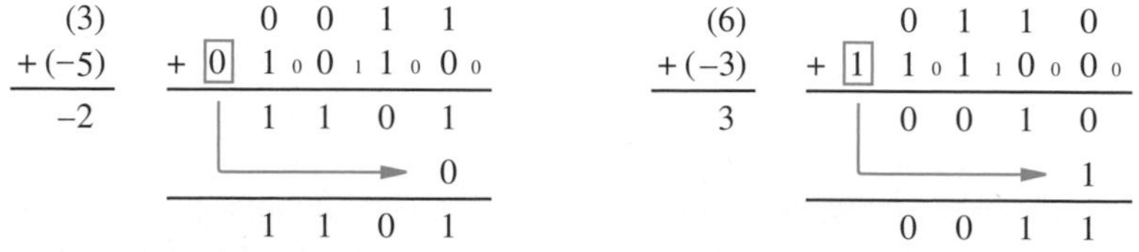

Figure P9.3   1's-complement addition used in Problem 9.31.

(*b*) What is the maximum representation error, *e*, involved in using only 5 significant bits after the binary point?

(*c*) Calculate the number of bits needed after the binary point so that the representation error *e* is less than 0.1, 0.01, or 0.001, respectively.

9.33 **[E]** Which of the four 6-bit answers to Problem 9.32(*a*) are not exact? For each of these cases, give the three 6-bit values that correspond to the three types of truncation defined in Section 9.7.2.

REFERENCES

1. A. D. Booth, "A Signed Binary Multiplication Technique," *Quarterly Journal of Mechanics and Applied Mathematics*, vol. 2, part 2, 1951, pp. 236-240.

2. C. S. Wallace, "A Suggestion for a Fast Multiplier," *IEEE Transactions on Electronic Computers*, vol. EC-13, February 1964, pp. 14-17.

3. M. R. Santoro and M. A. Horowitz, "SPIM: A Pipelined 64 × 64-bit Iterative Multiplier," *IEEE Journal of Solid-State Circuits*, vol. 24, No.2, April 1989, pp. 487-493.

4. Institute of Electrical and Electronics Engineers, *IEEE Standard for Binary Floating-Point Arithmetic*, ANSI/IEEE Standard 754-2008, August 2008.

10

EMBEDDED SYSTEMS

CHAPTER OBJECTIVES

In this chapter you will learn about:

- Embedded applications
- Microcontrollers for embedded systems
- Sensors and actuators
- Using the C language to control I/O devices
- Design issues

In previous chapters we discussed the concepts used in general-purpose computing systems. Now we will focus our discussion on systems that are intended to serve specific applications. A physical system that employs computer control for a specific purpose, rather than for general-purpose computation, is referred to as an *embedded system*. We will show how the general concepts presented earlier are applied in such systems.

An important aspect of software written for embedded systems is that it has to interact closely with the hardware. The term *reactive system* is often used to describe the fact that the points in time at which various routines are executed are determined by events external to the processor, such as the closing of a switch or the arrival of new data at an input port. The software designer must decide how this interaction will be achieved. The input/output techniques described in Chapter 3, based on polling and interrupts, are used for this purpose.

Microprocessor control is now commonly used in cameras, cell phones, display phones, point-of-sale terminals, kitchen appliances, cars, and many toys. Low cost and high reliability are the essential requirements in these applications. Small size and low power consumption are often of key importance. All of this can be achieved by placing on a single chip not only the processor circuitry, but also some memory, input/output interfaces, timer circuits, and other features to make it easy to implement a complete computer control system using very few chips. Microprocessor chips of this type are generally referred to as *microcontrollers*. In this chapter we will explore the main features of microcontroller-based embedded systems. In Chapter 11 we will discuss the system-on-a-chip approach for implementing such systems using Field Programmable Gate Array (FPGA) technology.

10.1   EXAMPLES OF EMBEDDED SYSTEMS

In this section we present three examples of embedded systems to illustrate the processing and control capability needed in a typical embedded application.

10.1.1   MICROWAVE OVEN

Many household appliances use computer control to govern their operation. A typical example is a microwave oven. This appliance is based on a magnetron power unit that generates the microwaves used to heat food in a confined space. When turned on, the magnetron generates its maximum power output. Lower power levels are achieved by turning the magnetron on and off for controlled time intervals. By controlling the power level and the total heating time, it is possible to realize a variety of user-selectable cooking options.

The specification for a microwave oven may include the following cooking options:

- Manual selection of the power level and cooking time
- Manual selection of the sequence of different cooking steps
- Automatic operation, where the user specifies the type of food (for example, meat, vegetables, or popcorn) and the weight of the food; then an appropriate power level and time are calculated by the controller
- Automatic defrosting of food by specifying the weight

The oven includes a display that can show:

- Time-of-day clock
- Decrementing clock timer while cooking
- Information messages to the user

An audio alert signal, in the form of a beep tone, is used to indicate the end of a cooking operation. An exhaust fan and oven light are provided. As a safety measure, a door interlock turns the magnetron off if the door of the oven is open. All of these functions can be controlled by a microcontroller.

The input/output capability needed to communicate with the user includes:

- Input keys that comprise a 0 to 9 number pad and function keys such as Reset, Start, Stop, Power Level, Auto Defrost, Auto Cooking, Clock Set, and Fan Control
- Visual output in the form of a liquid-crystal display, similar to the seven-segment display illustrated in Figure 3.17
- A small speaker that produces the beep tone

The computational tasks executed by a microcontroller to control a microwave oven are quite simple. They include maintaining the time-of-day clock, determining the actions needed for the various cooking options, generating the control signals needed to turn on or off devices such as the magnetron and the fan, and generating display information. The program needed to implement the desired actions is quite small. It is stored in a nonvolatile read-only memory, so that it will not be lost when the power is turned off. It is also necessary to have a small RAM for use during computations and to hold the user-entered data. The most significant requirement for the microcontroller is to have sufficient I/O capability for all of the input keys, displays, and output control signals. Parallel I/O ports provide a convenient mechanism for dealing with the external input and output signals.

Figure 10.1 shows a possible organization of the microwave oven. A simple processor with small ROM and RAM units is sufficient. Basic input and output interfaces are used to connect to the rest of the system. It is possible to realize most of this circuitry on a small microcontroller chip.

10.1.2 Digital Camera

Digital cameras provide an excellent example of a sophisticated embedded system in a small package. Figure 10.2 shows the main parts of a digital camera.

Traditional cameras use film to capture images. In a digital camera, an array of optical sensors is used to capture images. These sensors convert light into electrical charge. The intensity of light determines the amount of charge that is generated. Two different types of sensors are used in commercial products. One type is known as *charge-coupled devices* (CCDs). It is the type of sensing device used in the earliest digital cameras. It has since been refined to give high-quality images. More recently, sensors based on CMOS technology have been developed.

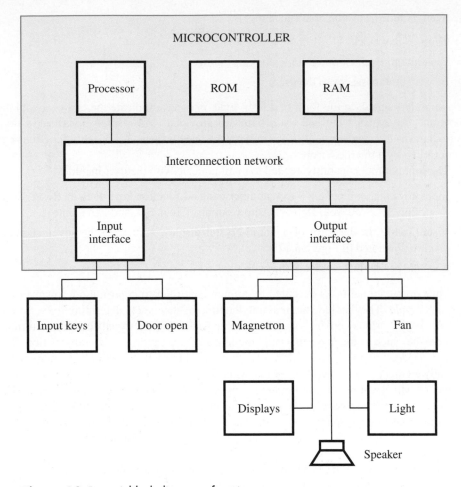

Figure 10.1   A block diagram of a microwave oven.

Each sensing element generates a charge that corresponds to one *pixel,* which is one point of a pictorial image. The number of pixels determines the quality of pictures that can be recorded and displayed. The charge is an analog quantity, which is converted into a digital representation using *analog-to-digital* (A/D) conversion circuits. A/D conversion produces a digital representation of the image in which the color and intensity of each pixel are represented by a number of bits. The digital form of the image can then be treated like any other data that can be manipulated using standard computer circuitry.

The processor and system controller block in Figure 10.2 includes a variety of interface circuits needed to connect to other parts of the system. The processor governs the operation of the camera. It processes the raw image data obtained from the A/D circuits to generate images represented in standard formats suitable for use in computers, printers, and display devices. The main formats used are TIFF (Tagged Image File Format) for uncompressed

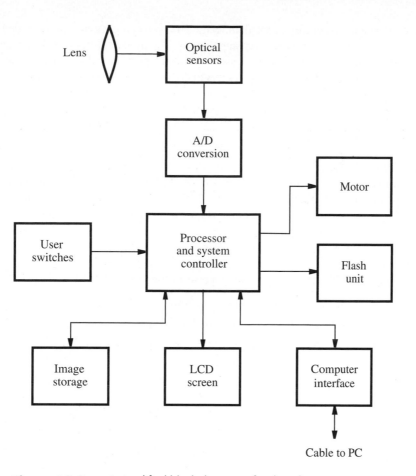

Figure 10.2 A simplified block diagram of a digital camera.

images and JPEG (Joint Photographic Experts Group) for compressed images. The processed images are stored in a larger image storage device. Flash memory cards, discussed in Section 8.3.5, are a popular choice for storing images.

A captured and processed image can be displayed on a liquid-crystal display (LCD) screen, which is included in the camera. This allows the user to decide whether the image is worth keeping. The number of images that can be saved depends on the size of the image storage unit. It also depends on the chosen quality of the images, namely on the number of pixels per image and on the degree of compression (for JPEG format).

A standard interface provides a mechanism for transferring the images to a computer or a printer. Typically, this is done using a USB cable. If Flash memory cards are used, images can also be transferred by physically transferring the card.

The system controller generates the signals needed to control the operation of the focusing mechanism and the flash unit. Some of the inputs come from switches activated by the user.

A digital camera requires a considerably more powerful processor than is needed for the previously discussed microwave oven application. The processor has to perform complex signal processing functions. Yet, it is essential that the processor does not consume much power because the camera is a battery-powered device. Typically, the processor consumes less power than the display and flash units of a camera.

10.1.3 HOME TELEMETRY

Microcontrollers are used in the home in a host of embedded applications. In Section 10.1.1, we considered the microwave oven example. Similar examples can be found in other equipment, such as washers, dryers, dishwashers, cooking ranges, furnaces, and air conditioners. Another notable example is the display telephone, in which an embedded processor enables a variety of useful features. In addition to the standard telephone features, a telephone with an embedded microcontroller can be used to provide remote access to other devices in the home.

Using the telephone one can remotely perform functions such as:

- Communicate with a computer-controlled home security system

- Set a desired temperature to be maintained by a furnace or an air conditioner

- Set the start time, the cooking time, and the temperature for food that has been placed in the oven at some earlier time

- Read the electricity, gas, and water meters, replacing the need for the utility companies to send an employee to the home to read the meters

All of this is easily implementable if each of these devices is controlled by a microcontroller. It is only necessary to provide a link, either wired or wireless, between the device microcontroller and the microprocessor in the telephone. Using signaling from a remote location to observe and control the state of equipment is often referred to as *telemetry*.

10.2 MICROCONTROLLER CHIPS FOR EMBEDDED APPLICATIONS

A microcontroller chip should be versatile enough to serve a wide variety of applications. Figure 10.3 shows the block diagram of a typical chip. The main part is a *processor core,* which may be a basic version of a commercially available microprocessor. It is prudent to choose a microprocessor architecture that has proven to be popular in practice, because for such processors there exist numerous CAD tools, good examples, and a large amount of experience and knowledge that facilitate the design of new products.

It is useful to include some memory on the chip, sufficient to satisfy the memory requirements found in small applications. Some of this memory has to be of RAM type to hold the data that change during computations. Some should be of the read-only type to hold the software, because an embedded system usually does not include a magnetic disk. To allow cost-effective use in low-volume applications, it is necessary to have a

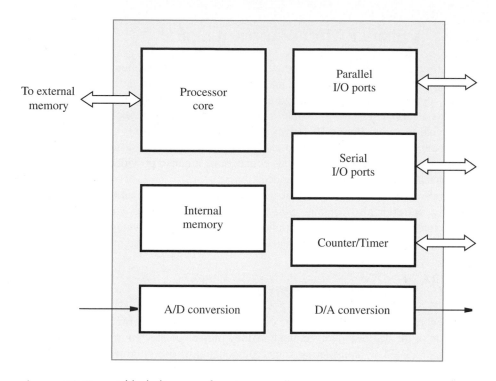

Figure 10.3   A block diagram of a microcontroller.

field-programmable type of ROM storage. Popular choices for realization of this storage are EEPROM and Flash memory.

Several I/O ports are usually provided for both parallel and serial interfaces, which allow easy implementation of standard I/O connections. In many applications, it is necessary to generate control signals at programmable time intervals. This task is achieved easily if a timer circuit is included in the microcontroller chip. Since the timer is a circuit that counts clock pulses, it can also be used for event-counting purposes, for example to count the number of pulses generated by a moving mechanical arm or a rotating shaft.

An embedded system may include some analog devices. To deal with such devices, it is necessary to be able to convert analog signals into digital representations, and vice versa. This is conveniently accomplished if the embedded controller includes A/D and D/A conversion circuits.

Many embedded processor chips are available commercially. Some of the better known examples are: Freescale's 68HC11 and 68K/ColdFire families, Intel's 8051 and MCS-96 families, all of which have CISC-style processor cores, and ARM microcontrollers which have a RISC-style processor. The nature of the processor core is not important to our discussion in this chapter. We will emphasize the system aspects of embedded applications to illustrate how the concepts presented in the previous chapters fit together in the design of a complete embedded computer system.

10.3   A SIMPLE MICROCONTROLLER

The input/output structure of a microcontroller has to be flexible enough to accommodate the needs of different applications and make good use of the pins available on the chip. For example, a parallel port may be configurable as either input or output.

In this section we discuss a possible organization of a simple microcontroller to illustrate some typical features. Figure 10.4 gives its block diagram. There is a processor core and some on-chip memory. Since the on-chip memory may not be sufficient to support all potential applications, the processor bus connections are also provided on the pins of the chip so that external memory can be added.

There are two 8-bit parallel interfaces, called port A and port B, and one serial interface. The microcontroller also contains a 32-bit counter/timer circuit, which can be used to generate internal interrupts at programmed time intervals, to serve as a system timer, to count the pulses on an input line, to generate square-wave output signals, and so on.

10.3.1   PARALLEL I/O INTERFACE

Embedded system applications require considerable flexibility in input/output interfaces. The nature of the devices involved and how they may be connected to the microcontroller can be appreciated by considering some components of the microwave oven shown in Figure 10.1. A sensor is needed to generate a signal with the value 1 when the door is open. This signal is sent to the microcontroller on one of the pins of an input interface. The same is true for the keys on the microwave's front panel. Each of these simple devices produces one bit of information.

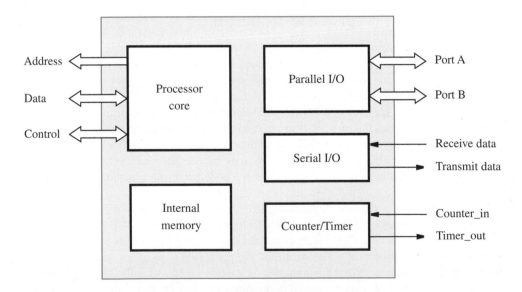

Figure 10.4   An example microcontroller.

Output devices are controlled in a similar way. The magnetron is controlled by a single output line that turns it on or off. The same is true for the fan and the light. The speaker may also be connected via a single output line on which the processor sends a square wave signal having an appropriate tone frequency. A liquid-crystal display, on the other hand, requires several bits of data to be sent in parallel.

One of the objectives of the design of input/output interfaces for a microcontroller is to reduce the need for external circuitry as much as possible. The microcontroller is likely to be connected to simple devices, many of which require only one input or output signal line. In most cases, no encoding or decoding is needed.

Each parallel port in Figure 10.4 has an associated eight-bit data direction register, which can be used to configure individual data lines as either input or output. Figure 10.5 illustrates the bidirectional control for one bit in port A. Port pin PA_i is treated as an input if the data direction flip-flop contains a 0. In this case, activation of the control signal Read_Port places the logic value on the port pin onto the data line D_i of the processor bus. The port pin serves as an output if the data direction flip-flop is set to 1. The value loaded into the output data flip-flop, under control of the Write_Port signal, is placed on the pin.

Figure 10.5 shows only the part of the interface that controls the direction of data transfer. In the input data path there is no flip-flop to capture and hold the value of the data signal provided by a device connected to the corresponding pin. A versatile parallel interface may include two possibilities: one where input data are read directly from the pins, and the other where the input data are stored in a register as in the interface in Figure 7.11. The choice is made by setting a bit in the control register of the interface.

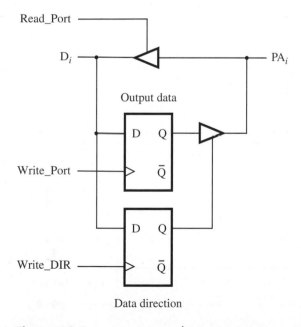

Figure 10.5   Access to one bit in port A in Figure 10.4.

Figure 10.6 depicts all registers in the parallel interface, as well as the addresses assigned to them. We have arbitrarily chosen addresses at the high end of a 32-bit address range.

The status register, PSTAT, contains the status flags. The PASIN flag is set to 1 when there are new data on port A. It is cleared to 0 when the processor accepts the data by reading the PAIN register. The PASOUT flag is set to 1 when the data in register PAOUT are accepted by the connected device, to indicate that the processor may now load new data into PAOUT. The interface uses a separate control line (described below) to signal the availability of new data to the connected device. The PASOUT flag is cleared to 0 when

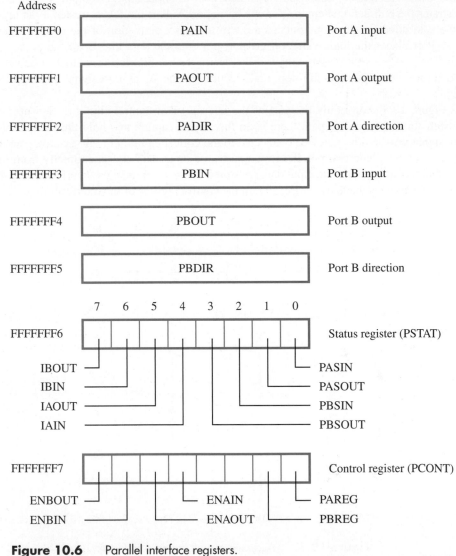

Figure 10.6   Parallel interface registers.

the processor writes data into PAOUT. The flags PBSIN and PBSOUT perform the same function for port B.

The status register also contains four interrupt flags. An interrupt flag, such as IAIN, is set to 1 when that interrupt is enabled and the corresponding I/O action occurs. The interrupt-enable bits are held in control register PCONT. An enable bit is set to 1 to enable the corresponding interrupt. For example, if ENAIN = 1 and PASIN = 1, then the interrupt flag IAIN is set to 1 and an interrupt request is raised. Thus,

$$\text{IAIN} = \text{ENAIN} \cdot \text{PASIN}$$

A single interrupt-request signal is used for all ports in the interface. In response to an interrupt request, the processor must examine the interrupt flags to determine the actual source of the request.

The information in the status and control registers is used for controlling data transfers to and from the devices connected to ports A and B. Port A has two control lines, CAIN and CAOUT, which can be used to provide an automatic signaling mechanism between the interface and the attached device, for devices that have this capability. For an input transfer, the device places new data on the port's pins and signifies this action by activating the CAIN line for one clock cycle. When the interface circuit sees CAIN = 1, it sets the status bit PASIN to 1. Later, this bit is cleared to 0 when the processor reads the input data. This action also causes the interface to send a pulse on the CAOUT line to inform the device that it may send new data to the interface. For an output transfer, the processor writes the data into the PAOUT register. The interface responds by clearing the PASOUT bit to 0 and sending a pulse on the CAOUT line to inform the device that new data are available. When the device accepts the data, it sends a pulse on the CAIN line, which in turn sets PASOUT to 1. This signaling mechanism is operational when all data pins of a port have the same orientation, that is, when the port serves as either an input or an output port. If some pins are selected as inputs and others as outputs, then the automatic mechanism is not used and neither the control lines nor the status and control registers contain meaningful information. In this case, the inputs are read directly from the pins.

Control register bits PAREG and PBREG are used to select the mode of operation of inputs to ports A and B, respectively. If set to 1, a register is used to store the input data; otherwise, a direct path from the pins is used as indicated in Figure 10.5. As an example of using the direct path, consider the operation of the microwave oven depicted in Figure 10.1. The microcontroller turns the magnetron on to start the cooking operation, but it may do so only if the oven door is closed. A simple sensor switch indicates whether the door is open by providing a signal that can be read as one bit of data. The sensor is connected to a pin in a microcontroller interface, enabling the microcontroller to determine the status of the door by reading the logic value of this input directly.

10.3.2 SERIAL I/O INTERFACE

The serial interface provides the UART (Universal Asynchronous Receiver/Transmitter) capability to transfer data based on the scheme described in Section 7.4.2. Double buffering is used in both the transmit and receive paths, as shown in Figure 10.7. Such buffering is needed to handle bursts in I/O transfers correctly.

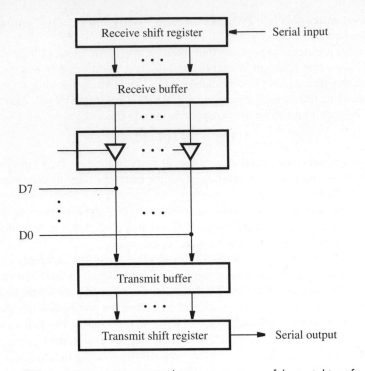

Figure 10.7   Receive and transmit structure of the serial interface.

Figure 10.8 shows the addressable registers of the serial interface. Input data are read from the 8-bit Receive buffer, and output data are loaded into the 8-bit Transmit buffer. The status register, SSTAT, provides information about the current status of the receive and transmit units. Bit $SSTAT_0$ is set to 1 when there are valid data in the receive buffer; it is cleared to 0 automatically upon a read access to the receive buffer. Bit $SSTAT_1$ is set to 1 when the transmit buffer is empty and can be loaded with new data. These bits serve the same purpose as the status flags KIN and DOUT discussed in Section 3.1. Bit $SSTAT_2$ is set to 1 if an error occurs during the receive process. For example, an error occurs if the character in the receive buffer is overwritten by a subsequently received character before the first character is read by the processor. The status register also contains the interrupt flags. Bit $SSTAT_4$ is set to 1 when the receive buffer becomes full and the receiver interrupt is enabled. Similarly, $SSTAT_5$ is set to 1 when the transmit buffer becomes empty and the transmitter interrupt is enabled. The serial interface raises an interrupt if either $SSTAT_4$ or $SSTAT_5$ is equal to 1. It also raises an interrupt if $SSTAT_6 = 1$, which occurs if $SSTAT_2 = 1$ and the error condition interrupt is enabled.

The control register, SCONT, is used to hold the interrupt-enable bits. Setting bits $SCONT_{6-4}$ to 1 or 0 enables or disables the corresponding interrupts, respectively. This register also indicates how the transmit clock is generated. If $SCONT_0 = 0$, then the transmit clock is the same as the system (processor) clock. If $SCONT_0 = 1$, then a lower-frequency transmit clock is obtained using a clock-dividing circuit.

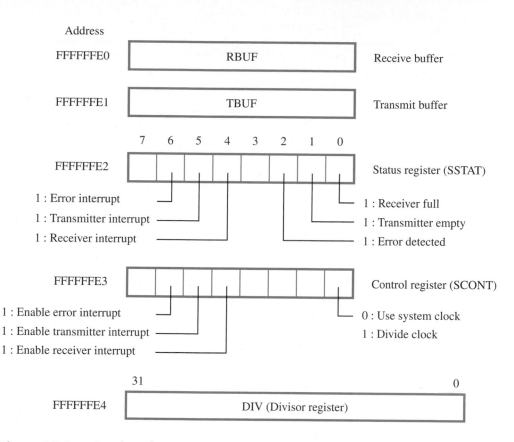

Figure 10.8   Serial interface registers.

The last register in the serial interface is the clock-divisor register, DIV. This 32-bit register is associated with a counter circuit that divides down the system clock signal to generate the serial transmission clock. The counter generates a clock signal whose frequency is equal to the frequency of the system clock divided by the contents of this register. The value loaded into this register is transferred into the counter, which then counts down using the system clock. When the count reaches zero, the counter is reloaded using the value in the DIV register.

10.3.3   COUNTER/TIMER

A 32-bit down-counter circuit is provided for use as either a counter or a timer. The basic operation of the circuit involves loading a starting value into the counter, and then decrementing the counter contents using either the internal system clock or an external clock signal. The circuit can be programmed to raise an interrupt when the counter contents reach zero. Figure 10.9 shows the registers associated with the counter/timer circuit. The

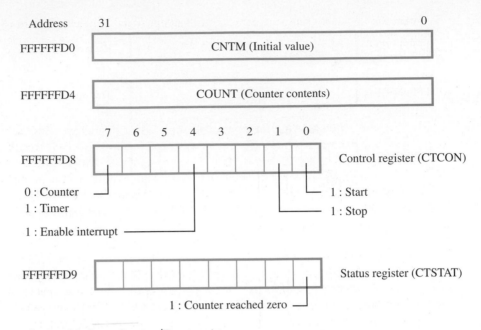

Figure 10.9   Counter/Timer registers.

counter/timer register, CNTM, can be loaded with an initial value, which is then transferred into the counter circuit. The current contents of the counter can be read by accessing memory address FFFFFFD4. The control register, CTCON, is used to specify the operating mode of the counter/timer circuit. It provides a mechanism for starting and stopping the counting process, and for enabling interrupts when the counter contents are decremented to 0. The status register, CTSTAT, reflects the state of the circuit.

Counter Mode

The counter mode is selected by setting bit $CTCON_7$ to 0. The starting value is loaded into the counter by writing it into register CNTM. The counting process begins when bit $CTCON_0$ is set to 1 by a program instruction. Once counting starts, bit $CTCON_0$ is automatically cleared to 0. The counter is decremented by pulses on the Counter_in line in Figure 10.4. Upon reaching 0, the counter circuit sets the status flag $CTSTAT_0$ to 1, and raises an interrupt if the corresponding interrupt-enable bit has been set to 1. The next clock pulse causes the counter to reload the starting value, which is held in register CNTM, and counting continues. The counting process is stopped by setting bit $CTCON_1$ to 1.

Timer Mode

The timer mode is selected by setting bit $CTCON_7$ to 1. This mode can be used to generate periodic interrupts. It is also suitable for generating a square-wave signal on the output line Timer_out in Figure 10.4. The process starts as explained above for the counter mode. As the counter counts down, the value on the output line is held constant. Upon reaching zero, the counter is reloaded automatically with the starting value, and the output signal on the line is inverted. Thus, the period of the output signal is twice the starting counter value multiplied by the period of the controlling clock pulse. In the timer mode, the counter is decremented by the system clock.

10.3.4 INTERRUPT-CONTROL MECHANISM

The processor in our example microcontroller has two interrupt-request inputs, IRQ and XRQ. The IRQ input is used for interrupts raised by the I/O interfaces within the microcontroller. The XRQ input is used for interrupts raised by external devices. If the IRQ input is asserted and interrupts are enabled, the processor executes an interrupt-service routine that uses the polling method to determine the source(s) of the interrupt request. This is done by examining the flags in the status registers PSTAT, SSTAT, and CTSTAT. The XRQ interrupts have higher priority than the IRQ interrupts.

The processor status register, PSR, has two bits for enabling interrupts. The IRQ interrupts are enabled if $PSR_6 = 1$, and the XRQ interrupts are enabled if $PSR_7 = 1$. When the processor accepts an interrupt, it disables further interrupts at the same priority level by clearing the corresponding PSR bit before the interrupt service routine is executed. A vectored interrupt scheme is used, with the vectors for IRQ and XRQ interrupts in memory locations 0x20 and 0x24, respectively. Each vector contains the address of the first instruction of the corresponding interrupt-service routine. This address is automatically loaded into the program counter, PC.

The processor has a Link register, LR, which is used for subroutine linkage as explained in Section 2.7. A subroutine Call instruction causes the updated contents of the program counter, which is the required return address, to be stored in LR prior to branching to the first instruction in the subroutine. There is another register, IRA, which saves the return address when an interrupt request is accepted. In this case, in addition to saving the return address in IRA, the contents of the processor status register, PSR, are saved in processor register IPSR.

Return from a subroutine is performed by a ReturnS instruction, which transfers the contents of LR into PC. Return from an interrupt is performed by a ReturnI instruction, which transfers the contents of IRA and IPSR into PC and PSR, respectively. Since there is only one IRA and IPSR register, nested interrupts can be implemented by saving the contents of these registers on the stack using instructions in the interrupt-service routine. Note that if the interrupt-service routine calls a subroutine, then it must save the contents of LR, because an interrupt may occur when the processor is executing another subroutine.

10.3.5 PROGRAMMING EXAMPLES

Having introduced the microcontroller hardware, we will now consider some software issues that arise when the microcontroller's interfaces are used to connect to I/O devices. Programs can be written either in assembly language or in a high-level language. The latter choice is preferable in most applications because the desired code is easier to generate and maintain, and development time is shorter. We will use the C programming language in the examples in this chapter.

The examples in this section are rudimentary and are intended to illustrate the possible approaches. In Section 10.4, we give a more elaborate example of a complete application.

Example 10.1 Consider the following task. A microcontroller is used to monitor the state of some mechanical equipment. The state information is available as binary signals provided on four wires. The 16 possible values of the state are to be displayed as a hexadecimal digit on a seven-segment display of the type shown in Figure 3.17.

The desired operation can be achieved by using the parallel interface illustrated in Figures 10.4 to 10.6. Let the four input wires be connected to the pins of port A and the seven data lines to the seven-segment display to port B. Then, the data direction registers, PADIR and PBDIR, must configure ports A and B as input and output, respectively. The input data can be read directly from the pins on port A.

Figure 10.10 gives a possible program. The *define* statements are used to associate the required address constants with the symbolic names of the pointers. Note that the PAIN

```
/* Define register addresses */
#define   PAIN      (volatile unsigned char *) 0xFFFFFFF0
#define   PADIR     (volatile unsigned char *) 0xFFFFFFF2
#define   PBOUT     (volatile unsigned char *) 0xFFFFFFF4
#define   PBDIR     (volatile unsigned char *) 0xFFFFFFF5
#define   PCONT     (volatile unsigned char *) 0xFFFFFFF7

/* Hex to 7-segment conversion table */
unsigned char table[16] = { 0x40, 0x79, 0x24, 0x30, 0x19, 0x12,
    0x02, 0x78, 0x00, 0x18, 0x08, 0x03, 0x46, 0x21, 0x06, 0x0E };
unsigned int current_value;

void main()
{
    /* Initialize ports A and B */
    *PADIR = 0x0;                       /* Configure Port A as input. */
    *PBDIR = 0xFF;                      /* Configure Port B as output. */
    *PCONT = 0x0;                       /* Read inputs directly from pins. */

    /* Read and display data. */
    while (1)                           /* Continuous loop. */
    {
        current_value = *PAIN & 0x0F;   /* Read the input from Port A. */
        *PBOUT = table[current_value];  /* Send the character to Port B. */
    }
}
```

Figure 10.10   C program for Example 10.1.

pointer is declared as *volatile*. This is necessary because the program only reads the contents of the corresponding location, but it neither writes any data into it, nor associates a specific value with it. An optimizing compiler may remove program statements that appear to have no impact. This includes statements involving variables whose values never change. Since the contents of register PAIN change under influences that are external to the program, it is essential to inform the compiler of this fact. The compiler will not remove the statements that contain variables that have been declared as volatile.

A table is used to translate a hex digit into a corresponding seven-segment pattern. The program uses a continuous loop to read and display new data. In an actual application, it is not likely that one would use a loop in this manner because other tasks would also be involved. We use the continuous loop merely to keep the example simple.

Example 10.2

Consider now the case of an I/O device that is capable of sending information in a bit-serial format that can be handled by the serial interface depicted in Figures 10.7 and 10.8. The device sends eight bits of information that is to be displayed as two hex digits on two 7-segment displays of the type in Figure 3.17. Let the I/O device be connected to the serial interface, and the 7-segment displays to parallel ports A and B. Thus, both A and B must be configured as output ports.

A possible program is presented in Figure 10.11. The polling method is used to determine when new data are available in the receive buffer of the serial interface. Bit $SSTAT_0$ serves as the flag that is polled. As described in Section 10.3.2, this bit is cleared when data are read from the buffer.

Figure 10.12 shows how interrupts can be used in accessing new data. Recall from Section 10.3.4 that the IRQ interrupt vector is in memory location 0x20. The address of the interrupt-service routine is loaded into this location. Bit $SCONT_4$ is set to 1 to enable receiver interrupts. To cause the processor to respond to IRQ interrupts, bit 6 in the processor status register, PSR, must be set to 1. Since PSR is not a location in the addressable space, it is necessary to use the *asm* directive for in-line insertion of the assembly-language instruction

$$\text{MoveControl} \quad \text{PSR, \#0x40}$$

Also, it is necessary to include the return-from-interrupt instruction in the object program to ensure a correct return to the interrupted program. The compiler will insert this instruction, because the *intserv* function definition includes the keyword *interrupt*. This manner of handling interrupts in a high-level language is explained in Section 4.6.

10.4 Reaction Timer—A Complete Example

Having introduced the basic features of the microcontroller, we will now show how it can be used in a simple embedded system that implements an easily understood task that exemplifies the term *reactive system*. We want to design a "reaction timer" that can be used to measure the speed of response of a person to a visual stimulus. The idea is to have the

```
                    /* Define register addresses */
#define   RBUF     (volatile unsigned char *) 0xFFFFFFE0
#define   SSTAT    (volatile unsigned char *) 0xFFFFFFE2
#define   PAOUT    (volatile unsigned char *) 0xFFFFFFF1
#define   PADIR    (volatile unsigned char *) 0xFFFFFFF2
#define   PBOUT    (volatile unsigned char *) 0xFFFFFFF4
#define   PBDIR    (volatile unsigned char *) 0xFFFFFFF5

        /* Hex to 7-segment conversion table */
        unsigned char table[16] = {0x40, 0x79, 0x24, 0x30, 0x19, 0x12,
            0x02, 0x78, 0x00, 0x18, 0x08, 0x03, 0x46, 0x21, 0x06, 0x0E};
        unsigned int current_value, low_digit, high_digit;

        void main()
        {
            /* Initialize the parallel ports */
            *PADIR = 0xFF;                   /* Configure Port A as output. */
            *PBDIR = 0xFF;                   /* Configure Port B as output. */

            /* Read and display data */
            while (1)                        /* Continuous loop. */
            {
                while ((*SSTAT & 0x1) == 0); /* Wait for new data. */
                current_value = *RBUF;       /* Read the 8-bit value. */
                low_digit = current_value & 0x0F;
                high_digit = (current_value >> 4) & 0x0F;
                *PAOUT = table[low_digit];   /* Send the two digits    */
                *PBOUT = table[high_digit];  /*  to 7-segment displays. */
            }
        }
```

Figure 10.11   C program for Example 10.2 that uses polling to read input data.

microcontroller turn on a light and then measure the reaction time that the subject takes to turn the light off by pressing a pushbutton key. Details of the system and its operation are as follows:

- There are two manual pushbutton keys, *Go* and *Stop,* a light-emitting diode (LED), and a three-digit seven-segment display.
- The system is activated by pressing the *Go* key.
- Upon activation, the seven-segment display is set to 000 and the LED is turned off.
- After a three-second delay, the LED is turned on and the timing process begins.
- When the *Stop* key is pressed, the timing process is stopped, the LED is turned off, and the elapsed time is displayed on the seven-segment display.

```
#define   RBUF     (volatile unsigned char *) 0xFFFFFFE0
#define   SCONT    (volatile unsigned char *) 0xFFFFFFE3
#define   PAOUT    (volatile unsigned char *) 0xFFFFFFF1
#define   PADIR    (volatile unsigned char *) 0xFFFFFFF2
#define   PBOUT    (volatile unsigned char *) 0xFFFFFFF4
#define   PBDIR    (volatile unsigned char *) 0xFFFFFFF5
#define   IVECT    (volatile unsigned int *) 0x20


/* Hex to 7-segment conversion table */
unsigned char table[16] = {0x40, 0x79, 0x24, 0x30, 0x19, 0x12,
    0x02, 0x78, 0x00, 0x18, 0x08, 0x03, 0x46, 0x21, 0x06, 0x0E};
unsigned int current_value, low_digit, high_digit;

interrupt void intserv();

void main()
{
    /* Initialize the parallel port */
    *PADIR = 0xFF;                          /* Configure Port A as output.  */
    *PBDIR = 0xFF;                          /* Configure Port B as output.  */

    /* Initialize the interrupt mechanism */
    *IVECT = (unsigned int *) &intserv;     /* Set the interrupt vector.  */
    asm ("MoveControl   PSR, #0x40");       /* Respond to IRQ interrupts.  */
    *SCONT = 0x10;                          /* Enable receiver interrupts.  */

    while (1);                              /* Continuous loop.  */
}

/* Interrupt service routine */
interrupt void intserv()
{
    current_value = *RBUF;                  /* Read the 8-bit value.  */
    low_digit = current_value & 0x0F;
    high_digit = (current_value > > 4) & 0x0F;
    *PAOUT = table[low_digit];              /* Send the two digits     */
    *PBOUT = table[high_digit];             /*   to 7-segment displays. */
}
```

Figure 10.12   C program for Example 10.2 that uses interrupts to read input data.

- The elapsed time is calculated and displayed in hundredths of a second. Since the display has only three digits, it is assumed that the elapsed time will be less than ten seconds.

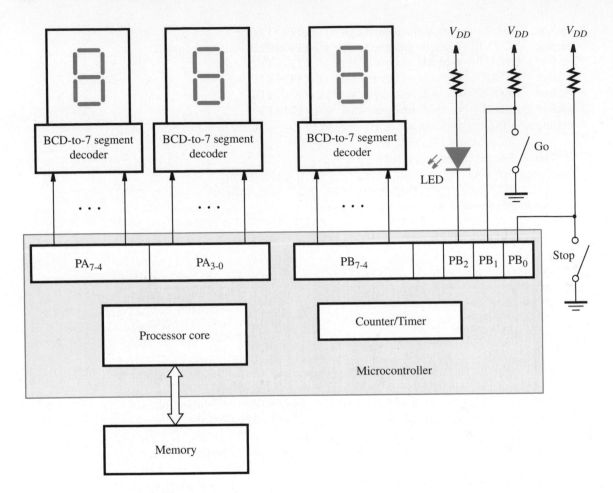

Figure 10.13   The reaction-timer circuit.

Figure 10.13 depicts the hardware that can implement the desired reaction timer. The microcontroller provides all hardware components except for the input keys and the output displays. In contrast with the examples in the preceding section, we assume that a BCD-to-7-segment decoder circuit is associated with each seven-segment display device, so that the microcontroller needs to send only a four-bit BCD code for each digit to be displayed. Our microcontroller does not have enough parallel ports to allow sending decoded seven-segment signals to three displays.

We will use the two parallel ports, A and B, for all input/output functions. The two most-significant BCD digits of the displayed time are connected to port A, and the least-significant digit is connected to the upper four bits of port B. The keys and the LED are connected to the lowest three bits of port B. The counter/timer circuit is used to measure the elapsed time. It is driven by the system clock, which we assume to have a frequency of 100 MHz.

A program to realize the required task can be based on the following approach:

- The user's intention to begin a test is monitored by means of a wait loop that polls the state of the *Go* key.

- Upon observing that the *Go* key has been pressed, that is, having detected $PB_1 = 0$, and after a further delay of three seconds, the LED is turned on.

- The counter is set to the initial value 0xFFFFFFFF and the process of decrementing the count on each clock pulse is started.

- A wait loop polls the state of the *Stop* key to detect when the user reacts by pressing it.

- When the *Stop* key is pressed, the LED is turned off, the counter is stopped, and the elapsed time is calculated.

- The measured delay is converted into a BCD number and sent to the seven-segment displays.

The addresses of various I/O registers in the microcontroller are as given in Figures 10.6 through 10.9. The program must configure ports A and B as required by the connections shown in Figure 10.13. All bits of port A and the high-order four bits of port B are configured as outputs. In the low-order three bits of port B, PB_0, and PB_1 are used as inputs, while PB_2 is an output. There is no need to use the control signals available on the two ports, because the input device consists of pushbutton keys that drive the port lines directly, and the output device is a display that directly follows any changes in signals on the port pins that drive it.

We will show how the required application can be implemented using the C programming language. The program performs the following tasks. After the *Go* key is pressed, a delay of three seconds is implemented by using the timer. Since the counter/timer circuit is clocked at 100 MHz, the counter is initialized to the hex value 11E1A300, which corresponds to the decimal value 300,000,000. The process of counting down is started by setting the $CTCONT_0$ bit to 1. When the count reaches zero, the LED is turned on to begin the reaction time test and the counter is set to 0xFFFFFFFF. Upon detecting that the *Stop* key has been pressed, the counting process is stopped by setting $CTCONT_1 = 1$. The total count is computed as

$$\text{Total count} = \text{0xFFFFFFFF} - \text{Present count}$$

Since this is the total number of clock cycles, the actual time in hundredths of seconds is

$$\text{Actual time} = (\text{Total count})/1000000$$

This binary integer can be converted to a decimal number by first dividing it by 100 to generate the most-significant digit. The remainder is then divided by 10 to generate the next digit. The final remainder is the least-significant digit.

Figure 10.14 gives a possible program. After first configuring ports A and B as required and turning off the display and LED, the program continuously polls the value on pin PB_1. After the *Go* key is pressed and PB_1 becomes equal to 0, a three-second delay is introduced. Then, the LED is turned on, and the reaction timing process starts. Another polling operation is used to wait for the *Stop* key to be pressed. When this key is pressed, the LED is turned off, the counter is stopped, and its contents are read. The computation of the elapsed time and the conversion to a decimal number are performed as explained above. The resulting

```c
/* Define register addresses */
#define PAOUT (volatile unsigned char *) 0xFFFFFFF1
#define PADIR (volatile unsigned char *) 0xFFFFFFF2
#define PBIN (volatile unsigned char *) 0xFFFFFFF3
#define PBOUT (volatile unsigned char *) 0xFFFFFFF4
#define PBDIR (volatile unsigned char *) 0xFFFFFFF5
#define CNTM (volatile unsigned int *) 0xFFFFFFD0
#define COUNT (volatile unsigned int *) 0xFFFFFFD4
#define CTCON (volatile unsigned char *) 0xFFFFFFD8

void main()
{
    unsigned int counter_value, total_count;
    unsigned int actual_time, seconds, tenths, hundredths;

    /* Initialize the parallel ports */
    *PADIR = 0xFF;              /* Configure Port A. */
    *PBDIR = 0xF4;              /* Configure Port B. */
    *PAOUT = 0x0;               /* Turn off the display */
    *PBOUT = 0x4;               /*   and LED. */

    /* Start the test. */
    while (1)                   /* Continuous loop. */
    {
        while ((*PBIN & 0x2) != 0);     /* Wait for the Go key to be pressed. */

        /* Wait 3 seconds and then turn LED on */
        *CNTM = 0x11E1A300;     /* Set timer value to 300,000,000. */
        *CTCONT = 0x1;          /* Start the timer. */
        while ((*CTSTAT & 0x1) == 0);   /* Wait until timer reaches zero. */
        *PBOUT = 0x0;           /* Turn the LED on. */

        /* Initialize the counting process */
        counter_value = 0;
        *CNTM = 0xFFFFFFFF;     /* Set the starting counter value. */
        *CTCONT = 0x1;          /* Start counting. */

        while ((*PBIN & 0x1) != 0);     /* Wait for the Stop key to be pressed. */

        /* The Stop key has been pressed - stop counting */
        *CTCONT = 0x2;          /* Stop the counter. */
        *PBOUT = 0x4;           /* Turn the LED off. */
        counter_value = *COUNT; /* Read the contents of the counter. */
```

Figure 10.14   C program for the reaction timer (Part a).

```
    /* Compute the total count */
    total_count = (0xFFFFFFFF – counter_value);

    /* Convert count to time */ ;
    actual_time = total_count / 1000000;        /* Time in hundredths of seconds */
    seconds = actual_time / 100;
    tenths = (actual_time – seconds * 100) / 10;
    hundredths = actual_time – (seconds * 100 + tenths * 10);

    /* Display the elapsed time */
    *PAOUT = ((seconds < < 4) | tenths);
    *PBOUT = ((hundredths < < 4) | 0x4);    /* Keep the LED turned off */
  }
}
```

Figure 10.14   C program for the reaction timer (Part b).

three BCD digits are written to the port data registers according to the arrangement depicted in Figure 10.13.

10.5   SENSORS AND ACTUATORS

An embedded computer interacts closely with its environment. So far, we have used switches and simple display devices to illustrate such interactions. There is a variety of other devices used in practical applications. To control a mechanical system, it is necessary to use devices that provide an interface between the mechanical domain and the digital electronics domain used in the computer. These devices enable the computer to sense, or monitor, the state of the controlled system. They also cause the actions ordered by the computer to be performed. Such devices are usually referred to as *sensors* and *actuators*. Collectively, they are referred to as *transducers*. In this section, we present a few examples of transducers that illustrate some of the basic principles used.

10.5.1   SENSORS

Depending on the nature of the controlled system, there may be many parameters that an embedded computer needs to monitor. Consider the cruise control system in a car. Its purpose is to maintain the speed as close as possible to a desired value, whether the road is level, uphill, or downhill. It is not sufficient to simply keep the gas throttle in a fixed position. The control system has to measure the speed of the car continuously and adjust the throttle opening to maintain the speed at the desired level. Thus, a sensor is needed to measure the speed of the car and express it in a digital form suitable for use by the computer.

The computer can then determine whether the throttle opening needs to be adjusted, and send commands to an actuator to cause this to happen. Many other sensors are found in cars. They include devices that measure the levels of various fluids, including gas, oil, and engine coolant. Sensors can be used to monitor the coolant temperature, tire pressure, and battery voltage.

Some sensors are simple, such as those that detect if a person or an animal walks under a closing garage door. Others may be very sophisticated. A few examples of sensors are given below.

Position Sensors

Consider an embedded computer that controls the movement of a robot's hand. The position of the hand is determined by the angular position of the shoulder, elbow, and wrist joints. To monitor the position of the hand, the computer has to measure the angular position of each of these joints.

A simple transducer for measuring the angular position of a shaft relative to its housing is a potentiometer. It consists of a resistor wound around a circular base attached to the housing and a slider contact attached to the shaft whose position is to be monitored. As the shaft rotates, the contact point on the resistor changes. When attached to a voltage source as shown in Figure 10.15, the two parts of the resistor on either side of the contact point form a voltage divider. The output voltage of this circuit is given by

$$V_{out} = \frac{R_2 V_{in}}{R_1 + R_2}$$

This voltage is fed to an A/D converter circuit to convert the analog value into a digital representation. The microcontroller in Figure 10.3 includes an A/D converter for use in such situations.

Some sensors produce a digital output directly. For example, a coded disc may be attached to a shaft whose position is to be monitored. The code on the disc is in the form of transparent and opaque areas organized in concentric annular regions, as shown in Figure 10.16. The disc is positioned between pairs of light-emitting diodes and photodetectors, with one pair for each annular region. Each photodetector is connected to a circuit that

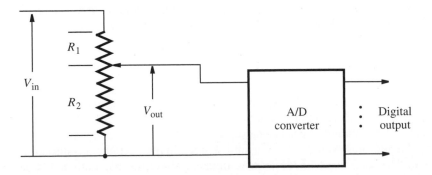

Figure 10.15   A sensor using a voltage divider.

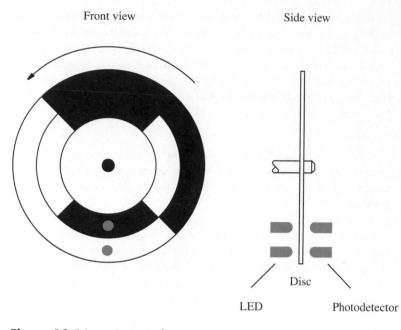

Front view   Side view

Disc

LED   Photodetector

Figure 10.16   An optical position sensor.

produces a logic signal 1 when light is detected and 0 otherwise. Thus, as the disc rotates, the two photodetectors shown in the figure produce the 2-bit binary numbers 00, 01, 10, and 11, representing the angular position of the shaft.

Temperature Sensors

Many types of sensors make use of changes in the properties of materials as the temperature or humidity changes, or as a result of deformation caused by stretching, compressing, or bending. The resistance of a conductor changes with temperature, and the effect is much more pronounced in some materials than others. Hence, using a voltage divider similar to that in Figure 10.15, a temperature sensor can be constructed by making resistor R_2 from a material with high sensitivity to temperature changes and exposing it to the environment whose temperature is to be measured. As the temperature changes, voltage V_{out} changes. Thus, after converting V_{out} into a digital representation, the value can be read by a computer as a measure of temperature. Other types of temperature sensors use capacitors as the sensing element. The capacitance of a capacitor changes as the properties of the dielectric (the insulating material) used to construct it changes. Some ceramic materials are also well suited for use in temperature sensors.

Pressure Sensors

A widely used sensor that is based on measuring changes in resistance is the strain gauge, which consists of a resistor deposited on a flexible film. The value of the resistance changes when the film is stretched.

Suppose that we wish to monitor the air pressure inside a closed container, such as a car tire. A pressure sensor can be constructed in the form of a small cylinder with a diaphragm attached to one end, and a strain gauge mounted on the diaphragm. The cylinder is inserted into the container such that the diaphragm blocks the air flow out of the container. As the container is pressurized, the diaphragm stretches, and the resistance of the strain gauge changes. This change in resistance can be measured using a circuit similar to that in Figure 10.15.

Speed Sensors

A small electrical generator attached to a rotating shaft produces a voltage that is proportional to the speed of rotation. The generator's output voltage can be converted into digital form and read by a computer as a measure of speed. Such a device is often referred to as a tachometer.

Another approach is to generate electrical pulses as the shaft rotates. For example, a toothed disc may be attached to the shaft. As the disc rotates, an appropriately placed electromagnetic or optical sensor produces an electrical pulse as each tooth passes the sensor. The speed of rotation is determined by counting the number of pulses generated during a fixed time period or by measuring the time delay between successive pulses.

10.5.2 ACTUATORS

An actuator is a device that causes a mechanical component to move after receiving a command. Figure 10.17 illustrates a basic principle that is used to construct a variety of actuators. An electrical wire is wound to form a coil around a cylinder that contains a movable core, called an armature. This structure is known as a solenoid. The armature is made of a magnetic material such as iron. It is held by a spring in a partially inserted position in the cylinder, as shown. When electrical current flows through the coil, it produces a magnetic field that pulls the armature into the cylinder. When current stops flowing, the armature is pulled back to its rest position by the spring. The movement of the armature can be used to open a water valve, or close an electrical switch that turns on a motor. This arrangement can be used in the starter motor of a car, for example.

A combination of a motor and a sensor can be used to move an object to a desired position. When the motor is turned on, the object begins to move. The computer can then use the sensor to repeatedly check whether the desired position has been reached. In a

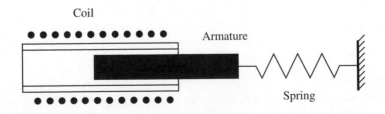

Figure 10.17   A solenoid actuator.

camera with an automatic focus the motor rotates the focusing mechanism. At the same time, the computer uses image analysis algorithms to check whether the image is focused properly. When the best focus is achieved, it stops the motor.

Another useful type of actuator is a stepper motor. This is a motor that rotates its shaft in response to commands in the form of pulses. Each pulse causes the motor shaft to rotate a predefined amount, such as a few degrees. A stepper motor is useful in applications requiring precise control of the position of an object, such as a robot arm.

The sensors and actuators presented above constitute the interface between the computer and the physical environment in which it is embedded. They provide the computer with the ability to monitor the state of various system components and to cause desired actions to take place. Sensors present the computer with information about the state of the system. Actuators accept commands to perform their function. The computer's task is to implement the control algorithms needed for the application. It also accepts commands from and displays information to the user.

10.5.3   APPLICATION EXAMPLES

We now consider briefly two applications to illustrate how sensors and actuators may be used.

Home Heating Control

Heating and air conditioning in the home are controlled by a device known as a thermostat. Let us focus on controlling the heating furnace. By including a microcontroller in the thermostat, it is possible to implement features such as changing the desired temperature automatically at different times of the day or on weekends. Such a thermostat includes:

- A temperature sensor
- A circuit that generates an output signal to turn the furnace on and off
- A timer to keep track of the time of day and day of the week
- Pushbutton keys for the user to enter the desired settings
- A display screen

We will only examine the temperature control mechanism in this discussion. Assume that the resistive temperature sensor described in Section 10.5.1 is used, and that its output voltage is connected to the A/D converter in the microcontroller. A solenoid is used to activate a switch that turns the furnace on or off. The control algorithm is implemented by a program in the microcontroller. Suppose that the desired temperature is set at T degrees. The actual temperature of the house is allowed to deviate from this setting by a small amount ΔT above or below the desired value. Then, the control task can be implemented by repeatedly performing the following actions:

1. Sample the temperature sensor to obtain the input voltage representing the temperature.
2. If the temperature is below $T - \Delta T$, turn the furnace on.
3. If temperature is above $T + \Delta T$, turn the furnace off.

The rest of the computer program deals with the tasks of using the timer to keep track of time, receiving the user's input through the pushbutton keys, and sending information to the display.

Cruise Control

The cruise control system found in many cars requires the following components:

- A sensor to measure the speed of the car's drive shaft
- An actuator to control the position of the gas throttle
- Input pushbuttons for the driver to activate the system and set the desired speed

This application differs from the home heating system in that the parameter to be controlled—the position of the throttle—varies continuously between two extremes, fully closed and fully open. The simple on/off control algorithm used in the previous example is not suitable. When controlling a varying quantity such as the position of the throttle, more sophisticated algorithms are needed, the discussion of which is beyond the scope of this text. However, the desired actions can be described briefly as follows. The computer repeatedly measures the speed of the car and compares it to the set value. The difference is an error, ϵ, which may be positive or negative. Depending on the value of ϵ, the computer makes a small adjustment to the position of the throttle. The objective is to maintain a value of ϵ that is as close to zero as possible. In effect, the computer mimics the decisions and actions of a driver who is operating the car manually and maintaining a constant speed.

10.6   MICROCONTROLLER FAMILIES

Having presented an example of a microcontroller in Section 10.3, we now briefly survey the broad range of commercially available microcontroller chips. Many embedded applications do not require a powerful processor. Certainly, the microwave oven discussed in Section 10.1.1 does not need a powerful microcontroller, because its computational requirements are rather modest and reaction times are not demanding. For such applications it is preferable to use a chip that has a simple processor but which contains sufficient memory and I/O resources to implement all controller functions. The digital camera, discussed in Section 10.1.2, has much more demanding computational requirements, and hence requires a more powerful processor.

Processors may be characterized by how many data bits they handle in parallel when accessing data in the memory. The most powerful microcontrollers are likely to be based on a 32-bit processor, with a 32-bit-wide data bus. Such is the case with some microcontrollers based on the ARM architecture. It is also possible to have a processor that has an internal 32-bit structure, but a 16-bit-wide data bus to memory. An example is Freescale's 68K/ColdFire family of microcontrollers. Some of the most popular microcontrollers are 8-bit chips. They are much cheaper, yet powerful enough to satisfy the requirements of a large number of embedded applications. There exist even smaller 4-bit chips, which are attractive because of their simplicity and extremely low cost.

10.6.1 MICROCONTROLLERS BASED ON THE INTEL 8051

In the early 1980s, Intel Corporation introduced a microcontroller chip called the 8051. This chip has the basic architecture of Intel's 8080 microprocessor family, which used 8-bit chips for general-purpose computing applications. The 8051 chip gained rapid popularity and has become one of the most widely used chips in practice. It has four 8-bit I/O ports, a UART, and two 16-bit counter/timer circuits. It also contains 4K bytes of ROM and 128 bytes of RAM storage. The EPROM version of the chip, in which there are 4K bytes of EPROM rather than ROM, is available under the name 8751.

A number of other chips based on the 8051 architecture are available; they provide various enhancements. For example, the 8052 chip has 8K bytes of ROM and 256 bytes of RAM, as well as an extra counter/timer circuit. Its EPROM version is called 8752.

The 8051 architecture was developed by Intel. Subsequently, a number of other semiconductor manufacturers have produced chips that are either identical to those in the 8051 family, or have some enhanced features but are otherwise fully compatible with the 8051.

10.6.2 FREESCALE MICROCONTROLLERS

Motorola had a dominant position as a manufacturer of microprocessor chips in the 1980s. Their most popular 8-bit microprocessors became the basis for their microcontrollers. Freescale Semiconductor Inc. is Motorola's successor in this area. Freescale manufactures a wide range of microcontrollers, based on different processor cores.

68HC11 Microcontroller

Motorola's most popular 8-bit microprocessors were the 6800 and the 6809. The 68HC11 was later introduced as a microcontroller chip that implements a superset of 6800 instructions. It has five I/O ports that can be used for a variety of purposes. The I/O structure includes two serial interfaces. There are also counter/timer circuits capable of operating in a number of different modes.

The amount of memory included in 68HC11 chips ranges from an 8K-byte ROM, a 512-byte EEPROM, and a 256-byte RAM in the original chip, to a 12K-byte ROM, a 512-byte EEPROM, and a 512-byte RAM in later chips.

68K Microcontrollers

A family of microcontrollers, known as 68K, is based on the 32-bit 68000 processor core. To reduce the number of pins, the external data bus is only 16 bits wide. These chips include parallel and serial ports, counter/timer capability, and A/D conversion circuits. The amount of on-chip memory depends on the particular chip. For example, the 68376 chip has an 8K-byte EEPROM and a 4K-byte RAM.

ColdFire Microcontrollers

The 68000 instruction set architecture provides the basis for the 32-bit ColdFire processor presented in Appendix C and the MCF5xxx microcontrollers, known as the ColdFire embedded processors. Their distinguishing feature is a pipelined structure that leads to enhanced performance. The external data bus width may be 16 bits or 32 bits, depending on the selected microcontroller chip. The ColdFire processor core is also intended for use in the system-on-a-chip environment, which is discussed in Chapter 11.

PowerPC Microcontrollers

Freescale's high-end 32-bit microprocessor family, known as PowerPC, is based on a RISC-style architecture. This processor architecture is also available in microcontroller form, in chips comprising the MPC5xx family.

10.6.3 ARM Microcontrollers

The ARM architecture, presented in Appendix D, is attractive for embedded systems where substantial computing capability is needed, and the cost and power consumption have to be relatively low. A key objective of the design of the ARM processor is to make it suitable for use in the system-on-a-chip environment. ARM microcontrollers are also available as separate chips.

There has been a progression of ARM processor cores intended for embedded applications, including ARM6, ARM7, ARM9, ARM10, and ARM Cortex. The basic ARM architecture uses a 32-bit organization and an instruction set in which all instructions are 32 bits long. There exists another version, known as Thumb, which uses 16-bit instructions and 16-bit data transfers. The Thumb version uses a subset of the ARM instructions, which are encoded to fit into a 16-bit format. It also has fewer registers than the ARM architecture. An advantage of Thumb is that a significantly smaller memory is needed to store programs that comprise highly encoded 16-bit instructions. At execution time, each Thumb instruction is expanded into a normal 32-bit ARM instruction. Thus, a Thumb-aware ARM core contains a *Thumb decompressor* in addition to its normal circuits.

10.7 Design Issues

The designer of an embedded system has to make many important decisions. The nature of the application or the product that has to be designed presents certain requirements and constraints. In this section, we will consider some of the most important issues that the designer faces.

Cost

The cost of electronics in many embedded applications has to be low. The least costly solution is realized if a single chip suffices for the implementation of all functions that must be provided. This is possible only if this chip provides sufficient I/O capability to meet the demands of the application and enough on-chip memory to hold the necessary programs and data.

I/O Capability

Microcontroller chips provide a variety of I/O resources, ranging from simple parallel and serial ports to counters, timers, and A/D and D/A conversion circuits. The number of available I/O lines is important. Without sufficient I/O lines it is necessary to use external circuitry to make up the shortfall. This is illustrated by the reaction-timer example in Figure 10.13, in which external decoder circuits are used to drive the 7-segment displays from the 4-bit BCD signals provided by the microcontroller. If the microcontroller had four parallel ports, rather than two, it would be possible to connect each 7-segment display to one port. The controlling program would then directly generate the seven bit signals needed to drive the seven individual segments in each display.

Size

Microcontroller chips come in various sizes. If an application can be handled adequately with an 8-bit microcontroller, then it makes no sense to use a 16- or 32-bit chip which is likely to be more expensive, physically larger, and consume more power. The majority of practical applications can be handled with relatively small chips.

Power Consumption

Power consumption is an important consideration in all computer applications. In high-performance systems the power consumption tends to be high, requiring some mechanism to dissipate the heat generated. In many embedded applications the consumed power is low enough so that heat dissipation is not a concern. However, these applications often involve battery-powered products, so the life of the battery, which depends on the power consumption, is a key factor.

On-Chip Memory

Inclusion of memory on a microcontroller chip allows single-chip implementations of simple embedded applications. The size and the type of memory have significant ramifications. A relatively small amount of RAM may be sufficient for storing data during computations. A larger read-only memory is needed to store programs. This memory may be of the ROM, PROM, EPROM, EEPROM, or Flash type. For high-volume products, the most economical choices are microcontrollers with ROM. However, this is also the least flexible choice because the contents of the ROM are permanently set at the time the chip is manufactured. The greatest flexibility is offered by EEPROM and Flash memories, which can be programmed multiple times.

For applications that have greater storage requirements, it is necessary to use an external memory. Some microcontrollers do not have any on-chip memory. They are typically intended for more sophisticated applications where a substantial amount of memory, which cannot be realized within the microcontroller chip, is needed.

Performance

Performance is not an important consideration when microcontrollers are used in applications such as home appliances and toys. Small and inexpensive chips can be chosen in these cases. But, in applications such as digital cameras, cell phones, and some hand-held video games, it is essential to have much higher performance. High performance requires more powerful chips and results in higher cost and greater power consumption. Since the application is often battery-powered, it is also important to minimize power consumption. Various tradeoffs are required to satisfy these conflicting goals.

Software

There are many advantages to using high-level computer languages for application programs. They facilitate the process of program development and make it easy to maintain and modify the software in the future. However, there are some instances when it may be prudent or necessary to resort to assembly language. A well-crafted assembly-language program is likely to generate object code that is 10 to 20 percent more compact (in terms of the amount of storage needed) than the code produced by a compiler. If an embedded application is based on a microcontroller that has limited on-chip memory, it is a major advantage if the necessary code can fit into the memory provided on the chip, avoiding the need for external memory.

The limited capacity of the available on-chip RAM is an important consideration for a system designer. This memory is used for storing dynamic data, as a temporary buffer, and for implementing a stack. When writing an application program in a high-level language such as C, care must be taken to ensure that the total amount of code and data does not exceed the available memory.

Instruction Set

Another significant issue is the nature of the instruction set of the processor used. CISC-style instructions lead to more compact code than RISC-style instructions. Thus, the choice of the processor has an impact on the size of the code. An interesting example of an approach that addresses this issue is provided by the Thumb version of the ARM architecture, where a RISC-style instruction set designed for 32-bit processors has been modified into a more highly encoded form using 16-bit instructions, as discussed in Section 10.6.3. Programs written for Thumb versions are up to 30 percent more compact than those written for the full ARM architecture.

Development Tools

Designers of digital systems rely heavily on development tools. These tools include software packages for computer-aided design (CAD), compilers, assemblers, and simulators for the processors. The range and availability of tools often depends on the choice of the embedded processor. It is also attractive to have third-party support, where alternate sources of tools and documentation exist. Good documentation and helpful advice from the manufacturer (if needed) are extremely valuable.

Testability and Reliability

Printed circuit boards are often difficult to test, particularly if they are densely populated with chips. The testing process is greatly simplified if the entire system is designed to be easily testable. A microcontroller chip can include circuitry that makes it easier to test printed circuit boards that contain this chip. For example, some microcontrollers include a *test access port* that is compatible with the IEEE 1149.1 standard for a testable architecture, known as the Test Access Port and Boundary-Scan Architecture standard [1].

Embedded applications demand robustness and reliability. The life cycle of a typical product is expected to be at least five years. This is in contrast with personal computers, which tend to be considered obsolete in a shorter time.

10.8 CONCLUDING REMARKS

This chapter has provided an introduction to the design of embedded computer systems. We have not used a specific commercially-available microcontroller for this discussion because the principles presented are general and deal with the key issues that face the designer of an embedded system.

It is particularly important to appreciate the close interaction of hardware and software. The design choices may involve trade-offs between polled I/O and interrupts, between different instruction sets in terms of functionality and compactness of code, between power consumption and performance, and so on.

In this chapter we discussed the use of microcontrollers in implementing embedded systems. In the next chapter we will show how FPGA chips can be used to realize such systems. In particular, we will focus on the system-on-a-chip approach, which attempts to implement an entire system on a single chip.

Finally, let us consider the characteristics of embedded systems that make them different from general-purpose computers. The basic principles are the same. A designer of embedded systems must have a good knowledge of computer organization, which includes a thorough understanding of instruction sets, execution of programs, input/output techniques, memory structures, and interfacing schemes for dealing with a variety of devices that may be included in the system. So, what is different?

A general-purpose computer executes arbitrary application programs, including those that are used to create or modify other programs. Each program normally runs for a limited period of time, as a consequence of either the processing algorithm or control by the user. There is a need for a large main memory that is external to the processor chip to meet the potentially large requirements of some application programs. Large secondary storage devices are needed to hold files containing programs and data. A sophisticated operating system is used to control all resources in the computer system.

In contrast, an embedded system typically executes a single application program that is not likely to be modified. The program begins executing automatically when the system is turned on, and execution is continuous until the system is turned off. Memory requirements tend to be modest. It is often possible to employ a microcontroller with adequate on-chip memory. Powerful operating system software is not needed. In many cases, there is no operating system software. The single application program executes continuously and has direct access to all processor, memory, and input/output resources.

Our discussion has been focused on low-end embedded systems, in which the computing requirements are relatively modest. Such systems embody the main principles of embedded applications. But, there are also many high-end embedded systems, such as those used in aircraft and high-speed trains, which require much more powerful computing capability. They are often implemented using multiple processors. Chapter 12 deals with the issues pertinent to multiprocessor systems.

PROBLEMS

10.1   **[M]** In Example 10.2, we assumed that the I/O device is capable of sending 8-bit data in a bit-serial manner. Consider now a similar device that uses eight lines to send the data in parallel. Thus, one of the parallel ports in the microcontroller has to be used to receive the data. This leaves only one parallel port to display two hexadecimal digits that represent the data. Hence, only one 7-segment display device of the type shown in Figure 3.17 can be used. To convey the received information, a single device can be used to display the digits one after another. Let the most-significant digit be displayed for one second, followed by a one-second blank period, and then the second digit is displayed for one second. After displaying the second digit, the display should show a "dash" for two seconds. This sequence is to be repeated continuously, reflecting the latest data received. Use the timer in Figure 10.9, and assume that it is driven by a 100-MHz clock. Show the necessary hardware connections and write a program to implement the required task. Use polling to check the timer status.

10.2   **[M]** Solve Problem 10.1 by using the timer's interrupt capability.

10.3   **[M]** The microcontroller described in Section 10.3 is used to control a system that includes a motor which can run at two speeds, fast and slow. A sensor associated with the motor uses a single signal line to indicate the current speed of the motor. For the fast speed, the sensor transmits a continuous square-wave signal that has a frequency of 100 kHz. For the slow speed it transmits a 50-kHz signal. It transmits no signal (i.e. a constant logic value 0) if the motor is not running. The microcontroller uses a 7-segment display of the type shown in Figure 3.17 to display the state of the motor as F, S, or 0. Show the necessary hardware connections and write a program to implement the required task. Use the timer in Figure 10.9 to generate the time intervals needed to test the frequency of the signal sent by the sensor. Assume that the timer is driven by a 100-MHz clock. Use polling to check the timer status.

10.4   **[M]** Solve Problem 10.3 by using the timer's interrupt capability.

10.5   **[D]** The microcontroller in Section 10.3 is used to receive decimal numbers on its serial port. Each number consists of two digits encoded as ASCII characters. In order to distinguish between successive two-digit numbers, a delimiter character H is used. Thus, if two successive numbers are 43 and 28, the received sequence will be H43H28. Each number is to be displayed on two 7-segment displays connected to parallel ports A and B. The delimiter character should not be displayed. The displayed number should change only when both digits of the next number have been received. Show the connections needed to accomplish this function. Label the segments of the display unit as indicated in Figure 3.17. Write a program to perform the required task. Use the serial interface in Figure 10.8. Use polling to detect the arrival of each ASCII character.

10.6   **[D]** Solve Problem 10.5 by using interrupts to detect the arrival of each ASCII character.

10.7   **[D]** The microcontroller in Section 10.3 is used to receive decimal numbers on its serial port. Each number consists of four digits encoded as ASCII characters. In order to distinguish between successive four-digit numbers, a delimiter character H is used. Thus, if two successive numbers are 2143 and 6292, the received sequence will be H2143H6292. Each number is to be displayed on four 7-segment display units. Assume that each display unit has a BCD-to-7-segment decoder circuit associated with it, as shown in Figure P10.1. Show the necessary connections to the microcontroller. Write a program to perform the required task. Use the serial interface in Figure 10.8. Use polling to detect the arrival of each ASCII character.

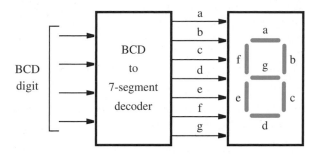

Figure P10.1   A 7-segment display with a BCD decoder.

10.8   [D] Solve Problem 10.7 by using interrupts to detect the arrival of each ASCII character.

10.9   [D] Repeat Problem 10.7, but assume that each 7-segment display unit has a 7-bit register associated with it, rather than a BCD-to-7-segment decoder. The register has a control input *Load,* such that the seven data bits are loaded into the register when $Load = 1$. Each bit in the register drives one segment of the associated display unit. Figure P10.2 shows the register-display arrangement. Arrange the microcontroller output connections such that parallel port A provides the data for all four display units.

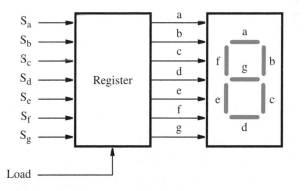

Figure P10.2   A 7-segment display with a register.

10.10 [D] Solve Problem 10.9 by using interrupts to detect the arrival of each ASCII character.

10.11 [E] Modify the reaction timer presented in Section 10.4 assuming that the tested person will always respond in less than one second. Thus, the elapsed reaction time can be displayed using only two digits representing hundredths of a second. Connect the two 7-segment display units to port A and modify the program in Figure 10.14 to implement the desired operation.

10.12 [M] In Figure 10.13, the 7-segment display unit for each digit incorporates a BCD-to-7-segment decoder; hence the microcontroller provides a 4-bit BCD code for each digit to be displayed. Suppose that instead of using the decoder, each 7-segment unit has a 7-bit register with a control input *Load,* such that the seven data bits are loaded into the register when *Load* = 1. Each bit in the register drives one segment of the associated display unit. Figure P10.2 shows the register-display arrangement. Modify the program in Figure 10.14 for use with this register-display circuit.

10.13 [M] Use the microcontroller in Section 10.3 to generate a "time of day" clock. The time (in hours and minutes) is to be displayed on four 7-segment display units. Assume that each display unit has a BCD-to-7-segment decoder associated with it, as shown in Figure P10.1. Assume also that a 100-MHz clock is used. Show the required hardware connections and write a suitable program.

10.14 [M] Repeat Problem 10.13 assuming that each 7-segment display unit has a register associated with it, as shown in Figure P10.2.

10.15 [E] In a system implemented on a single chip, the processor and the main memory reside on the same chip. Is there a need for a cache in this system? Explain.

REFERENCES

1. *Test Access Port and Boundary-Scan Architecture,* IEEE Standard 1149.1, May 1990.

chapter

11

SYSTEM-ON-A-CHIP—A CASE STUDY

CHAPTER OBJECTIVES

In this chapter you will learn about:

- Designing a system for implementation on an FPGA chip
- Using CAD tools
- Using parameterized modules
- Typical design considerations

In Chapter 10 we discussed the use of microcontrollers in embedded systems. In an embedded application, it is desirable to use as few chips as possible. Ideally, a single chip would realize the entire system. The term *System-on-a-Chip* (SOC) has been used to describe this technology. In simple applications, some commercially available microcontrollers can realize all of the necessary functions. This is unlikely to be the case in more complex applications.

Designing a microcontroller for a complex embedded application and implementing it in the form of a custom chip is both challenging and expensive. It is also time consuming. Yet, the development time for most consumer products has to be short. A chip that implements an entire system for a given application can be developed in a much shorter time if the designer has access to predesigned circuit modules that are available in a form that is easy to use. A processor circuit is one of the needed modules. Such circuits are called *processor cores* in technical literature. A variety of processor cores can be obtained, through a licensing agreement, from a number of companies. Other modules can be obtained to implement memory, input/output interfaces, A/D and D/A conversion circuits, or DSP (digital signal processing) circuits. The system developer then completes the design by using the available modules and designing the rest of the required circuitry that is specific to the application.

Providers of processor cores and other modules sell designs rather than chips. They provide *intellectual property* (IP) that can be used by others to design their own chips. To facilitate IP-based product development, a variety of computer-aided design (CAD) tools are available.

The cost of implementing a custom-designed chip is a major factor. Fabrication of such chips is expensive and, while they offer better performance and lower power consumption, their cost can be justified only if a large number of application-specific chips are needed. An alternative possibility is to use Field Programmable Gate Array (FPGA) technology.

11.1 FPGA IMPLEMENTATION

FPGAs provide an attractive platform for implementing systems on single chips. Unlike commercially available microcontroller chips, which provide a designer with a set of predefined functional units, FPGA devices allow complete freedom in the design process. They make it possible to include suitable IP modules and then build the rest of the system as desired. This can be accomplished with relative ease. Once the design is completed and tested, it can be implemented in an FPGA device immediately.

The capability of FPGAs has increased dramatically. A single FPGA chip can implement a system that comprises hundreds of thousands of logic gates. Such chips are large enough to implement the typical functionality of a microcontroller and other circuitry needed for a complex embedded application.

In this chapter we will examine the issues involved in using FPGAs in the embedded environment. To make the discussion as practical as possible, we will consider the technology provided by Altera Corporation, which is one of the major vendors of FPGA devices and supporting CAD software.

11.1.1   FPGA Devices

The basic structure of FPGAs is explained in Appendix A. FPGA devices contain a large number of logic elements and versatile wiring resources that can be used to interconnect them. They usually also contain a considerable amount of memory that can be used to implement the RAM and ROM portions of an embedded system if memory size requirements are not too large. Many FPGAs also include multiplier circuits, which are particularly useful in DSP applications.

An FPGA device has to be programmed to implement a particular design. The logic elements include programmable switches that have to be set to realize the desired logic functions. Typically, a logic element can be programmed to realize logic functions of four to six variables. The logic element also includes a flip-flop to make it possible to implement registers and finite-state machines. The interconnection wiring also contains programmable switches, which are used to interconnect the logic elements to implement a desired circuit. The programming process of setting the switches is referred to as *configuring* the FPGA device.

In most FPGA devices, the state of each programmable switch is set in an SRAM cell of the type discussed in Section 8.2.2. Since SRAM cells maintain their state only as long as the power supply to the FPGA is on, such FPGAs are volatile. If power is turned off, the device has to be reconfigured when power is turned on again. To configure the FPGA, the configuration information has to be loaded into the device. This is typically done by using another chip, called the *configuration device*, which keeps the required information in a memory of Flash type. Whenever the power is turned on, the configuration device automatically programs the FPGA.

Usually, the Flash memory in the configuration device is large enough to hold not only the configuration data for the circuits that have to be implemented in the FPGA, but also some additional information that may comprise data or code. If a processor core is implemented in the FPGA, then it is possible to store in the configuration device some code that the processor will execute.

11.1.2   Processor Choice

The key component of any system on a chip is the processor core. There exist two distinct alternatives for FPGA-based systems. One involves a processor that is defined in software and implemented in an FPGA in the same way as any other circuit. The other involves a specialized FPGA chip that has a processor core implemented on the chip at the time of manufacture.

Soft Processor Core

The most flexible solution is to provide a software module written in a hardware description language, such as Verilog or VHDL, which specifies a parameterized processor. The designer of an embedded system can set the parameters to obtain a processor with suitable features for the intended application. For example, one parameter pertains to the cache configuration, where the choices may be:

- No caches
- Instruction cache, but no data cache
- Both instruction and data caches

Another parameter may relate to the inclusion of multiplier and divider circuits in the processor. Multiplication and division operations can be implemented in hardware, but they can also be realized in software. Implementing them in hardware uses more of the FPGA resources, but improves performance considerably.

Hard Processor Core

An alternative to the soft processor core approach is to implement the processor directly as a hardware module on the chip, thus creating a specialized FPGA. This leads to a higher-performance system. The cost of such FPGAs is higher than the cost of regular FPGA devices.

11.2 COMPUTER-AIDED DESIGN TOOLS

Manufacturers of FPGA devices provide powerful CAD tools that make the task of designing embedded systems relatively easy. A variety of predefined modules are provided in a parameterized form. The designer creates a system by including these modules and specifying the parameters to suit the application requirements. Examples of such modules are:

- Processor cores
- Memory modules and interfaces
- Parallel I/O interfaces
- Serial I/O interfaces
- Timer/counter circuits

These modules may be sufficient to realize all functions needed in a desired embedded system. If they are not, then additional specialized circuits have to be designed and included in the system.

Typically, a subsystem that comprises a processor core and other parameterized modules is specified first. A CAD tool is used to generate a module that implements the subsystem. This module is defined in a hardware description language. It is then instantiated in the overall design, along with any additional application-specific circuits that have been created. Finally, a different CAD tool is used to synthesize and implement the overall design in a form that can be used to configure the FPGA device.

In addition to the FPGA device, it is necessary to include the external components needed to complete the system, such as switches, displays, and additional memory chips. Such components must be connected to the appropriate pins on the FPGA. We will discuss these issues in the context of a design example in Section 11.3.

To give the reader a specific example of CAD tools and modules for FPGA devices, we will briefly consider the tools provided by the Altera Corporation. All information about its technology and tools is available on Altera's web site [1].

11.2.1 ALTERA CAD TOOLS

The main CAD tools from Altera are known as Quartus II software. They include a full range of tools needed to design and implement a digital system in an FPGA device. One of these tools is called the SOPC Builder, which can be used to design systems that include a processor core. This tool includes a number of parameterized modules that can be used in the designed system. To illustrate their nature, we will consider four of these modules.

Nios II Processor

The Nios II processor is described in Appendix B. For implementation in FPGAs, it is provided in three versions: economy, standard, and fast. The economy version is the simplest and least expensive to implement (in terms of FPGA resources). It also has the lowest performance. It does not include any caches, it is not pipelined, and it does not use branch prediction. Better performance is achieved with the standard version, which includes an instruction cache, is pipelined, and uses static branch prediction. The best performance is achieved with the fast version, which includes both instruction and data caches, and uses dynamic branch prediction.

There are several parameters that a designer can specify, including the sizes of the instruction and data caches. Nios II processor cores are small enough to occupy only a small portion of an FPGA device. It is possible to implement as many as ten Nios II cores on a relatively small FPGA.

Memory

Memory blocks in an FPGA device can be used to implement caches and a portion of the main memory. The portion of the main memory that is realized in this way is referred to as the *on-chip memory*. This memory can be configured in various ways. It can be implemented as either RAM or ROM type of memory. Its size and wordlength can be specified at design time.

If the on-chip memory is not large enough to hold the software needed in an embedded application, then it is necessary to provide additional memory by using external memory chips. The SOPC Builder makes it easy to generate the controllers and interfaces needed to connect a system implemented in the FPGA to a variety of external memory components, such as SRAMs, SDRAMs, and Flash devices.

Parallel I/O Interface

A parallel interface, called PIO, is a parameterized module that can be used for both input and output purposes. Its data port can be selected at design time to serve as:

- an input port
- an output port
- a bidirectional port

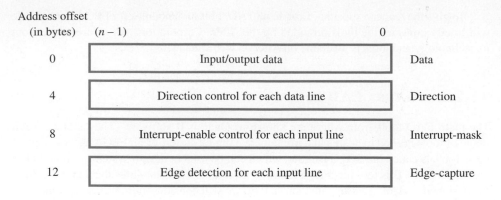

Figure 11.1   Registers in the PIO interface.

If the bidirectional option is chosen, then the PIO data lines must be connected to FPGA pins that have tristate capability.

The processor accesses a PIO as a memory-mapped interface, and communicates with it in the manner described in Chapter 3. The PIO registers are shown in Figure 11.1. The register size n is a parameter that is specified at design time, and can be in the range from 1 to 32. The registers are used as follows:

- The *Data* register holds the n bits of data that are transferred between the processor and the PIO interface.

- The *Direction* register determines the direction of transfer (input or output) for each of the n data lines when a bidirectional port is implemented.

- The *Interrupt-mask* register is used to enable interrupts from the input lines connected to the PIO. Individual interrupt requests can be raised on each of the n possible input lines.

- The *Edge-capture* register indicates changes in logic values detected in the signals on the input lines connected to the PIO. The type of edge (rising or falling) that is detected is specified at design time.

The lines that connect the PIO to an I/O device can be configured individually. If the PIO serves only as an input port, then all n lines are configured at design time as inputs. Similarly, for an output port, all lines are configured as outputs. In these cases, the Direction register is not needed, and it is not implemented in the generated circuit. For a bidirectional port the Direction register is included; when the value of its bit k is equal to 1 (0), line k of the port functions as an output (input) to (from) the connected I/O device.

When the PIO is used as an input port, its Data register contains the logic values that currently exist on the input lines. Changes in logic values on the input lines can be detected by using the Edge-capture register. At design time, it is possible to specify that the bits in this register be set to 1 when an edge on the input signal occurs. The edge can be specified as: rising, falling, or either edge. Bits in the Edge-capture register are cleared by a program instruction that writes a zero into the register.

The Interrupt-mask register allows enabling and disabling of interrupts. Writing a 1 into bit position k of the register enables interrupts caused by the activity on input line k. The interrupts can be:

- Level sensitive, in which case an interrupt request is raised when the signal on any enabled input line has the value 1

- Edge sensitive, in which case an interrupt request is raised when any enabled bit in the Edge-capture register is equal to 1

Note that the addresses of PIO registers in Figure 11.1 are offset by four, regardless of the length n. Thus, the register addresses are word-aligned.

Interval Timer

The timer module provides a capability similar to that of the timer described in Section 3.4. Its key component is a counter whose contents are decremented by one in each clock cycle. The counter can be specified to be either 32 or 64 bits long. In our discussion, we will assume that the counter has 32 bits. The Interval Timer interface has the registers depicted in Figure 11.2. Each register is 16 bits long. In the status register, only two bits are used:

- RUN is equal to 1 when the counter is running; otherwise, it is equal to 0. This bit is not affected if the processor writes to the status register.

- TO is the timeout bit. It is set to 1 when the counter reaches 0. It remains set at 1 until the processor clears it by writing a 0 into it.

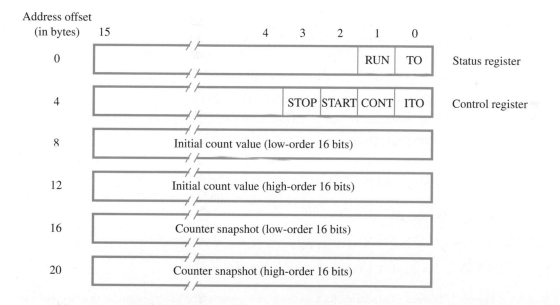

Figure 11.2   Registers in the Interval Timer interface.

In the control register, four bits are used:

- STOP is set to 1 to stop the counter.

- START is set to 1 to cause the counter to start running.

- CONT determines the behavior of the counter when it reaches 0. If CONT = 0, the counter stops running when it reaches 0. If CONT = 1, the counter reloads the initial count value and continues to run.

- ITO enables interrupts when set to 1.

The initial count value has to be loaded in two 16-bit write operations. The counter snapshot registers are used to take a snapshot of the contents of the counter while it is running. A write operation to either snapshot register causes a snapshot to be taken, which means that the current contents of the counter are loaded into the snapshot registers. Then, these registers can be read in the usual manner.

In addition to the capability of using the initial count value to define a timeout period, a default timeout period can be specified at design time. The default period time is used if the initial count value is zero.

An interrupt request is raised when TO = 1 and ITO is set to 1. To clear this request, the processor must write a 0 into TO.

In the next section, we will use the modules presented above in a complete design example.

11.3 ALARM CLOCK EXAMPLE

In this section we present a detailed example of an embedded system. We show how an alarm clock can be implemented using FPGA technology. The alarm clock, shown in Figure 11.3, has the following specifications:

- There are four 7-segment displays that indicate the time in hours and minutes.

- An on/off slider switch is used to activate the alarm feature.

- Two slider switches are used to enable setting of the actual time and the alarm time.

- Two pushbutton switches are used to set hours and minutes.

- An LED indicates that the alarm is set.

- Two LEDs, arranged vertically, create a colon that separates hours and minutes.

- A buzzing sound is produced when the alarm slider switch is activated and the alarm time is reached.

11.3.1 USER'S VIEW OF THE SYSTEM

Figure 11.3 shows the alarm clock as seen by the user. The seven-segment displays, of the type depicted in Figure 3.17, indicate the time. Time is displayed in the range 00:00 to 23:59. The operation of the clock is as follows:

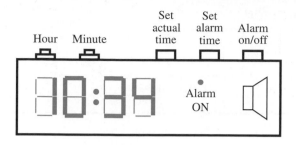

Figure 11.3   User's view of the alarm clock.

- When power is turned on, both the time-of-day and the alarm time are cleared to zero.

- The time-of-day is set by activating the *set-actual-time* slider switch and then setting the time by pressing the *Hour* and *Minute* pushbuttons. Each time a pushbutton is pressed, the displayed time is incremented by one.

- Alarm time is set in the same manner when the *set-alarm-time* switch is activated.

- The alarm is turned on by activating the *alarm-on/off* switch. This causes the corresponding LED to be turned on.

- The speaker emits a buzzing sound when the alarm time is reached with the alarm switch activated.

11.3.2   SYSTEM DEFINITION AND GENERATION

Our goal is to implement the alarm clock using an FPGA chip and the external components that comprise: slider switches, pushbutton switches, 7-segment displays, LEDs, and a speaker. Figure 11.4 depicts the desired system. The processor is Nios II. The on-chip memory is large enough to satisfy the needs of our application, even in very small FPGA chips. The external components are connected through PIO interfaces. There are two timers. One is designed to provide intervals of one minute, to be used in updating the time of day. The other is used to generate a square wave that produces a buzzing sound. The timers are implemented by using the Interval Timer module described in Section 11.2.1. We will assume that the slider switches generate a logic signal 1 when activated. The pushbutton switches are debounced, and they generate a logic signal 0 when pressed.

The system is implemented in the FPGA device by using the Quartus II software. The SOPC Builder is used to realize the blocks in the shaded area of Figure 11.4. The PIO blocks are configured as follows:

- PIO1 is a three-bit wide input port. Its data inputs are level sensitive.

- PIO2 is a two-bit wide input port. Its inputs are falling-edge sensitive, so that a bit in the Edge-capture register is set to 1 when the corresponding pushbutton is pressed.

- PIO3 is a 32-bit wide output port. Each byte will be connected to one 7-segment display, such that bits 0 to 6 of a byte drive one segment each, while bit 7 is not used.

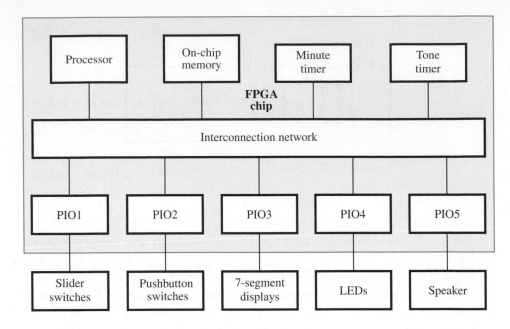

Figure 11.4   Block diagram of the alarm clock.

The low-order byte will be connected to the display for the low-order digit of minutes, and the high-order byte to the high-order digit of hours.

- PIO4 is a three-bit wide output port.
- PIO5 is a one-bit wide output port.

Using the SOPC Builder, this system is specified as depicted in Figure 11.5. Note that we gave the PIOs names that are indicative of their functions. The SOPC Builder assigns addresses to the various components in the system. The on-chip memory occupies the range 0 to 0x3FFF, while the timer and PIO interfaces have addresses starting at 0x5000. The designer can specify different addresses if so desired. Note also that the timers and the pushbutton switches can raise interrupt requests (IRQ). The last column in the figure indicates the bit positions in the Nios II control registers ctl3 and ctl4 that are associated with interrupts from these sources. The SOPC Builder generates the specified system by producing a module that describes the system in either Verilog or VHDL hardware description languages.

11.3.3 CIRCUIT IMPLEMENTATION

Quartus II software includes a compiler that accepts a specification of a digital system in a hardware description language. The compiler synthesizes a circuit that implements the system, and it determines how this circuit is to be implemented on the FPGA chip.

Conn...	Module Name	Description	Clock	Base	End	T...	IRQ
	⊟ **cpu**	Nios II Processor					
	instruction_master	Avalon Memory Mapped Master	clk				
	data_master	Avalon Memory Mapped Master		IRQ 0	IRQ 31		
	jtag_debug_module	Avalon Memory Mapped Slave		0x00004800	0x00004fff		
	⊟ **onchip_memory**	On-Chip Memory (RAM or ROM)					
	s1	Avalon Memory Mapped Slave	clk	0x00000000	0x00003fff		
	⊟ **minute_timer**	Interval Timer					
	s1	Avalon Memory Mapped Slave	clk	0x00005000	0x0000501f		0
	⊟ **tone_timer**	Interval Timer					
	s1	Avalon Memory Mapped Slave	clk	0x00005020	0x0000503f		2
	⊟ **sliders**	PIO (Parallel I/O)					
	s1	Avalon Memory Mapped Slave	clk	0x00005040	0x0000504f		
	⊟ **pushbuttons**	PIO (Parallel I/O)					
	s1	Avalon Memory Mapped Slave	clk	0x00005050	0x0000505f		1
	⊟ **display**	PIO (Parallel I/O)					
	s1	Avalon Memory Mapped Slave	clk	0x00005060	0x0000506f		
	⊟ **LEDs**	PIO (Parallel I/O)					
	s1	Avalon Memory Mapped Slave	clk	0x00005070	0x0000507f		
	⊟ **speaker**	PIO (Parallel I/O)					
	s1	Avalon Memory Mapped Slave	clk	0x00005080	0x0000508f		

Figure 11.5   System on the FPGA chip designed using the SOPC Builder.

Since external devices have to be connected to the FPGA pins, the designer must specify the desired connections. This is referred to as *pin assignment*. The compiler generates the final implementation in the form of a configuration file which is used to download the configuration information into the FPGA device.

Figure 11.4 does not show all components needed to implement the complete alarm clock. Missing are the power supply, the clock signal generator, and the configuration device needed to program the FPGA. We will assume that a 100-MHz external clock signal is provided. The FPGA pins typically cannot be connected directly to external devices such as switches, seven-segment displays, and LEDs. Each device has its own electrical characteristics, which usually means that components such as resistors have to be used, as in Figure 10.13.

In our design, the pushbuttons for setting hours and minutes are connnected to the corresponding PIO bits b_1 and b_0, respectively. The slider switches *set-actual-time*, *set-alarm-time*, and *alarm-on/off* are connected to the corresponding PIO bits b_2, b_1, and b_0, respectively. The minute-timer has a timeout period of 60 seconds. The tone-timer has a timeout period of 1 ms.

11.3.4   APPLICATION SOFTWARE

It is necessary to write a program that will run on the designed hardware to realize the alarm clock functions. We will write two programs, one in the C language and another in the Nios II assembly language, to illustrate how such programs may be written. The developed program has to be compiled into Nios II machine code. On power-up, this code would be loaded into the on-chip memory from the configuration device.

We use the following approach in writing the programs. The actual time and the alarm time are kept as 32-bit binary integers that represent the time in minutes. The actual time is incremented by one whenever the minute-timer reaches zero, which is indicated by the TO bit in its Status register being set to 1. When the actual time is incremented, it is necessary to check if it has reached 1440, which is the number of minutes in a day. In that case, the time must be cleared to zero to correspond to the transition from 23:59 to 00:00. A similar check is needed when setting the time by pressing the pushbuttons.

To display the time, the four decimal digits representing hours and minutes are computed by dividing the time by 600 to get the high-order hours digit, then dividing the remainder by 60 to get the low-order hours digit, and so on. A table is used to look up the corresponding segment patterns that are sent to the 7-segment displays.

We use the tone timer to create a square-wave signal of 500 Hz, which produces a buzzing sound when connected to a speaker. The tone timer is run in the continuous mode. Since it has a predefined timeout period of 1 ms, we could directly generate the 500-Hz signal by inverting the logic value of the signal at the end of each period of the timer. However, to illustrate how a different period may be defined in an application program, we will use the initial-count register to specify the desired period. In this case, the value of 0x30D40 is needed for the 500-Hz signal if the counter is driven by a 100-MHz clock.

When polling for the timeout of a timer, it is necessary to check the TO bit in its status register. Since the RUN bit is always equal to 1 when the counter is running, the polling task can be performed by checking if the contents of the status register are equal to 3. The TO bit can be cleared to 0 simply by writing a zero into the status register, because the state of the RUN bit is not affected by a write operation.

C Program

Figure 11.6 shows a possible C-language program. Our application is not demanding from a performance point of view, so we use the polling method to access all PIOs and timers. The comments in the program explain the meaning of various statements. Observe that the macro ADJUST defines an expression that increments the time properly in different situations.

Assembly-Language Program

Figure 11.7 presents a Nios II program. To illustrate the use of interrupts, the program uses interrupts to deal with the minute timer. Polling is used for the tone timer.

At design time, the SOPC Builder assigned 0x20 to be the address at which the interrupt handler starts when an interrupt request is accepted by the processor. The interrupt handler verifies that an interrupt caused by a device external to the Nios II processor has occurred, and adjusts the return address accordingly. (See Appendix B for a detailed explanation of the Nios II interrupt mechanism.) It then clears the TO bit in the minute timer and calls the interrupt-service routine. Note that the interrupt handler saves, and later restores, the contents of registers r2 and ra. It saves the contents of ra, which is the link register that holds the return address when a subroutine is called, because a timer interrupt may occur when some subroutine in the program is being executed. The interrupt handler also uses the

```
#define    minute_timer (volatile int *) 0x5000
#define    tone_timer (volatile int *) 0x5020
#define    sliders (volatile int *) 0x5040
#define    pushbuttons (volatile int *) 0x5050
#define    display (int *) 0x5060
#define    LEDs (int *) 0x5070
#define    speaker (int *) 0x5080
#define    ADJUST(t, x) ((t + x) > = 1440) ? (t + x − 1440) : (t + x)
int        actual_time, alarm_time, alarm_active, time;

/* Hex to 7-segment conversion table */
unsigned char table[16] = {0x40, 0x79, 0x24, 0x30, 0x19, 0x12, 0x02, 0x78,
    0x00, 0x18, 0x3F, 0x3F, 0x3F, 0x3F, 0x3F, 0x3F};

void initializeToneTimer()
{
    *(tone_timer + 2) = 0x0D40;    /* Set the timeout period     */
    *(tone_timer + 3) = 0x03;      /*   for continuous operation. */
    *(tone_timer + 1) = 0x6;       /* Start in continuous mode. */
}
void DISP(time)                    /* Get 7-segment patterns for display. */
{
    *display = table[time / 600] << 24 |
        table[(time % 600) / 60] << 16 |
        table[(time % 60) / 10] << 8 |
        table[(time % 10)];
}

main()
{
    actual_time = alarm_time = alarm_active = 0;
    initializeToneTimer();
    *(minute_timer + 1) = 0x6;     /* Run in continuous mode. */
    while (1)
    {
       if (*minute_timer == 3)     /* One minute elapsed. */
       {
           *minute_timer = 0;      /* Clear the TO bit. */
           actual_time = ADJUST(actual_time, 1);
       }

...continued in Part b
```

Figure 11.6   C program for the alarm clock (Part *a*).

```
        if ((*sliders & 1) != 0)              /* Check the alarm-on switch. */
        {
                *LEDs = 7;                     /* Turn on the alarm LED. */
                if (actual_time == alarm_time)
                    alarm_active = 1;          /* Start the alarm sound. */
                else
                    alarm_active = alarm_active & (*sliders & 1);
                if (*tone_timer == 3)          /* Generate the square wave. */
                {
                    *speaker = (*speaker ^ 1) & alarm_active;
                    *tone_timer = 0;           /* Clear the TO bit. */
                }
        }
        else
        {
                *LEDs = 6;                     /* Turn off the alarm LED. */
                alarm_active = 0;
        }
        if ((*sliders & 4) != 0)               /* Check the set-the-time-of-day switch. */
        {
                DISP(actual_time);             /* Display the time of day. */
                if ((*(pushbuttons + 3) & 1) != 0)    /* Set the minutes? */
                    actual_time = ADJUST(actual_time, 1);
                else if ((*(pushbuttons + 3) & 2) != 0)    /* Set the hours? */
                    actual_time = ADJUST(actual_time, 60);
                *(pushbuttons + 3) = 0;        /* Clear the edge-capture register. */
        }
        else if ((*sliders & 2) != 0)          /* Check the set-the-alarm-time switch. */
        {
                DISP(alarm_time);              /* Display the alarm time. */
                if ((*(pushbuttons + 3) & 1) != 0)    /* Set the minutes? */
                    alarm_time = ADJUST(alarm_time, 1);
                else if ((*(pushbuttons + 3) & 2) != 0)    /* Set the hours? */
                    alarm_time = ADJUST(alarm_time, 60);
                *(pushbuttons + 3) = 0;        /* Clear the edge-capture register. */
        }
        else
                DISP(actual_time);             /* Display the time of day. */
    }
}
```

Figure 11.6   C program for the alarm clock (Part *b*).

```
        .equ    minute_timer, 0x05000
        .equ    tone_timer, 0x5020
        .equ    sliders, 0x5040
        .equ    pushbuttons, 0x5050
        .equ    display, 0x5060
        .equ    LEDs, 0x5070
        .equ    speaker, 0x5080
        .equ    ACTUAL_TIME, 0x1000
        .equ    ALARM_TIME, 0x1010
        .equ    STACK, 0x2000
_start: br      MAIN

/*      Interrupt handler                                               */
        .org    0x20
        subi    sp, sp, 8       /* Save registers.                      */
        stw     r2, 0(sp)
        stw     ra, 4(sp)
        rdctl   et, ipending
        beq     et, r0, MAIN    /* Error if not an external             */
                                /*   interrupt, treat as reset.         */
        subi    ea, ea, 4       /* Decrement ea to execute the          */
                                /*   interrupted instruction upon       */
                                /*   return to the main program.        */
        movia   r2, minute_timer /* Clear the TO bit in the             */
        sthio   r0, (r2)        /*   minute-timer.                      */
        call    UPDATE_TIME     /* Call interrupt-service routine.      */
        ldw     r2, 0(sp)       /* Restore registers.                   */
        ldw     ra, 4(sp)
        addi    sp, sp, 8
        eret

/*      Main program                                                    */
MAIN:   movia   sp, STACK       /* Set up the stack pointer.            */
        movia   r2, ALARM_TIME  /* Clear the alarm-time buffer.         */
        stw     r0, (r2)
        movia   r2, ACTUAL_TIME /* Clear the actual-time buffer.        */
        stw     r0, (r2)
        movia   r2, sliders     /* Address of slider switches.          */
        movia   r3, LEDs        /* Address of LEDs.                     */
        movia   r4, display     /* Address of 7-segment displays.       */
        movia   r5, pushbuttons /* Address of pushbuttons.              */
```

...continued in Part *b*

Figure 11.7   Nios II program for the alarm clock (Part *a*).

```
           movi    r6, 6                 /* Turn on the two                    */
           stbio   r6, (r3)              /*   vertical LEDs.                    */
           movia   r6, tone_timer
           ori     r7, r0, 0x0D40        /* Set the tone-timer period.          */
           sthio   r7, 8(r6)
           ori     r7, r0, 0x03
           sthio   r7, 12(r6)
           movi    r7, 6                 /* Start the tone-timer.               */
           sthio   r7, 4(r6)
           movia   r6, minute_timer      /* Address of minute-timer.            */
           addi    r7, r0, 7             /* Start the timer.                    */
           sthio   r7, 4(r6)
           movi    r7, 1
           wrctl   ienable, r7           /* Enable timer interrupts.            */
           wrctl   status, r7            /* Enable external interrupts.         */
LOOP:      movia   r10, ACTUAL_TIME      /* Display the time of day.            */
           call    DISP
           ldbio   r7, (r2)
           andi    r11, r7, 1            /* Check if alarm switch is on.        */
           beq     r11, r0, NEXT
           movi    r11, 7                /* If yes, then turn on the            */
           stbio   r11, (r3)             /*   alarm LED.                        */
           movia   r9, ALARM_TIME
           ldw     r11, (r9)             /* Have to compare alarm-time          */
           ldw     r12, (r10)            /*   with actual-time.                 */
           bne     r11, r12, NEXT        /* Should the alarm ring?              */
           movia   r8, tone_timer
           movi    r12, 1
RING_LOOP:
           call    DISP
           ldbio   r7, (r2)
           andi    r13, r7, 1            /* Check if alarm switch is on.        */
           beq     r13, r0, NEXT
           ldhio   r9, (r8)              /* Read the tone-timer status.         */
           sthio   r0, (r8)              /* Clear the TO bit.                   */
           andi    r9, r9, 1             /* Check if counter reached 0.         */
           xor     r12, r9, r12          /* Generate the next square            */
           movia   r11, speaker          /*   wave half-cycle; send             */
           stbio   r12, (r11)            /*   signal to the speaker.            */
           br      RING_LOOP
```

...continued in Part *c*

Figure 11.7   Nios II program for the alarm clock (Part *b*).

```
NEXT:    movi    r11, 6                /* Turn off the alarm-on         */
         stbio   r11, (r3)             /*   LED indicator.              */
TEST_SLIDERS:
         ldbio   r7, (r2)
         andi    r11, r7, 2            /* Is set-alarm switch on?       */
         beq     r11, r0, SETACT       /* If not, test actual time.     */
         movia   r10, ALARM_TIME       /* Have to set the alarm time.   */
         br      SET_TIME
SETACT:
         andi    r11, r7, 4            /* Is set-time switch on?         */
         beq     r11, r0, LOOP         /* All sliders are off.           */
         movia   r10, ACTUAL_TIME
SET_TIME:
         call    DISP
         call    SETSUB
         br      TEST_SLIDERS

/*       Display the time on 7-segment displays.                         */
DISP:    subi    sp, sp, 24            /* Save registers.               */
         stw     r11, 0(sp)
         stw     r12, 4(sp)
         stw     r13, 8(sp)
         stw     r14, 12(sp)
         stw     r15, 16(sp)
         stw     r16, 20(sp)
         ldw     r11, (r10)            /* Load the time to be displayed. */
         movi    r12, 600              /* To determine the first digit of */
         divu    r13, r11, r12         /*   hours, divide by 600.       */
         ldb     r15, TABLE(r13)       /* Get the 7-segment pattern.    */
         slli    r15, r15, 8           /* Make space for next digit.    */
         mul     r14, r13, r12         /* Compute the remainder of the  */
         sub     r11, r11, r14         /*   division operation.         */
         movi    r12, 60               /* Divide the remainder by 60 to */
         divu    r13, r11, r12         /*   get the second digit of hours. */
         ldb     r16, TABLE(r13)       /* Get the 7-segment pattern,    */
         or      r15, r15, r16         /*   concatenate it to the first */
         slli    r15, r15, 8           /*   digit, and shift.           */
         mul     r14, r13, r12         /* Determine the minutes that have */
         sub     r11, r11, r14         /*   to be displayed.            */
```

...continued in Part *d*

Figure 11.7   Nios II program for the alarm clock (Part c).

```
        movi    r12, 10              /* To determine the first digit of    */
        divu    r13, r11, r12        /*   minutes, divide by 10.           */
        ldb     r16, TABLE(r13)      /* Get the 7-segment pattern,         */
        or      r15, r15, r16        /*   concatenate it to the first      */
        slli    r15, r15, 8          /*   two digits, and shift.           */
        mul     r14, r13, r12        /* Compute the remainder, which       */
        sub     r11, r11, r14        /*   is the last digit.               */
        ldb     r16, TABLE(r11)      /* Concatenate the last digit to      */
        or      r15, r15, r16        /*   the preceding 3 digits.          */
        movia   r11, display
        stw     r15, (r11)           /* Display the obtained pattern.      */
        ldw     r11, 0(sp)           /* Restore registers.                 */
        ldw     r12, 4(sp)
        ldw     r13, 8(sp)
        ldw     r14, 12(sp)
        ldw     r15, 16(sp)
        ldw     r16, 20(sp)
        addi    sp, sp, 24
        ret


/*      Set the desired time.        */
SETSUB:
        subi    sp, sp, 16           /* Save registers.                    */
        stw     r11, 0(sp)
        stw     r12, 4(sp)
        stw     r13, 8(sp)
        stw     r14, 12(sp)
        ldbio   r12, 12(r5)          /* Test pushbuttons.                  */
        stbio   r0, 12(r5)           /* Clear edge-detection register.     */
        andi    r13, r12, 1          /* Is minute pushbutton pressed?      */
        beq     r13, r0, HOURS       /* If not, check hours.               */
        ldw     r11, (r10)           /* Load present time.                 */
        movi    r12, 60              /* Divide by 60 to determine          */
        divu    r13, r11, r12        /*   the number of hours.             */
        mul     r14, r13, r12        /* Remainder of division operation    */
        sub     r11, r11, r14        /*   is the number of minutes.        */
        addi    r11, r11, 1          /* Increment minutes.                 */
        blt     r11, r12, SAVEM      /* Save if less than 60,              */
        mov     r11, r0              /*   otherwise set minutes to 00.     */
```

. . . continued in Part *e*

Figure 11.7   Nios II program for the alarm clock (Part *d*).

```
SAVEM:    add      r11, r14, r11        /* (hours x 60) + (updated minutes).   */
          stw      r11, (r10)           /* Save the new time.                  */
          br       DONE
HOURS:    andi     r13, r12, 2          /* Is hour pushbutton pressed?         */
          beq      r13, r0, DONE        /* If not, then return.                */
          ldw      r11, (r10)           /* Load present time in minutes.       */
          addi     r12, r11, 60         /* Add 60 minutes.                     */
          movi     r13, 1440            /* Have to check if updated time       */
          blt      r12, r13, SAVEH      /*   is less than 24:00.               */
          sub      r12, r12, r13        /* Roll over hours to 00.              */
SAVEH:    stw      r12, (r10)           /* Save the new time.                  */
DONE:
          ldw      r11, 0(sp)           /* Restore registers.                  */
          ldw      r12, 4(sp)
          ldw      r13, 8(sp)
          ldw      r14, 12(sp)
          addi     sp, sp, 16
          ret


/*        Interrupt-service routine that updates actual-time                   */
UPDATE_TIME:
          subi     sp, sp, 12           /* Save registers.                     */
          stw      r2, 0(sp)
          stw      r3, 4(sp)
          stw      r4, 8(sp)
          movia    r2, ACTUAL_TIME
          ldw      r3, (r2)             /* Load present time of day.           */
          addi     r3, r3, 1            /* Increment by one minute.            */
          movi     r4, 1440             /* Done if updated time is             */
          blt      r3, r4, SAVET        /*   less than 24:00.                  */
          mov      r3, r0               /* Otherwise, set to 00:00.            */
SAVET:    stw      r3, (r2)             /* Save updated time.                  */
          ldw      r2, 0(sp)            /* Restore registers.                  */
          ldw      r3, 4(sp)
          ldw      r4, 8(sp)
          addi     sp, sp, 12
          ret


/*        Hex-digit to 7-segment conversion table                             */
          .org     0x1050
TABLE:    .byte    0x40, 0x79, 0x24, 0x30, 0x19, 0x12, 0x02, 0x78
          .byte    0x00, 0x18, 0x3F, 0x3F, 0x3F, 0x3F, 0x3F, 0x3F
          .end
```

Figure 11.7   Nios II program for the alarm clock (Part e).

register ra for a call to the interrupt-service routine, UPDATE_TIME, which increments the actual time and clears the stored time to zero at midnight.

The main program starts by setting up the processor stack and clearing the memory locations that store time. As part of the initialization process, it sets the timeout period for the tone timer. It then starts both timers and enables interrupts from the minute timer.

The main loop, LOOP, checks the state of the slider switches and takes the necessary action. Subroutine DISP displays either actual time or alarm time, which are maintained in memory locations 0x1000 or 0x1010, on the seven-segment displays. Subroutine SETSUB is used in setting the values of minutes and hours when the corresponding pushbuttons are pressed. Every time a pushbutton is pressed, the value is incremented by one.

The table at the end of the program is used to convert a decimal digit into the corresponding seven-bit pattern to be displayed.

Comments in the program explain the meaning of various statements. Control registers ctl3 and ctl4 can also be referred to by the names ienable and ipending, respectively. These names are used in the program.

11.4   CONCLUDING REMARKS

The designer of an embedded system inevitably looks for the simplest and most cost-effective approach. A microcontroller chip that has the resources to implement an entire system may be the best choice. The situation is different if additional chips are needed to realize the system. Then, FPGA solutions are very attractive because they are likely to need fewer chips to implement the system.

Another consideration is the availability of predesigned modules. A microcontroller chip contains a number of different modules. Any feature that cannot be realized using these modules has to be implemented using additional chips. An FPGA device allows the designer to design any type of digital circuit. Very large and complex circuits can be implemented in modern FPGA devices.

Practical designs often involve circuits that perform commonly used tasks. Such circuits are usually available as library modules, as illustrated by the I/O interfaces and timer circuits used in the previous section. For signal-processing applications, the library includes typical filter circuits. If a system is to be connected to another computer using a standard interconnection scheme, such as PCI Express, the designer's task is much simpler if a PCI Express interface is available as a predesigned module.

PROBLEMS

11.1   **[E]** In Section 11.3.4, we mentioned that the 500-Hz square-wave signal can be generated simply by inverting the logic value of the signal at the end of each timeout period of the tone timer, which is designed to occur every millisecond. Modify the program in Figure 11.6 to exploit this fact.

11.2   **[E]** Repeat Problem 11.1 for the program in Figure 11.7.

11.3   **[M]** Consider the display format for the alarm clock in Section 11.3. Instead of displaying the time from 00:00 to 23:59, we wish to display it as 12:00 to 11:59 AM or PM. Assume that a fourth LED is provided and connected to bit b_3 of a four-bit wide PIO instead of the three-bit wide PIO used in Section 11.3. This LED indicates PM when turned on. Modify the program in Figure 11.6 to display the time in this manner.

11.4   **[M]** Repeat Problem 11.3 for the program in Figure 11.7.

11.5   **[E]** Suppose that only one timer, with a default timeout period of 1 ms, is used in the alarm clock in Section 11.3. Make appropriate changes in the program in Figure 11.6 to provide the required behavior.

11.6   **[E]** Repeat Problem 11.5 for the program in Figure 11.7.

11.7   **[E]** In Figure 11.7 we used interrupts to deal with the minute timer and polling for the tone timer. Modify the program to use interrupts for both timers.

11.8   **[M]** In the alarm clock in Section 11.3, the time is set by incrementing the current value each time a pushbutton is pressed. This could be tedious if a pushbutton has to be pressed many times. A better alternative would be to increment the time automatically every 0.5 second while a pushbutton is being pressed. What changes, if any, should be made in the hardware to provide this feature? Modify the program in Figure 11.6 to implement the feature.

11.9   **[M]** Repeat Problem 11.8 for the program in Figure 11.7.

11.10   **[M]** It is desired to make the two vertically-arranged LEDs in the alarm clock flash in one-second intervals when power is first turned on. They should stop flashing as soon as the user begins to set the time. Modify the program in Figure 11.6 to cause this behavior.

11.11   **[M]** Repeat Problem 11.10 for the program in Figure 11.7.

REFERENCES

1.   Altera's web site at *www.altera.com*

chapter

12

PARALLEL PROCESSING AND PERFORMANCE

CHAPTER OBJECTIVES

In this chapter you will learn about:

- Multithreading
- Vector processing in general-purpose and graphics processors
- Shared-memory multiprocessors
- Cache coherence for shared data
- Message passing in distributed-memory systems
- Parallel programming
- Mathematical modeling of performance

In Chapter 6, instruction pipelining and superscalar operation are described as processor design techniques aimed at increasing the rate of instruction execution, which therefore reduces execution time. In Chapter 8, caches are presented as a way to reduce the average latency in accessing instructions and data.

This chapter describes three additional techniques for improving performance, namely multithreading, vector processing, and multiprocessing. These techniques are implemented in the multicore processor chips that are used in general-purpose computers. They increase performance by improving the utilization of processing resources and by performing more operations in parallel.

12.1   HARDWARE MULTITHREADING

Operating system (OS) software enables multitasking of different programs in the same processor by performing context switches among programs. As explained in Section 4.9, a program, together with any information that describes its current state of execution, is regarded by the OS as an entity called a *process*. Information about the memory and other resources allocated by the OS is maintained with each process. Processes may be associated with applications such as Web-browsing, word-processing, and music-playing programs that a user has opened in a computer.

Each process has a corresponding thread, which is an independent path of execution within a program. More precisely, the term *thread* is used to refer to a thread of control whose state consists of the contents of the program counter and other processor registers. As we will discuss in Section 12.6, it is possible for multiple threads to execute portions of one program and run in parallel as if they correspond to separate programs. Two or more threads can be running on different processors, executing either the same part of a program on different data, or executing different parts of a program. Threads for different programs can also execute on different processors. All threads that are part of a single program run in the same address space and are associated with the same process.

In this section, we focus on multitasking where two or more programs run on the same processor and each program has a single thread. Section 4.9 describes the technique of time slicing, where the OS selects a process among those that are not presently blocked and allows this process to run for a short period of time. Only the thread corresponding to the selected process is active during the time slice. Context switching at the end of the time slice causes the OS to select a different process, whose corresponding thread becomes active during the next time slice. A timer interrupt invokes an interrupt-service routine in the OS to switch from one process to another.

To deal with multiple threads efficiently, a processor is implemented with several identical sets of registers, including multiple program counters. Each set of registers can be dedicated to a different thread. Thus, no time is wasted during a context switch to save and restore register contents. The processor is said to be using a technique called *hardware multithreading*.

With multiple sets of registers, context switching is simple and fast. All that is necessary is to change a hardware pointer in the processor to use a different set of registers to fetch and execute subsequent instructions. Switching to a different thread can be completed within one clock cycle. The state of the previously active thread is preserved in its own set of registers.

Switching to a different thread may be triggered at any time by the occurrence of a specific event, rather than at the end of a fixed time interval. For example, a cache miss may occur when a Load or Store instruction is being executed for the active thread. Instead of stalling while the slower main memory is accessed to service the cache miss, a processor can quickly switch to a different thread and continue to fetch and execute other instructions. This is called *coarse-grained* multithreading because many instructions may be executed for one thread before an event such as a cache miss causes a switch to another thread.

An alternative to switching between threads on specific events is to switch after every instruction is fetched. This is called *fine-grained* or *interleaved* multithreading. The intent is to increase the processor throughput. Each new instruction is independent of its predecessors from other threads. This should reduce the occurrence of stalls due to data dependencies. Thus, throughput may be increased by interleaving instructions from many threads, but it takes longer for a given thread to complete all of its instructions. A form of interleaved multithreading with only two threads is used in processors that implement the Intel IA-32 architecture described in Appendix E.

12.2   VECTOR (SIMD) PROCESSING

Many computationally demanding applications involve programs that use loops to perform operations on vectors of data, where a *vector* is an array of elements such as integers or floating-point numbers. When a processor executes the instructions in such a loop, the operations are performed one at a time on individual vector elements. As a result, many instructions need to be executed to process all vector elements.

A processor can be enhanced with multiple ALUs. In such a processor, it is possible to operate on multiple data elements in parallel using a single instruction. Such instructions are called *single-instruction multiple-data* (SIMD) instructions. They are also called *vector instructions*. These instructions can only be used when the operations performed in parallel are independent. This is known as *data parallelism*.

The data for vector instructions are held in *vector registers*, each of which can hold several data elements. The number of elements, L, in each vector register is called the *vector length*. It determines the number of operations that can be performed in parallel on multiple ALUs. If vector instructions are provided for different sizes of data elements using the same vector registers, L may vary. For example, the Intel IA-32 architecture has 128-bit vector registers that are used by instructions for vector lengths ranging from $L = 2$ up to $L = 16$, corresponding to integer data elements with sizes ranging from 64 bits down to 8 bits.

Some typical examples of vector instructions are given below to illustrate how vector registers are used. We assume that the OP-code mnemonic includes a suffix S which specifies the size of each data element. This determines the number of elements, L, in a vector. For instructions that access the memory, the contents of a conventional register are used in the calculation of the effective address.

The vector instruction

$$\text{VectorAdd.S} \quad Vi, Vj, Vk$$

computes L sums using the elements in vector registers Vj and Vk, and places the resulting sums in vector register Vi. Similar instructions are used to perform other arithmetic operations.

Special instructions are needed to transfer multiple data elements between a vector register and the memory. The instruction

$$\text{VectorLoad.S} \quad Vi, X(Rj)$$

causes L consecutive elements beginning at memory location $X + [Rj]$ to be loaded into vector register Vi. Similarly, the instruction

$$\text{VectorStore.S} \quad Vi, X(Rj)$$

causes the contents of vector register Vi to be stored as L consecutive elements in the memory.

Vectorization

In a source program written in a high-level language, loops that operate on arrays of integers or floating-point numbers are *vectorizable* if the operations performed in each pass are independent of the other passes. Using vector instructions reduces the number of instructions that need to be executed and enables the operations to be performed in parallel on multiple ALUs. A *vectorizing compiler* can recognize such loops, if they are not too complex, and generate vector instructions.

Vectorization of a loop is illustrated with the simple example of C-language code shown in Figure 12.1a. Assume that the starting locations in memory for arrays A, B, and C are in registers R2, R3, and R4. Using conventional assembly-language instructions, the compiler may generate the loop shown in Figure 12.1b. The loop body has nine instructions, hence a total of $9N$ instructions are executed for N passes through the loop.

To vectorize the loop, the compiler must recognize that the computation in each pass through the loop is independent of the other passes, and that the same operation can be performed simultaneously on multiple elements. Assume for simplicity that the number of passes, N, is evenly divisible by the vector length, L. The Load, Add, and Store instructions at the beginning of the loop are replaced by corresponding vector instructions that operate on L elements at a time. Consequently, the vectorized loop requires only N/L passes to process all of the data in the arrays. With L elements processed in each pass through the loop, the address pointers in registers R2, R3, and R4 are incremented by $4L$, and the count in register R5 is decremented by L. The vectorized loop is shown in Figure 12.1c. We assume that the assembler calculates the value of $4L$ for the expression given as the immediate operand in the Add instructions. There are still nine instructions in the loop body, but because the number of passes is now N/L, the total number of instructions that need to be executed is only $9N/L$.

Vectorizable loops exist in programs for applications such as computer graphics and digital signal processing. Such loops have many independent computations that can be performed simultaneously on several data elements. If a large portion of the execution time

for (i = 0; i < N; i++)
    A[i] = B[i] + C[i];

(a) A C-language loop to add vector elements

	Move	R5, #N	R5 is the loop counter.
LOOP:	Load	R6, (R3)	R3 points to an element in array B.
	Load	R7, (R4)	R4 points to an element in array C.
	Add	R6, R6, R7	Add a pair of elements from the arrays.
	Store	R6, (R2)	R2 points to an element in array A.
	Add	R2, R2, #4	Increment the three array pointers.
	Add	R3, R3, #4	
	Add	R4, R4, #4	
	Subtract	R5, R5, #1	Decrement the loop counter.
	Branch_if_[R5]> 0	LOOP	Repeat the loop if not finished.

(b) Assembly-language instructions for the loop

	Move	R5, #N	R5 counts the number of elements to process.
LOOP:	VectorLoad.S	V0, (R3)	Load L elements from array B.
	VectorLoad.S	V1, (R4)	Load L elements from array C.
	VectorAdd.S	V0, V0, V1	Add L pairs of elements from the arrays.
	VectorStore.S	V0, (R2)	Store L elements to array A.
	Add	R2, R2, #4*L	Increment the array pointers by L words.
	Add	R3, R3, #4*L	
	Add	R4, R4, #4*L	
	Subtract	R5, R5, #L	Decrement the loop counter by L.
	Branch_if_[R5]> 0	LOOP	Repeat the loop if not finished.

(c) Vectorized form of the loop

Figure 12.1   Example of loop vectorization.

for an application is spent executing loops of this type, then vectorization of these loops can significantly reduce the total execution time. The extent of the performance improvement is limited by the vector length L, which determines the number of ALUs that can operate in parallel. To obtain higher performance, support for vector (SIMD) processing can be implemented in another way, as the next section describes.

12.2.1   GRAPHICS PROCESSING UNITS (GPUs)

The increasing demands of processing for computer graphics has led to the development of specialized chips called *graphics processing units* (GPUs). The primary purpose of GPUs is to accelerate the large number of floating-point calculations needed in high-resolution three-dimensional graphics, such as in video games. Since the operations involved in these calculations are often independent, a large GPU chip contains hundreds of simple cores with floating-point ALUs to perform them in parallel.

A GPU chip and a dedicated memory for it are included on a video card. Such a card is plugged into an expansion slot of a host computer using an interconnection standard such as the PCIe standard discussed in Chapter 7. A small program is written for the processing cores in the GPU chip. A large number of cores execute this program in parallel. The cores execute the same instructions, but operate on different data elements. A separate controlling program runs in the general-purpose processor of the host computer and invokes the GPU program when necessary. Before initiating the GPU computation, the program in the host computer must first transfer the data needed by the GPU program from the main memory into the dedicated GPU memory. After the computation is completed, the resulting output data in the dedicated memory are transferred back to the main memory.

The processing cores in a GPU chip have a specialized instruction set and hardware architecture, which are different from those used in a general-purpose processor. An example is the *Compute Unified Device Architecture* (CUDA) that NVIDIA Corporation uses for the cores in its GPU chips. To facilitate writing programs that involve a general-purpose processor and a GPU, an extension to the C programming language, called CUDA C, has been developed by NVIDIA [1, 2]. This extension enables a single program to be written in C, with special keywords used to label the functions executed by the processing cores in a GPU chip. The compiler and related software tools automatically partition the final object program into the portions that are translated into machine instructions for the host computer and the GPU chip. Library routines are provided to allocate storage in the dedicated memory of a GPU-based video card and to transfer data between the main memory and the dedicated memory. An open standard called OpenCL has also been proposed by industry as a programming framework for systems that include GPU chips from any vendor [3].

12.3   SHARED-MEMORY MULTIPROCESSORS

A multiprocessor system consists of a number of processors capable of simultaneously executing independent tasks. The granularity of these tasks can vary considerably. A task may encompass a few instructions for one pass through a loop, or thousands of instructions executed in a subroutine.

In a shared-memory multiprocessor, all processors have access to the same memory. Tasks running in different processors can access shared variables in the memory using the same addresses. The size of the shared memory is likely to be large. Implementing a large memory in a single module would create a bottleneck when many processors make requests to access the memory simultaneously. This problem is alleviated by distributing the memory across multiple modules so that simultaneous requests from different processors are more likely to access different memory modules, depending on the addresses of those requests.

An interconnection network enables any processor to access any module that is a part of the shared memory. When memory modules are kept physically separate from the processors, all requests to access memory must pass through the network, which introduces latency. Figure 12.2 shows such an arrangement. A system which has the same network latency for all accesses from the processors to the memory modules is called a Uniform Memory Access (UMA) multiprocessor. Although the latency is uniform, it may be large for a network that connects many processors and memory modules.

For better performance, it is desirable to place a memory module close to each processor. The result is a collection of *nodes*, each consisting of a processor and a memory module. The nodes are then connected to the network, as shown in Figure 12.3. The network latency is avoided when a processor makes a request to access its local memory. However, a request to access a remote memory module must pass through the network. Because of the difference in latencies for accessing local and remote portions of the shared memory, systems of this type are called Non-Uniform Memory Access (NUMA) multiprocessors.

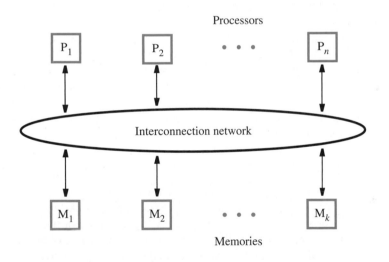

Figure 12.2   A UMA multiprocessor.

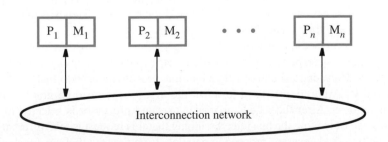

Figure 12.3   A NUMA multiprocessor.

12.3.1 INTERCONNECTION NETWORKS

The interconnection network must allow information transfer between any pair of nodes in the system. The network may also be used to broadcast information from one node to many other nodes. The traffic in the network consists of requests (such as read and write) and data transfers.

The suitability of a particular network is judged in terms of cost, bandwidth, effective throughput, and ease of implementation. The term *bandwidth* refers to the capacity of a transmission link to transfer data and is expressed in bits or bytes per second. The *effective throughput* is the actual rate of data transfer. This rate is less than the available bandwidth because a given link must also carry control information that coordinates the transfer of data.

Information transfer through the network usually takes place in the form of *packets* of fixed length and specified format. For example, a read request is likely to be a single packet sent from a processor to a memory module. The packet contains the node identifiers for the source and destination, the address of the location to be read, and a command field that indicates what type of read operation is required. A write request that writes one word in a memory module is also likely to be a single packet that includes the data to be written. On the other hand, a read response may involve an entire cache block requiring several packets for the data transfer.

Ideally, a complete packet would be handled in parallel in one clock cycle at any node or switch in the network. This implies having wide links, comprising many wires. However, to reduce cost and complexity, the links are often considerably narrower. In such cases, a packet must be divided into smaller pieces, each of which can be transmitted in one clock cycle.

The following sections describe a few of the interconnection networks that are commonly used in multiprocessors.

Bus

A *bus* is a set of lines (wires) that provide a single shared path for information transfer, as discussed in Chapter 7. Buses are most commonly used in UMA multiprocessors to connect a number of processors to several shared-memory modules. Arbitration is necessary to ensure that only one of many possible requesters is granted use of the bus at any time. The bus is suitable for a relatively small number of processors because of the contention for access to the bus and the increased propagation delays caused by electrical loading when many processors are connected.

A simple bus does not allow a new request to appear on the bus until the response for the current request has been provided. However, if the response latency is high, there may be considerable idle time on the bus.

Higher performance can be achieved by using a *split-transaction* bus, in which a request and its corresponding response are treated as separate events. Other transfers may take place between them. Consider a situation where multiple processors need to make read requests to the memory. Arbitration is used to select the first processor to be granted use of the bus for its request. After the request is made, a second processor is selected to make its request, instead of leaving the bus idle. Assuming that this request is to a different memory module, the two read accesses proceed in parallel. If neither module has finished with its access, a third processor is selected to make its request, and so on. Eventually, one memory module completes its read access. It is granted the use of the bus to transfer the data to the requesting processor. As other modules complete their accesses, the bus is used to transfer their responses. The actual length of time between each request and its corresponding response may vary as requests and responses for different transactions with the memory are interleaved on the bus to make efficient use of the available bandwidth.

The split-transaction bus requires a more complex bus protocol. The main source of complexity is the need to match each response with its corresponding request. This is usually handled by associating a unique tag with each request that appears on the bus. Each response then appears with the appropriate tag so that the source can match it to its original request.

Ring

A *ring* network is formed with point-to-point connections between nodes, as shown in Figure 12.4. A single ring is shown in Figure 12.4*a*. A long single ring results in high average latency for communication between any two nodes. This high latency can be mitigated in two different ways.

A second ring can be added to connect the nodes in the opposite direction. The resulting *bidirectional ring* halves the average latency and doubles the bandwidth. However, handling of communications is more complex.

Another approach is to use a *hierarchy* of rings. A two-level hierarchy is shown in Figure 12.4*b*. The upper-level ring connects the lower-level rings. The average latency for communication between any two nodes on lower-level rings is reduced with this arrangement. Transfers between nodes on the same lower-level ring need not traverse the upper-level ring. Transfers between nodes on diffcrent lower-level rings include a traversal on part of the upper-level ring. The drawback of the hierarchical scheme is that the upper-level ring may become a bottleneck when many nodes on different lower-level rings communicate with each other frequently.

(a) Single ring

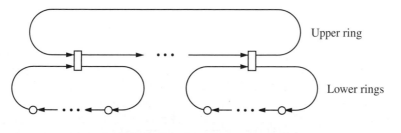

Upper ring

Lower rings

(b) Hierarchy of rings

Figure 12.4   Ring-based interconnection networks.

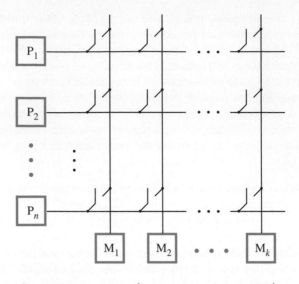

Figure 12.5   Crossbar interconnection network.

Crossbar

A *crossbar* is a network that provides a direct link between any pair of units connected to the network. It is typically used in UMA multiprocessors to connect processors to memory modules. It enables many simultaneous transfers if the same destination is not the target of multiple requests. For example, we can implement the structure in Figure 12.2 using a crossbar that comprises a collection of switches as in Figure 12.5. For n processors and k memories, $n \times k$ switches are needed.

Mesh

A natural way of connecting a large number of nodes is with a two-dimensional *mesh*, as shown in Figure 12.6. Each internal node of the mesh has four connections, one to each of its horizontal and vertical neighbors. Nodes on the boundaries and corners of the mesh

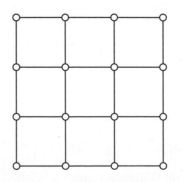

Figure 12.6   A two-dimensional mesh network.

have fewer neighbors and hence fewer connections. To reduce latency for communication between nodes that would otherwise be far apart in the mesh, wraparound connections may be introduced between nodes at opposite boundaries of the mesh. A network with such connections is called a *torus*. All nodes in a torus have four connections. Average latency is reduced, but the implementation complexity for routing requests and responses through a torus is somewhat higher than in the case of a simple mesh.

12.4   CACHE COHERENCE

A shared-memory multiprocessor is easy to program. Each variable in a program has a unique address location in the memory, which can be accessed by any processor. However, each processor has its own cache. Therefore, it is necessary to deal with the possibility that copies of shared data may reside in several caches. When any processor writes to a shared variable in its own cache, all other caches that contain a copy of that variable will then have the old, incorrect value. They must be informed of the change so that they can either update their copy to the new value or invalidate it. This is the issue of maintaining *cache coherence*, which requires having a consistent view of shared data in multiple caches.

In Chapter 8 we discussed two basic approaches for performing write operations on data in a cache. The write-through approach changes the data in both the cache and the main memory. The write-back approach changes the data only in the cache; the main memory copy is updated when a modified data block in the cache has to be replaced. Similar approaches can be used to address cache coherence in a multiprocessor system.

12.4.1   WRITE-THROUGH PROTOCOL

A write-through protocol can be implemented in one of two ways. One version is based on updating the values in other caches, while the second relies on invalidating the copies in other caches.

Let us consider the *update* protocol first. When a processor writes a new value to a block of data in its cache, the new value is also written into the memory module containing the block being modified. Since copies of this block may exist in other caches, these copies must be updated to reflect the change caused by the Write operation. The simplest way of doing this is to broadcast the written data to the caches of all processors in the system. As each processor receives the broadcast data, it updates the contents of the affected cache block if this block is present in its cache.

The second version of the write-through protocol is based on *invalidation* of copies. When a processor writes a new value into its cache, this value is also sent to the appropriate location in memory, and all copies in other caches are invalidated. Again, broadcasting can be used to send the invalidation requests throughout the system.

12.4.2   WRITE-BACK PROTOCOL

Maintaining coherence with the write-back protocol is based on the concept of ownership of a block of data in the memory. Initially, the memory is the owner of all blocks, and the memory retains ownership of any block that is read by a processor to place a copy in its cache.

If some processor wants to write to a block in its cache, it must first become the exclusive owner of this block. To do so, all copies in other caches must first be invalidated with a broadcast request. The new owner of the block may then modify the contents at will without having to take any other action.

When another processor wishes to read a block that has been modified, the request for the block must be forwarded to the current owner. The data are then sent to the requesting processor by the current owner. The data are also sent to the appropriate memory module, which reacquires ownership and updates the contents of the block in the memory. The cache of the processor that was the previous owner retains a copy of the block. Hence, the block is now shared with copies in two caches and the memory. Subsequent requests from other processors to read the same block are serviced by the memory module containing the block.

When another processor wishes to write to a block that has been modified, the current owner sends the data to the requesting processor. It also transfers ownership of the block to the requesting processor and invalidates its cached copy. Since the block is being modified by the new owner, the contents of the block in the memory are not updated. The next request for the same block is serviced by the new owner.

The write-back protocol has the advantage of creating less traffic than the write-through protocol. This is because a processor is likely to perform several writes to a cache block before this block is needed by another processor. With the write-back protocol, these writes are performed only in the cache, once ownership is acquired with an invalidation request. With the write-through protocol, each write must also be performed in the appropriate memory module and broadcast to other caches.

So far, we have assumed that update and invalidate requests in these protocols are broadcast through the interconnection network. Whether it is easy to implement such broadcasts depends largely on the structure of the interconnection network. The most natural network for supporting broadcasting is the single bus. In multiprocessors that connect a modest number of processors to the memory modules using a single bus, cache coherence can be realized using a scheme known as snooping.

12.4.3   SNOOPY CACHES

In a single-bus system, all transactions between processors and memory modules occur via requests and responses on the bus. In effect, they are broadcast to all units connected to the bus. Suppose that each processor cache has a controller circuit that observes, or *snoops*, all transactions on the bus. We now describe some scenarios for the write-back protocol and how cache coherence is enforced.

Consider a processor that has previously read a copy of a block from the memory into its cache. Before writing to this block for the first time, the processor must broadcast an *invalidation request* to all other caches, whose controllers accept the request and invalidate any copies of the same block. This action causes the requesting processor to become the new owner of the block. The processor may then write to the block and mark it as being modified. No further broadcasts are needed from the same processor to write to the modified block in its cache.

Now, if another processor broadcasts a *read request* on the bus for the same block, the memory must not respond because it is not the current owner of the block. The processor owning the requested block snoops the read request on the bus. Because it holds a modified copy of the requested block in its cache, it asserts a special signal on the bus to prevent the memory from responding. The owner then broadcasts a copy of the block on the bus, and marks its copy as clean (unmodified). The data response on the bus is accepted by the cache of the processor that issued the read request. The data response is also accepted by the memory to update its copy of the block. In this case, the memory reacquires ownership of the block, and the block is said to be in a shared state because copies of it are in the caches of two processors. Coherence is maintained because the two cached copies and the copy of the block in the memory contain the same data. Subsequent requests from any processor are serviced by the memory.

Consider now the situation in which two processors have copies of the same block in their respective caches, and both processors attempt to write to the same cache block at the same time. Since the block is in the shared state, the memory is the owner of the block. Hence, both processors request the use of the bus to broadcast an invalidation message. One of the processors is granted the use of the bus first. That processor broadcasts its invalidation request and becomes the new owner of the block. Through snooping, the copy of the block in the cache of the other processor is invalidated. When the other processor is later granted the use of the bus, it broadcasts a *read-exclusive request*. This request combines a read request and an invalidation request for the same block. The controller for the first processor snoops the read-exclusive request, provides a data response on the bus, and invalidates the copy in its cache. Ownership of the block is therefore transferred to the second processor making the request. The memory is not updated because the block is being modified again. Since the requests from the two processors are handled sequentially, cache coherence is maintained at all times.

The scheme just described is based on the ability of cache controllers to observe the activity on the bus and take appropriate actions. Such schemes are called *snoopy-cache* techniques.

For performance reasons, it is important that the snooping function not interfere with the normal operation of a processor and its cache. Such interference occurs if the cache controller accesses the tags of the cache for every request that appears on the bus. In most cases, the cache would not contain a valid copy of the block that is relevant to a request. To eliminate unnecessary interference, each cache can be provided with a set of duplicate tags, which maintain the same status information about the blocks in the cache but can be accessed separately by the snooping circuitry.

12.4.4 DIRECTORY-BASED CACHE COHERENCE

The concept of snoopy caches is easy to implement in single-bus systems. Large shared-memory multiprocessors use interconnection networks such as rings and meshes. In such systems, broadcasting every single request to the caches of all processors is inefficient. A scalable, but more complex, solution to this problem uses *directories* in each memory module to indicate which nodes may have copies of a given block in the shared state. If a block is modified, the directory identifies the node that is the current owner. Each request from a processor must be sent first to the memory module containing the relevant block. The directory information for that block is used to determine the action that is taken. A read request is forwarded to the current owner if the block is modified. In the case of a write request for a block that is shared, individual invalidations are sent only to nodes that may have copies of the block in question. The cost and complexity of the directory-based approach for enforcing cache coherence limits its use to large systems. Small multiprocessors, including current multicore chips, typically use snooping.

12.5 MESSAGE-PASSING MULTICOMPUTERS

A different way of using multiple processors involves implementing each node in the system as a complete computer with its own memory. Other computers in the system do not have direct access to this memory. Data that need to be shared are exchanged by sending messages from one computer to another. Such systems are called *message-passing multicomputers*.

Parallel programs are written differently for message-passing multicomputers than for shared-memory multiprocessors. To share data between nodes, the program running in the computer that is the source of the data must send a message containing the data to the destination computer. The program running in the destination computer receives the message and copies the data into the memory of that node.

To facilitate message passing, a special communications unit at each node is often responsible for the low-level details of formatting and interpreting messages that are sent and received, and for copying message data to and from the memory of the node. The computer in each node issues commands to the communications unit. The computer then continues performing other computations while the communications unit handles the details of sending and receiving messages.

12.6 PARALLEL PROGRAMMING FOR MULTIPROCESSORS

The preceding sections described hardware arrangements for shared-memory multiprocessors that can exploit parallelism in application programs. The available parallelism may be found in loops with independent passes, and also in independent higher-level tasks.

A source program written in a high-level language allows a programmer to express the desired computation in a manner that is easy to understand. It must be translated by the compiler and the assembler into machine-language representation. The hardware of the processor is designed to execute machine-language instructions in proper sequence to perform the computation desired by the programmer. It cannot automatically identify independent high-level tasks that could be executed in parallel. The compiler also has limitations in detecting and exploiting parallelism. It is therefore the responsibility of the programmer to explicitly partition the overall computation in the source program into tasks and to specify how they are to be executed on multiple processors.

Programming for a shared-memory multiprocessor is a natural extension of conventional programming for a single processor. A high-level source program is written using tasks that are executed by one processor. But it is also possible to indicate that certain tasks are to be executed simultaneously in different processors. Sharing of data is achieved by defining global variables that are read and written by different processors as they perform their assigned tasks. The multicore chips currently used in general-purpose computers, such as those implementing the Intel IA-32 architecture, are programmed in this manner.

To illustrate parallel programming, we consider the example of computing the dot product of two vectors, each containing N numbers. A C-language program for this task is shown in Figure 12.7. The details of initializing the contents of the two vectors are omitted to focus on the aspects relevant to parallel programming.

The loop accumulates the sum of N products. Each pass depends on the partial sum computed in the preceding pass, and the result computed in the final pass is the dot product. Despite the dependency, it is possible to partition the program into independent tasks for simultaneous execution by exploiting the associative property of addition. Each task computes a partial sum, and the final result is obtained by adding the partial sums.

```
#include    < stdio.h>     /* Routines for input/output. */

#define     N    100       /* Number of elements in each vector. */

double      a[N], b[N];    /* Vectors for computing the dot product. */

void        main (void)
{
            int i;
            double dot_product;

            < Initialize vectors a[ ], b[ ] – details omitted.>
            dot_product = 0.0;
            for (i = 0; i <  N; i++)
                dot_product = dot_product + a[i] * b[i];
            printf ("The dot product is %g\ n", dot_product);
}
```

Figure 12.7   C program for computing a dot product.

To implement a parallel program for computing the dot product, two questions need to be answered:

- How do we make multiple processors participate in parallel execution to compute the partial sums?

- How do we ensure that each processor has computed its partial sum before the final result for the dot product is computed?

Thread Creation

To answer the first question, we define the tasks that are assigned to different processors, and then we describe how execution of these tasks is initiated in multiple processors. We can write a parallel version of the dot product program using parameters for the number of processors, P, and the number of elements in each vector, N. We assume for simplicity that N is evenly divisible by P. The overall computation involves a sum of N products. For P processors, we define P independent tasks, where each task is the computation of a partial sum of N/P products.

When a program is executed in a single processor, there is one active thread of execution control. This thread is created implicitly by the operating system (OS) when execution of the program begins. For a parallel program, we require the independent tasks to be handled separately by multiple threads of execution control, one for each processor. These threads must be created explicitly. A typical approach is to use a routine named *create_thread* in a library that supports parallel programming. The library routine accepts an input parameter, which is a pointer to a subroutine to be executed by the newly created thread. An operating system service is invoked by the library routine to create a new thread with a distinct stack, so that it may call other subroutines and have its own local variables. All global variables are shared among all threads.

It is necessary to distinguish the threads from each other. One approach is to provide another library routine called *get_my_thread_id* that returns a unique integer between 0 and $P - 1$ for each thread. With that information, a thread can determine the appropriate subset of the overall computation for which it is responsible.

Thread Synchronization

The second question involves determining when threads have completed their tasks, so that the final result can be computed correctly. *Synchronization* of multiple threads is therefore required. There are several methods of synchronization, and they are often implemented in additional library routines for parallel programming. Here, we consider one method called a *barrier*.

The purpose of a barrier is to force threads to wait until they have all reached a specific point in the program where a call is made to the library routine for the barrier. Each thread that calls the barrier routine enters a busy-wait loop until the last thread calls the routine and enables all of the threads to continue their execution. This ensures that the threads have completed their respective computations preceding the barrier call.

Example Parallel Program

Having described the issues related to thread creation and synchronization, and typical library routines that are provided for thread management, we can now present a parallel dot product program as an example. Figure 12.8 shows a *main* routine, and another routine

```
#include    < stdio.h>          /* Routines for input/output. */
#include    "threads.h"         /* Routines for thread creation/synchronization. */

#define     N   100             /* Number of elements in each vector. */
#define     P   4               /* Number of processors for parallel execution. */

double      a[N], b[N];         /* Vectors for computing the dot product. */
double      partial_sums[P];    /* Array of results computed by threads. */
Barrier     bar;                /* Shared variable to support barrier synchronization. */

void        ParallelFunction (void)
{
            int my_id, i, start, end;
            double s;

            my_id = get_my_thread_id ();    /* Get unique identifier for this thread. */
            start = (N/P) * my_id;          /* Determine start/end using thread identifier. */
            end = (N/P) * (my_id + 1) – 1;  /* N is assumed to be evenly divisible by P .* /
            s = 0.0;
            for (i = start; i <= end; i++)
               s = s + a[i] * b[i];
            partial_sums[my_id] = s;        /* Save result in array. */
            barrier (&bar, P);              /* Synchronize with other threads. */
}

void        main (void)
{
            int i;
            double dot_product;

            < Initialize vectors a[ ], b[] – details omitted.>
            init_barrier (&bar);
            for (i = 1; i < P; i++)              /* Create P – 1 additional threads. */
               create_thread (ParallelFunction);
            ParallelFunction();                  /* Main thread also joins parallel execution. */
            dot_product = 0.0;                   /* After barrier synchronization, compute final result. */
            for (i = 0; i < P; i++)
               dot_product = dot_product + partial_sums[i];
            printf ("The dot product is %g\ n", dot_product);
}
```

Figure 12.8   Parallel program in C for computing a dot product.

called *ParallelFunction* that defines the independent tasks for parallel execution. When the program begins executing, there is only one thread executing the *main* routine. This thread initializes the vectors, then it initializes a shared variable needed for barrier synchronization. To initiate parallel execution, the *create_thread* routine is called $P - 1$ times from the *main* routine to create additional threads that each execute *ParallelFunction*. Then, the thread executing the *main* routine calls *ParallelFunction* directly so that a total of P threads are involved in the overall computation. The operating system software is responsible for distributing the threads to different processors for parallel execution.

Each thread calls *get_my_thread_id* from *ParallelFunction* to obtain a unique integer identifier in the range 0 to $P - 1$. Using this information, the thread calculates the *start* and *end* indices for the loop that generates the partial sum of that thread. After executing the loop, it writes the result to a separate element of the shared *partial_sums* array using its unique identifier as the array index. Then, the thread calls the library routine for barrier synchronization to wait for other threads to complete their computation.

After the last thread to complete its computation calls the barrier routine, all threads return to *ParallelFunction*. There is no further computation to perform in *ParallelFunction*, so the $P - 1$ threads created by the library call in the *main* routine terminate. The thread that called *ParallelFunction* directly from the *main* routine returns to compute the final result using the values in the *partial_sums* array.

The program in Figure 12.8 uses generic library routines to illustrate thread creation and synchronization. A large collection of routines for parallel programming in the C language is defined in the IEEE 1003.1 standard [4]. This collection is also known as the *POSIX threads* or *Pthreads* library. It provides a variety of thread management and synchronization mechanisms. Implementations of this library are available for widely-used operating systems to facilitate programming for multiprocessors.

12.7   PERFORMANCE MODELING

The most important measure of the performance of a computer is how quickly it can execute programs. When considering one processor, the speed with which instructions are fetched and executed is affected by the instruction set architecture and the hardware design. The total number of instructions that are executed is affected by the compiler as well as the instruction set architecture. Chapter 6 introduced the basic performance equation, which is a low-level mathematical model that reflects these considerations for one processor. The terms in that model include the number of instructions executed, the average number of cycles per instruction, and the clock frequency. This model enables the prediction of execution time, given sufficiently detailed information.

A higher-level model that relies on less detailed information can be used to assess potential improvements in performance. Consider a program whose execution time on some computer is T_{orig}. Our objective is to assess the extent to which the execution time can be reduced when a performance enhancement, such as parallel processing, is introduced.

Assume that a fraction f_{enh} of the execution time is affected by the enhancement. The remaining fraction, $f_{unenh} = 1 - f_{enh}$, is unchanged. Let p represent the factor by which the portion of time $f_{enh} \times T_{orig}$ is reduced due to the performance enhancement. The new execution time is

$$T_{new} = T_{orig} \; (f_{unenh} + f_{enh}/p)$$

The *speedup* is the ratio T_{orig}/T_{new} or

$$1/ \; (f_{unenh} + f_{enh}/p)$$

The above expression for speedup is known as *Amdahl's Law*. It is named after Gene Amdahl, who was the first to formalize the reasoning explained above. It is a way of stating the intuitive observation that the benefit of a given performance enhancement increases if it affects a larger portion of the execution time.

Once a breakdown of the original execution time has been determined, it is often useful to determine an upper bound on the possible speedup. To do so, we let $p \to \infty$ to reflect the ideal, but unrealistic, reduction of the fraction f_{enh} of execution time to zero. The resulting speedup is $1/f_{unenh}$, which means that the portion of execution time that is not enhanced is the limiting factor on performance. A smaller value of f_{unenh} gives a larger bound on the speedup. For example, $f_{unenh} = 0.1$ gives an upper bound of 10, but $f_{unenh} = 0.05$ gives a larger bound of 20. However, the expected speedup using a realistic value of p is normally well below the upper bound. For example, using $p = 16$ with $f_{unenh} = 0.05$ gives a speedup of only $1/(0.05 + 0.95/16) = 9.1$, well below the upper bound of 20.

The important conclusion from this discussion is that the unenhanced portion of the original execution time can significantly limit the achievable speedup, even if the enhanced portion is improved by an arbitrarily large factor. If a programmer can determine, even approximately, the fractions f_{unenh} and f_{enh} of execution time before applying a particular enhancement, Amdahl's Law can provide useful insight into the expected improvement. That information can be used to determine whether the expected gain in performance justifies the effort and expense to implement the enhancement.

12.8 CONCLUDING REMARKS

Fundamental techniques such as pipelining and caches are important ways of improving performance and are widely used in computers. The additional techniques of multithreading, vector (SIMD) processing, and multiprocessing provide the potential for further improvements in performance by making more efficient use of processing resources and by performing more operations in parallel. These techniques have been incorporated into general-purpose multicore processor chips.

PROBLEMS

12.1   [M] Assume that a bus transfer takes T seconds and memory access time is $4T$ seconds. A read request over a conventional bus then requires $6T$ seconds to complete. How many conventional buses are needed to equal or exceed the effective throughput of a split-transaction bus that operates with the same time delays? Consider only read requests, ignore memory conflicts, and assume that all memory modules are connected to all buses in the multiple-bus case. Does your answer increase or decrease if memory access time increases?

12.2   [M] Assume that a computation comprises $k + 1$ distinct tasks. In order to prepare a program for the desired computation, each of these tasks has been written as a function in the C language. The $k + 1$ functions are labeled T0(), T1(), ..., Tk(). Each function requires τ time units to execute. Due to data dependencies, functions T1() to Tk() must be executed after function T0(). There are no data dependencies among the functions T1() to Tk().

(a) Using the given functions, write a C program that executes on a single processor.

(b) Write an equivalent C program that executes on k processors.

(c) Derive an expression for the ideal speedup for the program in part (b) relative to the program in part (a).

12.3   [D] What are the arguments for and against invalidation and updating as strategies for maintaining cache coherence?

12.4   [D] The approaches of shared memory and message passing both support simultaneous execution of tasks that interact with each other. Which of these two approaches can emulate the action of the other more easily? Briefly justify your answer.

12.5   [E] With reference to Figure 12.1, assume an array size of $N = 32$. Let all instructions require one time unit to execute in a processor. Determine the speedup of vectorization for vector lengths of 4, 8, 16, and 32.

12.6   [M] For vectorization, efficiency is defined as the ratio of the speedup to the vector length. Determine the efficiency for each of the results in Problem 12.5. Comment on the variation of the efficiency with the vector length.

12.7   [M] In the parallel program in Figure 12.8 for computing the dot product, the sum of the partial products is computed by one processor after all threads have reached the barrier. Modify the program so that each thread adds its partial sum incrementally to a global sum for the dot product. To prevent two or more threads from trying to update the global sum at the same time, synchronization is required. One method is to use a shared counter variable whose value is the identifier of the thread that is granted exclusive access to the variable for the global sum. After the thread with exclusive access has updated the global sum, it can simply increment this counter to grant exclusive access to another thread.

12.8   [E] Assume that a multiprocessor has eight processors. Based on an existing program that runs on one processor, a parallel program is written to run on this multiprocessor. Assume that the workload of the parallel portion of the program can be distributed evenly over the eight processors. Use Amdahl's Law to determine the value of f_{enh} that would allow a speedup of 5.

REFERENCES

1. NVIDIA Corporation, *NVIDIA C CUDA Programming Guide*, Version 3.1.1, July 2010, available at http://www.nvidia.com.
2. D. Kirk and W.-M. Hwu, *Programming Massively Parallel Processors: A Hands-on Approach*, Morgan Kaufmann, Burlington, Massachusetts, 2010.
3. Khronos Group, *OpenCL Introduction and Overview*, June 2010, available at http://www.khronos.org/opencl.
4. IEEE, *1003.1 Standard for Information Technology—Portable Operating System Interface (POSIX): System Interfaces, Issue 6*, 2001, available at http://www.ieee.org.

appendix

A

Logic Circuits

Appendix Objectives

This appendix provides a concise presentation of logic
circuits. You will learn about:

- Synthesis of logic functions
- Flip-flops, registers, and counters
- Decoders and multiplexers
- Finite state machines
- Programmable logic devices
- Practical implementation of logic circuits

Information in digital computers is represented and processed by electronic networks called *logic circuits*. These circuits operate on *binary variables* that assume one of two distinct values, usually called 0 and 1. In this appendix we will give a concise presentation of logic functions and circuits for their implementation, including a brief review of integrated circuit technology.

A.1   BASIC LOGIC FUNCTIONS

It is helpful to introduce the topic of binary logic by examining a practical problem that arises in all homes. Consider a lightbulb whose on/off status is controlled by two switches, x_1 and x_2. Each switch can be in one of two possible positions, 0 or 1, as shown in Figure A.1a. It can thus be represented by a binary variable. We will let the switch names serve as the names of the associated binary variables. The figure also shows an electrical power supply and a lightbulb. The way the switch terminals are interconnected determines how the switches control the light. The light will be on only if a closed path exists from the power supply through the switch network to the lightbulb. Let a binary variable f represent the condition of the light. If the light is on, $f = 1$, and if the light is off, $f = 0$. Thus, $f = 1$ means that there is at least one closed path through the network, and $f = 0$ means that there is no closed path. Clearly, f is a function of the two variables x_1 and x_2.

Let us consider some possibilities for controlling the light. First, suppose that the light is to be on if either switch is in the 1 position, that is, $f = 1$ if

$$x_1 = 1 \quad \text{and} \quad x_2 = 0$$

or

$$x_1 = 0 \quad \text{and} \quad x_2 = 1$$

or

$$x_1 = 1 \quad \text{and} \quad x_2 = 1$$

The connections that implement this type of control are shown in Figure A.1b. A logic *truth table* that represents this situation is shown beside the wiring diagram. The table lists all possible switch settings along with the value of f for each setting. In logic terms, this table represents the OR function of the two variables x_1 and x_2. The operation is represented algebraically by a "+" sign or a "$\vee$" sign, so that

$$f = x_1 + x_2 = x_1 \vee x_2$$

We say that x_1 and x_2 are the *input* variables and f is the *output* function.

We should point out some basic properties of the OR operation. It is commutative, that is,

$$x_1 + x_2 = x_2 + x_1$$

It can be extended to n variables, so that

$$f = x_1 + x_2 + \cdots + x_n$$

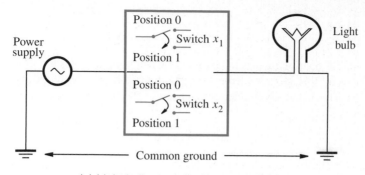

(a) Light bulb controlled by two switches

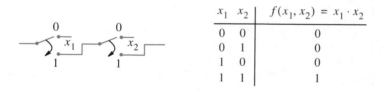

x_1	x_2	$f(x_1, x_2) = x_1 + x_2$
0	0	0
0	1	1
1	0	1
1	1	1

(b) Parallel connection (OR control)

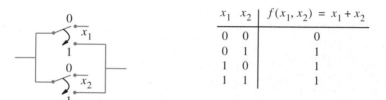

x_1	x_2	$f(x_1, x_2) = x_1 \cdot x_2$
0	0	0
0	1	0
1	0	0
1	1	1

(c) Series connection (AND control)

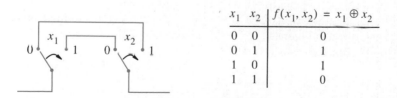

x_1	x_2	$f(x_1, x_2) = x_1 \oplus x_2$
0	0	0
0	1	1
1	0	1
1	1	0

(d) EXCLUSIVE-OR connection (XOR control)

Figure A.1   Light switch example.

has the value 1 if any variable x_i has the value 1. This represents the effect of connecting more switches in parallel with the two switches in Figure A.1b. Also, inspection of the truth table shows that

$$1 + x = 1$$

and

$$0 + x = x$$

Now, suppose that the light is to be on only when both switches are in the 1 position. The connections for this, along with the corresponding truth-table representation, are shown in Figure A.1c. This is the AND function, which uses the symbol "$\cdot$" or "$\wedge$" and is denoted as

$$f = x_1 \cdot x_2 = x_1 \wedge x_2$$

Some basic properties of the AND operation are

$$x_1 \cdot x_2 = x_2 \cdot x_1$$
$$1 \cdot x = x$$

and

$$0 \cdot x = 0$$

The AND function also extends to n variables, with

$$f = x_1 \cdot x_2 \cdots \cdot x_n$$

having the value 1 only if all the x_i variables have the value 1. This represents the case in which more switches are connected in series with the two switches in Figure A.1c.

The final possibility that we will discuss for the way the switches determine the light status is another common situation. If we assume that the switches are at the two ends of a stairway, it should be possible to turn the light on or off from either switch. That is, if the light is on, changing either switch position should turn it off; and if it is off, changing either switch position should turn it on. Assume that the light is off when both switches are in the 0 position. Then changing either switch to the 1 position should turn the light on. Now suppose that the light is on with $x_1 = 1$ and $x_2 = 0$. Switching x_1 back to 0 will obviously turn the light off. Furthermore, it must be possible to turn the light off by changing x_2 to 1, that is, $f = 0$ if $x_1 = x_2 = 1$. The connections to implement this type of control are shown in Figure A.1d. The corresponding logic operation is called the XOR (Exclusive-OR) function, which is represented by the symbol "$\oplus$". Some of its properties are

$$x_1 \oplus x_2 = x_2 \oplus x_1$$
$$1 \oplus x = \overline{x}$$

and

$$0 \oplus x = x$$

where $\overline{x}$ denotes the NOT function of the variable x. This single-variable function, $f = \overline{x}$, has the value 1 if $x = 0$ and the value 0 if $x = 1$. We say that the input x is being *inverted* or *complemented*.

A.1.1   Electronic Logic Gates

The use of switches, closed or open electrical paths, and lightbulbs to illustrate the idea of logic variables and functions is convenient because of their familiarity and simplicity. The logic concepts that have been introduced are equally applicable to the electronic circuits used to process information in digital computers. The physical variables are electrical voltages and currents instead of switch positions and closed or open paths. For example, consider a circuit that is designed to operate on inputs that are at either +5 or 0 volts. The circuit outputs are also at either +5 or 0 V. Now, if we say that +5 V represents logic 1 and 0 V represents logic 0, then we can describe what the circuit does by specifying the truth table for the logic operation that it performs.

With the help of transistors, it is possible to design simple electronic circuits that perform logic operations such as AND, OR, XOR, and NOT. It is customary to use the name *gates* for these basic logic circuits. Standard symbols for these gates are shown in Figure A.2. A somewhat more compact graphical notation for the NOT operation is used when inversion is applied to a logic gate input or output. In such cases, the inversion is denoted by a small circle.

The electronic implementation of logic gates will be discussed in Section A.5. We will now proceed to discuss how basic gates can be used to construct logic networks that implement more complex logic functions.

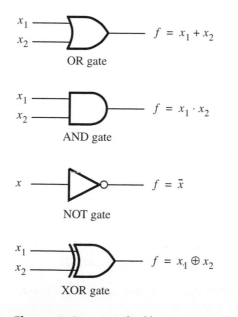

x_1
x_2
$f = x_1 + x_2$
OR gate

x_1
x_2
$f = x_1 \cdot x_2$
AND gate

x
$f = \bar{x}$
NOT gate

x_1
x_2
$f = x_1 \oplus x_2$
XOR gate

Figure A.2   Standard logic gate symbols.

A.2   Synthesis of Logic Functions

Consider the network composed of two AND gates and one OR gate that is shown in Figure A.3*a*. It can be represented by the expression

$$f = \bar{x}_1 \cdot x_2 + x_1 \cdot \bar{x}_2$$

The construction of the truth table for this expression is shown in Figure A.3*b*. First, the values of the AND terms are determined for each input valuation. Then the values of the function f are determined using the OR operation. The truth table for f is identical to the truth table for the XOR function, so the three-gate network in Figure A.3*a* is an implementation of the XOR function using AND, OR, and NOT gates. The logic expression $\bar{x}_1 \cdot x_2 + x_1 \cdot \bar{x}_2$ is called a *sum-of-products* form because the OR operation is sometimes called the "sum" function and the AND operation the "product" function.

We should note that it would be more proper to write

$$f = ((\bar{x}_1) \cdot x_2) + (x_1 \cdot (\bar{x}_2))$$

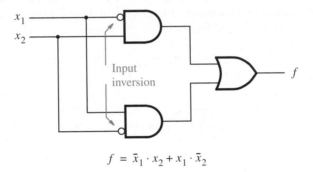

$$f = \bar{x}_1 \cdot x_2 + x_1 \cdot \bar{x}_2$$

(a) Network for the XOR function

x_1	x_2	$\bar{x}_1 \cdot x_2$	$x_1 \cdot \bar{x}_2$	$f = \bar{x}_1 \cdot x_2 + x_1 \cdot \bar{x}_2$ $= x_1 \oplus x_2$
0	0	0	0	0
0	1	1	0	1
1	0	0	1	1
1	1	0	0	0

(b) Truth table construction of $\bar{x}_1 \cdot x_2 + x_1 \cdot \bar{x}_2$

Figure A.3   Implementation of the XOR function using AND, OR, and NOT gates.

Table A.1 Two 3-variable functions.

x_1	x_2	x_3	f_1	f_2
0	0	0	1	1
0	0	1	1	1
0	1	0	0	1
0	1	1	1	0
1	0	0	0	1
1	0	1	0	1
1	1	0	0	0
1	1	1	1	0

to indicate the order of applying the operations in the expression. To simplify the appearance of such expressions, we define a hierarchy among the three operations AND, OR, and NOT. In the absence of parentheses, operations in a logic expression should be performed in the following order: NOT, AND, and then OR. Furthermore, it is customary to omit the "·" operator when there is no ambiguity.

Returning to the sum-of-products form, we will now explain how any logic function can be synthesized in this form directly from its truth table. Consider the truth table of Table A.1 and suppose we wish to synthesize the function f_1 using AND, OR, and NOT gates. For each row of the table in which $f_1 = 1$, we include a product (AND) term in the sum-of-products form. The product term includes all three input variables. The NOT operator is applied to these variables individually so that the term is 1 only when the variables have the particular valuation that corresponds to that row of the truth table. This means that if $x_i = 0$, then $\bar{x}_i$ is entered in the product term, and if $x_i = 1$, then x_i is entered. For example, the fourth row of the table has the function entry 1 for the input valuation

$$(x_1, x_2, x_3) = (0, 1, 1)$$

The product term corresponding to this is $\bar{x}_1 x_2 x_3$. Doing this for all rows in which the function f_1 has the value 1 leads to

$$f_1 = \bar{x}_1 \bar{x}_2 \bar{x}_3 + \bar{x}_1 \bar{x}_2 x_3 + \bar{x}_1 x_2 x_3 + x_1 x_2 x_3$$

The logic network corresponding to this expression is shown on the left side in Figure A.4. As another example, the sum-of-products expression for the XOR function can be derived from its truth table using this technique. This approach can be used to derive sum-of-products expressions and the corresponding logic networks for truth tables of any size.

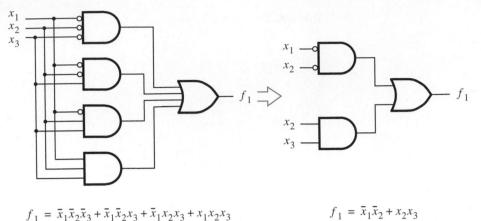

$$f_1 = \bar{x}_1\bar{x}_2\bar{x}_3 + \bar{x}_1\bar{x}_2 x_3 + \bar{x}_1 x_2 x_3 + x_1 x_2 x_3 \qquad\qquad f_1 = \bar{x}_1\bar{x}_2 + x_2 x_3$$

Figure A.4   A logic network for f_1 of Table A.1 and an equivalent minimal network.

A.3   MINIMIZATION OF LOGIC EXPRESSIONS

We have shown how to derive one sum-of-products expression for each truth table. In fact, there are many equivalent expressions and logic networks for any particular truth table. Two logic expressions or logic gate networks are equivalent if they have identical truth tables. An expression that is equivalent to the sum-of-products expression we derived for f_1 in the previous section is

$$\bar{x}_1\bar{x}_2 + x_2 x_3$$

To prove this, we construct the truth table for the simpler expression and show that it is identical to the truth table for f_1 in Table A.1. This is done in Table A.2. The construction of the table for $\bar{x}_1\bar{x}_2 + x_2 x_3$ is done in three steps. First, the value of the product term $\bar{x}_1\bar{x}_2$ is computed for each valuation of the inputs. Then $x_2 x_3$ is evaluated. Finally, these two columns are ORed together to obtain the truth table for the expression. This truth table is identical to the truth table for f_1 given in Table A.1.

To simplify logic expressions we perform a series of algebraic manipulations. The new logic rules that are used in these manipulations are the distributive rule

$$w(y + z) = wy + wz$$

and the identity

$$w + \bar{w} = 1$$

Table A.3 shows the truth-table proof of the distributive rule. It should now be clear that rules such as this can always be proved by constructing the truth tables for the left-hand side and the right-hand side to show that they are identical. Logic rules, such as the distributive rule, are sometimes called *identities*. Although we will not need to use it here, another form

Table A.2   Evaluation of the expression $\bar{x}_1\bar{x}_2 + x_2x_3$.

x_1	x_2	x_3	$\bar{x}_1\bar{x}_2$	x_2x_3	$\bar{x}_1\bar{x}_2 + x_2x_3 = f_1$
0	0	0	1	0	1
0	0	1	1	0	1
0	1	0	0	0	0
0	1	1	0	1	1
1	0	0	0	0	0
1	0	1	0	0	0
1	1	0	0	0	0
1	1	1	0	1	1

Table A.3   Truth-table technique for proving equivalence of expressions.

w	y	z	$y + z$	Left-hand side $w(y + z)$	wy	wz	Right-hand side $wy + wz$
0	0	0	0	0	0	0	0
0	0	1	1	0	0	0	0
0	1	0	1	0	0	0	0
0	1	1	1	0	0	0	0
1	0	0	0	0	0	0	0
1	0	1	1	1	0	1	1
1	1	0	1	1	1	0	1
1	1	1	1	1	1	1	1

of distributive rule that we should include for completeness is

$$w + yz = (w + y)(w + z)$$

The objective in logic minimization is to reduce the cost of implementation of a given logic function according to some criterion. More particularly, we wish to start with a sum-of-products expression derived from a truth table and simplify it to an equivalent *minimal sum-of-products* expression. To define the criterion for minimization, it is necessary to introduce a size or cost measure for a sum-of-products expression. The usual cost measure is a count of the total number of gates and gate inputs required in implementing the expression in the form shown in Figure A.4. For example, the larger expression in this figure has a cost of 21, composed of a total of 5 gates and 16 gate inputs. Input inversions are ignored in this counting process. The cost of the simpler expression is 9, composed of 3 gates and 6 inputs. We are now in a position to state that a sum-of-products expression is minimal if there is no other equivalent sum-of-products expression with a lower cost. In the simple examples that we will introduce, it is usually reasonably clear when we have arrived at a minimal expression. Thus, we will not give rigorous proofs of minimality.

The general strategy in performing algebraic manipulations to simplify a given expression is as follows. First, group product terms in pairs that differ only in that some variable appears complemented $(\bar{x})$ in one term and true (x) in the other. When the common subproduct consisting of the other variables is factored out of the pair by the distributive rule, we are left with the term $x + \bar{x}$, which has the value 1. Applying this procedure to the first expression for f_1, we obtain

$$
\begin{aligned}
f_1 &= \bar{x}_1\bar{x}_2\bar{x}_3 + \bar{x}_1\bar{x}_2x_3 + \bar{x}_1x_2x_3 + x_1x_2x_3 \\
&= \bar{x}_1\bar{x}_2(\bar{x}_3 + x_3) + (\bar{x}_1 + x_1)x_2x_3 \\
&= \bar{x}_1\bar{x}_2 \cdot 1 + 1 \cdot x_2x_3 \\
&= \bar{x}_1\bar{x}_2 + x_2x_3
\end{aligned}
$$

This expression is minimal. The network corresponding to it is shown in Figure A.4.

The grouping of terms in pairs so that minimization can lead to the simplest expression is not always as obvious as it is in the preceding example. A rule that is often helpful is

$$ w + w = w $$

This allows us to repeat product terms so that a particular term can be combined with more than one other term in the factoring process. As an example of this, consider the function f_2 in Table A.1. The sum-of-products expression that can be derived for it directly from the truth table is

$$ f_2 = \bar{x}_1\bar{x}_2\bar{x}_3 + \bar{x}_1\bar{x}_2x_3 + \bar{x}_1x_2\bar{x}_3 + x_1\bar{x}_2\bar{x}_3 + x_1\bar{x}_2x_3 $$

By repeating the first product term $\bar{x}_1\bar{x}_2\bar{x}_3$ and interchanging the order of terms (by the commutative rule), we obtain

$$ f_2 = \bar{x}_1\bar{x}_2\bar{x}_3 + \bar{x}_1\bar{x}_2x_3 + x_1\bar{x}_2\bar{x}_3 + x_1\bar{x}_2x_3 + \bar{x}_1\bar{x}_2\bar{x}_3 + \bar{x}_1x_2\bar{x}_3 $$

Grouping the terms in pairs and factoring yields

$$
\begin{aligned}
f_2 &= \bar{x}_1\bar{x}_2(\bar{x}_3 + x_3) + x_1\bar{x}_2(\bar{x}_3 + x_3) + \bar{x}_1(\bar{x}_2 + x_2)\bar{x}_3 \\
&= \bar{x}_1\bar{x}_2 + x_1\bar{x}_2 + \bar{x}_1\bar{x}_3
\end{aligned}
$$

Now, reducing the first pair of terms by factoring gives the minimal expression

$$ f_2 = \bar{x}_2 + \bar{x}_1\bar{x}_3 $$

This completes our discussion of algebraic simplification of logic expressions. The obvious practical application of this mathematical exercise stems from the fact that networks with fewer gates and inputs are cheaper and easier to implement. Therefore, it is of economic interest to be able to determine the minimal expression that is equivalent to a given expression. The rules that we have used in manipulating logic expressions are summarized in Table A.4. They are arranged in pairs to show their symmetry as they apply to both the AND and OR functions. So far, we have not had occasion to use either involution or de Morgan's rules, but they will be found to be useful in the next section.

Table A.4 Rules of binary logic.

Name	Algebraic identity	
Commutative	$w + y = y + w$	$wy = yw$
Associative	$(w + y) + z = w + (y + z)$	$(wy)z = w(yz)$
Distributive	$w + yz = (w + y)(w + z)$	$w(y + z) = wy + wz$
Idempotent	$w + w = w$	$ww = w$
Involution	$\overline{\overline{w}} = w$	
Complement	$w + \overline{w} = 1$	$w\overline{w} = 0$
de Morgan	$\overline{w + y} = \overline{w}\,\overline{y}$	$\overline{wy} = \overline{w} + \overline{y}$
	$1 + w = 1$	$0 \cdot w = 0$
	$0 + w = w$	$1 \cdot w = w$

A.3.1 Minimization using Karnaugh Maps

In our algebraic minimization of the functions f_1 and f_2 of Table A.1, it was necessary to guess the best way to proceed at certain points. For instance, the decision to repeat the term $\overline{x}_1\overline{x}_2\overline{x}_3$ as the first step in minimizing f_2 is not obvious. There is a geometric technique that can be used to quickly derive the minimal expression for a logic function of a few variables. The technique depends on a different form for presentation of the truth table, a form called the *Karnaugh map*. For a three-variable function, the map is a rectangle composed of eight squares arranged in two rows of four squares each, as shown in Figure A.5a. Each square of the map corresponds to a particular valuation of the input variables. For example, the third square of the top row represents the valuation $(x_1, x_2, x_3) = (1, 1, 0)$. Because there are eight rows in a three-variable truth table, the map obviously requires eight squares. The entries in the squares are the function values for the corresponding input valuations.

The key idea in the formation of the map is that horizontally and vertically adjacent squares correspond to input valuations that differ in only one variable. When two adjacent squares contain 1s, they indicate the possibility of an algebraic simplification. In the map for f_2 in Figure A.5a, the 1 values in the leftmost two squares of the top row correspond to the product terms $\overline{x}_1\overline{x}_2\overline{x}_3$ and $\overline{x}_1 x_2 \overline{x}_3$. The simplification

$$\overline{x}_1\overline{x}_2\overline{x}_3 + \overline{x}_1 x_2 \overline{x}_3 - \overline{x}_1\overline{x}_3$$

was performed earlier in minimizing the algebraic expression for f_2. This simplification can be obtained directly from the map by grouping the two 1s as shown. The product term that corresponds to a group of squares is the product of the input variables whose values are constant on these squares. If the value of input variable x_i is 0 for all 1s of a group, then $\overline{x}_i$ is entered in the product, but if x_i has the value 1 for all 1s of the group, then x_i is entered in the product. Adjacency of two squares includes the property that the left-end squares are adjacent to the right-end squares. Continuing with our discussion of f_2, the group of four 1s consisting of the left-end column and the right-end column simplifies to the single-variable term $\overline{x}_2$ because x_2 is the only variable whose value remains constant over the group. All four possible combinations of values of the other two variables occur in the group.

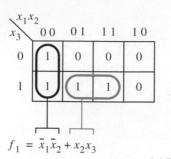

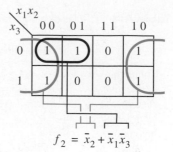

$$f_1 = \bar{x}_1\bar{x}_2 + x_2x_3$$

$$f_2 = \bar{x}_2 + \bar{x}_1\bar{x}_3$$

(a) Three-variable maps

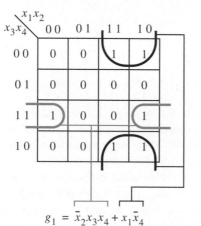

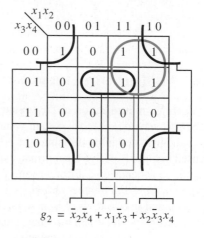

$$g_1 = \bar{x}_2x_3x_4 + x_1\bar{x}_4$$

$$g_2 = \bar{x}_2\bar{x}_4 + x_1\bar{x}_3 + x_2\bar{x}_3x_4$$

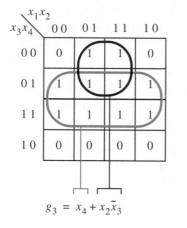

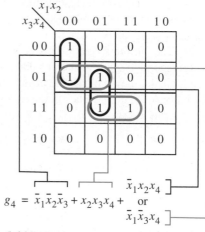

$$g_3 = x_4 + x_2\bar{x}_3$$

$$g_4 = \bar{x}_1\bar{x}_2\bar{x}_3 + x_2x_3x_4 + \begin{array}{l} \bar{x}_1x_2x_4 \\ \text{or} \\ \bar{x}_1\bar{x}_3x_4 \end{array}$$

(b) Four-variable maps

Figure A.5   Minimization using Karnaugh maps.

Karnaugh maps can be used for more than three variables. A Karnaugh map for four variables can be obtained from two 3-variable maps. Examples of four-variable maps are shown in Figure A.5b, along with minimal expressions for the functions represented by the maps. In addition to two- and four-square groupings, it is now possible to form eight-square groupings. Such a grouping is illustrated in the map for g_3. Note that the four corner squares constitute a valid group of four and are represented by the product term $\bar{x}_2\bar{x}_4$ in g_2. As in the case of three-variable maps, the term that corresponds to a group of squares is the product of the variables whose values do not change over the group. For example, the grouping of four 1s in the upper right-hand corner of the map for g_2 is represented by the product term $x_1\bar{x}_3$ because $x_1 = 1$ and $x_3 = 0$ over the group. The variables x_2 and x_4 have all the possible combinations of values over this group. It is also possible to use Karnaugh maps for five-variable functions. In this case, two 4-variable maps are used, one of them corresponding to the 0 value for the fifth variable and the other corresponding to the 1 value.

The general procedure for forming groups of two, four, eight, and so on in Karnaugh maps is readily derived. Two adjacent pairs of 1s can be combined to form a group of four. Similarly, two adjacent groups of four can be combined to form a group of eight. In general, the number of squares in any valid group must be equal to 2^k, where k is an integer.

We will now consider a procedure for using Karnaugh maps to obtain minimal sum-of-products expressions. As can be seen in the maps of Figure A.5, a large group of 1s corresponds to a small product term. Thus, a simple gate implementation results from covering all the 1s in the map with as few groups as possible. In general, we should choose the smallest set of groups, picking large ones wherever possible, that cover all the 1s in the map. Consider, for example, the function g_2 in Figure A.5b. As we have already seen, the 1s in the four corners constitute a group of four that is represented by the product term $\bar{x}_2\bar{x}_4$. Another group of four exists in the upper right-hand corner and is represented by the term $x_1\bar{x}_3$. This covers all the 1s in the map except for the 1 in the square where $(x_1, x_2, x_3, x_4) = (0, 1, 0, 1)$. The largest group of 1s that includes this square is the two-square group represented by the term $x_2\bar{x}_3x_4$. Therefore, the minimal expression for g_2 is

$$g_2 = \bar{x}_2\bar{x}_4 + x_1\bar{x}_3 + x_2\bar{x}_3x_4$$

Minimal expressions for the other functions shown in the figure can be derived in a similar manner. Note that in the case of g_4 there are two possible minimal expressions, one including the term $\bar{x}_1x_2x_4$ and the other including the term $\bar{x}_1\bar{x}_3x_4$. It is often the case that a given function has more than one minimal expression.

In all our examples, it is relatively easy to derive minimal expressions. In general, there are formal algorithms for this process, but we will not consider them here.

A.3.2 Don't-Care Conditions

In many situations, some valuations of the inputs to a digital circuit never occur. For example, consider the binary-coded decimal (BCD) number representation. Four binary variables b_3, b_2, b_1, and b_0 represent the decimal digits 0 through 9, as shown in Figure A.6. These four variables have a total of 16 distinct valuations, only 10 of which are used for representing the decimal digits. The remaining valuations are not used. Therefore, any

Decimal digit represented	Binary coding b_3 b_2 b_1 b_0	f
0	0 0 0 0	0
1	0 0 0 1	0
2	0 0 1 0	0
3	0 0 1 1	1
4	0 1 0 0	0
5	0 1 0 1	0
6	0 1 1 0	1
7	0 1 1 1	0
8	1 0 0 0	0
9	1 0 0 1	1
	1 0 1 0	d
	1 0 1 1	d
unused	1 1 0 0	d
	1 1 0 1	d
	1 1 1 0	d
	1 1 1 1	d

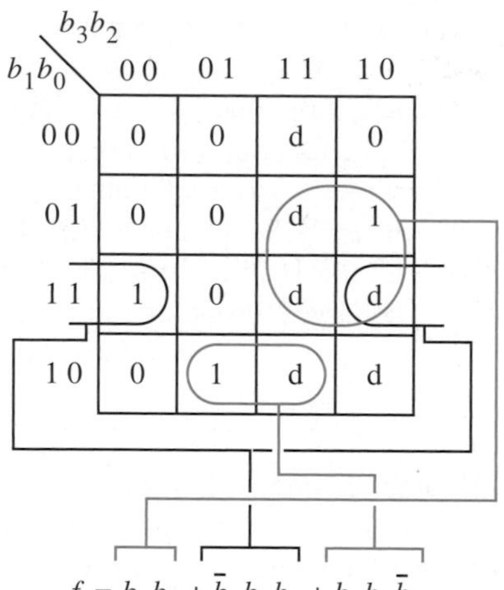

$$f = b_3 b_0 + \bar{b}_2 b_1 b_0 + b_2 b_1 \bar{b}_0$$

Figure A.6   Four-variable Karnaugh map illustrating don't cares.

logic circuit that processes BCD data will never encounter any of these six valuations at its inputs.

Figure A.6 gives the truth table for a particular function that may be performed on a BCD digit. We do not care what the function values are for the unused input valuations; hence, they are called *don't-cares* and are denoted as such by the letter "d" in the truth table. To obtain a circuit implementation, the function values corresponding to don't-care conditions can be arbitrarily assigned to be either 0 or 1. The best way to assign them is in a manner that will lead to a minimal logic gate implementation. We should interpret don't-cares as 1s whenever they can be used to enlarge a group of 1s. Because larger groups correspond to smaller product terms, minimization is enhanced by the judicious inclusion of don't-care entries.

The function in Figure A.6 represents the following processing on a decimal digit input: The output f is to have the value 1 whenever the inputs represent a nonzero digit that is evenly divisible by 3. Three groups are necessary to cover the three 1s of the map, and don't-cares have been used to enlarge these groups as much as possible.

A.4   SYNTHESIS WITH NAND AND NOR GATES

We will now consider two other basic logic gates called NAND and NOR, which are extensively used in practice because of their simple electronic realizations. The truth table for these gates is shown in Figure A.7. They implement the equivalent of the AND and OR functions followed by the NOT function, which is the motivation for the names and standard logic symbols for these gates. Letting the arrows "↑" and "↓" denote the NAND and NOR operators, respectively, and using de Morgan's rule in Table A.4, we have

$$x_1 \uparrow x_2 = \overline{x_1 x_2} = \bar{x}_1 + \bar{x}_2$$

and

$$x_1 \downarrow x_2 = \overline{x_1 + x_2} = \bar{x}_1 \bar{x}_2$$

NAND and NOR gates with more than two input variables are available, and they operate according to the obvious generalization of de Morgan's law as

$$x_1 \uparrow x_2 \uparrow \cdots \uparrow x_n = \overline{x_1 x_2 \cdots x_n} = \bar{x}_1 + \bar{x}_2 + \cdots + \bar{x}_n$$

x_1	x_2	f
0	0	1
0	1	1
1	0	1
1	1	0

x_1	x_2	f
0	0	1
0	1	0
1	0	0
1	1	0

$$f = x_1 \uparrow x_2 = \overline{x_1 x_2} = \bar{x}_1 + \bar{x}_2 \qquad f = x_1 \downarrow x_2 = \overline{x_1 + x_2} = \bar{x}_1 \bar{x}_2$$

(a) NAND   (b) NOR

Figure A.7   NAND and NOR gates.

and

$$x_1 \downarrow x_2 \downarrow \cdots \downarrow x_n = \overline{x_1 + x_2 + \cdots + x_n} = \overline{x}_1 \overline{x}_2 \cdots \overline{x}_n$$

Logic design with NAND and NOR gates is not as straightforward as with AND, OR, and NOT gates. One of the main difficulties in the design process is that the associative rule is not valid for NAND and NOR operations. We will expand on this problem later. First, however, let us describe a simple, general procedure for synthesizing any logic function using only NAND gates. There is a direct way to translate a logic network expressed in sum-of-products form into an equivalent network composed only of NAND gates. The procedure is easily illustrated with the aid of an example. Consider the following algebraic manipulation of a logic expression corresponding to a four-input network composed of three 2-input NAND gates:

$$\begin{aligned}
(x_1 \uparrow x_2) \uparrow (x_3 \uparrow x_4) &= \overline{(\overline{x_1 x_2})(\overline{x_3 x_4})} \\
&= \overline{\overline{x_1 x_2}} + \overline{\overline{x_3 x_4}} \\
&= x_1 x_2 + x_3 x_4
\end{aligned}$$

We have used de Morgan's rule and the involution rule in this derivation. Figure A.8 shows the logic network equivalent of this derivation. Since any logic function can be synthesized in a sum-of-products (AND-OR) form and because the preceding derivation is obviously reversible, we have the result that any logic function can be synthesized in NAND-NAND form. We can see that this result is true for functions of any number of variables. The required number of inputs to the NAND gates is obviously the same as the number of inputs to the corresponding AND and OR gates.

Let us return to the comment that the nonassociativity of the NAND operator can be an annoyance. In designing logic networks with NAND gates using the procedure illustrated in Figure A.8, a requirement for a NAND gate with more inputs than can be implemented in a given technology may arise. If this happens when one is using AND and OR gates, there

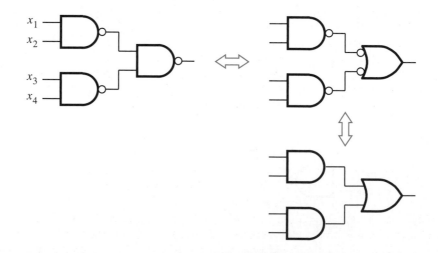

Figure A.8   Equivalence of NAND-NAND and AND-OR networks.

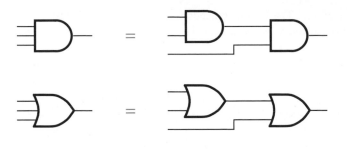

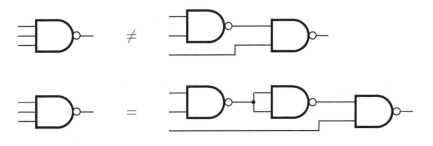

(a) Implementing three-input AND and OR functions with two-input gates

(b) Implementing a three-input NAND function with two-input gates

Figure A.9 Cascading of gates.

is no problem because the AND and OR operators are associative, and a straightforward cascade of such gates can be used. The case of implementing three-input AND and OR functions with two-input gates is shown in Figure A.9a. The solution is not as simple in the case of NAND gates. For example, a three-input NAND function cannot be implemented by a cascade of 2 two-input NAND gates. Three gates are needed, as shown in Figure A.9b.

A discussion of the implementation of logic functions using only NOR gates proceeds in a similar manner. Any logic function can be synthesized in a product-of-sums (OR-AND) form. Such networks can be implemented by equivalent NOR-NOR networks.

The preceding discussion introduced some basic concepts in logic design. Detailed discussion of the subject can be found in any of a number of textbooks (see References 1–7).

It is important for the reader to appreciate that many different realizations of a given logic function are possible. For practical reasons, it is useful to find realizations that minimize the cost of implementation. It is also often necessary to minimize the propagation delay through a logic network. We introduced the concept of minimization in the previous sections to give an indication of the nature of logic synthesis and the reductions in cost that may be achieved. For example, Karnaugh maps graphically show the manipulation possibilities that lead to optimal solutions. Although it is important to understand the principles of optimization of logic networks, it is not necessary to do the optimization by hand. Sophisticated *computer-aided design* (CAD) programs exist to perform logic synthesis and optimization. The designer needs to specify only the desired functional behavior, and the CAD software generates a cost-effective network that implements the required functionality.

A.5 PRACTICAL IMPLEMENTATION OF LOGIC GATES

Let us now turn our attention to the means by which logic variables can be represented and logic functions can be implemented in practice. The choice of a physical parameter to represent logic variables is obviously technology-dependent. In electronic circuits, either voltage or current levels can be used for this purpose.

To establish a correspondence between voltage levels and logic values or states, the concept of a *threshold* is used. Voltages above a given threshold are taken to represent one logic value, with voltages below that threshold representing the other. In practical situations, the voltage at any point in an electronic circuit undergoes small random variations for a variety of reasons. Because of this "noise," the logic state corresponding to a voltage level near the threshold cannot be reliably determined. To avoid such ambiguity, a "forbidden range" should be established, as shown in Figure A.10. In this case, voltages below $V_{0,max}$ represent the 0 value, and voltages above $V_{1,min}$ represent the 1 value. In subsequent discussion, we will often use the terms "low" and "high" to represent the voltage levels corresponding to logic values 0 and 1, respectively.

We will begin our discussion of electronic circuits that implement basic logic functions by considering simple circuits consisting of resistors and transistors that act as switches. Consider the circuits in Figure A.11. When switch S in Figure A.11a is closed, the output voltage V_{out} is equal to 0 (ground). When S is open, the output voltage V_{out} is equal to

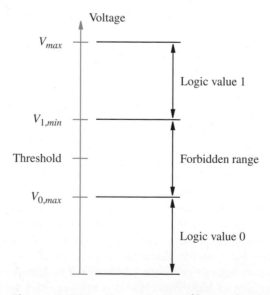

Figure A.10   Representation of logic values by voltage levels.

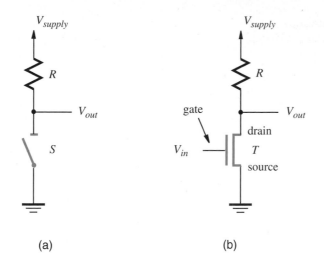

(a)   (b)

Figure A.11   An inverter circuit.

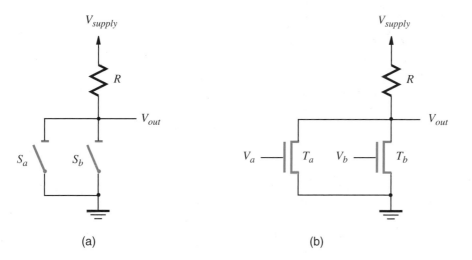

(a)   (b)

Figure A.12   A transistor circuit implementation of a NOR gate.

the supply voltage, V_{supply}. The same effect can be obtained in Figure A.11b, in which a transistor T is used to replace the switch S. When the input voltage applied to the gate of the transistor is 0 (that is, when $V_{in} = 0$), the transistor functions as an open switch, and $V_{out} = V_{supply}$. When V_{in} changes to V_{supply}, the transistor acts as a closed switch and the output voltage V_{out} is very close to 0. Thus, the circuit performs the function of a logic NOT gate.

We can now discuss the implementation of more complex logic functions. Figure A.12 shows a circuit realization for a NOR gate. In this case, V_{out} in Figure A.12a is high only when both switches S_a and S_b are open. Similarly, V_{out} in Figure A.12b is high only when

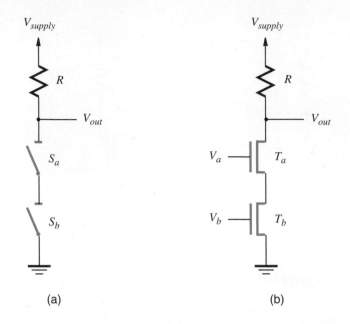

(a)   (b)

Figure A.13   A transistor circuit implementation of a NAND gate.

both inputs V_a and V_b are low. Thus, the circuit is equivalent to a NOR gate in which V_a and V_b correspond to two logic variables x_1 and x_2. We can easily verify that a NAND gate can be obtained by connecting the transistors in series as shown in Figure A.13. The logic functions AND and OR can be implemented using NAND and NOR gates, respectively, followed by the inverter of Figure A.11.

Note that NAND and NOR gates are simpler in their circuit implementations than AND and OR gates. Hence, it is not surprising to find that practical realizations of logic functions use NAND and NOR gates extensively. Many of the examples given in this book show circuits consisting of AND, OR, and NOT gates for ease of understanding. In practice, logic circuits contain all five types of gates.

A.5.1 CMOS CIRCUITS

Figures A.11 through A.13 illustrate the general structure of circuits implemented using *NMOS technology*. The name derives from the fact that the transistors used to realize the logic functions are of NMOS type. Two types of *metal-oxide semiconductor* (MOS) transistors are available for use as switches. An n-channel transistor is said to be of NMOS-type, and it behaves as a closed switch when its gate input is raised to the positive power supply voltage, V_{supply}, as indicated in Figure A.14a. The opposite behavior is achieved with a p-channel transistor, which is said to be of PMOS type. It acts as an open switch when the gate voltage, V_G, is equal to V_{supply}, and as a closed switch when $V_G = 0$, as indicated in Figure A.14b. Note that the graphical symbol for a PMOS transistor has a bubble on the gate input to indicate that its behavior is complementary to that of an NMOS transistor. Note

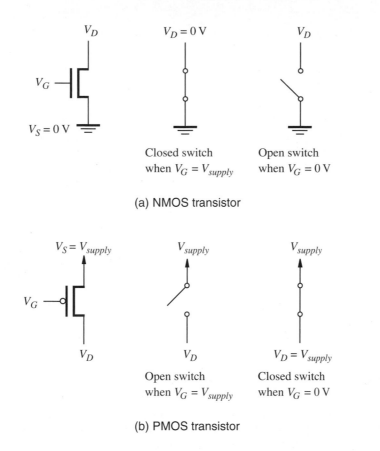

V_D

V_G —

$V_S = 0\,\text{V}$

$V_D = 0\,\text{V}$

Closed switch
when $V_G = V_{supply}$

V_D

Open switch
when $V_G = 0\,\text{V}$

(a) NMOS transistor

$V_S = V_{supply}$

V_G —

V_D

V_{supply}

V_D

Open switch
when $V_G = V_{supply}$

V_{supply}

$V_D = V_{supply}$

Closed switch
when $V_G = 0\,\text{V}$

(b) PMOS transistor

Figure A.14   NMOS and PMOS transistors in logic circuits.

also that the names source and drain are associated with the opposite terminals of PMOS transistors in comparison with NMOS transistors. The source of an NMOS transistor is connected to ground, while the source of a PMOS transistor is connected to V_{supply}. This naming convention is due to the nature of the current that flows through these transistors.

A drawback of the circuits in Figures A.11 through A.13 is their power consumption. In the state in which the switches are closed to provide a path between ground and the pull-up resistor R, there is current flowing from V_{supply} to ground. In the opposite state, in which switches are open, there is no path to ground and there is no current flowing. (In MOS transistors no current flows through the gate terminal.) Thus, depending on the states of its gates, there may be significant power consumption in a logic circuit.

An effective solution to the power consumption problem lies in using both NMOS and PMOS transistors to implement circuits that do not dissipate power when in a steady state. This approach leads to the CMOS (complementary metal-oxide semiconductor) technology. The basic idea of CMOS circuits is illustrated by the inverter circuit in Figure A.15. When $V_x = V_{supply}$, which corresponds to the input x having the logic value 1, transistor T_1 is

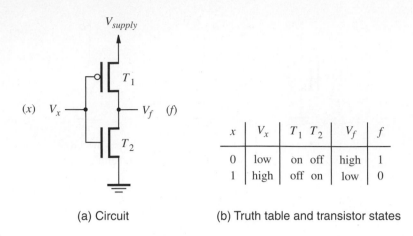

x	V_x	T_1	T_2	V_f	f
0	low	on	off	high	1
1	high	off	on	low	0

(a) Circuit   (b) Truth table and transistor states

Figure A.15   CMOS realization of a NOT gate.

turned off and T_2 is turned on. Thus, T_2 pulls the output voltage V_f down to 0. When V_x changes to 0, transistor T_1 turns on and T_2 turns off. Thus, T_1 pulls the output voltage V_f up to V_{supply}. Therefore, the logic values of x and f are complements of each other, and the circuit implements a NOT gate.

A key feature of this circuit is that transistors T_1 and T_2 operate in a complementary fashion; when one is on, the other is off. Hence, there is always a closed path from the output point f to either V_{supply} or ground. But, there is no closed path between V_{supply} and ground at any time except during a very short transition period when the transistors are changing their states. This means that the circuit does not dissipate appreciable power when it is in a steady state. It dissipates power only when it is switching from one logic state to another. Therefore, power dissipation in this circuit is dependent on the rate at which state changes take place.

We can now extend the CMOS concept to circuits that have n inputs, as shown in Figure A.16. NMOS transistors are used to implement the pull-down network, such that a closed path is established between the output point f and ground when a desired function $F(x_1, \ldots, x_n)$ is equal to 0. The pull-up network is built with PMOS transistors, such that a closed path is established between the output f and V_{supply} when $F(x_1, \ldots, x_n)$ is equal to 1. The pull-up and pull-down networks are functional complements of each other, so that in steady state there exists a closed path only between the output f and either V_{supply} or ground, but not both.

The pull-down network is implemented in the same way as shown in Figures A.11 through A.13. Figure A.17 gives the implementation of a NAND gate, and Figure A.18 gives a NOR gate. Figure A.19 shows how an AND gate is realized by inverting the output of a NAND gate.

In addition to low power dissipation, CMOS circuits have the advantage that MOS transistors can be implemented in very small sizes and thus occupy a very small area on an integrated circuit chip. This results in two significant benefits. First, it is possible to fabricate chips containing billions of transistors, which has led to the realization of modern

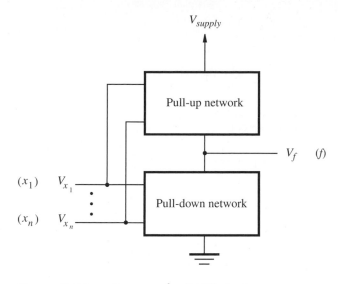

Figure A.16   Structure of a CMOS circuit.

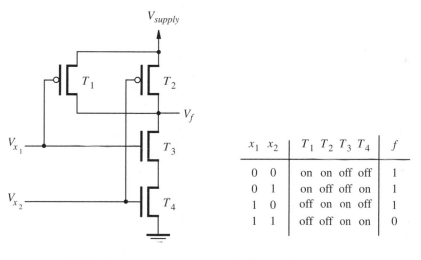

x_1 x_2	T_1 T_2 T_3 T_4	f
0 0	on on off off	1
0 1	on off off on	1
1 0	off on on off	1
1 1	off off on on	0

(a) Circuit   (b) Truth table and transistor states

Figure A.17   CMOS realization of a NAND gate.

processors and large memory chips. Second, the smaller the transistor, the faster it can be switched from one state to another. Thus, CMOS circuits can be operated at speeds in the gigahertz range.

Different CMOS circuits have been developed to operate with power supply voltages up to 15 V. The most commonly used power supplies are in the range from 1 V to 5 V.

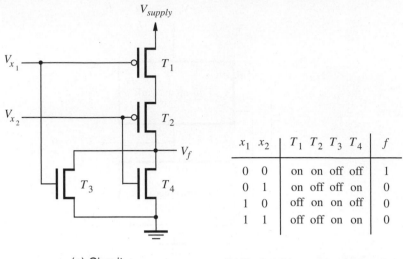

x_1 x_2	T_1 T_2 T_3 T_4	f
0 0	on on off off	1
0 1	on off off on	0
1 0	off on on off	0
1 1	off off on on	0

(a) Circuit

(b) Truth table and transistor states

Figure A.18   CMOS realization of a NOR gate.

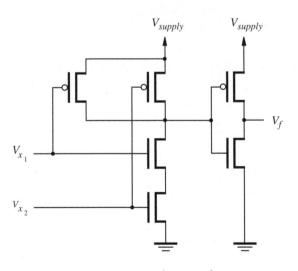

Figure A.19   CMOS realization of an AND gate.

Circuits that use lower power supply voltages dissipate much less power (power dissipation is proportional to V_{supply}^2), which means that more transistors can be placed on a chip without causing overheating. A drawback of lower power supply voltage is reduced noise immunity.

Transitions between low and high signal levels in a CMOS inverter are illustrated in more detail in Figure A.20. The blue curve, known as the *transfer characteristic*, shows the output voltage as a function of the input voltage. It indicates that a rather sharp transition

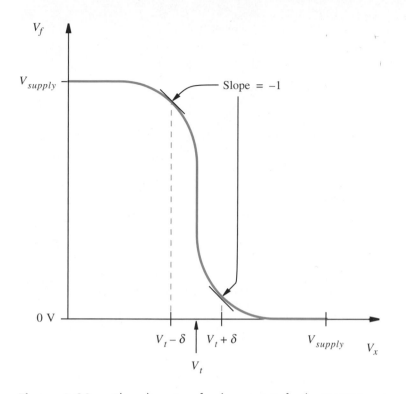

Figure A.20   The voltage transfer characteristic for the CMOS inverter.

in output voltage takes place when the input voltage passes through the value of about $V_{supply}/2$. There is a *threshold* voltage, V_t, and a small value δ such that $V_{out} \approx V_{supply}$ if $V_{in} < V_t - \delta$ and $V_{out} \approx 0$ if $V_{in} > V_t + \delta$. This means that the input signal need not be exactly equal to the nominal value of either 0 or V_{supply} to produce the correct output signal. There is room for some error, called *noise,* in the input signal that will not cause adverse effects. The amount of noise that can be tolerated is called the *noise margin.* This margin is $V_{supply} - (V_t + \delta)$ volts when the logic value of the input is 1, and it is $V_t - \delta$ when the logic value of the input is 0. CMOS circuits have excellent noise margins.

In this section, we have introduced the basic features of CMOS circuits. For a more detailed discussion of this technology the reader may consult References [1] and [8].

A.5.2   PROPAGATION DELAY

Logic circuits do not switch instantaneously from one state to another. Speed is measured by the rate at which state changes can take place. A related parameter is *propagation delay,* which is defined in Figure A.21. When a state change takes place at the input, a delay is encountered before the corresponding change at the output is observed. This propagation delay is usually measured between the 50-percent points of the transitions, as shown in the

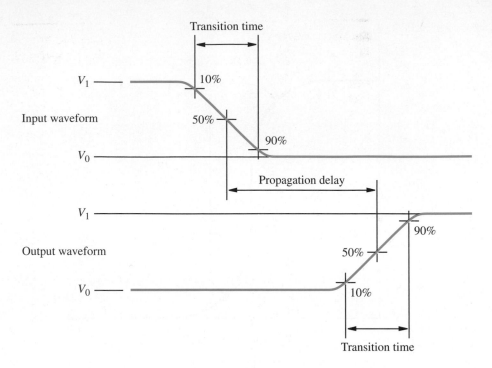

Figure A.21   Definition of propagation delay and transition time.

figure. Another important parameter is the *transition time,* which is normally measured between the 10- and 90-percent points of the signal swing, as shown. The maximum speed at which a logic circuit can be operated decreases as the propagation delay through different paths within that circuit increases. The delay along any path in a logic circuit is the sum of individual gate delays along this path.

A.5.3   FAN-IN AND FAN-OUT CONSTRAINTS

The number of inputs to a logic gate is called its *fan-in.* The number of gate inputs that the output of a logic gate drives is called its *fan-out.* Practical circuits do not allow large fan-in and fan-out because they both have an adverse effect on the propagation delay and hence the speed of the circuit.

    Each transistor in a CMOS gate contributes a certain amount of capacitance. As the capacitance increases, the circuit becomes slower and its signal levels and noise margins become worse. Therefore, it is necessary to limit the fan-in and fan-out, typically to a number less than ten. If the number of desired inputs exceeds the maximum fan-in, it is necessary to use an additional gate of the same type. Figure A.9*a* shows how two gates of the same type can be cascaded. If the number of outputs that have to be driven by a particular gate exceeds the acceptable fan-out, it is possible to use two copies of that gate.

A.5.4   TRI-STATE BUFFERS

In the logic gates discussed so far, it is not possible to connect the outputs of two gates together. This would make no sense from the logic point of view because if one gate generated an output value of 1 and the other an output of 0, it would be uncertain what the combined output signal would be. More importantly, in CMOS circuits, the gate that generates the output of 1 establishes a direct path from the output terminal to V_{supply}, while the gate that generates 0 establishes a path to ground. Thus, the two gates would provide a short circuit across the power supply, which would damage the gates.

Yet, in the design of computer systems, there are many cases where an input signal to a circuit may be derived from one of a number of different sources. This can be done using multiplexer logic circuits, which are discussed in Section A.10. It can also be done using special gates called *tri-state buffers*. A tri-state buffer has three states. Two of the states produce the normal 0 and 1 signals. The third state places the output terminal of the buffer into a high-impedance state in which the output is electrically disconnected from the input it is supposed to drive.

Figure A.22 depicts a tri-state buffer. The buffer has two inputs and one output. The *enable* input, e, controls the operation of the buffer. When $e = 1$, the output f has the same logic value as the input x. When $e = 0$, the output is placed in the high-impedance state, Z. An equivalent circuit is shown in Figure A.22b. The triangular symbol in this figure represents a noninverting driver. This is a circuit that performs no logic operation

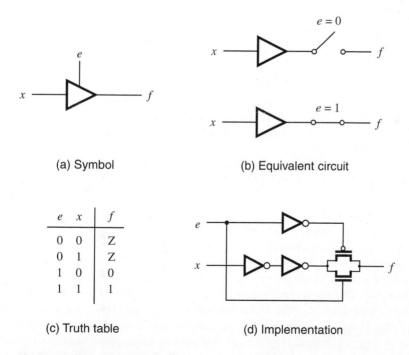

(a) Symbol   (b) Equivalent circuit

e	x	f
0	0	Z
0	1	Z
1	0	0
1	1	1

(c) Truth table   (d) Implementation

Figure A.22   Tri-state buffer.

because its output merely replicates the input signal. Its purpose is to provide additional electrical driving capability. When combined with the output switch shown in the figure, it behaves according to the truth table given in Figure A.22c. This table describes the required tri-state behavior. Figure A.22d shows a circuit implementation of the tri-state buffer. One NMOS and one PMOS transistor are connected in parallel to implement the switch, which is connected to the output of the driver. Because the two transistor types require complementary control signals at their gate inputs, an inverter is used as shown. When $e = 0$, both transistors are turned off, resulting in an open switch. When $e = 1$, both transistors are turned on, resulting in a closed switch.

The driver circuit may be required to drive a number of inputs of other gates whose combined capacitance exceeds the drive capability of an ordinary logic gate circuit. To provide a sufficient drive capability, the driver circuit needs larger transistors. Hence, the two cascaded NOT gates that realize the driver are implemented with transistors of larger size than in regular logic gates.

The reader may wonder why is it necessary to use the PMOS transistor in the output switch because from the logic function point of view the same behavior could be achieved using just the NMOS transistor. The reason is that these transistors have to "pass" the logic value generated by the driver circuit to the output f, and it turns out that NMOS transistors pass the logic value 0 well but the logic value 1 poorly, while PMOS transistors pass 1 well and 0 poorly. The parallel arrangement of NMOS and PMOS transistors passes both 1s and 0s well. For a more detailed discussion of this issue and tri-state buffers in general, the reader may consult Reference [1].

A.6   FLIP-FLOPS

The majority of applications of digital logic require the storage of information. For example, a circuit that controls a combination lock must remember the sequence in which the digits are dialed in order to determine whether to open the lock. Another important example is the storage of programs and data in the memory of a digital computer.

The basic electronic element for storing binary information is called a *latch*. Consider the two cross-coupled NOR gates in Figure A.23a. Let us examine this circuit, starting with the situation in which R = 1 and S = 0. Simple analysis shows that $Q_a = 0$ and $Q_b = 1$. Under this condition, both inputs to gate G_a are equal to 1. Thus, if R is changed to 0, no change will take place at the outputs Q_a and Q_b. If S is set to 1 with R equal to 0, Q_a and Q_b will become 1 and 0, respectively, and will remain in this state after S is returned to 0. Hence, this logic circuit constitutes a memory element, or a latch, that remembers which of the two inputs S and R was most recently equal to 1. A truth table for this latch is given in Figure A.23b. Some typical waveforms that characterize the latch are shown in Figure A.23c. The arrows in Figure A.23c indicate the cause-effect relationships among the signals. Note that when the R and S inputs change from 1 to 0 at the same time, the resulting state is undefined. In practice, the latch will assume one of its two stable states at random. The input valuation R = S = 1 is not used in most applications of such latches.

Because of the nature of the operation of the preceding circuit, the S and R lines are referred to as the *set* and *reset* inputs. Since the valuation R = S = 1 is normally not used,

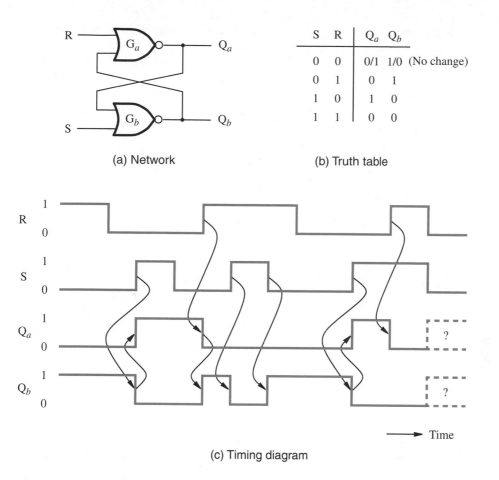

S	R	Q_a	Q_b	
0	0	0/1	1/0	(No change)
0	1	0	1	
1	0	1	0	
1	1	0	0	

(a) Network   (b) Truth table

(c) Timing diagram

Figure A.23 A basic latch implemented with NOR gates.

the Q_a and Q_b outputs are usually labeled as Q and $\overline{Q}$, respectively. However, $\overline{Q}$ should be regarded merely as a symbol representing the second output of the latch rather than as the complement of Q, because the input valuation R = S = 1 yields Q = $\overline{Q}$ = 0.

A.6.1 GATED LATCHES

Many applications require that the time at which a latch is set or reset be controlled from an input other than R and S, called a *clock* input. The resulting configuration is called a *gated SR latch*. A logic circuit, truth table, characteristic waveforms, and a graphical symbol for such a latch are given in Figure A.24. When the clock, *Clk,* is equal to 1, signals S' and R' follow the inputs S and R, respectively. On the other hand, when *Clk* = 0, signals S' and R' are equal to 0, and no change in the state of the latch can take place.

So far we have used truth tables to describe the behavior of logic circuits. A truth table gives the output of a network for various input valuations. Logic circuits whose outputs are

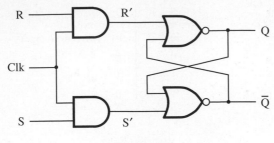

Clk	S	R	Q(t + 1)
0	x	x	Q(t) (no change)
1	0	0	Q(t) (no change)
1	0	1	0
1	1	0	1
1	1	1	x

(a) Circuit   (b) Truth table

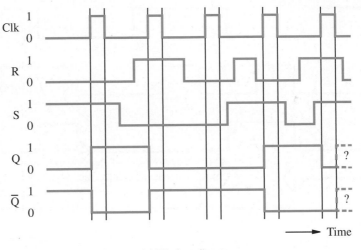

(c) Timing diagram

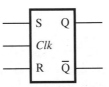

(d) Graphical symbol

Figure A.24   Gated SR latch.

uniquely defined for each input valuation are referred to as *combinational circuits*. This is the class of circuits discussed in Sections A.1 to A.4. When memory elements are present, a different class of circuits is obtained. The output of such circuits is a function not only of the present valuation of the input variables but also of their previous behavior. An example of this is shown in Figure A.24. Circuits of this type are called *sequential circuits*.

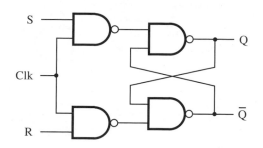

Figure A.25   Gated SR latch implemented with NAND gates.

Because of the memory property, the truth table for the latch has to be modified to show the effect of its present state. Figure A.24b describes the behavior of the gated SR latch, where $Q(t)$ denotes its present state. The transition to the next state, $Q(t + 1)$, occurs following a clock pulse. Note that for the input valuation $S = R = 1$, $Q(t + 1)$ is undefined for reasons discussed earlier.

The gated SR latch can be implemented using NAND gates as shown in Figure A.25. It is a useful exercise to show that this circuit is functionally equivalent to the circuit in Figure A.24a (see Problem A.20).

A second type of gated latch, called the *gated D latch,* is shown in Figure A.26. In this case, the two signals S and R are derived from a single input D. At a clock pulse, the Q output is set to 1 if $D = 1$ or is reset to 0 if $D = 0$. This means that the D flip-flop samples the D input at the time the clock is high and stores that information until the next clock pulse arrives.

A.6.2   MASTER-SLAVE FLIP-FLOP

In the circuit of Figure A.24, we assumed that while $Clk = 1$, the inputs S and R do not change. Inspection of the circuit reveals that the outputs will respond immediately to any change in the S or R input during this time. Similarly, for the circuit of Figure A.26, $Q = D$ while $Clk = 1$. This is undesirable in many cases, particularly in circuits involving counters and shift registers, which will be discussed later. In such circuits, immediate propagation of logic conditions from the data inputs (R, S, and D) to the latch outputs may lead to incorrect operation. The concept of a *master-slave* organization eliminates this problem. Two gated D latches can be connected to form a *master-slave D flip-flop,* as shown in Figure A.27a. The first, referred to as the master, is connected to the input line D when Clock $= 1$. A 1-to-0 transition of the clock isolates the master from the input and transfers the contents of the master stage to the slave stage. We can see that no direct path ever exists from the input D to the output Q.

It should be noted that while Clock $= 1$, the state of the master stage is immediately affected by changes in the input D. The function of the slave stage is to hold the value at the output of the flip-flop while the master stage is being set to the next-state value determined by the D input. The new state is transferred from the master to the slave after the 1-to-0

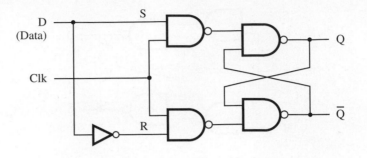

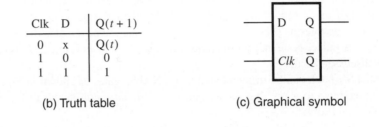

(a) Circuit

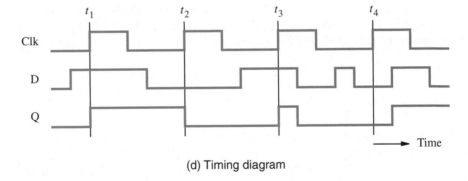

Clk	D	Q(t + 1)
0	x	Q(t)
1	0	0
1	1	1

(b) Truth table

(c) Graphical symbol

(d) Timing diagram

Figure A.26   Gated D latch.

transition on Clock. At this point, the master stage is isolated from the inputs so that further changes in the D input will not affect this transfer. Examples of state transitions are shown in the form of a timing diagram in Figure A.27b.

The term *flip-flop* refers to a storage element that changes its output state at the edge of a controlling clock signal. In the above master-slave D flip-flop, the observable change takes place at the negative (1-to-0) edge of the clock. The change is observable when it reaches the Q terminal of the slave stage. Note that in the circuit in Figure A.27 we could have used the complement of Clock to control the master stage and the uncomplemented Clock to control the slave stage. In that case, the changes in the flip-flop output Q would occur at the positive edge of the clock.

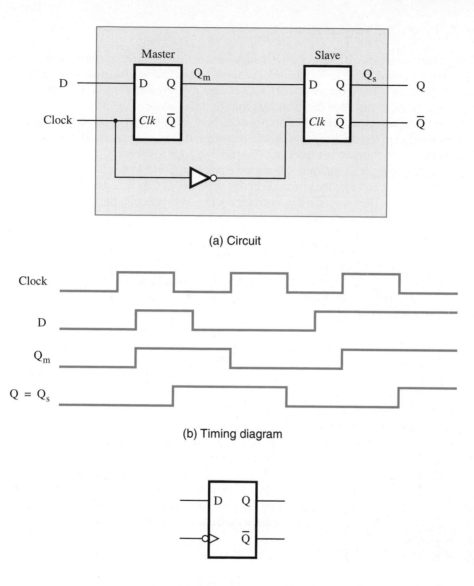

(a) Circuit

(b) Timing diagram

(c) Graphical symbol

Figure A.27   Master-slave D flip-flop.

A graphical symbol for a flip-flop is given in Figure A.27c. We have used an arrowhead, instead of the label *Clk,* to denote the clock input to the flip-flop. This is a standard way of denoting that the positive edge of the clock causes changes in the state of the flip-flop. In our figure it is the negative edge which causes changes, so a small circle is used (in addition to the arrowhead) on the clock input.

A.6.3 EDGE TRIGGERING

A flip-flop is said to be *edge triggered* if data present at the input are transferred to the output only at a transition in the clock signal. The input and output are isolated from each other at all other times. The terms *positive (leading) edge triggered* and *negative (trailing) edge triggered* describe flip-flops in which data transfer takes place at the 0-to-1 and the 1-to-0 clock transitions, respectively. For proper operation, edge-triggered flip-flops require the triggering edge of the clock pulse to be well defined and to have a very short transition time. The master-slave flip-flop in Figure A.27 is negative-edge triggered.

A different implementation for a negative-edge-triggered D flip-flop is given in Figure A.28a. Let us consider the operation of this flip-flop. If $Clk = 1$, the outputs of gates 2 and 3 are both 0. Therefore, the flip-flop outputs Q and $\overline{Q}$ maintain the current state of the flip-flop. It is easy to verify that during this period, points P3 and P4 immediately respond to changes at D. Point P3 is kept equal to $\overline{D}$, and P4 is maintained equal to D. When Clk drops to 0, these values are transmitted to P1 and P2 by gates 2 and 3, respectively. Thus, the output latch, consisting of gates 5 and 6, acquires the new state to be stored.

We now verify that while $Clk = 0$, further changes at D do not change points P1 and P2. Consider two cases. First, suppose $D = 0$ at the negative edge of Clk. The 1 at P2 maintains an input of 1 at each of the gates 2 and 4, holding P1 and P2 at 0 and 1, respectively, independent of further changes in D. Second, suppose $D = 1$ at the negative edge of Clk. The 1 at P1 means that further changes at D cannot affect the output of gate 1, which is maintained at 0.

When Clk goes to 1 at the start of the next clock pulse, points P1 and P2 are again forced to 0, isolating the output from the remainder of the circuit. Points P3 and P4 then follow changes at D, as we have previously described.

An example of the operation of this type of D flip-flop is shown in Figure A.28b. The state acquired by the flip-flop upon the 1 to 0 transition of Clk is equal to the value on the D input immediately preceding this transition. However, there is a critical time period T_{CR} around the negative edge of Clk during which the value on D should not change. This region is split into two parts, the *setup time* before the clock edge and the *hold time* after the clock edge, as shown in the figure. The timing diagram shows that the output Q changes slightly after the negative edge of the clock. This is the effect of the propagation delay through the NOR gates.

A.6.4 T FLIP-FLOP

The most commonly used flip-flops are the D flip-flops because they are useful for temporary storage of data. However, there are applications for which other types of flip-flops are convenient. Counter circuits, discussed in Section A.8, are implemented efficiently using T flip-flops. A *T flip-flop* changes its state every clock cycle if its input T is equal to 1. We say that it "toggles" its state.

Figure A.29 presents the T flip-flop. Its circuit is derived from a D flip-flop as shown in Figure A.29a. Its truth table, graphical symbol, and a timing diagram example are also given in the figure. Note that we have assumed a positive-edge-triggered flip-flop.

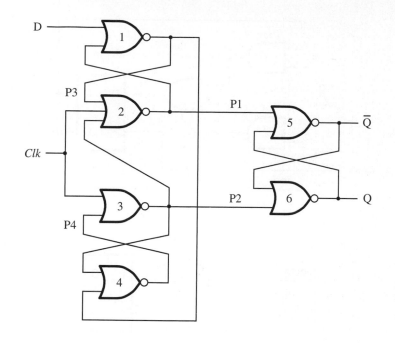

(a) Network

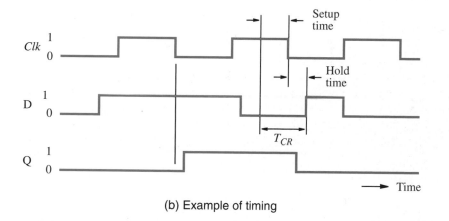

(b) Example of timing

Figure A.28 A negative-edge-triggered D flip-flop.

A.6.5 JK FLIP-FLOP

Another flip-flop that is sometimes encountered in practice is the *JK flip-flop,* which combines the behaviors of SR and T flip-flops. It is presented in Figure A.30. Its operation is defined by the truth table in Figure A.30b. The first three entries in this table define the

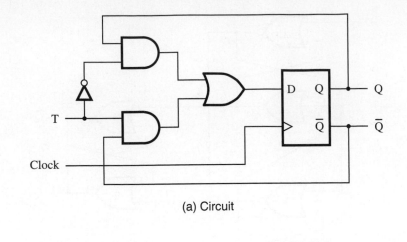

(a) Circuit

T	Q(t + 1)
0	Q(t)
1	Q̄(t)

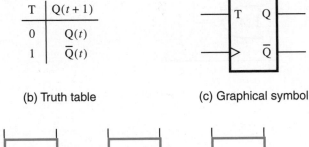

(b) Truth table

(c) Graphical symbol

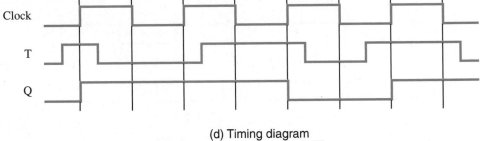

(d) Timing diagram

Figure A.29   T flip-flop.

same behavior as those in Figure A.24*b* (when *Clk* = 1), so that J and K correspond to S and R. For the input valuation J = K = 1, the next state is defined as the complement of the present state of the flip-flop. That is, when J = K = 1, the flip-flop functions as a *toggle,* reversing its present state.

A JK flip-flop can be implemented using a D flip-flop connected such that

$$D = J\overline{Q} + \overline{K}Q$$

The corresponding circuit is shown in Figure A.30*a*.

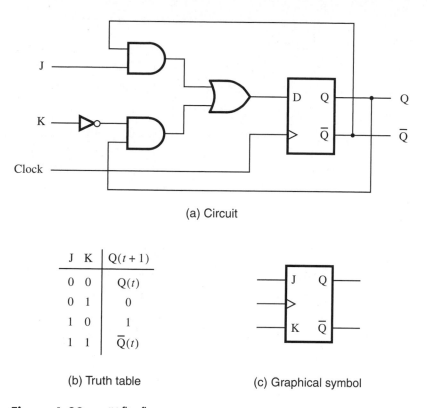

(a) Circuit

J	K	$Q(t+1)$
0	0	$Q(t)$
0	1	0
1	0	1
1	1	$\overline{Q}(t)$

(b) Truth table

(c) Graphical symbol

Figure A.30   JK flip-flop.

The JK flip-flop is versatile. It can be used to store data, just like the D flip-flop. It can also be used to build counters, because it behaves like the T flip-flop if its J and K input terminals are connected together.

A.6.6   FLIP-FLOPS WITH PRESET AND CLEAR

The state of a flip-flop is determined by its present state and the logic values on its input terminals. Sometimes it is desirable to force a flip-flop into a particular state, either 0 or 1, regardless of its present state and the values of the normal inputs. For example, when a computer is powered on, it is necessary to place all flip-flops into a known state. Usually, this means resetting their outputs to state 0. In some cases it is desirable to preset some flip-flops into state 1.

Figure A.31 illustrates how preset and clear control inputs can be added to a master-slave D flip-flop, to force the flip-flop into state 1 or 0 independent of the D input and the clock. These inputs are active low, as indicated by the overbars and bubbles in the figure. When both the $\overline{\text{Preset}}$ and $\overline{\text{Clear}}$ inputs are equal to 1, the flip-flop is controlled by the clock and D input in the normal way. When $\overline{\text{Preset}} = 0$, the flip-flop is forced to the 1 state, and

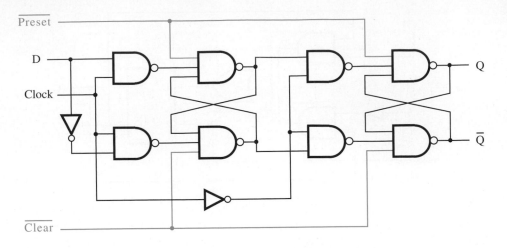

(a) Circuit

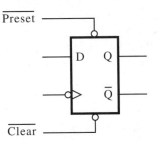

(b) Graphical symbol

Figure A.31   Master-slave D flip-flop with Preset and Clear.

when $\overline{\text{Clear}} = 0$, the flip-flop is forced to the 0 state. The preset and clear controls are also often incorporated in the other flip-flop types.

A.7   REGISTERS AND SHIFT REGISTERS

An individual flip-flop can be used to store one bit. However, in machines in which data are handled in words consisting of many bits (perhaps as many as 64), it is convenient to arrange a number of flip-flops into a common structure called a *register*. The operation of all flip-flops in a register is synchronized by a common clock. Thus, data are written (loaded) into or read from all flip-flops at the same time.

Processing of digital data often requires the capability to shift and rotate the data, so it is necessary to provide the hardware with this facility. A simple mechanism for realizing both operations is a register whose contents may be shifted to the right or left one bit position

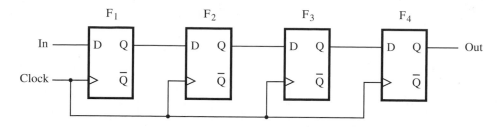

Figure A.32   A simple shift register.

at a time. As an example, consider the 4-bit shift register in Figure A.32. It consists of D flip-flops connected so that each clock pulse will cause the transfer of the contents (state) of F_i to F_{i+1}, effecting a "right shift." Data are shifted serially into and out of the register. A rotation of the data can be implemented by connecting Out to In.

Proper operation of a shift register requires that its contents be shifted exactly one position for each clock pulse. This places a constraint on the type of storage elements that can be used. Gated latches, depicted in Figure A.26, are not suitable for this purpose. While the clock is high, the value on the D input quickly propagates to the output. From there, the value propagates through the next gated latch in the same manner. Hence, there is no control over the number of shifts that will take place during a single clock pulse. This number depends on the propagation delays of the gated latches and the duration of the clock pulse. The solution to the problem is to use either master-slave or edge-triggered flip-flops.

A particularly useful form of a shift register is one that can be loaded and read in parallel. This can be accomplished with some additional gating as illustrated in Figure A.33, which shows a 4-bit register constructed with D flip-flops. The register can be loaded either serially or in parallel. When the register is clocked, a shift takes place if $\overline{\text{Shift/Load}} = 0$; otherwise, a parallel load is performed.

A.8   COUNTERS

In the preceding section, we discussed the applicability of flip-flops in the construction of shift registers. They are equally useful in the implementation of *counter* circuits. It is hardly necessary to justify the need for counters in digital machines. In addition to being hardware mechanisms for realizing ordinary counting functions, counters are also used to generate control and timing signals. A counter driven by a high-frequency clock can be used to produce signals whose frequencies are submultiples of the original clock frequency. In such applications a counter is said to be functioning as a *scaler*.

A simple three-stage (or 3-bit) counter constructed with T flip-flops is shown in Figure A.34. Recall that when the T input is equal to 1, the flip-flop acts as a toggle, that is, its state changes with each successive clock pulse. Thus, two clock pulses will cause Q_0 to change from the 1 state to the 0 state and back to the 1 state or from 0 to 1 to 0. This means

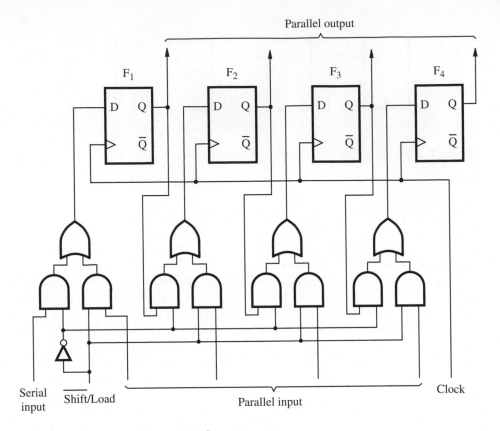

Figure A.33   Parallel-access shift register.

that the output waveform of Q_0 has half the frequency of the clock. Similarly, because the second flip-flop is driven by Q_0, the waveform at Q_1 has half the frequency of Q_0, or one-fourth the frequency of the clock. Note that we have assumed that the positive edge of the clock input to each flip-flop triggers the change of its state.

Such a counter is often called a *ripple counter* because the effect of an input clock pulse ripples through the counter. For example, the positive edge of pulse 4 will change the state of Q_0 from 1 to 0. This change in Q_0 will then force Q_1 from 1 to 0, which in turn forces Q_2 from 0 to 1. If each flip-flop introduces some delay Δ, then the delay in setting Q_2 is 3Δ. Such delays can be a problem when very fast operation of counter circuits is required. In many applications, however, these delays are small in comparison with the clock period and can be neglected.

With the addition of some extra logic gates, it is possible to construct a "synchronous" counter in which each stage is under the control of the common clock so that all flip-flops can change their states simultaneously. Such counters are capable of operation at higher speed because the total propagation delay is reduced considerably. In contrast, the counter in Figure A.34 is said to be "asynchronous."

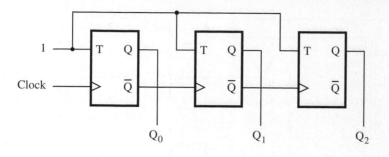

(a) Circuit

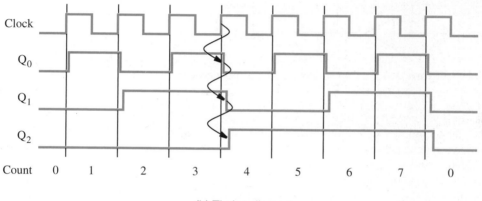

(b) Timing diagram

Figure A.34   A 3-bit up-counter.

A.9 DECODERS

Much of the information in computers is handled in a highly encoded form. In an instruction, an n-bit field may be used to denote 1 out of 2^n possible choices for the action to be taken. To perform the desired action, the encoded instruction must first be decoded. A circuit capable of accepting an n-variable input and generating the corresponding output signal on one out of 2^n output lines is called a *decoder*. A simple example of a two-input to four-output decoder is given in Figure A.35. One of the four output lines is selected by the inputs x_1 and x_2, as indicated in the figure. The selected output has the logic value 1, and the remaining outputs have the value 0.

Other useful types of decoders exist. For example, using information in BCD form often requires decoding circuits in which a four-variable BCD input is used to select 1 out of 10 possible outputs. As another specific example, let us consider a decoder suitable for driving a seven-segment display. Figure A.36 shows the structure of a seven-segment

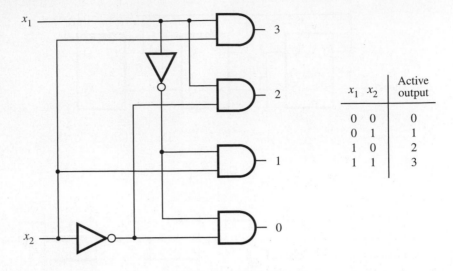

Figure A.35   A two-input to four-output decoder.

element used for display purposes. We can easily see that any decimal number from zero to nine can be displayed with this element simply by turning some segments on (light) while leaving others off (dark). The necessary functions are indicated in the table. They can be realized using the decoding circuit shown in the figure. Note that the circuit is constructed with NAND gates. We encourage the reader to verify that the circuit implements the required functions.

A.10   MULTIPLEXERS

In the preceding section, we saw that decoders select one output line on the basis of input signals. The selected output line has logic value 1, while the other outputs have the value 0. Another class of very useful selector circuits exists in which any one of n data inputs can be selected to appear as the output. The choice is governed by a set of "select" inputs. Such circuits are called *multiplexers*. An example of a multiplexer circuit is shown in Figure A.37. It has two select inputs, w_1 and w_2. Their four possible valuations are used to select one of four inputs, x_1, x_2, x_3, or x_4, to appear as the output z. A simple logic circuit that can implement the required operation is also given. Obviously, the same structure can be used to realize larger multiplexers, in which k select inputs are used to connect one of the 2^k data inputs to the output.

The obvious application of multiplexers is in the gating of data that may come from a number of different sources. For example, loading a 16-bit data register from one of four distinct sources can be accomplished with sixteen 4-input multiplexers.

No.	x_1	x_2	x_3	x_4	a	b	c	d	e	f	g
0	0	0	0	0	1	1	1	1	1	1	0
1	0	0	0	1	0	1	1	0	0	0	0
2	0	0	1	0	1	1	0	1	1	0	1
3	0	0	1	1	1	1	1	1	0	0	1
4	0	1	0	0	0	1	1	0	0	1	1
5	0	1	0	1	1	0	1	1	0	1	1
6	0	1	1	0	1	0	1	1	1	1	1
7	0	1	1	1	1	1	1	0	0	0	0
8	1	0	0	0	1	1	1	1	1	1	1
9	1	0	0	1	1	1	1	1	0	1	1

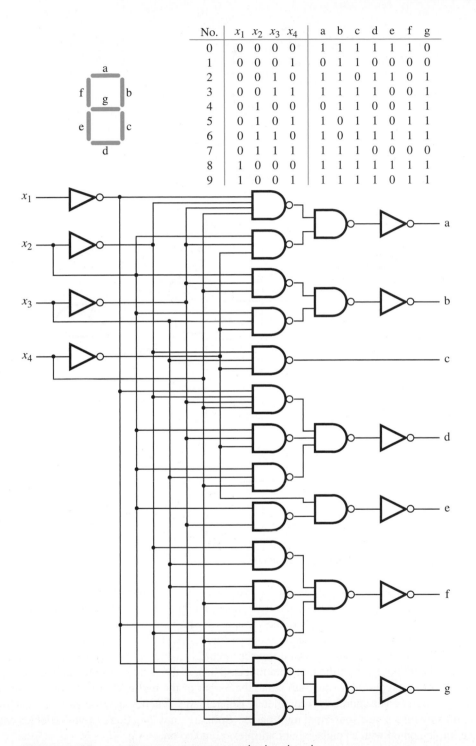

Figure A.36   A BCD to seven-segment display decoder.

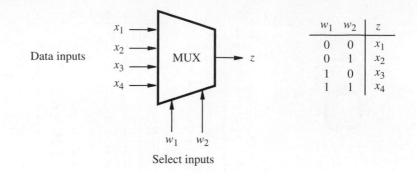

w_1	w_2	z
0	0	x_1
0	1	x_2
1	0	x_3
1	1	x_4

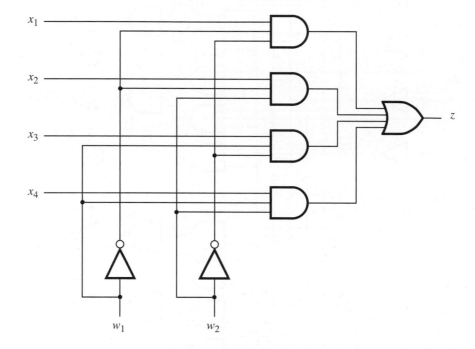

Figure A.37   A four-input multiplexer.

Multiplexers are also very useful as basic elements for implementing logic functions. Consider a function f defined by the truth table of Figure A.38. It can be represented as shown in the figure by factoring out the variables x_1 and x_2. Note that for each valuation of x_1 and x_2, the function f corresponds to one of four terms: 0, 1, x_3, or $\overline{x}_3$. This suggests the possibility of using a four-input multiplexer circuit, in which x_1 and x_2 are the two select inputs that choose one of the four data inputs. Then, if the data inputs are connected to 0, 1, x_3, or $\overline{x}_3$ as required by the truth table, the output of the multiplexer will correspond to the function f. The approach is completely general. Any function of three variables can be realized with a single four-input multiplexer. Similarly, any function of four variables can be implemented with an eight-input multiplexer, and so on.

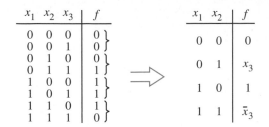

x_1	x_2	x_3	f
0	0	0	0
0	0	1	0
0	1	0	0
0	1	1	1
1	0	0	1
1	0	1	1
1	1	0	1
1	1	1	0

x_1	x_2	f
0	0	0
0	1	x_3
1	0	1
1	1	$\bar{x}_3$

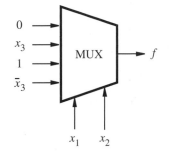

Figure A.38   Multiplexer implementation of a logic function.

A.11   PROGRAMMABLE LOGIC DEVICES (PLDS)

In previous sections we showed how logic circuits can be implemented using gates and flip-flops. In this section we will consider devices that can be used to implement circuits of various types, simply by programming them to perform the desired functions. They are called *programmable logic devices* (PLDs).

A.11.1   PROGRAMMABLE LOGIC ARRAY (PLA)

Any combinational logic function can be implemented in the sum-of-products form, as explained in Sections A.2 and A.3. A generalized circuit that can implement a variety of combinational functions may be organized as shown in Figure A.39. It has *n* input variables $(x_1, \ldots, x_n)$ and *m* output functions $(f_1, \ldots, f_m)$. Each function f_i is realized as a sum of product terms that involve the input variables. The variables $x_1, \ldots, x_n$ are presented in true and complemented form to the AND array, where up to *k* product terms are formed. These are then gated into the OR array, where the output functions are formed. To make this circuit customizable by a user, it is possible to use programmable connections to the AND and OR arrays.

A circuit in which connections to both the AND and the OR arrays can be programmed is called a *programmable logic array* (PLA). Figure A.40 illustrates the functional structure

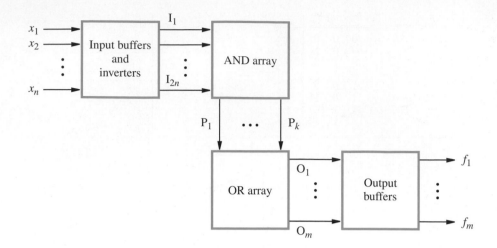

Figure A.39   A block diagram for a PLD.

of a PLA using a simple example. The programmable connections must be such that if no connection is made to a given input of an AND gate, the input behaves as if a logic value of 1 is driving it (that is, this input does not contribute to the product term realized by this gate). Similarly, if no connection is made to a given input of an OR gate, this input must have no effect on the output of the gate (that is, the input must behave as if a logic value of 0 is driving it).

Programmed connections may be realized in different ways. In one method, programming consists of blowing fuses in positions where connections are not required. This is done by applying higher-than-normal current. Another possibility is to use transistor switches controlled by erasable memory elements (see Section 8.3.3 on EPROM memory circuits) to provide the connections as desired. This allows the PLA to be reprogrammable.

The simple PLA in Figure A.40 can generate up to four product terms from three input variables. Two output functions may be implemented using these product terms. Some of the product terms may be used in more than one output function. The PLA is configured to realize the following two functions:

$$f_1 = x_1 x_2 + x_1 \bar{x}_3 + \bar{x}_1 \bar{x}_2 x_3$$
$$f_2 = x_1 x_2 + x_1 x_3 + \bar{x}_1 \bar{x}_2 x_3$$

Only four product terms are needed, because two terms can be shared by both functions.

Although Figure A.40 depicts clearly the basic functionality of a PLA, this style of presentation is awkward for describing a larger PLA. It is customary in technical literature to represent the product and sum terms by means of corresponding gate symbols that have only one symbolic input line. An × is placed on this line to represent each programmed connection. This drawing convention is used in Figure A.41 to represent the PLA example from Figure A.40. A programmable connection can be made at any crossing of a vertical line and a horizontal line in the diagram, to implement different functions of the input variables.

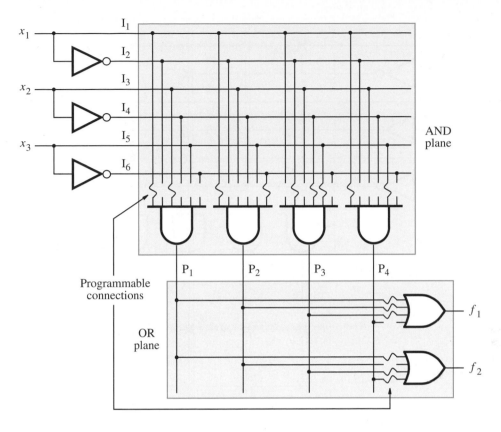

$$f_1 = x_1x_2 + x_1\bar{x}_3 + \bar{x}_1\bar{x}_2x_3$$
$$f_2 = x_1x_2 + \bar{x}_1\bar{x}_2x_3 + x_1x_3$$

Figure A.40   Functional structure of a PLA.

A.11.2 PROGRAMMABLE ARRAY LOGIC (PAL)

In a PLA, the inputs to both the AND array and the OR array are programmable. A similar circuit, in which the inputs to the AND array are programmable but the connections to the OR gates are fixed, provides enough flexibility for practical applications. Such circuits are known as *programmable array logic* (PAL) circuits.

Figure A.42 shows a simple example of a PAL that can implement two functions. The number of AND gates connected to each OR gate in a PAL determines the maximum number of product terms that can be realized in a sum-of-products representation of a given function. The AND gates are permanently connected to specific OR gates, which means that a particular product term cannot be shared among output functions.

The versatility of a PAL circuit may be enhanced further by including flip-flops in the outputs from the OR gates. Figure A.43 indicates the kind of flexibility that can be provided.

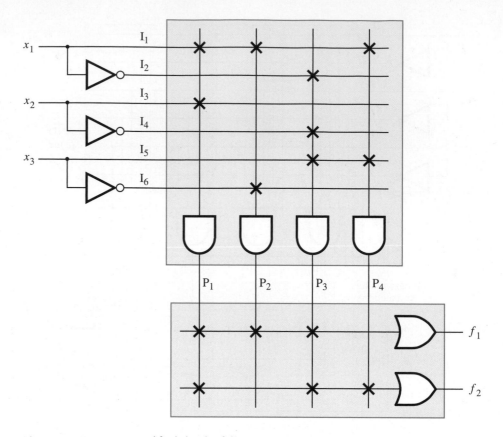

Figure A.41   A simplified sketch of the PLA in Figure A.40.

A multiplexer is used to choose whether a true, complemented, or stored (from the previous clock cycle) value of f is to be presented at the output terminal. The select inputs to the multiplexer are provided as programmable connections.

A.11.3 COMPLEX PROGRAMMABLE LOGIC DEVICES (CPLDs)

The PAL structure has been used within larger devices known as *complex programmable logic devices* (CPLDs). These devices comprise a number of PAL-like blocks and programmable interconnection wires. Figure A.44 indicates the organization of a CPLD chip. Each PAL-like block is connected to a number of input/output pins. Connections between PAL-like blocks are established by programming the switches associated with the interconnection wires.

The interconnection resource consists of horizontal and vertical wires. Each horizontal wire can be connected to some of the vertical wires by programming the corresponding switches. It is impractical to provide full connectivity, where each horizontal wire can be

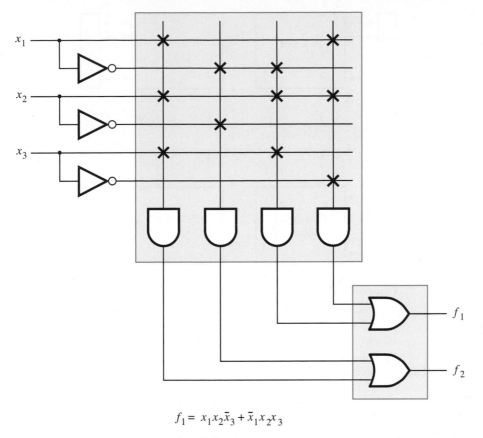

$$f_1 = x_1 x_2 \bar{x}_3 + \bar{x}_1 x_2 x_3$$

$$f_2 = \bar{x}_1 \bar{x}_2 + x_1 x_2 x_3$$

Figure A.42   An example of a PAL.

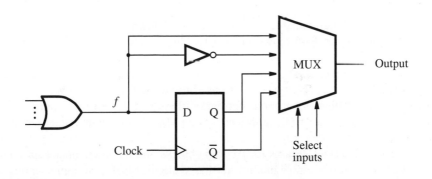

Figure A.43   Inclusion of a flip-flop in a PAL element.

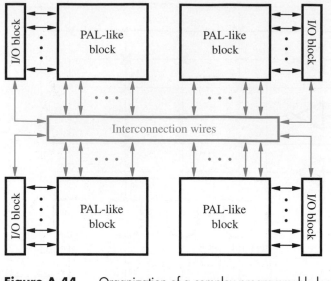

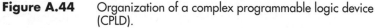

Figure A.44   Organization of a complex programmable logic device (CPLD).

connected to any of the vertical wires, because the number of required switches would be large. Satisfactory connectivity can be achieved with a much smaller number of switches.

Commercial CPLDs come in different sizes, ranging from 2 to more than 100 PAL-like blocks. A CPLD chip is programmed by loading the programming information into it as a serial stream of bits via a *JTAG port*. This is a 4-pin port that conforms to an IEEE standard developed by the Joint Test Action Group.

A.12   FIELD-PROGRAMMABLE GATE ARRAYS

The most versatile programmable logic devices are known as *field-programmable gate arrays* (FPGAs). Figure A.45 shows a conceptual block diagram of an FPGA. It consists of an array of logic blocks (indicated as black boxes) that can be connected by general interconnection resources. The *interconnect*, shown in blue, consists of wire segments and programmable switches. The switches are used to connect the logic blocks to the wire segments and to establish connections between different wire segments as desired. This allows a large degree of routing flexibility on the chip. Input and output buffers are provided for access to the pins of the chip.

There are a variety of designs for the logic blocks and the interconnect structure. A logic block may be just a simple multiplexer-based circuit capable of implementing logic functions as discussed in Section A.10. Another popular design uses a simple *lookup table* (LUT) as a logic block. For example, a four-input LUT can be implemented in the form of a 16-bit memory circuit in which the truth table of a logic function is stored. Each memory

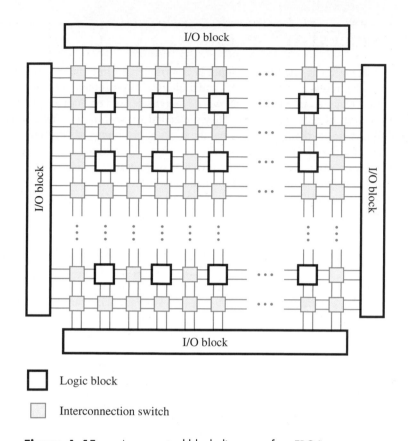

Logic block

Interconnection switch

Figure A.45   A conceptual block diagram of an FPGA.

bit corresponds to one combination of true or complemented values of the input variables. Such a lookup table can be programmed to implement any function of four variables. The logic blocks may contain flip-flops to provide additional flexibility of the type encountered in Figure A.43.

In addition to the logic blocks, many FPGA chips include a substantial number of memory cells (not shown in Figure A.45), which may be used to implement structures such as first-in first-out (FIFO) queues or RAM and ROM components in system-on-a-chip applications, which are discussed in Chapter 11.

FPGAs are available in a wide range of sizes. The largest devices contain billions of transistors and can be used to implement very large circuits. The growing popularity of FPGAs is due to the fact that they allow a designer to implement very complex logic circuits and large digital systems on a single chip without having to design and fabricate a custom VLSI chip, which is both expensive and time-consuming. Using CAD tools, it is possible to generate an FPGA design in a matter of days, rather than the months needed to produce a custom-designed VLSI chip. For an introductory discussion of designing circuits using FPGA devices and CAD tools the reader may consult Reference [1].

A.13 SEQUENTIAL CIRCUITS

A combinational circuit is one whose output is determined entirely by its present inputs. Examples of such circuits are the decoders and multiplexers presented in Sections A.9 and A.10. A different class of circuits are those whose outputs depend on both the present inputs and on the sequence of previous inputs. They are called *sequential circuits*. Such circuits can be in different *states,* depending on what the sequence of inputs has been up to a given time. The state of a circuit determines the behavior when various input patterns are applied to the circuit. We encountered two specific forms of such circuits in Sections A.7 and A.8, called shift registers and counters. In this section, we will introduce a general form for sequential circuits, and give a brief introduction to the design of these circuits.

A.13.1 DESIGN OF AN UP/DOWN COUNTER AS A SEQUENTIAL CIRCUIT

Figure A.34 shows the configuration of an up-counter, implemented with three T flip-flops, which counts in the sequence $0, 1, 2, \ldots, 7, 0, \ldots$. A similar circuit can be used to count in the down direction, that is, $0, 7, 6, \ldots, 1, 0, \ldots$ (see Problem A.26). These simple circuits are made possible by the toggle feature of T flip-flops.

We now consider the possibility of implementing such counters with D flip-flops. As a specific example, we will design a counter that counts either up or down, depending on the value of an external control input. To keep the example small, let us restrict the size to a mod-4 counter, which requires only two state bits to represent the four possible count values. We will show how this counter can be designed using general techniques for the synthesis of sequential circuits. The desired circuit will count up if an input signal x is equal to 0 and down if x is 1. Using the D flip-flops of the type presented in Figures A.27 and A.28, the count will change on the negative edge of the clock signal. Let us assume that we are particularly interested in the state when the count is equal to 2. Thus, an output signal, z, should be asserted when the count is equal to 2; otherwise $z = 0$.

The desired counter can be implemented as a sequential circuit. In order to determine what the new count will be when a clock pulse is applied, it is sufficient to know the value of x and the present count. It is not necessary to know what the actual sequence of previous input values was, as long as we know the present count that has been reached. This count value is said to determine the *present state* of the circuit, which is all that the circuit remembers about previous input values. If the present count is 2 and $x = 0$, the next count will be 3. It makes no difference whether the count of 2 was reached counting down from 3 or up from 1.

Before we show a circuit implementation, let us depict the desired behavior of the counter by means of a state diagram. The counter has four distinct states: S0, S1, S2, and S3. A *state diagram* is a graph in which states are represented as circles (sometimes called nodes). Transitions between states are indicated by labeled arrows. The label associated with an arrow specifies the value of the input x that will cause this particular transition to occur. We will design a circuit in which the value of the output is determined by the present state of the counter. Figure A.46 shows the state diagram of our up/down counter. For

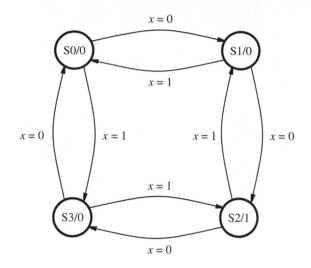

Figure A.46   State diagram of a mod-4 up/down counter that detects the count of 2.

Present state	Next state		Output z
	$x = 0$	$x = 1$	
S0	S1	S3	0
S1	S2	S0	0
S2	S3	S1	1
S3	S0	S2	0

Figure A.47   State table for the example of the up/down counter.

example, the arrow emanating from state S1 (count = 1) for an input $x = 0$ points to state S2, thus specifying the transition to state S2. An arrow from S2 to S3 specifies that when $x = 0$ the next clock pulse will cause a transition from S2 to S3. The output z should be 1 while the circuit is in state S2, and it should be 0 in states S0, S1, and S3. This is indicated inside each circle.

Note that the state diagram describes the functional behavior of the counter without any reference to how it is implemented. Figure A.46 can be used to describe an electronic digital circuit, a mechanical counter, or a computer program that behaves in this way. Such diagrams are a powerful means of describing any system that exhibits sequential behavior.

A different way of presenting the information in a state diagram is to use a *state table*. Figure A.47 gives the state table for the example in Figure A.46. The table indicates

Present state	Next state		Output z
	$x = 0$	$x = 1$	
$y_2 y_1$	$Y_2\ Y_1$	$Y_2\ Y_1$	
0 0	0 1	1 1	0
0 1	1 0	0 0	0
1 0	1 1	0 1	1
1 1	0 0	1 0	0

Figure A.48   State assignment for the example in Figure A.47.

transitions from all present states to the *next states,* as required by the applied input x. It also shows the value of the output signal, z, in each state.

Having specified the desired up/down counter in general terms, we will now consider its implementation. Two bits are needed to encode the four states that indicate the count. Let these bits be y_2 (high-order) and y_1 (low-order). The states of the counter are determined by the values of y_2 and y_1, which we will write in the form $y_2 y_1$. We will assign values to $y_2 y_1$ for each of the four states as follows: $S0 = 00$, $S1 = 01$, $S2 = 10$, and $S3 = 11$. We have chosen the assignment such that the binary number $y_2 y_1$ represents the count in an obvious way. The variables y_2 and y_1 are called the *state variables* of the sequential circuit. Using this *state assignment,* the state table for our example is as shown in Figure A.48. Note that we are using the variables Y_2 and Y_1 to denote the next state in the same manner as y_2 and y_1 are used to represent the present state.

It is important to note that we could have chosen a different assignment of $y_2 y_1$ values to the various states. For example, a possible state assignment is: $S0 = 10$, $S1 = 11$, $S2 = 01$, and $S3 = 00$. For a counter circuit, this assignment is less intuitive than the one in Figure A.48, but the resultant circuit will work properly. Different state assignments usually lead to different costs in implementing the circuit (see Problem A.30).

Our intention in this example is to use D flip-flops to store the values of the two state variables between successive clock pulses. The output, Q, of a flip-flop is the present-state variable y_i, and the input, D, is the next-state variable Y_i. Note that Y_i is a function of y_2, y_1, and x, as indicated in Figure A.48. From the figure, we see that

$$Y_2 = \overline{y}_2 y_1 \overline{x} + y_2 \overline{y}_1 \overline{x} + \overline{y}_2 \overline{y}_1 x + y_2 y_1 x$$
$$= y_2 \oplus y_1 \oplus x$$
$$Y_1 = \overline{y}_2 \overline{y}_1 \overline{x} + y_2 \overline{y}_1 \overline{x} + \overline{y}_2 \overline{y}_1 x + y_2 \overline{y}_1 x$$
$$= \overline{y}_1$$

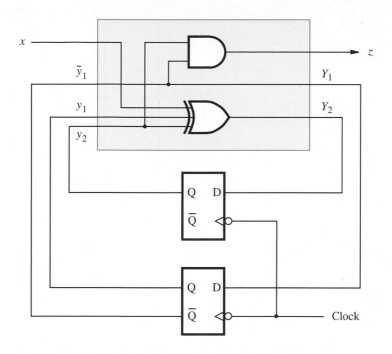

Figure A.49   Implementation of the up/down counter.

The output z is determined as

$$z = y_2\bar{y}_1$$

These expressions lead to the circuit shown in Figure A.49.

A.13.2 TIMING DIAGRAMS

To fully understand the operation of the counter circuit, it is useful to consider its timing diagram. Figure A.50 gives an example of a possible sequence of events. It assumes that state transitions (changes in flip-flop values) occur on the negative edge of the clock and that the counter starts in state S0. Since $x = 0$, the counter advances to state S1 at t_0, then to S2 at t_1, and to S3 at t_2. The output changes from 0 to 1 when the counter enters state S2. It goes back to 0 when state S3 is reached. At t_3, the counter goes to S0. We have assumed that at this time the input x changes to 1, causing the counter to count in the down sequence. When the count again reaches S2, at t_5, the output z goes to 1.

Note that all signal changes occur just after the negative edge of the clock, and signals do not change again until the negative edge of the next clock pulse. The delay from the clock edge to the time at which variables y_i change is the propagation delay of the flip-flops used to implement the counter circuit. It is important to note that the input x is also assumed to be controlled by the same clock, and it changes only near the beginning of a clock period.

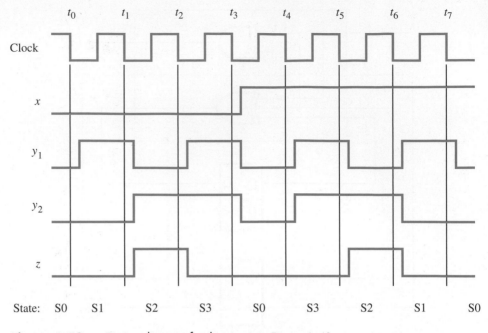

Figure A.50   Timing diagram for the circuit in Figure A.49.

These are essential features of circuits where all changes are controlled by a clock. Such circuits are called *synchronous sequential circuits*.

Another important observation concerns the relationship between the labels used in the state diagram in Figure A.46 and the timing diagram. For example, consider the clock period between t_1 and t_2. During this clock period, the machine is in state S2 and the input value is $x = 0$. This situation is described in the state diagram by the arrow emanating from state S2 labeled $x = 0$. Since this arrow points to state S3, the timing diagram shows y_2 and y_1 changing to the values corresponding to state S3 at the next clock edge, t_2.

A.13.3 THE FINITE STATE MACHINE MODEL

The specific example of the up/down counter implemented as a synchronous sequential circuit with flip-flops and combinational logic gates, as shown in Figure A.49, is easily generalized to the formal *finite state machine* model given in Figure A.51. In this model, the time delay through the delay elements is equal to the duration of the clock cycle. This is the time that elapses between changes in Y_i and the corresponding changes in y_i. The model assumes that the combinational logic block has no delay; hence, the outputs z, Y_1, and Y_2 are instantaneous functions of the inputs x, y_1, and y_2. In an actual circuit, some delay will be introduced by the flip-flops, as shown in Figure A.50. The circuit will work properly if the delay through the combinational logic block is short relative to the clock cycle. The next-state outputs Y_i must be available in time to cause the flip-flops to change to the desired next state at the end of the clock cycle.

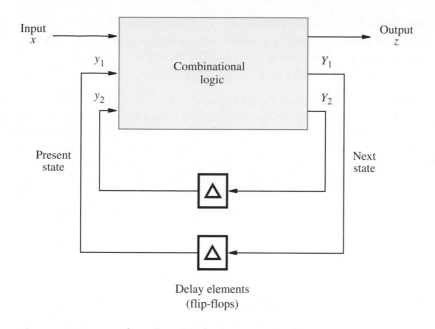

Figure A.51   A formal model of a finite state machine.

Inputs to the combinational logic block consist of the flip-flop outputs, y_i, which represent the present state, and the external input, x. The outputs of the block are the inputs to the flip-flops, which we have called Y_i, and the external output, z. When the active clock edge arrives marking the end of the present clock cycle, the values on the Y_i lines are loaded into the flip-flops. They become the next set of values of the state variables, y_i. Since these signals are connected to the input of the combinational block, they, along with the next value of the external input x, will produce new z and Y_i values. A clock cycle later, the new Y_i values are transferred to y_i, and the process repeats. In other words, the flip-flops constitute a feedback path from the output to the input of the combinational block, introducing a delay of one clock period.

Although we have shown only one external input, one external output, and two state variables in Figure A.51, it is clear that multiple inputs, outputs, and state variables are possible.

A.13.4   SYNTHESIS OF FINITE STATE MACHINES

Let us summarize how to design a synchronous sequential circuit having the general organization in Figure A.51. The design, or synthesis, process involves the following steps:

1.   Develop an appropriate state diagram or state table.
2.   Determine the number of flip-flops needed, and choose a suitable type of flip-flop.
3.   Determine the values to be stored in these flip-flops for each state in the state diagram. This is referred to as state assignment.

4. Develop the state-assigned state table.

5. Derive the next-state logic expressions needed to control the inputs of the flip-flops. Also, derive the expressions for the outputs of the circuit.

6. Use the derived expressions to implement the circuit.

Sequential circuits can easily be implemented with CPLDs and FPGAs because these devices contain flip-flops as well as combinational logic gates. Modern computer-aided design tools can be used to synthesize sequential circuits directly from a specification given in terms of a state diagram.

Our discussion of sequential circuits is based on the type of circuits that operate under the control of a clock. It is also possible to implement sequential circuits without using a clock. Such circuits are called *asynchronous sequential circuits*. Their design is not as straightforward as that of synchronous sequential circuits. For a complete treatment of both types of sequential circuits, consult one of the many books that specialize in logic design [1–7].

A.14 CONCLUDING REMARKS

The main purpose of this appendix is to acquaint the reader with the basic concepts in logic design and to provide an indication of the circuit configurations commonly used in the construction of computer systems. Familiarity with this material will lead to a much better understanding of the architectural concepts discussed in the main chapters of the book. As we have said in several places, the detailed design of logic circuits is done with the help of CAD tools. These tools take care of many details and can be used very effectively by a knowledgeable designer.

IC technology and CAD tools have revolutionized logic design. A variety of IC components are commercially available at ever-decreasing costs, and new developments and technological improvements are constantly occurring. In this appendix, we introduced some of the basic components that are useful in the design of digital systems.

PROBLEMS

A.1 **[E]** Implement the COINCIDENCE function in the sum-of-products form, where COINCIDENCE = $\overline{\text{XOR}}$.

A.2 **[M]** Prove the following identities by using algebraic manipulation and also by using truth tables.

(a) $\overline{a \oplus b} \oplus c = \overline{a}\overline{b}\overline{c} + ab\overline{c} + \overline{a}bc + a\overline{b}c$

(b) $x + w\overline{x} = x + w$

(c) $x_1\overline{x}_2 + \overline{x}_2x_3 + x_3\overline{x}_1 = x_1\overline{x}_2 + x_3\overline{x}_1$

A.3 **[E]** Derive minimal sum-of-products forms for the four 3-variable functions f_1, f_2, f_3, and f_4 given in Figure PA.1. Is there more than one minimal form for any of these functions? If so, derive all of them.

x_1	x_2	x_3	f_1	f_2	f_3	f_4
0	0	0	1	1	d	0
0	0	1	1	1	1	1
0	1	0	0	1	0	1
0	1	1	0	1	1	d
1	0	0	1	0	d	d
1	0	1	0	0	0	d
1	1	0	1	0	1	1
1	1	1	1	1	1	0

Figure PA.1   Logic functions for Problem A.3.

A.4 **[E]** Find the simplest sum-of-products form for the function f using the don't-care condition d, where

$$f = x_1(x_2\bar{x}_3 + x_2x_3 + \bar{x}_2\bar{x}_3x_4) + x_2\bar{x}_4(\bar{x}_3 + x_1)$$

and

$$d = x_1\bar{x}_2(x_3x_4 + \bar{x}_3\bar{x}_4) + \bar{x}_1\bar{x}_3x_4$$

A.5 **[M]** Consider the function

$$f(x_1, \ldots, x_4) = (x_1 \oplus x_3) + (x_1x_3 + \bar{x}_1\bar{x}_3)x_4 + x_1\bar{x}_2$$

(a) Use a Karnaugh map to find a minimum cost sum-of-products (SOP) expression for f.
(b) Find a minimum cost SOP expression for $\bar{f}$, which is the complement of f. Then, complement (using de Morgan's rule) this SOP expression to find an expression for f. The resulting expression will be in the product-of-sums (POS) form. Compare its cost with the SOP expression derived in part (a). Can you draw any general conclusions from this result?

A.6 **[E]** Find a minimum cost implementation of the function $f(x_1, x_2, x_3, x_4)$, where $f = 1$ if either one or two of the input variables have the logic value 1. Otherwise, $f = 0$.

A.7 **[M]** Figure A.6 defines the 4-bit encoding of BCD digits. Design a circuit that has four inputs labeled $b_3, \ldots, b_0$, and an output f, such that $f = 1$ if the 4-bit input pattern is a valid BCD digit; otherwise $f = 0$. Give a minimum cost implementation of this circuit.

A.8   **[M]** Two 2-bit numbers $A = a_1 a_0$ and $B = b_1 b_0$ are to be compared by a four-variable function $f(a_1, a_0, b_1, b_0)$. The function f is to have the value 1 whenever

$$v(A) \le v(B)$$

where $v(X) = x_1 \times 2^1 + x_0 \times 2^0$ for any 2-bit number. Assume that the variables A and B are such that $|v(A) - v(B)| \le 2$. Synthesize f using as few gates as possible.

A.9   **[M]** Repeat Problem A.8 for the requirement that $f = 1$ whenever

$$v(A) > v(B)$$

subject to the input constraint

$$v(A) + v(B) \le 4$$

A.10   **[E]** Prove that the associative rule does not apply to the NAND operator.

A.11   **[M]** Implement the following function with no more than six NAND gates, each having three inputs.

$$f = x_1 x_2 + x_1 x_2 x_3 + \bar{x}_1 \bar{x}_2 \bar{x}_3 x_4 + \bar{x}_1 \bar{x}_2 x_3 \bar{x}_4$$

Assume that both true and complemented inputs are available.

A.12   **[M]** Show how to implement the following function using six or fewer two-input NAND gates. Complemented input variables are not available.

$$f = x_1 x_2 + \bar{x}_3 + \bar{x}_1 x_4$$

A.13   **[E]** Implement the following function as economically as possible using only NAND gates. Assume that complemented input variables are not available.

$$f = (x_1 + x_3)(\bar{x}_2 + \bar{x}_4)$$

A.14   **[M]** A number code in which consecutive numbers are represented by binary patterns that differ only in one bit position is called a Gray code. A truth table for a 3-bit Gray code to binary code converter is shown in Figure PA.2a.

(a) Implement the three functions f_1, f_2, and f_3 using only NAND gates.

(b) A lower-cost network for performing this code conversion can be derived by noting the following relationships between the input and output variables.

$$f_1 = a$$
$$f_2 = f_1 \oplus b$$
$$f_3 = f_2 \oplus c$$

Using these relationships, specify the contents of a combinational network N that can be repeated, as shown in Figure PA.2b, to implement the conversion. Compare the total number of NAND gates required to implement the conversion in this form to the number required in part (a).

3-bit Gray code inputs			Binary code outputs		
a	b	c	f_1	f_2	f_3
0	0	0	0	0	0
0	0	1	0	0	1
0	1	1	0	1	0
0	1	0	0	1	1
1	1	0	1	0	0
1	1	1	1	0	1
1	0	1	1	1	0
1	0	0	1	1	1

(a) Three-bit Gray code to binary code conversion

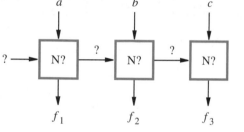

(b) Code conversion network

Figure PA.2   Gray code conversion example for Problem A.14.

A.15   [M] Implement the XOR function using only 4 two-input NAND gates.

A.16   [M] Figure A.36 defines a BCD to seven-segment display decoder. Give an implementation for this truth table using AND, OR, and NOT gates. Verify that the same functions are correctly implemented by the NAND gate circuits shown in the figure.

A.17   [M] In the logic network shown in Figure PA.3, gate 3 fails and produces the logic value 1 at its output F1 regardless of the inputs. Redraw the network, making simplifications wherever possible, to obtain a new network that is equivalent to the given faulty network and that contains as few gates as possible. Repeat this problem, assuming that the fault is at position F2, which is stuck at a logic value 0.

A.18   [M] Figure A.16 shows the structure of a general CMOS circuit. Derive a CMOS circuit that implements the function

$$f(x_1, \ldots, x_4) = \bar{x}_1\bar{x}_2 + \bar{x}_3\bar{x}_4$$

Use as few transistors as possible. (Hint: Consider series/parallel networks of transistors. Note the complementary series and parallel structure of the pull-up and pull-down networks in Figures A.17 and A.18.)

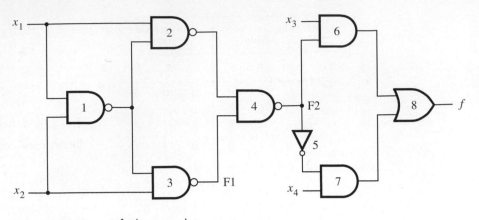

Figure PA.3   A faulty network.

A.19   **[E]** Draw the waveform for the output Q in the JK circuit of Figure A.30, using the input waveforms shown in Figure PA.4 and assuming that the flip-flop is initially in the 0 state.

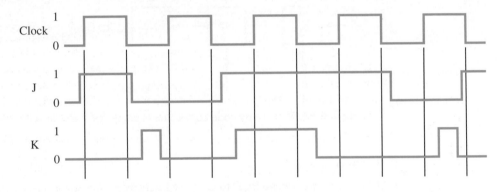

Figure PA.4   Input waveforms for a JK flip-flop.

A.20   **[E]** Derive the truth table for the NAND gate circuit in Figure PA.5. Compare it to the truth table in Figure A.23*b* and then verify that the circuit in Figure A.25 is equivalent to the circuit in Figure A.24*a*.

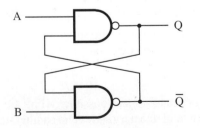

Figure PA.5   NAND latch.

A.21   **[M]** Compute both the setup time and the hold time in terms of NOR gate delays for the negative-edge-triggered D flip-flop shown in Figure A.28.

A.22   **[M]** In the circuit of Figure A.26a, replace all NAND gates with NOR gates. Derive a truth table for the resulting circuit. How does this circuit compare with the circuit in Figure A.26a?

A.23   **[M]** Figure A.32 shows a shift register network that shifts the data to the right one place at a time under the control of a clock signal. Modify this shift register to make it capable of shifting data either one or two places at a time under the control of the clock and an additional control input ONE/TWO.

A.24   **[D]** A 4-bit shift register that has two control inputs—INITIALIZE and RIGHT/LEFT—is required. When INITIALIZE is set to 1, the binary number 1000 should be loaded into the register independently of the clock input. When INITIALIZE $= 0$, pulses at the clock input should rotate this pattern. The pattern rotates right or left when the RIGHT/LEFT input is equal to 1 or 0, respectively. Give a suitable design for this register using D flip-flops that have preset and clear inputs as shown in Figure A.31.

A.25   **[M]** Derive a three-input to eight-output decoder network, with the restriction that the gates to be used cannot have more than two inputs.

A.26   **[D]** Figure A.34 shows a 3-bit up counter. A counter that counts in the opposite direction (that is, 7, 6, . . . , 1, 0, 7, . . .) is called a down counter. A counter capable of counting in both directions under the control of an UP/DOWN signal is called an up/down counter. Show a logic diagram for a 3-bit up/down counter that can also be preset to any state through parallel loading of its flip-flops from an external source. A LOAD/COUNT control is used to determine whether the counter is being loaded or is operating as a counter.

A.27   **[D]** Figure A.34 shows an asynchronous 3-bit up-counter. Design a 4-bit synchronous up-counter, which counts in the sequence 0, 1, 2, . . . , 15, 0 . . . . Use T flip-flops in your circuit. In the synchronous counter all flip-flops have to be able to change their states at the same time. Hence, the primary clock input has to be connected directly to the clock inputs of all flip-flops.

A.28   **[M]** A logic function to be implemented is described by the expression

$$f(x_1, x_2, x_3, x_4) = x_1 x_3 \bar{x}_4 + \bar{x}_1 \bar{x}_3 x_4 + \bar{x}_2 \bar{x}_3 \bar{x}_4$$

(a) Show an implementation of f in terms of an eight-input multiplexer circuit.

(b) Can f be realized with a four-input multiplexer circuit? If so, show how.

A.29   **[M]** Repeat Problem A.28 for

$$f(x_1, x_2, x_3, x_4) = x_1 \bar{x}_2 x_3 + x_2 x_3 x_4 + \bar{x}_1 \bar{x}_4$$

A.30   **[E]** Complete the design of the up/down counter in Figure A.46 by using the state assignment $S0 = 10$, $S1 = 11$, $S2 = 01$, and $S3 = 00$. How does this design compare with the one given in Section A.13.1?

A.31   [M] Design a 2-bit synchronous counter of the general form shown in Figure A.49 that counts in the sequence . . . , 0, 3, 1, 2, 0, . . . , using D flip-flops. This circuit has no external inputs, and the outputs are the flip-flop values themselves.

A.32   [M] Repeat Problem A.31 for a 3-bit counter that counts in the sequence . . . , 0, 1, 2, 3, 4, 5, 0, . . . , taking advantage of the unused count values 6 and 7 as don't-care conditions in designing the combinational logic.

A.33   [M] Finite state machines can be used to detect the occurrence of certain subsequences in the sequence of binary inputs applied to the machine. Such machines are called *finite state recognizers*. Suppose that a machine is to produce a 1 as its output whenever the input pattern 011 occurs.

(*a*) Draw the state diagram for this machine.

(*b*) Make a state assignment for the required number of flip-flops and construct the assigned state table, assuming that D flip-flops are to be used.

(*c*) Derive the logic expressions for the output and the next-state variables.

A.34   [M] Repeat part (*a*) only of Problem A.33 for a machine that is to recognize the occurrence of either of the subsequences 011 and 010 in the input sequence, including the cases where overlap occurs. For example, the input sequence 1101010110 . . . is to produce the output sequence 00000101010 . . . .

REFERENCES

1. S. Brown and Z. Vranesic, *Fundamentals of Digital Logic with VHDL Design*, 3rd ed., McGraw-Hill, Burr Ridge, IL, 2009.

2. M.M. Mano and M.D. Ciletti, *Digital Design*, 4th ed., Prentice-Hall, Upper Saddle River, NJ, 2007.

3. J. F. Wakerly, *Digital Design Principles and Practices*, 4th ed., Prentice-Hall, Englewood Cliffs, NJ, 2005.

4. R.H. Katz and G. Borriello, *Contemporary Logic Design*, 2nd ed., Pearson Prentice-Hall, Upper Saddle River, NJ, 2005.

5. C.H. Roth Jr., *Fundamentals of Logic Design*, 5th ed., Thomson/Brooks/Cole, Belmont, Ca., 2004.

6. D.D. Gajski, *Principles of Digital Design*, Prentice-Hall, Upper Saddle River, NJ, 1997.

7. J.P. Hayes, *Digital Logic Design,* Addison-Wesley, Reading, Mass., 1993.

8. A.S. Sedra and K.C. Smith, *Microelectronic Circuits*, 6th ed., Oxford, New York, 2009.

appendix

B

THE ALTERA NIOS II PROCESSOR

APPENDIX OBJECTIVES

In this appendix you will learn about the Altera Nios II
processor which has a RISC-style instruction set. The
discussion includes:

- Instruction set architecture
- Input/output capability
- Support for embedded applications

In Chapters 2 and 3 we introduced the basic concepts used in the design of instruction sets, mostly from the programmer's point of view. In this appendix we will examine the Nios II processor from the Altera Corporation as an example of a RISC-style commercial product that embodies the previously discussed concepts. The discussion follows closely the presentation of topics in Chapters 2 and 3.

The Nios II processor is intended for implementation in Field Programmable Gate Array (FPGA) devices (see Appendix A). It is provided in a software form that makes it easy to incorporate it into a computer system by using the Quartus II CAD (Computer-Aided Design) tools provided by Altera. The designed system is then downloaded into an FPGA device, thus resulting in an implementation that has the functionality of a typical computer.

The Quartus II software includes a tool called the SOPC Builder that can be used to design such systems. The SOPC Builder provides a variety of predesigned modules, called *IP cores*, which can be easily incorporated into a system. These modules include the Nios II processor, various I/O interfaces, and memory controllers. The modules are characterized by a variety of parameters which allow the user who is designing a custom system to specify the exact nature of the desired system. The Nios II processor can be configured to have a number of different features which require different amounts of logic circuitry for their implementation, thus affecting the performance and cost of the final system. Since the user can customize the design of the final circuit, we say that Nios II is a *soft* processor.

The ability to design a custom computer system, which can be implemented in a single FPGA chip, is attractive in embedded applications. We discuss such applications in Chapter 11.

B.1   NIOS II CHARACTERISTICS

The Nios II processor has a RISC-style architecture. Its features are very similar to those described in general terms in Chapter 2.

Data Sizes

The word length is 32 bits. Data are handled in 32-bit *words*, 16-bit *halfwords*, or 8-bit *bytes*. Byte addresses in a word are assigned in the little-endian arrangement, where the lower byte addresses are used for the less significant bytes.

Memory Access

Data in the memory are accessed only by Load and Store instructions, which load the data into general-purpose registers or store them from these registers. The Load and Store instructions can transfer data in word, halfword, and byte sizes.

Registers

There are 32 general-purpose registers and a number of control registers. All registers are 32 bits long.

Instructions

All instructions are 32 bits long. They have all of the RISC-style functionality presented in Chapter 2.

B.2   GENERAL-PURPOSE REGISTERS

Table B.1 presents the processor's 32 general-purpose registers. They are called r0 to r31, which are the names used in assembly-language instructions. Some registers are used for specific purposes and hence are also given names that are more indicative of their functionality, as shown in Table B.1. These names are also recognized by the assembler program. The registers intended for a specific purpose are:

- r0 always contains the constant 0. Reading this register returns the value 0; writing into it has no effect.
- r1 is used by the assembler as a temporary register. It should not be used in user programs.
- r24 and r29 are used for processing of exceptions.
- r25 and r30 are used exclusively by a debugging tool called the JTAG Debug Module.
- r26 is the global pointer to the data in a user program.
- r27 is the processor stack pointer.
- r28 is the frame pointer.
- r31 holds the return address when a subroutine is called.

The other registers are used for general purposes.

Table B.1   Nios II general-purpose registers.

Register	Name	Function
r0	zero	0x00000000
r1	at	Assembler Temporary
r2		
r3		
.	.	.
.	.	.
.	.	.
r23		
r24	et	Exception Temporary
r25	bt	Breakpoint Temporary
r26	gp	Global Pointer
r27	sp	Stack Pointer
r28	fp	Frame Pointer
r29	ea	Exception Return Address
r30	ba	Breakpoint Return Address
r31	ra	Return Address

Because register r0 always contains the value 0, it can be included as an operand in an instruction whenever the value 0 is needed. This can be exploited in several ways. For example, the instruction

add   r5, r0, r0

can be used to clear register r5. Similarly, r0 can be the source operand in a Store instruction to clear a memory location. In Compare and Branch instructions, it can be used when comparing a value in another register to 0. It can also be used in the Index address mode to provide a limited version of the Absolute address mode.

The Nios II processor also has a number of control registers. We will discuss these registers in Section B.9, because they are primarily used for input/output transfers.

B.3   ADDRESSING MODES

The Nios II processor supports five addressing modes:

- *Immediate mode*—A 16-bit operand is given explicitly in the instruction. This value is sign-extended to produce a 32-bit operand for instructions that perform arithmetic operations.
- *Register mode*—The operand is the contents of a general-purpose register.
- *Register indirect mode*—The effective address of the operand is the contents of a register.
- *Displacement mode*—The effective address of the operand is generated by adding the contents of a register and a signed 16-bit displacement value given in the instruction. This is the Index mode discussed in Chapter 2.
- *Absolute mode*—A 16-bit absolute address of an operand can be specified by using the Displacement mode with register r0.

The addressing modes and their assembler syntax are given in Table B.2. Note that the syntax of the Immediate mode differs from that given in Chapter 2 in that the number sign (#) is not used. Instead, the immediate specification is included in the mnemonic for the OP-code. For example, the instruction

addi   r3, r2, 24

adds the contents of r2 and the immediate decimal value 24, and places the result in r3.

Observe also that both Immediate and Absolute modes can be used only if the immediate value or the address can be represented in 16 bits. We will discuss the issue of 32-bit immediate values and addresses in Sections B.4.4 and B.4.5, respectively.

Table B.2   Nios II addressing modes.

Name	Assembler syntax	Addressing function
Immediate	Value	Operand = Value
Register	ri	EA = ri
Register indirect	(ri)	EA = [ri]
Displacement	X(ri)	EA = [ri] + X
Absolute	LOC(r0)	EA = LOC

EA = effective address
Value = a 16-bit signed number
X = a 16-bit signed displacement value

B.4   INSTRUCTIONS

The Nios II instruction set exemplifies all features discussed in the context of RISC-style processors in Chapter 2. All instructions are 32-bits long. Arithmetic and logic operations can be done only on operands in the general-purpose registers. Load and Store instructions are used to transfer data between memory and registers.

The instructions come in three basic forms. Those that specify three register operands have the form

Operation   dest_register, source1_register, source2_register

Instructions with an immediate operand have the form

Operation   dest_register, source_register, immediate_operand

The immediate operand is 16 bits long and it can be sign-extended to provide a 32-bit operand. The third form includes a 26-bit unsigned immediate value. It is used only in the subroutine-call instruction such as

call   LABEL

B.4.1   NOTATION

The notation used in assembly-language programs is governed by the constraints imposed by a particular assembler program that is used to assemble a source program into machine code that can be executed by the processor. In many assemblers it is assumed that the statements in a source program are case-insensitive. This means that the statements

ADD   R2, R3, R4

and

$$\text{add}\quad \text{r2, r3, r4}$$

are equivalent. However, this is not so in the Nios II assembler provided by Altera Corp. This assembler allows case-insensitive specification of OP-code mnemonics, but it requires lower-case specification of register names. Thus, registers must be identified by the names given in Table B.1. For example, we can use either r27 or sp to refer to the stack pointer, but not R2 or SP.

In Altera's documentation, lower-case letters are used to specify the OP-code mnemonics. To make it easier for the user to consult Altera's literature, we will use the same convention in this appendix.

The Nios II instruction set is quite extensive. In this appendix, we will present only a subset that is sufficient for developing an understanding of the capabilities of the Nios II processor. To make the presentation easier to follow, we will discuss the instructions in groups according to their functionality. We will also show how these instructions can be used to implement the programming examples in Chapters 2 and 3. For a full description of the instruction set, the reader can consult the *Nios II Processor Reference Handbook*, which is available in the literature section of the Altera Web site (altera.com).

B.4.2   LOAD AND STORE INSTRUCTIONS

Load and Store instructions move data between memory, or I/O interfaces, and the general-purpose registers. The Load Word instruction has the general form

$$\text{ldw}\quad \text{r}i,\text{ source\_operand}$$

For example, the instruction

$$\text{ldw}\quad \text{r2, 40(r3)}$$

uses the Displacement address mode to determine the effective address of a memory location by adding the decimal value 40 and the contents of register r3; then it loads the 32-bit operand from memory into r2. The effective address must be word-aligned, which means that it must be a multiple of four.

The Store Word instruction has the form

$$\text{stw}\quad \text{r}i,\text{ destination\_operand}$$

For example,

$$\text{stw}\quad \text{r2, 40(r3)}$$

stores the contents of r2 into the same memory location as above.

The assembler syntax requires the memory operand in all Load and Store instructions to be specified using the Displacement address mode, X(ri). This allows using the Register indirect mode as 0(ri), or simply (ri), as well as the Absolute mode as X(r0). However, the

Absolute mode cannot be specified by using only a label even if the value of the label is defined in an assembler directive. Thus, the statement

ldw   r2, LOCATION

would cause a syntax error.

In addition to word-sized operands, the Load and Store instructions can also handle byte- and halfword-sized operands. The size of the operand is indicated in the OP-code mnemonic. Such Load instructions are:

- ldb   (Load Byte)
- ldbu   (Load Byte Unsigned)
- ldh   (Load Halfword)
- ldhu   (Load Halfword Unsigned)

When a shorter operand is loaded into a 32-bit register, its value has to be adjusted to fit into the register. This is done by sign-extending the 8- or 16-bit value to 32 bits in the ldb and ldh instructions. In the ldbu and ldhu instructions the operand is zero-extended, because the value represents a positive integer.

The corresponding Store instructions are:

- stb (Store Byte), which stores the low-order byte of the source register into the memory byte specified by the effective address.
- sth (Store Halfword), which stores the low-order halfword of the source register into the memory halfword specified by the effective address (which must be halfword-aligned).

For each Load or Store instruction there is also a version intended for accessing locations in I/O interfaces. These instructions are:

- ldwio   (Load Word I/O)
- ldbio   (Load Byte I/O)
- ldbuio   (Load Byte Unsigned I/O)
- ldhio   (Load Halfword I/O)
- ldhuio   (Load Halfword Unsigned I/O)
- slwio   (Store Word I/O)
- stbio   (Store Byte I/O)
- sthio   (Store Halfword I/O)

The I/O versions of Load and Store instructions are needed when the Nios II processor is used with a *cache memory*, a concept that is discussed in Chapter 8. A cache is a relatively small memory that can be accessed faster than the main memory. It is typically loaded with recently used instructions and data from the main memory so that they may be accessed more quickly when they are needed again. This is advantageous for instructions and data that are normally found in the main memory. But, it is inappropriate if an address used to access a particular data item refers to a memory-mapped I/O interface, because input data in I/O interfaces may change at any time, and output data must always be sent directly to the I/O device. The I/O versions of Load and Store instructions bypass the cache, if one exists, and always access the I/O location.

B.4.3 ARITHMETIC INSTRUCTIONS

Arithmetic instructions operate on data that are either in the general-purpose registers or given as an immediate value in the instruction. The following instructions are included:

- add (Add Registers)
- addi (Add Immediate)
- sub (Subtract Registers)
- subi (Subtract Immediate)
- mul (Multiply)
- muli (Multiply Immediate)
- div (Divide)
- divu (Divide Unsigned)

The Add instruction

$$\text{add} \quad ri, rj, rk$$

adds the contents of registers rj and rk, and places the sum into register ri.

The Add Immediate instruction

$$\text{addi} \quad ri, rj, 85$$

adds the contents of register rj and the immediate value 85, and places the result into register ri. The immediate operand is represented in 16 bits in the instruction, and it is sign-extended to 32 bits prior to the addition.

The Subtract instruction

$$\text{sub} \quad ri, rj, rk$$

subtracts the contents of register rk from register rj, and places the result into register ri.

The Multiply instruction

$$\text{mul} \quad ri, rj, rk$$

multiplies the contents of registers rj and rk, and places the low-order 32 bits of the product into register ri. The multiplication treats the operands as unsigned numbers. The result in register ri is correct if the generated product can be represented in 32 bits, regardless of whether the operands are unsigned or signed. In the immediate version

$$\text{muli} \quad ri, rj, \text{Value16}$$

the 16-bit immediate operand Value16 is sign-extended to 32 bits.

The Divide instruction

$$\text{div} \quad \text{r}i, \text{r}j, \text{r}k$$

divides the contents of register rj by the contents of register rk and places the integer portion of the quotient into register ri. The operands are treated as signed integers. The divu instruction is performed in the same way except that the operands are treated as unsigned integers.

B.4.4 LOGIC INSTRUCTIONS

The logic instructions provide the AND, OR, XOR, and NOR operations. They operate on data that are either in the general-purpose registers or given as an immediate value in the instruction.

The AND instruction

$$\text{and} \quad \text{r}i, \text{r}j, \text{r}k$$

performs a bitwise logical AND of the contents of registers rj and rk, and stores the result in register ri. Similarly, the instructions or, xor, and nor perform the OR, XOR, and NOR operations, respectively.

The AND Immediate instruction

$$\text{andi} \quad \text{r}i, \text{r}j, \text{Value16}$$

performs a bitwise logical AND of the contents of register rj and the 16-bit immediate operand Value16 which is zero-extended to 32 bits, and stores the result in register ri. Similarly, the instructions ori, xori, and nori perform the OR, XOR, and NOR operations, respectively, using immediate operands.

It is also possible to use a 16-bit immediate operand as the 16 high-order bits in the logic operations, in which case the low-order 16 bits of the operand are zeros. This is achieved with the instructions:

- andhi   (AND High Immediate)
- orhi   (OR High Immediate)
- xorhi   (XOR High Immediate)

This provides a mechanism for loading a 32-bit immediate value into a register, by first placing the high-order 16 bits into the register using the orhi instruction and then ORing in the low-order 16 bits using the ori instruction.

B.4.5 MOVE INSTRUCTIONS

The Move instructions copy the contents of one register into another, or they place an immediate value into a register. These are *pseudoinstructions* provided as a convenience to the programmer, which the assembler implements by using other instructions. The instruction

$$\text{mov} \quad \text{r}i, \text{r}j$$

copies the contents of register rj into register ri. It is implemented as

$$\text{add} \quad \text{r}i, \text{r}j, \text{r0}$$

The Move Immediate instruction

$$\text{movi} \quad \text{r}i, \text{Value16}$$

sign-extends the 16-bit immediate Value16 to 32 bits and loads it into register ri. It is implemented as

$$\text{addi} \quad \text{r}i, \text{r0}, \text{Value16}$$

The Move Unsigned Immediate instruction

$$\text{movui} \quad \text{r}i, \text{Value16}$$

zero-extends the 16-bit immediate Value16 to 32 bits and loads it into register ri. It is implemented as

$$\text{ori} \quad \text{r}i, \text{r0}, \text{Value16}$$

The Move Immediate Address instruction

$$\text{movia} \quad \text{r}i, \text{LABEL}$$

loads a 32-bit value that corresponds to the address LABEL into register ri. The assembler implements this by using two instructions as

$$\text{orhi} \quad \text{r}i, \text{r0}, \text{LABEL\_HIGH}$$
$$\text{ori} \quad \text{r}i, \text{r}i, \text{LABEL\_LOW}$$

where LABEL_HIGH and LABEL_LOW are the high-order and low-order 16 bits of LABEL.

B.4.6 BRANCH AND JUMP INSTRUCTIONS

The flow of execution of a program is changed by using Branch or Jump instructions. The Unconditional Branch instruction

$$\text{br} \quad \text{LABEL}$$

transfers execution unconditionally to the instruction at address LABEL. The branch target is specified in the form of a signed 16-bit offset that is included in the instruction. The offset is the distance in bytes from the instruction that immediately follows br to the address LABEL.

Conditional transfer of execution is achieved with Conditional Branch instructions, which compare the contents of two general-purpose registers and cause a branch if the result satisfies the branch condition. For example, the Branch if Less Than Signed instruction

blt   ri, rj, LABEL

performs the comparison $[ri] < [rj]$, treating the contents of the registers as signed numbers.

The Branch if Less Than Unsigned instruction

bltu   ri, rj, LABEL

performs the comparison $[ri] < [rj]$, treating the contents of the registers as unsigned numbers.

The other Conditional Branch instructions of the same form are:

- beq   (Comparison $[ri] = [rj]$)
- bne   (Comparison $[ri] \neq [rj]$)
- bge   (Signed comparison $[ri] \geq [rj]$)
- bgeu   (Unsigned comparison $[ri] \geq [rj]$)
- bgt   (Signed comparison $[ri] > [rj]$)
- bgtu   (Unsigned comparison $[ri] > [rj]$)
- ble   (Signed comparison $[ri] \leq [rj]$)
- bleu   (Unsigned comparison $[ri] \leq [rj]$)

The target of any branch instruction must be within the range that can be specified in a 16-bit offset. For a target outside this range, it is necessary to use the Jump instruction

jmp   ri

which transfers execution unconditionally to the address contained in the specified register, ri.

To illustrate the use of Nios II instructions, let us consider the program in Figure 2.8 which adds a list of numbers. A Nios II version of this program, using the same register choices, is given in Figure B.1. The size of the list is loaded into register r2 from the memory location N using the Absolute address mode. This assumes that the address N can be expressed in 16 bits, because the Absolute mode is actually implemented as the Displacement mode that uses a 16-bit offset plus the contents of r0 to determine the effective address of the operand. Register r3 is cleared to zero by using the Add instruction that adds the zero contents of r0. The address NUM1 is loaded into r4 by specifying it as an immediate operand in an Add Immediate instruction. Observe that when an immediate operand is specified, this is done by simply giving its name (that is recognized by the assembler) or an actual value. The fact that it is an immediate operand is stated within the OP code addi. The conditional branch

Example B.1

instruction causes the execution to continue at LOOP if the contents of r2 are greater than zero. Finally, note that the label LOOP must be followed by a colon, and that the comments are delineated by the /* and */ characters.

```
        ldw    r2, N(r0)       /* Load the size of the list.              */
        add    r3, r0, r0      /* Initialize sum to 0.                    */
        addi   r4, r0, NUM1    /* Load address of the first number.       */
LOOP:   ldw    r5, (r4)        /* Get the next number.                    */
        add    r3, r3, r5      /* Add this number to sum.                 */
        addi   r4, r4, 4       /* Increment the pointer to the list.      */
        subi   r2, r2, 1       /* Decrement the counter.                  */
        bgt    r2, r0, LOOP    /* Loop back if not finished.              */
        stw    r3, SUM(r0)     /* Store the final sum.                    */
```

Figure B.1   Nios II implementation of the program in Figure 2.8.

Example B.2   In the program in Figure B.1, the addresses that correspond to labels N, NUM1, and SUM must be small enough to be representable in 16 bits. If this is not the case, then the program can be augmented as shown in Figure B.2. Here, the **movia** instructions are used to load 32-bit addresses into registers. Note also that the **mov** instruction is used to clear r3 to zero.

```
        movia  r2, N           /* Get the address N.                     */
        ldw    r2, (r2)        /* Load the size of the list.             */
        mov    r3, r0          /* Initialize sum to 0.                   */
        movia  r4, NUM1        /* Load address of the first number.      */
LOOP:   ldw    r5, (r4)        /* Get the next number.                   */
        add    r3, r3, r5      /* Add this number to sum.                */
        addi   r4, r4, 4       /* Increment the pointer to the list.     */
        subi   r2, r2, 1       /* Decrement the counter.                 */
        bgt    r2, r0, LOOP    /* Loop back if not finished.             */
        movia  r6, SUM         /* Get the address SUM.                   */
        stw    r3, (r6)        /* Store the final sum.                   */
```

Figure B.2   A more general Nios II implementation of the program in Figure 2.8.

Example B.3   Figure B.3 gives an implementation of the program in Figure 2.11, which sums the marks attained by students in different tests.

```
           movia   r2, LIST     /* Get the address LIST.              */
           mov     r3, r0       /* Clear r3.                          */
           mov     r4, r0       /* Clear r4.                          */
           mov     r5, r0       /* Clear r5.                          */
           movia   r6, N        /* Get the address N.                 */
           ldw     r6, (r6)     /* Load the value n.                  */
LOOP:      ldw     r7, 4(r2)    /* Add the mark for next student's    */
           add     r3, r3, r7   /*   Test 1 to the partial sum.       */
           ldw     r7, 8(r2)    /* Add the mark for that student's    */
           add     r4, r4, r7   /*   Test 2 to the partial sum.       */
           ldw     r7, 12(r2)   /* Add the mark for that student's    */
           add     r5, r5, r7   /*   Test 3 to the partial sum.       */
           addi    r2, r2, 16   /* Increment the pointer.             */
           subi    r6, r6, 1    /* Decrement the counter.             */
           bgt     r6, r0, LOOP /* Branch back if not finished.       */
           movia   r7, SUM1     /* Store the total for Test 1         */
           stw     r3, (r7)     /*   into location SUM1.              */
           movia   r7, SUM2     /* Store the total for Test 2         */
           stw     r4, (r7)     /*   into location SUM2.              */
           movia   r7, SUM3     /* Store the total for Test 3         */
           stw     r5, (r7)     /*   into location SUM3.              */
```

Figure B.3   Implementation of the program in Figure 2.11.

B.4.7 SUBROUTINE LINKAGE INSTRUCTIONS

Nios II has two instructions for calling subroutines. The Call Subroutine instruction

call   LABEL

includes a 26-bit unsigned immediate value. The instruction saves the return address (which is the address of the next instruction) in register r31. Then, it transfers control to the instruction at address LABEL. This jump address is determined by concatenating the four high-order bits of the Program Counter with the immediate value, Value26, and two low-order zeroes as follows

$$\text{Jump address} = PC_{31-28} : \text{Value26} : 00$$

The two least-significant bits are 0 because Nios II instructions must be aligned on word boundaries.

The Call Subroutine in Register instruction

callr   ri

saves the return address in register r31 and then transfers control to the instruction at the address contained in register r*i*.

Return from a subroutine is performed with the instruction

ret

This instruction transfers execution to the address contained in register r31.

Example B.4 Figure B.4 illustrates how the program of Figure B.2 can be written in the form of a subroutine, where the parameters are passed through processor registers.

Calling program

```
          movia   r2, N          /* Get the address N.                 */
          ldw     r2, (r2)       /* Load the size of the list.         */
          movia   r4, NUM1       /* Load address of the first number.  */
          call    LISTADD        /* Call subroutine.                   */
          movia   r6, SUM        /* Get the address SUM.               */
          stw     r3, (r6)       /* Store the final sum.               */
          :
```

Subroutine

```
LISTADD:  mov     r3, r0         /* Initialize sum to 0.               */
LOOP:     ldw     r5, (r4)       /* Get the next number.               */
          add     r3, r3, r5     /* Add this number to sum.            */
          addi    r4, r4, 4      /* Increment the pointer to the list. */
          subi    r2, r2, 1      /* Decrement the counter.             */
          bgt     r2, r0, LOOP   /* Loop back if not finished.         */
          ret                    /* Return to calling program.         */
```

Figure B.4   Program of Figure B.2 written as a subroutine; parameters passed through registers.

Example B.5 Figure B.5 shows how the program of Figure B.2 can be written as a subroutine where the parameters are passed on the processor stack.

```
          movia   r2, NUM1      /* Push parameters on the stack.    */
          subi    sp, sp, 4
          stw     r2, (sp)
          movia   r2, N
          ldw     r2, (r2)
          subi    sp, sp, 4
          stw     r2, (sp)
          call    LISTADD       /* Call subroutine.                 */
          ldw     r2, 4(sp)     /* Get the result from the stack    */
          movia   r3, SUM       /*   and save it in location SUM.   */
          stw     r2, (r3)
          addi    sp, sp, 8     /* Restore top of stack.            */
          :
LISTADD:  subi    sp, sp, 16    /* Save registers.                  */
          stw     r2, 12(sp)
          stw     r3, 8(sp)
          stw     r4, 4(sp)
          stw     r5, (sp)
          ldw     r2, 16(sp)    /* Initialize counter to n.         */
          ldw     r4, 20(sp)    /* Initialize pointer to the list.  */
          mov     r3, r0        /* Initialize sum to 0.             */
LOOP:     ldw     r5, (r4)      /* Get the next number.             */
          add     r3, r3, r5    /* Add this number to sum.          */
          addi    r4, r4, 4     /* Increment the pointer by 4.      */
          subi    r2, r2, 1     /* Decrement the counter.           */
          bgt     r2, r0, LOOP  /* Loop back if not finished.       */
          stw     r3, 20(sp)    /* Put result in the stack.         */
          ldw     r5, (sp)      /* Restore registers.               */
          ldw     r4, 4(sp)
          ldw     r3, 8(sp)
          ldw     r2, 12(sp)
          addi    sp, sp, 16
          ret                   /* Return to calling program.       */
```

Figure B.5   Program of Figure B.2 written as a subroutine; parameters passed on the stack.

Example B.6

When a Subroutine Call instruction is executed, the Nios II processor saves the return address in register r31 (ra). In the case of nested subroutines, this return address must be saved on the processor stack before the second subroutine is called. Figure B.6 indicates how nested subroutines may be implemented. It corresponds to the program in Figure 2.21.

```
              movia    r2, PARAM2      /* Place parameters on the stack.     */
              ldw      r2, (r2)
              subi     sp, sp, 4
              stw      r2, (sp)
              movia    r2, PARAM1
              ldw      r2, (r2)
              subi     sp, sp, 4
              stw      r2, (sp)
              call     SUB1            /* Call the subroutine.               */
              ldw      r2, (sp)        /* Get the result from the stack      */
              movia    r3, RESULT      /*    and save it in location RESULT. */
              stw      r2, (r3)
              addi     sp, sp, 8       /* Restore top of stack.              */
                :
    SUB1:     subi     sp, sp, 24      /* Save registers.                    */
              stw      ra, 20(sp)
              stw      fp, 16(sp)
              stw      r2, 12(sp)
              stw      r3, 8(sp)
              stw      r4, 4(sp)
              stw      r5, (sp)
              addi     fp, sp, 16      /* Initialize the frame pointer.      */
              ldw      r2, 8(fp)       /* Get first parameter.               */
              ldw      r3, 12(fp)      /* Get second parameter.              */
                :
              movia    r5, PARAM3      /* Get the parameter that has to be   */
              ldw      r4, (r5)        /*    passed to SUB2, and push it on  */
              subi     sp, sp, 4       /*    the stack.                      */
              stw      r4, (sp)
              call     SUB2
              ldw      r4, (sp)        /* Get result from SUB2.              */
              addi     sp, sp, 4
                :
              stw      r5, 8(fp)       /* Place answer on stack.             */
              ldw      r5, (sp)        /* Restore registers.                 */
              ldw      r4, 4(sp)
              ldw      r3, 8(sp)
              ldw      r2, 12(sp)
              ldw      fp, 16(sp)
              ldw      ra, 20(sp)
              addi     sp, sp, 24
              ret                      /* Return to Main program.            */
    ...continued in Part b
```

Figure B.6   Nested subroutines (Part *a*); implementation of the program in Figure 2.21*a*.

```
SUB2:   subi    sp, sp, 12    /* Save registers.              */
        stw     fp, 8(sp)
        stw     r2, 4(sp)
        stw     r3, (sp)
        addi    fp, sp, 8     /* Initialize the frame pointer. */
        ldw     r2, 4(fp)     /* Get the parameter.            */
          ⋮
        stw     r3, 4(fp)     /* Place SUB2 result on stack.   */
        ldw     r3, (sp)      /* Restore registers.            */
        ldw     r2, 4(sp)
        ldw     fp, 8(sp)
        addi    sp, sp, 12
        ret                   /* Return to SUB1.               */
```

...continued from Part *a*

Figure B.6   Nested subroutines (Part *b*); implementation of the program in Figure 2.21*b*.

B.4.8 COMPARISON INSTRUCTIONS

The Comparison instructions compare the contents of two registers or the contents of a register and an immediate value, and write either 1 (if true) or 0 (if false) into the result register.

The Compare Less Than Signed instruction

$$\text{cmplt} \quad ri, rj, rk$$

performs the comparison of signed numbers in registers rj and rk, $[rj] < [rk]$, and writes a 1 into register ri if the result is true; otherwise, it writes a 0.

The Compare Less Than Unsigned instruction

$$\text{cmpltu} \quad ri, rj, rk$$

performs the same function as the cmplt instruction, but it treats the operands as unsigned numbers.

Other instructions of this type are:

- cmpeq   (Comparison $[rj] = [rk]$)
- cmpne   (Comparison $[rj] \neq [rk]$)
- cmpge   (Signed comparison $[rj] \geq [rk]$)

- cmpgeu   (Unsigned comparison $[rj] \geq [rk]$)
- cmpgt   (Signed comparison $[rj] > [rk]$)
- cmpgtu   (Unsigned comparison $[rj] > [rk]$)
- cmple   (Signed comparison $[rj] \leq [rk]$)
- cmpleu   (Unsigned comparison $[rj] \leq [rk]$)

The immediate versions of the Comparison instructions include a 16-bit immediate operand. For example, the Compare Less Than Signed Immediate instruction

$$\text{cmplti} \quad ri, \, rj, \, \text{Value16}$$

compares the signed number in register rj with the sign-extended immediate operand. It writes a 1 into register ri if $[rj] < \text{Value16}$; otherwise, it writes a 0.

The Compare Less Than Unsigned Immediate instruction

$$\text{cmpltui} \quad ri, \, rj, \, \text{Value16}$$

compares the unsigned number in register rj with the zero-extended immediate operand. It writes a 1 into register ri if $[rj] < \text{Value16}$; otherwise, it writes a 0.

Other instructions of this type are:

- cmpeqi   (Comparison $[rj] = \text{Value16}$)
- cmpnei   (Comparison $[rj] \neq \text{Value16}$)
- cmpgei   (Signed comparison $[rj] \geq \text{Value16}$)
- cmpgeui   (Unsigned comparison $[rj] \geq \text{Value16}$)
- cmpgti   (Signed comparison $[rj] > \text{Value16}$)
- cmpgtui   (Unsigned comparison $[rj] > \text{Value16}$)
- cmplei   (Signed comparison $[rj] \leq \text{Value16}$)
- cmpleui   (Unsigned comparison $[rj] \leq \text{Value16}$)

B.4.9   SHIFT INSTRUCTIONS

The Shift instructions shift the contents of a specified register either to the right or to the left.

The Shift Right Logical instruction

$$\text{srl} \quad ri, \, rj, \, rk$$

shifts the contents of register rj to the right by the number of bit positions specified by the five least-significant bits (number in the range 0 to 31) in register rk, and stores the result in register ri. The vacated bits on the left side of the shifted operand are filled with zeros.

The Shift Right Logical Immediate instruction

$$\text{srli} \quad ri, \ rj, \ \text{Value5}$$

shifts the contents of register rj to the right by the number of bit positions specified by the five-bit unsigned value, Value5, given in the instruction, and stores the result in register ri. The vacated bits on the left side of the shifted operand are filled with zeros.

The other Shift instructions are:

* sra (Shift Right Arithmetic)
* srai (Shift Right Arithmetic Immediate)
* sll (Shift Left Logical)
* slli (Shift Left Logical Immediate)

The sra and srai instructions perform the same actions as the srl and srli instructions, except that the sign bit, rj_{31}, is replicated into the vacated bits on the left side of the shifted operand.

The sll and slli instructions are similar to the srl and srli instructions, but they shift the operand in register rj to the left and fill the vacated bits on the right side with zeros.

B.4.10 ROTATE INSTRUCTIONS

There are three Rotate instructions. The Rotate Right instruction

$$\text{ror} \quad ri, \ rj, \ rk$$

rotates the bits of register rj in the left-to-right direction by the number of bit positions specified by the five least-significant bits (number in the range 0 to 31) in register rk, and stores the result in register ri.

The Rotate Left instruction

$$\text{rol} \quad ri, \ rj, \ rk$$

is similar to the ror instruction, but it rotates the operand in the right-to-left direction.

The Rotate Left Immediate instruction

$$\text{roli} \quad ri, \ rj, \ \text{Value5}$$

rotates the bits of register rj in the right-to-left direction by the number of bit positions specified by the five-bit unsigned value, Value5, given in the instruction, and stores the result in register ri.

In Figure 2.24 we showed a program that packs two BCD digits into a byte. A Nios II version of that program is given in Figure B.7. **Example B.7**

```
movia    r2, LOC         /* r2 points to data.            */
ldb      r3, (r2)        /* Load first byte into r3.      */
slli     r3, r3, 4       /* Shift left by 4 bit positions. */
addi     r2, r2, 1       /* Increment the pointer.        */
ldb      r4, (r2)        /* Load second byte into r4.     */
andi     r4, r4, 0xF     /* Clear high-order bits to zero. */
or       r3, r3, r4      /* Concatenate the BCD digits.   */
movia    r2, PACKED      /* Store the result into         */
stb      r3, (r2)        /*   location PACKED.            */
```

Figure B.7   A routine that packs two BCD digits into a byte, corresponding to Figure 2.24.

B.4.11 CONTROL INSTRUCTIONS

There are two special instructions for reading and writing the control registers that will be discussed in Section B.9. The Read Control Register instruction

$$\text{rdctl} \quad ri, ctlj$$

copies the contents of control register ctl$j$ into the general purpose register ri.

The Write Control Register instruction

$$\text{wrctl} \quad ctlj, ri$$

copies the contents of general purpose register ri into the control register ctl$j$.

There are two instructions provided for dealing with exceptions: trap and eret. They are similar to the call and ret instructions, but they are used for exceptions. We will discuss them in Section B.10.2.

There are also instructions for management of cache memories: flushd (Flush Data Cache Line), flushi (Flush Instruction Cache Line), initd (Initialize Data Cache Line), and initi (Initialize Instruction Cache Line).

B.5 PSEUDOINSTRUCTIONS

For programming convenience, it is useful to have a variety of different instructions. From the hardware point of view, a large number of instructions requires more extensive circuitry for their implementation. Often, the action of some desired instructions can be achieved efficiently by using other instructions. If these desired instructions are not implemented in hardware, they are called *pseudoinstructions*. The assembler replaces pseudoinstructions with actual instructions that are implemented in hardware.

In Section B.4.5, we saw that the Move instructions are pseudoinstructions. This section describes some other pseudoinstructions.

The Subtract Immediate instruction

$$\text{subi} \quad ri, rj, \text{Value16}$$

is implemented as

$$\text{addi} \quad ri, rj, -\text{Value16}$$

The Branch Greater Than Signed instruction

$$\text{bgt} \quad ri, rj, \text{LABEL}$$

is implemented as the blt instruction by swapping the register operands.

When writing a program, the programmer need not be aware of pseudoinstructions. But, an awareness becomes important if one tries to examine the assembled code, perhaps during the debugging process.

B.6 ASSEMBLER DIRECTIVES

The Nios II assembler directives conform to those defined by the widely used GNU assembler, which is software available in the public domain. Assembler directives begin with a period. Some of the frequently used directives are described below.

.org *Value*

This is the ORIGIN directive discussed in Chapter 2.

.equ *LABEL, Value*

The name LABEL is equated with Value. For example,

$$\text{.equ} \quad \text{LIST, 0x1000}$$

assigns the hexadecimal number 1000 to LIST.

.byte *expressions*

Places byte-sized data items into the memory. Items are specified by expressions that are separated by commas. Each expression is assembled into the next byte. Examples of expressions are: 23, 6 + LABEL, and Z − 4.

.hword *expressions*

This is the same as .byte, except that the expressions are assembled into successive 16-bit halfwords.

.word   *expressions*

This is the same as .byte, except that the expressions are assembled into successive 32-bit words.

.skip   *Size*

This is the RESERVE directive discussed in Chapter 2. It reserves in the memory the number of bytes specified as Size.

.end

Indicates the end of the source-code file. Everything after this directive is ignored by the assembler.

Example B.8   Figure B.8 illustrates the use of some assembler directives. It corresponds to Figure 2.13.

```
                .org    100          /* Place this code at location 100.     */
                movia   r2, N        /* Get the address N.                   */
                ldw     r2, (r2)     /* Load the size of the list.           */
                mov     r3, r0       /* Initialize sum to 0.                 */
                movia   r4, NUM1     /* Load address of the first number.    */
      LOOP:     ldw     r5, (r4)     /* Get the next number.                 */
                add     r3, r3, r5   /* Add this number to sum.              */
                addi    r4, r4, 4    /* Increment the pointer to the list.   */
                subi    r2, r2, 1    /* Decrement the counter.               */
                bgt     r2, r0, LOOP /* Loop back if not finished.           */
                movia   r6, SUM      /* Get the address SUM.                 */
                stw     r3, (r6)     /* Store the final sum.                 */
                next instruction

                .org    200          /* Place data at location 200.          */
      SUM:      .skip   4
      N:        .word   150
      NUM1:     .skip   600
                .end
```

Figure B.8   A program that corresponds to Figure 2.13.

B.7 CARRY AND OVERFLOW DETECTION

When performing an arithmetic operation such as Add or Subtract, it is often important to know if the operation produced a carry from the most-significant bit position or if arithmetic overflow occurred. A processor that uses condition codes, as discussed in Section 2.10.2, automatically sets the C and V flags to indicate whether carry or overflow occurred. However, the Nios II processor does not include condition code flags. Its Add and Subtract instructions perform the corresponding operations in the same way for both signed and unsigned operands. Additional instructions have to be used to detect the occurrence of carry and overflow. The carry out from bit position 31 is of interest when unsigned numbers are added or subtracted. Overflow is of interest when signed operands are involved.

Carry and Overflow in Addition

Upon executing the instruction

$$\text{add} \quad \text{r4, r2, r3}$$

a possible occurrence of a carry can be detected by checking if the unsigned sum, in register r4, is less than either one of the unsigned operands. If this instruction is followed by

$$\text{cmpltu} \quad \text{r5, r4, r2}$$

the carry bit will be written into register r5.

If it is desired to continue execution at location CARRY when a carry of 1 is detected, this can be achieved by using

$$\text{add} \quad \text{r4, r2, r3}$$
$$\text{bltu} \quad \text{r4, r2, CARRY}$$

Arithmetic overflow can be detected by checking the signs of the source operands and the resulting sum. Overflow occurs if two positive numbers produce a negative sum, or if two negative numbers produce a positive sum. Exploiting this fact, the instruction sequence

```
add   r4, r2, r3
xor   r5, r4, r2
xor   r6, r4, r3
and   r5, r5, r6
blt   r5, r0, OVERFLOW
```

will cause a branch to OVERFLOW if the addition results in arithmetic overflow. The two xor instructions are used to compare the signs of the sum and each of the two summands. While these instructions perform the XOR on all 32 bits, it is only the sign position, b_{31}, that is considered in the subsequent branch instruction. This bit is set to 1 only if the sign bits of the sum and the summand are different. The and instruction causes bit $r5_{31}$ to be set to 1 only if the signs of both operands are the same, but the sign of the sum is different. The blt instruction causes a branch if the signed number in r5 is negative, which is indicated by $r5_{31}$ being equal to 1.

Carry and Overflow in Subtraction

Carry and overflow conditions in Subtract operations can be detected using a similar approach. A carry from the most-significant bit position of the generated difference can be detected by checking if the minuend is less than the subtrahend. For example, the instructions

```
sub   r4, r2, r3
bltu  r2, r3, CARRY
```

will cause execution to branch to location CARRY if a carry is generated in the subtraction.

Arithmetic overflow occurs if the minuend and subtrahend have different signs and the sign of the generated difference is not the same as the sign of the minuend. This condition can be detected by the instruction sequence

```
sub   r4, r2, r3
xor   r5, r2, r3
xor   r6, r2, r4
and   r5, r5, r6
blt   r5, r0, OVERFLOW
```

The two xor instructions compare the sign of the minuend with the signs of the subtrahend and the generated difference. The and instruction causes the bit $r5_{31}$ to be set to 1 only if the above stated condition for overflow is true.

Example B.9   Consider the task of adding two integers that are too big to fit into 32-bit registers. This can be done by loading the numbers into two different registers and then performing the addition with carry detection as explained above. We will use hexadecimal numbers to make it easy to see how a number can be represented in two registers. Let $A = 10A72C10F8$ and $B = 4A5C00FE04$. Then $C = A + B$ can be computed as shown in Figure B.9. Registers r2 and r3 are loaded with the low- and high-order 32 bits of A, respectively. Registers r4 and

```
orhi    r2, r0, 0xA72C    /* r2 now contains A72C0000.  */
ori     r2, r2, 0x10F8    /* r2 now contains A72C10F8.  */
ori     r3, r0, 0x10      /* r3 now contains 10.        */
orhi    r4, r0, 0x5C00    /* r4 now contains 5C000000.  */
ori     r4, r4, 0xFE04    /* r4 now contains 5C00FE04.  */
ori     r5, r0, 0x4A      /* r5 now contains 4A.        */
add     r6, r2, r4        /* Add low-order 32 bits.     */
cmpltu  r7, r6, r2        /* Check if carry occurred.   */
add     r7, r7, r3        /* Add the carry plus the     */
add     r7, r7, r5        /*   high-order bits.         */
```

Figure B.9   Program for Example B.9.

r5 are used to hold B in the same way. Note that the 32-bit values in registers r2 and r4 are loaded using two 16-bit immediate operands, as explained in Section B.4.4. After the addition of the low-order 32 bits of A and B, the carry out is included in the addition of the high-order 32 bits. The generated sum $C = 5B032D0EFC$ is placed in registers r6 and r7.

B.8 EXAMPLE PROGRAMS

In Section 2.11, we presented two example programs. A Nios II version of the program that computes the dot product of two vectors is given in Figure B.10; it corresponds to Figure 2.27. A program that searches for a matching string is shown in Figure B.11; it corresponds to Figure 2.30.

	movia	r2, AVEC	/* r2 points to vector A.	*/
	movia	r3, BVEC	/* r3 points to vector B.	*/
	movia	r4, N	/* Get the address N.	*/
	ldw	r4, (r4)	/* r4 serves as a counter.	*/
	mov	r5, r0	/* r5 accumulates the dot product.	*/
LOOP:	ldw	r6, (r2)	/* Get next element of vector A.	*/
	ldw	r7, (r3)	/* Get next element of vector B.	*/
	mul	r8, r6, r7	/* Compute the product of next pair.	*/
	add	r5, r5, r8	/* Add to previous sum.	*/
	addi	r2, r2, 4	/* Increment pointer to vector A.	*/
	addi	r3, r3, 4	/* Increment pointer to vector B.	*/
	subi	r4, r4, 1	/* Decrement the counter.	*/
	bgt	r4, r0, LOOP	/* Loop again if not done.	*/
	movia	r2, DOTPROD	/* Store dot product	*/
	stw	r5, (r2)	/* in memory.	*/

Figure B.10   A program for computing the dot product of two vectors, corresponding to Figure 2.27.

B.9 CONTROL REGISTERS

So far, we have considered only the use of general-purpose registers. Prior to discussing the Nios II input/output schemes, we need to introduce the control registers. In Chapter 3, we explained the use of control registers in handling interrupts. Figure 3.7 depicts four registers that typify the functionality needed for this task. The same functionality is found in the Nios II control registers. In the basic configuration of a Nios II processor, there are six control registers. Additional control registers are provided when advanced hardware modules, such as the Memory Management Unit or the External Interrupt Controller, are implemented.

```
                movia    r2, T             /* Get the address of T (0).        */
                movia    r3, P             /* Get the address of P (0).        */
                movia    r4, N             /* Get the address N.               */
                ldw      r4, (r4)          /* Read the value n.                */
                movia    r5, M             /* Get the address M.               */
                ldw      r5, (r5)          /* Read the value m.                */
                sub      r4, r4, r5        /* Compute n − m.                   */
                add      r4, r2, r4        /* The address of T (n − m).        */
                add      r5, r3, r5        /* The address of P (m).            */
LOOP1:          mov      r6, r2            /* Scan through string T.           */
                mov      r7, r3            /* Scan through string P.           */
LOOP2:          ldb      r8, (r6)          /* Compare a pair of                */
                ldb      r9, (r7)          /*   characters in                  */
                bne      r8, r9, NOMATCH   /*   strings T and P.               */
                addi     r6, r6, 1         /* Point to next character in T.    */
                addi     r7, r7, 1         /* Point to next character in P.    */
                bgt      r5, r7, LOOP2     /* Loop again if not done.          */
                movia    r9, RESULT        /* Store the address of T (i)       */
                stw      r2, (r9)          /*   in location RESULT.            */
                br       DONE
NOMATCH:        addi     r2, r2, 1         /* Point to next character in T.    */
                bge      r4, r2, LOOP1     /* Loop back if not done.           */
                movi     r8, −1            /* Write −1 into location           */
                movia    r9, RESULT        /*   RESULT to indicate that        */
                stw      r8, (r9)          /*   no match was found.            */
DONE:           next instruction
```

Figure B.11   A string-search program corresponding to Figure 2.30.

The basic control registers are indicated in Table B.3. They are called ctl0 to ctl5. They also have the alternate names shown in the table which indicate their functionality. Both sets of names are recognized by the assembler. The control registers are read and written by the special instructions rdctl and wrctl. They are used as follows:

- Register ctl0 is the status register which indicates the current state of the processor. In the basic configuration, only two bits are used:

    - *PIE* is the processor interrupt-enable bit. The processor will accept interrupt requests from I/O devices when $PIE = 1$, and it will ignore them when $PIE = 0$.

    - *U* is the User/Supervisor mode bit. It is 0 for Supervisor mode and 1 for User mode.

- Register ctl1 is used to automatically save the contents of the status register when an interrupt- or exception-service routine is being executed. Bits *EU* and *EPIE* are the saved status bits *U* and *PIE*.

Table B.3 Nios II basic control registers.

Register	Name	$b_{31} \cdots b_2$	b_1	b_0
ctl0	status	Reserved	U	PIE
ctl1	estatus	Reserved	EU	EPIE
ctl2	bstatus	Reserved	BU	BPIE
ctl3	ienable	Interrupt-enable bits		
ctl4	ipending	Pending-interrupt bits		
ctl5	cpuid	Processor identifier		

- Register ctl2 is used to save the contents of the status register during debug break processing. Bits *BU* and *BPIE* are the saved status bits *U* and *PIE*.

- Register ctl3 is used to enable individual interrupts from I/O devices. Each bit corresponds to one of the interrupts *irq0* to *irq31*. The bit values 1 and 0 enable and disable each interrupt, respectively.

- Register ctl4 indicates which interrupt requests are pending. The value of a given bit, $ctl4_k$, is set to 1 if the interrupt *irqk* is active and also enabled by the interrupt-enable bit $ctl3_k$ being equal to 1.

- Register ctl5 is used to hold a value that uniquely identifies the processor when it is a part of a multiprocessor system.

Operating Modes

The Nios II processor can operate in two different modes:

- *Supervisor mode*, in which the processor can execute all instructions and perform all available functions. This mode is entered when the processor is reset.

- *User mode*, in which some control instructions cannot be executed.

In a basic configuration of a Nios II processor, all programs are run in the Supervisor mode. The User mode is available when the processor is configured to include the Memory Management Unit. Its sole purpose is to support operating systems, so that the OS software can run in the Supervisor mode while the application programs run in the User mode.

B.10 INPUT/OUTPUT

The general concepts dealing with input/output transfers, which are discussed in Chapter 3, apply fully to the Nios II processor. I/O devices are memory-mapped, and I/O transfers are performed either under program control or by using the interrupt mechanism.

```
        .equ    KBD_DATA, 0x4000   /*  Specify addresses for keyboard          */
        .equ    DISP_DATA, 0x4010  /*    and display data registers.           */
        movia   r2, LOC            /*  Location where line will be stored.      */
        movia   r3, KBD_DATA       /*  r3 points to keyboard data register.     */
        movia   r4, DISP_DATA      /*  r4 points to display data register.      */
        addi    r5, r0, 0x0D       /*  Load ASCII code for Carriage Return.     */
READ:   ldbio   r6, 4(r3)          /*  Read keyboard status register.           */
        andi    r6, r6, 2          /*  Check the KIN flag.                      */
        beq     r6, r0, READ
        ldbio   r7, (r3)           /*  Read character from keyboard.            */
        stb     r7, (r2)           /*  Write character into main memory         */
        addi    r2, r2, 1          /*    and increment the pointer.             */
ECHO:   ldbio   r6, 4(r4)          /*  Read display status register.            */
        andi    r6, r6, 4          /*  Check the DOUT flag.                     */
        beq     r6, r0, ECHO
        stbio   r7, (r4)           /*  Send the character to display.           */
        bne     r5, r7, READ       /*  Loop back if character is not CR.        */
```

Figure B.12   Program that reads a line of characters and displays it, corresponding to Figure 3.4.

B.10.1 PROGRAM-CONTROLLED I/O

Section 3.1.2 explains the concept of program-controlled I/O. A RISC-style program that reads a line of characters from a keyboard and sends it to a display device is given in Figure 3.4. A Nios II implementation of this program is presented in Figure B.12. It assumes that the keyboard and display interfaces have the registers shown in Figure 3.3. The names of these registers are associated with the addresses indicated in Figure 3.3. Note that the I/O registers are accessed by using the ldbio and stbio instructions. As explained in Section B.4.2, these instructions are used to bypass the cache memory that may exist in a given Nios II system.

B.10.2 INTERRUPTS AND EXCEPTIONS

Using interrupts is an efficient way of performing I/O transfers. Section 3.2 describes this approach in general terms. The Nios II implementation of interrupts conforms to this description.

A Nios II system can deal with two types of interruptions. A request for service from an I/O device is considered to be a *hardware interrupt*. Any other interruption is not called an interrupt; instead, it is called an *exception*. In fact, the term exception is used generally to describe any hardware-initiated or software-initiated deviation from normal execution.

An exception in the normal flow of program execution can be caused by:

- Hardware interrupt
- Software trap
- Unimplemented instruction

In response to an exception, the Nios II processor performs the following actions:

1. Saves the existing processor status information by copying the contents of the **status** register (ctl0) into the **estatus** register (ctl1).

2. Clears the *U* bit in the **status** register, to ensure that the processor is in the Supervisor mode.

3. Clears the *PIE* bit in the **status** register, which prevents further external processor interrupts.

4. Writes the return address, which is the address of the instruction after the exception, into the **ea** register (r29).

5. Transfers execution to the address of the *exception handler*, which determines the cause of the exception and calls the required *exception-service routine* to respond to the exception.

The address of the exception handler is specified when a Nios II system is designed, and it cannot be changed by software at run time. This address can be provided by the designer; otherwise, the default address is at an offset of 0x20 from the starting address of the main memory. For example, if the memory starts at address 0, then the default address of the exception handler is 0x20.

Hardware Interrupts

An I/O device requests an interrupt by asserting one of the processor's 32 interrupt-request inputs, *irq0* through *irq31*. An interrupt is generated only if the following three conditions are true:

- The *PIE* bit in the **status** register is set to 1.
- An interrupt-request input, *irqk*, is asserted.
- The corresponding interrupt-enable bit, $ctl3_k$, is set to 1.

The contents of the **ipending** register (ctl4) indicate which interrupt requests are pending. The exception handler determines which of the pending interrupts has the highest priority, and calls the corresponding interrupt-service routine.

Upon completion of the interrupt-service routine, execution control is returned to the interrupted program by means of the **eret** (Exception Return) instruction. The Nios II processor starts servicing a hardware interrupt without first completing the instruction that is being executed when the interrupt request occurs. (This is different from our discussion in Chapter 3, where we assumed that the execution of the current instruction will be completed.) Therefore, the interrupted instruction must be re-executed upon return from the interrupt-service routine. To achieve this, the exception handler has to adjust the contents of the **ea** register which are at this time pointing to the next instruction of the interrupted program.

Therefore, the address in the ea register has to be decremented by 4 prior to executing the eret instruction.

Figure B.13 shows how interrupts can be used to read a line of characters from a keyboard and display it using polling. The program corresponds to the general scheme presented in Figure 3.8. To keep the example simple, we do not use the exception handler, but only the necessary interrupt-service routine. This assumes that the keyboard is the only source of exceptions, so that when an interrupt request arrives the program automatically treats it as having come from the keyboard.

Observe that we defined the addresses KBD and DISPLAY as 0x4000 and 0x4010, which are the actual addresses of KBD_DATA and DISP_DATA registers in Figure 3.3. The program accesses the other registers in the keyboard and display interfaces by using the Displacement mode. The 32-bit addresses KBD and DISPLAY, as well as the addresses of memory locations PNTR, EOL, and LINE are loaded into processor registers by using the pseudoinstruction movia.

Note also that the exception return address in register ea is adjusted prior to returning to the interrupted program.

Software Trap

A software exception occurs when a trap instruction is executed in a program. This causes the address of the next instruction to be saved in the ea register (r29). Then, interrupts are disabled and execution is transferred to the exception handler.

The last instruction in the exception-service routine is eret, which returns execution control to the instruction that follows the trap instruction that caused the exception. The return address is the contents of register ea. The eret instruction restores the previous status of the processor by copying the contents of the estatus register into the status register.

A common use of the software trap is to transfer control to a different program, such as an operating system, as explained in Chapter 4.

Unimplemented Instructions

An exception occurs when the processor encounters a valid instruction that is not implemented in hardware. For example, a Nios II processor may be configured without hardware circuits that perform multiplication and division. In this case, an exception will occur if the mul or div instruction is encountered. The exception handler may call a routine that implements the required operation in software.

Exception Handler

The exception handler is a program that deals with exceptions. It is loaded in a predetermined location in memory to which execution control is transferred when an exception occurs. As mentioned above, in a Nios II system, a default location for the exception handler is 0x20.

Figure B.14 gives an outline of the exception handler. The routine starts by saving all registers used by it, as well as the subroutine-linkage register ra, as explained in Example 3.3 in Chapter 3. Then, it must determine the source of an exception request. First, it checks if the request is a hardware interrupt. It reads the ipending control register, and tests the

```
            .equ    KBD, 0x4000       /* Address for keyboard.             */
            .equ    DISPLAY, 0x4010   /* Address for display.              */
            .equ    PNTR, 0x2000      /* Buffer pointer in memory.         */
            .equ    EOL, 0x2004       /* End-of-line indicator.            */
            .equ    LINE, 0x2008      /* Address of start of buffer.       */
```

Interrupt-service routine

```
            .org    0x020
ILOC:       subi    sp, sp, 16        /* Save registers.                   */
            stw     r2, 12(sp)
            stw     r3, 8(sp)
            stw     r4, 4(sp)
            stw     r5, (sp)
            movia   r2, PNTR
            ldw     r3, (r2)          /* Load address pointer.             */
            movia   r4, KBD
            ldbio   r5, (r4)          /* Read character from keyboard.     */
            stb     r5, (r3)          /* Write the character into memory   */
            addi    r3, r3, 1         /*    and increment the pointer.     */
            stw     r3, (r2)          /* Update the pointer in memory.     */
            movia   r2, DISPLAY
ECHO:       ldbio   r3, 4(r2)         /* See if display is ready.          */
            andi    r3, r3, 4         /* Check the DOUT flag.              */
            beq     r3, r0, ECHO
            stbio   r5, (r2)          /* Display the character just read.  */
            addi    r3, r0, 0x0D      /* ASCII code for Carriage Return.   */
            bne     r5, r3, RTRN      /* Return if character is not CR.    */
            movi    r3, 1
            movia   r5, EOL
            stw     r3, (r5)          /* Indicate end of line.             */
            stbio   r0, 8(r4)         /* Disable interrupts in KBD interface. */
RTRN:       ldw     r5, (sp)          /* Restore registers.                */
            ldw     r4, 4(sp)
            ldw     r3, 8(sp)
            ldw     r2, 12(sp)
            addi    sp, sp, 16
            subi    ea, ea, 4         /* Adjust the return address.        */
            eret                      /* Return from exception.            */
```

...continued in Part *b*.

Figure B.13 Program that reads a line of characters using interrupts and displays it using polling, corresponding to Figure 3.8 (Part *a*).

Main program

```
START:    movia    r2, LINE
          movia    r3, PNTR
          stw      r2, (r3)      /* Initialize buffer pointer.          */
          movia    r2, EOL
          stw      r0, (r2)      /* Clear end-of-line indicator.        */
          movia    r2, KBD
          movi     r3, 2         /* Enable interrupts in                */
          stbio    r3, 8(r2)     /*   the keyboard interface.           */
          rdctl    r2, ienable
          ori      r2, r2, 2     /* Enable keyboard interrupts in       */
          wrctl    ienable, r2   /*   the processor control register.   */
          rdctl    r2, status
          ori      r2, r2, 1
          wrctl    status, r2    /* Set PIE bit in status register.     */
          next instruction
```

Figure B.13   Program that reads a line of characters using interrupts and displays it using polling, corresponding to Figure 3.8 (Part *b*).

bits of this word, one at a time, to find a bit that is set to 1. The order in which these bits are tested determines the priority assigned to the various sources of interrupts. Upon finding a bit set to 1, the corresponding interrupt-service routine is executed. Although there may be as many as 32 different interrupt sources, in a typical system the number of I/O devices is much smaller. If the request is not a hardware interrupt, then other exceptions are checked and serviced as necessary. Prior to returning to the interrupted program, the saved registers are restored.

The main program must initialize the settings needed to attain a desired interrupt behavior of I/O devices. This is similar to the initialization illustrated in Figure B.13.

Reset

A Nios II system has to include a *reset* capability to make it possible to recover from an erroneous state that cannot be handled as an exception. This may be done by providing a reset key. When the key is pressed, the processor is reset and an appropriate program is executed. If the memory starts at address 0, then it is natural to use this address as the reset location, which can be done when the Nios II system is being implemented. When the processor is reset, the program counter and control registers are cleared to zero. Thus, execution starts with the instruction at address 0. To execute the main program after reset, it is only necessary to place a Branch instruction at address 0 with first instruction of the main program as the branch target.

```
            .org    0
RESET:      br      START           /* Branch to the Main program.          */
```

Exception handler

```
            .org    0x020
ELOC:       subi    sp, sp, 12      /* Save registers.                      */
            stw     ra, 8(sp)
            stw     et, 4(sp)
            stw     r2, (sp)
            . . .
            rdctl   et, ipending    /* Get pending interrupt requests.      */
            beq     et, r0, OTHER   /* Not an external interrupt.           */
            subi    ea, ea, 4       /* Adjust the return address.           */
IRQ0:       andi    r2, et, 1       /* Check if irq0 is active.             */
            beq     r2, r0, IRQ1    /* If not, check irq1.                  */
            call    ISR0            /* Service the irq0 request.            */
IRQ1:       andi    r2, et, 2       /* Check if irq1 is active.             */
            beq     r2, r0, IRQ2    /* If not, check irq2.                  */
            call    ISR1            /* Service the irq1 request.            */
            ⋮
IRQ31:      orhi    r2, r0, 0x8000  /* Pattern to test bit 31.              */
            and     r2, et, r2      /* Check if irq31 is active.            */
            beq     DONE            /* If not, finished external interrupts.*/
            call    ISR31           /* Service the irq31 request.           */
            br      DONE            /* Finished with external interrupts.   */
OTHER:      . . .
            Instructions that check for other exceptions and
              call the required exception-service routines.
            . . .
DONE:       ldw     r2, (sp)        /* Restore registers.                   */
            ldw     et, 4(sp)
            ldw     ra, 8(sp)
            addi    sp, sp, 12
            eret                    /* Return to interrupted program.       */
```

Interrupt-service routine for irq0

```
ISR0:       . . .
            ⋮
            ret
```

Interrupt-service routine for irq31

```
ISR31:      . . .
            ⋮
            ret
```

Main program

```
START:      . . .
```

Figure B.14   An outline of the exception handler.

B.11   ADVANCED CONFIGURATIONS OF NIOS II PROCESSOR

In the previous sections we discussed the features found in the basic configurations of a Nios II processor. It is possible to implement larger Nios II processors that include additional hardware modules that provide enhanced capability. In this section we consider three of the possible enhancements.

B.11.1   EXTERNAL INTERRUPT CONTROLLER

Section B.10.2 describes the mechanism used by the internal interrupt controller, in which software is used to determine the priority of interrupt requests. This scheme is simple to implement, but it may lead to unacceptably long latency in servicing of interrupts in some applications. To reduce the latency, it is possible to include an external interrupt controller circuit that uses vectored interrupts. In this case, the controller provides the address of the interrupt-service routine for each interrupt request.

To further reduce the interrupt latency, the processor can include shadow registers for the 32 general-purpose registers. Several sets of shadow registers can be implemented and associated with different interrupts. The external interrupt controller identifies the shadow-register set to be used with an incoming interrupt request. Then, the identified set is used instead of the normal register set. This obviates the need for saving the contents of registers that are used in the interrupt-service routine.

Priority levels are associated with different interrupts. When the processor is servicing an interrupt of a given priority level, it can be interrupted only by another interrupt that has a higher priority level. The current priority level of the processor and an indication of the active shadow-register set are a part of the processor state, which is kept in the status control register, $ctl0$. This information is kept in the "reserved" bits indicated for this register in Table B.3.

When a Nios II processor is defined, it is configured with either the internal interrupt controller or the external interrupt controller.

B.11.2   MEMORY MANAGEMENT UNIT

A Nios II system can include a memory management unit (MMU), which provides the functionality discussed in Section 8.8. The MMU is intended to support operating systems that use the memory management capability. A system that incorporates an MMU can use both the Supervisor and User modes of operation. The MMU is an optional unit which has to be specified for inclusion in a system at design time.

B.11.3   FLOATING-POINT HARDWARE

The Nios II architecture makes a provision for *custom* instructions. These instructions can be used to define a variety of operations, which may require using additional circuits.

A set of predefined custom instructions is available for implementation of floating-point arithmetic operations. The necessary hardware is included in a Nios II system at design time if floating-point operations are desired.

B.12 Concluding Remarks

In this appendix, we described the main features of the basic implementations of Nios II processors. The basic configurations provide a powerful processor that can be used in a broad range of applications. In Section B.11, we indicated the kind of hardware that can be included in a Nios II system to provide additional capability. Since Nios II is a soft processor, a designer of a system can tailor the capability of the system to suit the desired usage.

The Nios II processor is mainly intended for commercial and industrial applications, but it is also very attractive for use in teaching environments. The FPGA technology for implementing Nios II processors is affordable and easy to use. Altera Corp. has developed a set of Development and Education boards that provide an excellent platform for introducing students to digital technology. These boards comprise the typical components found in a computer system. They make it easy for students to investigate both the hardware and software aspects of computer organization.

Extensive literature on Nios II processors and systems is available on Altera's Web site:

http://www.altera.com

B.13 Solved Problems

This section presents some examples of problems that a student may be asked to solve, and shows how such problems can be solved.

Problem: Assume that there is a string of ASCII-encoded characters stored in memory   **Example B.10** starting at address STRING. The string ends with the Carriage Return (CR) character. Write a Nios II program to determine the length of the string.

Solution: Figure B.15 presents a possible program. Each character in the string is compared to CR (ASCII code 0x0D), and a counter is incremented until the end of the string is reached. The result is stored in location LENGTH.

Problem: We want to find the smallest number in a list of non-negative 32-bit integers.   **Example B.11** Storage for data begins at address $(1000)_{16}$. The word at this address must hold the value of the smallest number after it has been found. The next word contains the number of entries, n, in the list. The following n words contain the numbers in the list. Write a Nios II program to find the smallest number and include the assembler directives needed to organize the data as stated.

Solution: The program in Figure B.16 accomplishes the required task. Comments in the program explain how this task is performed. A few sample numbers are included as entries in the list.

	movia	r2, STRING	/* r2 points to the start of the string.	*/
	add	r3, r0, r0	/* r3 is a counter that is cleared to 0.	*/
	addi	r4, r0, 0x0D	/* Load ASCII code for Carriage Return.	*/
LOOP:	ldb	r5, (r2)	/* Get the next character.	*/
	beq	r5, r4, DONE	/* Finished if character is CR.	*/
	addi	r2, r2, 1	/* Increment the string pointer.	*/
	addi	r3, r3, 1	/* Increment the counter.	*/
	br	LOOP	/* Not finished, loop back.	*/
DONE:	movia	r2, LENGTH	/* Store the count in memory	*/
	stw	r3, (r2)	/* location LENGTH.	*/

Figure B.15   Program for Example B.10.

	.equ	LIST, 0x1000	/* Starting address of the list.	*/
	movia	r2, LIST	/* r2 points to the start of the list.	*/
	ldw	r3, 4(r2)	/* r3 is a counter, initialize it with *n*.	*/
	addi	r4, r2, 8	/* r4 points to the first number.	*/
	ldw	r5, (r4)	/* r5 holds the smallest number found so far.	*/
LOOP:	subi	r3, r3, 1	/* Decrement the counter.	*/
	beq	r3, r0, DONE	/* Finished if r3 is equal to 0.	*/
	addi	r4, r4, 4	/* Increment the list pointer.	*/
	ldw	r6, (r4)	/* Get the next number.	*/
	ble	r5, r6, LOOP	/* Check if smaller number found.	*/
	add	r5, r6, r0	/* Update the smallest number found.	*/
	br	LOOP		
DONE:	stw	r5, (r2)	/* Store the smallest number into SMALL.	*/
	.org	0x1000		
SMALL:	.skip	4	/* Space for the smallest number found.	*/
N:	.word	7	/* Number of entries in the list.	*/
ENTRIES:	.word	4,5,3,6,1,8,2	/* Entries in the list.	*/
	.end			

Figure B.16   Program for Example B.11.

Problem: Write a Nios II program that converts an n-digit decimal integer into a binary **Example B.12** number. The decimal number is given as n ASCII-encoded characters, as would be the case if the number is entered by typing it on a keyboard.

Solution: Consider a four-digit decimal number, $D = d_3d_2d_1d_0$. The value of this number is $((d_3 \times 10 + d_2) \times 10 + d_1) \times 10 + d_0$. This representation of the number is the basis for the conversion technique used in the program in Figure B.17. Note that each ASCII-encoded character is converted into a Binary Coded Decimal (BCD) digit before it is used in the computation.

	movia	r2, N	/* r2 is a counter, initialize	*/
	ldw	r2, (r2)	/* it with n.	*/
	movia	r3, DECIMAL	/* r3 points to the ASCII digits.	*/
	add	r4, r0, r0	/* r4 will hold the binary number.	*/
LOOP:	ldb	r5, (r3)	/* Get the next ASCII digit.	*/
	andi	r5, r5, 0x0F	/* Form the BCD digit.	*/
	add	r4, r4, r5	/* Add to the intermediate result.	*/
	addi	r3, r3, 1	/* Increment the digit pointer.	*/
	subi	r2, r2, 1	/* Decrement the counter.	*/
	beq	r2, r0, DONE		
	muli	r4, r4, 10	/* Multiply by 10.	*/
	br	LOOP	/* Loop back if not done.	*/
DONE:	movia	r5, BINARY	/* Store the result in	*/
	stw	r4, (r5)	/* memory location BINARY.	*/

Figure B.17   Program for Example B.12.

Problem: Consider an array of numbers $A(i,j)$, where $i = 0$ through $n - 1$ is the row index, **Example B.13** and $j = 0$ through $m - 1$ is the column index. The array is stored in the memory of a computer one row after another, with elements of each row occupying m successive word locations. Write a Nios II subroutine for adding column x to column y, element by element, leaving the sum elements in column y. The indices x and y are passed to the subroutine in registers r2 and r3. The parameters n and m are passed to the subroutine in registers r4 and r5, and the address of element $A(0,0)$ is passed in register r6.

Solution: A possible program is given in Figure B.18. We assumed that the values x, y, n, and m are stored in memory locations X, Y, N, and M. Also, the elements of the array are stored in successive words that begin at location ARRAY, which is the address of the element $A(0,0)$. Comments in the program indicate the purpose of individual instructions.

```
            movia   r2, X
            ldw     r2, (r2)        /* Load the value x.                      */
            movia   r3, Y
            ldw     r3, (r3)        /* Load the value y.                      */
            movia   r4, N
            ldw     r4, (r4)        /* Load the value n.                      */
            movia   r5, M
            ldw     r5, (r5)        /* Load the value m.                      */
            movia   r6, ARRAY       /* Load the address of A(0,0).            */
            call    SUB
            next instruction
            ⋮

SUB:        subi    sp, sp, 4
            stw     r7, (sp)        /* Save register r7.                      */
            slli    r5, r5, 2       /* Determine the distance in bytes        */
                                    /*    between successive elements         */
                                    /*    in a column.                        */
            sub     r3, r3, r2      /* Form y − x.                            */
            slli    r3, r3, 2       /* Form 4(y − x).                         */
            slli    r2, r2, 2       /* Form 4x.                               */
            add     r6, r6, r2      /* r6 points to A(0,x).                   */
            add     r7, r6, r3      /* r7 points to A(0,y).                   */
LOOP:       ldw     r2, (r6)        /* Get the next number in column x.       */
            ldw     r3, (r7)        /* Get the next number in column y.       */
            add     r2, r2, r3      /* Add the numbers and                    */
            stw     r2, (r7)        /*    store the sum.                      */
            add     r6, r6, r5      /* Increment pointer to column x.         */
            add     r7, r7, r5      /* Increment pointer to column y.         */
            subi    r4, r4, 1       /* Decrement the row counter.             */
            bgt     r4, r0, LOOP    /* Loop back if not done.                 */
            ldw     r7, (sp)        /* Restore r7.                            */
            addi    sp, sp, 4
            ret                     /* Return to the calling program.         */
```

Figure B.18   Program for Example B.13.

Example B.14   **Problem:** Assume that a memory location BINARY contains a 32-bit pattern. It is desired to display these bits as eight hexadecimal digits on a display device that has the interface depicted in Figure 3.3. Write a Nios II program that accomplishes this task.

Solution: First it is necessary to convert the 32-bit pattern into hex digits that are represented as ASCII-encoded characters. The conversion can be done by using the table-lookup approach. A 16-entry table has to be constructed to provide the ASCII code for each possible hex digit. Then, for each four-bit segment of the pattern in BINARY, the corresponding character can be looked up in the table and stored in eight consecutive byte locations starting at location HEX. Finally, the eight characters are sent to the display. Figure B.19 gives a possible program.

```
              movia    r2, BINARY         /* Get address of binary number.          */
              ldw      r2, (r2)           /* Load the binary number.                */
              movi     r3, 8              /* r3 is a digit counter that is set to 8. */
              movia    r4, HEX            /* r4 points to the hex digits.           */
LOOP:         roli     r2, r2, 4          /* Rotate high-order digit                */
                                          /*   into low-order position.             */
              andi     r5, r2, 0xF        /* Extract next digit.                    */
              ldb      r6, TABLE(r5)      /* Get ASCII code for the digit           */
              stb      r6, (r4)           /*   and store it HEX buffer.             */
              subi     r3, r3, 1          /* Decrement the digit counter.           */
              addi     r4, r4, 1          /* Increment the pointer to hex digits.   */
              bgt      r3, r0, LOOP       /* Loop back if not the last digit.       */
DISPLAY:      movi     r3, 8
              movia    r4, HEX
              movia    r2, DISP_DATA
DLOOP:        ldbio    r5, 4(r2)          /* Check if the display is ready          */
              andi     r5, r5, 4          /*   by testing the DOUT flag.            */
              beq      r5, r0, DLOOP
              ldb      r6, (r4)           /* Get the next ASCII character           */
              stbio    r6, (r2)           /*   and send it to the display.          */
              subi     r3, r3, 1          /* Decrement the counter.                 */
              addi     r4, r4, 1          /* Increment the character pointer.       */
              bgt      r3, r0, DLOOP      /* Loop until all characters displayed.   */
              next instruction

              .org     1000
HEX:          .skip    8                  /* Space for ASCII-encoded digits.        */
TABLE:        .byte    0x30,0x31,0x32,0x33  /* Table for conversion                 */
              .byte    0x34,0x35,0x36,0x37  /*   to ASCII code.                     */
              .byte    0x38,0x39,0x41,0x42
              .byte    0x43,0x44,0x45,0x46
```

Figure B.19   Program for Example B.14.

PROBLEMS

B.1   [E] Write a program that computes the expression SUM = 580 + 68400 + 80000.

B.2   [E] Write a program that computes the expression ANSWER = A × B + C × D.

B.3   [M] Write a program that finds the number of negative integers in a list of n 32-bit integers and stores the count in location NEGNUM. The value n is stored in memory location N, and the first integer in the list is stored in location NUMBERS. Include the necessary assembler directives and a sample list that contains six numbers, some of which are negative.

B.4   [E] Write an assembly-language program in the style of Figure B.8 for the program in Figure B.3. Assume the data layout of Figure 2.10.

B.5   [M] Write a Nios II program to solve Problem 2.10 in Chapter 2.

B.6   [E] Write a Nios II program for the problem described in Example 2.5 in Chapter 2.

B.7   [M] Write a Nios II program for the problem described in Example 3.5 in Chapter 3.

B.8   [E] Write a Nios II program for the problem described in Example 3.6 in Chapter 3.

B.9   [E] Write a Nios II program for the problem described in Example 3.6 in Chapter 3, but assume that the address of TABLE is 0x10100.

B.10 [E] Write a program that displays the contents of 10 bytes of the main memory in hexadecimal format on a line of a video display. The byte string starts at location LOC in the memory. Each byte has to be displayed as two hex characters. The displayed contents of successive bytes should be separated by a space.

B.11 [M] Assume that a memory location BINARY contains a 16-bit pattern. It is desired to display these bits as a string of 0s and 1s on a display device that has the interface depicted in Figure 3.3. Write a program that accomplishes this task.

B.12 [M] Using the seven-segment display in Figure 3.17 and the timer circuit in Figure 3.14, write a program that flashes decimal digits in the repeating sequence $0, 1, 2, \ldots, 9, 0, \ldots$. Each digit is to be displayed for one second. Assume that the counter in the timer circuit is driven by a 100-MHz clock.

B.13 [D] Using two 7-segment displays of the type shown in Figure 3.17, and the timer circuit in Figure 3.14, write a program that flashes numbers in the repeating sequence $0, 1, 2, \ldots, 98, 99, 0, \ldots$. Each number is to be displayed for one second. Assume that the counter in the timer circuit is driven by a 100-MHz clock.

B.14 [D] Write a program that computes real clock time and displays the time in hours (0 to 23) and minutes (0 to 59). The display consists of four 7-segment display devices of the type shown in Figure 3.17. A timer circuit that has the interface given in Figure 3.14 is available. Its counter is driven by a 100-MHz clock.

B.15 [M] Write a Nios II program to solve Problem 2.22 in Chapter 2.

B.16 [D] Write a Nios II program to solve Problem 2.24 in Chapter 2.

B.17   **[M]** Write a Nios II program to solve Problem 2.25 in Chapter 2.

B.18   **[M]** Write a Nios II program to solve Problem 2.26 in Chapter 2.

B.19   **[M]** Write a Nios II program to solve Problem 2.27 in Chapter 2.

B.20   **[M]** Write a Nios II program to solve Problem 2.28 in Chapter 2.

B.21   **[M]** Write a Nios II program to solve Problem 2.29 in Chapter 2.

B.22   **[M]** Write a Nios II program to solve Problem 2.30 in Chapter 2.

B.23   **[M]** Write a Nios II program to solve Problem 2.31 in Chapter 2.

B.24   **[D]** Write a Nios II program to solve Problem 2.32 in Chapter 2.

B.25   **[D]** Write a Nios II program to solve Problem 2.33 in Chapter 2.

B.26   **[M]** Write a Nios II program to solve Problem 3.19 in Chapter 3.

B.27   **[M]** Write a Nios II program to solve Problem 3.21 in Chapter 3.

B.28   **[D]** Write a Nios II program to solve Problem 3.23 in Chapter 3.

B.29   **[D]** Write a Nios II program to solve Problem 3.25 in Chapter 3.

THE COLDFIRE PROCESSOR

APPENDIX OBJECTIVES

In this appendix you will learn about the ColdFire processor, which is representative of CISC-style architecture. The discussion includes:

- Memory organization and register structure
- Addressing modes and types of instructions
- Example programs for computing tasks and I/O
- Extensions for floating-point operations

The ColdFire processor is produced by Freescale Semiconductor, Inc., which was formerly a part of Motorola, Inc. ColdFire was introduced in the mid-1990s. It is derived from the Motorola 68000 processor. ColdFire has been enhanced several times since its introduction with various extensions and new functionality. Processors that implement the ColdFire instruction set are available either as prefabricated chips or as software designs that can be implemented in field-programmable gate-array (FPGA) chips. Both types of implementations are commonly used in embedded applications.

We have selected ColdFire as an example of CISC-style processor design discussed in Sections 2.9 and 2.10. ColdFire includes many instructions that combine memory accesses with arithmetic and logic operations. This increased functionality for individual instructions permits computing tasks to be performed with fewer instructions, thereby reducing the size of programs in memory. A variety of addressing modes enable individual instructions to use both register and memory operands. This increases the flexibility in developing programs, but it adds to the complexity of implementing the instruction set in hardware.

This appendix describes the basic ColdFire instruction set (Revision A as defined in the *ColdFire Family Programmer's Reference Manual* by Freescale Semiconductor [1]). We describe the memory organization, the register structure, the addressing modes for operands, and the various types of instructions. We illustrate the use of ColdFire instructions by implementing the computing tasks presented in Chapters 2 and 3. We also provide a brief overview of floating-point extensions to the basic instruction set.

C.1   MEMORY ORGANIZATION

The ColdFire wordlength is 16 bits. Data are handled in 8-bit *bytes*, 16-bit *words*, and 32-bit *longwords*. Addresses consist of 32 bits and the memory is byte-addressable. From the point of view of the instruction set, the memory is organized as indicated in Figure C.1. The big-endian address assignment is used for the bytes in a word or a longword.

C.2   REGISTERS

Figure C.2 shows the ColdFire registers. There are eight *data registers* and eight *address registers*, each 32 bits long. The data registers, D0 to D7, serve as general-purpose registers for arithmetic/logic operations and other uses. The address registers, A0 to A7, are used primarily to hold information that is needed in determining the addresses of operands in memory. One address register, A7, is dedicated to serving as the processor *stack pointer* (SP).

There is also a *status register* (SR) with the four condition code flags—N, V, Z, and C—discussed in Section 2.3.7. These flags are set or cleared based on the results of arithmetic, logic, or data-transfer operations. There is an additional flag called X (Extend), which is set or cleared in the same way as the C flag, but it is not affected by as many instructions. It is used as an extended carry-in/carry-out bit for addition or subtraction operations on numbers that are larger than the data register size of 32 bits, as explained in Section C.3.3. The remaining bits in the status register are used to control the behavior of the processor and will be discussed in Section C.6.

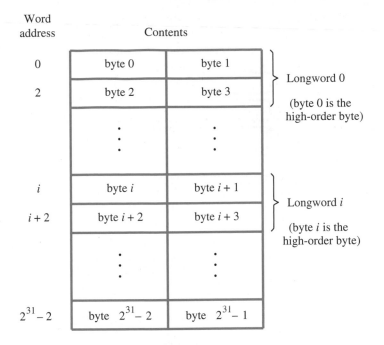

Figure C.1   Big-endian memory layout of bytes for a ColdFire processor.

C.3 INSTRUCTIONS

ColdFire instructions may consist of 16, 32, or 48 bits that are stored as one, two, or three consecutive words in memory. The first word is the *OP-code* word that specifies the operation to be performed. The OP-code word also provides some addressing information. If more addressing information is required for a given type of instruction, it is provided in one or possibly two *extension* words.

Most arithmetic, logic, and data-movement instructions have two operands and are written in assembly language as

$$\text{OP} \quad \text{source, destination}$$

where the operation OP is performed using the operands and the result is placed in the destination location, overwriting its original value. Note that the destination is the second operand. This order is different from the order that is discussed in Chapter 2 for CISC-style instructions.

In assembly language, the OP code is given as a mnemonic that indicates the operation to be performed, along with a length specifier that indicates the size of the data operands. The length specifier can be L, W, or B for longword, word, or byte size, respectively. For

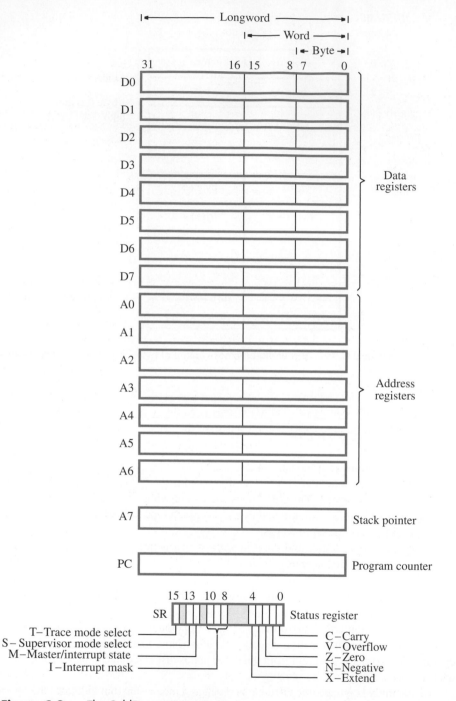

Figure C.2   The ColdFire register structure.

example, the instruction

ADD.L   LOC, D1

adds the 32-bit operands in memory location LOC and processor register D1, and places the sum in D1. Not all sizes are available for all instructions; addition is only supported for the longword size.

Assembly-language specification of instructions must conform to the constraints imposed by the assembler program that is used for generating executable machine-language code. The assembler provided by Freescale Semiconductor is case-insensitive for instruction mnemonics and register names. The technical documentation for ColdFire [1] uses upper-case characters consistently. To conform to this presentation style, and to make example programs easier to read, we will use upper-case characters for all instruction mnemonics and register names.

C.3.1 ADDRESSING MODES

The operands for instructions may be in processor registers, in memory, or included as immediate values within instructions. The following addressing modes are available.

Immediate mode—The operand is a constant value that is contained within the instruction. Four sizes of immediate operands can be specified. Small 3-bit numbers can be included in the OP-code word of certain instructions. Byte, word, and longword operands are found in one or two extension words that follow the OP-code word.

Absolute mode—The memory address of an operand is given in the instruction immediately after the OP-code word. There are two versions of this mode—long and short. In the long mode, a full 32-bit address is specified in two extension words. In the short mode, a 16-bit value is given in one extension word. This value is used as the low-order 16 bits of a full 32-bit address. To determine the high-order 16 bits, the sign bit of the short value is extended. Therefore, the short form can only access two 32-Kbyte regions in memory: 0 to 7FFF, or FFFF8000 to FFFFFFFF.

Register mode—The operand is in a processor register, An or Dn, that is specified in the instruction.

Register indirect mode—The effective address of the operand is in an address register, An, that is specified in the instruction.

Autoincrement mode—The effective address of the operand is in an address register, An, that is specified in the instruction. After the operand is accessed, the contents of An are incremented by 1, 2, or 4, depending on whether the operand is a byte, a word, or a longword.

Autodecrement mode—The contents of an address register, An, that is specified in the instruction are first decremented by 1, 2, or 4, depending on whether the operand is a byte, a word, or a longword. The effective address of the operand is then given by the decremented contents of An.

Basic index mode—A 16-bit signed offset and an address register, An, are specified in the instruction. The offset is sign-extended to 32 bits, and the sum of the sign-extended offset and the 32-bit contents of An is the effective address of the operand.

Full index mode—An 8-bit signed offset, an address register An, and an index register Rk (either an address or a data register) are given in the instruction. The effective address of the operand is the sum of the sign-extended offset, the contents of register An, and the signed contents of register Rk.

Basic relative mode—This mode is the same as the Basic index mode, except that the program counter (PC) is used instead of an address register, An.

Full relative mode—This mode is the same as the Full index mode, except that the program counter (PC) is used instead of an address register, An.

The addressing modes and their assembler syntax are summarized in Table C.1. The Basic and Full index modes correspond to the Index addressing mode discussed in Section 2.4.3. The two relative modes are versions of the index modes that use the program counter instead

Table C.1   ColdFire addressing modes.

Name	Assembler syntax	Addressing function
Immediate	#Value	Operand = Value
Absolute Short	Value	EA = Sign Extended WValue
Absolute Long	Value	EA = Value
Register	Rn	EA = R_n that is, Operand = $[R_n]$
Register Indirect	(An)	EA = $[A_n]$
Autoincrement	(An)+	EA = $[A_n]$; Increment A$_n$
Autodecrement	−(An)	Decrement A$_n$; EA = $[A_n]$
Basic index	WValue(An)	EA = WValue + $[A_n]$
Full index	BValue(An, Rk)	EA = BValue + $[A_n]$ + $[R_k]$
Basic relative	WValue(PC)	EA = WValue + [PC]
Full relative	BValue(PC, Rk)	EA = BValue + [PC] + $[R_k]$

EA = effective address
Value = a number given either explicitly or represented by a label
BValue = an 8-bit Value
WValue = a 16-bit Value
A$_n$ = an address register
R$_n$ = an address register or a data register

of an address register. In these cases, the offset represents the distance between the memory location of the desired operand and the location following that of the instruction accessing it.

Finally, it is important to note that not all instructions support all addressing modes or all operand sizes. Some of the restrictions on addressing modes and operand sizes are indicated later in this appendix for different categories of instructions. The technical documentation on the ColdFire processor provides full details on the valid combinations for individual instructions [1].

C.3.2 MOVE INSTRUCTION

The MOVE instruction transfers data between memory, or I/O interfaces, and the processor registers. The direction of the transfer is from source to destination. The value being transferred by a MOVE instruction causes the condition code flags Z or N in the status register to be set to 1 if the value is zero or negative, respectively. This instruction can be used with all three operand sizes. The source operand can use all of the available addressing modes. As for the destination operand, all modes except Immediate and Relative are permitted. To ensure that the size of the instruction does not exceed three words, certain combinations of addressing modes for the source and destination are not permitted. For example, the Absolute mode (short or long) cannot be used for both operands.

To illustrate how different addressing modes and different operand sizes may be specified, consider the instruction

$$\text{MOVE.L} \quad \text{D0, (A2)}$$

which writes a 32-bit value from register D0 into the memory location whose address is given by the contents of register A2. Similarly, the instruction

$$\text{MOVE.B} \quad \text{CHARACTER, D3}$$

transfers an 8-bit value from memory location CHARACTER into register D3. Only the low-order byte of register D3 is modified by this transfer; the remaining bits are not affected.

Transfers between registers are possible, as in

$$\text{MOVE.W} \quad \text{D5, D7}$$

which transfers the 16-bit value in the low-order bits of register D5 to the low-order bits in register D7. The high-order bits of D7 are not affected.

Direct transfers between memory locations are also possible, as in

$$\text{MOVE.L} \quad \text{(A2), 16(A4)}$$

which transfers a 32-bit value from the memory location whose address is given by the contents of register A2 to the memory location whose effective address is obtained by adding 16 to the value in register A4.

An immediate value can be loaded into a register or a memory location by an instruction such as

$$\text{MOVE.L} \quad \text{\#\$2A4C80, D7}$$

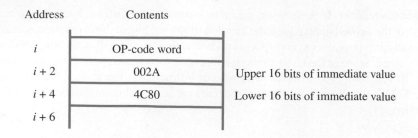

Address   Contents

i   OP-code word

i + 2   002A   Upper 16 bits of immediate value

i + 4   4C80   Lower 16 bits of immediate value

i + 6

Figure C.3   The instruction MOVE.L #$2A4C80, D7 in memory.

which loads the specified hexadecimal value into register D7. Note that the '$' character is used to denote a hexadecimal value. All 32 bits of the destination are affected because of the L size specifier, hence the resulting value in D7 will be 002A4C80. Figure C.3 shows how this instruction would be stored in memory. The OP-code word indicates that it is a MOVE instruction and specifies the operand size. It also specifies the addressing modes for the source and destination operands, including the fact that register D7 is the destination location. The two extension words following the OP-code word contain the 32-bit immediate value for the source operand.

There are two specialized versions of the MOVE instruction. The MOVEQ (Move Quick) instruction is used when the source operand is an immediate value that is small enough to fit in 8 bits and the destination operand is a data register. This instruction is only one word in size. The MOVEA instruction is used when the destination location is an address register. Only word and longword operands are permitted for MOVEA. The condition codes in the status register are not affected by this instruction. The ColdFire assembler replaces the normal MOVE instruction with MOVEQ or MOVEA where applicable.

There is also an instruction, MOVEM (Move Multiple Registers), which performs multiple transfers involving several registers. It is used in subroutine linkage as discussed in Section C.3.7.

C.3.3   ARITHMETIC INSTRUCTIONS

This category of instructions includes arithmetic operations as well as comparison, sign-extension, negation, and clear operations. The operands can be in memory, in data registers, or included as immediate values within instructions. All but four of the arithmetic instructions discussed in this section permit only longword size for operands. All but one of the instructions require at least one register operand.

Addition, Subtraction, Comparison, and Negation
The instructions of this type are:

*   ADD.L   (Add)
*   ADDI.L   (Add immediate)
*   ADDA.L   (Add address)

- SUB.L (Subtract)
- SUBI.L (Subtract immediate)
- SUBA.L (Subtract address)
- CMP.L (Compare)
- CMPI.L (Compare immediate)
- CMPA.L (Compare address)
- NEG.L (Negate; single data-register operand)
- ADDX.L (Add extended; two data-register operands)
- SUBX.L (Subtract extended; two data-register operands)
- NEGX.L (Negate extended; single data-register operand)

The ADD and SUB instructions perform the specified arithmetic operation on two longword operands and place the result in the destination location. The SUB instruction subtracts the source operand from the destination operand. All of the condition code flags are affected, based on the result.

The CMP instruction is used for comparing longword values. The destination operand must be in a register. The instruction performs the same operation as the SUB instruction, but does not change the destination operand. The result affects all condition code flags, except the X flag.

There are specialized versions of the ADD, SUB, and CMP instructions for two cases: when the source operand is an immediate value (ADDI, SUBI, and CMPI), and when the destination operand is an address register (ADDA, SUBA, and CMPA). The ColdFire assembler replaces the normal versions of these instructions with the specialized versions where applicable.

Consider the following examples. The instruction

$$\text{ADD.L} \quad \text{D4, (A1)+}$$

adds the longword in register D4 to the longword at the memory address given by the contents of register A1 and places the sum in the same memory location. The value in register A1 is incremented by four. The instruction

$$\text{SUBI.L} \quad \text{\#256, D7}$$

subtracts the value 256 from the contents of register D7 and places the result in D7. Note that the instruction

$$\text{CMPI.L} \quad \text{\#256, D7}$$

performs the same subtraction, but the contents of register D7 are not changed. All condition code flags except X are affected in the same manner as for the SUB instruction.

The NEG.L instruction is used to negate a longword operand in a data register. Negation is achieved by subtracting the value in the data register from zero. All of the condition code flags are affected, based on the result. The instruction

$$\text{NEG.L} \quad \text{D3}$$

```
MOVE.L    #$A72C10F8, D2      D2 contains A72C10F8.
MOVE.L    #$10, D3            D3 contains 10.
MOVE.L    #$5C00FE04, D4      D4 contains 5C00FE04.
MOVE.L    #$4A, D5            D5 contains 4A.
ADD.L     D2, D4             Add low-order 32 bits; carry-out sets X and C flags.
ADDX.L    D3, D5             Add high-order bits with X flag as carry-in bit.
```

Figure C.4   Program to add numbers larger than 32 bits using the ADDX instruction.

negates the longword in register D3 and overwrites the original value with the negated value.

To facilitate arithmetic operations on values that are larger than 32 bits, the ADDX.L, SUBX.L, and NEGX.L instructions use the X flag as a carry-in bit. All operands must be in data registers. All of the condition code flags are affected. For example, Figure C.4 shows how the ADDX instruction is used to add numbers that are too large to fit into 32-bit registers. The two hexadecimal values to be added are 10A72C10F8 and 4A5C00FE04. Registers D2 and D3 are loaded with the low- and high-order bits of 10A72C10F8, respectively. Similarly, registers D4 and D5 are loaded with the low- and high-order bits of 4A5C00FE04. The ADD.L instruction is used to add the low-order 32 bits. This addition generates a carry-out of 1 that causes the X and C flags to be set. The ADDX.L instruction then uses the new value of the X flag as the carry-in bit when adding the high-order bits. The low- and high-order bits of the sum are in registers D4 and D5. The C and X flags are both affected by the result of the ADDX.L instruction, but in this example, they will not be used because the desired 64-bit addition has been completed.

Multiplication

Multiplication is performed by using the MULS and MULU instructions for signed and unsigned operands, respectively. The operand size can be word or longword. The destination operand must be in a data register.

The instruction

$$\text{MULS.W} \quad \text{\#1340, D5}$$

multiplies 1340 by the signed 16-bit value in the low-order bits of register D5, and places the 32-bit product in D5.

The instruction

$$\text{MULS.L} \quad \text{D2, D5}$$

multiplies the longwords in registers D2 and D5, truncates the product to 32 bits, and places it in D5.

The MULU.W and MULU.L instructions perform the same operations on unsigned operands. As a result of multiplication, the N and Z condition code flags are set or cleared based on the value of the product, while the V and C flags are cleared to zero.

MOVE.W   #$FFFF, D2   The low-order word of D2 is treated as −1.
MOVE.W   #$0001, D3   The low-order word of D3 contains 1.
MULS.W   D2, D3   The signed longword result in D3 is −1
                        or $FFFFFFFF, hence the N flag is set.

(a) Signed computation of −1 × 1 = −1

MOVE.W   #$FFFF, D2   The low-order word of D2 is treated as 65535.
MOVE.W   #$0001, D3   The low-order word of D3 contains 1.
MULU.W   D2, D3   The unsigned longword result in D3 is 65535
                        or $0000FFFF, hence the N flag is cleared.

(b) Unsigned computation of 65535 × 1 = 65535

Figure C.5   Signed versus unsigned multiplication.

Figure C.5 shows how different results are obtained for signed and unsigned multiplication of the same pair of word operands, $FFFF and $0001. The MULS.W instruction in Figure C.5a treats the low-order word value of $FFFF in register D2 as −1. The longword result for the signed multiplication is $FFFFFFFF representing −1, and the N flag is set. In contrast, the MULU.W instruction in Figure C.5b treats $FFFF as the unsigned number 65535, and the longword result for the unsigned multiplication is $0000FFFF representing 65535, which causes the N flag to be cleared.

Division

Division is performed by using the DIVS and DIVU instructions for signed and unsigned operands, respectively. The operand size can be word or longword. The destination operand must be in a data register.

The instruction

DIVS.W   #2500, D1

divides the 32-bit value in register D1 by the 16-bit immediate operand 2500. The 16-bit quotient is placed in the low-order bits of D1, and the 16-bit remainder is placed in the high-order bits of D1.

The instruction

DIVS.L   D2, D1

divides the value in D1 by the value in D2, and places the quotient in D1. The remainder is discarded.

The DIVU.W and DIVU.L instructions perform the same operations on unsigned operands. As a result of division, the N and Z condition code flags are set or cleared based on the value of the quotient, while the V and C flags are cleared to zero.

Since the remainder is discarded in the DIVS.L and DIVU.L operations, there exist two other instructions that can be used to obtain the remainder when needed. The instruction

$$\text{REMS.L} \quad \text{D2, D1:D4}$$

divides the value in D1 by the value in D2, places the 32-bit remainder in register D4, and leaves the contents of D1 unchanged. Thus, both the remainder and the quotient can be obtained if this instruction is followed by

$$\text{DIVS.L} \quad \text{D2, D1}$$

Note that a third operand, delineated by a colon, must be specified in the REMS.L instruction.

The REMU.L instruction performs the same operation as REMS.L, but on unsigned operands. It also requires three operands.

Other Arithmetic Instructions

The EXT (Sign extend) instruction is provided to extend the sign bit when increasing the number of bits used to represent a number. It has a single operand that must be in a data register. The size specified determines how the operation is performed. The EXT.L instruction sign-extends the low-order word to a longword, the EXT.W instruction sign-extends the low-order byte to a word, and the EXT.B instruction sign-extends the low-order byte to a longword. For all three instructions, the N and Z condition code flags are affected, based on the result, and the V and C flags are cleared.

The CLR (Clear) instruction is provided to clear bits in a specified operand. The size specifier indicates whether a longword, word, or byte is to be cleared. The operand may be in memory or in a data register. The Z flag is set by this instruction, and the N, V, and C flags are cleared.

C.3.4   BRANCH AND JUMP INSTRUCTIONS

Conditional branch instructions have the format

$$\text{B}cc \quad \text{LABEL}$$

where cc specifies the condition code. Table C.2 summarizes the condition codes and the corresponding combinations of the condition code flags that are tested. For example, the BEQ (Branch-if-equal) instruction causes a branch if the Z flag is set, whereas BGE (Branch-if-greater-than-or-equal) depends on the state of the N and V flags. There is also an unconditional branch instruction, BRA, where the branch is always taken.

Branch instructions specify a signed offset that is added to the value of the program counter to determine the target address. Three types of offsets are provided, based on the distance between the location following the branch instruction and the target of the branch. In the first type, a small offset of 8 bits is included in the OP-code word when the distance is within ±127 bytes. In the second type, a larger 16-bit offset is specified in the extension word that follows the OP-code word when the distance is up to ±32 Kbytes. In the third

Table C.2   Condition codes for Bcc instructions.

Condition suffix cc	Name	Test condition
HI	High	$C \vee Z = 0$
LS	Low or same	$C \vee Z = 1$
CC	Carry clear	$C = 0$
CS	Carry set	$C = 1$
NE	Not equal	$Z = 0$
EQ	Equal	$Z = 1$
VC	Overflow clear	$V = 0$
VS	Overflow set	$V = 1$
PL	Plus	$N = 0$
MI	Minus	$N = 1$
GE	Greater or equal	$N \oplus V = 0$
LT	Less than	$N \oplus V = 1$
GT	Greater than	$Z \vee (N \oplus V) = 0$
LE	Less or equal	$Z \vee (N \oplus V) = 1$

type, a 32-bit offset can be specified in two extension words when the distance to the target of the branch exceeds the range supported by a 16-bit offset.

The JMP (Jump) instruction performs an unconditional jump to a specified location for the next instruction to be executed. A single operand specifies the target address. The addressing modes that can be used in the JMP instruction are Absolute, Indirect, Basic and Full index, and Basic and Full relative. For example, the instruction

$$\text{JMP} \quad (A3)$$

jumps to the location given by the contents of address register A3.

To illustrate the use of a branch instruction in a loop, Figure C.6 shows a ColdFire version of the loop program in Figure 2.26 for adding numbers in a list. The Autoincrement addressing mode is used in the ADD.L instruction to automatically increment the pointer to the entries in the list. The BGT (Branch-if-greater-than) instruction checks the condition code flags that are set or cleared as a result of the execution of the SUBQ.L instruction. This is the instruction that decrements the count of the number of elements in the list remaining to be processed. It is a version of the SUBI instruction that is used when the immediate value can be represented with 3 bits.

Figure C.7 shows the format of a conditional branch instruction with a small offset and how the three instructions in the loop of the program in Figure C.6 would appear when stored in the memory. The BGT instruction requires a negative offset that is computed as

$$\text{Offset} = \text{TargetAddress} - [\text{PC}]$$

```
          MOVEA.L   #NUM1, A2    Put the address NUM1 in A2.
          MOVE.L    N, D1        Put the number of entries n in D1.
          CLR.L     D0
LOOP:     ADD.L     (A2)+, D0    Accumulate sum in D0.
          SUBQ.L    #1, D1
          BGT       LOOP
          MOVE.L    D0, SUM      Store the result when finished.
```

Figure C.6   A ColdFire version of the list-summing program in Figure 2.26.

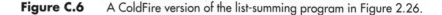

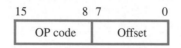

Branch address = [updated PC] + offset

(a) Short-offset branch instruction format

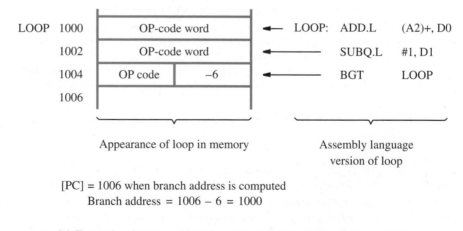

Appearance of loop in memory   Assembly language
                                   version of loop

[PC] = 1006 when branch address is computed
Branch address = 1006 − 6 = 1000

(b) Example of using a branch instruction in the loop of Figure C.6

Figure C.7   Branch instruction format and appearance in memory.

The target address is 1000. At the time that the BGT instruction is executed, the value in the PC will be 1006 because the PC is incremented after fetching the OP-code word for the BGT instruction. Hence, the offset is $1000 - 1006 = -6$. An 8-bit offset is sufficient for this small value, which means that this BGT instruction can be encoded using a single word.

```
          MOVEA.L    #LIST, A2    Get the address LIST.
          CLR.L      D3
          CLR.L      D4
          CLR.L      D5
          MOVE.L     N, D6        Load the value n.
LOOP:     ADD.L      4(A2), D3    Add current student mark for Test 1.
          ADD.L      8(A2), D4    Add current student mark for Test 2.
          ADD.L      12(A2), D5   Add current student mark for Test 3.
          ADDA.L     #16, A2      Increment the pointer.
          SUBQ.L     #1, D6       Decrement the counter.
          BGT        LOOP         Loop back if not finished.
          MOVE.L     D3, SUM1     Store the total for Test 1.
          MOVE.L     D4, SUM2     Store the total for Test 2.
          MOVE.L     D5, SUM3     Store the total for Test 3.
```

Figure C.8   A ColdFire version of the program in Figure 2.11 for summing test scores.

A more involved example that also illustrates some other aspects of instructions is shown in Figure C.8. It is a ColdFire version of the program in Figure 2.11, which computes the sum of all scores for three tests taken by a group of students. The availability of the Basic index mode in the ADD instructions to access memory operands obviates the need for the Load instructions within the loop body in Figure 2.11.

C.3.5   LOGIC INSTRUCTIONS

Logic instructions require longword operands and at least one operand must be in a data register. The following instructions are available:

- AND.L   (Bitwise Logical AND)
- ANDI.L   (Bitwise Logical AND; source operand is an immediate value)
- OR.L   (Bitwise Logical OR)
- ORI.L   (Bitwise Logical OR; source operand is an immediate value)
- EOR.L   (Bitwise Logical Exclusive-OR; source operand must be in a data register)
- EORI.L   (Bitwise Logical Exclusive-OR; source operand is an immediate value)
- NOT.L   (Bitwise Complement; single data-register operand)

All logic instructions affect the N and Z condition code flags, based on the result; the V and C flags are cleared.

For example, the instruction

$$\text{ANDI.L} \quad \#\$FF, D5$$

performs a bitwise logical AND of the hexadecimal value 000000FF and the longword in data register D5, and places the result in D5. The instruction

$$\text{EOR.L} \quad \text{D3, (A6)+}$$

performs a bitwise logical Exclusive-OR of the longword in register D3 with the longword at the memory address given by the contents of register A6. The result is placed at the same address. The contents of register A6 are then incremented by four.

C.3.6   SHIFT INSTRUCTIONS

Shift instructions have two operands: the destination operand must be in a data register holding the longword value to be shifted, and the source operand specifies the shift amount either as an immediate value or as the contents of a data register. The immediate value must be between 1 and 8, which is encoded in the instruction. If the shift amount is in a data register, its value is interpreted modulo 64, even though the data register size is only 32 bits.

For all shift instructions, the last bit that is shifted out of the destination data register is copied into the C and X condition code flags. Each bit that is shifted into the destination data register is zero, except for arithmetic shifts to the right where the value of the sign in bit b_{31} is preserved. Each of these cases is shown in Figure 2.23. Based on the final result after shifting, the N and Z flags are affected. The V flag is cleared.

The available shift instructions are:

- LSL.L   (Logical Shift Left)
- LSR.L   (Logical Shift Right)
- ASL.L   (Arithmetic Shift Left)
- ASR.L   (Arithmetic Shift Right; sign bit is preserved)

The following examples illustrate the differences between shift operations. Assume that data register D4 initially contains hexadecimal 80000000 (bit b_{31} is one and all other bits are zero). The instruction

$$\text{LSR.L} \quad \text{\#6, D4}$$

shifts the value in D4 to the right by 6 bits, inserting zero bits into the left end. The result in D4 is hexadecimal 02000000. The C and X flags are cleared because the last bit shifted out of D4 is zero.

For the same initial value in D4, the instruction

$$\text{ASR.L} \quad \text{\#6, D4}$$

also shifts the value in D4 to the right by 6 bits, but it preserves the sign in bit b_{31}. Therefore, the bits shifted into the data register on the left end are 1s. The result in D4 is FE000000. The C and X flags are cleared because the last bit shifted out is zero.

MOVEA.L	#LOC, A0	A0 points to two consecutive bytes.
MOVE.B	(A0)+, D0	Load first byte into D0.
LSL.L	#4, D0	Shift left by 4 bit positions.
MOVE.B	(A0), D1	Load second byte into D1.
ANDI.L	#$F, D1	Clear all high-order bits in D1.
OR.L	D0, D1	Concatenate the digits.
MOVE.B	D1, PACKED	Store the result.

Figure C.9   Use of logic and shift instructions in packing BCD digits.

Consider the BCD digit-packing program of Figure 2.24. The ColdFire version of this program is shown in Figure C.9. The two ASCII-encoded characters in consecutive memory byte locations are brought into registers D0 and D1. The LSL instruction shifts the first byte in D0 four bit positions to the left, filling the low-order four bits with zeros. The ANDI instruction clears all of the high-order bits in register D1 to zero. The 4-bit patterns that are the desired BCD codes are subsequently combined in D1 with the OR instruction. Finally, the byte of interest, which is the rightmost byte in register D1, is placed in memory location PACKED. Note that the LSL, AND, and OR instructions affect all 32 bits in the register operand, but the desired packed byte is generated properly in the lower-most 8 bits of D1.

Example C.1

C.3.7 SUBROUTINE LINKAGE INSTRUCTIONS

ColdFire provides instructions and a processor stack to support subroutines and parameter passing in the manner outlined in Section 2.7. Address register A7 serves as the stack pointer, and it must always have a value that is longword-aligned, that is, a multiple of 4. This register should not be used for any other purpose. The stack grows in the direction of decreasing memory addresses. The stack pointer value in register A7 is decremented by 4 to push new information onto the stack, and incremented by 4 to pop information off the stack.

There are two subroutine call instructions, BSR (Branch-to-subroutine) and JSR (Jump-to-subroutine). The BSR instruction specifies the address of a subroutine with an 8-bit, 16-bit, or 32-bit offset in the same manner as other branch instructions. The JSR instruction may use the Absolute, Indirect, Basic and Full index, or Basic and Full relative addressing modes to generate the target address. Both BSR and JSR automatically push the return address onto the processor stack, rather than saving it in a link register as described in Section 2.7.

At the end of a subroutine, the RTS (Return-from-subroutine) instruction is used to return to the calling program. The RTS instruction pops the return address off the top of the stack and loads it into the program counter.

Parameter Passing

Section 2.7.2 discusses two different methods of parameter passing, which are illustrated by using the example program in Figure 2.26 for adding numbers in a list. Figure C.6 provides a ColdFire version of this program. It will be the basis for the discussion that follows.

Figure C.10 is a ColdFire version of the program in Figure 2.17 for passing parameters through registers. The starting address of the list of values to be added is passed to the subroutine by placing it in register A2. The number of elements in the list is passed to the subroutine in register D1. After adding all of the elements in the list, the subroutine returns the sum in register D0.

Figure C.11 shows a ColdFire version of the program in Figure 2.18 for passing parameters via the processor stack. Prior to calling the subroutine, the starting address of the list and the number of elements are pushed onto the stack. The subroutine retrieves these values from the stack. Upon completion of the subroutine, the result being returned is placed on the stack to be retrieved by the calling program.

The program in Figure C.11 also illustrates how the MOVEM (Move Multiple Registers) instruction is used to save or restore registers to or from consecutive locations in memory. The MOVEM instruction has two operands, and the order of the operands dictates whether register values are written to or read from memory. One operand is a list of individual registers or ranges of registers, e.g., D0–D1/A2. The other operand is the starting address for the values in memory, which must be specified with either the Indirect mode

---

Calling program

MOVEA.L	#NUM1, A2	Put the address NUM1 in A2.
MOVE.L	N, D1	Put the number of elements n in D1.
BSR	LISTADD	Call subroutine LISTADD.
MOVE.L	D0, SUM	Store the sum in SUM.
next instruction		

$\vdots$

Subroutine

LISTADD:	CLR.L	D0	
LOOP:	ADD.L	(A2)+, D0	Accumulate sum in D0.
	SUBQ.L	#1, D1	
	BGT	LOOP	
	RTS		

Figure C.10   Program of Figure C.6 written as a subroutine; parameters passed through registers.

(Assume that the top of stack is initially at level 1 in the diagram below.)

Calling program

MOVE.L	#NUM1, –(A7)	Push parameters onto stack.
MOVE.L	N, –(A7)	
BSR	LISTADD	
MOVE.L	4(A7), D0	Get result from the stack.
MOVE.L	D0, SUM	Save result.
ADDA.L	#8, A7	Restore top of stack.

⋮

Subroutine

LISTADD:	ADDA.L	#–12, A7	Adjust stack pointer to allocate space.
	MOVEM.L	D0–D1/A2, (A7)	Save registers D0, D1, and A2.
	MOVE.L	16(A7), D1	Initialize counter to n.
	MOVEA.L	20(A7), A2	Initialize pointer to the list.
	CLR.L	D0	Initialize sum to 0.
LOOP:	ADD.L	(A2)+, D0	Add entry from list.
	SUBQ.L	#1, D1	
	BGT	LOOP	
	MOVE.L	D0, 20(A7)	Put result on the stack.
	MOVEM.L	(A7), D0–D1/A2	Restore registers.
	ADDA.L	#12, A7	Adjust stack pointer to deallocate space.
	RTS		

(a) Calling program and subroutine

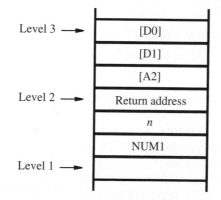

(b) Stack contents at different times

Figure C.11 Program of Figure C.6 written as a subroutine; parameters passed on the stack.

or Basic index mode. The MOVEM instruction writes or reads memory in the direction of increasing addresses from the given starting location.

At the beginning of the subroutine, the ADDA.L instruction adjusts the stack pointer from Level 2 to Level 3 in Figure C.11b. This allocates space for saving the contents of three registers. The MOVEM instruction then writes the contents of registers D0, D1, and A2 into the allocated space. At the end of the subroutine, these values are read from the stack and loaded back into the registers with a similar MOVEM instruction, except that the source/destination order is reversed. The final step before returning from the subroutine is to readjust the stack pointer from Level 3 to Level 2 to deallocate the space that was previously allocated for saving the registers.

Stack Frames for Nested Subroutines

For nested subroutine calls using either BSR or JSR instructions, the return address for each call is automatically pushed onto the processor stack. Subsequently, RTS instructions are executed when subroutines in the nested sequence are completed. As each RTS instruction is executed, the corresponding return address is popped from the stack.

As discussed in Section 2.7.3, *stack frames* provide workspaces in memory for each subroutine in a nested sequence. In addition to the stack pointer A7, another address register can be used as the *frame pointer* within a subroutine to identify the current stack frame.

ColdFire provides two special instructions for managing stack frames. The instruction

LINK   Ai, #disp

is used at the beginning of a subroutine to allocate a stack frame. It performs the following operations:

1. Pushes the contents of register Ai, the frame pointer, onto the processor stack

2. Copies the contents of the stack pointer, A7, into the frame pointer, Ai

3. Adds the specified displacement value to the stack pointer, A7

The displacement value is a negative number so that the stack grows to allocate additional space for local variables in the subroutine. These variables can be accessed with the Basic index or Full index addressing modes using register Ai, the frame pointer. The displacement can also be used to allocate space for saving the values of registers used by the subroutine.

The second special instruction

UNLK   Ai

is used at the end of a subroutine to deallocate the stack frame. It reverses the actions of the LINK instruction. It loads A7 from Ai, thus lowering the top of the stack to its original position, where it was before adding the displacement value. Then it pops the saved contents of register Ai off the stack and loads them back into Ai.

To illustrate the use of the LINK and UNLK instructions, Figure C.12 provides ColdFire code for the program with nested subroutine calls presented in Figure 2.21. The stack frames for subroutines SUB1 and SUB2 are shown in Figure C.13. The execution flow is as follows:

• The calling program pushes parameters param2 and param1 onto the stack for use by subroutine SUB1. When SUB1 is called by the BSR instruction, the return address 2014

Memory location	Instructions		Comments

Calling program

$\vdots$

2000	MOVE.L	PARAM2, −(A7)	Place parameters on stack.
2006	MOVE.L	PARAM1, −(A7)	
2012	BSR	SUB1	
2014	MOVE.L	(A7), RESULT	Store result.
2020	ADDA.L	#8, A7	Restore stack level.
2024	next instruction		

$\vdots$

First subroutine

2100	SUB1:	LINK	A6, #−16	Set frame pointer and allocate stack space.
2104		MOVEM.L	D0−D2/A0,(A7)	Save registers.
		MOVEA.L	8(A6), A0	Load parameters.
		MOVE.L	12(A6), D0	

$\vdots$

		MOVE.L	PARAM3, −(A7)	Place a parameter on stack.
2160		BSR	SUB2	
2164		MOVE.L	(A7)+, D1	Pop result from SUB2 into D1.

$\vdots$

		MOVE.L	D2, 8(A6)	Place result on stack.
		MOVEM.L	(A7), D0−D2/A0	Restore registers.
		UNLK	A6	Restore frame pointer and deallocate stack space.
		RTS		Return.

Second subroutine

3000	SUB2:	LINK	A6, #−8	Set frame pointer and allocate stack space.
		MOVEM.L	D0−D1,(A7)	Save registers.
		MOVE.L	8(A6), D0	Load parameter.

$\vdots$

		MOVE.L	D1, 8(A6)	Place result on stack.
		MOVEM.L	(A7), D0−D1	Restore registers.
		UNLK	A6	Restore frame pointer and deallocate stack space.
		RTS		Return.

Figure C.12   Nested subroutines.

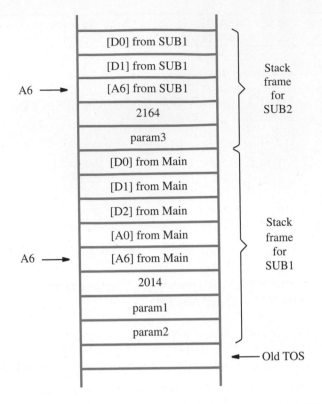

[D0] from SUB1
[D1] from SUB1
[A6] from SUB1
2164
param3
[D0] from Main
[D1] from Main
[D2] from Main
[A0] from Main
[A6] from Main
2014
param1
param2

A6 → (points to [A6] from SUB1)

A6 → (points to [A6] from Main)

Stack frame for SUB2

Stack frame for SUB1

← Old TOS

Figure C.13   Stack frames for program in Figure C.12.

is pushed onto the stack. The address 2100 for SUB1 is within 128 bytes of the BSR instruction, hence an 8-bit offset may be used and the BSR instruction requires only the OP-code word.

• Subroutine SUB1 begins by allocating a stack frame with the instruction

$$\text{LINK} \quad \text{A6, \#}-16$$

which saves the current value of A6 on the stack, writes the value of A7 into A6 to define the new frame pointer, and then adjusts the value of A7 to allocate space on the stack by an amount sufficient to save four registers to be used by SUB1.

• The current values of the four registers to be used by SUB1 are saved on the stack using the MOVEM instruction.

• SUB1 then retrieves the values of param1 and param2 from the stack using the Basic index mode with the frame pointer. After performing some computation, SUB1 pushes param3 onto the stack and calls subroutine SUB2. The return address 2164 is pushed on the stack. The subroutine address 3000 is separated by more than 128 bytes from the BSR instruction, hence a 16-bit offset is included in the instruction in one extension word.

- SUB2 begins with its own LINK instruction to allocate a new stack frame with space for saving register values, followed by the MOVEM instruction that writes the values of two registers on the stack. The value of param3 is then retrieved from the stack.

- After performing its computation, SUB2 places its result on the stack, overwriting param3. The two saved registers, D0 and D1, are restored from the stack, and the UNLK instruction deallocates the current stack frame and restores the previous frame pointer before returning to SUB1.

- Execution within SUB1 resumes at the return address 2164. The result from SUB2 is popped off the stack. SUB1 completes its computation and places its result on the stack, overwriting param1. The four saved registers are restored from the stack, and the UNLK instruction prepares for the return to the calling program.

- The main program resumes execution at the return address 2014. The result from SUB1 is retrieved from the stack. Finally, the ADDA instruction adjusts the value of register A7 to point to the initial top-of-stack element, labeled as Old TOS in Figure C.13.

C.4   ASSEMBLER DIRECTIVES

The assembler directives discussed in Section 2.5 can be used in ColdFire programs with only small differences in notation. The assembler provided by Freescale Semiconductor requires that each directive begins with a period to distinguish it from instruction mnemonics.

- The starting address of a block of instructions or data is specified with the ORG directive.

- The EQU directive equates names with numerical values.

- Data constants are inserted into an object program using the DC (Define Constant) directive. Several items may be defined in a single DC directive. The size of the items is indicated by the suffix L, W, or B. For example, the statements

```
        .ORG    100
ITEMS:  .DC.B   23,$4F,%10110101
```

result in byte-sized hexadecimal values 17 (23_{10}), 4F, and B5 being placed into memory locations 100, 101, and 102, respectively. The label ITEMS is assigned the value 100. Note that the '$' character denotes a hexadecimal value and the '%' character denotes a binary value.

- A block of uninitialized memory can be reserved for data by means of the DS (Define Storage) directive, with a suffix to indicate the data size. For example, the statement

```
ARRAY:  .DS.L   200
```

reserves 200 longwords and associates the label ARRAY with the address of the first longword.

The use of assembler directives is illustrated in Figure C.14, which corresponds to the list-summing program in Figure C.6.

```
            .ORG        100          Instructions begin at address 100.
            MOVEA.L     #NUM1, A2    Put the address NUM1 in A2.
            MOVE.L      N, D1        Put the number of entries n in D1.
            CLR.L       D0
    LOOP:   ADD.L       (A2)+, D0    Accumulate sum in D0.
            SUBQ.L      #1, D1
            BGT         LOOP
            MOVE.L      D0, SUM      Store the result when finished.

            .ORG        200          Data begins at address 200.
    SUM:    .DS.L       1            One longword reserved for sum.
    N:      .DC.L       150          There are N=150 longwords in list.
    NUM1:   .DS.L       150          Reserve memory for 150 longwords.
```

Figure C.14   A ColdFire program that corresponds to Figure 2.13.

C.5 EXAMPLE PROGRAMS

In this section, we show ColdFire versions of the programs for dot product and string search that are described in Chapter 2.

C.5.1 VECTOR DOT PRODUCT PROGRAM

The program in Figure 2.28 computes the dot product of two vectors, AVEC and BVEC. The ColdFire version is shown in Figure C.15. We have assumed that the vector elements are represented as signed 16-bit words. The MULS.W instruction multiplies two, signed,

```
            MOVEA.L     #AVEC, A1         Address of first vector.
            MOVEA.L     #BVEC, A2         Address of second vector.
            MOVE.L      N, D0             Set counter to number of elements.
            CLR.L       D1                Use D1 as accumulator.
    LOOP:   MOVE.W      (A1)+, D2         Get element from vector A.
            MULS.W      (A2)+, D2         Multiply element from vector B.
            ADD.L       D2, D1            Accumulate product.
            SUBQ.L      #1, D0            Decrement counter.
            BGT         LOOP              Repeat if counter is greater than zero.
            MOVE.L      D1, DOTPROD       Save the result when finished.
```

Figure C.15   A program for computing the dot product of two vectors.

16-bit numbers and produces a 32-bit product. The result of each multiplication is then accumulated into a 32-bit sum.

C.5.2   String Search Program

The program in Figure 2.31 determines the first matching instance of a pattern string P in a given target string T. The ColdFire version is shown in Figure C.16.

Recall that the CMP instruction is restricted to longword operands. Therefore, it is not possible to perform a byte-sized comparison between a register value and a memory operand with one instruction in the manner shown in Figure 2.31. Instead, the two characters to be compared must first be brought into registers D0 and D1 using separate MOVE.B instructions, as shown in Figure C.16, and then they are compared using CMP.L. Because the MOVE.B instruction affects only the low-order byte of the destination register, it is also necessary to clear all 32 bits of registers D0 and D1 before entering the main loop so that the result of the comparison is correct in each loop iteration.

	MOVEA.L	#T, A2	A2 points to string T.
	MOVEA.L	#P, A3	A3 points to string P.
	MOVEA.L	N, A4	Get the value n.
	MOVEA.L	M, A5	Get the value m.
	SUBA.L	A5, A4	Compute $n - m$.
	ADDA.L	A2, A4	A4 is the address of $T(n - m)$.
	ADDA.L	A3, A5	A5 is the address of $P(m)$.
	CLR.L	D0	Clear data registers that
	CLR.L	D1	will be used in comparisons.
LOOP1:	MOVEA.L	A2, A0	Use A0 to scan through string T.
	MOVEA.L	A3, A1	Use A1 to scan through string P.
LOOP2:	MOVE.B	(A0)+, D0	Compare a pair of
	MOVE.B	(A1)+, D1	characters in
	CMP.L	D0, D1	strings T and P.
	BNE	NOMATCH	
	CMPA.L	A1, A5	Check if at $P(m)$.
	BGT	LOOP2	Loop again if not done.
	MOVE.L	A2, RESULT	Store the address of $T(i)$.
	BRA	DONE	
NOMATCH:	ADDA.L	#1, A2	Point to next character in T.
	CMPA.L	A2, A4	Check if at $T(n - m)$.
	BGE	LOOP1	Loop again if not done.
	MOVE.L	#−1, RESULT	No match was found.
DONE:	next instruction		

Figure C.16   A program for string search.

C.6   MODE OF OPERATION AND OTHER CONTROL FEATURES

So far, we have described the normal execution of instructions that use operands in the address/data registers and in memory. We have also presented programs that implement simple computing tasks. Input/output operations and other tasks may require additional capabilities, such as interrupts, that alter normal execution behavior. Such behavior can be controlled by using certain bits in the status register shown in Figure C.2. This section describes these bits.

- The S bit selects one of two possible modes of operation. In *supervisor mode*, the S bit is set to one, and the processor can execute all instructions and access all available functions, including certain *privileged* features. For example, a MOVE instruction with the status register (SR) as the source or the destination is a privileged instruction because it accesses the S bit and the other bits that control the behavior of the processor. The supervisor mode is entered when the processor is reset. System software, which includes interrupt-service routines, executes in this mode. *User mode*, on the other hand, is intended for normal application programs. The S bit is equal to zero in this mode, which prevents the use of any privileged features. Switching from user mode to supervisor mode occurs only when entering an interrupt-service routine. Switching from supervisor mode to user mode can be done directly by executing a privileged instruction that modifies the status register or by returning from an interrupt-service routine.

- The three bits, b_{10-8}, represent the current *interrupt priority level* of the processor. These bits form the *interrupt mask*, which has a value between 0 and 7. Various interrupt sources are assigned different priority levels between 1 and 7. The interrupt mask setting prevents the processor from responding to an interrupt request from any source whose priority level is the same as or lower than the current mask level. Clearing the mask bits to 0 enables all interrupts. Setting these bits to 7 disables all interrupts, except for *non-maskable* interrupt requests at level 7. This approach, based on an interrupt mask, differs significantly from the discussion in Section 3.2.1 where a single IE bit in the status register of Figure 3.7 is used to enable all interrupts.

- The M bit is automatically cleared by the processor when an interrupt-service routine is entered. This feature is intended for use by system software and is not relevant for normal application programs.

- The T bit is used for debugging. When it is set to 1, a special interrupt is triggered after the execution of every instruction to allow system software to trace the execution of an application program.

All of the bits described above may be modified only when operating in the supervisor mode. A privileged version of the MOVE instruction allows all of the bits in the status register to be read or written. In user mode, a non-privileged version of the MOVE instruction allows only the condition code flags in the status register to be read or written.

C.7 INPUT/OUTPUT

Chapter 3 described I/O operations based on polling and interrupts using the example of displaying characters that are read from a keyboard. Using the same example and the I/O interface registers shown in Figure 3.3, we now show how ColdFire instructions are used for I/O operations.

Figure C.17 provides a ColdFire version of the program in Figure 3.5 with polling for both input and output of characters. The BTST.B instruction corresponds to the TestBit instruction in Figure 3.5. The use of an immediate operand to specify the bit to be checked by a BTST.B instruction places restrictions on the available addressing modes for the destination operands. The Absolute mode is not available, hence the program in Figure C.17 initializes address registers A3 and A4 with the locations of the status registers for the two I/O interfaces so that the BTST.B instructions can use the Indirect mode. Furthermore, the

	MOVEA.L	#LOC, A2	Initialize register A2 to point to the address of the first location in main memory where the characters are to be stored.
	MOVEA.L	#KBD_STATUS, A3	Initialize register A3 to point to the address of the status register for the keyboard.
	MOVEA.L	#DISP_STATUS, A4	Initialize register A4 to point to the address of the status register for the display.
	CLR.L	D0	Clear the data register to be used for characters.
READ:	BTST.B	#1, (A3)	Wait for a character to be entered
	BEQ	READ	in the keyboard buffer.
	MOVE.B	KBD_DATA, D0	Read the character from KBD_DATA into register D0 (this clears KIN to 0).
	MOVE.B	D0, (A2)+	Transfer the character into main memory and increment the pointer to store the next character.
ECHO:	BTST.B	#2, (A4)	Wait for the display to become ready.
	BEQ	ECHO	
	MOVE.B	D0, DISP_DATA	Move the character just read to the display buffer register (this clears DOUT to 0).
	CMPI.L	#CR, D0	Check if the character just read is CR (carriage return). If it is not CR, then
	BNE	READ	branch back and read another character.

Figure C.17 A ColdFire version of the polling-based program in Figure 3.5.

CMP instruction is restricted to longword operands, hence register D0 is cleared before executing the loops in Figure C.17. Each character is read from the keyboard interface into register D0 for later comparison with the carriage-return character, CR. As each character is stored in the memory from register D0, the pointer in register A2 is incremented.

To demonstrate how interrupts are used for I/O operations, Figure C.18 uses ColdFire instructions to implement the example in Figure 3.10. It is assumed that the initialization code in the main program of Figure C.18 is executed with the processor in supervisor mode. Two privileged MOVE instructions access the status register (SR). They are used with the ANDI instruction to clear the interrupt mask bits to 0 and thereby enable all interrupts. Because it is desirable to leave the other bits unchanged, the current contents of the status register are first read into a data register, then only the bits corresponding to the interrupt

---

Interrupt-service routine

ILOC:	MOVE.L	A2, −(A7)	Save registers.
	MOVE.L	D0, −(A7)	
	MOVEA.L	PNTR, A2	Load address pointer from the memory.
	CLR.L	D0	Clear register to hold character.
	MOVE.B	KBD_DATA, D0	Read character from keyboard.
	MOVE.B	D0, (A2)+	Write to memory and increment pointer.
	MOVE.L	A2, PNTR	Update pointer in the memory.
	MOVEA.L	#DISP_STATUS, A2	Set A2 with address of status register.
ECHO:	BTST.B	#2, (A2)	Wait for the display to become ready.
	BEQ	ECHO	
	MOVE.B	D0, DISP_DATA	Display the character just read.
	CMPI.L	#CR, D0	Check if the character just read is CR.
	BNE	RTRN	Return if not CR.
	ADDQ.L	#1, EOL	Indicate end of line.
	MOVEA.L	#KBD_CONT, A2	Set A2 with address of control register.
	BCLR.B	#1, (A2)	Disable interrupts in keyboard interface.
RTRN:	MOVE.L	(A7)+, D0	Restore registers.
	MOVEA.L	(A7)+, A2	
	RTE		Return from interrupt.

Main program

START:	MOVEA.L	#LINE, A0	Initialize buffer pointer.
	MOVE.L	A0, PNTR	
	CLR.L	EOL	Clear end-of-line indicator.
	MOVEA.L	#KBD_CONT, A0	Set A0 with address of control register.
	BSET.B	#1, (A0)	Enable interrupts in keyboard interface.
	MOVE.W	SR, D0	Read contents of status register into D0.
	ANDI.L	#$F8FF, D0	Clear priority mask to enable interrupts.
	MOVE.W	D0, SR	Write value of D0 to status register.

Figure C.18   A ColdFire version of the interrupt-based program in Figure 3.10.

priority level mask are cleared with the ANDI instruction. Finally, the modified contents are written into the status register.

C.8   FLOATING-POINT OPERATIONS

Floating-point operations are included in an extension of the basic ColdFire instruction set [1]. A hardware implementation of a processor with this extension incorporates a separate *floating-point unit* (FPU) with additional registers. The FPU permits concurrent execution of floating-point operations with other instructions. This section provides a brief summary of the floating-point features of ColdFire. Floating-point number representation is introduced in Chapter 1, and floating-point arithmetic is discussed in Chapter 9.

All floating-point operations are performed internally on 64-bit double-precision numbers. Eight 64-bit floating-point data registers, FP0 to FP7, are provided in the FPU for this purpose. There are also additional control and status registers for the FPU (for details, consult the ColdFire technical documentation [1]). The floating-point status register (FPSR) has condition code flags such as N and Z, as well as additional flags specific to floating-point operations, that are affected by data movement, arithmetic, and comparison operations involving floating-point numbers.

The floating-point registers always hold 64-bit double-precision numbers. Memory may contain numbers in either 32-bit single-precision representation or 64-bit double-precision representation. Single-precision representation reduces the storage requirements when large amounts of floating-point data are involved but very high precision is not needed. The FPU automatically converts any single-precision operands from memory to double-precision numbers before performing arithmetic operations. If desired, double-precision numbers may also be converted to single-precision numbers when transferring them to memory.

The FPU also converts between integer and double-precision floating-point representations, as explained below. Implementing this capability in hardware reduces execution time and code size by eliminating the need for software to perform the conversions.

The floating-point extension of the basic instruction set necessitates additional size specifiers in assembly language. The suffix D is used with floating-point instructions to indicate double-precision operands, and the suffix S indicates single-precision operands.

C.8.1   FMOVE INSTRUCTION

The FMOVE instruction transfers data between a memory location and a floating-point register, or between registers. A suffix specifies the operand size, and conversion to or from double-precision representation is performed as required. The source operand may be in a floating-point register (FP0–FP7), a data register (D0–D7), or a memory location specified with the Indirect, Autoincrement, Autodecrement, Basic index, or Basic relative addressing modes. The permitted modes for the destination operand are the same, except that the Basic relative mode is not available. Either the source operand or the destination operand must be contained in a floating-point register. When the destination operand is in a floating-point register, flags such as N and Z in the floating-point status register (FPSR) are affected according to the final 64-bit double-precision result. When the destination operand is in a data register (D0–D7) or a memory location, the FPSR is not affected.

When the size specifier is D, a 64-bit double-precision floating-point number is transferred without modification from a floating-point register to memory, from memory to a floating-point register, or between two floating-point registers. For example, the instruction

$$\text{FMOVE.D} \quad (A3), \text{FP5}$$

loads the double-precision number from the memory location specified by address register A3 into floating-point register FP5. Similarly, the instruction

$$\text{FMOVE.D} \quad \text{FP2, 16(A5)}$$

stores the double-precision number from register FP2 into the memory location given by adding 16 to the contents of register A5. The instruction

$$\text{FMOVE.D} \quad \text{FP3, FP4}$$

transfers a double-precision number from FP3 to FP4.

When any other operand-size suffix is specified for FMOVE, an automatic conversion is made either to or from double-precision representation for the information being transferred. For example, the instruction

$$\text{FMOVE.S} \quad \text{FP1, (A4)}$$

converts the 64-bit double-precision floating-point number in register FP1 into a 32-bit single-precision floating-point number, then writes the converted number into the location in memory given by the contents of register A4. The instruction

$$\text{FMOVE.L} \quad \text{16(A2), FP3}$$

reads a longword from memory using indexed addressing, converts this 32-bit integer into a 64-bit double-precision floating-point number, and places the converted number in register FP3. Finally, the instruction

$$\text{FMOVE.W} \quad \text{FP7, D2}$$

converts the 64-bit double-precision floating-point number in register FP7 into a 16-bit integer, and then places this converted number in the low-order bits of register D2. Clearly, there is potential for loss of precision when converting from floating-point to integer representation.

C.8.2   FLOATING-POINT ARITHMETIC INSTRUCTIONS

The basic instructions for performing arithmetic operations on floating-point numbers are FADD, FSUB, FMUL, and FDIV. In all cases, the destination operand must be in a floating-point register. The condition code flags such as N and Z in the FPSR are affected by the final 64-bit double-precision result. The source operand may be in a floating-point register, a data register, or a memory location specified with Indirect, Autoincrement, Autodecrement, Basic index, or Basic relative addressing modes. A suffix is required to indicate the format of the source operand. For any suffix other than D, the source operand is automatically converted to double-precision representation before performing the specified arithmetic operation. For example, the instruction

FADD.W   (A2)+, FP6

reads a 16-bit integer from the memory location given by address register A2, automatically increments A2 by two, converts the 16-bit integer to a 64-bit double-precision floating-point number, then adds the converted number to the number in register FP6.

C.8.3   COMPARISON AND BRANCH INSTRUCTIONS

Comparison of two floating-point numbers may be performed with the FCMP instruction. The outcome of the comparison affects flags such as N and Z in the FPSR for later use by branch instructions. The destination operand for the FCMP instruction must be in a floating-point register. The source operand may be in a floating-point register, a data register, or a memory location specified with the Indirect, Autoincrement, Autodecrement, Basic index, or Basic relative modes. A suffix must be included to specify the source operand size, and a conversion to double-precision representation is performed for the source operand as required. For example, the instruction

FCMP.S   (A1), FP3

reads the 32-bit single-precision floating-point number at the memory location given by the contents of register A1, converts this number to 64-bit double-precision representation, subtracts the converted number from the contents in register FP3, and sets the flags in the FPSR based on the result of the subtraction. Register FP3 is not modified.

Floating-point conditional branch instructions have the format

FB*cc*   LABEL

where *cc* specifies the floating-point condition code. Tests such as EQ, NE, LT, and GT can be specified for *cc*, corresponding to different combinations of the condition code flags in the FPSR. For the branch target that is used when the condition is true, the FB*cc* instruction specifies an offset relative to the PC value at execution time. Depending on the distance to the branch target from the FB*cc* instruction, the offset may be represented in either 16 or 32 bits.

Since floating-point arithmetic instructions such as FADD and FSUB affect the flags in the FPSR, an FCMP instruction may not be needed in some cases before an FB*cc* instruction. An example program in Section C.8.5 shows how a floating-point arithmetic instruction can be immediately followed by a floating-point branch instruction.

C.8.4   ADDITIONAL FLOATING-POINT INSTRUCTIONS

The FPU supports additional instructions such as square root (FSQRT), negation (FNEG), and absolute value (FABS). These instructions may specify one or two operands. For a single operand, it must be in a floating-point register. For two operands, the destination location must be a floating-point register, and the valid addressing modes for the source operand are the same as the source addressing modes in the basic floating-point arithmetic instructions. Condition code flags in the FPSR are affected by the result for each of these instructions. Number conversions are performed as required for the source operand, based on the format specifier that is appended to the instruction mnemonic.

C.8.5 EXAMPLE FLOATING-POINT PROGRAM

An example program is shown in Figure C.19. Given a pair of points (x_0, y_0) and (x_1, y_1), the program determines the slope m and y-axis intercept b of a line passing through those points, except when the points lie on a vertical line.

The coordinates for the two points are assumed to be 64-bit double-precision floating-point numbers stored consecutively in memory as x_0, y_0, x_1, and y_1 beginning at the location COORDS. The program places the computed slope and intercept as double-precision numbers in memory locations called SLOPE and INTERCEPT. The formula for the slope of a line is given by $m = (y_1 - y_0)/(x_1 - x_0)$, hence the program must check for a zero in the denominator before performing the division. When the denominator is zero, the points lie on a vertical line. The program writes a value of one to a separate variable in memory called VERT_LINE to reflect this case and to indicate that the values in memory locations SLOPE and INTERCEPT are not valid, and no further computation is done. Otherwise, the program computes the value of the slope and stores it in memory. With a valid slope, the intercept

	MOVEA.L	#COORDS, A2	A2 points to list of coordinates.
	FMOVE.D	(A2), FP0	FP0 contains x_0.
	FMOVE.D	8(A2), FP1	FP1 contains y_0.
	FMOVE.D	16(A2), FP2	FP2 contains x_1.
	FMOVE.D	24(A2), FP3	FP3 contains y_1.
	FSUB.D	FP0, FP2	Compute $x_1 - x_0$; may set Z flag in FPSR.
	FBEQ	NO_SLOPE	If denominator is zero, m is undefined.
	FSUB.D	FP1, FP3	Compute $y_1 - y_0$.
	FDIV.D	FP2, FP3	Compute $m = (y_1 - y_0)/(x_1 - y_0)$.
	MOVEA.L	#SLOPE, A2	A2 points to memory location SLOPE.
	FMOVE.D	FP3, (A2)	Store the slope to memory.
	FMUL.D	FP3, FP0	Compute $m \cdot x_0$.
	FSUB.D	FP1, FP0	Compute $b = y_0 - m \cdot x_0$.
	MOVEA.L	#INTERCEPT, A2	A2 points to memory location INTERCEPT.
	FMOVE.D	FP1, (A2)	Store the intercept to memory.
	MOVEQ.L	#0, D0	Indicate that line is not vertical.
	BRA	DONE	
NO_SLOPE:	MOVEQ.L	#1, D0	Indicate that line is vertical.
DONE:	MOVE.L	D0, VERT_LINE	

Figure C.19   Floating-point program to compute the slope and intercept of a line.

is then computed as $b = y_0 - m \cdot x_0$ and also stored in memory. Finally, a zero is written to the location VERT_LINE in memory to indicate that the slope and intercept are valid.

C.9 CONCLUDING REMARKS

ColdFire implements a CISC-style instruction set that combines arithmetic/logic operations and memory accesses in many of its instructions. This approach reduces the number of instructions that must be executed to perform a given computing task. Instructions are encoded into one, two, or three 16-bit words in memory, depending on the complexity of the operation to be performed and the amount of information needed to generate the effective addresses of the required operands. A variety of addressing modes are supported. In addition to the integer instructions, a floating-point extension is also defined for ColdFire. Automatic conversion between integer and floating-point number representations is a feature of the floating-point extension.

C.10 SOLVED PROBLEMS

This section presents some examples of problems that a student may be asked to solve, and shows how such problems can be solved.

Problem: Assume that there is a string of ASCII-encoded characters stored in memory starting at address STRING. The string ends with the Carriage Return (CR) character. Write a ColdFire program to determine the length of the string.

Example C.2

Solution: Figure C.20 presents a possible program. Each character in the string is compared to CR (ASCII code 0D), and a counter is incremented until the end of the string is reached. The result is stored in location LENGTH.

```
        MOVEA.L   #STRING, A2    A2 points to the start of the string.
        CLR.L     D3             D3 is a counter that is cleared to 0.
        CLR.L     D5             D5 is cleared for longword comparison.
LOOP:   MOVE.B    (A2)+, D5      Get the next character and increment the pointer.
        CMPI.L    #$0D, D5       Compare character with CR.
        BEQ       DONE           Finished if it matches.
        ADDQ.L    #1, D3         Increment the counter.
        BRA       LOOP           Not finished, loop back.
DONE:   MOVE.L    D3, LENGTH     Store the count in memory location LENGTH.
```

Figure C.20   Program for Example C.2.

Example C.3   **Problem:** We want to find the smallest number in a list of non-negative 32-bit integers. Storage for all data related to this problem begins at address $(1000)_{16}$. The longword at this address must hold the value of the smallest number after it has been found. The next longword at $(1004)_{16}$ contains the number of entries, n, in the list. The following n longwords beginning at address $(1008)_{16}$ contain the numbers in the list. Write a program to find the smallest number and include the assembler directives needed to organize the data as stated.

Solution: The program in Figure C.21 accomplishes the required task. Comments in the program explain how this task is performed. The program assumes that $n \geq 1$. A few sample numbers are included as entries in the list.

LIST:	.EQU	$1000	Starting address of list.
	MOVEA.L	#LIST, A2	A2 points to the start of the list.
	MOVE.L	4(A2), D3	D3 is a counter, initialize it with n.
	MOVEA.L	A2, A4	A4 points to the first number
	ADDA.L	#8, A4	after adjusting its value.
	MOVE.L	(A4), D5	D5 holds the smallest number so far.
LOOP:	SUBQ.L	#1, D3	Decrement the counter.
	BEQ	DONE	Finished if D3 is zero.
	MOVE.L	(A4)+, D6	Get the next number and increment the pointer.
	CMP.L	D6, D5	Compare next number and smallest so far.
	BLE	LOOP	If next number not smaller, loop again.
	MOVE.L	D6, D5	Otherwise, update smallest number so far.
	BRA	LOOP	Loop again.
DONE:	MOVE.L	D5, (A2)	Store the smallest number into SMALL.
	.ORG	$1000	
SMALL:	.DS.L	1	Space for the smallest number found.
N:	.DC.L	7	Number of entries in list.
ENTRIES:	.DC.L	4, 5, 3, 6, 1, 8, 2	Entries in the list.

Figure C.21   Program for Example C.3.

Example C.4   **Problem:** Write a ColdFire program that converts an n-digit decimal integer into a binary number. The decimal number is given as n ASCII-encoded characters, as would be the case if the number is entered by typing it on a keyboard.

Solution: Consider a four-digit decimal number, D, which is represented by the digits $d_3 d_2 d_1 d_0$. The value of this number is $((d_3 \times 10 + d_2) \times 10 + d_1) \times 10 + d_0$. This representation of the number is the basis for the conversion technique used in the program in Figure C.22. Note that each ASCII-encoded character is converted into a Binary Coded Decimal (BCD) digit with the ANDI instruction before it is used in the computation.

	MOVE.L	N, D2	D2 is a counter, initialize it with n.
	MOVEA.L	#DECIMAL, A3	A3 points to the ASCII digits.
	CLR.L	D4	D4 will hold the binary number.
	MOVEQ.L	#10, D6	D6 will be used to multiply by 10.
LOOP:	MOVE.B	(A3)+, D5	Get the next ASCII digit and increment the pointer.
	ANDI.L	#$0F, D5	Form the BCD digit.
	ADD.L	D5, D4	Add to the intermediate result.
	SUBQ.L	#1, D2	Decrement the counter.
	BEQ	DONE	Exit loop if finished.
	MULU.L	D6, D4	Multiply by 10.
	BRA	LOOP	Loop back if not done.
DONE:	MOVE.L	D5, BINARY	Store the result in memory location BINARY.

Figure C.22 Program for Example C.4.

Problem: Consider a two-dimensional array of numbers $A(i,j)$, where $i = 0$ through $n - 1$ is the row index, and $j = 0$ through $m - 1$ is the column index. The array is stored in the memory of a computer one row after another, with elements of each row occupying m successive word locations. Write a subroutine for adding column x to column y, element by element, leaving the sum elements in column y. The indices x and y are passed to the subroutine in registers D2 and D3. The parameters n and m are passed to the subroutine in registers D4 and D5, and the address of element $A(0,0)$ is passed in register A0.

Example C.5

Solution: A possible program is given in Figure C.23. We assume that the values x, y, n, and m are stored in memory locations X, Y, N, and M. Also, the elements of the array are stored in successive words that begin at location ARRAY, which is the address of the element $A(0,0)$. Comments in the program indicate the purpose of individual instructions.

Problem: Assume that a memory location BINARY contains a 32-bit pattern. It is desired to display these bits as eight hexadecimal digits on a display device that has the interface depicted in Figure 3.3. Write a program that accomplishes this task.

Example C.6

	MOVE.L	X, D2	Load the value x.
	MOVE.L	Y, D3	Load the value y.
	MOVE.L	N, D4	Load the value n.
	MOVE.L	M, D5	Load the value m.
	MOVEA.L	#ARRAY, A0	Load the address of A(0,0).
	JSR	SUB	
	next instruction		
	$\vdots$		
SUB:	MOVE.L	A1, −(A7)	Save register A1.
	LSL.L	#2, D5	Determine the distance in bytes between successive elements in a column.
	SUB.L	D2, D3	Form $y - x$.
	LSL.L	#2, D3	Form $4(y - x)$.
	LSL.L	#2, D2	Form $4x$.
	ADDA.L	D2, A0	A0 points to A(0, x).
	MOVEA.L	A0, A1	
	ADDA.L	D3, A1	A1 points to A(0, y).
LOOP:	MOVE.L	(A0), D2	Get the next number in column x.
	MOVE.L	(A1), D3	Get the next number in column y.
	ADD.L	D3, D2	Add the numbers and store the sum.
	MOVE.L	D2, (A1)	
	ADDA.L	D5, A0	Increment pointer to column x.
	ADDA.L	D5, A1	Increment pointer to column y.
	SUBQ.L	#1, D4	Decrement the row counter.
	BGT	LOOP	Loop back if not done.
	MOVE.L	(A7)+, A1	Restore A1.
	RTS		Return to the calling program.

Figure C.23   Program for Example C.5.

Solution: First it is necessary to convert the 32-bit pattern into hex digits that are represented as ASCII-encoded characters. The conversion can be done by using the table-lookup approach. A 16-entry table has to be constructed to provide the ASCII code for each possible hex digit. Then, for each four-bit segment of the pattern in BINARY, the corresponding character can be looked up in the table and stored in consecutive byte locations in memory beginning at address HEX. Finally, the eight characters beginning at address HEX are sent to the display. Figure C.24 gives a possible program. Because ColdFire does not include a rotate instruction, four pairs of LSL and ADDX instructions are used to achieve the effect of rotating the value in a register by four bits.

	MOVE.L	BINARY, D2	Load the binary number.
	MOVE.L	#8,D3	D3 is a digit counter that is set to 8.
	MOVEA.L	#HEX, A4	A4 points to the hex digits.
	MOVEA.L	#TABLE, A6	A6 points to table for ASCII conversion.
	CLR.L	D0	D0 is zero; needed for rotate below.
LOOP:	LSL.L	#1, D2	Rotate high-order digit into low-order position
	ADDX.L	D0, D2	by using X flag and adding zero (4 times).
	LSL.L	#1, D2	
	ADDX.L	D0, D2	
	LSL.L	#1, D2	
	ADDX.L	D0, D2	
	LSL.L	#1, D2	
	ADDX.L	D0, D2	
	MOVE.L	D2, D5	Copy current value to another register.
	ANDI.L	#$0F, D5	Extract next digit.
	MOVE.B	(A6,D5), D6	Get ASCII code for the digit,
	MOVE.B	D6, (A4)+	store it HEX buffer,
			and increment the digit pointer.
	SUBQ.L	#1, D3	Decrement the digit counter.
	BGT	LOOP	Loop back if not the last digit.
DISPLAY:	MOVEQ.L	#8, D3	
	MOVEA.L	#HEX, A4	
	MOVEA.L	#DISP_DATA, A2	
DLOOP:	MOVE.L	4(A2), D5	Check if the display is ready
	ANDI.L	#4, D5	by testing the DOUT flag.
	BEQ	DLOOP	
	MOVE.B	(A4)+, (A2)	Get the next ASCII character,
			increment the character pointer,
			and send it to the display.
	SUBQ.L	#1, D3	Decrement the counter.
	BGT	DLOOP	Loop until all characters displayed.
	next instruction		
	.ORG	1000	
HEX:	.DS.B	8	Space for ASCII-encoded digits.
TABLE:	.DC.B	$30, $31, $32, $33	Table for conversion
	.DC.B	$34, $35, $36, $37	to ASCII code.
	.DC.B	$38, $39, $41, $42	
	.DC.B	$43, $44, $45, $46	

Figure C.24   Program for Example C.6.

PROBLEMS

C.1   **[E]** Write a program that computes the expression SUM = 580 + 68400 + 80000.

C.2   **[E]** Write a program that computes the expression ANSWER = A × B + C × D.

C.3   **[M]** Write a program that finds the number of negative integers in a list of n 32-bit integers and stores the count in location NEGNUM. The value n is stored in memory location N, and the first integer in the list is stored in location NUMBERS. Include the necessary assembler directives and a sample list that contains six numbers, some of which are negative.

C.4   **[E]** Write an assembly-language program in the style of Figure C.14 for the program in Figure C.8. Assume the data layout of Figure 2.10.

C.5   **[M]** Write a ColdFire program to solve Problem 2.10 in Chapter 2.

C.6   **[M]** Write a ColdFire program for the problem described in Example 2.5 in Chapter 2.

C.7   **[M]** Write a ColdFire program for the problem described in Example 3.5 in Chapter 3.

C.8   **[M]** Write a ColdFire program for the problem described in Example 3.6 in Chapter 3.

C.9   **[M]** Write a ColdFire program for the problem described in Example 3.6 in Chapter 3, but assume that the address of TABLE is 0x10100.

C.10   **[M]** Write a program that displays the contents of 10 bytes of the main memory in hexadecimal format on a line of a video display. The byte string starts at location LOC in the memory. Each byte has to be displayed as two hex characters. The displayed contents of successive bytes should be separated by a space.

C.11   **[M]** Assume that a memory location BINARY contains a 16-bit pattern. It is desired to display these bits as a string of 0s and 1s on a display device that has the interface depicted in Figure 3.3. Write a ColdFire program that accomplishes this task.

C.12   **[M]** Using the seven-segment display in Figure 3.17 and the timer circuit in Figure 3.14, write a program that flashes decimal digits in the sequence 0, 1, 2, . . . , 9, 0, ... Each digit is to be displayed for one second. Assume that the counter in the timer circuit is driven by a 100-MHz clock.

C.13   **[M]** Using two 7-segment displays of the type shown in Figure 3.17, and the timer circuit in Figure 3.14, write a program that flashes numbers 0, 1, 2, . . . , 98, 99, 0, ... Each number is to be displayed for one second. Assume that the counter in the timer circuit is driven by a 100-MHz clock.

C.14   **[M]** Write a program that computes real clock time and displays the time in hours (0 to 23) and minutes (0 to 59). The display consists of four 7-segment display devices of the type shown in Figure 3.17. A timer circuit that has the interface given in Figure 3.14 is available. Its counter is driven by a 100-MHz clock.

C.15   **[M]** Write a ColdFire program to solve Problem 2.23 in Chapter 2.

C.16   **[D]** Write a ColdFire program to solve Problem 2.24 in Chapter 2.

C.17 **[M]** Write a ColdFire program to solve Problem 2.25 in Chapter 2.

C.18 **[M]** Write a ColdFire program to solve Problem 2.26 in Chapter 2.

C.19 **[D]** Write a ColdFire program to solve Problem 2.27 in Chapter 2.

C.20 **[M]** Write a ColdFire program to solve Problem 2.28 in Chapter 2.

C.21 **[M]** Write a ColdFire program to solve Problem 2.29 in Chapter 2.

C.22 **[M]** Write a ColdFire program to solve Problem 2.30 in Chapter 2.

C.23 **[M]** Write a ColdFire program to solve Problem 2.31 in Chapter 2.

C.24 **[D]** Write a ColdFire program to solve Problem 2.32 in Chapter 2.

C.25 **[D]** Write a ColdFire program to solve Problem 2.33 in Chapter 2.

C.26 **[D]** Write a ColdFire program to solve Problem 3.20 in Chapter 3.

C.27 **[D]** Write a ColdFire program to solve Problem 3.22 in Chapter 3.

C.28 **[D]** Write a ColdFire program to solve Problem 3.24 in Chapter 3.

C.29 **[D]** Write a ColdFire program to solve Problem 3.26 in Chapter 3.

C.30 **[D]** The function $sin(x)$ can be approximated with reasonable accuracy as $x - x^3/6 + x^5/120 = x(1 - x^2(1/6 - x^2(1/120)))$ when $0 \leq x \leq \pi/2$. Write a subroutine called SIN that accepts an input parameter representing x in a floating-point register and computes the approximated value of $sin(x)$ using the second expression above involving only terms in x and x^2. The computed value should be returned in a floating-point register. Any registers used by the subroutine, including floating-point registers, should be saved and restored as needed.

REFERENCES

1. Freescale Semiconductor, Inc., *ColdFire Family Programmer's Reference Manual*, Document Number CFPRM Rev. 3, March 2005. Available at http://www.freescale.com.

THE ARM PROCESSOR

APPENDIX OBJECTIVES

In this appendix you will learn about the ARM processor. The discussion includes:

- Instruction set architecture
- Input/output capability
- Support for embedded applications

In Chapter 2 we introduced the basic concepts used in the design of instruction sets and addressing modes. Chapter 3 discussed I/O operations. In this appendix we will show how those concepts are implemented in the ARM processor. The generic programs given in Chapters 2 and 3 are presented in the ARM assembly language.

Advanced RISC Machines (ARM) Limited has designed a family of RISC-style processors. ARM licences these designs to other companies for chip fabrication, together with software tools for system development and simulation. The main use for ARM processors is in low-power and low-cost embedded applications such as mobile telephones, communication modems, and automotive engine management systems.

All ARM processors share a basic machine instruction set. The ISA version used here is called version 4 by ARM [1]. Later versions add extensions that are not needed for the level of discussion in this appendix. However, we will briefly summarize some of them in a later section. The book by Furber [2] is a source of information on ARM processors and their design rationale. The book by Hohl [3] describes the ARM assembly language.

D.1   ARM CHARACTERISTICS

ARM word length is 32 bits, memory is byte-addressable using 32-bit addresses, and the processor registers are 32 bits long. Three operand lengths are used in moving data between the memory and the processor registers: byte (8 bits), half word (16 bits), and word (32 bits). Word and half-word addresses must be aligned, that is, they must be multiples of 4 and 2, respectively. Both little-endian and big-endian memory addressing schemes are supported. The choice is determined by an external input control line to the processor.

In most respects, the ARM ISA reflects a RISC-style architecture, but it has some CISC-style features.

RISC-style Aspects

- All instructions have a fixed length of 32 bits.
- Only Load and Store instructions access memory.
- All arithmetic and logic instructions operate on operands in processor registers.

CISC-style Aspects

- Autoincrement, Autodecrement, and PC-relative addressing modes are provided.
- Condition codes (N, Z, V, and C) are used for branching and for conditional execution of instructions. Their meaning was explained in Section 2.10.2.
- Multiple registers can be loaded from a block of consecutive memory words, or stored in a block, using a single instruction.

D.1.1   UNUSUAL ASPECTS OF THE ARM ARCHITECTURE

The ARM architecture has a number of features not generally found in modern processors.

Conditional Execution of Instructions

An unusual feature of ARM processors is that all instructions are conditionally executed. An instruction is executed only if the current values of the condition code flags satisfy the condition specified in a 4-bit field of the instruction. Otherwise, the processor proceeds to the next instruction. One of the possible conditions specifies that the instruction is always executed. The usefulness of conditional execution will be seen in an example in Section D.9. For now, we will ignore this feature and assume that the condition field of the instruction specifies the "always-executed" code.

No Shift or Divide Instructions

Shift instructions are not provided explicitly. However, an immediate value or one of the register operands in arithmetic, logic, and move instructions can be shifted by a prescribed amount before being used in an operation, as explained in Section D.4.2. This feature can also be used to implement shift instructions implicitly.

There are a number of different Multiply instructions, with many of the variations intended for use in signal-processing applications. But there are no hardware Divide instructions. Division must be implemented in software.

D.2   REGISTER STRUCTURE

There are sixteen 32-bit processor registers for user application programs, labeled R0 through R15, as shown in Figure D.1. They comprise fifteen general-purpose registers

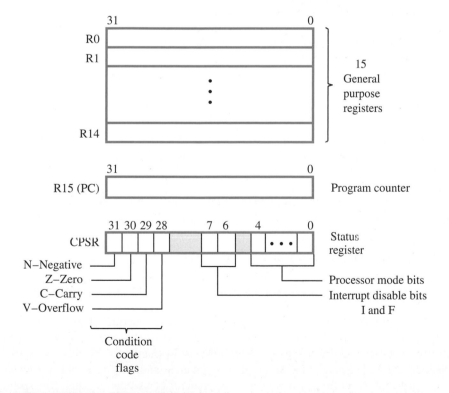

Figure D.1   ARM register structure.

(R0 through R14) and the Program Counter (PC), which is register R15. The general-purpose registers can hold either memory addresses or data operands. Registers R13 and R14 have dedicated uses related to the management of the processor stack and subroutines. This is discussed in Section D.4.8.

The Current Program Status Register (CPSR), or simply the Status register, also shown in Figure D.1, holds the condition code flags (N, Z, C, V), interrupt-disable bits, and processor mode bits. There are a total of seven processor modes of operation. Application programs run in User mode. The other six modes are used to handle I/O device interrupts, processor powerup/reset, software interrupts, and memory access violations. Processor modes and the use of interrupt-disable bits are described in Sections D.7 and D.8. Initially, we will assume that the processor is in User mode, executing an application program.

There are a number of additional general-purpose registers called *banked* registers. They are duplicates of some of the R0 to R14 registers. Different banked registers are used when the processor switches from User mode into other modes of operation. The use of banked registers avoids the need to save and restore some of the User-mode register contents on mode switches. Saved copies of the Status register are also available in the non-User modes. The banked registers, along with Status register copies, are discussed in Section D.7.

D.3   ADDRESSING MODES

The Immediate, Register, Absolute, Indirect, and Index addressing modes discussed in Section 2.4 are all available in some form. In addition to these basic modes, which are usually available in RISC processors, the Relative mode and variants of the Autoincrement and Autodecrement modes described in Section 2.10.1 are also provided. In the ARM architecture, many of these modes are derived from different forms of indexed addressing modes.

D.3.1   BASIC INDEXED ADDRESSING MODE

The basic method for addressing memory operands is an indexed addressing mode, defined as

Pre-indexed mode—The effective address of the operand is the sum of the contents of a base register, Rn, and a signed offset.

We will use Load and Store instructions, with assembly-language mnemonics LDR and STR, which load a word from memory into a register, or store a word from a register into memory, to show how the indexed addressing modes operate. The format of these instructions is shown in Figure D.2. In all ARM instructions, the high-order four bits specify a condition that determines whether or not the instruction is executed, as explained in Section D.1.1. The magnitude of the offset is given as an immediate value contained in the low-order 12 bits of the instruction or as the contents of a second register, Rm, specified

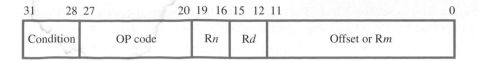

Figure D.2   Format for Load and Store instructions.

in the low-order four bits of the instruction. A bit in the OP-code field distinguishes between these two cases. The sign (direction) of the offset is specified by another bit in the OP-code field. In assembly language, the sign is given with the offset specification.

The Load instruction

$$\text{LDR} \quad \text{R}d, [\text{R}n, \#\text{offset}]$$

specifies the offset (expressed as a signed number) in the immediate mode and performs the operation

$$\text{R}d \leftarrow [[\text{R}n] + \text{offset}]$$

The instruction

$$\text{LDR} \quad \text{R}d, [\text{R}n, \text{R}m]$$

performs the operation

$$\text{R}d \leftarrow [[\text{R}n] + [\text{R}m]]$$

Since the contents of $\text{R}m$ are the magnitude of the offset, $\text{R}m$ is preceded by a minus sign if a negative offset is desired. Note that square brackets are used in the ARM assembly language instead of parentheses to denote indirection. These two versions of the Pre-indexed addressing mode are the same as the Index and Base with index modes, respectively, defined in Section 2.4.3.

An offset of zero does not have to be specified explicitly in assembly language. Hence, the instruction

$$\text{LDR} \quad \text{R}d, [\text{R}n]$$

performs the operation

$$\text{R}d \leftarrow [[\text{R}n]]$$

This is defined as the Indirect mode in Section 2.4.2.

D.3.2   RELATIVE ADDRESSING MODE

The Program Counter, PC, may be used as the Base register $\text{R}n$, along with an immediate offset, in the Pre-indexed addressing mode. This, in effect, is the Relative addressing mode, as described in Section 2.10.1. The programmer simply places the desired address label in the operand field to indicate this mode. Thus, the instruction

LDR   R1, ITEM

loads the contents of memory location ITEM into register R1. The assembler determines the immediate offset as the difference between the address of the operand and the contents of the updated PC. When the effective address is calculated at instruction execution time, the contents of the PC will have been updated to the address two words (8 bytes) forward from the instruction containing the Relative addressing mode. The reason for this is that the ARM processor will have already fetched the next instruction. This is due to pipelined instruction execution, which is described in Chapter 6.

D.3.3   INDEX MODES WITH WRITEBACK

In the Pre-indexed addressing mode, the original contents of register Rn are not changed in the process of generating the effective address of the operand. There is a variation of this mode, called Pre-indexed with *writeback*, in which the contents of Rn are changed. Another mode, called Post-indexed, also results in changing the contents of register Rn. These modes are generalizations of the Autodecrement and Autoincrement addressing modes, respectively, that were introduced in Section 2.10.1. They are defined as follows:

Pre-indexed with writeback mode—The effective address of the operand is generated in the same way as in the Pre-indexed mode, then the effective address is written back into Rn.

Post-indexed mode—The effective address of the operand is the contents of Rn. The offset is then added to this address and the result is written back into Rn.

Table D.1 specifies the assembly language syntax for all of the addressing modes, and gives expressions for the calculation of the effective address, EA. It also shows how writeback operations are specified. In the Pre-indexed mode, the exclamation character '!' signifies that writeback is to be done. The Post-indexed mode always involves writeback, so the exclamation character is not needed.

As can be seen in Table D.1, pre- and post-indexing are distinguished by the way the square brackets are used. When only the base register is enclosed in square brackets, its contents are used as the effective address. The offset is added to the register contents after the operand is accessed. In other words, post-indexing is specified. When both the base register and the offset are placed inside the square brackets, their sum is used as the effective address of the operand, that is, pre-indexing is used. If writeback is to be performed, it must be indicated by the exclamation character.

D.3.4   OFFSET DETERMINATION

In all three indexed addressing modes, the offset may be given as an immediate value in the range ±4095. Alternatively, the magnitude of the offset may be specified as the contents of

Table D.1   ARM indexed addressing modes.

Name	Assembler syntax	Addressing function
With immediate offset:		
Pre-indexed	[Rn, #offset]	EA = [Rn] + offset
Pre-indexed with writeback	[Rn, #offset]!	EA = [Rn] + offset; Rn ← [Rn] + offset
Post-indexed	[Rn], #offset	EA = [Rn]; Rn ← [Rn] + offset
With offset magnitude in Rm:		
Pre-indexed	[Rn, ± Rm, shift]	EA = [Rn] ± [Rm] shifted
Pre-indexed with writeback	[Rn, ± Rm, shift]!	EA = [Rn] ± [Rm] shifted; Rn ← [Rn] ± [Rm] shifted
Post-indexed	[Rn], ± Rm, shift	EA = [Rn]; Rn ← [Rn] ± [Rm] shifted
Relative (Pre-indexed with immediate offset)	Location	EA = Location = [PC] + offset

EA = effective address
offset = a signed number contained in the instruction
shift = direction #integer
    where direction is LSL for left shift or LSR for right shift; and
    integer is a 5-bit unsigned number specifying the shift amount
±Rm = the offset magnitude in register Rm can be added to or subtracted from the
    contents of base register Rn

the Rm register, with the sign (direction) of the offset specified by a ± prefix on the register name. For example, the instruction

$$\text{LDR} \quad R0, [R1, -R2]!$$

performs the operation

$$R0 \leftarrow [[R1] - [R2]]$$

The effective address of the operand, [R1] − [R2], is then loaded into R1 because writeback is specified.

When the offset is given in a register, it may be scaled by a power of 2 before it is used by shifting it to the right or to the left. This is indicated in assembly language by placing the shift direction (LSL for left shift or LSR for right shift) and the shift amount after the register name, Rm, as shown in Table D.1. The amount of the shift is specified by an immediate value in the range 0 to 31. The direction and amount of shifting are encoded in the same field of the instruction that specifies Rm, as shown in Figure D.2. For example, the contents of R2 in the example above may be multiplied by 16 before being used as an offset by modifying the instruction as follows:

$$\text{LDR} \quad \text{R0, [R1, } -\text{R2, LSL \#4]!}$$

This instruction performs the operation

$$\text{R0} \leftarrow [[\text{R1}] -16 \times [\text{R2}]]$$

and then loads the effective address into R1 because writeback is specified.

D.3.5   REGISTER, IMMEDIATE, AND ABSOLUTE ADDRESSING MODES

The Register addressing mode is the main way for accessing operands in arithmetic and logic instructions, which are discussed in Section D.4. Constants may also be used in these instructions. They are provided as 8-bit immediate values.

A limited form of Absolute addressing for accessing memory operands is obtained if the base register in the Pre-indexed mode contains the value zero. In this case, the 12-bit offset value is the effective address.

The Immediate and Absolute addressing modes described here involve only 8-bit and 12-bit values, respectively. The generation and use of 32-bit values as immediate operands or memory addresses are described in Section D.5.1.

D.3.6   ADDRESSING MODE EXAMPLES

An example of the Relative mode is shown in Figure D.3a. The address of the operand, given symbolically in the instruction as ITEM, is 1060. There is no Absolute addressing mode available in the ARM architecture, other than the limited form described in the previous section. Therefore, when the address of a memory location is specified by placing an address label in the operand field, the assembler uses the Relative addressing mode. This is implemented by the Pre-indexed mode with an immediate offset, using PC as the base register. As shown in the figure, the offset calculated by the assembler is 52, because the updated PC will contain 1008 when the offset is added to it during program execution. The effective address generated by this instruction is $1060 = 1008 + 52$. The operand must be within a distance of 4095 bytes forward or backward from the updated PC. If the operand address is outside this range, an error is indicated by the assembler and a different addressing mode must be used to access the operand.

Figure D.3b shows an example of the Pre-indexed mode with the offset contained in register R6 and the base value contained in R5. The Store instruction (STR) stores the contents of R3 into the word at memory location 1200.

The examples shown in Figure D.4 illustrate the usefulness of the writeback feature in the Post-indexed and Pre-indexed addressing modes. Figure D.4a shows the first three numbers of a list of 25 numbers, starting at memory address 1000 and spaced 25 words apart. They comprise the first row of a 25 × 25 matrix of numbers that is stored in column order. Memory locations 1000, 1004, 1008, . . . , 1096 contain the first column of the matrix. The

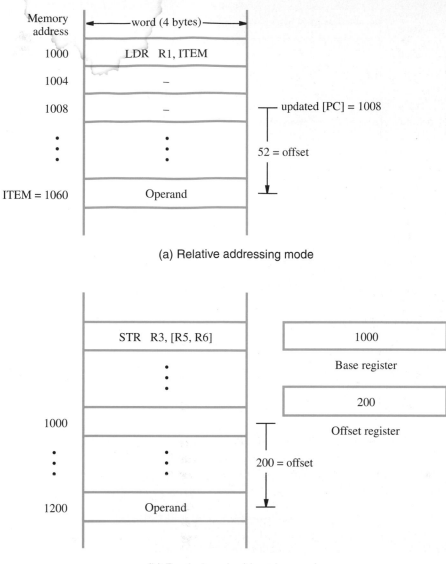

(a) Relative addressing mode

(b) Pre-indexed addressing mode

Figure D.3 Examples of memory addressing modes.

first number of the first row of the matrix is stored in word location 1000, and the numbers at addresses 1100, 1200, ..., 3400 are the successive numbers of the first row. The numbers in the first row of the matrix can be accessed conveniently in a program loop by using the Post-indexed addressing mode, with the offset contained in a register. Suppose that R2 is used as the base register and that it contains the initial address value 1000. Suppose also that register R10 is used to hold the offset, and that it is loaded with the value 25. The

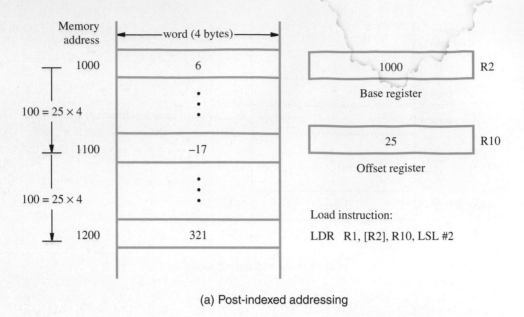

(a) Post-indexed addressing

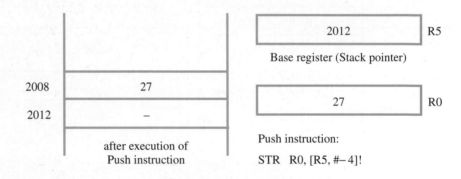

Push instruction:

STR   R0, [R5, #− 4]!

after execution of
Push instruction

(b) Pre-indexed addressing with writeback

Figure D.4   Memory addressing modes involving writeback.

instruction

$$\text{LDR} \quad \text{R1, [R2], R10, LSL \#2}$$

can be used in the body of a program loop to load register R1 with successive elements of the first row of the matrix in successive passes through the loop.

Let us examine how this works, step by step. The first time that the Load instruction is executed, the effective address is [R2] = 1000. Therefore, the number 6 at this address is loaded into R1. Then, the writeback operation changes the contents of R2 from 1000 to 1100 so that it points to the second number, -17. It does this by shifting the contents, 25, of the offset register R10 left by two bit positions and then adding the shifted value to the contents of R2. The contents of R10 are not changed in this process. The left shift is equivalent to multiplying 25 by 4, generating the required offset of 100. When the Load instruction is executed on the second pass through the loop, the second number, -17, is loaded into R1. The third number, 321, is loaded into R1 on the third pass, and so on.

This example involved adding the shifted contents of the offset register to the contents of the base register. As indicated in Table D.1, the shifted offset can also be subtracted from the contents of the base register. Any shift amount in the range 0 through 31 can be selected, and either right or left shifting can be specified.

Figure D.4*b* shows an example of pushing the contents of register R0, which are 27, onto a programmer-defined stack. Register R5 is used as the stack pointer. Initially, it contains the address 2012 of the current TOS (top-of-stack) element. The Pre-indexed addressing mode with writeback can be used to perform the Push operation with the instruction

STR   R0, [R5, #−4]!

The immediate offset -4 is added to the contents of R5 and the new value is written back into R5. Then, this address value of the new top of the stack, 2008, is used as the effective address for the Store operation. The contents of register R0 are then stored at this location.

D.4   INSTRUCTIONS

Each instruction in the ARM architecture is encoded into a 32-bit word. Access to memory is provided only by Load and Store instructions. All arithmetic and logic instructions operate on processor registers.

D.4.1   LOAD AND STORE INSTRUCTIONS

In the previous section on addressing modes, we used versions of the Load and Store instructions that move single word operands between the memory and registers. The OP-code mnemonics LDR and STR are used for these instructions.

Byte and half-word values can also be transferred between memory and registers. If the operand is a byte, it is located in the low-order byte position of the register. If the operand is a half word, it is located in the low-order half of the register. For Load instructions, byte and half-word values are zero-extended to the 32-bit register length by using the instruction mnemonics LDRB and LDRH or are sign-extended by using LDRSB and LDRSH. The byte and half-word Store instructions have the mnemonics STRB and STRH.

Loading and Storing Multiple Operands

There are two instructions for loading and storing multiple operands. They are called Block Transfer instructions. Any subset of the general-purpose registers can be loaded or stored. Only word operands are allowed. The OP codes used are LDM (Load Multiple) and STM (Store Multiple). The memory operands must be in successive word locations.

All of the forms of pre- and post-indexing with and without writeback are available. They operate on a base address register Rn specified in the instruction in the position shown in Figure D.2. The offset magnitude is always 4 in these instructions, so it does not have to be specified explicitly in the instruction. The list of registers must appear in increasing order in the assembly-language representation of the instruction, but they do not need to be contiguous. They are specified in bits b_{15-0} of the encoded machine instruction, with bit $b_i = 1$ if register Ri is in the list.

As an example, assume that register R10 is the base register and that it contains the value 1000 initially. The instruction

$$\text{LDMIA} \quad \text{R10!, \{R0, R1, R6, R7\}}$$

transfers the words from locations 1000, 1004, 1008, and 1012 into registers R0, R1, R6, and R7, leaving the address value 1016 in R10 after the last transfer, because writeback is indicated by the exclamation character. The suffix IA in the OP code indicates "Increment After," corresponding to post-indexing. We will discuss the use of Load/Store Multiple instructions for saving/restoring registers in subroutines in Section D.4.8.

D.4.2 ARITHMETIC INSTRUCTIONS

The ARM instruction set has a number of instructions for arithmetic operations on operands that are either contained in the general-purpose registers or given as immediate operands in the instruction itself. The format for these instructions is the same as that shown in Figure D.2 for Load and Store instructions, except that the field label "Offset or Rm" is replaced by the label "Immediate or Rm" for the second source operand.

The basic assembly-language format for arithmetic instructions is

$$\text{OP} \quad \text{R}d, \text{R}n, \text{R}m$$

where the operation specified by the OP code is performed on the source operands in general-purpose registers Rn and Rm. The result is placed in destination register Rd.

Addition and Subtraction

The instruction

$$\text{ADD} \quad \text{R0, R2, R4}$$

performs the operation

$$\text{R0} \leftarrow [\text{R2}] + [\text{R4}]$$

The instruction

$$\text{SUB} \quad \text{R0, R6, R5}$$

performs the operation

$$\text{R0} \leftarrow [\text{R6}] - [\text{R5}]$$

The second source operand can be specified in the immediate mode. Thus,

$$\text{ADD} \quad \text{R0, R3, \#17}$$

performs the operation

$$\text{R0} \leftarrow \text{[R3]} + 17$$

The immediate operand is an 8-bit value contained in bits b_{7-0} of the encoded machine instruction. It is an unsigned number in the range 0 to 255. The assembly language allows negative values to be used as immediate operands. If the instruction

$$\text{ADD} \quad \text{R0, R3, \#}-17$$

is used in a program, the assembler replaces it with the instruction

$$\text{SUB} \quad \text{R0, R3, \#17}$$

Shifting or Rotation of the Second Source Operand

When the second source operand is specified as the contents of a register, they can be shifted or rotated before being used in the operation. Logical shift left (LSL), logical shift right (LSR), arithmetic shift right (ASR), and rotate right (ROR), as described in Section 2.8.2 of Chapter 2, are available. The carry bit, C, is not involved in these operations. Shifting or rotation is specified after the register name for the second source operand. For example, the instruction

$$\text{ADD} \quad \text{R0, R1, R5, LSL \#4}$$

is executed as follows. The second source operand, which is contained in register R5, is shifted left 4 bit positions (equivalent to $\text{[R5]} \times 16$), then added to the contents of register R1. The sum is placed in register R0. The shift or rotation amount can also be specified as the contents of a fourth register.

If the second source operand is specified in an assembly-language instruction as an immediate value in the range 0 to 255, it is obtained directly from the low-order byte of the encoded machine instruction word, as described above. It is also possible for the programmer to specify a limited number of 32-bit values. They are generated by manipulating an 8-bit immediate value contained in the low-order byte of the machine instruction in the following manner at the time the instruction is executed. The 8-bit value is first zero-extended to 32 bits. It is then rotated right an even number of bit positions to generate the desired value. Both the 8-bit value and the rotation amount are determined by the assembler from the immediate value specified by the programmer. These two quantities are encoded into the low-order 12 bits of the instruction. If it is not possible to generate the desired value in this way, an error is reported and the programmer must use some other way of generating the desired value, as described in Section D.5.1.

Multiple-Word Operands

The carry flag, C, can be used to facilitate addition and subtraction operations that involve multiple-word numbers. Separate instructions are available for this purpose. Their assembly language mnemonics are ADC (Add with carry) and SBC (Subtract with carry). For example, suppose that two 64-bit operands are to be added. Assume that the first operand is contained in the register pair R3, R2, and that the second operand is contained in the register pair R5, R4. The high-order word of each operand is contained in the higher-numbered register. These 64-bit operands can be added by using the instruction

$$\text{ADDS} \quad \text{R6, R2, R4}$$

followed by the instruction

$$\text{ADC} \quad \text{R7, R3, R5}$$

producing the 64-bit sum in the register pair R7, R6. The carry output from the ADDS operation is used as a carry input in the ADC operation to execute the 64-bit addition. The S suffix on the ADD instruction is needed to set the C flag.

Multiplication

Two basic versions of a Multiply instruction are provided. The first version multiplies the contents of two registers and places the low-order 32-bits of the product in a third register. The high-order bits of the product are discarded. If the operands are 2's-complement numbers, and if their product can be represented in 32 bits, then the retained low-order 32 bits of the product represent the correct result.

For example, the instruction

$$\text{MUL} \quad \text{R0, R1, R2}$$

performs the operation

$$\text{R0} \leftarrow [\text{R1}] \times [\text{R2}]$$

The second version of the basic Multiply instruction specifies a fourth register whose contents are added to the product before the result is stored in the destination register. Hence, the instruction

$$\text{MLA} \quad \text{R0, R1, R2, R3}$$

performs the operation

$$\text{R0} \leftarrow ([\text{R1}] \times [\text{R2}]) + [\text{R3}]$$

This is called a Multiply-Accumulate operation. It is often used in signal-processing applications.

Multiply and Multiply-Accumulate instructions that generate double-length (64-bit) products are also provided. There are different versions of these instructions for signed and unsigned operands.

There are no provisions for shifting or rotating any of the operands before they are used in multiplication operations.

D.4.3 MOVE INSTRUCTIONS

It is often necessary to copy the contents of one register into another or to load an immediate value into a register. The Move instruction

$$\text{MOV} \quad \text{R}d, \text{R}m$$

copies the contents of register Rm into register Rd. The instruction

$$\text{MOV} \quad \text{R}d, \#\text{value}$$

loads an 8-bit immediate value into the destination register.

A second version of the Move instruction, called Move Negative, with the OP-code mnemonic MVN, forms the bit-complement of the source operand before it is placed in the destination register. Recall that an 8-bit immediate value is an unsigned number in the range 0 to 255. The MVN instruction can be used to load negative values in 2's-complement representation as follows. Suppose we wish to load -5 into register R0. The instruction

$$\text{MVN} \quad \text{R0}, \#4$$

achieves the desired result because the bit-complement of 4 is the 2's-complement representation for -5. In general, to load $-c$ into a register, the MVN instruction can be used with an immediate source operand value of $c - 1$. For the convenience of the programmer, the assembler program accepts an instruction such as

$$\text{MOV} \quad \text{R0}, \#-5$$

and replaces it with the instruction

$$\text{MVN} \quad \text{R0}, \#4$$

A MOV instruction with a negative immediate source operand is an example of a pseudoinstruction. The assembler replaces it with an actual machine instruction that achieves the desired result.

The source operand in Move instructions can be shifted, as described in Section D.4.2, before it is written into the destination register.

Implementing Shift and Rotate Instructions

ARM processors do not have explicit instructions for shifting or rotating register contents as described in Section 2.8.2 of Chapter 2. However, the ability to shift or rotate the source register operand in a Move instruction provides the same capability. For example, the instruction

$$\text{MOV} \quad \text{R}i, \text{R}j, \text{LSL} \#4$$

achieves the same result as the generic instruction

$$\text{LShiftL} \quad \text{R}i, \text{R}j, \#4$$

described in Section 2.8.2.

D.4.4   LOGIC AND TEST INSTRUCTIONS

The logic operations AND, OR, XOR, and Bit-Clear are implemented by instructions with the OP codes AND, ORR, EOR, and BIC, respectively. They have the same format as arithmetic instructions. The instruction

$$\text{AND} \quad Rd, Rn, Rm$$

performs a bitwise logical AND of the operands in registers Rn and Rm and places the result in register Rd. For example, if register R0 contains the hexadecimal pattern 02FA62CA and R1 contains the pattern 0000FFFF, then the instruction

$$\text{AND} \quad \text{R0, R0, R1}$$

will result in the pattern 000062CA being placed in register R0.

The Bit Clear instruction, BIC, is closely related to the AND instruction. It complements each bit in operand Rm before ANDing them with the bits in register Rn. Using the same R0 and R1 bit patterns as in the above example, the instruction

$$\text{BIC} \quad \text{R0, R0, R1}$$

results in the pattern 02FA0000 being placed in R0.

Digit-Packing Program

Figure D.5 illustrates the use of logic instructions in an ARM program for packing two 4-bit decimal digits into a memory byte location. The generic version of this program is shown in Figure 2.24 and described in Section 2.8.2. The decimal digits, represented in ASCII code, are stored in byte locations LOC and LOC + 1. The program packs the corresponding 4-bit BCD codes into a single byte location PACKED.

In writing the program for this task, we need to load a 32-bit address into a register. ARM instructions consist of a single 32-bit word, so the address cannot be represented by an immediate value in a Move instruction.

LDR	R0, =LOC	Load address LOC into R0.
LDRB	R1, [R0]	Load ASCII characters
LDRB	R2, [R0, #1]	into R1 and R2.
AND	R2, R2, #&F	Clear high-order 28 bits of R2.
ORR	R2, R2, R1, LSL #4	Shift contents of R1 left, perform logical OR with contents of R2, and place result into R2.
STRB	R2, PACKED	Store packed BCD digits into PACKED.

Figure D.5   A program for packing two 4-bit decimal digits into a byte.

The assembler accepts an instruction of the form

LDR   R*i*, =ADDRESS

to load the address value ADDRESS into register R*i*. This does not represent a real machine instruction. It is another example of a pseudoinstruction. The way in which the assembler implements the above instruction is discussed later in Section D.5. We will normally use this pseudoinstruction in program examples whenever it is necessary to load an address value into a register.

The first instruction in the program in Figure D.5 loads the address LOC into register R0. The two ASCII characters containing the BCD digits in their low-order four bits are loaded into the low-order byte positions of registers R1 and R2 by the next two Load instructions. The AND instruction clears the high-order 28 bits of R2 to zero, leaving the second BCD digit in the four low-order bit positions. The '&' character in this instruction signifies hexadecimal notation for the immediate value. The ORR instruction then shifts the first BCD digit in R1 to the left four positions and places it to the left of the second BCD digit in R2. The two digits packed into the low-order byte of R2 are then stored into location PACKED.

Test Instructions

Instructions called Test (TST) and Test Equivalence (TEQ) perform the logical AND and XOR operations, respectively, on their word operands, then set condition code flags based on the result. They do not store the result in a register. These instructions can be used to test how an unknown bit pattern matches up against a known bit pattern, and can then be followed by a Branch instruction that is conditioned on the result.

For example, the Test instruction

TST   R*n*, #1

performs an AND operation to test whether the low-order bit of register R*n* is equal to 1. If the result of the test is positive, that is, if the low-order bit of the contents of register R*n* is equal to 1, then the result of the AND operation is 1, and the Z bit is cleared to zero. Status bits in I/O device registers can be checked with this type of instruction.

The Test Equivalence instruction

TEQ   R*n*, #5

performs an XOR operation to test whether register R*n* contains the value 5. If it does, then the result of the bit-by-bit XOR operation will be zero, and the Z bit will be set to 1.

D.4.5 COMPARE INSTRUCTIONS

The Compare instruction

CMP   R*n*, R*m*

performs the operation

$$[Rn] - [Rm]$$

and sets the condition code flags based on the result of the subtraction operation. The result itself is discarded.

The Compare Negative instruction

$$\text{CMN} \quad \text{R}n, \text{R}m$$

performs the operation

$$[\text{R}n] + [\text{R}m]$$

and sets the condition code flags based on the result of the operation. The result of the operation is discarded.

In both of these instructions, the second operand can be an immediate value instead of the contents of a register. Either version of the second operand can be shifted as described in Section D.4.2.

D.4.6 SETTING CONDITION CODE FLAGS

The Compare and Test instructions always update the condition code flags. They are usually followed by conditional branch instructions, which are described in the next section. The arithmetic, logic, and Move instructions affect the condition code flags only if explicitly specified to do so by a bit in the OP-code field. This is indicated by appending the suffix S to the assembly language OP-code mnemonic. For example, the instruction

$$\text{ADDS} \quad \text{R0, R1, R2}$$

sets the condition code flags, but

$$\text{ADD} \quad \text{R0, R1, R2}$$

does not.

D.4.7 BRANCH INSTRUCTIONS

Conditional branch instructions contain a 24-bit 2's-complement value that is used to generate a branch offset as follows. When the instruction is executed, the value in the instruction is shifted left two bit positions (because all branch target addresses are word-aligned), then sign-extended to 32 bits to generate the offset. This offset is added to the updated contents of the Program Counter to generate the branch target address. An example is given in Figure D.6. The BEQ instruction (Branch if Equal to 0) causes a branch if the Z flag is set to 1. The appropriate 24-bit value in the instruction is computed by the assembler. In this case, it would be $92/4 = 23$.

The condition to be tested to determine whether or not branching should take place is specified in the high-order four bits, b_{31-28}, of the instruction word. A Branch instruction is executed in the same way as any other ARM instruction; that is, the branch is taken only if the current state of the condition code flags corresponds to the condition specified in the Condition field of the instruction. The full set of conditions is given in Table D.2. The

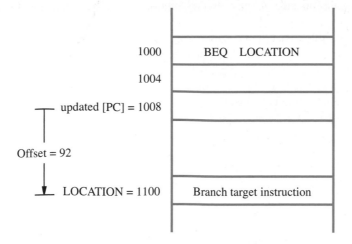

Figure D.6 Determination of the target address for a branch instruction.

Table D.2 Condition field encoding in ARM instructions.

Condition field $b_{31} \dots b_{28}$	Condition suffix	Name	Condition code test
0 0 0 0	EQ	Equal (zero)	$Z = 1$
0 0 0 1	NE	Not equal (nonzero)	$Z = 0$
0 0 1 0	CS/HS	Carry set/Unsigned higher or same	$C = 1$
0 0 1 1	CC/LO	Carry clear/Unsigned lower	$C = 0$
0 1 0 0	MI	Minus (negative)	$N = 1$
0 1 0 1	PL	Plus (positive or zero)	$N = 0$
0 1 1 0	VS	Overflow	$V = 1$
0 1 1 1	VC	No overflow	$V = 0$
1 0 0 0	HI	Unsigned higher	$\overline{C} \vee Z = 0$
1 0 0 1	LS	Unsigned lower or same	$\overline{C} \vee Z = 1$
1 0 1 0	GE	Signed greater than or equal	$N \oplus V = 0$
1 0 1 1	LT	Signed less than	$N \oplus V = 1$
1 1 0 0	GT	Signed greater than	$Z \vee (N \oplus V) = 0$
1 1 0 1	LE	Signed less than or equal	$Z \vee (N \oplus V) = 1$
1 1 1 0	AL	Always	
1 1 1 1		not used	

assembler accepts the OP code B as an unconditional branch. It is not necessary to use the suffix AL.

At the time the branch target address is computed, the contents of the PC will have been updated to contain the address of the instruction that is two words beyond the Branch instruction itself. This is due to pipelined instruction execution, as explained in Section D.3.2. If the Branch instruction is at address location 1000 and the branch target address is 1100, as shown in Figure D.6, then the offset is 92, because the contents of the updated PC will be $1000 + 8 = 1008$ when the branch target address 1100 is computed.

A Program for Adding Numbers

We have now described enough ARM instructions to enable us to present some of the programs that are given in generic form in Chapter 2. Figure D.7 shows a program for adding a list of numbers, patterned after the program in Figure 2.26. Location N contains the number of entries in the list, and location SUM is used to store the sum. The Load and Store operations performed by the first and last instructions use the Relative addressing mode. This assumes that the memory locations N and SUM are within the range reachable by offsets relative to the PC. The address NUM1 of the first of the numbers to be added is loaded into register R2 by the second instruction. The Post-indexed addressing mode, which includes writeback, is used in the first instruction of the loop. This mode achieves the same effect as the Autoincrement addressing mode in Figure 2.26.

A Program for Adding Test Scores

The flexibility available in ARM indexed addressing modes can be used to write an efficient version of the program for addition of student test scores shown in Figure 2.11. We assume the same data layout in memory as shown in Figure 2.10.

The program is shown in Figure D.8. The address N is loaded into register R2 at the beginning of the program. Register R2 serves as the index register for the Post-indexed addressing mode used to access test scores in successive student records. Note how the offsets 8, 4, and 4, along with writeback, cause the contents of register R2 to be increased correctly to skip over student ID locations in each pass through the loop, including the first pass. The combination of flexibility in the offset values, along with the writeback feature,

```
        LDR    R1, N          Load count into R1.
        LDR    R2, =NUM1      Load address NUM1 into R2.
        MOV    R0, #0         Clear accumulator R0.
LOOP    LDR    R3, [R2], #4   Load next number into R3.
        ADD    R0, R0, R3     Add number into R0.
        SUBS   R1, R1, #1     Decrement loop counter R1.
        BGT    LOOP           Branch back if not done.
        STR    R0, SUM        Store sum.
```

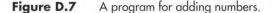

Figure D.7   A program for adding numbers.

```
        LDR    R2, =N         Load address N into R2.
        MOV    R3, #0
        MOV    R4, #0
        MOV    R5, #0
        LDR    R6, N          Load the value n.
LOOP    LDR    R7, [R2, #8]!  Add current student mark
        ADD    R3, R3, R7        for Test 1 to partial sum.
        LDR    R7, [R2, #4]!  Add current student mark
        ADD    R4, R4, R7        for Test 2 to partial sum.
        LDR    R7, [R2, #4]!  Add current student mark
        ADD    R5, R5, R7        for Test 3 to partial sum.
        SUBS   R6, R6, #1     Decrement the counter.
        BGT    LOOP           Loop back if not finished.
        STR    R3, SUM1       Store the total for Test 1.
        STR    R4, SUM2       Store the total for Test 2.
        STR    R5, SUM3       Store the total for Test 3.
```

Figure D.8   An ARM version of the program in Figure 2.11 for summing test scores.

means that the last Add instruction in the program in Figure 2.11 is not needed to increment the pointer register R2 at the end of each pass through the loop.

D.4.8   SUBROUTINE LINKAGE INSTRUCTIONS

The Branch and Link (BL) instruction is used to call a subroutine. It operates in the same way as other branch instructions, with one added step. The return address, which is the address of the next instruction after the BL instruction, is loaded into register R14, which acts as the link register. Since subroutines may be nested, the contents of the link register must be saved on the processor stack before a nested call to another subroutine is made. Register R13 is used as the processor stack pointer.

Figure D.9 shows the program of Figure D.7 rewritten as a subroutine. Parameters are passed through registers. The calling program passes the size of the number list and the address of the first number to the subroutine in registers R1 and R2. The subroutine passes the sum back to the calling program in register R0. The subroutine also uses register R3. Therefore, its contents, along with the contents of the link register R14, are saved on the stack by the STMFD instruction. The suffix FD in this instruction specifies that the stack grows toward lower addresses and that the stack pointer R13 is to be predecremented before pushing words onto the stack. The LDMFD instruction restores the contents of register R3 and pops the saved return address into the PC (R15), performing the return operation automatically.

Calling program

```
        LDR     R1, N
        LDR     R2, =NUM1
        BL      LISTADD
        STR     R0, SUM
        ⋮
```

Subroutine

```
LISTADD STMFD   R13!, {R3, R14}   Save R3 and return address in R14 on
                                  stack, using R13 as the stack pointer.
        MOV     R0, #0
LOOP    LDR     R3, [R2], #4
        ADD     R0, R0, R3
        SUBS    R1, R1, #1
        BGT     LOOP
        LDMFD   R13!, {R3, R15}   Restore R3 and load return address
                                  into PC (R15).
```

Figure D.9   Program of Figure D.7 written as a subroutine; parameters passed through registers.

Figure D.10a shows the program of Figure D.7 rewritten as a subroutine with parameters passed on the processor stack. The parameters NUM1 and *n* are pushed onto the stack by the first four instructions of the calling program. Registers R0 to R3 serve the same purpose inside the subroutine as in Figure D.7. Their contents are saved on the stack by the first instruction of the subroutine along with the return address in R14. The contents of the stack at various times are shown in Figure D.10b. After the parameters have been pushed and the Call instruction (BL) has been executed, the top of the stack is at level 2. It is at level 3 after all registers have been saved by the first instruction of the subroutine. The next two instructions load the parameters into registers R1 and R2 using offsets of 20 and 24 bytes into the stack to access the values *n* and NUM1, respectively. When the sum has been accumulated in R0, it is written into the stack by the Store instruction (STR), overwriting NUM1.

The final example of subroutines is the case of handling nested calls. Figure D.11 shows the ARM code for the program of Figure 2.21. The stack frames corresponding to the first and second subroutines are shown in Figure D.12. Register R12 is used as the frame pointer. Symbolic names are used for some of the registers in this example to aid program readability. Registers R12 (frame pointer), R13 (stack pointer), R14 (link register), and R15 (program counter), are labeled as FP, SP, LR, and PC, respectively. The assembler

(Assume top of stack is at level 1 below.)

Calling program

LDR	R0, =NUM1	Push NUM1
STR	R0, [R13, #−4]!	on stack.
LDR	R0, N	Push *n*
STR	R0, [R13, #−4]!	on stack.
BL	LISTADD	
LDR	R0, [R13, #4]	Move the sum into
STR	R0, SUM	memory location SUM.
ADD	R13, R13, #8	Remove parameters from stack.

⋮

Subroutine

LISTADD	STMFD	R13!, {R0−R3, R14}	Save registers.
	LDR	R1, [R13, #20]	Load parameters
	LDR	R2, [R13, #24]	from stack.
	MOV	R0, #0	
LOOP	LDR	R3, [R2], #4	
	ADD	R0, R0, R3	
	SUBS	R1, R1, #1	
	BGT	LOOP	
	STR	R0, [R13, #24]	Place sum on stack.
	LDMFD	R13!, {R0−R3, R15}	Restore registers and return.

(a) Calling program and subroutine

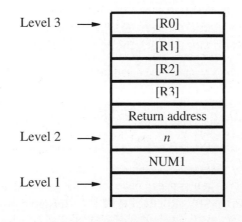

(b) Top of stack at various times

Figure D.10 Program of Figure D.7 written as a subroutine; parameters passed on the stack.

Memory location		Instructions	Comments
Main program			
		⋮	
2000	LDR	R10, PARAM2	Place parameters on stack.
2004	STR	R10, [SP, #–4]!	
2008	LDR	R10, PARAM1	
2012	STR	R10, [SP, #–4]!	
2016	BL	SUB1	
2020	LDR	R10, [SP]	Store SUB1 result.
2024	STR	R10, RESULT	
2028	ADD	SP, SP, #8	Remove parameters from stack.
2032	next instruction		
		⋮	
First subroutine			
2100 SUB1	STMFD	SP!, {R0–R3, FP, LR}	Save registers.
2104	ADD	FP, SP, #16	Load frame pointer.
2108	LDR	R0, [FP, #8]	Load parameters.
2112	LDR	R1, [FP, #12]	
		⋮	
	LDR	R2, PARAM3	Place parameter on stack.
	STR	R2, [SP, #–4]!	
2160	BL	SUB2	
2164	LDR	R2, [SP], #4	Pop SUB2 result into R2.
		⋮	
	STR	R3, [FP, #8]	Place result on stack.
	LDMFD	SP!, {R0–R3, FP, PC}	Restore registers and return.
Second subroutine			
3000 SUB2	STMFD	SP!, {R0, R1, FP, LR}	Save registers.
	ADD	FP, SP, #8	Load frame pointer.
	LDR	R0, [FP, #8]	Load parameter.
		⋮	
	STR	R1, [FP, #8]	Place result on stack.
	LDMFD	SP!, {R0, R1, FP, PC}	Restore registers and return.

Figure D.11   Nested subroutines.

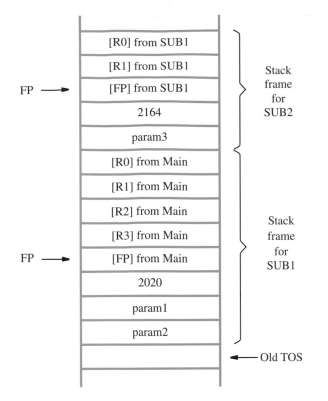

Figure D.12 Stack frames for Figure D.11.

predefines LR and PC for this use, and the assembler directive RN can be used to define the names FP and SP, as explained in Section D.5.

The structure of the calling program and the subroutines is the same as in Figure 2.21. Aspects that are specific to ARM are as follows. Both the return address and the old contents of the frame pointer are saved on the stack by the first instruction in each subroutine. The second instruction sets the frame pointer to point to its saved value, as shown in Figure D.12. This is consistent with the frame pointer position in Figures 2.20 and 2.22. The parameters are then referenced at offsets of 8, 12, and so on. The last instruction in each subroutine restores the saved value of the frame pointer as well as the saved values of other registers, and pops the return address from the stack into the PC.

D.5 ASSEMBLY LANGUAGE

The ARM assembly language has assembler directives to reserve storage space, assign numerical values to address labels and constant symbols, define where program and data blocks are to be placed in memory, and specify the end of the source program text. The general forms for such directives are described in Section 2.5.1.

	Memory address label	Operation	Addressing or data information
Assembler directives		AREA	CODE
		ENTRY	
Statements that		LDR	R1, N
generate		LDR	R2, POINTER
machine		MOV	R0, #0
instructions	LOOP	LDR	R3, [R2], #4
		ADD	R0, R0, R3
		SUBS	R1, R1, #1
		BGT	LOOP
		STR	R0, SUM
Assembler directives		AREA	DATA
	SUM	DCD	0
	N	DCD	5
	POINTER	DCD	NUM1
	NUM1	DCD	3, −17, 27, −12, 322
		END	

Figure D.13   Assembly-language source program for the program in Figure D.7.

We illustrate some of the ARM directives in Figure D.13, which gives a complete source program for the program of Figure D.7. The AREA directive, which uses the argument CODE or DATA, indicates the beginning of a block of memory that contains either program instructions or data. Other parameters are required to specify the placement of code and data blocks into specific memory areas. The ENTRY directive specifies that program execution is to begin at the following LDR instruction.

In the data area, which follows the code area, the DCD directives are used to label and initialize the data operands. The word locations SUM and N are initialized to 0 and 5, respectively, by the first two DCD directives. The address NUM1 is placed in the location POINTER by the next DCD directive. The combination of the instruction

LDR   R2, POINTER

and the data declaration

POINTER   DCD   NUM1

is one of the ways that the pseudoinstruction

$$\text{LDR} \quad \text{R2, =NUM1}$$

in Figure D.7 can be implemented, as described in Section D.5.1. The last DCD directive specifies that the five numbers to be added are placed in successive memory word locations, starting at NUM1.

Constants in hexadecimal notation are identified by the prefix '&', and constants in base n, for n between two and nine, are identified with a prefix indicating the base. For example, 2_101100 denotes a binary constant, and 8_70375 denotes an octal constant. Base ten constants do not need a prefix.

An EQU directive can be used to declare symbolic names for constants. For example, the statement

$$\text{TEN} \quad \text{EQU} \quad 10$$

allows TEN to be used in a program instead of the decimal constant 10.

It is convenient to use symbolic names for registers, relating to their usage. The RN directive is used for this purpose. For example,

$$\text{COUNTER} \quad \text{RN} \quad 3$$

establishes the name COUNTER for register R3. The register names R0 to R15, PC (for R15), and LR (for R14) are predefined by the assembler.

D.5.1   PSEUDOINSTRUCTIONS

A *pseudoinstruction* is an assembly-language instruction that performs some desired operation but does not correspond directly to an actual machine instruction. The assembler accepts such an instruction and replaces it with an actual machine instruction that performs the desired operation. In some cases, a short sequence of actual machine instructions may be needed. Pseudoinstructions are provided for the convenience of the programmer.

We have already seen examples of pseudoinstructions in Sections D.4.3 and D.4.4. Here, we will give a more complete discussion of pseudoinstructions that can be used to load a 32-bit number or address value into a register.

Loading 32-bit Values

The pseudoinstruction

$$\text{LDR} \quad \text{R}d, \text{=value}$$

can be used to load any 32-bit value into a register. The equal sign in front of the value distinguishes this instruction from an actual Load instruction. If the value can be formed and loaded into Rd by a MOV or MVN instruction, then that is the choice that will be made by the assembler. If this is not possible, the assembler will use the Relative addressing mode in an actual LDR instruction to load the value from a memory location that is in a data area allocated by the assembler.

For example, the instruction

$$\text{LDR} \quad \text{R3, =127}$$

will be replaced by the instruction

MOV   R3, #127

But the instruction

LDR   R3, =&A123B456

will be replaced with

LDR   R3, MEMLOC

where the hexadecimal value A123B456 is the contents of memory location MEMLOC, accessed using the Relative addressing mode.

The value of an address label can also be loaded into a register in this way, as we have done in most of the program examples in this appendix.

Loading Address Values

In addition to the method just described, a more efficient way can be used to load an address into a register when the address is close to the current value of the program counter PC (R15). This alternative approach avoids the need to place the desired address value in a data area.

The pseudoinstruction

ADR   Rd, LOCATION

loads the 32-bit address represented by LOCATION into Rd. The ADR instruction is implemented as follows. The assembler computes the offset from the current value in PC to LOCATION. If LOCATION is in the forward direction, then ADR is implemented with the instruction

ADD   Rd, R15, #offset

If LOCATION is in the backward direction, then

SUB   Rd, R15, #offset

is used.

In either case, the offset is an unsigned 8-bit number in the range 0 to 255, as described earlier for arithmetic instructions. A limited number of larger offset values can also be generated by rotation of an 8-bit value, as described in Section D.4.2.

D.6   EXAMPLE PROGRAMS

In this section, we give ARM versions of the generic programs for vector dot product and string search that are presented in Section 2.12. We will describe only those aspects of the ARM code that differ from the generic programs.

	LDR	R1, =AVEC	R1 points to vector A.
	LDR	R2, =BVEC	R2 points to vector B.
	LDR	R3, N	R3 is the loop counter.
	MOV	R0, #0	R0 accumulates the dot product.
LOOP	LDR	R4, [R1], #4	Load A component.
	LDR	R5, [R2], #4	Load B component.
	MLA	R0, R4, R5, R0	Multiply components and
			accumulate into R0.
	SUBS	R3, R3, #1	Decrement the counter.
	BGT	LOOP	Branch back if not done.
	STR	R0, DOTPROD	Store dot product.

Figure D.14   A dot product program.

D.6.1 VECTOR DOT PRODUCT

A program that calculates the dot product of two vectors A and B is given in Figure D.14. The first two instructions load the starting addresses of the vectors, AVEC and BVEC, into registers R1 and R2. The Relative addressing mode is used to access the contents of N and DOTPROD, and the Post-indexed addressing mode (which always includes writeback) is used in the first two instructions of the loop. The Multiply-Accumulate instruction (MLA) performs the necessary arithmetic operations. It multiplies the vector elements in R4 and R5 and accumulates their product into R0.

D.6.2 STRING SEARCH

The ARM program in Figure D.15 follows the generic program in Figure 2.30 very closely. There are two differences worth noting. The Post-indexed addressing mode used in the first two instructions of LOOP2 in the ARM program avoids the need for the two Add instructions in LOOP2 of the generic program; and the three pairs of ARM instructions CMP/BNE, CMP/BGT, and CMP/BGE are needed to implement the three generic Branch_if instructions.

D.7 OPERATING MODES AND EXCEPTIONS

The ARM processor has seven operating modes. Application programs run in User mode. There are five exception modes. One of them is entered when an exception occurs. The seventh operating mode is the System mode. It can only be entered from one of the exception modes, as discussed in Section D.7.3.

	LDR	R2, =T	Load address T into R2.
	LDR	R3, =P	Load address P into R3.
	LDR	R4, N	Get the value n.
	LDR	R5, M	Get the value m.
	SUB	R4, R4, R5	Compute $n - m$.
	ADD	R4, R2, R4	R4 is the address of $T(n - m)$.
	ADD	R5, R3, R5	R5 is the address of $P(m)$.
LOOP1	MOV	R6, R2	Use R6 to scan through string T.
	MOV	R7, R3	Use R7 to scan through string P.
LOOP2	LDRB	R8, [R6], #1	Compare a pair of
	LDRB	R9, [R7], #1	characters in
	CMP	R8, R9	strings T and P.
	BNE	NOMATCH	
	CMP	R5, R7	Check if at $P(m)$.
	BGT	LOOP2	Loop again if not done.
	STR	R2, RESULT	Store the address of $T(i)$.
	B	DONE	
NOMATCH	ADD	R2, R2, #1	Point to next character in T.
	CMP	R4, R2	Check if at $T(n - m)$.
	BGE	LOOP1	Loop again if not done.
	MOV	R8, #−1	No match was found.
	STR	R8, RESULT	
DONE	next instruction		

Figure D.15   A string search program.

The five exception modes and the exceptions that cause them to be entered are summarized as follows:

- Fast interrupt (FIQ) mode is entered when an external device raises a fast-interrupt request to obtain urgent service.

- Ordinary interrupt (IRQ) mode is entered when an external device raises a normal interrupt request.

- Supervisor (SVC) mode is entered on powerup or reset, or when a user program executes a Software Interrupt instruction (SWI) to call for an operating system routine to be executed.

- Memory access violation (Abort) mode is entered when an attempt by the current program to fetch an instruction or a data operand causes a memory access violation.

- Unimplemented instruction (Undefined) mode is entered when the current program attempts to execute an unimplemented instruction.

The interrupt-disable bits I and F in the Status register determine whether the processor is interrupted when an interrupt request is raised on the corresponding lines (IRQ and FIQ). The processor is not interrupted if the disable bit is 1; it is interrupted if the disable bit is 0.

The five exception modes and the System mode are *privileged* modes. When the processor is in a privileged mode, access to the Status register (CPSR in Figure D.1) is allowed so that the mode bits and the interrupt-disable bits can be manipulated. This is done with instructions that are not available in User mode, which is an *unprivileged* mode.

D.7.1 BANKED REGISTERS

When the processor is operating in either the User or System mode, the normal sixteen processor registers shown in Figure D.1 are in use. When an exception occurs and a switch is made from User mode to one of the five exception modes, some of these sixteen registers are replaced by an equal number of *banked* registers, as described in Section D.2. The contents of the replaced registers are left unchanged. There is a different set of banked registers for each of the five exception modes, shown in blue in Figure D.16.

When an exception occurs, the following actions are taken on the switch from User mode to the appropriate exception mode:

1. The contents of the Program Counter (R15) are loaded into the banked Link register (R14_mode) of the exception mode.

2. The contents of the Status register (CPSR) are loaded into the banked Saved Status register (SPSR_mode).

3. The mode bits of CPSR are changed to represent the appropriate exception mode, and the interrupt-disable bits I and F are set appropriately.

4. The Program Counter (R15) is loaded with the dedicated vector address for the exception, and the instruction at that address is fetched and executed to begin the exception-service routine.

The active stack pointer register (R13_mode) always points to the top element of a processor stack in an area of memory that has been allocated for the relevant exception mode. The contents of R13_mode are initialized by the operating system.

When the exception-service routine has been completed, it is necessary to return to the User mode to continue execution of the interrupted program. This is accomplished by transferring the contents of the mode link register (R14_mode) to the program counter and transferring the contents of the Saved Status register (SPSR_mode) to the Status register (CPSR).

The actions just described for switching from User mode to an exception mode and then back again to User mode have been presented in general terms. The details vary somewhat depending on the actual exception and the mode entered. These details are described further in the following sections.

General-purpose registers and program counter

User/System	FIQ	IRQ	Supervisor	Abort	Undefined
R0	R0	R0	R0	R0	R0
R1	R1	R1	R1	R1	R1
R2	R2	R2	R2	R2	R2
R3	R3	R3	R3	R3	R3
R4	R4	R4	R4	R4	R4
R5	R5	R5	R5	R5	R5
R6	R6	R6	R6	R6	R6
R7	R7	R7	R7	R7	R7
R8	R8_fiq	R8	R8	R8	R8
R9	R9_fiq	R9	R9	R9	R9
R10	R10_fiq	R10	R10	R10	R10
R11	R11_fiq	R11	R11	R11	R11
R12	R12_fiq	R12	R12	R12	R12
R13	R13_fiq	R13_irq	R13_svc	R13_abt	R13_und
R14	R14_fiq	R14_irq	R14_svc	R14_abt	R14_und
R15	R15	R15	R15	R15	R15

Processor status register

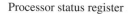

CPSR	CPSR	CPSR	CPSR	CPSR	CPSR
	SPSR_fiq	SPSR_irq	SPSR_svc	SPSR_abt	SPSR_und

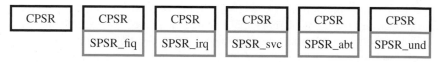

Figure D.16   Accessible registers in different modes of the ARM processor.

D.7.2 EXCEPTION TYPES

There are seven possible exceptions. They are listed in Table D.3 along with the processor mode that is entered when they occur. The exception vector addresses are also listed. These word locations at the low end of the address space must contain branch instructions to the start of the exception-service routines. The fast interrupt routine could start immediately

Table D.3   Exceptions and processor modes.

Exception	Processor mode entered	Vector address	Priority (Highest = 1)
Fast interrupt	FIQ	28	3
Ordinary interrupt	IRQ	24	4
Software interrupt	Supervisor (SVC)	8	–
Powerup/reset	Supervisor (SVC)	0	1
Data access violation	Abort	16	2
Instruction access violation	Abort	12	5
Unimplemented instruction	Undefined	4	6

without the need for a branch instruction because its vector address (28) is last in the list. When multiple exceptions occur at the same time, the priority order in which they are serviced is shown in the last column of Table D.3.

A more detailed description of the exceptions is as follows:

• Fast (FIQ) and ordinary (IRQ) interrupts—Input/output devices use one of two interrupt request lines to request service. The FIQ interrupt is intended for one device or a small number of devices that require rapid response. The banked registers for the FIQ processor mode shown in Figure D.16 include five general-purpose registers R8_fiq through R12_fiq in addition to the stack pointer register R13_fiq and the link register R14_fiq. If the five general-purpose registers provide enough working space for the FIQ interrupt-service routine, then none of the other User-mode registers need to be saved and restored. All other I/O devices use the IRQ interrupt line to request service.

• Software interrupts—A user program requests operating system services by executing the SWI instruction. This is an exception that causes entry into the Supervisor mode. A parameter field in the instruction specifies the requested service and is accessible from the Supervisor routines.

• Powerup/reset—This is the highest priority exception. It places the processor into a known initial state so that operating system software can begin or restart operation properly. Any program executing when this exception occurs is abandoned.

• Data and instruction access violations—Processor implementations may include a memory management unit that restricts programs to valid areas of the address space for their instructions and data. Such a unit is necessary to implement virtual memory as described in Chapter 8. If the processor issues an address for an instruction fetch or data operand access outside these areas, an exception occurs and the Abort mode is entered. This mode also handles the case where the address is valid but is not currently mapped into main memory and needs to be transferred from secondary storage.

• Unimplemented instruction—If the processor tries to execute an instruction that is not implemented in hardware, an exception is raised and the Undefined mode is entered. For example, a floating-point arithmetic operation that can be supported by special hardware may not be implemented in the current processor. In this case, the exception can cause a software implementation of the operation to be executed.

D.7.3   SYSTEM MODE

The System mode is a privileged mode that uses the same registers as those used in the User mode. It can only be entered from another exception mode. Its purpose is to facilitate linkage to subroutines during exception handling without overwriting the link register R14_mode. When in System mode, subroutine Call instructions use the normal link register R14. After returning from all subroutine calls, the original exception mode is reentered, regaining access to the link register R14_mode.

D.7.4   HANDLING EXCEPTIONS

The general actions needed to switch from User mode to the appropriate exception mode and then back again after an exception occurs have been described briefly in Section D.7.1. The actions vary in detail, depending upon the exception and the exception mode entered. Here, we consider some of those details.

Pipelined Execution, the Program Counter, and the Status Register

The ARM processor overlaps the fetching and execution of successive instructions in order to increase instruction throughput. This technique is called pipelined instruction execution. It is described in Chapter 6. During pipelined execution of instructions, updating of the program counter is done as follows. Suppose that the processor fetches instruction I_1 from address A. The contents of PC are incremented to A+4, then execution of I_1 is begun. Before the execution of I_1 is completed, the processor fetches instruction I_2 from address A+4, then increments PC to A+8.

Now assume that at the end of execution of I_1 the processor detects that an ordinary interrupt request (IRQ) has been received. The processor performs the actions described in Section D.7.1 to enter the IRQ exception mode to service the interrupt. It copies the contents of CPSR into SPSR_irq and copies the contents of PC, which are now A+8, into the link register R14_irq. Instruction I_2, which has been fetched but not yet fully executed, is discarded. This is the instruction to which the interrupt-service routine must return. The interrupt-service routine must subtract 4 from R14_irq before using its contents as the return address. The saved copy of the Status register must also be restored. The required actions are carried out by the single instruction

$$\text{SUBS} \quad \text{PC, R14\_irq, \#4}$$

which subtracts 4 from R14_irq and stores the result into PC. The suffix S in the OP code normally means "set condition codes." But when the target register of the instruction is PC, the S suffix causes the processor to copy the contents of SPSR_irq into CPSR, thus completing the actions needed to return to the interrupted program.

Table D.4   Address correction during return from exception.

Exception	Saved address*	Desired return address	Return instruction
Undefined instruction	PC+4	PC+4	MOVS PC, R14_und
Software interrupt	PC+4	PC+4	MOVS PC, R14_svc
Instruction Abort	PC+4	PC	SUBS PC, R14_abt, #4
Data Abort	PC+8	PC	SUBS PC, R14_abt, #8
IRQ	PC+4	PC	SUBS PC, R14_irq, #4
FIQ	PC+4	PC	SUBS PC, R14_fiq, #4

*PC is the address of the instruction that caused the exception. For IRQ and FIQ, it is the address of the first instruction not executed because of the interrupt.

In the case of a software interrupt triggered by execution of the SWI instruction, the value saved in R14_svc is the correct return address. Return from a software interrupt can be accomplished using the instruction

$$\text{MOVS} \quad \text{PC, R14\_svc}$$

that also copies the contents of SPSR_svc into CPSR.

Table D.4 gives the correct return-address value and the instruction that can be used to return to the interrupted program for each of the exceptions in Table D.3, except for powerup/reset, which abandons any currently executing program. Note that for a data access or instruction access violation, the return address is the address of the instruction that caused the exception, because it must be re-executed after the cause of the violation has been resolved.

Manipulating Status Register Bits

When the processor is running in a privileged mode, special Move instructions, MRS and MSR, can be used to transfer the contents of the current or saved processor status registers to or from a general-purpose register. For example,

$$\text{MRS} \quad \text{R}d, \text{CPSR}$$

copies the contents of CPSR into register Rd. Similarly,

$$\text{MSR} \quad \text{SPSR, R}m$$

copies the contents of register Rm into SPSR_mode.

After status register contents have been loaded into a register, logic instructions can be used to manipulate individual bits. Then, the register contents can be copied back into the status register to effect the desired changes. For example, these steps can be used to set or clear interrupt-disable bits in an exception-service routine. We will see this done in Section D.8 in the handling of I/O device interrupts.

Nesting Exception-Service Routines

Recall that nesting of subroutines is facilitated by storing the contents of the link register in the stack frame associated with a subroutine that calls another subroutine. This action is not needed when an exception-service routine is interrupted by a higher-priority exception whose service routine runs in a different processor mode. This is because each mode has its own banked link register.

For example, suppose that an ordinary interrupt is being serviced by an IRQ-mode routine when an interrupt that requires fast servicing is received. The first routine is interrupted and the FIQ mode is entered to service the second interrupt. The return address for the program that was interrupted to service the IRQ interrupt remains unchanged in link register R14_irq. The return address for the IRQ routine is stored in R14_fiq. Hence, the use of banked registers avoids overwriting saved return addresses, and these addresses do not need to be placed on the stack when nesting of exception routines occurs. However, if different exceptions are serviced in the same processor mode, then their return addresses will need to be saved if nesting is allowed.

D.8 INPUT/OUTPUT

The ARM architecture uses the memory-mapped I/O approach as described in Section 3.1. Reading a character from a keyboard or sending a character to a display can be done using program-controlled I/O as described in Section 3.1.2. It is also possible to use interrupt-driven I/O as described in Section 3.2. Both of these options will be illustrated in this section by presenting program examples that show how the generic programs in Chapter 3, which involve keyboard and display devices, can be implemented in ARM assembly language.

D.8.1 PROGRAM-CONTROLLED I/O

We begin by giving short instruction sequences for reading a character from a keyboard and writing a character to a display.

Keyboard Character Input

Assume that the data, status, and control registers in the keyboard interface are arranged as shown in Figure 3.3*a*. Also, assume that address KBD_DATA (0x4000) has been loaded into register R1. The instruction sequence

```
READWAIT    LDRB    R3, [R1, #4]
            TST     R3, #2
            BEQ     READWAIT
            LDRB    R3, [R1]
```

reads a character into register R3 when a key has been pressed on the keyboard. The test (TST) instruction performs the bitwise logical AND operation on its two operands and sets the condition code flags based on the result. The immediate operand, 2, has a single one in the b_1 bit position. Therefore, the result of the TST operation will be zero until KIN = 1, which signifies that a character is available in KBD_DATA. The BEQ instruction branches back to READWAIT if KIN = 0. This results in looping until a key is pressed, which causes KIN to be set to one. Then, the branch is not taken, and the character is loaded into register R3.

Display Character Output

Assuming that address DISP_DATA has been loaded into register R2, the instruction sequence

```
WRITEWAIT    LDRB    R4, [R2, #4]
             TST     R4, #4
             BEQ     WRITEWAIT
             STRB    R3, [R2]
```

sends the character in register R3 to the DISP_DATA register when the display is ready to receive it.

Complete Input/Output Program

The two routines just described can be used to read a line of characters from a keyboard, store them in the memory, and echo them back to a display, as shown in the program in Figure D.17. This program is patterned after the generic program in Figure 3.4. Register R0 is assumed to contain the address of the first byte in the memory area where the line is to be stored. Registers R1 through R4 have the same usage as in the READWAIT and WRITEWAIT loops just described. The first Store instruction (STRB) stores the character read from the keyboard into the memory. The Post-indexed addressing mode with writeback is used in this instruction to step through the memory area. The Test Equivalence (TEQ) instruction tests whether or not the two operands are equal and sets the Z condition code flag accordingly.

```
READ    LDRB    R3, [R1, #4]    Load KBD_STATUS byte and
        TST     R3, #2               wait for character.
        BEQ     READ
        LDRB    R3, [R1]        Read the character and
        STRB    R3, [R0], #1      store it in memory.
ECHO    LDRB    R4, [R2, #4]    Load DISP_STATUS byte and
        TST     R4, #4               wait for display
        BEQ     ECHO                to be ready.
        STRB    R3, [R2]        Send character to display.
        TEQ     R3, #CR         If not carriage return,
        BNE     READ                read more characters.
```

Figure D.17   A program that reads a line of characters and displays it.

D.8.2 INTERRUPT-DRIVEN I/O

The ARM interrupt facility described in Section D.7 can be used to read a line of characters typed on a keyboard under interrupt-driven control. We assume that the keyboard device has its interrupt-request line attached to the IRQ interrupt input to the processor.

There may be a number of devices that are enabled to raise interrupts on the IRQ line. If this is the case, software polling of these devices in some priority order can be used in the IRQ interrupt-service routine to identify the first device with an interrupt raised. For simplicity, we will assume that the keyboard is the only device that can raise an interrupt request on the IRQ line.

A generic program that uses interrupts for reading a line of characters until a carriage-return character (CR) is encountered is given in Figure 3.8. The interrupt-service routine also sends the characters to a display, as they are read from the keyboard, using program-controlled I/O. We will implement this task on the ARM processor. The Status register, CPSR, and the Saved Status register in the IRQ processor mode, SPSR_irq, are the processor control registers that are relevant for handling interrupts.

The following memory locations are needed in this example I/O program:

- PNTR is a pointer location that contains the address where the next character read from the keyboard is to be loaded into memory.

- LINE is the memory byte location where the first character of the line is to be placed.

- EOL is a memory location containing a binary variable that indicates to the main program when a complete line has been read.

Figure D.18 shows an ARM IRQ interrupt-service routine and a main program that correspond to those in Figure 3.8. The main program is assumed to be running in Supervisor mode. The first six instructions initialize PNTR with the address LINE, clear the EOL indicator, and enable interrupts in the keyboard control register, KBD_CONT. The last instruction clears the IRQ disable bit (I) and switches the processor to User mode by using the MSR instruction to load the hexadecimal value 50 into CPSR.

The IRQ interrupt-service routine follows the pattern of the generic program in Figure 3.8 very closely. Many of the Load and Store instructions use the Relative addressing mode for simplicity, assuming that both the memory locations and device registers named are within the range reachable by an offset from the Program Counter.

D.9 CONDITIONAL EXECUTION OF INSTRUCTIONS

The conditional execution of all ARM instructions permits shorter routines to be written in place of routines written for conventional RISC machines where there are a number of branch instructions.

Consider the following example. A loop component of a routine for finding the greatest common divisor (GCD) of two, non-zero, positive integers [4] using RISC-style instructions is shown in Figure D.19a. The two numbers are contained in registers R2 and R3 when the routine is entered. At the beginning of each pass through the loop, if the numbers are not equal, then the routine subtracts the smaller number from the larger number and returns to

Interrupt-service routine

IRQLOC	STMFD	R13!, {R2, R3}	Save R2 and R3 on the stack.
	LDR	R2, PNTR	Load address pointer.
	LDRB	R3, KBD_DATA	Read character from keyboard.
	STRB	R3, [R2], #1	Write character into memory
			and increment pointer.
	STR	R2, PNTR	Update pointer in memory.
ECHO	LDRB	R2, DISP_STATUS	Wait for display to be ready.
	TST	R2, #4	
	BEQ	ECHO	
	STRB	R3, DISP_DATA	Send character to display.
	CMP	R3, #CR	Check if character is Carriage Return
	BNE	RTRN	and return if not CR.
	MOV	R2, #1	If CR, indicate end of line.
	STR	R2, EOL	
	MOV	R2, #0	Disable interrupts in
	STRB	R2, KBD_CONT	keyboard interface.
RTRN	LDMFD	R13!, {R2, R3}	Restore registers
	SUBS	R15, R14, #4	and return from interrupt.

Main program

LDR	R2, =LINE	Initialize buffer pointer.
STR	R2, PNTR	
MOV	R2, #0	Clear end-of-line indicator.
STR	R2, EOL	
MOV	R2, #2	Enable interrupts in keyboard interface.
STRB	R2, KBD_CONT	
MOV	R2, #&50	Enable IRQ interrupts
MSR	CPSR, R2	and switch to User mode.
next instruction		

Figure D.18   A program that reads an input line from a keyboard using interrupts, and displays the line using polling.

the beginning of the loop. If the numbers are the same, an exit from the loop is taken to location NEXT, and the GCD is contained in both registers.

An ARM routine for this task is shown in Figure D.19b. The Compare instruction sets the condition codes. The suffix in the OP code of each Subtract instruction specifies the condition under which it is to be executed. The first Subtract instruction is executed only if the contents of register R2 are greater than those of register R3, and the second Subtract instruction is executed only if the contents of register R3 are greater than those of register

```
LOOP        Branch_if_[R2]=[R3]     NEXT
            Branch_if_[R2]>[R3]     REDUCE
            Subtract                R3, R3, R2
            Branch                  LOOP
REDUCE      Subtract                R2, R2, R3
            Branch                  LOOP
NEXT        next instruction
```

(a) GCD algorithm using RISC-style instructions

```
LOOP    CMP     R2, R3
        SUBGT   R2, R2, R3
        SUBLT   R3, R3, R2
        BNE     LOOP
NEXT    next instruction
```

(b) GCD algorithm using ARM instructions

Figure D.19   Conditional execution of instructions.

R2. On each pass through the loop when the contents of the two registers are not equal, only one of the Subtract instructions is executed. When the contents of the two registers are equal, which may be the case initially, neither of the two Subtract instructions is executed, and the branch back to LOOP is not taken.

The shorter ARM code sequences that result from cases such as this are most effective when there is a relatively high density of Branch instructions in conventional code. The code space savings are important in small embedded system applications.

D.10   COPROCESSORS

Hardware units called *coprocessors* can be connected to an ARM processor. They are used to perform operations that are not included in the basic ARM instruction set. One example is a hardware unit for performing arithmetic operations on floating-point numbers. Other examples include application-specific processing on digital signals or video data. Writing programs that use coprocessors is facilitated by including extensions to the ARM instruction set that are of three types:

- Data operations in the coprocessor
- Transfers between ARM and coprocessor registers
- Load and Store transfers between memory and the coprocessor registers

Software that defines a coprocessor unit in a form that can be used to synthesize a hardware realization can be combined with software that defines a basic ARM processor to synthesize a single chip that integrates the coprocessor unit with the ARM processor.

D.11   EMBEDDED APPLICATIONS AND THE THUMB ISA

Low-cost and low-power embedded systems, such as mobile telephones, are a major application area for ARM processors. Designers of such systems strive to minimize the size of the on-chip memory space needed to store the required programs. In Section D.9, we saw that conditional execution of instructions can lead to reduced code space. Block Transfer instructions, which are used to transfer words between multiple registers and a block of memory words, also reduce code space.

Code space can be reduced further by using a subset of the most commonly used ARM instructions that are provided in a format that uses only 16 bits for each instruction. This subset is called the *Thumb* instruction set. Thumb instructions are executed as follows. First, they are fetched from memory. Then, they are decompressed (expanded) from their 16-bit encoded format into corresponding 32-bit ARM instructions and executed in the usual way.

Bit b_5 in the Status register (CPSR), labeled T, determines whether the incoming instruction stream consists of Thumb (T = 1) or standard 32-bit ARM instructions (T = 0). A program can contain a mix of Thumb routines and standard instruction routines. Special instructions are needed to manipulate the T bit when switching between such routines.

There are two main differences between Thumb and standard instructions. First, many Thumb instructions use a two-operand format in which the destination register is also one of the source operand registers. Second, conditional execution, which applies to all standard ARM instructions, is used mainly for branches in the Thumb set. These differences lead to savings in instruction encoding bit space.

D.12   CONCLUDING REMARKS

The ARM processor has achieved significant commercial success in the embedded system market. Its design is licensed to a number of companies that make hand-held communication devices. The 16-bit Thumb version of the instruction set is particularly suitable for low-cost and low-power applications because it allows for compact programs. The flexible Index addressing modes and the Block Transfer instructions of the full 32-bit ISA are useful for many applications. While these two features reflect CISC-style attributes, ARM is generally considered to have a Load/Store RISC-style architecture.

D.13   SOLVED PROBLEMS

This section presents some examples of the types of problems that a student may be asked to solve, and shows how such problems can be solved.

Example D.1   **Problem:** Assume that there is a byte-string of ASCII-encoded characters stored in memory starting at location STRING. It is terminated by the Carriage-Return character (CR). Write an ARM program to determine the length of the string and store the length in location LENGTH.

Solution: Figure D.20 presents a possible program. The characters in the string are compared to CR (ASCII code &0D), and a counter is incremented until the end of the string is reached.

```
           LDR     R2, =STRING     Load address of start of string.
           MOV     R3, #0          Load length of string as 0.
           MOV     R4, #&0D        Load Carriage-Return character code.
   LOOP    LDRB    R5, [R2], #1    Load next character.
           CMP     R4, R5          Check for Carriage Return and finish,
           BEQ     DONE               or increment length count and go back.
           ADD     R3, R3, #1
           B       LOOP
   DONE    STR     R3, LENGTH      Store length of string.
```

Figure D.20   Program for Example D.1.

Example D.2   **Problem:** Write an ARM program to find the smallest number in a list of non-negative 32-bit integers. Successive memory word locations SMALL and N in the data area of the program are used to store the smallest number and the size of the list, respectively. These two locations are followed by the list, with the first number stored at location ENTRIES. Include the assembler directives needed to organize the program and data areas as specified. Use a small list of 7 integers as an example.

Solution: The program instructions and data are shown in Figure D.21. Comments are included to explain how the program accomplishes the required task. Note that the method for loading the address ENTRIES into register R2 is the way that the assembler would replace the pseudoinstruction used in earlier program examples, and explained in Section D.5.1.

```
            AREA    CODE
            ENTRY
            LDR     R2, POINTER      R2 points to list at ENTRIES.
            LDR     R3, [R2, #-4]    Counter R3 initialized to n.
            LDR     R5, [R2]         R5 holds smallest number so far.
LOOP        SUBS    R3, R3, #1       Decrement counter.
            BEQ     DONE             If R3 contains 0, done.
            LDR     R6, [R2, #4]!    Increment list pointer
                                       and get next number.

            CMP     R5, R6           Check if smaller number found,
            BLE     LOOP               branch back if not smaller;
            MOV     R5, R6             otherwise, move it into R5,
            B       LOOP               then branch back.
DONE        STR     R5, SMALL        Store smallest number into SMALL.

            AREA    DATA
POINTER     DCD     ENTRIES          Pointer to start of list.
SMALL       DCD     0                Location for smallest number.
N           DCD     7                Number of entries in list.
ENTRIES     DCD     4, 5, 3, 6, 1, 8, 2    List of numbers.
            END
```

Figure D.21   Program for Example D.2.

Problem: An ARM program is required to convert an n-digit decimal integer into a binary   **Example D.3**
number. The decimal number is given as n ASCII-encoded characters. They are stored
in successive byte locations in the memory, starting at location DECIMAL. The converted
number is to be stored at location BINARY. Location N contains the value n.

Solution: Consider a four-digit decimal number $D = d_3d_2d_1d_0$. Its value can be given by
the expression $((d_3 \times 10 + d_2) \times 10 + d_1) \times 10 + d_0$. This expression is used as the basis
for the conversion technique used in the program in Figure D.22. Each ASCII-encoded
character is converted into a Binary-Coded-Decimal (BCD) digit before it is used in the
computation. It is assumed that the converted binary value can be represented in no more
than 32 bits.

Problem: Consider an array of numbers A(i,j), where $i = 0$ through $n - 1$ is the row index,   **Example D.4**
and $y = 0$ through $m - 1$ is the column index. The array is stored in memory one row after

```
              LDR    R2, N              Initialize counter R2 with n.
              LDR    R3, =DECIMAL       R3 points to ASCII digits.
              MOV    R4, #0             R4 will hold the binary number.
              MOV    R6, #10            R6 will hold constant 10.
     LOOP     LDRB   R5, [R3], #1       Get next ASCII character
                                           and increment pointer.
              AND    R5, R5, #&0F       Form BCD digit.
              ADD    R4, R4, R5         Add to intermediate result.
              SUBS   R2, R2, #1         Decrement the counter.
              BEQ    DONE               Store result if done.
              MUL    R4, R6, R4         Multiply intermediate result by 10
              B      LOOP                  and loop back.
     DONE     STR    R4, BINARY         Store result in BINARY.
```

Figure D.22   Program for Example D.3.

another, with each row occupying *m* successive word locations. Write an ARM subroutine for adding column *x* to column *y*, element by element, and storing the sum elements in column *y*. The indices *x* and *y* are passed to the subroutine through registers R2 and R3. The parameters *n* and *m* are passed to the subroutine through registers R4 and R5. The address of element A(0,0) is passed to the subroutine through register R6.

Solution: A possible main program and subroutine for this task are given in Figure D.23. We have assumed that the values *x*, *y*, *n*, and *m*, are stored in memory locations X, Y, N, and M. The address of element A(0,0) is ARRAY. The comments in the program explain how the task is accomplished. It is interesting to compare the number of instructions in the ARM subroutine with the number of instructions in the generic RISC-style subroutine given in Figure 2.36. The shorter ARM subroutine is possible because of the flexibility and features provided by the ARM Index addressing modes and the availability of Block Transfer instructions.

Example D.5   **Problem:** Assume that memory location BINARY contains a 32-bit pattern. It is desired to display these bits as eight hexadecimal digit characters on a display device that has the interface depicted in Figure 3.3. Write an ARM program that accomplishes this task using program-controlled I/O to display the characters.

Solution: Figure D.24 shows a possible program. First, the hexadecimal digits are converted to ASCII characters by using a table lookup into a 16-entry table. The eight ASCII

Main program

	LDR	R2, X	Load the value x.
	LDR	R3, Y	Load the value y.
	LDR	R4, N	Load the value n.
	LDR	R5, M	Load the value m.
	LDR	R6, =ARRAY	Load address ARRAY of element A(0,0).
	BL	SUB	Call subroutine.

Subroutine

SUB	STMFD	R13!, {R10, R11, R14}	Save registers R10, R11, and Link (R14), on stack.
	ADD	R2, R6, R2, LSL #2	Load address of A(0,x) into R2.
	ADD	R3, R6, R3, LSL #2	Load address of A(0,y) into R3.
LOOP	LDR	R10, [R2], R5, LSL #2	Load x-column value into R10 and increment column address.
	LDR	R11, [R3]	Load y-column value into R11.
	ADD	R11, R11, R10	Add column values.
	STR	R11, [R3], R5, LSL #2	Store sum into y-column and increment column address.
	SUBS	R4, R4, #1	Decrement row counter and
	BGT	LOOP	loop back if not done.
	LDMFD	R13!, {R10, R11, R15}	Restore registers R10, R11, and program counter (R15), and return from subroutine.

Figure D.23   Program for Example D.4.

characters to be displayed are stored in a block of memory bytes starting at location HEX. Then, the characters are sent to the display. The comments describe the detailed actions taken in the program. Note the ORR instruction at location LOOP. It implements a right rotation operation on the contents of register R2. Each rotation moves the 4-bit hexadecimal digit that is to be converted next into the low-order 4-bit position of R2. Also note the use of the ADR pseudoinstruction for loading address values into registers. The ADR instruction is explained in Section D.5.1.

	AREA	CODE	
	ENTRY		
	MOV	R0, #0	Needed for ORR instruction.
	LDR	R2, BINARY	Load binary pattern.
	ADR	R3, TABLE	R3 points to ASCII table.
	ADR	R4, HEX	R4 points to hexadecimal characters.
	MOV	R5, #8	Load digit count.
LOOP	ORR	R2, R0, R2, ROR #28	Rotate next digit into low-order 4 bits.
	AND	R6, R2, #&F	Extract digit and load into R6.
	LDRB	R7, [R3, +R6]	Load ASCII code for digit.
	STRB	R7, [R4], #1	Store digit in character string, and increment pointer.
	SUBS	R5, R5, #1	Decrement digit counter.
	BGT	LOOP	Loop back if not done.
DISPLAY	MOV	R5, #8	Load digit count for display routine.
	ADR	R4, HEX	R4 points to hexadecimal characters.
	ADR	R2, DISP_DATA	R2 points to device registers.
SENDCHAR	LDRB	R3, [R2, #4]	Check if the display is ready
	TST	R3, #4	by testing DOUT flag.
	BEQ	SENDCHAR	
	LDRB	R6, [R4], #1	Get next ASCII character, and increment pointer.
	STRB	R6, [R2]	Send character to display.
	SUBS	R5, R5, #1	Decrement digit counter.
	BGT	SENDCHAR	Loop until all characters displayed.
	next instruction		
	AREA	DATA	
BINARY	DCD	&A123B456	Binary pattern.
HEX	SPACE	8	Space for ASCII-encoded digits.
TABLE	DCB	&30,&31,&32,&33	Table for conversion to ASCII code.
	DCB	&34,&35,&36,&37	
	DCB	&38,&39,&41,&42	
	DCB	&43,&44,&45,&46	

Figure D.24   Program for Example D.5.

PROBLEMS

D.1 [E] Assume the following register and memory contents in an ARM computer. Registers R0, R1, R2, R6, and R7 contain the values 1000, 2000, 1016, 20, and 30, respectively. The numbers 1, 2, 3, 4, 5, and 6 are stored in successive word locations starting at memory address 1000. What is the effect of executing each of the following two instruction blocks, starting each time with the given initial values?

(*a*) LDR   R8, [R0]
       LDR   R9, [R0, #4]
       ADD   R10, R8, R9

(*b*) STR   R6, [R1, #−4]!
       STR   R7, [R1, #−4]!
       LDR   R8, [R1], #4
       LDR   R9, [R1], #4
       SUB   R10, R8, R9

D.2 [M] Which of the following ARM instructions will cause the assembler to issue a syntax error message? Why?

(*a*) ADD   R2, R2, R2
(*b*) SUB   R0, R1, [R2, #4]
(*c*) MOV   R0, #2_1010101
(*d*) MOV   R0, #257
(*e*) ADD   R0, R1, R11, LSL #8

D.3 [M] Write an ARM program to reverse the order of bits in register R2. For example, if the starting pattern in R2 is 1110...0100, the final result in R2 should be 0010...0111. (Hint: Use shift and rotate operations.)

D.4 [M] Consider the program in Figure D.7. List the contents of registers R0, R1, and R2 after each of the first three executions of the BGT instruction. Present the results in a table that has the three registers as column headers. Use three rows to list the contents of the registers after each execution of the BGT instruction. The program data are as given in Figure D.13.

D.5 [M] Write an ARM program that compares the corresponding bytes of two lists of bytes and places the larger byte in a third list. The two lists start at byte locations X and Y, and the larger-byte list starts at LARGER. The length of the lists is stored in memory location N.

D.6 [M] Write an ARM program that generates the first n numbers of the Fibonacci series. In this series, the first two numbers are 0 and 1, and each subsequent number is generated by adding the preceding two numbers. For example, for $n = 8$, the series is 0, 1, 1, 2, 3, 5, 8, 13. Your program should store the numbers in successive memory word locations starting at MEMLOC. Assume that the value n is stored in location N.

D.7 [M] Write an ARM program to convert a word of text from lowercase to uppercase. The word consists of ASCII characters stored in successive byte locations in the memory, starting at location WORD and ending with a space character. (See Table 1.1 in Chapter 1 for the ASCII code.)

D.8   **[M]** The list of student marks shown in Figure 2.10 is changed to contain j test scores for each student. Assume that there are n students. Write an ARM program for computing the sums of the scores on each test and store these sums in the memory word locations at addresses SUM, SUM + 4, SUM + 8, ... The number of tests, j, is larger than the number of registers in the processor, so the type of program shown in Figure D.8 for the 3-test case cannot be used. Use two nested loops. The inner loop should accumulate the sum for a particular test, and the outer loop should run over the number of tests, j. Assume that j is stored in memory location J, placed just before location N in Figure 2.10.

D.9   **[E]** Write an ARM program that computes the expression SUM $= 580 + 68400 + 80000$.

D.10 **[E]** Write an ARM program that computes the expression ANSWER $= A \times B + C \times D$.

D.11 **[M]** Write an ARM program that finds the number of negative integers in a list of n 32-bit integers and stores the count in location NEGNUM. The value n is stored in memory location N, and the first integer in the list is stored in location NUMBERS. Include the necessary assembler directives and a sample list that contains six numbers, some of which are negative.

D.12 **[M]** Write an ARM program for the byte-sorting program described in Example 2.5 in Chapter 2.

D.13 **[M]** Write an ARM program to solve Problem 2.22 in Chapter 2.

D.14 **[D]** Write an ARM program to solve Problem 2.24 in Chapter 2.

D.15 **[M]** Write an ARM program to solve Problem 2.25 in Chapter 2.

D.16 **[M]** Write an ARM program to solve Problem 2.26 in Chapter 2.

D.17 **[M]** Write an ARM program to solve Problem 2.27 in Chapter 2.

D.18 **[M]** Write an ARM program to solve Problem 2.28 in Chapter 2.

D.19 **[M]** Write an ARM program to solve Problem 2.29 in Chapter 2.

D.20 **[M]** Write an ARM program to solve Problem 2.30 in Chapter 2.

D.21 **[M]** Write an ARM program to solve Problem 2.31 in Chapter 2.

D.22 **[D]** Write an ARM program to solve Problem 2.32 in Chapter 2.

D.23 **[D]** Write an ARM program to solve Problem 2.33 in Chapter 2.

D.24 **[M]** Write an ARM program that reads n characters from a keyboard and echoes them back to a display after pushing them onto a user stack as they are read. Use register R6 as the stack pointer. The count value n is contained in memory word location N.

D.25 **[M]** Assume that the average time taken to fetch and execute an instruction in the program in Figure D.17 is 5 nanoseconds. If keyboard characters are entered at the rate of 10 per second, approximately how many times is the   BEQ   READ   instruction executed per character entered? Assume that the time taken to display each character is much less than the time between the entry of successive characters at the keyboard.

D.26   **[M]** Rewrite the program in Figure D.17 in the form of a main program that calls a subroutine named GETCHAR to read a single character and calls another subroutine named PUTCHAR to display a single character. The address KBD_STATUS is passed to GETCHAR in register R1, and the main program expects to get the character passed back in register R3. The address DISP_STATUS and the character to be displayed are passed to PUTCHAR in registers R2 and R3, respectively. Any other registers used by either subroutine must be saved and restored by the subroutine using a stack whose pointer is register R13. Storing the characters in memory and checking for the end-of-line character CR is to be done in the main program.

D.27   **[M]** Repeat Problem D.26 using the stack to pass parameters.

D.28   **[M]** Write an ARM program to accept three decimal digits from a keyboard. Each digit is represented in the ASCII code (see Table 1.1 in Chapter 1). Assume that these three digits represent a decimal integer in the range 0 to 999. Convert the integer into a binary number representation. The high-order digit is received first. To aid in this conversion, two tables of words are stored in the memory. Each table has 10 entries. The first table, starting at word location TENS, contains the binary representations for the decimal values 0, 10, 20, . . . , 90. The second table starts at word location HUNDREDS and contains the decimal values 0, 100, 200, . . . , 900 in binary representation.

D.29   **[M]** The decimal-to-binary conversion program of Problem D.28 is to be implemented using two nested subroutines. The main program that calls the first subroutine passes two parameters by pushing them onto the stack whose pointer register is R13. The first parameter is the address of a 3-byte memory buffer area for storing the input decimal-digit characters. The second parameter is the address of the location where the converted binary value is to be stored. The first subroutine reads the three characters from the keyboard, then calls the second subroutine to perform the conversion. The necessary parameters are passed to this subroutine via the processor registers. Both subroutines must save the contents of any registers that they use on the stack.

(*a*) Write the two subroutines for the ARM processor.
(*b*) Give the contents of the stack immediately after the execution of the instruction that calls the second subroutine.

D.30   **[M]** Write an ARM program that displays the contents of 10 bytes of the main memory in hexadecimal format on a line of a video display. The byte string starts at location LOC in the memory. Each byte has to be displayed as two hex characters. The displayed contents of successive bytes should be separated by a space.

D.31   **[M]** Assume that a memory location BINARY contains a 16-bit pattern. It is desired to display these bits as a string of 0s and 1s on a display device that has the interface depicted in Figure 3.3. Write an ARM program that accomplishes this task.

D.32   **[M]** Using the seven-segment display in Figure 3.17 and the timer circuit in Figure 3.14, write an ARM program that flashes decimal digits in the repeating sequence 0, 1, 2, . . . , 9, 0, ... Each digit is to be displayed for one second. Assume that the counter in the timer circuit is driven by a 100-MHz clock.

D.33 **[D]** Using two 7-segment displays of the type shown in Figure 3.17, and the timer circuit in Figure 3.14, write an ARM program that flashes numbers in the repeating sequence $0, 1, 2, \ldots, 98, 99, 0, \ldots$. Each number is to be displayed for one second. Assume that the counter in the timer circuit is driven by a 100-MHz clock.

D.34 **[D]** Write an ARM program that computes real clock time and displays the time in hours (0 to 23) and minutes (0 to 59). The display consists of four 7-segment display devices of the type shown in Figure 3.17. A timer circuit that has the interface given in Figure 3.14 is available. Its counter is driven by a 100-MHz clock.

D.35 **[M]** Write an ARM program for the problem described in Example 3.5 in Chapter 3.

D.36 **[M]** Write an ARM program for the problem described in Example 3.6 in Chapter 3.

D.37 **[M]** Write an ARM program to solve Problem 3.19 in Chapter 3.

D.38 **[M]** Write an ARM program to solve Problem 3.21 in Chapter 3.

D.39 **[M]** Write an ARM program to solve Problem 3.23 in Chapter 3.

D.40 **[M]** Write an ARM program to solve Problem 3.25 in Chapter 3.

REFERENCES

1. ARM Limited, *ARM7TDMI Technical Reference Manual—revision r4p1*, Document number ARM DDI 0210C, November 2004. Available at http://www.arm.com.

2. Steve Furber, *ARM System-on-chip Architecture*, 2nd Ed., Addison Wesley, Harlow, England, 2000.

3. William Hohl, *ARM Assembly Language: Fundamentals and Techniques*, CRC Press, 2009.

4. ARM Limited, *The ARM Instruction Set—V1.0*, ARM University Program.

appendix

E

THE INTEL IA-32 ARCHITECTURE

APPENDIX OBJECTIVES

In this appendix you will learn about the features of the Intel
IA-32 architecture:

- Memory organization and register structure
- Addressing modes and types of instructions
- Input/output capability
- Scalar floating-point operations
- Multimedia operations
- Vector floating-point operations

The Intel Corporation uses the generic name Intel Architecture (IA) for the instruction sets of processors in its product line. We will describe the IA-32 instruction set for processors that operate with 32-bit memory addresses and 32-bit data operands. The IA-32 instruction set is very large. In addition to providing typical integer and floating-point instructions, it includes specialized instructions for multimedia applications and for vector data processing. We will restrict our attention to the basic instructions and addressing modes. Reference [1] provides a comprehensive overview of the IA-32 architecture, and the Intel website (http://www.intel.com) provides additional technical documentation with full details.

E.1   MEMORY ORGANIZATION

In the IA-32 architecture, memory is byte-addressable using 32-bit addresses, and instructions typically operate on data operands of 8 or 32 bits. These operand sizes are called *byte* and *doubleword* in Intel terminology. A 16-bit operand was called a *word* in earlier 16-bit Intel processors. There is also a larger 64-bit operand size called a *quadword* for double-precision floating-point numbers and packed integer data. Little-endian addressing is used, as described in Section 2.1.2. Multiple-byte data operands may start at any byte address location. They need not be aligned with any particular address boundaries in the memory.

E.2   REGISTER STRUCTURE

The processor registers are shown in Figure E.1. There are eight 32-bit general-purpose registers, which can hold either integer data operands or addressing information. Rather than being numbered consecutively, they are identified by unique names that are described later in this section. Eight additional registers are available for floating-point instructions. They are discussed in Section E.9. These registers are also used by the multimedia instructions described in Section E.10. There is another set of registers that is not shown in Figure E.1; these registers are used by vector-processing instructions discussed in Section E.11.

The IA-32 architecture has different models for accessing the memory. The *segmented* memory model associates different areas of the memory, called *segments*, with different usages. The *code segment* holds the instructions of a program. The *stack segment* contains the processor stack, and four *data segments* are provided for holding data operands. The six segment registers shown in Figure E.1 contain selector values that identify where these segments begin in the memory address space. The detailed function of these registers is not discussed in this appendix. Instead, the *flat* memory model of the IA-32 architecture is assumed, where a 32-bit address can access a memory location anywhere in the code, processor stack, or data areas. In this case, the segment registers are initialized with selector values that point to address 0 in the memory.

The two registers shown at the bottom of Figure E.1 are the Instruction Pointer, which serves as the program counter and contains the address of the next instruction to be executed,

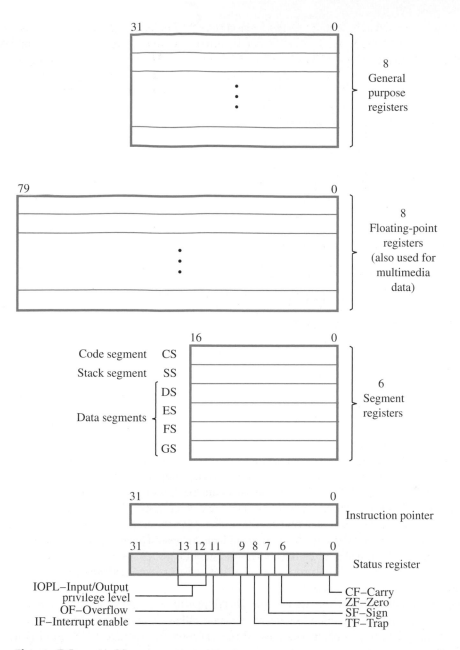

Figure E.1 IA-32 register structure.

and the status register, which holds the condition code flags (CF, ZF, SF, OF). These flags contain information about the results of arithmetic operations. The program execution mode bits (IOPL, IF, TF) are associated with input/output operations and interrupts.

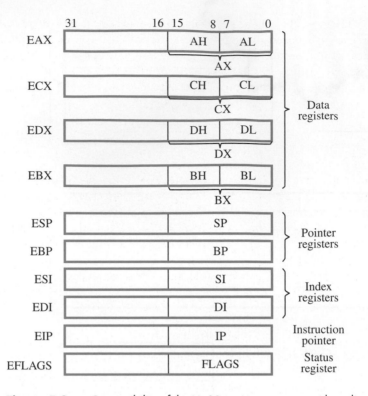

Figure E.2 Compatibility of the IA-32 register structure with earlier Intel processor register structures.

The IA-32 general-purpose registers allow for compatibility with the registers of earlier 8-bit and 16-bit Intel processors. In those processors, there are some restrictions regarding the use of certain registers. Figure E.2 shows the association between the IA-32 registers and the registers in earlier processors. The eight general-purpose registers are grouped into three different types: data registers for holding operands, pointer registers for holding addresses, and index registers for holding address indices. The pointer and index registers are used to determine the effective address of a memory operand.

In Intel's original 8-bit processors, the data registers were called A, B, C, and D. In later 16-bit processors, these registers were labeled AX, BX, CX, and DX. The high- and low-order bytes in each register are identified by suffixes H and L. For example, the two bytes in register AX are referred to as AH and AL. In IA-32 processors, the prefix E is used to identify the corresponding *extended* 32-bit registers: EAX, EBX, ECX, and EDX. The E-prefix labeling is also used for the other 32-bit registers shown in Figure E.2. They are the extended versions of the corresponding 16-bit registers used in earlier processors.

This register labeling is used in Intel technical documents [1] and in other descriptions of Intel processors. The reason that the historical labeling has been retained is that Intel has maintained upward compatibility over its processor line. That is, programs in machine language representation developed for the earlier 16-bit processors will run correctly on current IA-32 processors without change if the processor state is set to do so. We will use the E-prefix register labeling in giving examples of assembly language programs because these mnemonics are used in current versions of the assembly language for IA-32 processors. The AL, BL, etc. labeling will also be used for byte operands when they are held in the low-order eight bits of the corresponding 32-bit register.

E.3 ADDRESSING MODES

The IA-32 architecture has a large and flexible set of addressing modes. They are designed to access individual data items, or data items that are members of an ordered list that begins at a specified memory address. The basic addressing modes are the same as those available in most processors, as described in Section 2.4. They are: Immediate, Absolute, Register, and Register indirect. Intel uses the term Direct for the Absolute mode, so we will do the same here. There are also several addressing modes that provide more flexibility in accessing data operands in the memory. The most flexible mode described in Section 2.4 is the Index mode that has the general notation $X(Ri,Rj)$. The effective address of the operand, EA, is calculated as

$$EA = [Ri] + [Rj] + X$$

where Ri and Rj are general-purpose registers and X is a constant. Registers Ri and Rj are called *base* and *index* registers, respectively, and the constant X is called a *displacement*. The IA-32 addressing modes include this mode and simpler variations of it.

The full set of IA-32 addressing modes is defined as follows:

Immediate mode—The operand is contained in the instruction. It is a signed 8-bit or 32-bit number, with the length being specified by a bit in the OP code of the instruction. This bit is 0 for the short version and 1 for the long version.

Direct mode—The memory address of the operand is given by a 32-bit value in the instruction.

Register mode—The operand is contained in one of the eight general-purpose registers specified in the instruction.

Register indirect mode—The memory address of the operand is contained in one of the eight general-purpose registers specified in the instruction.

Base with displacement mode—An 8-bit or 32-bit signed displacement and one of the eight general-purpose registers to be used as a base register are specified in the instruction. The effective address of the operand is the sum of the contents of the base register and the displacement.

Index with displacement mode—A 32-bit signed displacement, one of the eight general-purpose registers to be used as an index register, and a scale factor of 1, 2, 4, or 8, are specified in the instruction. To obtain the effective address of the operand, the contents of the index register are multiplied by the scale factor and then added to the displacement.

Base with index mode—Two of the eight general-purpose registers and a scale factor of 1, 2, 4, or 8, are specified in the instruction. The registers are used as base and index registers. The effective address of the operand is determined by first multiplying the contents of the index register by the scale factor and then adding the result to the contents of the base register.

Base with index and displacement mode—An 8-bit or 32-bit signed displacement, two of the eight general-purpose registers, and a scale factor of 1, 2, 4, or 8, are specified in the instruction. The registers are used as base and index registers. The effective address of the operand is determined by first multiplying the contents of the index register by the scale factor and then adding the result to the contents of the base register and the displacement.

The IA-32 addressing modes and the way that they are expressed in assembly language are given in Table E.1. The calculation of the effective address of the operand is also shown in the table. As indicated in the footnotes, register ESP cannot be used as an index register. This is because it is used as the processor stack pointer.

Table E.1   IA-32 addressing modes.

Name	Assembler syntax	Addressing function
Immediate	Value	Operand = Value
Direct	Location	EA = Location
Register	Reg	EA = Reg that is, Operand = [Reg]
Register indirect	[Reg]	EA = [Reg]
Base with displacement	[Reg + Disp]	EA = [Reg] + Disp
Index with displacement	[Reg * S + Disp]	EA = [Reg] × S + Disp
Base with index	[Reg1 + Reg2 * S]	EA = [Reg1] + [Reg2] × S
Base with index and displacement	[Reg1 + Reg2 * S + Disp]	EA = [Reg1] + [Reg2] × S + Disp

Value = an 8- or 32-bit signed number
Location = a 32-bit address
Reg, Reg1, Reg2 = one of the general purpose registers EAX, EBX, ECX, EDX, ESP, EBP, ESI, EDI, with the exception that ESP cannot be used as an index register.
Disp = an 8- or 32-bit signed number, except that in the Index with displacement mode it can only be 32 bits.
S = a scale factor of 1, 2, 4, or 8

Instructions have zero, one, or two operands. In two-operand instructions, the source (src) and destination (dst) operands are specified in assembly language in the order

OP   dst, src

This ordering is the same as in Chapter 2.

It is convenient to use the Move instruction to illustrate the IA-32 addressing modes and their notation in assembly language. The instruction

MOV   EAX, 25

uses the Immediate addressing mode for the source operand to move the decimal value 25 into the destination register EAX, which is specified with the Register addressing mode.

When a numeric constant appears alone as an operand, it is assumed to represent an immediate value. Numeric constants may be expressed in decimal format using the digits 0 through 9. Depending on the assembler used, hexadecimal numbers are specified using the prefix 0x or the suffix H. In the latter case, numbers that begin with digits A to F also require a prefix 0 so that the assembler can distinguish a hexadecimal number from a label. Some assemblers also allow binary numbers to be specified using the suffix B.

Symbolic names may also be used as operands. If the name LOCATION has been defined as an address label, the instruction

MOV   EAX, LOCATION

implicitly uses the Direct addressing mode to move the doubleword at memory address LOCATION into register EAX. The Direct addressing mode can also be made explicit. The instruction

MOV   EAX, DWORD PTR LOCATION

uses the keywords DWORD PTR to indicate that the label LOCATION should be interpreted as the address of a 32-bit operand.

When it is necessary to treat an address label as an immediate operand, the keyword OFFSET is used. For example, the instruction

MOV   EBX, OFFSET LOCATION

moves the value of the address label LOCATION into the EBX register using the Immediate addressing mode.

Once an address is loaded into a register, the Register indirect mode can be used to access the operand in memory. The instruction

MOV   EAX, [EBX]

moves the contents of the memory location whose address is contained in register EBX into register EAX.

The above examples illustrate the basic addressing modes: Immediate, Direct, Register, and Register indirect. The remaining four addressing modes provide more flexibility in accessing data operands in the memory.

The Base with displacement mode is illustrated in Figure E.3*a*. Register EBP is used as the base register. A doubleword operand at address 1060, which is 60 byte locations away from the base address of 1000, can be moved into register EAX by the instruction

$$\text{MOV} \quad \text{EAX, [EBP + 60]}$$

Instructions can operate on byte operands as well as doubleword operands. For example, still assuming that the base register EBP contains the address 1000, the byte operand at address 1010 can be loaded into the low-order byte position in the EAX register by the instruction

$$\text{MOV} \quad \text{AL, [EBP + 10]}$$

The assembler selects the version of the Move OP code for byte data because the destination, AL, is the low-order byte position of the EAX register.

The addressing mode that provides the most flexibility is the Base with index and displacement mode. An example is shown in Figure E.3*b*, using EBP and ESI as the base and index registers. This example shows how the mode is used to access a particular doubleword operand in a list of doubleword operands. The list begins at a displacement of 200 away from the base address 1000. Using a scale factor of 4 on the index register contents, successive doubleword operands at addresses 1200, 1204, 1208, ... can be accessed by using the sequence of indices 0, 1, 2, ... in the index register ESI. In the example shown in the figure, the doubleword at address 1360 (that is, $1000 + 200 + 4 \times 40$) is accessed when the index register contains 40. This operand can be loaded into register EAX by the instruction

$$\text{MOV} \quad \text{EAX, [EBP + ESI * 4 + 200]}$$

The use of a scale factor of 4 in this addressing mode makes it easy to access successive doubleword operands of the list in a program loop by simply incrementing the index register by 1 on each pass through the loop. Having discussed these two modes in some detail, the closely related Index with displacement mode and Base with index mode should be easy to understand.

Before leaving this discussion of addressing modes, it is useful to comment on two of the modes described in Table E.1. It may appear that the Base with displacement mode is redundant because the same effect can be obtained by using the Index with displacement mode with a scale factor of 1. But the former mode is useful because it is encoded with one less byte. In addition, the displacement size in the Index with displacement mode can only be 32 bits, whereas it can also be 8 bits for the Base with displacement mode.

E.4 INSTRUCTIONS

The IA-32 instruction set is extensive. It is encoded in a variable-length instruction format that does not have a fully regular layout. Most instructions have either one or two operands. In the two-operand case, only one of the operands can be in the memory. The other must either be in a processor register or be an immediate value in the instruction. Instructions are provided for moving data between the memory and the processor registers,

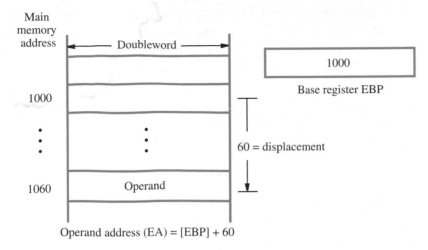

Operand address (EA) = [EBP] + 60

(a) Base with displacement mode, expressed as [EBP + 60]

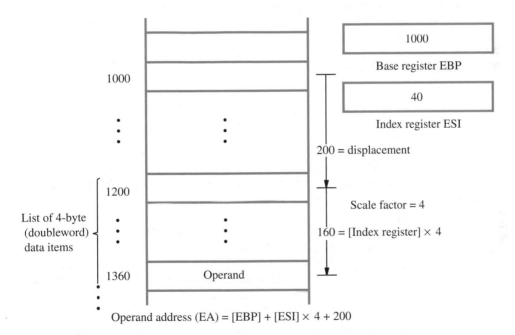

Operand address (EA) = [EBP] + [ESI] × 4 + 200

(b) Base with displacement and index mode, expressed as [EBP + ESI * 4 + 200]

Figure E.3   Examples of addressing modes in the IA-32 architecture.

performing arithmetic operations, and performing logical and shift/rotate operations. Jump instructions and subroutine call/return instructions are included. Push and pop operations for manipulating the processor stack are also directly supported in the instruction set.

OP code	Addressing mode	Displacement	Immediate
1 or 2 bytes	1 or 2 bytes	1 or 4 bytes	1 or 4 bytes

Figure E.4   IA-32 instruction format.

E.4.1 MACHINE INSTRUCTION FORMAT

The general format for machine instructions is shown in Figure E.4. The instructions are variable in length, ranging from 1 to 12 bytes and consisting of up to four fields. The OP-code field consists of one or two bytes, with most instructions requiring only one byte. The addressing mode information is contained in one or two bytes immediately following the OP code.

For instructions that involve the use of only one register in generating the effective address of an operand in memory, only one byte is needed in the addressing mode field. Two bytes are needed for encoding the last two addressing modes in Table E.1. Those modes use two registers to generate the effective address of a memory operand.

If a displacement value is needed in computing an effective address for a memory operand, it is encoded into either one or four bytes in a field that immediately follows the addressing mode field. If one of the operands is an immediate value, then it is placed in the last field of an instruction and it occupies either one or four bytes.

Some simple instructions, such as those that increment or decrement a register, occupy only one byte. For example, the instruction

INC   EDI

increments the contents of register EDI. In this case, the register operand is specified by a 3-bit code in the OP-code byte. However, for most instructions and addressing modes, the registers used are specified in the addressing mode field.

E.4.2 ASSEMBLY-LANGUAGE NOTATION

Some aspects of assembly-language notation have been introduced with the addressing modes in Section E.3. This section provides a summary of the notation used, with additional details on addresses and immediate values, operand sizes, and the use of upper-case characters in assembly language.

The keywords DWORD PTR preceding a name of an operand indicate that the name is to be interpreted as an address for a 32-bit operand. Similarly, the keywords BYTE PTR preceding a name specify that the name should be interpreted as the address of an 8-bit operand. On the other hand, the keyword OFFSET preceding a name indicates that the name is to be interpreted as an immediate value.

Each assembly-language instruction must contain sufficient information for the assembler to determine the operand size. In the case of the Register addressing mode, the register name provides the necessary information. For example, register EAX given as an operand in an instruction implies a size of 32 bits, whereas register AL implies an operand size of 8 bits. The assembler generates an OP code that corresponds to the implied operand size.

In cases that do not involve the Register addressing mode, the assembler requires additional information. For example, a one-operand instruction may specify a memory operand using an indirect or displacement addressing mode. To specify the operand size, it is necessary to include the keywords DWORD PTR or BYTE PTR.

Many IA-32 assemblers are case-insensitive for instruction mnemonics and register names. The Intel technical documentation uses upper-case characters consistently [1]. To conform to this presentation style, we will use upper-case characters for all instruction mnemonics and register names.

E.4.3 MOVE INSTRUCTION

The MOV instruction transfers data between memory or I/O interfaces and the processor registers. The direction of the transfer is from source to destination. The condition code flags in the status register are not affected by the execution of a MOV instruction.

The examples in Section E.3 show how MOV instructions transfer data from memory to registers. Register contents may also be transferred to memory or to another register. The instruction

$$\text{MOV} \quad \text{LOCATION, ECX}$$

moves the doubleword in register ECX into the memory location at address LOCATION. The instruction

$$\text{MOV} \quad \text{EBP, EDI}$$

moves the doubleword in register EDI to register EBP. The contents in register EDI are not changed.

The MOV instruction cannot be used with two memory operands, but it can be used to move an immediate value into a memory location, as in

$$\text{MOV} \quad \text{DWORD PTR [EAX + 16], 100}$$

Note that the assembler requires the keywords DWORD PTR (or BYTE PTR) to specify the operand size in this instruction.

E.4.4 LOAD-EFFECTIVE-ADDRESS INSTRUCTION

Section E.3 describes how the MOV instruction can be used to load an address into a register by using the keyword OFFSET. Alternatively, the LEA (Load-effective-address) instruction may be used. For example, if the name LOCATION is defined as an address label, the instruction

$$\text{LEA} \quad \text{EAX, LOCATION}$$

has exactly the same effect as the instruction

MOV   EAX, OFFSET LOCATION

The LEA instruction can be used to load an effective address that is computed at execution time. For example, suppose it is desired to use register EBX as a pointer to a data operand in memory. Assume that the desired operand is an element of an array, located at an offset of 12 bytes from the start of the array. If register EBP contains the starting address of the array, the instruction

LEA   EBX, [EBP + 12]

computes the desired effective address and places it in register EBX. The operand can then be accessed by a Move or other instruction using the Register indirect mode with EBX.

E.4.5 ARITHMETIC INSTRUCTIONS

This category of instructions includes arithmetic operations as well as comparison and negation operations. The operands can be in memory, in registers, or specified as immediate values (for two-operand instructions). The operand size may be doubleword or byte.

Addition, Subtraction, Comparison, and Negation

Two-operand arithmetic instructions are:

- ADD   (Add)
- ADC   (Add with carry; for multiple-precision arithmetic)
- SUB   (Subtract)
- SBB   (Subtract with borrow; for multiple-precision arithmetic)
- CMP   (Compare; value of destination operand remains unchanged)

These instructions affect all of the condition code flags based on the result of the operation that is performed. The instruction

ADD   EAX, EBX

performs the 32-bit operation

$$EAX \leftarrow [EAX] + [EBX]$$

The instruction

CMP   [EBX + 10], AL

performs the 8-bit operation

$$[[EBX] + 10] - [AL]$$

Using register AL implies an operand size of one byte. The condition code flags are set based on whether the subtraction caused overflow or a carry, and whether the result is negative or zero. The result of the subtraction is discarded.

One-operand arithmetic instructions are:

- INC (Increment)
- DEC (Decrement)
- NEG (Negate)

The NEG instruction affects all condition code flags, but the INC and DEC instructions do not affect the CF flag. These instructions must include keywords to specify the operand size unless the Register mode is used for the operand. The instruction

INC   DWORD PTR [EDX]

increments the doubleword at the memory location whose address is contained in register EDX.

Multiplication

The signed integer multiplication instruction, IMUL, performs 32-bit multiplication. Depending on the form of the instruction that is used, the destination may be implicit and the 64-bit product may be truncated to 32 bits.

One form of this instruction is

IMUL   src

which implicitly uses the EAX register as the multiplicand. The multiplier specified by src can be in a register or in the memory. The full 64-bit product is placed in registers EDX (high-order half) and EAX (low-order half).

A second form of this instruction is

IMUL   REG, src

The destination operand, REG, must be one of the eight general-purpose registers. The source operand can be in a register or in the memory. The product is truncated to 32 bits before it is placed in the destination register REG.

For both forms, the CF and OF flags are set if there are any 1s (including sign bits) in the high-order half of the 64-bit product. Otherwise, the CF and OF flags are cleared. The other flags are undefined.

Division

The integer divide instruction, IDIV, operates on a 64-bit dividend and a 32-bit divisor to generate a 32-bit quotient and a 32-bit remainder. The format of the instruction is

IDIV   src

The source operand is the divisor. The 64-bit dividend is formed by the contents of register EDX (high-order half) and register EAX (low-order half). After performing the division, the quotient is placed in EAX and the remainder is placed in EDX. All of the condition code flags are undefined. Division by zero causes an exception.

If the dividend value is represented by 32 bits, it must first be placed in EAX, and then sign-extended to the required 64-bit operand size in registers EAX and EDX. This is done by the instruction CDQ (convert doubleword to quadword), which has no operands because the source and destination are implicitly registers EAX and EDX, respectively.

E.4.6 JUMP AND LOOP INSTRUCTIONS

In IA-32 terminology, all branch instructions are called Jumps. Conditional and unconditional Jump instructions are provided. Such instructions can be used to implement loops. Often, a counter variable is decremented in each pass through a loop, and a conditional Jump instruction tests whether the count is still larger than zero to perform more passes through the loop. Because this approach is common, a special Loop instruction is also provided to combine the decrement and conditional Jump operations.

Conditional Jump Instructions and Condition Code Flags

The conditional Jump instructions test the four condition code flags in the status register. The instruction

$$\text{JG} \quad \text{LABEL}$$

is an example of a conditional Jump instruction. The condition is *greater-than* as indicated by the G suffix in the OP code. Table E.2 summarizes the conditional Jump instructions and the corresponding combinations of the condition code flags that are tested. The Jump instructions that test the sign flag (SF) are used when the operands of a preceding arithmetic or comparison instruction are signed numbers. For example, the JG instruction tests for the greater-than condition when signed numbers are involved, and it considers the SF flag. When unsigned numbers are involved, the JA (jump-above) instruction tests for the greater-than condition without considering the SF flag.

Table E.2   IA-32 conditional jump instructions.

Mnemonic	Condition name	Condition test
JS	Sign (negative)	$SF = 1$
JNS	No sign (positive or zero)	$SF = 0$
JE/JZ	Equal/Zero	$ZF = 1$
JNE/JNZ	Not equal/Not zero	$ZF = 0$
JO	Overflow	$OF = 1$
JNO	No overflow	$OF = 0$
JC/JB	Carry/Unsigned below	$CF = 1$
JNC/JAE	No carry/Unsigned above or equal	$CF = 0$
JA	Unsigned above	$CF \vee ZF = 0$
JBE	Unsigned below or equal	$CF \vee ZF = 1$
JGE	Signed greater than or equal	$SF \oplus OF = 0$
JL	Signed less than	$SF \oplus OF = 1$
JG	Signed greater than	$ZF \vee (SF \oplus OF) = 0$
JLE	Signed less than or equal	$ZF \vee (SF \oplus OF) = 1$

When the assembler generates machine code, a conditional Jump instruction is encoded with an offset relative to the address of the instruction that immediately follows the Jump instruction. This address reflects the updated contents of the Instruction Pointer after the Jump instruction is fetched. If the offset is in the range -128 through $+127$, then a single byte is sufficient, and the total number of bytes used to encode a conditional Jump instruction is two, including the OP-code byte. When the distance to the jump target exceeds this range, a four-byte offset is used.

Unconditional Jump Instruction

An unconditional Jump instruction, JMP, causes a branch to the instruction at the target address. In addition to using short (one-byte) or long (four-byte) relative signed offsets to determine the target address, as is done in conditional Jump instructions, the JMP instruction also allows the use of other addressing modes. This flexibility in generating the target address can be very useful. Consider the Case statement that is found in many high-level languages. It is used to perform one of a number of alternative computations at some point in a program. Each of these alternatives is referred to as a case. Suppose that for each case, a routine is defined to perform the corresponding computation. Suppose also that the 4-byte starting addresses of the routines are stored in a table in the memory, beginning at a location labeled JUMPTABLE. The cases are numbered with indices $0, 1, 2, \ldots$. At execution time, the index of the selected case is loaded into index register ESI. A jump to the routine for the selected case is performed by executing the instruction

$$\text{JMP} \quad [\text{JUMPTABLE} + \text{ESI} * 4]$$

which uses the Index with displacement addressing mode.

Loop Instruction

Loops often rely on a counter variable that is decremented in each pass through the loop. Maintaining the counter in a register reduces execution time. When an instruction that decrements the register for the counter affects the condition code flags, an explicit comparison is not required before a conditional branch instruction. A loop can be implemented as

```
            MOV   ECX, NUM_PASSES
START:
              ⋮
            DEC   ECX
            JG    START
```

Loops of this form can be expressed in a more compact manner by using the LOOP instruction. It combines the functionality of the DEC and JG instructions, and it also implicitly uses register ECX for the counter variable. Using this instruction, the loop can be implemented as

```
            MOV   ECX, NUM_PASSES
START:
              ⋮
            LOOP  START
```

Condition code flags are not affected by the LOOP instruction.

Example E.1   Using the instructions introduced thus far, we can now give a program for adding numbers using a loop, similar to the program in Figure 2.26. Assume that memory location N contains the number of 32-bit integers in a list that starts at memory location NUM1. The assembly-language program shown in Figure E.5a can be used to add the numbers and place their sum in memory location SUM.

Register EBX is loaded with the address value NUM1. It is used as the base register in the Base with index addressing mode in the instruction at the location STARTADD, which is the first instruction of the loop. Register EDI is used as the index register. It is cleared by loading it with zero before the loop is entered. On the first pass through the loop, the first number at address NUM1 is added into the EAX register, which was initially cleared to zero. The index register is then incremented by 1. On the second pass, the scale factor of 4 in the ADD instruction causes the second 32-bit number, at address NUM1 + 4, to be added into EAX. The numbers at addresses NUM1 + 8, NUM1 + 12, . . . are added in subsequent passes. Register ECX is used as a counter register. It is initially loaded with the contents of memory location N in the second instruction of the program and is decremented by 1 during each pass through the loop. The conditional branch instruction JG causes a

	LEA	EBX, NUM1	Use EBX as base register.
	MOV	ECX, N	Use ECX as counter register.
	MOV	EAX, 0	Use EAX as accumulator register.
	MOV	EDI, 0	Use EDI as index register.
STARTADD:	ADD	EAX, [EBX + EDI * 4]	Add next number into EAX.
	INC	EDI	Increment index register.
	DEC	ECX	Decrement counter register.
	JG	STARTADD	Branch back if [ECX] > 0.
	MOV	SUM, EAX	Store sum in memory.

(a) Straightforward approach

	LEA	EBX, NUM1	Load base register EBX and
	SUB	EBX, 4	adjust to hold NUM1 − 4.
	MOV	ECX, N	Initialize counter/index register ECX.
	MOV	EAX, 0	Use EAX as accumulator register.
STARTADD:	ADD	EAX, [EBX + ECX * 4]	Add next number into EAX.
	LOOP	STARTADD	Decrement ECX and branch back if [ECX] > 0.
	MOV	SUM, EAX	Store sum in memory.

(b) More compact program

Figure E.5   Implementation of the program in Figure 2.26.

branch back to STARTADD while [ECX] > 0. When the contents of ECX reach zero, all the numbers have been added. The branch is not taken, and the MOV instruction writes the sum in register EAX into memory location SUM.

A more compact program for the same task can be developed by making two observations on the program in Figure E.5a. The first observation is that the two-instruction sequence

DEC   ECX
JG   STARTADD

can be replaced with the single instruction

LOOP   STARTADD

It decrements the ECX register and then branches to the target address STARTADD if the contents of ECX have not reached zero. The second observation is that we have used two registers, EDI and ECX, as counters. If we scan the list of numbers to be added in the opposite direction, starting with the last number in the list, only one counter register is needed. We will use register ECX because it is the register referenced implicitly by the LOOP instruction. Assuming $[N] = n$, the first program accesses the numbers using the address sequence NUM1, NUM1 + 4, NUM1 + 8, . . . , NUM1 + 4(n − 1), as EDI contains the sequence of values 0, 1, 2, . . . , (n − 1). The new program, shown in Figure E.5b, uses the address sequence (NUM1 − 4) + 4n, (NUM1 − 4) + 4(n − 1), . . . , (NUM1 − 4) + 4(1), as ECX contains the sequence n, n −1, . . . , 1. Hence, the value in the base register EBX needs to be changed from NUM1 to NUM1 − 4 in the new program in order to account for the difference between the EDI sequence and the ECX sequence. On the last pass through the loop in the new program, before the LOOP instruction is executed, [ECX] = 1 and the last number to be added is accessed at memory location NUM1.

The program in Figure 2.11 computes the sum of all scores for three tests taken by a group of students. Load instructions are used in the program to fetch the operands from memory. Figure E.6 shows an IA-32 version of that program. The availability of the Base with displacement addressing mode for the ADD instructions makes it unnecessary to use separate instructions to access memory operands.

Example E.2

E.4.7 LOGIC INSTRUCTIONS

The IA-32 architecture has instructions that perform the logic operations AND, OR, and XOR. The operation is performed bitwise on two operands, and the result is placed in the destination location. For example, suppose register EAX contains the hexadecimal pattern 0000FFFF and register EBX contains the pattern 02FA62CA. The instruction

AND   EBX, EAX

clears the left half of EBX to all zeroes, and leaves the right half unchanged. The result in EBX will be 000062CA.

	MOV	EAX, OFFSET LIST	Get the address LIST.
	MOV	EBX, 0	
	MOV	ECX, 0	
	MOV	EDX, 0	
	MOV	EDI, N	Load the value n.
LOOP:	ADD	EBX, [EAX + 4]	Add current student mark for Test 1.
	ADD	ECX, [EAX + 8]	Add current student mark for Test 2.
	ADD	EDX, [EAX + 12]	Add current student mark for Test 3.
	ADD	EAX, 16	Increment the pointer.
	DEC	EDI	Decrement the counter.
	JG	LOOP	Loop back if not finished.
	MOV	SUM1, EBX	Store the total for Test 1.
	MOV	SUM2, ECX	Store the total for Test 2.
	MOV	SUM3, EDX	Store the total for Test 3.

Figure E.6   Implementation of the program in Figure 2.11.

There is also a NOT instruction which generates the logical complement of all bits of the operand, that is, it changes all 1s to 0s and all 0s to 1s.

E.4.8 SHIFT AND ROTATE INSTRUCTIONS

An operand can be shifted right or left, using either logical or arithmetic shifts, by a number of bit positions determined by a specified count. The format of the shift instructions is

OP   dst, count

where the destination operand to be shifted is specified using any addressing mode and the count is given either as an 8-bit immediate value or is contained in the 8-bit register CL. There are four shift instructions:

• SHL   (Shift left logical)
• SHR   (Shift right logical)
• SAL   (Shift left arithmetic; operation is identical to SHL)
• SAR   (Shift right arithmetic)

Shift operations are discussed in Section 2.8.2 and illustrated in Figure 2.23.

In addition to the shift instructions, there are also four rotate instructions:

• ROL   (Rotate left without the carry flag CF)
• ROR   (Rotate right without the carry flag CF)
• RCL   (Rotate left including the carry flag CF)
• RCR   (Rotate right including the carry flag CF)

All four operations are illustrated in Figure 2.25. The rotate instructions require the count argument to be either an 8-bit immediate value or the 8-bit contents of register CL.

Consider the BCD digit-packing program shown in Figure 2.24, which uses shift and logic instructions. The IA-32 code for this routine is shown in Figure E.7. Two ASCII bytes are loaded into registers AL and BL. The SHL instruction shifts the byte in AL four bit positions to the left, filling the low-order four bits with zeros. The AND instruction sets the high-order four bits of the second byte to zero. Finally, the 4-bit patterns that are the desired BCD codes are combined in AL with the OR instruction and then stored in memory byte location PACKED.

Example E.3

LEA	EBP, LOC	EBP points to first byte.
MOV	AL, [EBP]	Load first byte into AL.
SHL	AL, 4	Shift left by 4 bit positions.
MOV	BL, [EBP+1]	Load second byte into BL.
AND	BL, 0FH	Clear high-order 4 bits to zero.
OR	AL, BL	Concatenate the BCD digits.
MOV	PACKED, AL	Store the result.

Figure E.7   A routine that packs two BCD digits into a byte, corresponding to Figure 2.24.

E.4.9 SUBROUTINE LINKAGE INSTRUCTIONS

The use of the processor stack for subroutine linkage is described in Section 2.7. In the IA-32 architecture, register ESP is used as the stack pointer. It points to the current top element (TOS) in the processor stack. The stack grows toward lower numbered addresses. The width of the stack is 32 bits, that is, all stack entries are doublewords.

There are two instructions for pushing and popping individual elements onto and off the stack. The instruction

PUSH   src

decrements ESP by 4, and then stores the doubleword at location src into the memory location pointed to by ESP. The instruction

POP   dst

reverses this process by retrieving the TOS doubleword from the location pointed to by ESP, storing it at location dst, and then incrementing ESP by 4. These instructions implicitly use ESP as the stack pointer. The source and destination operands are specified using the IA-32 addressing modes.

There are also two more instructions that push or pop the contents of multiple registers. The instruction

PUSHAD

pushes the contents of all eight general-purpose registers EAX through EDI onto the stack, and the instruction

POPAD

pops them off in the reverse order. When POPAD reaches the old stored value of ESP, it discards those four bytes without loading them into ESP and continues to pop the remaining values into their respective registers. These two instructions are used to efficiently save and restore the contents of all registers as part of implementing subroutines.

The list-addition program in Figure E.5*a* can be written as a subroutine as shown in Figure E.8*a*. Parameters are passed through registers. Memory address NUM1 of the first number in the list is loaded into register EBX by the calling program. The number of entries in the list, contained in memory location N, is loaded into register ECX. The calling program expects to get the final sum passed back to it in register EAX. Thus, registers EBX, ECX, and EAX are used for passing parameters. Register EDI is used by the subroutine as an index register in performing the addition, so its contents have to be saved and restored in the subroutine by PUSH and POP instructions.

The subroutine is called by the instruction

CALL   LISTADD

which first pushes the return address onto the stack and then jumps to LISTADD. The return address is the address of the MOV instruction that immediately follows the CALL instruction. The subroutine saves the contents of register EDI on the stack. Figure E.8*b* shows the stack contents at this point. After executing the loop, the saved contents of register EDI are restored. The instruction RET returns execution control to the calling program by popping the TOS element into the Instruction Pointer (register EIP).

Figure E.9*a* shows the program of Figure E.5*a* rewritten as a subroutine with parameters passed on the stack. The parameters NUM1 and *n* are pushed onto the stack by the two PUSH instructions in the calling program. Note that the keyword OFFSET is required for pushing the address represented by NUM1 on the stack. The top of the stack is at level 2 in Figure E.9*b* after the CALL instruction has been executed. Registers EDI, EAX, EBX, and ECX serve the same purpose in this subroutine as in the subroutine in Figure E.8. After their values are saved, they are loaded with initial values and parameters by the first eight instructions in the subroutine. At this point, the top of the stack is at level 3. When the numbers have been added by the four-instruction loop, the sum is placed into the stack, overwriting parameter NUM1. After the RET instruction is executed, the ADD and POP instructions in the calling program remove parameter *n* from the stack and pop the returned sum into memory location SUM. The top of the stack is therefore restored to level 1.

We also have to consider the case of nested subroutines. Figure E.10 shows the IA-32 code for the program in Figure 2.21. The stack frames corresponding to the first and second subroutines are shown in Figure E.11. Register EBP is used as the frame pointer. Instead of using the PUSHAD and POPAD instructions to push and pop all eight general-purpose registers, we have chosen to use individual PUSH and POP instructions in Figure E.10 because only half of the register set is used by the subroutines.

Calling program

```
                            ⋮
        LEA    EBX, NUM1              Load parameters
        MOV    ECX, N                    into EBX, ECX.
        CALL   LISTADD                Branch to subroutine.
        MOV    SUM, EAX               Store sum into memory.
                            ⋮
```

Subroutine

```
LISTADD:   PUSH  EDI                     Save EDI.
           MOV   EDI, 0                  Use EDI as index register.
           MOV   EAX, 0                  Use EAX as accumulator register.

STARTADD:  ADD   EAX, [EBX + EDI * 4]    Add next number.
           INC   EDI                     Increment index.
           DEC   ECX                     Decrement counter.
           JG    STARTADD                Branch back if [ECX] > 0.
           POP   EDI                     Restore EDI.
           RET                           Return to calling program.
```

(a) Calling program and subroutine

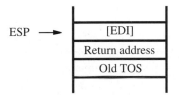

(b) Stack contents after saving EDI in subroutine

Figure E.8   Program of Figure E.5a written as a subroutine; parameters passed through registers.

E.4.10   OPERATIONS ON LARGE NUMBERS

Section E.4.5 described various arithmetic instructions, including those suitable for operations on numbers whose size exceeds the 32-bit width of a single general-purpose register. The ADC and SBB instructions use the CF flag in the status register as a carry-in bit. These instructions are useful for multiple-precision arithmetic.

(Assume top of stack is at level 1 below.)

Calling program

PUSH	OFFSET NUM1	Push parameters onto the stack.
PUSH	N	
CALL	LISTADD	Branch to the subroutine.
ADD	ESP, 4	Remove *n* from the stack.
POP	SUM	Pop the sum into SUM.

Subroutine

LISTADD:	PUSH	EDI	Save registers.
	PUSH	EAX	
	PUSH	EBX	
	PUSH	ECX	
	MOV	EDI, 0	Use EDI as index register.
	MOV	EAX, 0	Use EAX to accumulate the sum.
	MOV	EBX, [ESP + 24]	Load address NUM1.
	MOV	ECX, [ESP + 20]	Load count *n*.
STARTADD:	ADD	EAX, [EBX + EDI * 4]	Add next number.
	INC	EDI	Increment index.
	DEC	ECX	Decrement counter.
	JG	STARTADD	Branch back if not done.
	MOV	[ESP + 24], EAX	Overwrite NUM1 in stack with sum.
	POP	ECX	Restore registers.
	POP	EBX	
	POP	EAX	
	POP	EDI	
	RET		Return.

(a) Calling program and subroutine

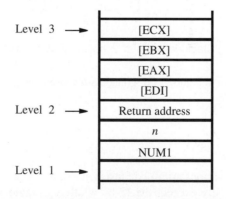

(b) Stack contents at different times

Figure E.9   Program of Figure E.5*a* written as a subroutine; parameters passed on the stack.

Address	Instructions		Comments

Calling program

⋮

2000	PUSH	PARAM2	Place parameters
2006	PUSH	PARAM1	on stack.
2012	CALL	SUB1	
2017	POP	RESULT	Store result.
	ADD	ESP, 4	Restore stack level.

⋮

First subroutine

2100	SUB1:	PUSH	EBP	Save frame pointer register.
		MOV	EBP, ESP	Load frame pointer.
		PUSH	EAX	Save registers.
		PUSH	EBX	
		PUSH	ECX	
		PUSH	EDX	
		MOV	EAX, [EBP + 8]	Get first parameter.
		MOV	EBX, [EBP + 12]	Get second parameter.

⋮

		PUSH	PARAM3	Place parameter on stack.
2160		CALL	SUB2	
2165		POP	ECX	Pop SUB2 result into ECX.

⋮

		MOV	[EBP + 8], EDX	Place answer on stack.
		POP	EDX	Restore registers.
		POP	ECX	
		POP	EBX	
		POP	EAX	
		POP	EBP	Restore frame pointer register.
		RET		Return to Main program.

Second subroutine

3000	SUB2:	PUSH	EBP	Save frame pointer register.
		MOV	EBP, ESP	Load frame pointer.
		PUSH	EAX	Save registers.
		PUSH	EBX	
		MOV	EAX, [EBP + 8]	Get parameter.

⋮

		MOV	[EBP + 8], EBX	Place SUB2 result on stack.
		POP	EBX	Restore registers.
		POP	EAX	
		POP	EBP	Restore frame pointer register.
		RET		Return to first subroutine.

Figure E.10   Nested subroutines; implementation of the program in Figure 2.21.

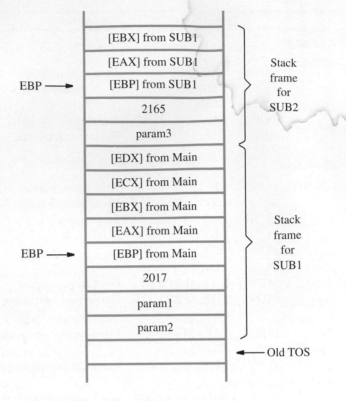

[EBX] from SUB1	
[EAX] from SUB1	
EBP → [EBP] from SUB1	Stack frame for SUB2
2165	
param3	
[EDX] from Main	
[ECX] from Main	
[EBX] from Main	
[EAX] from Main	Stack frame for SUB1
EBP → [EBP] from Main	
2017	
param1	
param2	
	← Old TOS

Figure E.11   Stack frames for Figure E.10.

Example E.4   The use of the ADC instruction to add numbers too large to fit into 32-bit registers is shown in Figure E.12. The two hexadecimal values to be added are 10A72C10F8 and 4A5C00FE04. Registers EAX and EBX are loaded with the low- and high-order bits of 10A72C10F8, respectively. Similarly, registers ECX and EDX are loaded the low- and high-order bits

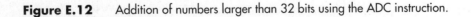

```
MOV   EAX, 0A72C10F8H    EAX contains A72C10F8.
MOV   EBX, 10H           EBX contains 10.
MOV   ECX, 5C00FE04H     ECX contains 5C00FE04.
MOV   EDX, 4AH           EDX contains 4A.
ADD   EAX, ECX           Add low-order 32 bits; carry-out sets CF flag.
ADC   EBX, EDX           Add high-order bits with CF flag as carry-in bit.
```

Figure E.12   Addition of numbers larger than 32 bits using the ADC instruction.

of 4A5C00FE04. The ADD instruction is used to add the low-order 32 bits. The addition generates a carry-out of 1 that causes the CF flag to be set. The ADC instruction then uses this flag as the carry-in bit when adding the high-order bits. The low- and high-order bits of the sum are in registers EAX and EBX.

E.5   ASSEMBLER DIRECTIVES

As discussed in Section 2.5.1, assembler directives are needed to define the data area of a program and to define the correspondence between symbolic names for data locations and the actual physical address values.

A complete assembly language program for the program in Figure E.5b is shown in Figure E.13. It corresponds to the program in Figure 2.13. The directives shown in Figure E.13 conform to those defined by the widely used Microsoft MASM assembler. The .CODE and .DATA directives define the beginning of the code and data sections of the program. In the data section, the DD directives allocate storage for doubleword-sized data. The label SUM is assigned the address of the location containing the doubleword for the sum that is computed; it is initialized to 0. The label N is assigned the address of the location containing the number 150. Finally, the storage is allocated for the list of numbers. The DUP keyword is used to initialize a specified number of consecutive locations in memory to a specified value. In this case, 150 consecutive locations are initialized to 0. Other assembler directives are also available, such as DB which allocates storage for byte-sized data and EQU which assigns a constant value to a label.

```
            .CODE
            LEA     EBX, NUM1
            SUB     EBX, 4
            MOV     ECX, N
            MOV     EAX, 0
STARTADD:   ADD     EAX, [EBX + ECX * 4]
            LOOP    STARTADD
            MOV     SUM, EAX

            .DATA
SUM         DD      0                    One doubleword reserved for sum.
N           DD      150                  There are N=150 doublewords in list.
NUM1        DD      150 DUP(0)           Reserve memory for 150 doublewords.
            END
```

Figure E.13   A program that corresponds to Figure 2.13.

E.6   EXAMPLE PROGRAMS

This section presents the IA-32 code for the example programs described in Section 2.12.

E.6.1   VECTOR DOT PRODUCT PROGRAM

Figure E.14 shows a program for computing the dot product of two vectors of numbers stored in the memory starting at addresses AVEC and BVEC. It corresponds to the program in Figure 2.28. The Base with index addressing mode is used to access successive elements of each vector. Register EDI is used as the index register. A scale factor of 4 is used because the vector elements are assumed to be doubleword (4-byte) numbers. Register ECX is used as the loop counter; it is initialized to n. This allows the use of the LOOP instruction, which first decrements ECX and then branches conditionally to the target address LOOPSTART if the contents of ECX have not reached zero. The product of two vector elements is assumed to fit into a doubleword, so the Multiply instruction IMUL explicitly specifies the desired destination register EDX, as discussed in Section E.4.5.

E.6.2   STRING SEARCH PROGRAM

Figure E.15 provides an IA-32 version of the program in Figure 2.31. It determines the first matching instance of a pattern string P in a given target string T. Because there are only eight general-purpose registers, the doubleword contents of EAX are saved in memory location TMP, so that the byte-sized register AL can be used in the loop. The saved doubleword is restored to EAX when that value is needed again.

	LEA	EBP, AVEC	EBP points to vector A.
	LEA	EBX, BVEC	EBX points to vector B.
	MOV	ECX, N	ECX is the loop counter.
	MOV	EAX, 0	EAX accumulates the dot product.
	MOV	EDI, 0	EDI is an index register.
LOOPSTART:	MOV	EDX, [EBP + EDI $*$ 4]	Compute the product
	IMUL	EDX, [EBX + EDI $*$ 4]	of next components.
	INC	EDI	Increment index.
	ADD	EAX, EDX	Add to previous sum.
	LOOP	LOOPSTART	Branch back if not done.
	MOV	DOTPROD, EAX	Store dot product in memory.

Figure E.14   A program for computing the dot product of two vectors.

```
                  MOV   EAX, OFFSET T              EAX points to string T.
                  MOV   EBX, OFFSET P              EBX points to string P.
                  MOV   ECX, N                     Get the value n.
                  MOV   EDX, M                     Get the value m.
                  SUB   ECX, EDX                   Compute n − m.
                  ADD   ECX, EAX                   ECX is the address of T(n − m).
                  ADD   EDX, EBX                   EBX is the address of P(m).
LOOP1:            MOV   ESI, EAX                   Use ESI to scan through string T.
                  MOV   EDI, EBX                   Use EDI to scan through string P.
                  MOV   DWORD PTR TMP, EAX         Save EAX in memory to allow use of AL.
LOOP2:            MOV   AL, [ESI]                  Get character from string T.
                  CMP   AL, [EDI]                  Compare with character from string P.
                  JNE   NOMATCH
                  INC   ESI                        Advance string T pointer.
                  INC   EDI                        Advance string P pointer.
                  CMP   EDX, EDI                   Check if at P(m).
                  JG    LOOP2                       Loop again if not done.
                  MOV   EAX, DWORD PTR TMP         Restore EAX after temporary use.
                  MOV   DWORD PTR RESULT, EAX      Store the address of T(i).
                  JMP   DONE
NOMATCH:          MOV   EAX, DWORD PTR TMP         Restore EAX after temporary use.
                  ADD   EAX, 1                     Point to next character in T.
                  CMP   ECX, EAX                   Check if at T(n − m).
                  JGE   LOOP1                       Loop again if not done.
                  MOV   DWORD PTR RESULT, −1       No match was found.
DONE:             next instruction
```

Figure E.15   A string-search program.

E.7 INTERRUPTS AND EXCEPTIONS

Processors implementing the IA-32 architecture use two interrupt-request lines, a nonmaskable interrupt, NMI, and a maskable interrupt, also called the user interrupt request, INTR. Interrupt requests on NMI are always accepted by the processor. Requests on INTR are accepted only if they have a higher privilege level than the program currently running. INTR interrupts can be enabled or disabled by setting an interrupt-enable bit, IF, in the status register.

In addition to external interrupts, there are other events that arise during program execution that can cause an exception. These include invalid OP codes, division by zero, and overflow. They also include trace and breakpoint interrupts.

The occurrence of any of these events causes the processor to branch to an interrupt-service routine. Each interrupt or exception is assigned a vector number. In the case of INTR, the vector number is sent by the I/O device over the bus when the interrupt request is acknowledged. For all other exceptions, the vector number is preassigned. Based on the vector number, the processor determines the starting address of the interrupt-service routine from a table called the Interrupt Descriptor Table.

An IA-32 processor relies on a companion Advanced Programmable Interrupt Controller (APIC). Various I/O devices are connected to the processor through this controller. The interrupt controller implements a priority structure among different devices and sends an appropriate vector number to the processor for each device.

The status register, shown in Figure E.1, contains the Interrupt Enable Flag (IF), the Trap flag (TF) and the I/O Privilege Level (IOPL). When IF = 1, INTR interrupts are accepted. The Trap flag enables trace interrupts after every instruction.

Interrupts are particularly important in the context of an operating system. The IA-32 architecture defines a sophisticated privilege structure, whereby different parts of the operating system execute at one of four levels of privilege. A different segment in the processor address space is used for each level. Switching from one level to another involves a number of checks implemented in a mechanism called a *gate*. This enables a highly secure OS to be constructed. It is also possible for the processor to run in a simple mode in which no privileges are implemented and all programs run in the same segment. We will only discuss the simple mode here.

When an interrupt request is received or when an exception occurs, the processor performs the following actions:

1. It pushes the status register, the Code Segment register (CS), and the Instruction Pointer (EIP) onto the processor stack.

2. In the case of an exception resulting from an abnormal execution condition, it pushes a code on the stack describing the cause of the exception.

3. It clears the corresponding interrupt-enable flag so that further interrupts from the same source are disabled.

4. It fetches the starting address of the interrupt-service routine from the Interrupt Descriptor Table based on the vector number of the interrupt, loads this value into EIP, and then resumes execution.

After servicing the interrupt request, the interrupt-service routine returns to the interrupted program using the return-from-interrupt instruction, IRET. This instruction pops EIP, CS, and the status register from the stack into the corresponding registers, thus restoring the processor state.

As in the case of subroutines, the interrupt-service routine may create a temporary work space by saving registers or using the stack frame for local variables. It must restore any saved registers and ensure that the stack pointer ESP is pointing to the return address, before executing the IRET instruction.

E.8   INPUT/OUTPUT EXAMPLES

This section uses the I/O examples and interface registers described in Chapter 3 to show how IA-32 instructions are used for polling and interrupt-based I/O operations.

Figure E.16 provides an IA-32 version of the program in Figure 3.5 with polling for both input and output operations. The BT instruction corresponds to the TestBit instruction in Figure 3.5. It copies the value of the specified bit into the CF flag of the status register. Each character is read from the keyboard interface into register AL for later comparison with the carriage-return character, CR. As each character is stored in the memory from register AL, register EBX is incremented to advance the pointer.

To illustrate how interrupts are used for I/O operations, Figure E.17 implements the example in Figure 3.10. The BTS instruction in the initialization code sets the interrupt-enable bit in the keyboard interface. The STI instruction enables the processor to respond to interrupt requests by setting the IF flag in the status register to 1. The BTR instruction in the interrupt-service routine clears the interrupt-enable bit in the keyboard interface. The pointer is maintained in a memory location and incremented for each character that is processed by the interrupt-service routine. We have assumed that the keyboard sends an interrupt request with a specific vector number i and that the corresponding entry i

	LEA	EBX, LOC	Initialize register EBX to point to the address of the first location in main memory where the characters are to be stored.
READ:	BT	KBD_STATUS, 1	Wait for a character to be entered
	JNC	READ	in the keyboard buffer KBD_DATA.
	MOV	AL, KBD_DATA	Transfer character into AL (this clears KIN to 0).
	MOV	[EBX], AL	Store the character in memory
	INC	EBX	and increment pointer.
ECHO:	BT	DISP_STATUS, 2	Wait for the display to become ready.
	JNC	ECHO	
	MOV	DISP_DATA, AL	Move the character just read to the display buffer register (this clears DOUT to 0).
	CMP	AL, CR	If it is not CR, then
	JNE	READ	branch back and read another character.

Figure E.16   Program that reads a line of characters and displays it.

Interrupt-service routine

READ:	PUSH	EAX	Save register EAX on stack.
	PUSH	EBX	Save register EBX on stack.
	MOV	EBX, PNTR	Load address pointer.
	MOV	AL, KBD_DATA	Transfer character into AL.
	MOV	[EBX], AL	Write the character into memory
	INC	DWORD PTR PNTR	and increment the pointer.
ECHO:	BT	DISP_STATUS, 2	Wait for the display to become ready.
	JNC	ECHO	
	MOV	DISP_DATA, AL	Display the character just read.
	CMP	AL, CR	Check if the character just read is CR.
	JNE	RTRN	Return if not CR.
	MOV	DWORD PTR EOL, 1	Indicate end of line.
	BTR	KBD_CONT, 1	Disable interrupts in keyboard interface.
RTRN:	POP	EBX	Restore registers.
	POP	EAX	
	IRET		Return from interrupt.

Main program

MOV	DWORD PTR PNTR, OFFSET LINE	Initialize buffer pointer.
MOV	DWORD PTR EOL, 0	Clear end-of-line indicator.
BTS	KBD_CONT, 1	Enable interrupts in keyboard interface.
STI		Set interrupt flag in processor register.
next instruction		

Figure E.17   A program that reads a line of characters using interrupts and displays it using polling.

in the Interrupt Descriptor Table has been loaded with the starting address READ of the interrupt-service routine.

E.9   SCALAR FLOATING-POINT OPERATIONS

The IA-32 architecture defines many instructions for floating-point operations. They are performed by a separate *floating-point unit* (FPU) which contains additional registers. The FPU permits concurrent execution of floating-point operations with other instructions. This section provides a summary of the floating-point features of the IA-32 architecture and some of its floating-point instructions. Floating-point number representation is introduced in Chapter 1, and floating-point arithmetic is discussed in Chapter 9.

All floating-point operations are performed internally on 80-bit double extended-precision numbers. Eight 80-bit floating-point data registers, shown in Figure E.1, are provided for this purpose. Performing operations internally on extended-precision numbers held in these registers reduces the size of accumulated round-off errors in a sequence of calculations, as explained in Section 9.7. There are also additional control and status registers in the FPU, whose details can be found in the Intel technical documentation [1].

A unique feature of the FPU is that the eight floating-point data registers are treated as a stack. Certain instructions that perform arithmetic or data transfer operations involving these registers may also perform push or pop operations. A pointer to the top of the register stack is maintained internally by the FPU. No particular initialization is required for the pointer. Push and pop operations adjust the pointer modulo 8 to cause it to wrap around when necessary.

In assembly language, floating-point register operands are identified using the notation $ST(i)$, where i is an index relative to the top of the register stack ($0 \le i \le 7$). For example, $ST(0)$ refers to the register that is the current top of the register stack, $ST(1)$ refers to the next register in the stack, and so on until $ST(7)$, which refers to the last register. When writing programs in assembly language, the programmer needs to keep track of the push and pop operations performed in a sequence of floating-point instructions to correctly identify the operands of each instruction.

Floating-point load instructions have one explicit operand that specifies the source location in the memory. They push the value read from the memory onto the register stack. The destination location is implicitly the register identified as $ST(7)$ at the time the load instruction is executed. After completing the load instruction, that register becomes $ST(0)$, the new top of the register stack. This is because the pointer to the top of the register stack is adjusted modulo 8. The previous register $ST(0)$ becomes $ST(1)$, the previous register $ST(1)$ becomes $ST(2)$, and so on.

For floating-point store instructions, the source operand is implicitly in register $ST(0)$. One explicit operand specifies the destination location in the memory into which the value of register $ST(0)$ is written. Some store instructions leave the register stack unchanged. Other store instructions also pop $ST(0)$. The pointer to the top of the register stack is adjusted modulo 8 in the opposite direction than for load instructions. After completing the pop operation, the previous register $ST(0)$ becomes $ST(7)$, the previous register $ST(1)$ becomes $ST(0)$, and so on.

Floating-point arithmetic instructions must have either the source operand or the destination operand in register $ST(0)$. For some instructions, register $ST(0)$ is implicitly the destination location. Only the source operand needs to be specified explicitly, which must be in the memory. Other instructions specify two operands explicitly. One must be in register $ST(0)$, which can be either the source or the destination. The other one may be in any register $ST(i)$. A few instructions require no explicit operands because they implicitly use register $ST(0)$ for both source and destination locations.

The floating-point registers always hold 80-bit double extended-precision numbers. The memory may contain numbers in either 32-bit single-precision or 64-bit double-precision representation. Single-precision representation reduces the storage requirements when large amounts of floating-point data are involved but very high precision is not needed. The FPU automatically converts single-precision or double-precision operands from the memory to double extended-precision numbers before performing arithmetic operations. Double extended-precision numbers are converted to either single-precision or double-precision representation when transferring them to the memory. The FPU also converts between integer and double extended-precision floating-point representations for transfers to or from the memory. Implementing the conversion capability in hardware reduces execution time and code size by eliminating the need for software to perform this task.

E.9.1   LOAD AND STORE INSTRUCTIONS

The FLD instruction loads a floating-point number from a memory location and pushes the value onto the floating-point register stack. The keywords DWORD PTR are used to indicate single-precision operand size, and the keywords QWORD PTR are used to indicate double-precision operand size. In either case, the value read from the memory is converted to the 80-bit double extended-precision format. For example, the instruction

$$\text{FLD   DWORD PTR [EAX]}$$

reads a single-precision floating-point number from the memory location [EAX], converts the number to the 80-bit format, and pushes it onto the register stack.

The FST instruction writes the floating-point number in ST(0) into the memory. The pointer to the top of the register stack is not affected in this case. The appropriate keywords, DWORD PTR or QWORD PTR, must be used to specify the desired size for the value to be written into the memory. This determines whether the 80-bit representation in ST(0) is to be converted to either single-precision or double-precision format. For example, the instruction

$$\text{FST   QWORD PTR [EDX + 8]}$$

converts the 80-bit floating-point number in ST(0) to 64-bit double-precision format, and writes this converted value into memory location [EDX] + 8.

There are instructions to load and store 32-bit integer operands. These instructions perform automatic conversion to and from the 80-bit floating-point format. The FILD instruction reads a 32-bit integer from the memory, converts it to an 80-bit floating-point number, and pushes the result onto the register stack. The FIST instruction converts the 80-bit floating-point number in register ST(0) to a 32-bit integer, then writes the result into the memory. It does not change the pointer to the top of the register stack.

Finally, there are store instructions that pop ST(0) after writing the contents of that register (with appropriate conversion) into the memory. This means that the previous register ST(0) becomes ST(7), the previous register ST(1) becomes ST(0), and so on. The FSTP instruction performs the same operation as the FST instruction, but it also pops ST(0). Similarly, the FISTP instruction combines the operation of the FIST instruction with a pop operation.

E.9.2 Arithmetic Instructions

The basic instructions for performing arithmetic operations on floating-point numbers are FADD, FSUB, FMUL, and FDIV. For instructions that explicitly specify one operand, it is the source operand and it must be in the memory. The destination operand is implicitly in register ST(0). The operand from the memory is converted to the 80-bit double extended-precision format before the arithmetic operation is performed. For example, the instruction

$$\text{FADD} \quad \text{QWORD PTR [EAX]}$$

reads the 64-bit double-precision number from memory location [EAX], converts it to the 80-bit double extended-precision representation, adds the converted value to the current value in register ST(0), and places the sum in ST(0).

For instructions that specify two operands explicitly, both must be in registers and one of the registers must be ST(0). For example, the instruction

$$\text{FMUL} \quad \text{ST(0), ST(3)}$$

multiplies the values in ST(0) and ST(3), and places the product in ST(0).

The instructions FADDP, FSUBP, FMULP, and FDIVP are used to pop the top of the register stack after performing an arithmetic operation. These instructions must specify two operands in registers. It is appropriate to use ST(1) as the destination location for these instructions. After the pop operation is completed, the result is in the register that is the new top of the register stack. For example, the instruction

$$\text{FSUBP} \quad \text{ST(1), ST(0)}$$

subtracts the value in ST(0) from ST(1), places the result in ST(1), then pops ST(0). Hence, the result is now at the top of the stack in ST(0).

The instructions FIADD, FISUB, FIMUL, and FIDIV specify a single explicit operand, which is a 32-bit integer in the memory. The destination operand is implicitly in register ST(0). The 32-bit integer is automatically converted to 80-bit double extended-precision representation before the arithmetic operation is performed. For example, the instruction

$$\text{FIDIV} \quad \text{DWORD PTR [ECX + 4]}$$

reads a 32-bit integer from memory location [ECX] + 4, converts the value into 80-bit floating-point representation, divides the value in ST(0) by the converted value, and places the result in ST(0).

For subtraction and division operations, the order of the operands is significant. Because the floating-point registers are organized as a stack, it may sometimes be useful to reverse the order of operands for these arithmetic operations so that a particular result or operand can later be popped from the stack. The instructions FSUBR and FDIVR are provided for this purpose. For example, the instruction

$$\text{FSUBR} \quad \text{ST(3), ST(0)}$$

performs the operation $ST(3) \leftarrow [ST(0)] - [ST(3)]$. In contrast, the instruction

$$\text{FSUB} \quad \text{ST(3), ST(0)}$$

performs the operation $ST(3) \leftarrow [ST(3)] - [ST(0)]$.

E.9.3   COMPARISON INSTRUCTIONS

Floating-point comparison instructions can be used to set the condition code flags in the status register. The conditional Jump instructions in Table E.2 can then be used to test different conditions. The FUCOMI and FUCOMIP instructions compare two floating-point operands in registers. The destination operand must be in ST(0). The FUCOMIP instruction also pops ST(0) after the comparison is performed. For example, the instruction

$$\text{FUCOMI} \quad \text{ST(0), ST(4)}$$

performs the subtraction [ST(0)] − [ST(4)] and sets the ZF and CF flags in the status register based on the result, which is then discarded. A subsequent Jump instruction can be used to test the appropriate condition: JE for ST(0) = ST(4), JA for ST(0) > ST(4), and JB for ST(0) < ST(4).

E.9.4   ADDITIONAL INSTRUCTIONS

There are additional instructions such as square root (FSQRT), change sign (FCHS), absolute value (FABS), sine (FSIN), and cosine (FCOS). These instructions require no explicit operands because they implicitly use ST(0) as both the source and destination. In other words, the value in the register at the top of the register stack is replaced with the result of the operation, and the pointer to the top of the register stack is unchanged.

There are also instructions that are used to push commonly used floating-point constants onto the stack. FLDZ pushes 0.0 onto the register stack. FLD1 pushes 1.0 onto the register stack. FLDPI pushes the double extended-precision floating-point representation of π, accurate to 19 decimal digits, onto the register stack. No explicit operands are required for these instructions.

E.9.5   EXAMPLE FLOATING-POINT PROGRAM

An example program is shown in Figure E.18. Given a pair of points (x_0,y_0) and (x_1,y_1), the program determines the slope m and intercept b of a line passing through these points, except when the points lie on a vertical line.

The coordinates for the two points are assumed to be 64-bit double-precision floating-point numbers stored consecutively in the memory as x_0, y_0, x_1, and y_1 beginning at location COORDS. The program places the computed slope and intercept as double-precision numbers in memory locations SLOPE and INTERCEPT. The slope of a line is given by $m = (y_1 - y_0)/(x_1 - x_0)$, hence the program must check for a zero in the denominator before performing the division. When the denominator is zero, the points lie on a vertical line. The program writes a value of one into memory location VERT_LINE to reflect this case and to indicate that the values in memory locations SLOPE and INTERCEPT are not valid, and no further computation is done. Otherwise, the program computes the value of the slope and stores it in the memory. With a valid slope, the intercept is computed as $b = y_0 - m \cdot x_0$, which is then written into the memory. The subtraction in this case uses the FSUBR instruction, which reverses the order of operands. Finally, a zero is written into memory location VERT_LINE to indicate that the slope and intercept are valid.

	MOV	EAX, OFFSET COORDS	EAX points to list of coordinates.
	FLD	QWORD PTR [EAX + 24]	Push y_1 on register stack.
	FLD	QWORD PTR [EAX + 16]	Push x_1 on register stack.
	FLD	QWORD PTR [EAX + 8]	Push y_0 on register stack.
	FLD	QWORD PTR [EAX]	Push x_0 on register stack.
	FSUBP	ST(2), ST(0)	Compute $x_1 - x_0$; pop x_0.
	FLDZ		Push 0.0 on stack.
	FUCOMIP	ST(0), ST(2)	Determine whether denominator is zero.
	JE	NO_SLOPE	If so, slope m is undefined.
	FSUBP	ST(2), ST(0)	Compute $y_1 - y_0$; pop y_0.
	FDIVP	ST(1), ST(0)	Compute $m = (y_1 - y_0)/(x_1 - x_0)$.
	MOV	EBX, OFFSET SLOPE	EBX points to memory location SLOPE.
	FST	QWORD PTR [EBX]	Store the slope to memory.
	FLD	QWORD PTR [EAX + 8]	Push y_0 on register stack.
	FLD	QWORD PTR [EAX]	Push x_0 on register stack.
	FMULP	ST(2), ST(0)	Compute $m \cdot x_0$; pop x_0.
	FSUBRP	ST(1), ST(0)	Compute $b = y_0 - m \cdot x_0$; pop y_0.
	MOV	EBX, OFFSET INTERCEPT	EBX points to memory location INTERCEPT.
	FSTP	QWORD PTR [EBX]	Store the intercept to memory; pop top of stack.
	MOV	EBX, 0	Indicate that line is not vertical.
	JMP	DONE	
NO_SLOPE:	MOV	EBX, 1	Indicate that line is vertical.
DONE:	MOV	DWORD PTR VERT_LINE, EBX	

Figure E.18   Floating-point program to compute the slope and intercept of a line.

E.10   MULTIMEDIA EXTENSION (MMX) OPERATIONS

A two-dimensional graphic or video image can be represented by a large array of sampled image points, called *pixels*. The color and brightness of each point can be encoded into an 8-bit data item. Processing of such data has two main characteristics. The first is that manipulations of individual pixels often involve very simple arithmetic or logic operations. The second is that very high computational performance is needed for some real-time display applications. The same characteristics apply to sampled audio signals or speech processing, where a sequence of signed numbers represents samples of a continuous analog signal taken at periodic intervals.

In such applications, processing efficiency is achieved if the individual data items, which are usually bytes or 16-bit words, are packed into small groups whose elements can be processed in parallel. Vector or single-instruction multiple-data (SIMD) instructions for this form of parallel processing are described in Chapter 12. The IA-32 instruction set includes a number of SIMD instructions, which are called *multimedia extension* (MMX) instructions. They perform the same operation simultaneously on multiple data elements, packed into 64-bit quadwords. The operands for MMX instructions can be in the memory, or in the eight floating-point registers. Thus, these registers serve a dual purpose. They can hold either floating-point numbers or MMX operands. When used by MMX instructions, the registers are referred to as MM0 through MM7, and only the lowermost 64 bits of each 80-bit register are relevant for MMX operations. Unlike the floating-point instructions in Section E.9, the MMX instructions do not manage this shared register set as a stack.

The MOVQ instruction is provided for transferring 64-bit quadword operands between the memory and the MMX registers. For example, the instruction

MOVQ   MM0, [EAX]

loads the quadword from the memory location whose address is in register EAX into register MM0. The MOVQ instruction can also be used to transfer data between MMX registers. For example, the instruction

MOVQ   MM3, MM4

transfers the contents of register MM4 to register MM3.

Instructions are provided to perform arithmetic and logic operations in parallel on multiple elements of a packed quadword operand. The source can be in the memory or in an MMX register, but the destination must be an MMX register. For most MMX instructions, a suffix is used to indicate the size (and number) of data elements within a packed quadword: B for byte (8 elements), W for word (4 elements), D for doubleword (2 elements), and Q for quadword (1 element). For example, the instruction

PADDB   MM2, [EBX]

adds eight corresponding bytes of the quadwords in register MM2 and in the memory location pointed to by register EBX. The eight sums are computed in parallel. The results are placed in register MM2.

Other instructions are provided for subtraction (PSUB), multiplication (PMUL), combined multiplication and addition (PMADD), logic operations (PAND, POR, and PXOR), and a large number of other operations on packed quadword operands.

E.11   Vector (SIMD) Floating-Point Operations

Section E.9 described instructions for operating on individual floating-point numbers. Vector (SIMD) instructions are also provided to perform operations simultaneously on multiple floating-point numbers. In Intel terminology, these instructions are called *streaming SIMD extension* (SSE) instructions. They handle packed 128-bit double quadwords, each consisting of four 32-bit floating-point numbers. Eight additional 128-bit registers, XMM0 to XMM7, are available for holding these operands.

The MOVAPS and MOVUPS instructions transfer a packed double quadword between memory and the XMM registers, or between XMM registers. The PS suffix indicates packed single-precision floating-point values in the double quadword. The A or U designation determines whether a memory address must be aligned to a 16-bit word boundary or may be unaligned. The instruction

$$\text{MOVUPS} \quad \text{XMM3, [EAX]}$$

loads a 128-bit double quadword from the memory location pointed to by register EAX into register XMM3. The instruction

$$\text{MOVUPS} \quad \text{XMM4, XMM5}$$

transfers the double quadword in register XMM5 into register XMM4.

The basic arithmetic operations are performed simultaneously on four pairs of 32-bit floating-point numbers from two double-quadword operands. The source can be in the memory or in an XMM register, but the destination must be an XMM register. Instructions include ADDPS, SUBPS, MULPS, and DIVPS. For example, the instruction

$$\text{ADDPS} \quad \text{XMM0, XMM1}$$

adds the four corresponding pairs of floating-point numbers in registers XMM0 and XMM1 and places the four sums in register XMM0.

E.12   EXAMPLES OF SOLVED PROBLEMS

This section presents some examples of the types of problems that a student may be asked to solve, and shows how such problems can be solved.

Problem: Assume that there is a string of ASCII-encoded characters stored in memory **Example E.5** starting at address STRING. The string ends with the Carriage Return (CR) character. Write an IA-32 program to determine the length of the string.

Solution: Figure E.19 presents a possible program. Each character in the string is compared to CR (ASCII code 0D), and a counter is incremented until the end of the string is reached. The result is stored in location LENGTH.

```
        MOV   EAX, OFFSET STRING        EAX points to the start of the string.
        MOV   EDI, 0                    EDI is a counter that is cleared to 0.
LOOP:   MOV   BL, BYTE PTR [EAX + EDI]  Load next character into lowest byte of EBX.
        CMP   BL, 0DH                   Compare character with CR.
        JE    DONE                      Finished if it matches.
        INC   EDI                       Increment the counter.
        JMP   LOOP                      Not finished, loop back.
DONE:   MOV   DWORD PTR LENGTH, EDI     Store the count in memory location LENGTH.
```

Figure E.19   Program for Example E.5.

Example E.6 **Problem:** We want to find the smallest number in a list of non-negative 32-bit integers. Storage for data begins at address 1000. The doubleword at this address must hold the value of the smallest number after it has been found. The next doubleword contains the number of entries, n, in the list. The following n doublewords contain the numbers in the list. Write a program to find the smallest number and include the assembler directives needed to organize the data as stated.

Solution: The program in Figure E.20 accomplishes the required task. It assumes that $n \geq 1$. A few sample numbers are included as entries in the list.

LIST	EQU	1000	Starting address of list.
	.CODE		
	MOV	EAX, OFFSET LIST	EAX points to the start of the list.
	MOV	EDI, [EAX + 4]	EDI is a counter, initialize it with n.
	MOV	EBX, EAX	EBX points to the first number
	ADD	EBX, 8	after adjusting its value.
	MOV	ECX, [EBX]	ECX holds the smallest number so far.
LOOP:	DEC	EDI	Decrement the counter.
	JZ	DONE	Finished if EDI is zero.
	MOV	EDX, [EBX]	Get the next number.
	ADD	EBX, 4	Increment the pointer.
	CMP	ECX, EDX	Compare next number and smallest so far.
	JLE	LOOP	If next number not smaller, loop again.
	MOV	ECX, EDX	Otherwise, update smallest number so far.
	JMP	LOOP	Loop again.
DONE:	MOV	[EAX], ECX	Store the smallest number into SMALL.
	.DATA		
	ORG	1000	
SMALL	DD	0	Space for the smallest number found.
N	DD	7	Number of entries in list.
ENTRIES	DD	4, 5, 3, 6, 1, 8, 2	Entries in the list.

Figure E.20 Program for Example E.6.

Example E.7 **Problem:** Write a program that converts an n-digit decimal integer into a binary number. The decimal number is given as n ASCII-encoded characters, as would be the case if the number is entered by typing it on a keyboard.

Solution: Consider a four-digit decimal number, D, which is represented by the digits $d_3d_2d_1d_0$. The value of this number is $((d_3 \times 10 + d_2) \times 10 + d_1) \times 10 + d_0$. This representation of the number is the basis for the conversion technique used in the program in Figure E.21. Note that each ASCII-encoded character is converted into a Binary Coded Decimal (BCD) digit with the AND instruction before it is used in the computation.

	MOV	ECX, DWORD PTR N	ECX is a counter, initialize it with n.
	MOV	ESI, OFFSET DECIMAL	ESI points to the ASCII digits.
	MOV	EBX, 0	EBX will hold the binary number.
	MOV	EDI, 10	EDI will be used to multiply by 10.
LOOP:	MOV	DL, [ESI]	Get the next ASCII digit.
	AND	EDX, 0FH	Form the BCD digit.
	ADD	EBX, EDX	Add to the intermediate result.
	DEC	ECX	Decrement the counter.
	JZ	DONE	Exit loop if finished.
	IMUL	EBX, EDI	Multiply by 10.
	INC	ESI	Increment the pointer.
	JMP	LOOP	Loop back if not done.
DONE:	MOV	DWORD PTR BINARY, EBX	Store result in memory location BINARY.

Figure E.21 Program for Example E.7.

Problem: Consider an array of numbers $A(i,j)$, where $i = 0$ through $n - 1$ is the row index, and $j = 0$ through $m - 1$ is the column index. The array is stored in the memory of a computer one row after another, with elements of each row occupying m successive word locations. Write a subroutine for adding column x to column y, element by element, leaving the sum elements in column y. The indices x and y are passed to the subroutine in registers EAX and EBX. The parameters n and m are passed to the subroutine in registers ECX and EDX, and the address of element $A(0,0)$ is passed in register EDI.

Example E.8

Solution: A possible program is given in Figure E.22. We assumed that the values x, y, n, and m are stored in memory locations X, Y, N, and M. Also, the elements of the array are stored in successive words that begin at location ARRAY, which is the address of the element $A(0,0)$. Comments in the program indicate the purpose of individual instructions.

Problem: Assume that a memory location BINARY contains a 32-bit pattern. It is desired to display these bits as eight hexadecimal digits on a display device that has the interface depicted in Figure 3.3. Write a program that accomplishes this task.

Example E.9

```
              MOV    EAX, DWORD PTR X        Load the value x.
              MOV    EBX, DWORD PTR Y        Load the value y.
              MOV    ECX, DWORD PTR N        Load the value n.
              MOV    EDX, DWORD PTR M        Load the value m.
              MOV    EDI, OFFSET ARRAY       Load the address of A(0,0).
              CALL   SUB
              next instruction
              ⋮

SUB:          PUSH   ESI                     Save register ESI.
              SHL    EDX, 2                  Determine the distance in bytes
                                                between successive elements
                                                in a column.
              SUB    EBX, EAX                Form y − x.
              SHL    EBX, 2                  Form 4(y − x).
              SHL    EAX, 2                  Form 4x.
              ADD    EDI, EAX                EDI points to A(0,x).
              MOV    ESI, EDI
              ADD    ESI, EBX                ESI points to A(0,y).
LOOP:         MOV    EAX, [EDI]              Get the next number in column x.
              MOV    EBX, [ESI]              Get the next number in column y.
              ADD    EAX, EBX                Add the numbers and store the sum.
              MOV    [ESI], EAX
              ADD    EDI, EDX                Increment pointer to column x.
              ADD    ESI, EDX                Increment pointer to column y.
              DEC    ECX                     Decrement the row counter.
              JG     LOOP                    Loop back if not done.
              POP    ESI                     Restore ESI.
              RET                            Return to the calling program.
```

Figure E.22   Program for Example E.8.

Solution: First it is necessary to convert the 32-bit pattern into hex digits that are represented as ASCII-encoded characters. The conversion can be done by using the table-lookup approach. A 16-entry table has to be constructed to provide the ASCII code for each possible hex digit. Then, for each four-bit segment of the pattern in BINARY, the corresponding character can be looked up in the table and stored in consecutive byte locations in memory beginning at address HEX. Finally, the eight characters beginning at address HEX are sent to the display. Figure E.23 gives a possible program.

```
            .CODE
            MOV     EAX, DWORD PTR BINARY      Load the binary number.
            MOV     ECX, 8                     ECX is a digit counter that is set to 8.
            MOV     EDI, OFFSET HEX            EDI points to the hex digits.
            MOV     ESI, OFFSET TABLE          ESI points to table for ASCII conversion.
LOOP:       ROL     EAX, 4                     Rotate high-order digit into low-order position.
            MOV     EBX, EAX                   Copy current value to another register.
            AND     EBX, 0FH                   Extract next digit.
            MOV     DL, [ESI + EBX]            Get ASCII code for the digit, store it in the
            MOV     [EDI], DL                    HEX buffer and increment the digital pointer.
            INC     EDI
            DEC     ECX                        Decrement the digit counter.
            JG      LOOP                       Loop back if not the last digit.
DISPLAY:    MOV     ECX, 8
            MOV     EDI, OFFSET HEX
            MOV     ESI, OFFSET DISP_DATA
DLOOP:      MOV     EDX, [ESI + 4]             Check if the display is ready by
            AND     EDX, 4                       testing the DOUT flag.
            JZ      DLOOP
            MOV     DL, [EDI]                  Get the next ASCII character,
            INC     EDI                          increment the character pointer,
            MOV     [ESI], DL                    and send it to the display.
            DEC     ECX                        Decrement the counter.
            JG      DLOOP                      Loop until all characters displayed.
            next instruction

            .DATA
            ORG     1000
HEX         DB      8 DUP (0)                  Space for ASCII-encoded digits.
TABLE       DB      30H, 31H, 32H, 33H         Table for conversion to ASCII code.
            DB      34H, 35H, 36H, 37H
            DB      38H, 39H, 41H, 42H
            DB      43H, 44H, 45H, 46H
```

Figure E.23   Program for Example E.9.

E.13   CONCLUDING REMARKS

The IA-32 instruction set is an example of a very extensive CISC design. It supports a broad range of operations on different types of data such as individual integers and floating-point numbers, as well as vectors of packed integers and floating-point numbers. Despite the challenges associated with such a large instruction set, it is implemented in high-performance processors.

PROBLEMS

E.1   **[E]** Write a program that computes the expression SUM = 580 + 68400 + 80000.

E.2   **[E]** Write a program that computes the expression ANSWER = A × B + C × D.

E.3   **[M]** Write a program that finds the number of negative integers in a list of n 32-bit integers and stores the count in location NEGNUM. The value n is stored in memory location N, and the first integer in the list is stored in location NUMBERS. Include the necessary assembler directives and a sample list that contains six numbers, some of which are negative.

E.4   **[E]** Write an assembly-language program in the style of Figure E.13 for the program in Figure E.6. Assume the data layout of Figure 2.10.

E.5   **[M]** Write an IA-32 program to solve Problem 2.10 in Chapter 2.

E.6   **[E]** Write an IA-32 program for the problem described in Example 2.5 in Chapter 2.

E.7   **[M]** Write an IA-32 program for the problem described in Example 3.5 in Chapter 3.

E.8   **[E]** Write an IA-32 program for the problem described in Example 3.6 in Chapter 3.

E.9   **[E]** Write an IA-32 program for the problem described in Example 3.6 in Chapter 3, but assume that the address of TABLE is 0x10100.

E.10   **[E]** Write a program that displays the contents of 10 bytes of the main memory in hexadecimal format on a line of a video display. The byte string starts at location LOC in the memory. Each byte has to be displayed as two hex characters. The displayed contents of successive bytes should be separated by a space.

E.11   **[M]** Assume that a memory location BINARY contains a 16-bit pattern. It is desired to display these bits as a string of 0s and 1s on a display device that has the interface depicted in Figure 3.3. Write a program that accomplishes this task.

E.12   **[M]** Using the seven-segment display in Figure 3.17 and the timer circuit in Figure 3.14, write a program that flashes decimal digits in the sequence 0, 1, 2, . . . , 9, 0, ... Each digit is to be displayed for one second. Assume that the counter in the timer circuit is driven by a 100-MHz clock.

E.13   **[D]** Using two 7-segment displays of the type shown in Figure 3.17, and the timer circuit in Figure 3.14, write a program that flashes numbers 0, 1, 2, . . . , 98, 99, 0, ... Each number is to be displayed for one second. Assume that the counter in the timer circuit is driven by a 100-MHz clock.

E.14 **[D]** Write a program that computes real clock time and displays the time in hours (0 to 23) and minutes (0 to 59). The display consists of four 7-segment display devices of the type shown in Figure 3.17. A timer circuit that has the interface given in Figure 3.14 is available. Its counter is driven by a 100-MHz clock.

E.15 **[M]** Write an IA-32 program to solve Problem 2.22 in Chapter 2. Assume that the element to be pushed/popped is located in register EAX, and that register EBX serves as the stack pointer for the user stack.

E.16 **[M]** Write an IA-32 program to solve Problem 2.24 in Chapter 2.

E.17 **[M]** Write an IA-32 program to solve Problem 2.25 in Chapter 2.

E.18 **[M]** Write an IA-32 program to solve Problem 2.26 in Chapter 2.

E.19 **[M]** Write an IA-32 program to solve Problem 2.27 in Chapter 2.

E.20 **[M]** Write an IA-32 program to solve Problem 2.28 in Chapter 2.

E.21 **[M]** Write an IA-32 program to solve Problem 2.29 in Chapter 2.

E.22 **[M]** Write an IA-32 program to solve Problem 2.30 in Chapter 2.

E.23 **[M]** Write an IA-32 program to solve Problem 2.31 in Chapter 2.

E.24 **[D]** Write an IA-32 program to solve Problem 2.32 in Chapter 2.

E.25 **[D]** Write an IA-32 program to solve Problem 2.33 in Chapter 2.

E.26 **[M]** Write an IA-32 program to solve Problem 3.20 in Chapter 3.

E.27 **[M]** Write an IA-32 program to solve Problem 3.22 in Chapter 3.

E.28 **[D]** Write an IA-32 program to solve Problem 3.24 in Chapter 3.

E.29 **[D]** Write an IA-32 program to solve Problem 3.26 in Chapter 3.

E.30 **[D]** The function $sin(x)$ can be approximated with reasonable accuracy as $x - x^3/6 + x^5/120 = x(1 - x^2(1/6 - x^2(1/120)))$ when $0 \leq x \leq \pi/2$. Write a subroutine called SIN that accepts an input parameter that is a pointer to the floating-point value of x in the memory and computes the approximated value of $sin(x)$ using the second expression above involving only terms in x and x^2. The computed value should be returned in the same memory location as the input parameter x. Any integer registers used by the subroutine should be saved and restored as needed. The accuracy of the approximation used by this subroutine can be explored by comparing its results with results obtained with the FSIN instruction that is included in the IA-32 instruction set.

REFERENCES

1. Intel Corporation, *Intel 64 and IA-32 Architectures Software Developer's Manual – Volume 1: Basic Architecture*, Document number 253665-033US, December 2009. Available at http://www.intel.com.

INDEX